World Economic and Financial Surveys

D1709376

World Economic Outlook
October 2016

Subdued Demand
Symptoms and Remedies

· ·

I N T E R N A T I O N A L   M O N E T A R Y   F U N D

Cover and Design: Luisa Menjivar and Jorge Salazar
Composition: AGS, An RR Donnelley Company

Cataloging-in-Publication Data

Joint Bank-Fund Library

Names: International Monetary Fund.
Title: World economic outlook (International Monetary Fund)
Other titles: WEO | Occasional paper (International Monetary Fund) | World economic and financial surveys.
Description: Washington, DC : International Monetary Fund, 1980- | Semiannual | Some issues also have thematic titles. | Began with issue for May 1980. | 1981-1984: Occasional paper / International Monetary Fund, 0251-6365 | 1986-: World economic and financial surveys, 0256-6877.
Identifiers: ISSN 0256-6877 (print) | ISSN 1564-5215 (online)
Subjects: LCSH: Economic development—Periodicals. | International economic relations—Periodicals. | Debts, External—Periodicals. | Balance of payments—Periodicals. | International finance—Periodicals. | Economic forecasting—Periodicals.
Classification: LCC HC10.W79

HC10.80

ISBN 978-1-51359-954-0 (paper)
      978-1-47553-996-7 (PDF)
      978-1-47553-981-3 (ePub)
      978-1-47553-998-1 (Mobi)

The *World Economic Outlook* (WEO) is a survey by the IMF staff published twice a year, in the spring and fall. The WEO is prepared by the IMF staff and has benefited from comments and suggestions by Executive Directors following their discussion of the report on September 23, 2016. The views expressed in this publication are those of the IMF staff and do not necessarily represent the views of the IMF's Executive Directors or their national authorities.

Recommended citation: International Monetary Fund. 2016. *World Economic Outlook: Subdued Demand: Symptoms and Remedies.* Washington, October.

Publication orders may be placed online, by fax, or through the mail:
International Monetary Fund, Publication Services
P.O. Box 92780, Washington, DC 20090, U.S.A.
Tel.: (202) 623-7430 Fax: (202) 623-7201
E-mail: publications@imf.org
www.imfbookstore.org
www.elibrary.imf.org

CONTENTS

Tables

Online Tables

Figures

ASSUMPTIONS AND CONVENTIONS

A number of assumptions have been adopted for the projections presented in the *World Economic Outlook* (WEO). It has been assumed that real effective exchange rates remained constant at their average levels during July 22 to August 19, 2016, except for those for the currencies participating in the European exchange rate mechanism II (ERM II), which are assumed to have remained constant in nominal terms relative to the euro; that established policies of national authorities will be maintained (for specific assumptions about fiscal and monetary policies for selected economies, see Box A1 in the Statistical Appendix); that the average price of oil will be $42.96 a barrel in 2016 and $50.64 a barrel in 2017 and will remain unchanged in real terms over the medium term; that the six-month London interbank offered rate (LIBOR) on U.S. dollar deposits will average 1.0 percent in 2016 and 1.3 percent in 2017; that the three-month euro deposit rate will average –0.3 percent in 2016 and –0.4 percent in 2017; and that the six-month Japanese yen deposit rate will yield on average 0.0 percent in 2016 and –0.1 percent in 2017. These are, of course, working hypotheses rather than forecasts, and the uncertainties surrounding them add to the margin of error that would in any event be involved in the projections. The estimates and projections are based on statistical information available through September 16, 2016.

The following conventions are used throughout the WEO:

. . .   to indicate that data are not available or not applicable;

–   between years or months (for example, 2015–16 or January–June) to indicate the years or months covered, including the beginning and ending years or months; and

/   between years or months (for example, 2015/16) to indicate a fiscal or financial year.

"Billion" means a thousand million; "trillion" means a thousand billion.

"Basis points" refers to hundredths of 1 percentage point (for example, 25 basis points are equivalent to ¼ of 1 percentage point).

Data refer to calendar years, except in the case of a few countries that use fiscal years. Please refer to Table F in the Statistical Appendix, which lists the economies with exceptional reporting periods for national accounts and government finance data for each country.

For some countries, the figures for 2015 and earlier are based on estimates rather than actual outturns. Please refer to Table G in the Statistical Appendix, which lists the latest actual outturns for the indicators in the national accounts, prices, government finance, and balance of payments indicators for each country.

In the tables and figures, the following conventions apply:

- If no source is listed on tables and figures, data are drawn from the WEO database.
- When countries are not listed alphabetically, they are ordered on the basis of economic size.
- Minor discrepancies between sums of constituent figures and totals shown reflect rounding.

As used in this report, the terms "country" and "economy" do not in all cases refer to a territorial entity that is a state as understood by international law and practice. As used here, the term also covers some territorial entities that are not states but for which statistical data are maintained on a separate and independent basis.

Composite data are provided for various groups of countries organized according to economic characteristics or region. Unless noted otherwise, country group composites represent calculations based on 90 percent or more of the weighted group data.

The boundaries, colors, denominations, and any other information shown on the maps do not imply, on the part of the International Monetary Fund, any judgment on the legal status of any territory or any endorsement or acceptance of such boundaries.

FURTHER INFORMATION AND DATA

This version of the *World Economic Outlook* (WEO) is available in full through the IMF eLibrary (www.elibrary.imf.org) and the IMF website (www.imf.org). Accompanying the publication on the IMF website is a larger compilation of data from the WEO database than is included in the report itself, including files containing the series most frequently requested by readers. These files may be downloaded for use in a variety of software packages.

The data appearing in the *World Economic Outlook* are compiled by the IMF staff at the time of the WEO exercises. The historical data and projections are based on the information gathered by the IMF country desk officers in the context of their missions to IMF member countries and through their ongoing analysis of the evolving situation in each country. Historical data are updated on a continual basis as more information becomes available, and structural breaks in data are often adjusted to produce smooth series with the use of splicing and other techniques. IMF staff estimates continue to serve as proxies for historical series when complete information is unavailable. As a result, WEO data can differ from those in other sources with official data, including the IMF's *International Financial Statistics*.

The WEO data and metadata provided are "as is" and "as available," and every effort is made to ensure their timeliness, accuracy, and completeness, but it cannot be guaranteed. When errors are discovered, there is a concerted effort to correct them as appropriate and feasible. Corrections and revisions made after publication are incorporated into the electronic editions available from the IMF eLibrary (www.elibrary.imf.org) and on the IMF website (www.imf.org). All substantive changes are listed in detail in the online tables of contents.

For details on the terms and conditions for usage of the WEO database, please refer to the IMF Copyright and Usage website (www.imf.org/external/terms.htm).

Inquiries about the content of the *World Economic Outlook* and the WEO database should be sent by mail, fax, or online forum (telephone inquiries cannot be accepted):

World Economic Studies Division
Research Department
International Monetary Fund
700 19th Street, N.W.
Washington, D.C. 20431, U.S.A.
Fax: (202) 623-6343
Online Forum: www.imf.org/weoforum

PREFACE

The analysis and projections contained in the *World Economic Outlook* are integral elements of the IMF's surveillance of economic developments and policies in its member countries, of developments in international financial markets, and of the global economic system. The survey of prospects and policies is the product of a comprehensive interdepartmental review of world economic developments, which draws primarily on information the IMF staff gathers through its consultations with member countries. These consultations are carried out in particular by the IMF's area departments—namely, the African Department, Asia and Pacific Department, European Department, Middle East and Central Asia Department, and Western Hemisphere Department—together with the Strategy, Policy, and Review Department, the Monetary and Capital Markets Department, and the Fiscal Affairs Department.

The analysis in this report was coordinated in the Research Department under the general direction of Maurice Obstfeld, Economic Counsellor and Director of Research. The project was directed by Gian Maria Milesi-Ferretti, Deputy Director, Research Department; Oya Celasun, Division Chief, Research Department; and Helge Berger, Division Chief, Research Department and Head of the IMF's Spillover Task Force.

The primary contributors to this report were Rabah Arezki, Aqib Aslam, Claudia Berg, Samya Beidas-Strom, Patrick Blagrave, Christian Bogmans, Emine Boz, Luis Catão, Eugenio Cerutti, Sangyup Choi, Davide Furceri, Bertrand Gruss, Zsóka Kóczán, Ksenia Koloskova, Toh Kuan, Weicheng Lian, Akito Matsumoto, Malhar Nabar, Marcos Poplawski-Ribeiro, Sweta Saxena, Petia Topalova, and Esteban Vesperoni.

Other contributors include Jaebin Ahn, Emre Alper, Michal Andrle, Elif Arbatli, Gavin Asdorian, Felicia Belostecinic, Diego Cerdeiro, Kevin Clinton, Vanessa Diaz Montelongo, Romain Duval, Rupa Duttagupta, Angela Espiritu, Rachel Yuting Fan, Emily Forrest, Mitko Grigorov, Refet Gürkaynak, Mahnaz Hemmati, Christian Henn, Benjamin Hilgenstock, Niko Hobdari, Ava Yeabin Hong, Keiko Honjo, Benjamin Hunt, Gabi Ionescu, Zoltan Matyas Jakab, Hao Jiang, Alimata Kini-Kaboré, Sinem Kılıç Çelik, Douglas Laxton, Andrei Levchenko, Olivia Ma, Trevor Charles Meadows, Juan Angel Garcia Morales, Brent Neiman, Emory Oakes, Evgenia Pugacheva, Rachel Szymanski, Daniel Te Kaat, Sheng Tibung, Nicholas Tong, Ali Uppal, Hou Wang, Niklas Westelius, Jilun Xing, Yuan Zeng, Fan Zhang, and Qiaoqiao Zhang.

Joseph Procopio from the Communications Department led the editorial team for the report, with support from Michael Harrup and Christine Ebrahimzadeh and editorial assistance from Linda Kean, Lucy Scott Morales, Lorraine Coffey, Gregg Forte, EEI Communications, and AGS (an RR Donnelley Company).

The analysis has benefited from comments and suggestions by staff members from other IMF departments, as well as by Executive Directors following their discussion of the report on September 23, 2016. However, both projections and policy considerations are those of the IMF staff and should not be attributed to Executive Directors or to their national authorities.

When I arrived at the International Monetary Fund about a year ago, our worries focused on China's growth prospects amid domestic rebalancing, the struggles of primary commodity exporters, and the timing and impact of the Federal Reserve's first interest rate increase since 2006. Today, stable growth performance has reduced near-term concerns about China, commodity prices have partially recovered, and the Federal Reserve's initial interest rate hike is behind us. Global asset markets seem placid after these developments, with advanced economy equity prices at high levels, market-based volatility measures low, and renewed capital inflows to emerging market economies. And our baseline forecast sees improving world growth in the years ahead. That projected improvement is driven by emerging market and developing economies: as conditions in economies under stress gradually normalize, China's growth rate—while declining—remains high, and the recovery is gaining traction elsewhere.

A closer look, however, gives cause for disquiet. China's growth stability owes much to macroeconomic stimulus measures that slow needed adjustments in both its real economy and financial sector. Commodity exporters still struggle with past investment overhangs in extractive sectors, along with the challenges of fiscal adjustment and longer-term economic diversification. And the Federal Reserve, despite an ever-strengthening U.S. job market, has so far judged a second interest rate rise to be too risky, several times citing worrisome economic developments abroad.

Asset prices and emerging market capital inflows are supported by ultra-low interest rates in advanced economies that now seem poised to persist considerably longer than they did last October. But while lower-for-longer interest rates have their upsides, they also reflect difficult economic realities. Our expectations for future global growth and productivity have fallen in light of recent disappointing outcomes. Deflation pressures persist. And policy uncertainty in the global economy, as reflected in news-based measures, is elevated. The current outlook remains subdued.

Political tensions have now made advanced economies a major locus of policy uncertainty. Most dramatically, the unexpected vote for Brexit on June 23 leaves unclear the future shape of the United Kingdom's

trade and financial relations with the remaining 27 European Union (EU) members, introducing political and economic uncertainties that threaten to dampen investment and hiring throughout Europe. Alongside economic anxiety and other factors, the Brexit vote reflects a resentment of cross-border migration that has fueled nationalist sentiment in Europe and called into question the way forward for EU integration. These trends are exacerbated by the difficulties of absorbing a large volume of refugees who have fled tragic events in the Middle East. In general, centrifugal political forces across the continent are making it harder to advance or even maintain economic reforms. Similar tensions afflict the U.S. political scene, where anti-immigrant and anti-trade rhetoric have been prominent from the start of the current presidential election round. Across the world, protectionist trade measures have been on the rise.

Inside the *World Economic Outlook*

Not coincidentally, the chapters in this new *World Economic Outlook* focus on several of these concerns. After Chapter 1's summary of the global outlook, Chapter 2 analyzes the forces behind the recent growth slowdown in the volume of international trade. A major driver is slower growth in aggregate demand, particularly in investment, which is especially apt to generate international trade flows in the form of capital goods and intermediate inputs. But key roles are also played by the slowing momentum of trade liberalization measures, the return of some protectionist measures, and the (possibly related) retraction of global value chains. Some of the trade slowdown may reflect a natural maturation of the tendencies that propelled trade growth in the past, but it also seems likely that more worrisome pressures are at work, and that these may in turn reduce business dynamism and productivity growth.

The topic of Chapter 3 is the persistently low inflation in many economies and its relationship to falling commodity prices, remaining output gaps, global excess capacity, and possibly de-anchored inflation expectations. The chapter finds that medium-term measures of inflation expectations generally remain reasonably close to central bank targets so far, but also shows that for countries with policy interest rates at their effective lower bounds, expectations of medium-term inflation have become more sensitive to weaker-than-expected inflation outcomes. The danger is that expectations will diverge downward from targets, raising real interest rates and thereby reducing monetary policy effectiveness while dragging these economies into low inflation or deflation traps.

Finally, Chapter 4 focuses on two salient cross-border economic spillovers that have driven recent global economic and political developments: repercussions from China's slowing growth and migration. Spillovers from China's economy have increased markedly since the mid-1990s, operating primarily through trade linkages and through the impact of China growth shocks on global commodity prices. China's growing global role makes it all the more important for it to address its internal imbalances so as to approach smoothly a more sustainable consumption- and service-oriented growth framework. Regarding migration, Chapter 4 finds that both sending and receiving countries are impacted. Most striking, perhaps, is the result that low-skilled and high-skilled migrants alike contribute to positive long-term productivity effects in receiving advanced economies. Moreover, these effects raise per capita income broadly across the income distribution. Demands to reduce immigration would foreclose these income gains, while accentuating the negative effects of workforce aging.

Policy Implications

A common thread connecting the chapters of this *World Economic Outlook* is the still weak and precarious nature of the global recovery, and the threats it faces. Especially in a low-demand environment where key policy interest rates are near effective lower bounds, tepid growth risks becoming self-perpetuating as investment falls, productivity growth declines, labor markets become less dynamic, and human capital erodes. Moreover, declining growth rates, along with increased income inequality and concerns about the impact of migration, contribute to political tensions that block constructive economic reforms and threaten a rollback of trade integration. These tensions will only worsen as governments struggle more and more to make good on social entitlements in the face of shrinking tax bases.

Some argue that current economic growth rates are acceptable, being consistent with past historical averages, and that they appear even more favorable when viewed in per capita terms. This argument ignores the still sizable slack in many advanced economies and the large number of emerging market and developing economies in recession or with stagnant per capita incomes. True, exogenous factors such as demographics likely weigh even on per capita growth, as does China's necessary rebalancing. But significant opportunities for boosting jobs and incomes around

the world are being lost today through short-sighted policy approaches.

What can be done to close remaining output gaps, fight deflation, and lift potential output?

A comprehensive, three-pronged policy approach that supports overstretched monetary policies with fiscal policy (where fiscal space allows) and structural reforms is essential. Even where fiscal space is limited, there is scope to change the composition of spending and revenues in a way that supports near-term growth and future productive capacity. One cause of economic uncertainty, however, is the fear that each of these three tools faces economic or political constraints, which could prevent policymakers from responding aggressively to a new global slowdown. Policy space can be created, however, if policy is based on consistent frameworks that communicate to markets how instruments will be used to attain objectives over time, exploiting their synergies while safeguarding medium-term inflation goals and fiscal sustainability. This is intranational policy coordination. International coordination can create even more policy space, thanks to positive, mutually reinforcing spillovers between different countries' demand support measures. Both intranational and international coordination make the whole greater than the sum of its parts.

The policy framework should include measures that mitigate the adverse income-distribution effects of economic changes, whether due to technology, globalization forces, or other developments. Educational investments that equip people with adaptable skills, as well as better social insurance mechanisms and appropriate income tax regimes, can enhance risk sharing and resilience for all, not just those with access to sophisticated financial markets.

It is vitally important to defend the prospects for increasing trade integration. A global environment hostile to trade will make it impossible for commodity exporters and low-income countries in general to develop new export models and gradually narrow income gaps with richer countries. It will also broadly deter global productivity growth, the spread of knowledge and technology, and investment. In short, turning back the clock on trade can only deepen and prolong the world economy's current doldrums.

The need for international cooperation extends to a much broader set of international public-good problems—refugees, climate, infectious disease, security, corporate taxation, and financial stability, for example. An increasingly interdependent world will achieve more growth and stability if governments engage cooperatively around the many areas where their interests intersect.

Maurice Obstfeld
Economic Counsellor

EXECUTIVE SUMMARY

Global growth is projected to slow to 3.1 percent in 2016 before recovering to 3.4 percent in 2017. The forecast, revised down by 0.1 percentage point for 2016 and 2017 relative to April, reflects a more subdued outlook for advanced economies following the June U.K. vote in favor of leaving the European Union (Brexit) and weaker-than-expected growth in the United States. These developments have put further downward pressure on global interest rates, as monetary policy is now expected to remain accommodative for longer. Although the market reaction to the Brexit shock was reassuringly orderly, the ultimate impact remains very unclear, as the fate of institutional and trade arrangements between the United Kingdom and the European Union is uncertain. Financial market sentiment toward emerging market economies has improved with expectations of lower interest rates in advanced economies, reduced concern about China's near-term prospects following policy support to growth, and some firming of commodity prices. But prospects differ sharply across countries and regions, with emerging Asia in general and India in particular showing robust growth and sub-Saharan Africa experiencing a sharp slowdown. In advanced economies, a subdued outlook subject to sizable uncertainty and downside risks may fuel further political discontent, with anti-integration policy platforms gaining more traction. Several emerging market and developing economies still face daunting policy challenges in adjusting to weaker commodity prices. These worrisome prospects make the need for a broad-based policy response to raise growth and manage vulnerabilities more urgent than ever.

The current outlook is shaped by a complex confluence of ongoing realignments, long-term trends, and new shocks. These factors imply a generally subdued baseline for growth, but also substantial uncertainty about future economic prospects. The main unforeseen development in recent months was the U.K. vote in favor of leaving the European Union. Brexit is very much an unfolding event—the long-term shape of relations between the United Kingdom and the European Union, and the extent to which their mutual trade and financial flows will be curtailed, will likely become clear only after several years. Adding to the uncertainty is the impact of the referendum results on political sentiment in other EU members, as well as on global pressure to adopt populist, inward-looking policies.

Important ongoing realignments—particularly salient for emerging market and developing economies—include rebalancing in China and the macroeconomic and structural adjustment of commodity exporters to a long-term decline in their terms of trade. Slow-moving changes that are playing an important role in the outlook for advanced economies (as well as for some emerging market economies) include demographic and labor-market trends, but also an ill-understood protracted slowdown in productivity, which is hampering income growth and contributing to political discontent.

In the *World Economic Outlook* (WEO) baseline scenario, global growth is projected to decline to 3.1 percent in 2016, and to rebound next year to 3.4 percent. The 2016 forecast reflects weaker-than-expected U.S. activity in the first half of the year as well as materialization of an important downside risk with the Brexit vote. Although financial market reaction to the result of the U.K. referendum has been contained, the increase in economic, political, and institutional uncertainty and the likely reduction in trade and financial flows between the United Kingdom and the rest of the European Union over the medium term is expected to have negative macroeconomic consequences, especially in the United Kingdom. As a result, the 2016 growth forecast for advanced economies has been marked down to 1.6 percent.

Growth in emerging market and developing economies is expected to strengthen slightly in 2016 to 4.2 percent after five consecutive years of decline, accounting for over three-quarters of projected world growth this year. However, the outlook for these economies is uneven and generally weaker than in the past. While external financing conditions have eased with expectations of lower interest rates in advanced economies, other factors are weighing on activity.

These include a slowdown in China, whose spillovers are magnified by its lower reliance on import- and resource-intensive investment; commodity exporters' continued adjustment to lower revenues; spillovers from persistently weak demand in advanced economies; and domestic strife, political discord, and geopolitical tensions in several countries. While growth in emerging Asia and especially India continues to be resilient, the largest economies in sub-Saharan Africa (Nigeria, South Africa, Angola) are experiencing sharp slowdowns or recessions as lower commodity prices interact with difficult domestic political and economic conditions. Brazil and Russia continue to face challenging macroeconomic conditions, but their outlook has strengthened somewhat relative to last April.

The recovery is projected to pick up in 2017 as the outlook improves for emerging market and developing economies and the U.S. economy regains some momentum, with a fading drag from inventories and a recovery in investment. Although longer-term prospects for advanced economies remain muted, given demographic headwinds and weak productivity growth, the forecast envisages a further strengthening of growth in emerging market and developing economies over the medium term. But as noted in previous WEOs, this forecast depends on a number of important assumptions:

• A gradual normalization of conditions in economies currently under stress, with a general pickup in growth in commodity exporters, albeit to levels more modest than in the past
• A gradual slowdown and rebalancing of China's economy with medium-term growth rates that—at close to 6 percent—remain higher than the average for emerging market and developing economies
• Resilient growth in other emerging market and developing economies

Both economic and noneconomic factors threaten to keep these assumptions from being realized and imperil the baseline outlook more generally. In particular, some risks flagged in recent WEOs have become more prominent in recent months. The first is *political discord and inward-looking policies.* The Brexit vote and the ongoing U.S. presidential election campaign have highlighted a fraying consensus about the benefits of cross-border economic integration. Concerns about the impact of foreign competition on jobs and wages in a context of weak growth have enhanced the appeal of protectionist policy approaches, with potential

ramifications for global trade flows and integration more broadly. Concerns about unequal (and widening) income distribution are rising, fueled by weak income growth as productivity dynamics remain disappointing. Uncertainty about the evolution of these trends may lead firms to defer investment and hiring decisions, thus slowing near-term activity, while an inward-looking policy shift could also stoke further cross-border political discord.

A second risk is *stagnation in advanced economies.* As global growth remains sluggish, the prospect of an extended shortfall in private demand leading to permanently lower growth and low inflation becomes ever more tangible, particularly in some advanced economies where balance sheets remain impaired. At the same time, a protracted period of weak inflation in advanced economies risks unmooring inflation expectations, causing expected real interest rates to rise and spending to decline, eventually feeding back to even weaker overall growth and inflation.

Other risks flagged in previous WEOs remain important potential influences on the outlook. *China's ongoing adjustment and associated spillovers* continue to be pertinent, even as near-term sentiment regarding China has appeared to recover from the acute anxiety at the start of the year. The economy's transition away from reliance on investment, industry, and exports in favor of greater dependence on consumption and services could become bumpier than expected at times, with important implications for commodity and machinery exporters as well as for countries indirectly exposed to China through financial contagion channels. That risk is heightened by the current short-term growth-promoting measures on which China is relying, as a still-rising credit-to-GDP ratio and lack of decisive progress in addressing corporate debt and governance concerns in state-owned enterprises raise the risk of a disruptive adjustment. More generally, although *financial conditions in emerging markets* have continued to improve in recent months, underlying vulnerabilities remain among some large emerging market economies. High corporate debt, declining profitability, weak bank balance sheets—together with the need to rebuild policy buffers, particularly in commodity exporters—leave these economies still exposed to sudden shifts in investor confidence. *A range of additional noneconomic factors* continues to influence the outlook in various regions—the protracted effects of a drought in eastern and southern Africa; civil war and domestic conflict in parts of the Middle East and Africa and the tragic plight of refugees in neighboring countries and in Europe; multiple acts of terror worldwide; and the spread of the Zika virus in Latin America and the Caribbean, the southern United States, and southeast Asia. If these factors intensify, they could collectively take a large toll on market sentiment, hurting demand and activity.

Upside developments include the orderly repricing in financial markets after the initial shock of the Brexit vote; sustained improvements in the U.S. labor market; and a modest recent uptick in commodity prices, which should ease some of the pressure on commodity exporters. These developments point to the possibility of a better-than-envisaged pickup in momentum, which could be even stronger if countries adopt comprehensive frameworks to lift actual and potential output.

While the baseline forecast for the global economy points to a pickup in growth over the rest of the forecast horizon from its subdued pace this year, the potential for setbacks to this outlook is high, as underscored by repeated growth markdowns in recent years. Against this backdrop, policy priorities differ across individual economies depending on the specific objectives of improving growth momentum, combating deflation pressures, or building resilience. But a common theme is that urgent action relying on all policy levers is needed to head off further growth disappointments and combat damaging perceptions that policies are ineffective in boosting growth or that the rewards accrue only to those at the higher end of the income distribution.

In *advanced economies*, output gaps are still negative, wage pressures are generally muted, and the risk of persistent low inflation (or deflation, in some cases) has risen. Monetary policy therefore must remain accommodative, relying on unconventional strategies as needed. But accommodative monetary policy alone cannot lift demand sufficiently, and fiscal support—calibrated to the amount of space available and oriented toward policies that protect the vulnerable and lift medium-term growth prospects—therefore remains essential for generating momentum and avoiding a lasting downshift in medium-term inflation expectations. In countries facing rising public debt and social entitlement outlays, credible commitments to medium-term consolidation can generate additional space for near-term support. And fiscal policy should

concentrate outlays on uses that most strongly support demand and longer-term potential growth. More broadly, accommodative macroeconomic policies must be accompanied by structural reforms that can counteract waning potential growth—including efforts to boost labor force participation, improve the matching process in labor markets, and promote investment in research and development and innovation. As discussed in Chapter 3 of the April 2016 WEO, comprehensive policies that combine demand support with reforms targeting a country's structural needs, anchored in coherent and well-communicated policy frameworks, can fire up both short-term activity and medium-term potential output.

Across *emerging market and developing economies*, the broad common policy objectives are continued convergence to higher incomes by reducing distortions in product, labor, and capital markets and giving people a better chance in life by investing wisely in education and health care. These goals can only be realized in an environment safe from financial vulnerability and the risk of reversals. Economies with large and rising nonfinancial debt, unhedged foreign liabilities, or heavy reliance on short-term borrowing to fund longer-term investments must adopt stronger risk management practices and contain currency and balance sheet mismatches.

For countries hardest hit by the slump in commodity prices, adjustment to reestablish macroeconomic stability is urgent. This implies fully allowing the exchange rate to absorb pressures for countries not relying on an exchange rate peg, tightening monetary policy where needed to tackle sharp increases in inflation, and ensuring that needed fiscal consolidation is as growth friendly as possible.

Low-income developing economies must rebuild fiscal buffers while continuing to spend on critical capital needs and social outlays, strengthen debt management, and implement structural reforms—including in education—that pave the way for economic diversification and higher productivity.

While essential at the country level, these policies for all country groups would be even more effective if adopted broadly throughout the world, with due attention to country-specific priorities.

With growth weak and policy space limited in many countries, continued *multilateral effort* is required in several areas to minimize risks to financial stability and sustain global improvements in living standards. This effort must proceed simultaneously on a number of fronts. Policymakers must address the backlash against global trade by refocusing the discussion on the long-term benefits of economic integration and ensuring that well-targeted social initiatives help those who are adversely affected and facilitate, through retraining, their absorption into expanding sectors. Effective banking resolution frameworks, both national and international, are vital, and emerging risks from nonbank intermediaries must be addressed. A stronger global safety net is more important than ever to protect economies with robust fundamentals that may nevertheless be vulnerable to cross-border contagion and spillovers, including strains that are not economic.

CHAPTER 1

GLOBAL PROSPECTS AND POLICIES

Recent Developments and Prospects

The forces shaping the global outlook—both those operating over the short term and those operating over the long term—point to subdued growth for 2016 and a gradual recovery thereafter, as well as to downside risks. These forces include new shocks, such as Brexit—the June 23, 2016, U.K. referendum result in favor of leaving the European Union; ongoing realignments, such as rebalancing in China and the adjustment of commodity exporters to a protracted decline in the terms of trade; and slow-moving trends, such as demographics and the evolution of productivity growth; as well as noneconomic factors, such as geopolitical and political uncertainty. The subdued recovery also plays a role in explaining the weakness in global trade (discussed in Chapter 2) and persistently low inflation (discussed in Chapter 3).

Relative to the global outlook envisaged in the April 2016 *World Economic Outlook* (WEO), the main changes relate to the downward revision to U.S. growth (mostly reflecting weaker-than-expected growth in the second quarter of 2016), further confirmation that the economies of Brazil and Russia are closer to exiting from recession, and the outcome of the U.K. referendum. Brexit is an unfolding event— the long-term arrangements in relations between the United Kingdom and the European Union will be uncertain for a protracted period of time. And the vote is not only a symptom of fraying consensus on the benefits of cross-border economic integration amid weak growth, but could catalyze pressures for inward-looking policies elsewhere as well.

On the positive side, beyond a sharp depreciation of the pound, broader market reaction to the Brexit vote has generally been contained, with equity valuations and risk appetite recovering after an initial drop, as discussed elsewhere in this chapter. Bank stocks, however, remain under pressure, especially in countries with more fragile banking systems. Based on preliminary readings, business and consumer sentiment were generally resilient in July, immediately following the referendum, except in the United Kingdom. Sentiment has improved regarding emerging market and developing economies, reflecting reduced concerns about China's near-term prospects following policy support for growth, mildly favorable macroeconomic news from other emerging market economies in the past few months, some recovery in commodity prices, and expectations of lower interest rates in advanced economies. But with very limited post-Brexit macroeconomic data so far, uncertainty about the impact of Brexit on macroeconomic outcomes remains, especially in Europe.

Growth is projected to pick up from 2017 onward, almost entirely on account of developments in emerging market and developing economies. This reflects primarily two factors: the gradual normalization of macroeconomic conditions in several countries experiencing deep recessions and the increasing weight of fast-growing countries in this group in the world economy (Box 1.1).

The World Economy in Recent Months

Global Activity Remains Sluggish

Based on preliminary data, global growth is estimated at 2.9 percent in the first half of 2016, slightly weaker than in the second half of 2015 and lower than projected in the April 2016 WEO. Global industrial production remained subdued, but has shown signs of a pickup in recent months, and trade volumes retreated in the quarter through June after several months of sustained recovery from the trough of early 2015 (Figure 1.1). The recent weak momentum is mostly a product of softer activity in advanced economies.

• The U.S. economy has lost momentum over the past few quarters, and the expectation of a pickup in the second quarter of 2016 has not been realized, with growth estimated at 1.1 percent at a seasonally adjusted annual rate. Consumption growth (at about 3.0 percent on average in the first half of the year) has remained strong, supported by a firm labor market and expanding payrolls, but continued weakness in nonresidential investment together with a sizable drawdown of inventories has weighed on the

Table 1.1. Overview of the *World Economic Outlook* Projections
(Percent change, unless noted otherwise)

	2015	Projections		Difference from July 2016 *WEO Update*[1]		Difference from April 2016 WEO[1]	
		2016	2017	2016	2017	2016	2017
World Output	**3.2**	**3.1**	**3.4**	**0.0**	**0.0**	**−0.1**	**−0.1**
Advanced Economies	**2.1**	**1.6**	**1.8**	**−0.2**	**0.0**	**−0.3**	**−0.2**
United States	2.6	1.6	2.2	−0.6	−0.3	−0.8	−0.3
Euro Area	2.0	1.7	1.5	0.1	0.1	0.2	−0.1
Germany	1.5	1.7	1.4	0.1	0.2	0.2	−0.2
France	1.3	1.3	1.3	−0.2	0.1	0.2	0.0
Italy	0.8	0.8	0.9	−0.1	−0.1	−0.2	−0.2
Spain	3.2	3.1	2.2	0.5	0.1	0.5	−0.1
Japan	0.5	0.5	0.6	0.2	0.5	0.0	0.7
United Kingdom	2.2	1.8	1.1	0.1	−0.2	−0.1	−1.1
Canada	1.1	1.2	1.9	−0.2	−0.2	−0.3	0.0
Other Advanced Economies[2]	2.0	2.0	2.3	0.0	0.0	−0.1	−0.1
Emerging Market and Developing Economies	**4.0**	**4.2**	**4.6**	**0.1**	**0.0**	**0.1**	**0.0**
Commonwealth of Independent States	−2.8	−0.3	1.4	0.3	−0.1	0.8	0.1
Russia	−3.7	−0.8	1.1	0.4	0.1	1.0	0.3
Excluding Russia	−0.5	0.9	2.3	−0.1	−0.2	0.0	0.0
Emerging and Developing Asia	6.6	6.5	6.3	0.1	0.0	0.1	0.0
China	6.9	6.6	6.2	0.0	0.0	0.1	0.0
India[3]	7.6	7.6	7.6	0.2	0.2	0.1	0.1
ASEAN-5[4]	4.8	4.8	5.1	0.0	0.0	0.0	0.0
Emerging and Developing Europe	3.6	3.3	3.1	−0.2	−0.1	−0.2	−0.2
Latin America and the Caribbean	0.0	−0.6	1.6	−0.2	0.0	−0.1	0.1
Brazil	−3.8	−3.3	0.5	0.0	0.0	0.5	0.5
Mexico	2.5	2.1	2.3	−0.4	−0.3	−0.3	−0.3
Middle East, North Africa, Afghanistan, and Pakistan	2.3	3.4	3.4	0.0	0.1	0.3	−0.1
Saudi Arabia	3.5	1.2	2.0	0.0	0.0	0.0	0.1
Sub-Saharan Africa	3.4	1.4	2.9	−0.2	−0.4	−1.6	−1.1
Nigeria	2.7	−1.7	0.6	0.1	−0.5	−4.0	−2.9
South Africa	1.3	0.1	0.8	0.0	−0.2	−0.5	−0.4
Memorandum							
European Union	2.3	1.9	1.7	0.0	0.1	0.1	−0.2
Low-Income Developing Countries	4.6	3.7	4.9	−0.1	−0.2	−1.0	−0.6
Middle East and North Africa	2.1	3.2	3.2	−0.1	0.1	0.3	−0.1
World Growth Based on Market Exchange Rates	2.6	2.4	2.8	−0.1	0.0	−0.1	−0.1
World Trade Volume (goods and services)	**2.6**	**2.3**	**3.8**	**−0.4**	**−0.1**	**−0.8**	**0.0**
Imports							
Advanced Economies	4.2	2.4	3.9	−0.4	−0.3	−1.0	−0.2
Emerging Market and Developing Economies	−0.6	2.3	4.1	−0.4	0.0	−0.7	0.4
Exports							
Advanced Economies	3.6	1.8	3.5	−0.5	−0.1	−0.7	0.0
Emerging Market and Developing Economies	1.3	2.9	3.6	−0.2	−0.2	−0.9	−0.3
Commodity Prices (U.S. dollars)							
Oil[5]	−47.2	−15.4	17.9	0.1	1.5	16.2	0.0
Nonfuel (average based on world commodity export weights)	−17.5	−2.7	0.9	1.1	1.5	6.7	1.6
Consumer Prices							
Advanced Economies	0.3	0.8	1.7	0.1	0.1	0.1	0.2
Emerging Market and Developing Economies[6]	4.7	4.5	4.4	−0.1	0.0	0.0	0.2
London Interbank Offered Rate (percent)							
On U.S. Dollar Deposits (six month)	0.5	1.0	1.3	0.1	0.1	0.1	−0.2
On Euro Deposits (three month)	0.0	−0.3	−0.4	0.0	0.0	0.0	0.0
On Japanese Yen Deposits (six month)	0.1	0.0	−0.1	0.0	0.1	0.1	0.2

Note: Real effective exchange rates are assumed to remain constant at the levels prevailing during July 22–August 19, 2016. Economies are listed on the basis of economic size. The aggregated quarterly data are seasonally adjusted.

[1]Difference based on rounded figures for the current, July 2016 *World Economic Outlook Update*, and April 2016 *World Economic Outlook* forecasts.

[2]Excludes the G7 (Canada, France, Germany, Italy, Japan, United Kingdom, United States) and euro area countries.

[3]For India, data and forecasts are presented on a fiscal year basis and GDP from 2011 onward is based on GDP at market prices with fiscal year 2011/12 as a base year.

[4]Indonesia, Malaysia, Philippines, Thailand, Vietnam.

Table 1.1 *(continued)*

	Year-over-Year				Q4-over-Q4[7]			
			Projections				Projections	
	2014	2015	2016	2017	2014	2015	2016	2017
World Output	**3.4**	**3.2**	**3.1**	**3.4**	**3.2**	**3.1**	**3.1**	**3.5**
Advanced Economies	**1.9**	**2.1**	**1.6**	**1.8**	**1.9**	**1.8**	**1.7**	**1.8**
United States	2.4	2.6	1.6	2.2	2.5	1.9	2.0	1.9
Euro Area	1.1	2.0	1.7	1.5	1.2	2.0	1.6	1.6
Germany	1.6	1.5	1.7	1.4	1.6	1.3	1.7	1.6
France	0.6	1.3	1.3	1.3	0.6	1.3	1.3	1.5
Italy	−0.3	0.8	0.8	0.9	−0.4	1.1	0.7	1.2
Spain	1.4	3.2	3.1	2.2	2.1	3.5	2.6	2.1
Japan	0.0	0.5	0.5	0.6	−0.9	0.8	0.8	0.8
United Kingdom	3.1	2.2	1.8	1.1	3.5	1.8	1.4	0.8
Canada	2.5	1.1	1.2	1.9	2.4	0.3	1.5	1.9
Other Advanced Economies[2]	2.8	2.0	2.0	2.3	2.7	2.0	2.1	2.4
Emerging Market and Developing Economies	**4.6**	**4.0**	**4.2**	**4.6**	**4.4**	**4.2**	**4.3**	**5.0**
Commonwealth of Independent States	1.1	−2.8	−0.3	1.4	−0.9	−3.3	−0.3	2.1
Russia	0.7	−3.7	−0.8	1.1	−0.2	−3.8	−0.3	2.4
Excluding Russia	2.0	−0.5	0.9	2.3	. . .	. . .	. . .	. . .
Emerging and Developing Asia	6.8	6.6	6.5	6.3	6.6	6.8	6.3	6.3
China	7.3	6.9	6.6	6.2	7.0	6.9	6.4	6.1
India[3]	7.2	7.6	7.6	7.6	7.1	8.1	7.4	7.4
ASEAN-5[4]	4.6	4.8	4.8	5.1	4.9	4.8	4.4	5.8
Emerging and Developing Europe	2.8	3.6	3.3	3.1	2.9	4.1	2.9	2.9
Latin America and the Caribbean	1.0	0.0	−0.6	1.6	0.3	−1.2	−0.4	2.3
Brazil	0.1	−3.8	−3.3	0.5	−0.7	−5.9	−1.2	1.1
Mexico	2.2	2.5	2.1	2.3	2.6	2.4	1.8	2.4
Middle East, North Africa, Afghanistan, and Pakistan	2.7	2.3	3.4	3.4	. . .	. . .	. . .	. . .
Saudi Arabia	3.6	3.5	1.2	2.0	2.4	1.8	1.0	2.5
Sub-Saharan Africa	5.1	3.4	1.4	2.9	. . .	. . .	. . .	. . .
Nigeria	6.3	2.7	−1.7	0.6	. . .	. . .	. . .	. . .
South Africa	1.6	1.3	0.1	0.8	1.4	0.2	0.1	1.3
Memorandum								
European Union	1.6	2.3	1.9	1.7	1.8	2.3	1.9	1.6
Low-Income Developing Countries	6.0	4.6	3.7	4.9	. . .	. . .	. . .	. . .
Middle East and North Africa	2.6	2.1	3.2	3.2	. . .	. . .	. . .	. . .
World Growth Based on Market Exchange Rates	2.7	2.6	2.4	2.8	2.5	2.3	2.5	2.8
World Trade Volume (goods and services)	**3.9**	**2.6**	**2.3**	**3.8**	. . .	. . .	. . .	. . .
Imports								
Advanced Economies	3.8	4.2	2.4	3.9	. . .	. . .	. . .	. . .
Emerging Market and Developing Economies	4.5	−0.6	2.3	4.1	. . .	. . .	. . .	. . .
Exports								
Advanced Economies	3.8	3.6	1.8	3.5	. . .	. . .	. . .	. . .
Emerging Market and Developing Economies	3.5	1.3	2.9	3.6	. . .	. . .	. . .	. . .
Commodity Prices (U.S. dollars)								
Oil[5]	−7.5	−47.2	−15.4	17.9	−28.7	−43.4	14.6	6.8
Nonfuel (average based on world commodity export weights)	−4.0	−17.5	−2.7	0.9	−7.4	−19.1	6.8	−1.2
Consumer Prices								
Advanced Economies	1.4	0.3	0.8	1.7	1.0	0.4	1.0	1.8
Emerging Market and Developing Economies[6]	4.7	4.7	4.5	4.4	4.2	4.6	4.2	3.9
London Interbank Offered Rate (percent)								
On U.S. Dollar Deposits (six month)	0.3	0.5	1.0	1.3	. . .	. . .	. . .	. . .
On Euro Deposits (three month)	0.2	0.0	−0.3	−0.4	. . .	. . .	. . .	. . .
On Japanese Yen Deposits (six month)	0.2	0.1	0.0	−0.1	. . .	. . .	. . .	. . .

[5]Simple average of prices of U.K. Brent, Dubai Fateh, and West Texas Intermediate crude oil. The average price of oil in U.S. dollars a barrel was $50.79 in 2015; the assumed price based on futures markets is $42.96 in 2016 and $50.64 in 2017.
[6]Excludes Argentina and Venezuela. See country-specific notes for Argentina in the "Country Notes" section of the Statistical Appendix.
[7]For World Output, the quarterly estimates and projections account for approximately 90 percent of annual world output at purchasing-power-parity weights. For Emerging Market and Developing Economies, the quarterly estimates and projections account for approximately 80 percent of annual emerging market and developing economies' output at purchasing-power-parity weights.

Figure 1.1. Global Activity Indicators

Global growth weakened slightly in the first half of 2016, mostly due to softer activity in advanced economies, while emerging market and developing economies picked up modestly. Global trade contracted in the second quarter of 2016, while industrial production remained subdued for the most part, but has risen in recent months.

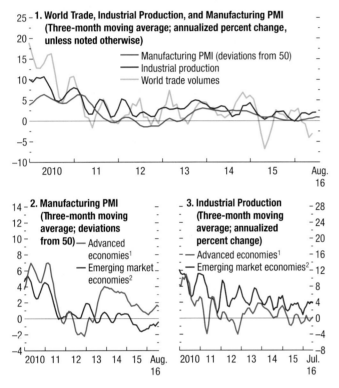

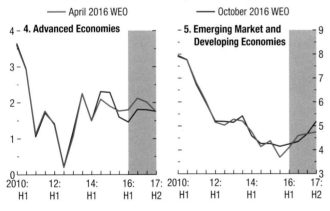

Sources: CPB Netherlands Bureau for Economic Policy Analysis; Haver Analytics; Markit Economics; and IMF staff estimates.
Note: IP = industrial production; PMI = purchasing managers' index.
[1]Australia, Canada, Czech Republic, Denmark, euro area, Hong Kong SAR (IP only), Israel, Japan, Korea, New Zealand, Norway (IP only), Singapore, Sweden (IP only), Switzerland, Taiwan Province of China, United Kingdom, United States.
[2]Argentina (IP only), Brazil, Bulgaria (IP only), Chile (IP only), China, Colombia (IP only), Hungary, India, Indonesia, Latvia (IP only), Lithuania (IP only), Malaysia (IP only), Mexico, Pakistan (IP only), Peru (IP only), Philippines (IP only), Poland, Romania (IP only), Russia, South Africa, Thailand (IP only), Turkey, Ukraine (IP only), Venezuela (IP only).

headline growth number. The weakness in business fixed investment appears to reflect the continued (albeit moderating) decline in capital spending in the energy sector, the impact of recent dollar strength on investment in export-oriented industries, and possibly also the financial market volatility and recession fears of late 2015 and early 2016. Nonfarm labor productivity declined 0.6 percent at a seasonally adjusted annualized rate in the second quarter, the third consecutive negative reading.

- Growth in the euro area declined to 1.2 percent at a seasonally adjusted annualized rate in the second quarter, after mild weather and consequent strong construction activity helped boost growth in the first quarter to 2.1 percent. Domestic demand, notably investment, decelerated in some of the larger euro area economies after successive quarters of stronger-than-expected growth. High-frequency data and corporate survey indicators for July point to a muted impact of the Brexit vote on confidence and activity thus far.

- In the United Kingdom, a strong start to the second quarter lifted GDP growth to 2.4 percent at a seasonally adjusted annualized rate (from 1.8 percent in the first quarter of 2016). A breakdown of high-frequency data within the quarter suggests that momentum had begun to weaken over May and June leading up to the referendum. Survey indicators for July and August point to a sharp post-referendum retrenchment in manufacturing activity followed by a rebound, while retail sales have held up so far.

- In Japan, growth decelerated in the second quarter to 0.7 percent at a seasonally adjusted annualized rate, from 2.1 percent in the first quarter. In part this reflects payback after an unusually strong first quarter, during which the outturn—particularly for consumer spending—was driven in part by leap-year effects. In addition, weaker external demand and corporate investment weighed on activity in the second quarter.

- Elsewhere, among advanced economies whose prospects are closely linked to systemic economies, momentum in Hong Kong Special Administrative Region and Taiwan Province of China improved in the second quarter as adverse financial and economic spillovers from China abated after the turbulence at the start of the year. Growth in Canada, by contrast, has been negatively affected by weaker-than-expected outcomes in the United States, compounding the setbacks stemming from one-off events such as the wildfires in Alberta.

Despite subdued activity in advanced economies and associated spillovers, emerging market and developing economies as a group recorded a slight pickup in momentum over the first half of 2016, broadly in line with the April 2016 WEO projection. Emerging Asia continued to register strong growth, and the situation improved slightly for stressed economies such as Brazil and Russia. Many economies in the Middle East and sub-Saharan Africa, however, continued to face challenging conditions.

- In emerging Asia, growth in China in the first half of the year stabilized close to the middle of the authorities' target range of 6½ –7 percent for 2016 on policy support and strong credit growth. Robust consumption and a further rotation in activity from industry to services indicate that rebalancing is progressing along the dimensions of internal demand and supply-side structure. India's economy continued to recover strongly, benefiting from a large improvement in the terms of trade, effective policy actions, and stronger external buffers, which have helped boost sentiment.

- In Latin America, Brazil's economy remains in recession, but activity appears to be close to bottoming out as the effects of past shocks—the decline in commodity prices, the administered-price adjustments of 2015, and political uncertainty—wear off.

- Russia's economy shows signs of stabilization as it is adjusting to the dual shock from oil prices and sanctions, and financial conditions eased after bank capital buffers were replenished with public funds. Macroeconomic performance elsewhere in emerging Europe was broadly stable, although the situation in Turkey became more uncertain in the aftermath of the attempted coup in July.

- Activity weakened in sub-Saharan Africa, led by Nigeria, where production was disrupted by shortages of foreign exchange, militant activity in the Niger Delta, and electricity blackouts. Momentum in South Africa was flat, despite the improvements in the external environment—notably stabilization in China. Elsewhere, resilience in Côte d'Ivoire, Kenya, Senegal, and Tanzania partially offset generally softer activity across the region.

- The Middle East continues to confront difficult challenges with subdued oil prices, the fallout from geopolitical tensions, and civil conflict in some countries.

Inflation Remains Low

In 2015, consumer price inflation in advanced economies was, at 0.3 percent, the lowest it had been since the global financial crisis. It edged up to about 0.5 percent in the first half of 2016 as the drag from oil prices diminished (Figure 1.2). Core consumer price inflation is higher than headline inflation but differs across major advanced economies. It averaged slightly above 2 percent in the first half of the year in the United States, which may reflect temporary factors or seasonality, while it was lower at about ¾ percent in the euro area and Japan. Inflation has held steady in emerging market and developing economies as exchange rates remained broadly stable—or appreciated—in many countries and the effects of past exchange rate depreciations began to fade.

A Partial Recovery in Commodity Prices

The IMF's Primary Commodities Price Index has increased by 22 percent since February 2016—that is, between the reference periods for the April 2016 and the current WEO report (Figure 1.3). The strongest price increases were for fuels, in particular for oil and coal:

- After hitting a 10-year low in January 2016, oil prices rallied by 50 percent, to $45 in August, mostly due to involuntary production outages that brought balance to the oil market.

- Natural gas prices are declining—the average price for Europe, Japan, and the United States is down by 6 percent since February 2016. The previous decline in oil prices, abundant natural gas production in Russia, and weak demand in Asia (particularly in Japan) have contributed to that decline. In the United States, natural gas prices have instead edged higher on account of stronger demand from the power sector, reflecting warmer-than-expected weather.

- Coal prices have rebounded, with the average of Australian and South African prices 32 percent higher than levels in February 2016.

Nonfuel commodity prices have also increased, with metals and agricultural commodity prices rising by 12 percent and 9 percent, respectively.

- Metal prices had been gradually declining because of a slowdown in and a shift away from commodity-intensive investment in China, but the recent stimulus has provided some support to prices.

Figure 1.2. Global Inflation

(Year-over-year percent change, unless noted otherwise)

Headline inflation inched up in advanced economies as the drag from lower commodity prices faded. In emerging market and developing economies, headline inflation has held steady as currencies remained broadly stable, or appreciated in some cases.

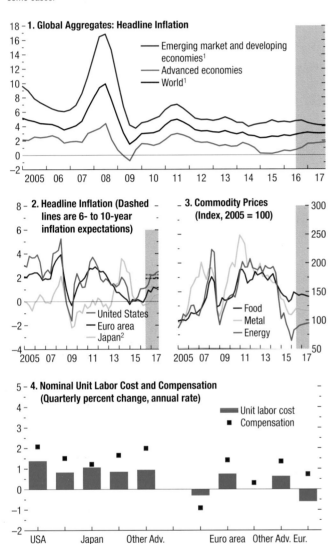

Sources: Consensus Economics; Haver Analytics; IMF, Primary Commodity Price System; and IMF staff estimates.
Note: Other Adv. = other advanced economies; Other Adv. Eur. = other advanced Europe; USA = United States.
[1]Excludes Venezuela.
[2]In Japan, the increase in inflation in 2014 reflects, to a large extent, the increase in the consumption tax.

Figure 1.3. Commodity and Oil Markets

Oil prices have rebounded from the 10-year low recorded in January 2016, due in large part to involuntary production shutdowns. Metal prices increased modestly in the first half of 2016 with slightly stronger demand from emerging market and developing economies, while food prices ticked up for most items, in large part due to adverse weather shocks.

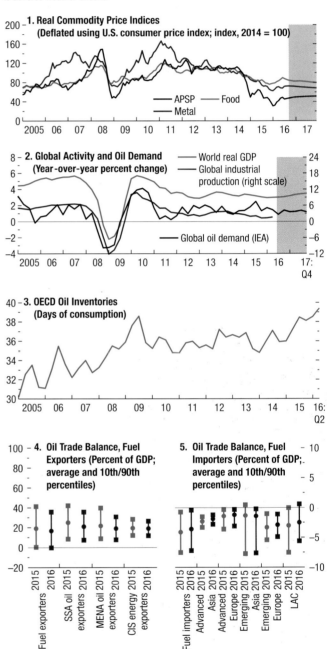

Sources: IMF, Primary Commodity Price System; International Energy Agency (IEA); Organisation for Economic Co-operation and Development (OECD); and IMF staff estimates.
Note: APSP = average petroleum spot price; CIS = Commonwealth of Independent States; LAC = Latin America and the Caribbean; MENA = Middle East and North Africa; SSA = sub-Saharan Africa.

- Among agricultural commodities, food prices rose by 7 percent, with increases in most items, except for a few such as corn and wheat. International prices have not fully reflected the adverse weather shock until recently, but El Niño and a potential La Niña have started to take a toll on international food markets. In addition, Brazil—a big food producer—has been experiencing a prolonged drought. Wheat prices have come down with the expectation of higher stocks following favorable production in the United States, the European Union, and Russia.

Exchange Rates and Capital Flows

Relative to the spring, the dollar and the euro remain broadly unchanged in real effective terms (Figure 1.4, first panel). The largest movements across the currencies of advanced economies as of the end of mid-September 2016 were the depreciation of the pound following Brexit (about 9 percent since the spring and over 10 percent since the June 23 referendum) and the appreciation of the Japanese yen (around 10 percent). Across emerging market currencies, the Chinese renminbi continued to depreciate gradually, by over 4 percent (Figure 1.4, panel 2). The currencies of commodity exporters—including the Brazilian real, the Russian ruble, and the South African rand—have generally appreciated, reflecting some recovery in commodity prices and a more general strengthening of financial market sentiment vis-à-vis emerging market economies, related in part to expectations of even lower interest rates in advanced economies.[1]

Capital flows to emerging market economies have recovered after the sharp downturn in the second half of 2015 and a weak start to 2016, on the back of the same factors supporting exchange rate valuations (Figure 1.5). In particular, purchases of shares in funds specializing in emerging market portfolio instruments have picked up (Figure 1.5, panel 1). Data from the few countries that have released full balance of payments data for the second quarter confirm an increase in capital inflows, especially in portfolio instruments. China has continued to experience capital outflows and some loss in foreign exchange reserves, but at

---

[1]Exceptions include the Mexican peso, which has weakened in recent weeks on U.S. electoral uncertainty, and especially the Nigerian naira, which depreciated sharply after the central bank initiated greater flexibility in the exchange rate in June.

Figure 1.4. Real Effective Exchange Rate Changes, March 2016–September 2016
(Percent)

Since March 2016 advanced economy currencies have remained mostly stable, or appreciated modestly, with the exception of the British pound (which depreciated sharply after the June 23 U.K. referendum vote to leave the European Union) and the Japanese yen (which has appreciated close to 10 percent). Currencies of commodity exporters have generally appreciated with the recovery in commodity prices.

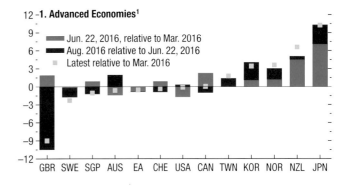

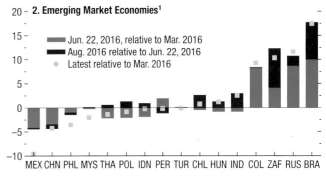

Source: IMF staff calculations.
Note: EA = euro area. Data labels in the figure use International Organization for Standardization (ISO) country codes.
[1]Latest data available are for September 16, 2016.

a much more modest pace than in the second half of 2015 and early 2016.

Monetary Policy and Financial Conditions

Asset prices and risk sentiment have generally recovered after the declines in the aftermath of the U.K. referendum (Figure 1.6). Equity prices reached record highs in the United States in August and picked up in other advanced economies as well. A notable exception are bank stocks, reflecting expectations of weakened future bank profitability, as interest rates are now expected to stay very low even longer, as well as balance sheet concerns in some countries

Figure 1.5. Emerging Market Economies: Capital Flows

Following a large decline in the second half of 2015 and early 2016, capital flows to emerging markets have recovered since February amid a growing sense in financial markets that advanced economy central banks will maintain accommodative monetary policy for even longer, the firming of commodity prices, and signs of stabilization in key emerging markets.

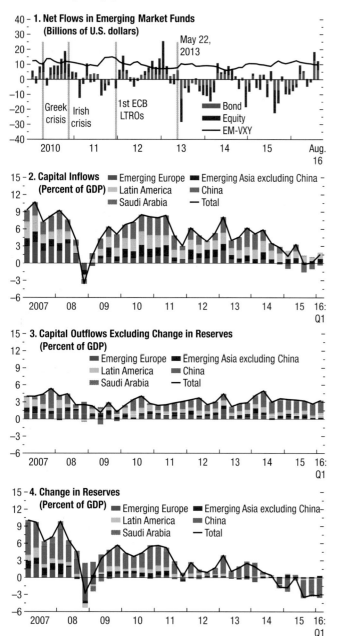

Sources: Bloomberg L.P.; EPFR Global; Haver Analytics; IMF, *International Financial Statistics;* and IMF staff calculations.
Note: Capital inflows are net purchases of domestic assets by nonresidents. Capital outflows are net purchases of foreign assets by domestic residents. Emerging Asia excluding China comprises India, Indonesia, Malaysia, the Philippines, and Thailand; emerging Europe comprises Poland, Romania, Russia, and Turkey; Latin America comprises Brazil, Chile, Colombia, Mexico, and Peru. ECB = European Central Bank; EM-VXY = J.P. Morgan Emerging Market Volatility Index; LTROs = longer-term refinancing operations.

with more vulnerable banking systems, such as Italy and Portugal.

In response to persistently weak inflation and lackluster data on economic activity, markets expect central banks in major advanced economies to remain dovish for longer than previously thought (Figure 1.6, panels 1 and 2). In particular, markets now expect only one further rate increase in the United States during 2016. The shift in expectations was particularly notable in the United Kingdom, where the Bank of England cut the policy rate, boosted quantitative easing, and undertook a number of other initiatives to support sentiment following the referendum. Term premiums have also compressed further, with long-term interest rates in advanced economies declining again (Figure 1.6, panel 3). As of late August, yields on 10-year U.S. and German government bonds had declined by 25 to 30 basis points since March, while the yields on U.K. 10-year gilts had declined by 90 basis points. Yields have increased modestly in September.

A large stock of advanced economy sovereign bonds is now trading at negative yields, as discussed in the October 2016 *Global Financial Stability Report* (GFSR). Meanwhile, credit to nonfinancial firms and households continues to expand (albeit at a decelerating pace) in the United States, and in the euro area as a whole (Figure 1.7).

Sentiment toward emerging market economies has generally improved, with a compression in spreads, declining long-term real interest rates, and a recovery in equity valuations (Figures 1.8 and 1.9). A number of emerging markets have eased monetary policy rates since the spring, including several economies in Asia where inflation has been muted (notably Indonesia and Malaysia) as well as Russia and Turkey. Exceptions to this trend are Mexico, where the policy rate was raised by 50 basis points after the exchange rate came under pressure immediately following the Brexit vote, and Colombia and South Africa, where policy rates were raised in order to keep inflation expectations around target.

Forces Weighing on the Outlook

Economic growth in recent years has fallen short of expectations in both advanced and emerging market economies. As the world economy moves further away from the global financial crisis, the factors affecting global economic performance are becoming more complex. They reflect a combination of global forces—demographic trends, a persistent decline in produc-

Figure 1.6. Advanced Economies: Monetary and Financial Market Conditions

(Percent, unless noted otherwise)

Markets expect advanced economy central banks to maintain low rates for even longer as economic activity has stayed sluggish and inflation pressures remain muted. Financial market sentiment has generally recovered after the initial short-lived negative reaction to the June 23 U.K. referendum vote to leave the European Union.

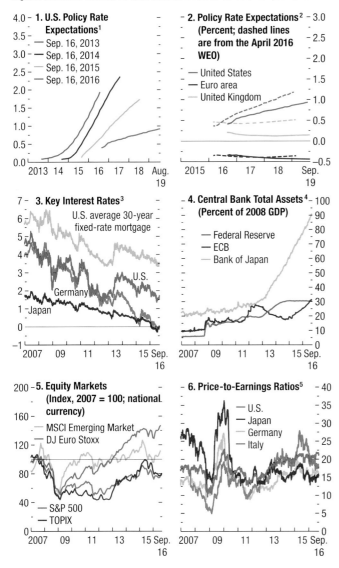

Figure 1.7. Advanced Economies: Credit, House Prices, and Balance Sheets

Credit to nonfinancial firms and households continues to grow in the United States and the euro area as a whole. Household net worth has generally continued to improve as a share of disposable income in Japan and the euro area, while stabilizing in the United States.

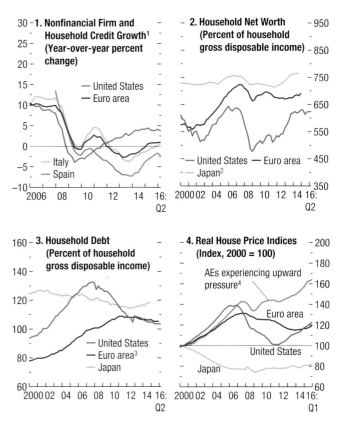

Sources: Bank of England; Bank of Spain; Bloomberg L.P.; European Central Bank (ECB); Haver Analytics; Organisation for Economic Co-operation and Development; and IMF staff calculations.
[1] Flow-of-funds data are used for the euro area, Spain, and the United States. Italian bank loans to Italian residents are corrected for securitizations.
[2] Interpolated from annual net worth as a percentage of disposable income.
[3] Includes subsector employers (including self-employed workers).
[4] Upward-pressure countries are those with a residential real estate vulnerability index above the median for advanced economies (AEs): Australia, Austria, Belgium, Canada, Denmark, France, Hong Kong SAR, Israel, Korea, Luxembourg, New Zealand, Norway, Portugal, Spain, Sweden, and the United Kingdom.

Sources: Bank of Spain; Bloomberg L.P.; Haver Analytics; Thomson Reuters Datastream; and IMF staff calculations.
Note: DJ = Dow Jones; ECB = European Central Bank; MSCI = Morgan Stanley Capital International; S&P = Standard & Poor's; TOPIX = Tokyo Stock Price Index; WEO = *World Economic Outlook*.
[1] Expectations are based on the federal funds rate futures.
[2] Expectations are based on the federal funds rate futures for the United States, the sterling overnight interbank average rate for the United Kingdom, and the euro interbank offered forward rate for the euro area. Current data are for September 16, 2016; April 2016 WEO data are for March 24, 2016.
[3] Interest rates are 10-year government bond yields, unless noted otherwise. Data are through September 16, 2016.
[4] Data are through September 16, 2016. ECB calculations are based on the Eurosystem's weekly financial statement.
[5] Data are through September 16, 2016.

Figure 1.8. Emerging Market Economies: Interest Rates

Financial conditions in emerging market economies have eased since February with expectations of a more persistent dovish monetary policy stance in advanced economies, an uptick in commodity prices, and signs of stabilization in emerging market economies currently in recession. Sovereign yields have declined and spreads have narrowed.

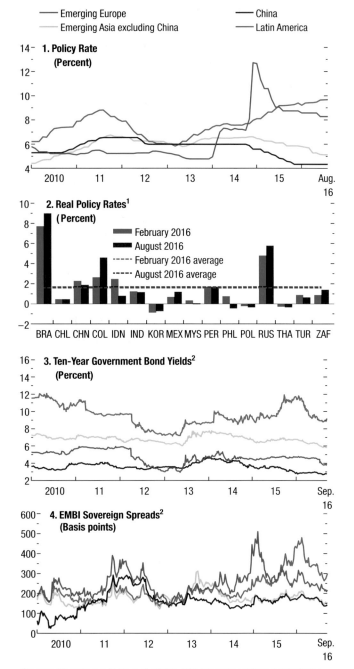

Figure 1.9. Emerging Market Economies: Equity Markets and Credit

Equity prices have generally firmed up in recent months, reflecting improvements in the operating environment for corporates in emerging market economies with the pickup in commodity prices and lower borrowing costs. Vulnerabilities, however, continue to accumulate in some cases as the credit-to-GDP ratio remains on an upward path.

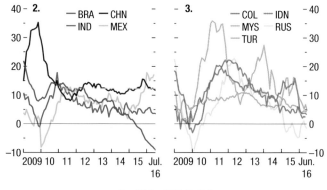

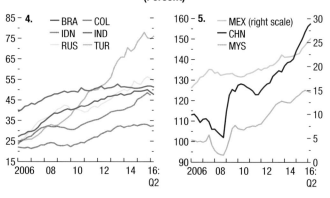

Sources: Bloomberg L.P.; Haver Analytics; IMF, *International Financial Statistics;* and IMF staff calculations.
Note: Emerging Asia excluding China comprises India, Indonesia, Malaysia, the Philippines, and Thailand; emerging Europe comprises Poland, Romania, Russia, and Turkey; Latin America comprises Brazil, Chile, Colombia, Mexico, and Peru. EMBI = J.P. Morgan Emerging Markets Bond Index. Data labels in the figure use International Organization for Standardization (ISO) country codes.
[1]Deflated by two-year-ahead *World Economic Outlook* inflation projections.
[2]Data are through September 16, 2016.

Sources: Bloomberg, L.P.; Haver Analytics; IMF, International Financial Statistics (IFS) database; and IMF staff calculations.
Note: Data labels in the figure use International Organization for Standardization (ISO) country codes.
[1]Credit is other depository corporations' claims on the private sector (from IFS), except in the case of Brazil, for which private sector credit is from the Monetary Policy and Financial System Credit Operations published by Banco Central do Brasil.

tivity growth, the adjustment to lower commodity prices—and shocks driven by domestic and regional factors. These are discussed in turn for advanced and emerging market and developing economies.

Advanced Economies

Advanced economies were at the epicenter of the global financial crisis. Eight years after the collapse of Lehman Brothers, significant progress has been made in repairing the macroeconomic damage from the crisis. But the progress is uneven, and the crisis scars still quite visible, especially in some countries. The first panel of Figure 1.10 documents deviations of main macroeconomic aggregates from their precrisis *trends* (based on the 1996–2005 period) and precrisis *levels*. For selected euro area countries more severely affected by the crisis, GDP and especially domestic demand and investment remain in 2016 well below their precrisis levels, and even more distant from their precrisis trends. As noted in the October 2016 GFSR, many banks in the euro area continue to struggle with a high volume of impaired assets, which has potentially held back lending and suppressed investment. In other advanced economies demand, GDP, and investment are generally above precrisis levels, but still well below precrisis trends.

Relative to the depth of the crisis, progress is more visible in output gaps (Figure 1.10, panel 2). Output gaps remain negative virtually across the board, a clear symptom of weak global demand, but economic slack has declined substantially since its postcrisis peak.[2] The extent of progress—and of cross-country heterogeneity—is also evident in the behavior of unemployment, which has declined sizably since its peak but remains higher than its precrisis level in most countries. For the aggregate of advanced economies, the unemployment rate is less than 1 percentage point above its 2007 level. In some countries (such as the United States) the decline in unemployment to precrisis levels somewhat overstates the recovery in employment, given the decline in labor force participation. This has not, however, been the case in other advanced economies, where in many cases participation rates are above precrisis levels (Figure 1.10, panel 4).

This uneven progress in macroeconomic repair across advanced economies is overlaid on underlying trends related to population aging and weaker productivity growth. The combination of these deeper factors may have contributed to diminished expectations of future potential output growth and profitability and to weak current demand and a lower equilibrium real interest rate. Lower equilibrium rates, in turn, limit the extent to which low policy rates can stimulate demand.

Other factors have also played a role in shaping prospects for advanced economies. One example is the slowdown and rebalancing in China, discussed further below and in Chapter 4, which implies more modest growth in demand for advanced economies' exports. This slowdown, together with the weakening in the growth rate of global trade discussed in Chapter 2, had a notable impact on prospects for advanced Asian economies (Hong Kong SAR, Korea, Singapore, Taiwan Province of China) that are very open and have strong trade ties to China. Also at play is the decline in commodity prices, which, as discussed more extensively in Chapter 1 of the April 2016 WEO, implies windfall gains for most advanced economies but sizable losses in disposable income for commodity exporters such as Australia, Canada, and Norway.

Demographic Trends and Migration

With low fertility rates, population growth in advanced economies has declined over the past decade and is projected to decline further over the next five years and beyond (Figure 1.11, panel 1).[3] Slowing population growth has been accompanied by aging—the working-age population (between the ages of 15 and 64) is projected to decline over the next five years (Figure 1.11, panel 2). These trends are common to "old" advanced economies (considered advanced since at least the mid-1990s) but also to "new" advanced economies,[4] which are actually experiencing a faster and sharper demographic transition. In addition, the share of workers ages 55 to 64 has increased sizably in advanced economies over the past two decades (Figure 1.11, panel 3). Population aging is set to increase pressure on pension and health care systems

---

[2]Downward revisions to potential growth and reassessment of precrisis potential output imply estimated negative output gaps that are much smaller in absolute terms than a comparison of pre- and postcrisis growth outcomes would suggest.

[3]The decline has been more moderate than demographic projections suggested a decade ago, given the strong increase in immigration.

[4]These include the Baltic countries (Estonia, Latvia, Lithuania), Cyprus, the Czech Republic, Hong Kong S.A.R., Israel, Korea, Macao S.A.R., Puerto Rico, San Marino, Singapore, the Slovak Republic, and Slovenia.

Figure 1.10. Domestic Demand, Output Gap, Unemployment, and Labor Force Participation in Advanced Economies

In advanced economies, uneven progress has been made in repairing the macroeconomic damage from the global financial crisis. Domestic demand and investment are still below precrisis levels in some euro area countries. Economic slack and unemployment rates have fallen from their postcrisis peaks, but remain high in a few cases.

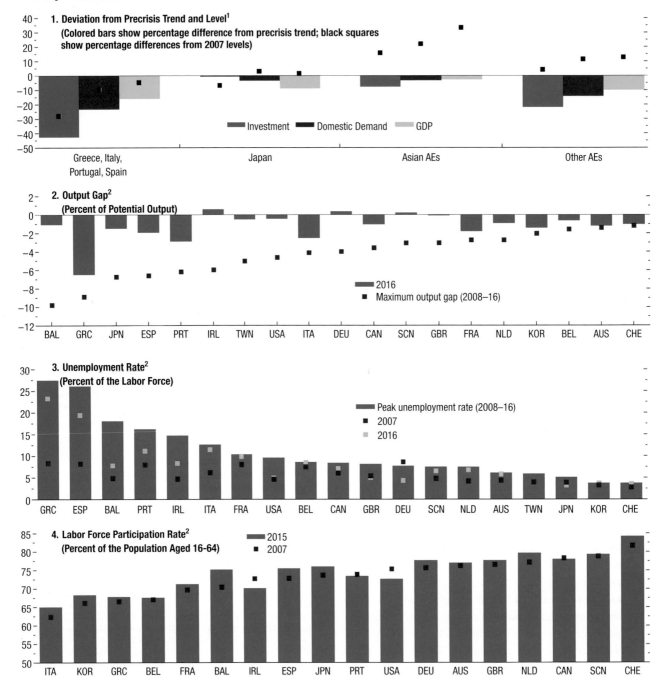

Sources: Organisation for Economic Co-operation and Development labor statistics; and IMF staff estimates.
[1]Investment, domestic demand, and GDP are in real terms. For all countries except Japan, precrisis trends are linear regression trends fitted for each variable using data for 1996–2005. For Japan, trends are fitted for 2001–05 given the sharp drop in investment in 1997–98. Asian AEs = Australia, Hong Kong SAR, Korea, Macao SAR, New Zealand, Singapore, Taiwan Province of China; Other AEs = Austria, Belgium, Canada, Cyprus, Czech Republic, Denmark, Estonia, Finland, France, Germany, Iceland, Israel, Latvia, Lithuania, Luxembourg, Malta, Netherlands, New Zealand, Norway, San Marino, Slovak Republic, Slovenia, Sweden, Switzerland, United Kingdom, United States.
[2]BAL = Estonia, Latvia, Lithuania; SCN = Denmark, Finland, Iceland, Norway, Sweden. Other labels in the figure use International Organization for Standardization (ISO) country codes.

and worsen debt dynamics, especially as the workforce starts to shrink.

Migration from emerging market and developing economies over the past few decades has alleviated the impact of aging on the labor force in advanced economies, as discussed in more detail in Chapter 4. The share of migrants in the advanced-economy population almost doubled from 6 to 11 percent between 1990 and 2015. As the majority of migrants tend to be of working age, migration contributed about half of the increase in the working-age population between 1990 and 2010.

Receiving migrants, however, also creates challenges for advanced economies, especially in a context of weak economic growth. Concerns about the impact on wages and possible displacement of native workers and short-term fiscal costs can potentially add to social tensions. These concerns can in turn spur a political backlash, as demonstrated by the current U.S. presidential election campaign and the campaign preceding the Brexit vote in the United Kingdom. However, once integrated into the labor force, migrants tend to benefit recipient economies. Previous studies find positive long-term effects of immigration on per capita income and labor productivity and little impact on the employment rates and wages of native workers. A number of studies do, however, find negative effects on lower-wage groups. Immigrants can help alleviate the fiscal challenges of aging societies by reducing dependency ratios (and accordingly, the burden of health care and social security spending), even if they weigh on fiscal balances in the short run.

More recently, the civil war in Syria and unrest throughout the Middle East have led to a resurgence of refugees in advanced economies, particularly in Europe, boosting the refugees' share in global migration flows to about 50 percent in 2014–15. Efficient and swift integration of refugees into the local workforce will be crucial for unlocking the potential net benefits of these inflows in recipient economies. Gainful employment opportunities for refugees would also help reduce potential social tensions and meet the humanitarian challenge of absorbing traumatized populations.

Weak Productivity Growth and Low Interest Rates

A second important trend—with much more uncertainty surrounding its causes and likely persistence—is weak productivity growth. For instance, the October 2015 WEO documented that labor

Figure 1.11. Demographics

The growth rates of total population and of the working-age population have declined, notably in advanced economies. The share of older workers has been on a steady upward trend in advanced economies for close to two decades. A similar pattern has formed in emerging market and developing economies in the past 10 years, although the share of older workers remains below that in advanced economies.

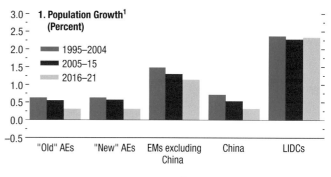
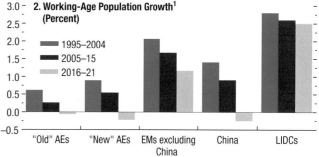
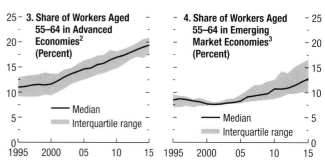

Sources: United Nations Population and Development database; and IMF staff estimates.
Note: Calculations were performed using a weighted average based on population shares; LIDCs = low-income developing countries.
[1] Working-age population is defined here as the number of people aged between 15 and 64. "Old" AEs = countries considered advanced economies in 1996, comprising Australia, Austria, Belgium, Canada, Denmark, Finland, France, Germany, Greece, Iceland, Ireland, Italy, Japan, Luxembourg, Netherlands, New Zealand, Norway, Portugal, Spain, Sweden, Switzerland, United Kingdom, and United States. "New" AEs = Cyprus, Czech Republic, Estonia, Hong Kong SAR, Israel, Korea, Latvia, Lithuania, Macao SAR, Malta, Singapore, Slovak Republic, Slovenia.
[2] Advanced Economies (AEs) = Australia, Austria, Belgium, Canada, Czech Republic, Denmark, Estonia, Finland, France, Germany, Greece, Iceland, Ireland, Israel, Italy, Japan, South Korea, Latvia, Lithuania, Luxembourg, Netherlands, New Zealand, Norway, Portugal, Slovak Republic, Slovenia, Spain, Sweden, Switzerland, United Kingdom, United States.
[3] Emerging Market Economies (EMs) = Brazil, Chile, China, Colombia, Costa Rica, Hungary, India, Indonesia, Mexico, Poland, Russia, South Africa, Turkey.

Figure 1.12. Advanced Economies: Growth, Investment, and Employment in Recent WEO Vintages

In advanced economies, GDP and investment have in recent years grown more slowly than projected, whereas employment has grown faster, pointing to weaker-than-expected labor productivity growth. Persistent weakness in productivity growth has contributed to lower estimates of potential growth. Long-term interest rates are also expected to be lower than previously projected, reflecting a possible decline in the real interest rate and weaker inflation forecasts.

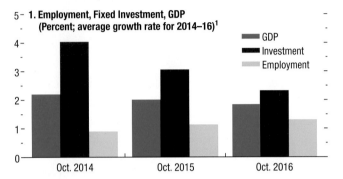

1. Employment, Fixed Investment, GDP
   (Percent; average growth rate for 2014–16)[1]

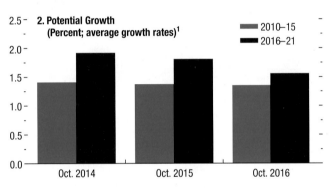

2. Potential Growth
   (Percent; average growth rates)[1]

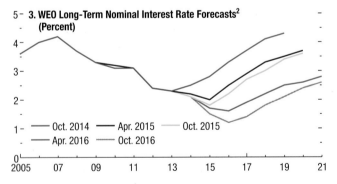

3. WEO Long-Term Nominal Interest Rate Forecasts[2]
   (Percent)

Source: IMF staff estimates.
[1]Simple averages of annual growth rates calculated for each respective *World Economic Outlook* (WEO) forecast vintage.
[2]Weighted average of long-term nominal interest rates for advanced economies using a three-year moving average of GDP in U.S. dollars as weights.

productivity growth for the 2008–14 period had been below precrisis trends for all but one of a sample of some 30 advanced economies. The causes for the productivity slowdown remain uncertain. It may partly reflect crisis legacies and prolonged weak investment, as well as the exhaustion of productivity gains from the information and communications technology revolution, as discussed in detail by Fernald (2015) and Gordon (2015) for the United States. Productivity measurement issues are severe for some parts of the economy, but recent research suggests that they are unlikely to account for a sizable part of the slowdown (Byrne, Fernald, and Reinsdorf 2016; Syverson 2016).

Disappointing productivity growth was a main factor behind what proved to be overoptimism in growth forecasts for advanced economies in the period after the crisis.[5] These forecasts generally projected productivity growth to return to rates close to those prevailing before the crisis. Even though projections for output and productivity growth have been gradually revised downward since 2011, growth in advanced economies has continued to disappoint even relative to the diminished forecasts. For instance, during 2014–16 it has been weaker than projected in the October 2014 WEO (about 0.4 percentage point a year) and subsequent WEOs (Figure 1.12, panel 1, blue bars), despite the sizable favorable terms-of-trade shock associated with the decline in commodity prices. The weakness in growth relative to past forecasts, which is common across advanced economies and regions, was accompanied by fixed investment falling short of expectations, especially in the United States, commodity exporters, and advanced Asian economies (panel 1, maroon bars). In contrast, employment growth (panel 1, yellow bars) has generally been stronger than expected (almost ½ percentage point), and unemployment in many countries is lower than predicted in earlier forecasts. These findings point again to weaker labor productivity growth—and the lion's share of the downward revisions to labor productivity growth estimates reflects lower-than-expected growth in total factor productivity.

The protracted weakness in total factor productivity growth has led to further downward revisions to potential growth over the medium term (Figure 1.12,

[5]Overoptimism in postcrisis growth forecasts was discussed in Box 1.2 of the October 2014 WEO.

panel 2), which compound the decline due to the demographic factors highlighted earlier in the chapter. Both demographics and expectations of lower future growth in productivity (and hence disposable income) are putting downward pressure on investment rates today, as lower investment is required to maintain a stable capital-output ratio. But feedback mechanisms may be at play as well—expectations of weak future demand growth that hinder investment can take a toll on future potential output both directly (through lower installed productive capacity) and indirectly (through weaker total factor productivity growth, to the extent that new technologies are embodied in capital).

Another salient feature of the change in the outlook for advanced economies is the very sharp decline in the levels and expected path of policy rates (Figure 1.6, panels 1 and 2) and especially long-term interest rates (Figure 1.12, panel 3). As discussed further in the October 2016 GFSR, the decline in long-term interest rates reflects both expectations of lower future short-term rates and a further compression in the term premium (Hördahl, Sobrun, and Turner 2016). Inflation forecasts have also come down, as discussed further in Chapter 3; however, the lion's share of the decline in interest rates reflects a decline in real rates. Estimates of the natural rate of interest—defined as the interest rate at which the economy would operate at full employment without inflationary pressures—have declined substantially (see, for instance, Laubach and Williams 2015; and Pescatori and Turunen 2015).

On a conceptual note, a persistent decline in productivity growth reduces the rate of return on capital and results in a lower real interest rate. As discussed in Chapter 3 of the April 2014 WEO, lower long-term interest rates are driven in part by demographic factors (since demand for investment falls as growth in the workforce declines) and an increase in desired saving following the global financial crisis. An increase in demand for safe assets is an additional factor putting downward pressure on long-term government bond yields. This increase is driven by higher risk aversion in the wake of the global financial crisis, in part related to financial regulatory changes, central bank purchases of long-term government bonds, and increased demand for safe fixed-income assets stemming from demographic factors. While there is uncertainty regarding the evolution of some of these factors, those related to demographics and arguably to financial regulation

are likely to be very persistent, which implies that the natural rate of interest may well stay compressed over the medium term.

An implication of the decline in the natural interest rate is that the extent of monetary accommodation provided by record-low policy rates may actually be lower than previously thought. To the extent that the decline is persistent, this would have significant bearing on the stabilization role of monetary policy and on appropriate monetary policy frameworks more generally.[6]

Emerging Market and Developing Economies

The growth rates of emerging market and developing economies have been even more varied than those of advanced economies, and prospects remain diverse across countries and regions. Indeed, while fast growth in countries such as China and India has sustained global growth, deep recessions in a handful of emerging market and developing economies have implied a particularly strong drag on global activity over 2015 and 2016 (see Box 1.1). Factors that have shaped the growth rates of this country group include the generalized slowdown in advanced economies, discussed earlier in this section; rebalancing in China; the adjustment to lower commodity prices; an uncertain external environment, with sizable changes in risk sentiment over time; and geopolitical tension and strife in several countries and regions. Longer-term issues include an important demographic transition, especially in emerging market economies, as well as prospects for export diversification and convergence.

The Rebalancing in China and Its Cross-Border Implications

China's transition to a more consumption- and service-based economy continues to influence other emerging market economies, notably commodity producers and countries exposed to China's manufacturing sector. As previously noted (see, for example, the IMF's 2016 Asia and Pacific *Regional Economic Outlook*), spillovers to global trade and growth from China's rebalancing and gradual slowdown have been significant—not surprising given that as of 2015 China's GDP at market exchange rates exceeded the aggregate GDP of the next 12 largest emerging market and developing economies combined.

[6]See Williams 2016 for a recent discussion.

But developments in China increasingly affect a wider range of emerging market economies through financial sentiment and cross-border contagion (as explored in detail in the Spillover Chapter in this report). As seen in the emerging market sell-off episodes of August 2015 and January 2016, the spikes in risk aversion vis-à-vis emerging markets coincided with policy-induced shifts in China's exchange rate that raised questions for investors about China's policy objectives and the underlying strength of its economy. As a corollary, greater clarity on policy objectives and more transparent communication by key policymakers in China in recent months have helped stabilize near-term sentiment regarding China and, by extension, toward emerging markets exposed to China. Nevertheless, the medium-term outlook for China remains clouded by the high stock of corporate debt—a large fraction of which is considered at risk (see the analysis in the April 2016 GFSR). And vulnerabilities continue to accumulate with the economy's rising dependence on credit, which complicates the difficult task of rebalancing the economy across multiple fronts (shifting from investment to consumption; switching from industry to services; reining in credit—see the IMF 2016 China Article IV Staff Report and Selected Issues Papers). In light of these factors, external financial conditions and the outlook for emerging market and developing economies will continue to be shaped to a significant extent by market perceptions of China's prospects for successfully restructuring and rebalancing its economy.

Adjustment to Lower Commodity Prices

The adjustment to lower commodity prices in commodity exporters continues. The macroeconomic implications of the terms-of-trade shock were discussed in detail in Chapter 2 of the October 2015 WEO. The April 2016 WEO showed the extent of cross-border income redistribution arising from terms-of-trade fluctuations and its strong correlation with macroeconomic outcomes. Figure 1.13 provides an update to the size of the windfall income gains and losses in the largest emerging market and developing economies as a result of changes in commodity prices, in light of the revised baseline for such prices.[7] The figure clearly illustrates the extent

of the income losses in 2015, concentrated in oil exporters. The forecasts for windfall gains and losses in 2016–17 are much smaller than those for 2015 and have declined since the spring with the modest strengthening in commodity prices. At the same time, these are gains and losses *relative to the previous year*, so they imply a further decline in income in countries already severely affected by the previous year's shock. The "acute" phase of the shock might be over for several commodity exporters (especially those where exchange rates adjusted), but further adjustments lie ahead, particularly in the fiscal sphere, which implies a subdued outlook for domestic demand, and notably for investment, given the high capital intensity of extractive industries.

The link between commodity prices and exchange rate movements since the spring of this year is illustrated in the third panel of Figure 1.13. The panel shows that real effective exchange rate movements between March 2016 and July 2016 are positively correlated with changes in the forecast of income gains and losses over 2016 and 2017 resulting from changes in the terms of trade (the difference between the yellow dots and red diamonds in panels 1 and 2). But commodity price changes have been much less dramatic than those during 2014–15. As a result, the exchange rate responses have generally been more muted than those seen over the previous year.

Demographics and Convergence

As Figure 1.11 shows, many emerging market economies are also experiencing a demographic transition, with a decline in population growth rates that is even sharper for the working-age population than for the population overall. The transition is particularly rapid for China, where the population growth rate over the next five years is expected to decline to ¼ percent (from ½ percent in the past decade). Even more dramatic is the decline in the growth rate of China's working-age population, which is projected to turn negative over the next five years.[8] In low-income countries, population growth rates remain much higher—over double the rate for emerging economies

---

$\left(\Delta p_t^A x_{t-1} - \Delta p_t^B m_{t-1} \right) / Y_{t-1}$, in which Δp_t^A and Δp_t^B are the percentage changes in the prices of A and B between year $t-1$ and year t, and Y is GDP in year $t-1$ in U.S. dollars. See also Gruss 2014.

[8]By contrast, demographic trends in India are relatively more favorable, and the working-age ratio is projected to increase in the decades ahead (Aiyar and Mody 2011).

[7]The windfall is an estimate of the change in disposable income arising from commodity price changes. The windfall gain in year t for a country exporting x U.S. dollars of commodity A and importing m U.S. dollars of commodity B in year $t-1$ is defined as

Figure 1.13. Emerging Markets: Terms-of-Trade Windfall Gains and Losses and Real Exchange Rates

With the recent stabilization and strengthening in commodity prices, terms-of-trade windfall gains and losses in 2016–17 are expected to be smaller than those registered in 2015. Exchange rate adjustments over recent months have been positively correlated with changes in expected terms-of-trade windfall gains and losses for 2016–17.

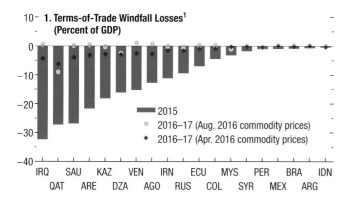

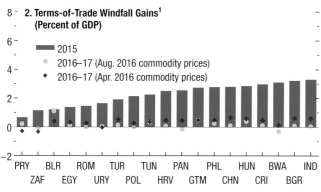

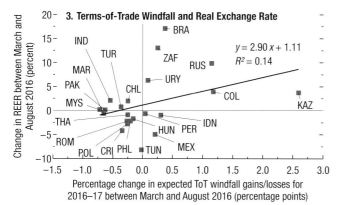

Source: IMF staff estimates.
Note: REER = real effective exchange rate; ToT = terms of trade. Data labels in the figure use International Organization for Standardization (ISO) country codes.
[1]Gains (losses) for 2016–17 are simple averages of annual incremental gains (losses) for 2016 and 2017. For details of the calculations see footnote 7 in the chapter text.

Figure 1.14. Real per Capita Growth Rates and Convergence (1995–2020)

Emerging market economies and low-income countries narrowed the income gap relative to advanced economies at a much faster pace over 2005–15 than during the preceding decade, but the average pace of convergence is expected to be lower over the next five years.

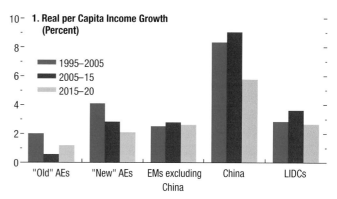

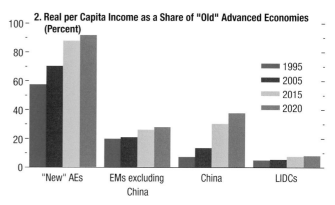

Source: IMF staff estimates.
Note: LIDCs = low-income developing countries.
[1]"Old"AEs = only countries considered advanced economies in 1996, comprising Australia, Austria, Belgium, Canada, Denmark, Finland, France, Germany, Greece, Iceland, Ireland, Italy, Japan, Luxembourg, Netherlands, New Zealand, Norway, Portugal, Spain, Sweden, Switzerland, United Kingdom, and United States. "New" AEs = Cyprus, Czech Republic, Estonia, Hong Kong SAR, Israel, Korea, Latvia, Lithuania, Macao SAR, Malta, Singapore, Slovak Republic, Slovenia, Taiwan Province of China.

excluding China.[9] This variation across countries, regions, and levels of development must be taken into account when translating GDP growth rates into assessments of the evolution of income per capita or per worker and convergence of incomes toward advanced economy levels.

Figure 1.14 looks at growth in income per capita across these same country groups. Real income per capita in the group overall increased by 50 percent between 2005 and 2015, with gains spread unevenly: it surged by almost 140 percent in China and increased by about 45 percent in low-income developing economies and by about 30 percent in other emerging market economies. Over this time period, real per capita income in the "older" advanced economies—economies classified as advanced since at least the mid-1990s—increased by only about 5 percent. As a result of their growth advantage, the developing parts of the world narrowed the income gap relative to advanced economies over the 10 years through 2015: real per capita income went from about 13 percent to 30 percent of those of "older" advanced economy levels in China, from 21 percent to 26 percent in other emerging market economies, and from 6 percent to 8 percent in low-income developing economies. For all three groups, these gains were three to five times larger than those in the prior decade, between 1995 and 2005.

Looking ahead, the per capita growth differential for most emerging market and developing economies relative to the advanced economies is projected to stay well below that of the past decade, and the pace of convergence will become more uneven. Over the next five years, low-income developing economies—many of which are experiencing a stark slowdown in output growth yet have very high population growth rates—are expected to close the gap between their and advanced economy income levels by barely more than half a percentage point, other emerging market economies by only 2 percentage points, and China by a still strong 7 percentage points. The new advanced economies, which have maintained remarkably high growth over the past decade despite starting from a relatively high level of per capita income (about 70 percent of that of old advanced economy incomes in 2005) are

projected to further reduce their gap with advanced economy levels by about 4 percentage points, following a gain of 17 percentage points in the previous decade.

The Forecast

Policy Assumptions

Fiscal policy is projected to provide mild support to economic activity in advanced economies as a whole in 2016, slightly more than projected in the April 2016 WEO (Figure 1.15). The fiscal policy stance (measured by the fiscal impulse)[10] is forecast to be expansionary in Canada (over 1 percentage point) and Germany (0.8 percentage point) and to a lesser extent in Italy and the United States (½ percentage point). It is forecast to be broadly neutral in Japan and contractionary in the United Kingdom (0.8 percentage point). In emerging market and developing economies, structural government balances are in the aggregate projected to remain broadly unchanged for 2016—but with marked differences across countries and regions.

Monetary policy in advanced economies is expected to tighten more slowly than envisioned in the April 2016 WEO. The policy rate in the United States is projected to rise gradually but steadily, reaching a long-term equilibrium rate of 2¾ percent by 2020—much lower than before the crisis. Very low policy interest rates are expected to remain in place for longer in the United Kingdom, the euro area, and Japan, with short-term rates projected to remain below zero in the euro area and Japan through 2020. The monetary policy assumptions underlying the forecasts for emerging market economies vary, given the different circumstances these economies are facing.

Other Assumptions

The baseline global growth forecasts for 2016 and 2017 reflect broadly accommodative financial conditions, a partial recovery in commodity prices, and an easing in geopolitical tensions in 2017 and beyond. Arrangements between the European Union and the United Kingdom are assumed to settle so as to avoid a large increase in economic barriers, and the political fallout from Brexit is assumed to be limited. The process of monetary policy normalization in the United

---

[9]Sub-Saharan Africa, in particular, will see a continued pronounced increase in the share of the working-age population in the next few decades (see Chapter 2 of the IMF's sub-Saharan Africa 2015 *Regional Economic Outlook*).

[10]The fiscal impulse is defined as minus the change in the ratio of the structural fiscal balance to potential output.

States is expected to proceed smoothly, without protracted increases in financial market volatility or sharp movements in long-term interest rates. Financial conditions in emerging markets are forecast to be slightly more accommodative than assumed in the April 2016 WEO, in light of the partial decline in interest rate spreads and the recovery in equity prices in recent months (Figure 1.8). Oil prices are expected to increase gradually over the forecast horizon, from an average of $43 a barrel in 2016 to $51 a barrel in 2017. As in the April 2016 WEO forecast, geopolitical tensions in some countries in the Middle East are assumed to remain elevated for the remainder of the year, before easing in 2017, allowing for a gradual economic recovery in the most severely affected economies.

Global Outlook for 2016 and 2017

Global growth is projected to remain modest at 3.1 percent in 2016, slightly weaker than projected in the April 2016 WEO (Table 1.1). This forecast incorporates somewhat weaker-than-expected activity through the second quarter of 2016 in advanced economies, as well as the implications of the U.K. referendum outcome in favor of leaving the European Union. The recovery is expected to gather some pace in 2017 and beyond, driven primarily by emerging market and developing economies, as conditions in stressed economies gradually normalize.

Growth in emerging market and developing economies is expected to strengthen in 2016 to 4.2 percent after five consecutive years of decline, accounting for over three-quarters of projected world growth in 2016. However, despite an improvement in external financing conditions, their outlook is uneven and generally weaker than in the past. A combination of factors can account for this weakness: a slowdown in China, whose spillovers are magnified by its lower reliance on import- and resource-intensive investment; continued adjustment to structurally lower commodity revenues in a number of commodity exporters; spillovers from persistently weak demand from advanced economies; and domestic strife, political discord, and geopolitical tensions in a number of countries.

In major advanced economies, the recovery is forecast to slow this year, with growth projected at 1.6 percent in 2016, ½ percentage point lower than in 2015. Their subdued outlook is shaped by a number of common forces, including legacies of the global financial crisis (high debt—as discussed in the Octo-

Figure 1.15. Fiscal Indicators
(Percent of GDP, unless noted otherwise)

Fiscal policy is projected to be mildly expansionary in 2016 in advanced economies in the aggregate, and broadly neutral for emerging market and developing economies as a whole, but with differences across countries.

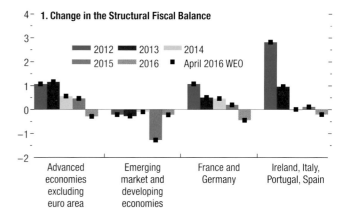

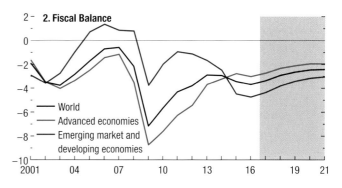

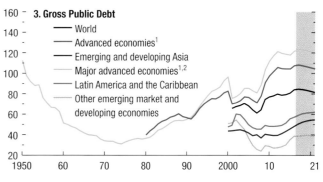

Source: IMF staff estimates.
Note: WEO = *World Economic Outlook.*
[1]Data through 2000 exclude the United States.
[2]Canada, France, Germany, Italy, Japan, United Kingdom, United States.

ber 2016 *Fiscal Monitor*; financial sector vulnerabilities, as described in the October 2016 GFSR; and low investment) and low productivity growth, as discussed previously in this chapter. Economic, political, and institutional uncertainty following the Brexit vote is also expected to have some negative macroeconomic consequences, especially in advanced European economies.

The projected increase in global growth in 2017 to 3.4 percent hinges crucially on rising growth in emerging market and developing economies, where the waning of downward pressures on activity in countries in recession in 2016 such as Brazil, Nigeria, and Russia is expected to more than make up for the steady slowdown in growth in China. In advanced economies, growth is projected to pick up modestly to 1.8 percent (0.2 percentage point less than in the April 2016 WEO), reflecting primarily a strengthening of the recovery in the United States and Canada and a rebound in Japan due to the recent fiscal stimulus. In contrast, growth is projected to be lower in the euro area and the United Kingdom, due to the macroeconomic repercussions of heightened uncertainty in the aftermath of the U.K. referendum.

As discussed elsewhere in the chapter, the sluggish global growth outlook implies a waning pace of improvement in global living standards. This trend can be illustrated by the distribution of world population by per capita growth rates. With the growth rates of emerging market and developing economies projected to remain well below those over the past decade, the share of the world population living in areas with greater than 2 percent annual real per capita growth is set to decline by almost 10 percentage points between 2005–10 and 2016–21.

Global Outlook for the Medium Term

Beyond 2017, global growth is projected to gradually increase to 3.8 percent by the end of the forecast horizon. This recovery in global activity—which is expected to be driven entirely by emerging market and developing economies—is premised on the normalization of growth rates in countries and regions under stress or growing well below potential in 2016–17 (such as Nigeria, Russia, South Africa, Latin America, parts of the Middle East), China maintaining its transition toward consumption- and services-based growth, and continued resilience in other countries. It also reflects the increasing weight in the world economy of

large emerging market economies, such as China and India, that are growing well above the world average. As shown in Box 1.1, these two factors account for the bulk of the projected pickup in world growth. The pace of economic activity in advanced economies is projected to remain subdued in line with their diminished potential, as populations age, but growth in GDP per worker is projected to reach levels broadly in line with its average over the past 20 years. Within the group of emerging market and developing economies, growth is projected to pick up over the medium term in low-income developing countries but to remain below the pace of the past decade, both in absolute and in per capita terms.

Economic Outlook for Individual Countries and Regions

Advanced Economies

- In the *United Kingdom* slower growth is expected since the referendum as uncertainty in the aftermath of the Brexit vote weighs on firms' investment and hiring decisions and consumers' purchases of durable goods and housing. Growth is forecast at 1.8 percent in 2016 and 1.1 percent in 2017, based on the assumptions of smooth post-Brexit negotiations and a limited increase in economic barriers. Medium-term growth forecasts have also been revised down to 1.9 percent (0.2 percentage point lower than the April 2016 WEO forecast) as greater impediments to trade, migration, and capital flows are expected to erode growth potential.

- Softer-than-expected activity in the second half of 2015 and the first half of 2016 points to some loss in momentum in the *United States*, despite a mildly supportive fiscal stance and a slower projected pace of monetary policy normalization. Job creation has been healthy, the housing market is improving, and consumer spending remains robust. However, a prolonged inventory correction cycle and weak business investment has prompted a downward revision of the 2016 forecast to 1.6 percent. The weakness in capital spending reflects in part still-negative energy investment, dollar appreciation, financial turbulence earlier in the year, and heightened policy uncertainty related to the electoral cycle. In 2017, growth is expected to pick up to 2.2 percent, as the drag from lower energy prices and past appreciation of the U.S. dollar fades. Medium-term potential growth, projected at 1.8 percent, is held down by an aging population and a continu-

ation of the recent trend of low total factor productivity growth.
• The *euro area* recovery is expected to proceed at a
slightly lower pace in 2016–17 relative to 2015.[11]
Low oil prices, a modest fiscal expansion in 2016,
and easy monetary policy will support growth,
while weaker investor confidence on account of
uncertainty following the Brexit vote will weigh on
activity. Growth for the area as a whole is projected to
decline slightly to 1.7 percent in 2016 and 1.5 percent
in 2017. In *Germany* growth is forecast to pick up this
year to 1.7 percent, before softening to 1.4 percent
in 2017. In *France*, growth is expected to stabilize at
1.3 percent in 2016 and 2017. In *Spain*, growth is
expected to remain broadly stable in 2016 and moderate from 3.1 percent to 2.2 percent in 2017. In *Italy*
growth is projected to notch up slightly from 0.8 percent in 2016 to 0.9 percent in 2017. Medium-term
potential growth in the *euro area* is projected at
1.4 percent, held back by unfavorable demographics;
crisis legacies of high unemployment, debt, and, in
some countries, impaired bank balance sheets; and
deep-rooted structural impediments that are holding
back total factor productivity growth.
• *Japan*'s growth is projected to remain weak, in line
with potential, at 0.5 percent in 2016, before rising
to 0.6 percent in 2017.[12] Postponement of the consumption hike, the recently announced growth-enhancing measures, including the supplementary
budget, and additional monetary easing will support
private consumption in the near term, offsetting
some of the drag from the increase in uncertainty,
the recent appreciation of the yen, and weak global
growth. Japan's medium-term prospects remain
weak, primarily reflecting a shrinking population.

[11]Ireland's GDP growth for 2014–15 was revised upward by
more than 20 percentage points over two years, largely reflecting
operations of multinational companies that had a limited impact on
the underlying Irish economy. Specifically, corporate restructuring
through the relocation to Ireland of companies' entire balance sheets,
the shifting of assets to Irish subsidiaries, and the takeover of foreign
companies by entities domiciled in Ireland have led to a sizable level
shift in the stock of capital assets in Ireland (as well as a substantial
negative revision of Ireland's net international investment position
due to higher liabilities to nonresidents). The relocation of companies was also associated with an increase in Ireland's net exports and
GDP. As a consequence, growth for the euro area in 2015 was also
revised upward by more than 0.3 percentage point.

[12]The forecast does not reflect the adjustment to the Bank of
Japan's monetary policy framework announced on September 21,
2016, which includes a zero interest rate target on 10-year government bonds (JGBs) and a commitment to temporarily overshoot the
2 percent inflation target.

• The prospects of other advanced economies are
mixed. The recovery in *Sweden* will remain strong,
with growth projected at 3.6 percent in 2016 and 2.6
in 2017, supported by expansionary monetary policy,
higher residential investment, and fiscal spending due
to the refugee inflows. Economic activity is expected
to pick up modestly in *Switzerland*, with growth
forecast at 1 percent in 2016 and 1.3 percent in 2017
as the effect of the Swiss franc appreciation wanes.
The decline in commodity revenues and reduced
resource-related investment are taking a toll on the
Norwegian economy, with 2016 growth forecast at
only 0.8 percent. Activity is expected to accelerate in 2017 supported by expansionary fiscal and
monetary policy, a more competitive currency, and
a gradual upturn in oil prices. Growth is projected
to rebound starting in 2016 in other advanced
commodity exporters, supported by exchange rate
depreciation and accommodative policies. In *Canada*,
growth is projected at 1.2 percent in 2016, held back
by the severe impact of wildfires in Alberta on oil
output in the second quarter, before rising to 1.9 percent in 2017, while in *Australia*, growth is expected
to hover around 2.8 percent in both years. Among
other advanced economies in Asia, growth in 2016
is expected to soften in *Singapore* (1.7 percent) and
Hong Kong Special Administrative Region (1.4 percent)
and pick up modestly in *Korea* (to 2.7 percent) and
Taiwan Province of China (to 1 percent). Growth in
all four of these very open economies is expected to
pick up more robustly from 2017 onward as strengthening global trade improves their export prospects.

Emerging Market and Developing Economies

• In *China*, the economy is expected to grow by
6.6 percent in 2016 on the back of policy support,
slowing to 6.2 percent in 2017 absent further stimulus. The medium-term forecast assumes that the
economy will continue to rebalance from investment
to consumption and from industry to services, on
the back of reforms to strengthen the social safety
net and deregulation of the service sector. However,
nonfinancial debt is expected to continue rising
at an unsustainable pace, which—together with a
growing misallocation of resources—casts a shadow
over the medium-term outlook.
• Elsewhere in emerging and developing Asia, growth is
projected to remain strong. *India*'s GDP will continue
to expand at the fastest pace among major economies,
with growth forecast at 7.6 percent in 2016–17.

Large terms-of-trade gains, positive policy actions, structural reforms—including the introduction of an important tax reform and formalization of the inflation-targeting framework—and improved confidence are expected to support consumer demand and investment. In the near term, however, private investment will likely be constrained by weakened corporate and public bank balance sheets. Among the ASEAN-5 economies (*Indonesia, Malaysia, Philippines, Thailand, Vietnam*), *Malaysia* and *Vietnam* are expected to slow this year (to 4.3 and 6.1 percent, respectively) partly due to weaker external demand, while growth in *Indonesia,* the *Philippines,* and *Thailand* is forecast to pick up relative to 2015 (to 4.9, 6.4, and 3.2 percent, respectively). Growth in all members of the ASEAN-5 is expected to strengthen further in 2017 and thereafter.

- Economic activity in *Latin America and the Caribbean* continues to slow, with a contraction of 0.6 percent projected for 2016 (0.1 percentage point more severe than the April forecast). A recovery is expected to take hold in 2017, with growth reaching 1.6 percent (0.1 percentage point stronger than forecast in April). However, as highlighted in the April 2016 WEO, the region's aggregate growth masks substantial heterogeneity: although several countries are mired in recession, most economies in the region will continue to expand in 2016.

  o Confidence appears to have bottomed out in *Brazil,* and growth is forecast at –3.3 percent for 2016 and 0.5 percent in 2017, on the assumption of declining political and policy uncertainty and the waning effects of past economic shocks. This forecast is about ½ percentage point stronger for both years when compared with April. *Argentina* has begun an important and much needed transition to a more consistent and sustainable economic policy framework, which has proven costlier than envisaged in 2016, with growth projected at –1.8 percent (compared with –1 percent forecast in April). Growth is expected to strengthen to 2.7 percent in 2017 on the back of moderating inflation and more supportive monetary and fiscal policy stances. The economic crisis in *Venezuela* is projected to deepen in 2016 and 2017 (growth forecast of –10 percent and –4.5 percent, respectively), as the decline in oil prices since mid-2014 has exacerbated domestic macroeconomic imbalances and balance of payments pressures. *Ecuador* continues to face a challenging outlook given the

reduced value of its oil exports and its dollarized economy. With the partial recovery in global oil prices and a more favorable external financing outlook, its projected contraction in activity for 2016 and 2017 is less severe than projected in April, at –2.3 percent and –2.7 percent, respectively.

  o Most of the remaining commodity exporters in the region will experience some deceleration in activity in 2016. In *Colombia,* growth is expected to ease to 2.2 percent in 2016 (from 3.1 percent in 2015), reflecting tighter macroeconomic policies. Similarly, the protracted decline in the price of copper and policy uncertainties are weighing on *Chile's* outlook, with growth declining to 1.7 percent in 2016 from 2.3 percent in 2015. In both countries, growth is forecast to strengthen in 2017 and gradually rise to potential thereafter. Unlike most of its peers, *Peru* is expected to grow faster this year and next, with growth rising to 3.7 percent and 4.1 percent in 2016 and 2017, respectively, on the back of expanding activity in the mining sector and higher public investment.

  o Growth in *Mexico* is projected to decline to 2.1 percent in 2016 due to weak export performance in the first half of the year. It is expected to accelerate modestly to 2.3 percent in 2017 as external demand recovers and to 2.9 percent over the medium term as the structural reforms take hold.

- The economic outlook for the *Commonwealth of Independent States* remains lackluster. The modest improvement in the region's growth outlook since April mostly reflects the firming in oil prices. Higher oil export revenues are providing some relief to the region's oil exporters and to the *Russian* economy in particular, where the decline in GDP this year (0.8 percent) is now projected to be milder than envisaged in the April 2016 WEO. The somewhat improved outlook for Russia is expected to support activity elsewhere in the region, especially in oil importers, given linkages through trade and remittances. Nonetheless, Russia's growth outlook for 2017 and beyond remains subdued given long-standing structural bottlenecks and the impact of sanctions on productivity and investment. Among oil importers, *Ukraine's* economy is estimated to have returned to positive growth in 2016 after very sharp contractions in 2014 and 2015 and is expected to accelerate as the external economic environment improves and domestic economic reforms bear fruit. The pace of contraction in activity in

Belarus is expected to ease in 2017, with a recovery taking hold in 2018. Among oil exporters, the economies of *Azerbaijan* and *Kazakhstan* are projected to contract in 2016 amid a drop in export revenues, with the Azeri economy shrinking by 2.4 percent and that of Kazakhstan by about 0.8 percent. Growth in these countries is projected to rise gradually, supported by increased hydrocarbon production in Kazakhstan and nonhydrocarbon activities in Azerbaijan, as well as some recovery in oil prices and more competitive currencies.

- Growth in *emerging and developing Europe* is projected to remain robust at slightly above 3 percent in 2016 and beyond, with exports expanding at a strong clip despite sluggish growth in the euro area, the main trading partner for most economies in the region. *Hungary* is estimated to be growing faster than potential and is projected to return to more sustainable rates of growth over the medium term. In *Turkey,* growth in 2016 and 2017 will be held back by the heightened uncertainty in the aftermath of recent terrorist attacks and the failed coup attempt, though macroeconomic policy easing will support economic activity.

- The picture for *sub-Saharan Africa* is increasingly one of multispeed growth. While growth projections were revised down substantially in the region, they mostly reflect challenging macroeconomic conditions in its largest economies, which are adjusting to lower commodity revenues. In *Nigeria*, economic activity is now projected to contract 1.7 percent in 2016, reflecting temporary disruptions to oil production, foreign currency shortages resulting from lower oil receipts, lower power generation, and weak investor confidence. In *South Africa*, where policy uncertainty is making the adjustment to weaker terms of trade more difficult, GDP is projected to remain flat in 2016, with only a modest recovery next year as the commodity and drought shocks dissipate and power supply improves. *Angola* is similarly adjusting to a sharp drop in oil export receipts. It is not expected to grow this year and will experience only feeble growth next year. By contrast, several of the region's nonresource exporters, including *Côte d'Ivoire, Ethiopia, Kenya,* and *Senegal,* are expected to continue to expand at a very robust pace of more than 5 percent this year, benefiting from low oil prices and enjoying healthy private consumption and investment growth rates.

- In the Middle East, the recent modest recovery in oil prices is projected to have little impact on growth in oil-exporting countries. Most continue to tighten fiscal policy in response to structurally lower oil revenues, and financial sector liquidity continues to decline. Many countries in the region also remain affected by strife and conflict. The largest economy, Saudi Arabia, is projected to grow at a modest 1.2 percent this year in the face of fiscal consolidation, before picking up to 2 percent growth next year. Growth rates in most other countries of the Gulf Cooperation Council are similarly projected to be held back by ongoing fiscal adjustment. In Iraq, higher-than-expected oil production has pushed up the projected growth rate for 2016. Growth in 2017 and beyond is expected to be held back by continued security challenges and lower investment in the oil sector limiting gains in oil production. The Islamic Republic of Iran's outlook has been boosted by higher oil production this year following the unwinding of sanctions. However, growth dividends are likely to materialize only gradually with reintegration into global financial markets and domestic reforms proceeding slowly. Recent reforms and lower oil prices have helped improve macroeconomic stability in the oil-importing countries of the region. Yet growth remains fragile due to security concerns, social tensions, and lingering structural impediments. Continued reform, progress, less fiscal drag, and gradual improvements in external demand are expected to support the recovery.

Inflation Outlook

Inflation rates in advanced economies are projected to pick up to about 0.8 percent in 2016, from 0.3 percent in 2015, mostly reflecting a reduced drag from energy prices. Inflation is expected to rise over the next few years as fuel prices increase modestly and output gaps gradually shrink, reaching central bank targets around 2020. By contrast, excluding Argentina (where high inflation is a byproduct of an ongoing and necessary liberalization process) and Venezuela (where inflation this year is expected to surge to close to 500 percent), inflation in emerging market and developing economies is expected to soften, to 4.5 percent this year from 4.7 percent last year, reflecting the waning effect of earlier currency depreciations. However, there is considerable diversity in the inflation rates within both groups.

- In the *United States*, consumer price inflation is picking up relatively strongly, from 0.1 percent last year to 1.2 percent this year, and is projected to reach 2.3 percent next year. This reflects a rapid easing of previous disinflationary forces—the dollar appreciation in 2015 and the drop in fuel prices—as well as well-anchored medium-term inflation expectations.

- Inflation is also picking up in the *euro area*, but more slowly and from a lower level, to 0.3 percent in 2016 from about zero in 2015. The increase is projected to remain gradual going forward, with inflation remaining below the European Central Bank's target through 2021, reflecting the gradual closing of output gaps and firming of inflation expectations. Inflation is expected to increase only slowly in *Japan* as well, staying well below the Bank of Japan's target throughout the forecast horizon, as inflation expectations slowly rise.

- The depreciation of the pound is projected to push inflation in the *United Kingdom* up to about 0.7 percent this year, with a further sharp increase expected for next year, to about 2.5 percent, before gradually reaching the Bank of England's target of 2 percent in the next few years.

- Inflation rates remain subdued in most other advanced economies. In *Korea*, *Sweden*, and *Taiwan Province of China*, inflation is expected to pick up this year and gradually reach central bank targets in the following years. *Singapore* and *Switzerland* are projected to experience another year of deflation this year, although milder than last year, and shift to positive inflation rates gradually over the forecast horizon.

- Inflation in *China* is expected to pick up to 2.1 percent this year and to 3 percent over the medium term as slack in the industrial sector and downward pressure on goods prices diminish. In most other large emerging market economies, such as *Brazil*, *Russia*, and *Turkey*, inflation rates are above central bank targets and are expected to decline gradually as the effects of past exchange rate depreciations dissipate. By contrast, *Mexico*'s inflation rate is projected to remain close to the central bank's target, while *Hungary*'s and *Poland*'s rates are projected to recover slowly from very weak levels in 2015.

- Inflation is back at double-digit levels in a few large economies in sub-Saharan Africa, reflecting the pass-through of large depreciations.

External Sector Outlook

The growth rate in world trade volumes in 2016 (about 2.3 percent, which is slightly weaker than its 2015 level) is projected to remain very weak, both in absolute terms and in relation to world GDP growth. As discussed extensively in Chapter 2, the composition of global demand—and in particular the weakness in investment—plays an important role in explaining subdued global trade. Global trade growth is forecast to pick up to about 4.3 percent over the medium term, reflecting the projected recovery in economic activity and investment in emerging market and developing economies and, to a lesser extent, in advanced economies.

The evolution of global current account imbalances during 2016 continues to be affected by the very large decline in oil prices during the previous two years, as well as by sizable differences in the growth rate of domestic demand in different regions of the world. The size of global current account deficits and surpluses in relation to world GDP, which had expanded modestly in 2015 for the first time since 2010 (as discussed in the 2016 *External Sector Report*—IMF 2016), is projected to fall slightly this year (Figure 1.16, panel 1), reflecting some decline in surpluses in China and advanced European economies, together with some further decline in deficits in Latin American countries. Global current account imbalances are projected to shrink further in the medium term, to levels last seen in the mid-1990s, on the back of a further compression of surpluses in China and Germany, as well as some moderation of deficits (for instance in Latin America and the United Kingdom).

In contrast to shrinking current account imbalances, the size of cross-border creditor and debtor positions in relation to world GDP has continued to rise (Figure 1.16, panel 2). Forecasting the evolution of these positions is particularly difficult, given their sensitivity to difficult-to-predict exchange rate and asset price movements, in addition to future patterns of net borrowing and lending. Assuming for simplicity no valuation effect, projections for current account balances and GDP growth would imply a broad medium-term stabilization of creditor and debtor positions in relation to world GDP at levels modestly higher than those prevailing in 2016. Across creditor countries, the position of advanced European economies—especially Germany—would improve further, while the position of oil exporters would deteriorate to some extent. The persistence of large debtor positions despite the substantial adjustment in current account balances in recent years is related to slow growth in domestic demand and GDP in a number of debtor countries. It underscores the importance of rebalancing global demand to boost growth in those countries, which would facilitate external adjustment and reduce external risks.

With this perspective in mind, Figure 1.17 looks at three factors affecting the extent of global rebalancing over the 2014–16 period: GDP growth, the contribution of net external demand to GDP growth, and windfall gains and losses from terms-of-trade shocks. Creditor countries have grown faster than debtor countries and are projected to do so again in 2016. This differential reflects entirely the strong growth rate of China—excluding China, creditor countries are now growing more slowly than debtor countries, reflecting weak growth in oil exporters and Japan (Figure 1.17, panel 1). The positive growth differential in 2015 between creditor and debtor countries also reflected the former's reliance on net external demand, in contrast with rebalancing needs. This was due mainly to growth dynamics in oil exporters, which had to compress domestic demand in response to the decline in the terms of trade. For 2016, the forecast envisages a broadly neutral contribution of net external demand to growth in creditor and debtor countries, albeit with significant cross-regional differences. The second panel of Figure 1.17 shows that windfall gains and losses from terms-of-trade shocks (primarily related to commodity prices) have been a major driver of shifts in current account balances across regions. As also discussed in the 2016 *External Sector Report*, terms-of-trade changes have affected various creditor and debtor country groups differently (strengthening the current account balance of creditor and debtor countries and regions that import commodities and weakening the balance of commodity exporters).

There is of course no normative presumption that current account deficits and surpluses should be compressed. However, as discussed in the 2016 *External Sector Report*, current account imbalances in a number of the world's largest economies appear too large relative to a country-specific norm consistent with underlying fundamentals and desirable policies. Current account balances are expected to move in a direction consistent with a narrowing of these excess imbalances. The first panel of Figure 1.18 depicts on the horizontal

Figure 1.16. External Sector

After increasing slightly in 2015, global imbalances are expected to fall this year and continue to shrink into the medium term, reflecting differences in the growth rate of domestic demand across countries.

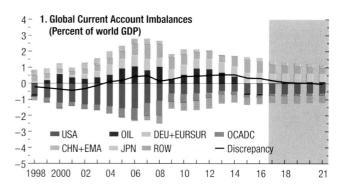

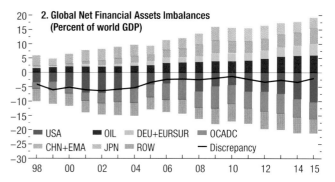

Source: IMF staff estimates.
Note: CHN+EMA = China and emerging Asia (Hong Kong SAR, Indonesia, Korea, Malaysia, Philippines, Singapore, Taiwan Province of China,Thailand); DEU+EURSUR = Germany and other advanced European surplus economies (Austria, Denmark, Luxembourg, Netherlands, Sweden, Switzerland); OCADC = other European countries with precrisis current account deficits (Greece, Ireland, Italy, Portugal, Spain, United Kingdom, *World Economic Outlook* (WEO) group of emerging and developing Europe); OIL = Norway and WEO group of emerging market and developing economy fuel exporters; ROW = rest of the world. Data labels in the figure use International Organization for Standardization (ISO) country codes.

axis the gap between the 2015 current account balance and its norm and on the vertical axis the projected movement in current account balances over the next five years. It shows a strong negative correlation (–0.7), with current account balances expected to go in the direction of reducing gaps vis-à-vis the 2015 current account norm, especially over a longer-horizon.[13] During the past few months exchange rate movements have been more muted than in 2015. As the second

[13]The correlation of 2015 current account gaps with the change in current account balances between 2015 and 2016 is also negative but weaker (–0.15). Of course current account and exchange rate norms may also shift in the future as economic fundamentals and policies change.

Figure 1.17. Creditors versus Debtors

Excluding China, creditor countries are projected to grow at a slower pace than debtor countries over 2015–16, mainly reflecting subdued domestic demand in oil exporters in response to the adverse terms of trade shock. Windfall gains and losses from shifts in terms of trade account for a large portion of the projected changes in current account balances across countries and regions.

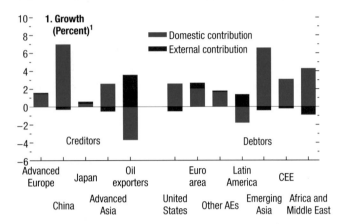

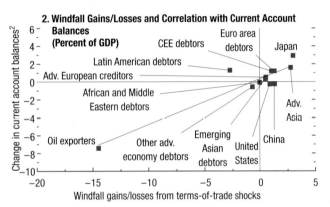

Source: IMF staff estimates.
Note: Adv. = advanced; AEs = advanced economies; CEE = central and eastern Europe.
[1]Average, 2015–16.
[2]Indicates change from 2014 to 2016.

Figure 1.18. Current Account Gaps and Real Exchange Rates

Projected changes in current account balances are consistent with a narrowing of excess external imbalances identified in the *2016 External Sector Report*.

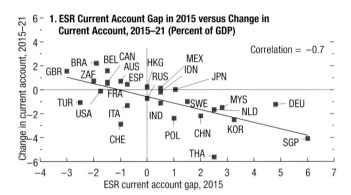

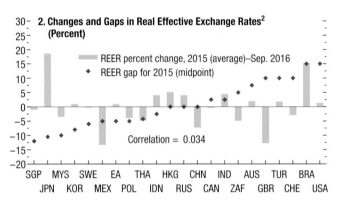

Sources: Global Insight; IMF, *2016 External Sector Report* (ESR); IMF, *International Financial Statistics*; and IMF staff calculations.
Note: Data labels in the figure use International Organization for Standardization (ISO) country codes. EA = euro area; REER = real effective exchange rate; ToT = terms of trade.
[1]Data for the euro area are an average for France, Germany, Italy, and Spain.
[2]REER gaps and classifications are based on the IMF's *2016 External Sector Report*.

panel of Figure 1.18 illustrates, these exchange rate changes are not systematically correlated with the exchange rate gaps for 2015 identified in the 2016 *External Sector Report*.

Risks

Some risks flagged in recent WEO reports have become more pronounced in recent months, including those associated with political discord and inward-looking policies, or secular stagnation in advanced economies. Other risks, such as rising financial turbulence and capital pullbacks from emerging

market economies, seem to have become less prominent, but they still remain. On balance, downside risks continue to dominate.

Risks Stemming from the Policy and Institutional Domain

The U.K. vote to leave the European Union and the ongoing U.S. presidential election campaign have brought to the fore issues related to labor mobility and migration, global trade integration, and cross-border regulation. Institutional arrangements long in place are now potentially up for renegotiation—arrangements that have shaped how businesses organize their production and hiring, sourcing of raw materials and financing, and distribution channels across borders. Additional questions loom regarding possible follow-up referenda in other EU economies. More generally, concerns about the impact of foreign competition on jobs and wages in a context of weak economic growth have enhanced the appeal of protectionist policy platforms, with potential ramifications for global trade flows. Ambiguity about how these trends will evolve may lead firms to defer long-term projects, limit job creation, and slow near-term activity.

Institutional uncertainty interacting with hardening political divisions within countries can make solutions to structural challenges even more elusive. As these challenges—ranging from product and labor market deregulation to balance sheet repair, entitlement reform, and the integration of migrants into the labor force— become seemingly more intractable, perceptions of policy ineffectiveness could become more firmly rooted and the coordinating role of policy could diminish. As such, if any of the risks outlined below were to materialize, the toll on sentiment could be amplified by concerns that policy action will fail to offset the shock decisively.

Increasing pressure for inward-looking policies are a particular threat to the global outlook—a theme also discussed in Chapter 2. Scenario Box 1 discusses the potential economic consequences of an increase in protectionism. It first highlights the implications of a unilateral increase in tariffs by one country on another country—as well as the consequences of retaliation by the second country. The model simulations illustrate how GDP, consumption, and investment of *both* countries are negatively affected by the unilateral tariff increase. A second scenario illustrates the implications for the global economy of a generalized increase in protectionism, taking the form of higher tariff and nontariff barriers. The result is not just a collapse in trade flows, but also a sharp decline in global output. The negative repercussions for the global economy could be even larger because the disruption in international economic linkages drive a more generalized decline in cross-border cooperation.

Debilitating Cycles: Weak Demand–Weak Inflation; Low Productivity–Low Investment

One common thread running through several recent WEO reports is the prospect of secular stagnation—an

extended shortfall in private demand leading to permanently lower output and low inflation.[14] As the world economy continues to struggle to generate widespread, durable momentum, this prospect becomes ever more tangible, particularly in some advanced economies. At the same time, a protracted period of weak inflation risks dislodging inflation expectations, causing expected real interest rates to rise and expenditure on capital goods and consumer durables to decline, eventually feeding back to weaker overall growth and inflation. And in economies with a large debt overhang, an extended period of low nominal growth would add to debt service difficulties, complicate the task of deleveraging, and further weigh on growth (as discussed in the October 2016 *Fiscal Monitor*).

A second debilitating cycle relates to possible feedback effects between low productivity growth and low investment. As noted earlier in the chapter, total factor productivity and labor productivity growth have declined markedly in many economies. At the same time, investment has slowed globally and is below long-term average growth rates in several advanced and emerging market and developing economies. To the extent that low productivity growth translates into expectations of weak profitability, investment could be negatively affected. The resulting deceleration in capital deepening would harm the adoption of capital-embodied technological change, further weigh on total factor and labor productivity, reinforce expectations of diminishing profitability, and spiral back to weak investment.

China's Ongoing Adjustment and Associated Spillovers

China's economy continues to support global growth, but its adjustment to a more sustainable pace of expansion has at times turned bumpier than

---

[14]As discussed in Box 1.1 of the October 2015 WEO, a number of mechanisms could generate lower output paths after recessions. For instance, a prolonged period of high unemployment could lead some workers to drop out or become unemployable. Reduced research and development could hurt the level—or even the growth rate—of productivity. Financial crises could trigger institutional changes such as tougher capital requirements, weighing on investment. A number of studies have provided empirical evidence supporting these hypotheses. For instance, Blanchard, Cerutti, and Summers (2015) find that, even for recessions triggered by intentional disinflation, the proportion of recessions followed by lower output relative to the prerecession trend was substantial. Likewise, Reifschneider, Wascher, and Wilcox (2015) find that the financial crisis of 2008 and the ensuing recession put the productive capacity of the U.S. economy on a lower trajectory than prior to 2007, with a significant portion of the damage to the supply side of the economy resulting from the weakness in aggregate demand.

expected. Recent months have seen a fading of the capital outflow pressure and domestic equity market turbulence that contributed to large sell-offs in global financial markets in August 2015 and January 2016. Nevertheless, China's transition to a services and consumption-based economy less dependent on commodity and machinery imports will continue to have an impact on prices, trade volumes, and profits across a swath of global industries, with associated effects on asset prices, international portfolio allocations, and investor sentiment.

China confronts a difficult trade-off in its transition—restructuring the economy, reducing its reliance on credit, and accepting slower near-term growth in return for higher and more sustainable long-term growth. The baseline assumes limited progress in tackling the corporate debt problem and reining in credit, and a preference for maintaining relatively high near-term growth, which raises the risk of an eventual disruptive adjustment (see the China IMF 2016 Article IV Staff Report). Against this backdrop, relatively mild triggers such as negative surprises in China's high-frequency indicators or a modest adjustment in domestic asset prices and the exchange rate could catalyze an outsized reaction in global sentiment.

Adverse Turn in Financial Conditions for Emerging Markets

Despite the unexpected outcome of the Brexit vote, financial conditions in emerging markets have continued to improve in recent months, with some firming of commodity prices and growing conviction among investors that monetary policy in advanced economies will remain highly accommodative into 2017 and beyond. As noted in the October 2016 GFSR, external developments appear to have played an important role in the recent pickup in capital flows to emerging market economies. Underlying vulnerabilities among some large emerging market economies (including high corporate debt, declining profitability, and weak bank balance sheets in some cases)—together with the need to rebuild policy buffers, particularly in commodity exporters—leave emerging market and developing economies still exposed to sudden shifts in investor confidence. Such shifts could materialize, for example, if incoming inflation data for the United States point to an earlier hike in the policy interest rate than anticipated. Investor sentiment could also shift if emerging market and developing economies fail to take advantage of the relative stability

in external conditions to press ahead with structural reforms, tackle debt overhangs, and credibly advance fiscal adjustment, where needed.

Breakdown of Correspondent Banking Relationships

In the aftermath of the crisis, large global banks have been forced to reassess their business models as they rebuild capital buffers, strengthen their risk management practices, and face compressed net interest margins. As a consequence, correspondent banking relationships—large global banks' provision of payment and deposit-taking services on behalf of other banks, often located in smaller countries—have declined with global banks' withdrawal from transactions with smaller, vulnerable economies in Africa, the Caribbean, central Asia, and the Pacific Islands. An intensification of this trend would imperil the access of some of these economies to cross-border remittances, undermine their ability to finance activity, and weaken their response to natural disasters. Although the direct impact on global GDP might be relatively small, the social and economic ramifications could extend beyond the borders of the affected economies—for example, if they add to outward migration.

Conflict, Health, and Climate Factors

A range of additional factors continues to influence the outlook in various regions—for example, the drought in east and southern Africa; civil war and domestic conflict in parts of the Middle East and Africa; the unfolding migrant situation in Jordan, Lebanon, Turkey, and Europe; multiple acts of terror worldwide; and the spread of the Zika virus in Latin America and the Caribbean, the southern United States, and southeast Asia. Each of these factors inflicts both immeasurable humanitarian and direct economic costs. Recurrent incidents of terrorism, protracted civil conflict that spreads to contiguous regions, and a worsening public health crisis from Zika could collectively take a large toll on market sentiment, with negative repercussions for demand and activity.

Upside Risks

Despite the abundance of downside risks flagged in previous WEOs, the world economy had begun to record slightly stronger-than-expected growth in the first quarter of 2016. Several signs point to prospects of a more robust pickup in momentum than currently envisaged, including the resilience and orderly repricing in financial markets after the initial shock of the Brexit vote; sustained improvements in the U.S. labor market; the modest uptick in commodity prices, which should ease some of the pressure on commodity exporters without severely hurting net importers; and fading headwinds from rapid currency depreciations and capital flows out of stressed emerging markets. Additional momentum could follow if countries intensify efforts to lift actual and potential output through targeted and well-sequenced structural reforms, demand support, and balance sheet repair.

Fan Chart

A fan chart analysis—based on financial and commodity market data as well as inflation and term spread forecasts—suggests reduced dispersion of outcomes around the central scenario. As visible in Figure 1.19, the width of the 90 percent confidence interval has narrowed slightly for both the 2016 and 2017 growth forecasts relative to those in the October 2015 WEO, but remain wider than the estimates of the October 2014 WEO. Risks remain tilted to the downside for 2016 and 2017.

The probability of a recession over a four-quarter horizon (2016:Q3–2017:Q2) in most regions has declined relative to the probability computed in March 2016 (for 2016:Q1–2016:Q4; Figure 1.20). In Japan, the recently announced fiscal stimulus measures have lowered the probability of recession relative to the April 2016 estimates. The slightly improved outlook for commodity prices and financial conditions relative to April have helped lower the probability of a recession in Latin America, although the risk remains high. Deflation risks—as measured by the four-quarter-ahead probability of deflation—have also declined relative to April 2016 for the United States and the euro area, primarily owing to the strengthening in commodity prices and the associated firming in projected headline consumer price inflation. By contrast, the probability of deflation has increased in Japan owing to weak momentum in consumer prices and the recent appreciation of the yen.

Policy Priorities

While the outlook for the global economy discussed above points to a projected pickup in growth

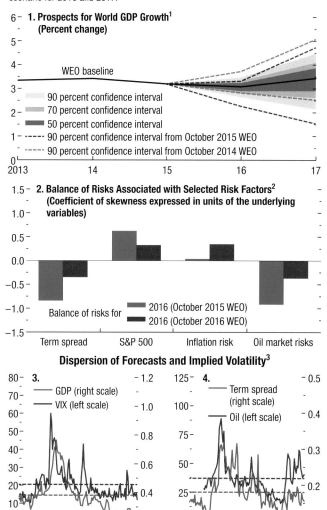

Figure 1.19. Risks to the Global Outlook

The balance of risks points to growth weaker than envisaged in the central scenario for 2016 and 2017.

Sources: Bloomberg L.P.; Chicago Board Options Exchange (CBOE); Consensus Economics; Haver Analytics; and IMF staff estimates.
[1]The fan chart shows the uncertainty around the *World Economic Outlook* (WEO) central forecast with 50, 70, and 90 percent confidence intervals. As shown, the 70 percent confidence interval includes the 50 percent interval, and the 90 percent confidence interval includes the 50 and 70 percent intervals. See Appendix 1.2 of the April 2009 WEO for details. The 90 percent intervals for the current-year and one-year-ahead forecasts from the October 2015 WEO and October 2014 WEO are shown.
[2]The bars depict the coefficient of skewness expressed in units of the underlying-variables. The values for inflation risks and oil price risks enter with the opposite sign since they represent downside risks to growth.
[3]GDP measures the purchasing-power-parity-weighted average dispersion of GDP growth forecasts for the G7 economies (Canada, France, Germany, Italy, Japan, United Kingdom, United States), Brazil, China, India, and Mexico. VIX is the Chicago Board Options Exchange Volatility Index. Term spread measures the average dispersion of term spreads implicit in interest rate forecasts for Germany, Japan, the United Kingdom, and the United States. Oil is the CBOE crude oil volatility index. Forecasts are from Consensus Economics surveys. Dashed lines represent the average values from 2000 to the present.

Figure 1.20. Recession and Deflation Risks
(Percent)

The probability of recession over a four-quarter horizon spanning 2016:Q3 through 2017:Q2 has generally declined in most regions relative to the probabilities computed in the April 2016 WEO for the period 2016:Q1 through 2016:Q4. The risk of deflation remains high in the euro area and Japan.

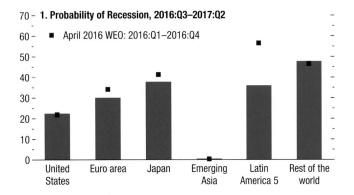

1. Probability of Recession, 2016:Q3–2017:Q2

■ April 2016 WEO: 2016:Q1–2016:Q4

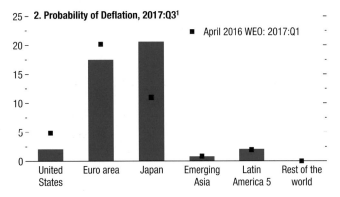

2. Probability of Deflation, 2017:Q3[1]

■ April 2016 WEO: 2017:Q1

Source: IMF staff estimates.
Note: Emerging Asia comprises China, Hong Kong SAR, India, Indonesia, Korea, Malaysia, Philippines, Singapore, Taiwan Province of China, and Thailand; Latin America 5 comprises Brazil, Chile, Colombia, Mexico, and Peru; Rest of the world comprises Argentina, Australia, Bulgaria, Canada, the Czech Republic, Denmark, Israel, New Zealand, Norway, Russia, South Africa, Sweden, Switzerland, Turkey, the United Kingdom, and Venezuela. April 2016 WEO data refer to simulations run in March 2016.
[1]Deflation is defined as a fall in the price level on a year-over-year basis in the quarter indicated in the figure.

over the rest of the forecast horizon, as seen in Box 1.1, a significant portion of this improvement arises from weights shifting toward large emerging market economies projected to grow at rates above the global average and from the normalization of conditions in some countries experiencing growth downturns or outright recessions. The potential for setbacks to this outlook is high. Against this backdrop, policy priorities differ across individual economies depending on the specific objectives for improving growth momentum,

combating deflation pressure, or building resilience. A common theme, though, is that urgent policy action is needed on multiple fronts to head off repeated growth disappointments and combat damaging perceptions that policies are ineffective in boosting growth and that the rewards accrue only to those at the higher end of the income distribution.

Where room to loosen fiscal or monetary policy appears more limited, coordinated, comprehensive responses that exploit complementarities between structural and demand management policies may help strengthen the efficacy of the overall policy package. And coherent frameworks that embed near-term responses in the context of clearly articulated medium-term targets can boost confidence and create more room for policy maneuvering to combat near-term shocks. While essential at the country level, these policies would be even more effective if adopted broadly, with due attention to country-specific priorities.

Policies—Advanced Economies

Advanced economies as a group continue to experience a modest recovery characterized by generally weak productivity growth, low investment, and low inflation. These features are products of the interplay between subdued demand, diminished growth expectations, and declining potential output growth. Policy action must therefore continue to support demand while implementing measures that will lift potential growth.

With output gaps still negative, wage pressures muted, and inflation expectations for the next few years below central bank targets, monetary policy must steer an accommodative course. As the post-Brexit referendum experience has demonstrated thus far, central banks' readiness to act with unconventional tools has lowered the risk of a systemic liquidity crunch, facilitated orderly market repricing, and helped boost investor sentiment. Further monetary policy loosening through asset purchases and, in some cases, negative deposit rates, will ensure that long-term rates remain contained, help lift inflation expectations, and lower the real costs of borrowing for households and firms. As discussed in Box 3.5 and in Chapter 3 more generally, transparent inflation-forecast frameworks allow for economic stimulus—even when policy rates are close to their effective lower bounds—through temporary overshooting of the target.

As the past several years' experience with unconventional strategies has however also shown, accommodative monetary policy alone cannot lift demand and may, in some cases, generate undesirable side effects (as discussed in the October 2016 GFSR). This is especially true in an environment in which the natural rate of interest is persistently low, since this implies less monetary policy accommodation even at record-low interest rates. Fiscal support therefore remains essential for lifting momentum where there is slack and avoiding a lasting downshift in medium-term inflation expectations. It should be calibrated to the amount of space available and, where adjustment is warranted, oriented toward policies that protect the vulnerable and are conducive to lifting medium-term growth prospects. Such growth-friendly tax and expenditure policies include reforming labor taxes and social benefits to incentivize labor force participation; reforming corporate income taxes and providing well-targeted tax incentives to boost research and development investment (as discussed in the April 2016 *Fiscal Monitor*); increasing productive capacity through infrastructure investment where there are clear shortfalls; and facilitating improvements in human capital by investing in education and health care. In countries facing rising public debt burdens and social entitlement outlays, credible commitments to medium-term consolidation strategies can generate additional space for near-term support.

Support for near-term demand must be accompanied, in some cases, by efforts to repair bank balance sheets (addressing legacy nonperforming loans and strengthening operational efficiency, as discussed in the October 2016 GFSR), as well as structural reform policies to address waning potential growth, thus bolstering longer-term income prospects. Better income prospects, in turn, would lift private demand in the short term and help contain increases in debt-to-GDP ratios in the medium term. Although employment has grown more strongly than expected in recent years, unfavorable demographic trends in advanced economies point to limits to the extent potential growth can recover on the back of an expanding labor force. Specific priorities vary across countries, ranging from measures to boost labor force participation rates, to reforms that eliminate product and labor market distortions, to steps that address corporate debt overhangs and facilitate restructuring, to policies that lift research and development investment and encourage innovation. Some structural reforms can also raise near-term activity, thereby amplifying the effects of demand sup-

port policies in countries with slack. Other structural reforms require supportive macroeconomic policies to lessen possible dampening effects they may have on near-term growth and inflation (see Chapter 3 of the April 2016 WEO).

Country-Specific Priorities

- In the *United Kingdom*, the Bank of England's August announcement of a suite of accommodative measures—including a 25 basis point cut in the policy rate, a new "term funding scheme" to transmit the lower policy rate to retail borrowing costs, and resumption of quantitative easing—signals its commitment to limit post-Brexit downside risks and maintain confidence. These measures, together with the reduction in banks' countercyclical capital buffers announced immediately after the referendum, are appropriately geared toward ensuring that lending conditions remain supportive as the U.K. economy begins to adjust to the new institutional arrangements. On the fiscal front, automatic stabilizers should be allowed to operate freely. As greater clarity emerges on the macroeconomic impact of the Brexit vote, the need for further near-term discretionary fiscal policy easing and the appropriateness of the medium-term deficit target should be assessed, possibly in the context of the upcoming November fiscal review.

- In the *euro area*, with inflation expectations still below target, several economies operating with slack, and uncertainty clouding prospects for sustained momentum in activity, the European Central Bank should maintain its current appropriately accommodative stance. Additional easing through expanded asset purchases may be needed if inflation fails to pick up. Fiscal policy should also be used to support the recovery in the near term by funding investment and other priorities in countries where space permits and by accelerating deployment of centrally funded investment. Countries with high debt burdens should undertake gradual fiscal consolidation. Centrally funded investment programs should be expanded, with access subject to compliance with the Stability and Growth Pact and implementation of recommended structural reforms. Demand support should be reinforced with product, labor market, and public administration reforms to encourage firms' entry and exit, raise labor participation rates, and address labor market duality. Action in these areas, which could be encouraged through outcome-based reform benchmarks, along with steps to boost infrastructure investment and complete the single market in services, energy, digital commerce, transportation, and capital, would lift potential growth and productivity. Faster bank and corporate balance sheet repair, a common deposit insurance scheme, and a fiscal backstop for the banking union remain critical in order to weaken bank-sovereign links, contain risks to financial stability, improve policy transmission, and facilitate consolidation and restructuring of the banking sector. Refugee integration into the workforce through swift processing of asylum applications and enhanced training and placement services is essential in countries that face this pressing concern.

- In the *United States*, despite the steady decline in the unemployment rate to less than 5 percent and the pace of job creation over the past year, exceeding the average of the precrisis boom years, wage growth and consumer price inflation have remained subdued. The Federal Reserve's pause after the December 2015 increase in the federal funds rate is thus an appropriate response to these developments as well as to risks stemming from the global environment. Further increases should be gradual and tied to clear signs that wages and prices are firming durably. On the fiscal side, the moderately expansionary near-term stance is appropriate. Over the long term, however, public finances are on an unsustainable path given the anticipated increases in health and pension outlays as the population ages and potential output slows. Instituting a credible deficit and debt-reduction strategy would create room to lift productive capacity by increasing infrastructure investment; boosting labor force participation (through expansion in child care assistance and the earned income tax credit, combined with an increase in the minimum wage for low-income workers) and enhancing human capital (through higher spending on early childhood education and skills-enhancing vocational training). Complementing this consolidation plan, a comprehensive reform of the tax code geared toward simplification and fewer exemptions would incentivize job creation, widen the revenue base, and enhance fiscal sustainability.

- In *Japan*, with growth below potential and inflation weakening this year following the yen appreciation, the Bank of Japan's monetary easing through asset purchases and negative deposit rates has been critical to preventing the economy from tipping back into deflation. The fiscal stimulus announced in August will lessen the drag from the expiration of previous measures and reduce the risk of a slide in near-term activity. In order to secure a durable increase in inflation and growth, however, a comprehensive policy approach is required that enhances demand support with actions to lift medium-term growth expectations and boost wages. Elements of such a package would include reforms to diminish labor market duality and increase labor force participation by women and older workers, while admitting more foreign workers; measures to boost private investment, including lowering entry barriers in retail trade and services, improvements in the provision of capital for new ventures, and stronger corporate governance to discourage companies from accumulating excess cash reserves; and income policies that motivate profitable companies to raise wages in line with the Bank of Japan's inflation target and productivity growth. Together with this comprehensive package, a credible long-term fiscal consolidation plan based on a preannounced schedule of a gradual increase in the consumption tax, social security reform, and efforts to broaden the tax base would place public finances on a more sustainable footing, create additional space for fiscal policy to respond to near-term setbacks, and boost confidence in the overall policy approach.

Policies—Emerging Market and Developing Economies

Emerging market and developing economies have experienced a period of relative calm in recent months. External financial conditions are benign compared with the start of 2016, and there are signs that macroeconomic distress in some key countries may be easing. As discussed earlier in the chapter, China's adjustment to a slower growth path and the subdued outlook for commodity prices remain potent forces shaping prospects for many of these economies. Most tangibly, these two large reconfigurations have burdened the operating environment for emerging market and developing economy businesses, many of which are saddled with high debt after the credit boom of 2002–12.

Despite the diverse range of country circumstances and levels of development within this group, the broad common policy objectives confronting emerging market and developing economies are to maintain convergence to higher income ranges and to strengthen resilience. The former requires structural reforms that facilitate technology diffusion and job creation, appropriately harnessing the existing skills in the economy while minimizing inefficiencies from resource misallocation. And to continue making progress up the value-added ladder, a key imperative is to enhance the quality of human capital through adequate investment in education and health care.

Strengthening resilience requires action on several fronts. In stressed emerging market economies where activity appears to be bottoming out, it is imperative to continue facilitating the recovery by avoiding premature and excessive tightening of fiscal and monetary policy. More broadly, as the considerable aftershocks of the global financial crisis have demonstrated, periods of relative calm in external financial conditions for emerging market and developing economies can quickly take an adverse turn. Recent instances of rapid asset price and exchange rate movements appear to have had largely localized and short-lived effects in exposed economies. Nevertheless, the prospect of large repercussions in economies with unhedged foreign liabilities, and where short-term borrowing is channeled into longer-term, less liquid investments, requires that these economies strengthen their defenses against potential financial turbulence by containing currency and balance sheet mismatches. Exchange rate flexibility and permitting market forces to guide movements in the currency can help absorb shocks and provide some insulation from protracted external pressure, but at times foreign exchange intervention may be needed to maintain orderly market conditions and prevent disruptive overshooting. Commodity exporters with large fiscal imbalances face the additional challenge of adjusting their public finances to an environment with lower revenue and potentially less favorable financing conditions compared with those in the past decade. Against this backdrop, they need to ensure that fiscal consolidation is as growth friendly as possible.

Country-Specific Priorities

- *China* continues to make progress with the complex tasks of rebalancing its economy toward consumption and services and permitting market forces a greater role. But the economy's dependence on credit is increasing at a dangerous pace, intermediated through an increasingly opaque and complex financial sector. The high and rising credit dependence reflects a combination of factors—the pursuit of unsustainably high growth targets, efforts to prop up unviable state-owned enterprises to preserve employment and defer loss recognition, and opportunistic lending by financial intermediaries in the belief that all debt is implicitly guaranteed by the government. By maintaining high near-term growth momentum in this manner, the economy faces a growing misallocation of resources and risks an eventual disruptive adjustment. This would undermine the impressive reform progress made so far with financial sector liberalization, the opening of the capital account, and a strengthened framework for local government finances. The priorities are therefore to address the corporate debt problem by separating viable from unviable state-owned enterprises, hardening budget constraints and improving governance in the former while shutting down the latter and absorbing the related welfare costs through targeted funds; apportioning losses among creditors and recapitalizing banks as needed; allowing credit expansion to slow and accepting the associated slower GDP growth; strengthening the financial system by closely monitoring credit quality and funding stability, including in the nonbank sector; continuing to make progress toward an effectively floating exchange rate regime; and further improving data quality and transparency in communications. Avoiding a further buildup of excess capacity among unviable state-owned enterprises in China would also help ease deflation pressures in advanced economies grappling with the risk of persistently low inflation.

- *India's* economy has benefited from the large terms of trade gain triggered by lower commodity prices, and inflation has declined more than expected. Nevertheless, underlying inflationary pressures arising from bottlenecks in the food storage and distribution sector point to the need for further structural reforms to ensure that consumer price inflation remains within the target band over the medium term. Important policy actions toward the implementation of the goods and services tax have been taken, which will be positive for investment and growth. This tax reform and the elimination of poorly targeted subsidies are needed to widen the revenue base and expand the fiscal envelope to support investment in infrastructure, education, and health care. More broadly, while several positive measures have been undertaken over the past two years, additional measures to enhance efficiency in the mining sector and increase electricity generation are required to boost productive capacity. Additional labor market reforms to reduce rigidities are essential for maximizing the employment potential of the demographic dividend and making growth more inclusive. Continued efforts by the Reserve Bank of India to strengthen bank balance sheets through full recognition of losses and increasing bank capital buffers remain critical for improving the quality of domestic financial intermediation.

- In *Brazil*, the economy continues to contract, albeit at a more moderate pace, inflation is above the central bank's tolerance band, and policy credibility has been severely dented by events leading up to the regime transition. There is an overarching need to boost confidence and lift investment by strengthening policy frameworks. Adopting the proposed spending rule and laying out a coherent medium-term fiscal consolidation framework would send a strong signal of policy commitment. Further imperatives for lifting investment include simplifying the tax code, reducing barriers to trade, and addressing infrastructure shortfalls to reduce the cost of doing business.

- *South Africa's* economy is still grappling with the decline in commodity prices, over a quarter of the workforce is unemployed, and the outlook is clouded by policy uncertainty and political risks. A comprehensive structural reform package that fosters greater product market competition, more inclusive labor market policies and industrial relations, and improved education and training, as well as reducing infrastructure gaps is critical to boost growth, create more jobs, and reduce inequality. Measures to improve state-owned enterprises' efficiency and governance, including through greater private participation, are a particularly important element of the needed reform package to lift growth prospects and reduce contingent fiscal risks. While some of these reforms may take time to yield positive growth effects, immediate benefits can stem from improved confidence and signaling of policy consistency.

- In *Russia,* the combined effects of lower oil prices, sanctions, and diminished access of firms to international capital markets have forced the economy into recession since the end of 2014. Although the economy is projected to return to growth in 2016, excessive fiscal tightening should be avoided from a cyclical perspective. Anchoring fiscal policy to a medium-term consolidation program and reinstituting the three-year framework based on an updated

outlook for oil prices would enhance transparency, increase confidence, and help the economy adjust to a revised environment for commodity prices. With inflationary pressures remaining contained, monetary easing should continue to support the adjustment. Improvements to financial supervision and regulation, comprehensive asset quality reviews with a view toward publicly funded bank recapitalizations as needed, and a stronger resolution framework would boost the resilience of the financial system, improve the efficiency of credit allocation, and raise medium-term growth prospects.

Policies—Low-Income Developing Economies

Among low-income economies, those dependent on commodity exports continue to face a different outlook than the others. With commodity prices much below their 2014 peaks, subdued global growth, and a further tightening in their financial conditions, economic growth has significantly weakened for commodity-dependent low-income developing countries, particularly fuel exporters. Indeed, many of the risks highlighted in Box 1.2 of the April 2016 WEO are now materializing for this group of economies. In contrast, growth expectations for relatively diversified low-income developing countries are still solid, broadly in line with the projections in the April 2016 WEO. Some of these economies have, however, also been hit by nonmacroeconomic shocks, including conflicts and difficult security situations (Afghanistan, South Sudan, Yemen, the Sahel region) and droughts and natural disasters (Ethiopia, Lesotho, Malawi, Mozambique, Myanmar), exacerbating already weak macroeconomic conditions.

Policies in commodity-dependent countries have been slow to adjust to the difficult economic conditions. After widening sharply in 2015, current account deficits are expected to narrow slightly in 2016, helped in part by exchange rate depreciation. But exchange rate depreciations have also raised inflation for some (for example, Mozambique, Nigeria, and Zambia) or increased external debt liabilities. Fiscal deficits are likely to remain elevated through 2016 as weaker revenues offset cutbacks in spending.

Among diversified economies, fiscal and external current account positions have not improved despite continued strong economic growth, reflecting limited progress in adopting countercyclical policies—particularly with current spending outpacing revenue in some cases.

Against this backdrop, while the overarching priority for low-income developing countries remains to deliver on their United Nations Sustainable Development Goals, actions to deal with near-term macroeconomic challenges will also help meet these long-term objectives. In particular, efforts to create fiscal space by enhancing domestic resource mobilization and improving the efficiency of government spending; steps to reorient fiscal spending to protect the vulnerable and address infrastructure gaps to foster inclusive growth; and measures to improve financial sector resilience through stronger prudential regulation, along with steps to deepen financial inclusion, will help achieve macroeconomic stabilization as well as overall economic resilience, sustained growth, and development.

Specific near-term policy priorities for low-income developing countries differ based on their degree of dependence on commodity exports:

- The ongoing adjustment in macroeconomic policies must continue and in some cases accelerate in *commodity-dependent low-income developing countries.* Specifically, fiscal policy adjustment needs to be better balanced with efforts to raise the contribution of the noncommodity sector in fiscal revenue collection. In the sub-Saharan African economies hit hard by the slump in commodity prices, especially oil exporters, the adjustment has started but remains far from sufficient and continues to rely on unsustainable features, such as the drawdown of reserves, central bank financing, and accumulation of arrears. Instead, a sustainable adjustment is needed, based on a comprehensive and internally consistent set of policies. With most countries facing limited fiscal space, spending needs to be rationalized—to the extent possible by preserving priority capital expenditures and social sector spending and containing current expenditures. The side effects of exchange rate flexibility and depreciation will need to be better managed through a tighter monetary policy stance in some countries and stronger monetary policy frameworks that anchor inflation expectations. Enhanced financial sector regulation and supervision will be required to manage foreign currency exposures in balance sheets. Medium-term priorities to improve economic resilience by rebuilding fiscal buffers when commodity prices recover, and structural reforms to achieve economic diversification and higher productivity, remain relevant.
- For *relatively diversified low-income developing countries,* while growth remains strong, it is imperative to

focus on adopting countercyclical macroeconomic policies, in particular to rebuild fiscal buffers. Strong debt management will also help those exposed to global financial markets better cope with volatility in capital inflows.

Multilateral Policies

With growth weak and policy space limited in many countries, multilateral actions acquire even greater relevance to sustain global improvements in living standards. Continued multilateral effort is required on several levels, including financial regulatory reform, trade, and the global financial safety net.

- *Financial Regulatory Reform*—Steady progress has been made on building bank capital and liquidity buffers, but more work is needed on implementing effective resolution frameworks and addressing emerging risks from nonbank intermediaries. Closer cross-border regulatory cooperation is also required to limit the withdrawal of correspondent banking relationships that provide vulnerable low-income countries a gateway into the international payments system.
- *Trade*—With the seeming backlash against global trade in advanced economies, there is a pressing need for policymakers to refocus the discussion toward the benefits of integration and to ensure that those who bear the brunt of the adjustment costs in an open trading system are adequately supported through well-targeted social initiatives. As Chapter 2 finds, the diminishing pace of new trade reforms in recent years, together with a rise in protectionist measures, appears to have contributed in part to the global slowdown in trade. Going forward the process of trade liberalization should be revived in order to support trade growth and lift productivity. There is substantial scope to further reduce trade costs through cutting tariffs where they remain elevated, ratifying and fully implementing commitments made under the Trade Facilitation Agreement, and establishing a way forward in the post-Doha trade agenda. The next generation of trade reforms would need to focus on areas most relevant to the contemporary global economy, such as reducing barriers to e-commerce and trade in services, improving regulatory cooperation, and leveraging complementarities between investment and trade. Reforms should be coupled with measures to mitigate the costs to those who are adversely affected. In particular, as noted

in Chapter 2, specific trade adjustment assistance programs and effective support for retraining, skill building, and occupational and geographic mobility could play an important role in certain cases.

- *Strengthening the global financial safety net*—The combination of still-moderate global growth and pronounced downside risks underscores the importance of strengthening the global financial safety net to help economies with robust fundamentals that may nevertheless be vulnerable to cross-border contagion and spillovers. Risks stemming from noneconomic factors with cross-border ramifications, such as the ongoing refugee crisis, further demonstrate the case for instituting globally funded vehicles to help the exposed economies absorb the strains.

Scenario Box 1. Tariff Scenarios

The Global Integrated Monetary and Fiscal Model (GIMF) is used here to illustrate the macroeconomic implications of trade protectionism. Two scenarios are used to illustrate how one country may have an incentive to impose tariffs, particularly if it believes there will be no retaliation. However, once a tariff has been imposed on a country's exports, it is in that country's best interest to retaliate, and when it does, both countries end up worse off. Further, a scenario is used to illustrate the negative implications for global output, trade, and inflation should an increase in global protectionism become a reality.

Consider first the scenarios presented in Scenario Figure 1. The blue line traces out some key macro outcomes when country A (left column in figure) imposes a tariff of 10 percent on imports from country B (right column in figure) and country B does not retaliate. Countries A and B are of similar size and have a similar degree of openness. It is assumed that the revenue generated by the tariff is returned to households in country A via transfers.[1] The higher cost of imports from country B leads households and firms in country A to demand fewer of them. With country A's import demand lower, it does not need to export as much to maintain external balance and its currency appreciates, lowering foreign demand for its exports. Household consumption in country A rises as the currency appreciation makes imports from all other countries cheaper, and the higher cost of country B imports is returned to households in the form of transfers. However, because country A exports less, firms reduce investment (not shown) and overall output in country A declines.

When there is no retaliation, lower export demand from country A means that to maintain external balance, country B's currency needs to depreciate to increase demand for its exports in other countries. However, it does not fully offset the impact of the decline in export demand from country A, and exports fall below their pre-tariff level in country B. Imports in country B also decline notably owing to both its currency depreciation, which leads to higher import prices, and the decline in consumption and investment

[1]If the tariff revenue is used for infrastructure investment rather than transferred back to households, GDP in country A will be higher. However, higher tariffs are not the most efficient way to fund infrastructure investment as output rises more if government consumption expenditure is reduced instead or if consumption taxes are increased.

Scenario Figure 1. Unilateral and Bilateral Imposition of Tariffs on Imported Goods
(Percent difference from baseline)

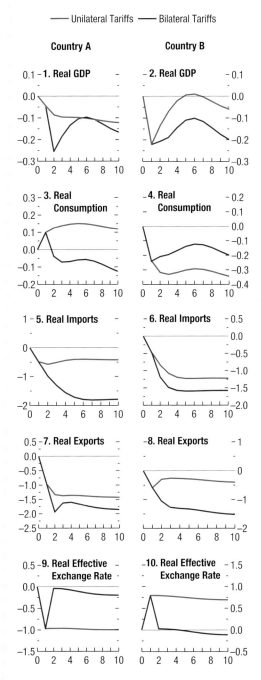

Source: IMF staff estimates.

Scenario Box 1. Tariff Scenarios *(continued)*

demand (not shown) owing to the hit to country B's income from lower foreign demand for its exports. The result is an improvement in country B's net export position, which helps moderate the decline in GDP from lower domestic demand.

Facing trade barriers on its exports, it is in its households' best interest for country B to retaliate and impose a tariff of 10 percent on imports from country A. As illustrated by the red line in Scenario Figure 1, when country B retaliates with its own tariff in the second year, consumption in country B rises relative to the case of no retaliation. First, the higher cost of imports from country A reduces import demand in country B. This means that country B does not need to export as much to maintain external balance and the currency depreciation is unwound. Imports from countries other than A are now cheaper and some of the demand is substituted away from country A. In addition, households receive back tariff revenues in the form of transfers from the government and, consequently, they can afford to support a higher level of consumption. Investment in country B declines further as the currency appreciation makes its exports more expensive, reducing foreign demand. Lower investment and a relatively weaker net export position more than offset the impact of higher consumption and GDP in country B falls below the level when there is no retaliation.

In country A, the retaliation lowers demand for its exports, which means it no longer needs the currency appreciation to maintain external balance. The resulting higher price of imports, plus the decline in household income resulting from the reduction in foreign demand, means that households can no longer afford the previous level of consumption and it falls back below the original baseline level. Although country A's net export position improves relative to the no retaliation case, this is more than offset by lower consumption and investment and GDP declines. In the end, both country A and country B are left worse off by the increase in protectionism.

A similar exercise is examined at the global level in Scenario Figure 2 where it is assumed that a growing level of protectionism in all countries raises tariff and nontariff barriers gradually over the first three years such that import prices everywhere rise by 10 percent. It is assumed that half of the increase in import prices is from tariffs, the revenue from which is returned to households via transfers, and half is from an

Scenario Figure 2. A Worldwide Increase in Protectionism
(Percent difference from baseline, unless noted otherwise)

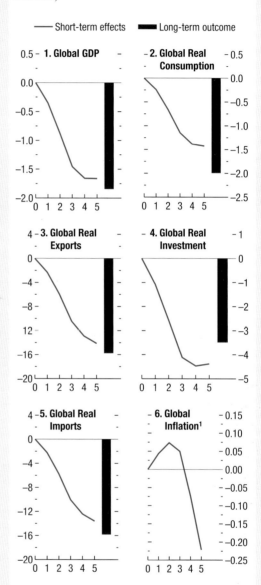

Source: IMF staff estimates.
[1]Global inflation shown in percentage point difference.

Scenario Box 1. Tariff Scenarios *(continued)*

increase in nontariff barriers. The higher cost of traded goods lowers global output by almost 1¾ percent after five years and by almost 2 percent in the long run. Global consumption falls by a similar amount, with global investment falling by even more. Global trade however takes the biggest hit, with imports and exports down by 15 percent after five years and 16

percent in the long run. Although rising import prices help raise global inflation marginally during the period of rising protectionism, once trade restrictions are no longer increasing in year 4, the decline in demand starts to dominate and inflation falls below baseline, resulting in a lower level of prices in the long run globally.

Box 1.1. World Growth Projections over the Medium Term

This box discusses the factors explaining the evolution of medium-term growth projections for the global economy and how the projections compare with historical averages. For that purpose, it is useful to recall how the world growth rate g_t^W for a generic year t is calculated. Specifically, $g_t^W = \sum_i \omega_{it} g_{it}$ where ω_{it} is country i's weight in global output for year t (calculated at purchasing power parity) and g_{it} is country i's growth rate in year t. It follows that the change in the world growth rate between year t and year T (in this case, 2016 and 2021) can be written as follows:

$$g_T^W - g_t^W = \sum_i \omega_{it}(g_{iT} - g_{it}) + \sum_i (\omega_{iT} - \omega_{it}) g_{iT}$$

That is, the change in the world growth rate can be decomposed into two terms:
- The weighted sum of changes in individual growth rate forecasts between 2016 and 2021 (using 2016 weights)
- The impact of changes in country weights between 2016 and 2021, measured by the difference between the 2021 world growth rate evaluated at 2021 weights and 2016 weights

The results of this decomposition are displayed in the first panel of Figure 1.1.1. The change in country weights (reflecting the increase in weights for emerging market and developing economies growing faster than the world average—primarily China and India) explains about one-third of the ¾ percentage point increase in global growth whereas the weighted sum of changes in growth forecasts explains the remaining two-thirds. A large part of the latter (0.36 percentage points) is explained by a normalization of conditions in a handful of emerging market and developing economies experiencing a recession in 2016 (Argentina, Brazil, Nigeria, Russia, South Africa, and Venezuela). The aggregate GDP growth rate of these economies is projected to be –2.3 percent in 2016, and about 2 percent in 2021.[1] Higher growth in advanced economies explains only 0.10 percentage point, with the remainder explained by faster growth elsewhere in emerging market and developing economies.

The second panel of Figure 1.1.1 puts the medium-term growth forecast in perspective by comparing it to average growth rates over the past 20 years.

Figure 1.1.1. World Growth Projections over the Medium Term
(Percent, unless noted otherwise)

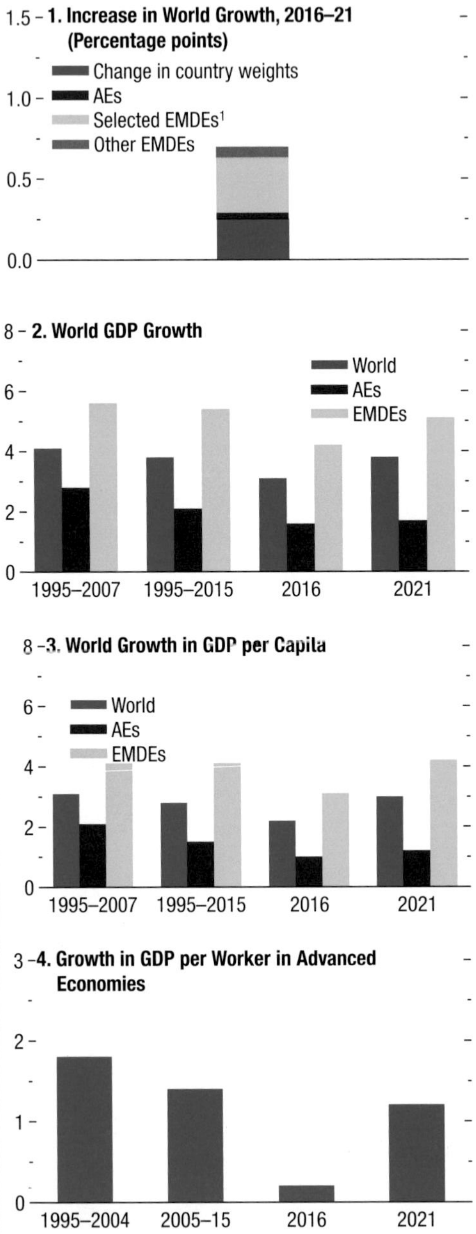

1. Increase in World Growth, 2016–21
(Percentage points)
- Change in country weights
- AEs
- Selected EMDEs[1]
- Other EMDEs

2. World GDP Growth
- World
- AEs
- EMDEs

3. World Growth in GDP per Capita
- World
- AEs
- EMDEs

4. Growth in GDP per Worker in Advanced Economies

Source: IMF staff estimates.
Note: AEs = advanced economies; EMDEs = emerging market and developing economies.
[1]Selected EMDEs = Argentina, Brazil, Nigeria, Russia, South Africa, Venezuela.

[1]The negative impact on world growth from recessions in emerging market economies in 2015 (2016) was more than three (two) times its median value over the past 20 years.

Box 1.1 *(continued)*

While the growth forecast for 2016 is considerably lower than historical averages, world growth in 2021 is projected to be broadly in line with its average over the past two decades.[2] The figure also illustrates the role played by shifts in weights between advanced economies and emerging market and developing economies: while the projected growth rate for 2021 for both country groups is below their 1995–2015 average, the increased weight on (faster-growing) emerging market and developing economies implies that world growth is roughly unchanged. The shift in weights also affects the aggregate growth rate for the emerging market and developing economies group: that growth rate for 2021 would be 0.6 percentage points lower if it were calculated with precrisis (2007) weights.

However, as highlighted in this chapter, the world is undergoing an important demographic transition. Hence, the third panel of Figure 1.1.1 provides the same comparison for growth in GDP per capita. It shows that by 2021 world growth is projected to exceed its average of the past two decades, again reflecting shifts in weights: per capita growth is projected to be in line with its 20-year average for emerging market and developing economies (also reflecting

shifts in weights within the group, as mentioned above), and below historical averages for advanced economies.

The aging process implies not only a decline in population growth rates, but an even sharper decline in the growth rate of the workforce. To account for this factor, the fourth panel of Figure 1.1.1 compares growth in GDP per worker for advanced economies (the only ones for which historical data and projections for employment are available). The figure shows that growth is projected to pick up relative to its average over the past decade, but to remain below its precrisis average.

In sum, this box highlights three main points. First, the projected increase in global GDP growth over the next five years reflects to an important extent the normalization of conditions in a few large emerging market and developing economies currently in a recession, as well as the increased global weight of emerging market and developing economies as a whole. Second, taking into account the impact of the demographic transition on population growth rates, the projections for medium-term growth for the global economy are actually broadly in line with precrisis averages. Third, shifts in relative weights across emerging market and developing economies play an important role in explaining growth resilience for the country group as a whole, as the relative importance of countries growing faster than average is increasing.

[2]The 2021 growth forecast is marginally higher than estimated potential growth for that year given that output gaps are on average still slightly negative in 2020.

Annex Table 1.1.1. Europe: Real GDP, Consumer Prices, Current Account Balance, and Unemployment
(Annual percent change, unless noted otherwise)

| | Real GDP | | | Consumer Prices[1] | | | Current Account Balance[2] | | | Unemployment[3] | | |
| | | Projections | | | Projections | | | Projections | | | Projections | |
	2015	2016	2017	2015	2016	2017	2015	2016	2017	2015	2016	2017
Europe	**2.4**	**2.0**	**1.8**	**0.6**	**0.9**	**1.8**	**2.3**	**2.3**	**2.3**	...	...	...
Advanced Europe	**2.2**	**1.7**	**1.5**	**0.1**	**0.4**	**1.3**	**2.7**	**2.7**	**2.8**	**9.5**	**8.7**	**8.5**
Euro Area[4,5]	2.0	1.7	1.5	0.0	0.3	1.1	3.2	3.4	3.1	10.9	10.0	9.7
Germany	1.5	1.7	1.4	0.1	0.4	1.5	8.4	8.6	8.1	4.6	4.3	4.5
France	1.3	1.3	1.3	0.1	0.3	1.0	−0.2	−0.5	−0.4	10.4	9.8	9.6
Italy	0.8	0.8	0.9	0.1	−0.1	0.5	2.2	2.2	1.9	11.9	11.5	11.2
Spain	3.2	3.1	2.2	−0.5	−0.3	1.0	1.4	1.9	1.7	22.1	19.4	18.0
Netherlands	2.0	1.7	1.6	0.2	0.1	0.9	8.6	9.1	8.2	6.9	6.7	6.5
Belgium	1.4	1.4	1.4	0.6	2.1	1.6	0.0	0.1	0.4	8.5	8.4	8.3
Austria	0.9	1.4	1.2	0.8	0.9	1.5	2.6	2.6	2.7	5.7	6.2	6.4
Greece	−0.2	0.1	2.8	−1.1	−0.1	0.6	0.0	0.0	0.0	25.0	23.3	21.5
Portugal	1.5	1.0	1.1	0.5	0.7	1.1	0.4	0.0	−0.7	12.4	11.2	10.7
Ireland	26.3	4.9	3.2	0.0	0.3	1.2	10.2	9.5	9.1	9.5	8.3	7.7
Finland	0.2	0.9	1.1	−0.2	0.4	1.2	0.1	0.1	0.2	9.3	9.1	8.9
Slovak Republic	3.6	3.4	3.3	−0.3	−0.2	1.1	−1.3	−1.0	−0.6	11.5	9.9	8.8
Lithuania	1.6	2.6	3.0	−0.7	0.5	1.2	−1.7	−1.6	−2.8	9.1	7.8	7.6
Slovenia	2.3	2.3	1.8	−0.5	−0.3	1.0	5.2	7.7	7.2	9.0	8.2	7.9
Luxembourg	4.8	3.5	3.1	0.1	0.2	1.0	5.5	4.4	4.3	6.9	6.4	6.3
Latvia	2.7	2.5	3.4	0.2	0.2	1.7	−1.2	−2.0	−1.2	9.9	9.4	9.2
Estonia	1.1	1.5	2.5	0.1	0.5	1.4	2.1	0.6	0.0	6.1	5.6	5.5
Cyprus[5]	1.5	2.8	2.2	−1.5	−1.0	0.5	−3.6	−0.9	−3.7	14.9	13.0	11.6
Malta	6.2	4.1	3.4	1.2	1.2	1.5	9.9	6.2	5.8	5.4	4.8	4.9
United Kingdom[5]	2.2	1.8	1.1	0.1	0.7	2.5	−5.4	−5.9	−4.3	5.4	5.0	5.2
Switzerland	0.8	1.0	1.3	−1.1	−0.4	0.0	11.4	9.2	9.0	3.2	3.5	3.4
Sweden	4.2	3.6	2.6	0.7	1.1	1.4	5.2	5.0	5.3	7.4	6.9	6.7
Norway	1.6	0.8	1.2	2.2	3.2	2.3	9.0	7.0	7.6	4.4	4.7	4.5
Czech Republic	4.5	2.5	2.7	0.3	0.6	1.9	0.9	1.5	1.0	5.0	4.1	4.1
Denmark	1.0	1.0	1.4	0.5	0.4	1.1	7.0	6.7	6.6	6.2	6.0	5.8
Iceland	4.0	4.9	3.8	1.6	1.7	3.1	4.2	2.9	1.9	4.0	3.4	3.5
San Marino	0.5	1.0	1.2	0.1	0.6	0.7	...	...	...	8.4	7.9	7.3
Emerging and Developing Europe[6]	**3.6**	**3.3**	**3.1**	**2.9**	**3.1**	**4.2**	**−1.9**	**−2.0**	**−3.0**	...	...	...
Turkey	4.0	3.3	3.0	7.7	8.4	8.2	−4.5	−4.4	−5.6	10.3	10.2	10.2
Poland	3.6	3.1	3.4	−0.9	−0.6	1.1	−0.2	−0.1	−1.0	7.5	6.3	6.2
Romania	3.8	5.0	3.8	−0.6	−1.5	1.7	−1.1	−2.0	−2.8	6.8	6.4	6.2
Hungary	2.9	2.0	2.5	−0.1	0.4	1.9	4.4	4.9	4.6	6.8	6.0	5.8
Bulgaria[5]	3.0	3.0	2.8	−1.1	−1.6	0.6	1.4	0.8	0.0	9.2	8.2	7.1
Serbia	0.7	2.5	2.8	1.4	1.3	3.2	−4.8	−4.2	−3.9	18.5	18.6	18.7
Croatia	1.6	1.9	2.1	−0.5	−1.0	0.8	5.2	3.0	2.2	16.9	16.4	15.9

Note: Data for some countries are based on fiscal years. Please refer to Table F in the Statistical Appendix for a list of countries with exceptional reporting periods.
[1]Movements in consumer prices are shown as annual averages. Year-end to year-end changes can be found in Tables A6 and A7 in the Statistical Appendix.
[2]Percent of GDP.
[3]Percent. National definitions of unemployment may differ.
[4]Current account position corrected for reporting discrepancies in intra-area transactions.
[5]Based on Eurostat's harmonized index of consumer prices.
[6]Includes Albania, Bosnia and Herzegovina, Kosovo, FYR Macedonia, and Montenegro.

Annex Table 1.1.2. Asia and Pacific: Real GDP, Consumer Prices, Current Account Balance, and Unemployment
(Annual percent change, unless noted otherwise)

	Real GDP			Consumer Prices[1]			Current Account Balance[2]			Unemployment[3]		
		Projections			Projections			Projections			Projections	
	2015	2016	2017	2015	2016	2017	2015	2016	2017	2015	2016	2017
Asia	5.4	5.4	5.3	2.3	2.5	2.9	2.8	2.6	1.9	. . .	. . .	. . .
Advanced Asia	1.2	1.3	1.6	0.8	0.5	1.2	4.1	4.4	3.8	3.7	3.6	3.5
Japan	0.5	0.5	0.6	0.8	−0.2	0.5	3.3	3.7	3.3	3.4	3.2	3.2
Korea	2.6	2.7	3.0	0.7	1.0	1.9	7.7	7.2	5.9	3.6	3.6	3.3
Australia	2.4	2.9	2.7	1.5	1.3	2.1	−4.7	−3.5	−3.9	6.1	5.7	5.7
Taiwan Province of China	0.6	1.0	1.7	−0.3	1.1	1.1	14.6	15.0	14.4	3.8	3.9	4.0
Singapore	2.0	1.7	2.2	−0.5	−0.3	1.1	19.8	19.3	19.3	1.9	2.0	2.0
Hong Kong SAR	2.4	1.4	1.9	3.0	2.5	2.6	3.1	2.8	2.9	3.3	3.2	3.1
New Zealand	3.0	2.8	2.7	0.3	0.7	1.6	−3.2	−3.0	−3.5	5.4	5.3	5.5
Macao SAR[4]	−20.3	−4.7	0.2	4.6	2.6	2.8	28.0	28.4	29.2	1.9	1.9	2.0
Emerging and Developing Asia	6.6	6.5	6.3	2.7	3.1	3.3	2.1	1.6	0.8	. . .	. . .	. . .
China	6.9	6.6	6.2	1.4	2.1	2.3	3.0	2.4	1.6	4.1	4.1	4.1
India[5]	7.6	7.6	7.6	4.9	5.5	5.2	−1.1	−1.4	−2.0	. . .	. . .	. . .
ASEAN-5	4.8	4.8	5.1	3.3	2.5	3.4	1.5	1.2	0.7	. . .	. . .	. . .
Indonesia	4.8	4.9	5.3	6.4	3.7	4.2	−2.1	−2.3	−2.3	6.2	5.6	5.7
Thailand	2.8	3.2	3.3	−0.9	0.3	1.6	7.8	9.6	7.7	0.9	0.8	0.7
Malaysia	5.0	4.3	4.6	2.1	2.1	3.0	3.0	1.2	1.5	3.2	3.2	3.2
Philippines	5.9	6.4	6.7	1.4	2.0	3.4	2.9	1.8	1.4	6.3	5.9	5.7
Vietnam	6.7	6.1	6.2	0.6	2.0	3.6	0.5	0.4	0.1	2.4	2.4	2.4
Other Emerging and Developing Asia[6]	6.0	6.0	6.3	6.0	6.3	6.7	−1.5	−2.4	−3.5	. . .	. . .	. . .
Memorandum												
Emerging Asia[7]	6.7	6.5	6.3	2.6	3.0	3.2	2.2	1.7	1.0	. . .	. . .	. . .

Note: Data for some countries are based on fiscal years. Please refer to Table F in the Statistical Appendix for a list of countries with exceptional reporting periods.
[1]Movements in consumer prices are shown as annual averages. Year-end to year-end changes can be found in Tables A6 and A7 in the Statistical Appendix.
[2]Percent of GDP.
[3]Percent. National definitions of unemployment may differ.
[4]Macao SAR is classified as an advanced economy. It is a Special Administrative Region of China, but its statistical data are maintained on a separate and independent basis.
[5]See country-specific notes for India in the "Country Notes" section of the Statistical Appendix.
[6]Other Emerging and Developing Asia comprises Bangladesh, Bhutan, Brunei Darussalam, Cambodia, Fiji, Kiribati, Lao P.D.R., Maldives, Marshall Islands, Micronesia, Mongolia, Myanmar, Nepal, Palau, Papua New Guinea, Samoa, Solomon Islands, Sri Lanka, Timor-Leste, Tonga, Tuvalu, and Vanuatu.
[7]Emerging Asia comprises the ASEAN-5 (Indonesia, Malaysia, Philippines, Thailand, Vietnam) economies, China, and India.

Annex Table 1.1.3. Western Hemisphere: Real GDP, Consumer Prices, Current Account Balance, and Unemployment
(Annual percent change, unless noted otherwise)

	Real GDP			Consumer Prices[1]			Current Account Balance[2]			Unemployment[3]		
		Projections			Projections			Projections			Projections	
	2015	2016	2017	2015	2016	2017	2015	2016	2017	2015	2016	2017
North America	**2.5**	**1.6**	**2.2**	**0.4**	**1.4**	**2.4**	**−2.6**	**−2.6**	**−2.7**	**...**	**...**	**...**
United States	2.6	1.6	2.2	0.1	1.2	2.3	−2.6	−2.5	−2.7	5.3	4.9	4.8
Canada	1.1	1.2	1.9	1.1	1.6	2.1	−3.2	−3.7	−3.1	6.9	7.0	7.1
Mexico	2.5	2.1	2.3	2.7	2.8	3.3	−2.9	−2.7	−2.8	4.4	4.1	3.9
Puerto Rico[4]	0.0	−1.8	−1.4	−0.8	−0.2	1.1	...	...	...	12.0	11.9	11.9
South America[5]	**−1.3**	**−2.0**	**1.1**	**...**	**...**	**...**	**−3.7**	**−2.0**	**−2.0**	**...**	**...**	**...**
Brazil	−3.8	−3.3	0.5	9.0	9.0	5.4	−3.3	−0.8	−1.3	8.5	11.2	11.5
Argentina[6]	2.5	−1.8	2.7	...	...	23.2	−2.5	−2.3	−3.2	...	9.2	8.5
Colombia	3.1	2.2	2.7	5.0	7.6	4.1	−6.4	−5.2	−4.2	8.9	9.7	9.6
Venezuela	−6.2	−10.0	−4.5	121.7	475.8	1,660.1	−7.8	−3.4	−0.9	7.4	18.1	21.4
Chile	2.3	1.7	2.0	4.3	4.0	3.0	−2.0	−1.9	−2.4	6.2	7.0	7.6
Peru	3.3	3.7	4.1	3.5	3.6	2.5	−4.4	−3.8	−3.1	6.0	6.0	6.0
Ecuador	0.3	−2.3	−2.7	4.0	2.4	1.1	−2.2	−1.5	−0.9	4.8	6.1	6.9
Bolivia	4.8	3.7	3.9	4.1	3.9	5.1	−5.8	−6.6	−4.9	4.0	4.0	4.0
Uruguay	1.0	0.1	1.2	8.7	10.2	8.7	−3.5	−2.9	−3.1	7.5	7.9	8.5
Paraguay	3.1	3.5	3.6	3.1	4.1	4.1	−1.7	0.6	−0.5	6.1	5.9	5.5
Central America[7]	**4.2**	**3.9**	**4.1**	**1.4**	**2.5**	**3.0**	**−4.0**	**−3.7**	**−3.7**	**...**	**...**	**...**
Caribbean[8]	**3.9**	**3.4**	**3.6**	**2.2**	**3.5**	**4.5**	**−4.3**	**−4.5**	**−4.6**	**...**	**...**	**...**
Memorandum												
Latin America and the Caribbean[9]	0.0	−0.6	1.6	5.5	5.8	4.2	−3.6	−2.3	−2.3	...	...	...
East Caribbean Currency Union[10]	2.3	2.2	2.6	−0.9	0.3	2.2	−12.1	−12.6	−13.8	...	...	...

Note: Data for some countries are based on fiscal years. Please refer to Table F in the Statistical Appendix for a list of countries with exceptional reporting periods.
[1]Movements in consumer prices are shown as annual averages. Year-end to year-end changes can be found in Tables A6 and A7 in the Statistical Appendix.
[2]Percent of GDP.
[3]Percent. National definitions of unemployment may differ.
[4]The Commonwealth of Puerto Rico is classified as an advanced economy. It is a territory of the United States, but its statistical data are maintained on a separate and independent basis.
[5]Includes Guyana and Suriname. Data for Argentina and Venezuela's consumer prices are excluded. See country-specific notes for Argentina in the "Country Notes" section of the Statistical Appendix.
[6]See country-specific notes for Argentina in the "Country Notes" section of the Statistical Appendix.
[7]Central America comprises Belize, Costa Rica, El Salvador, Guatemala, Honduras, Nicaragua, and Panama.
[8]The Caribbean comprises Antigua and Barbuda, The Bahamas, Barbados, Dominica, Dominican Republic, Grenada, Haiti, Jamaica, St. Kitts and Nevis, St. Lucia, St. Vincent and the Grenadines, and Trinidad and Tobago.
[9]Latin America and the Caribbean comprises Mexico and economies of the Caribbean, Central America, and South America. Data for Argentina and Venezuela's consumer prices are excluded. See country-specific notes for Argentina in the "Country Notes" section of the Statistical Appendix.
[10]Eastern Caribbean Currency Union comprises Antigua and Barbuda, Dominica, Grenada, St. Kitts and Nevis, St. Lucia, and St. Vincent and the Grenadines, as well as Anguilla and Montserrat, which are not IMF members.

Annex Table 1.1.4. Commonwealth of Independent States: Real GDP, Consumer Prices, Current Account Balance, and Unemployment

(Annual percent change, unless noted otherwise)

	Real GDP			Consumer Prices[1]			Current Account Balance[2]			Unemployment[3]		
		Projections			Projections			Projections			Projections	
	2015	2016	2017	2015	2016	2017	2015	2016	2017	2015	2016	2017
Commonwealth of Independent States[4]	−2.8	−0.3	1.4	15.5	8.4	6.3	3.0	1.3	1.9	. . .	. . .	. . .
Net Energy Exporters	**−2.4**	**−0.4**	**1.3**	**13.7**	**7.9**	**5.8**	**3.6**	**1.9**	**2.5**	. . .	. . .	. . .
Russia	−3.7	−0.8	1.1	15.5	7.2	5.0	5.2	3.0	3.5	5.6	5.8	5.9
Kazakhstan	1.2	−0.8	0.6	6.5	13.1	9.3	−2.4	−2.2	0.0	5.0	5.0	5.0
Uzbekistan	8.0	6.0	6.0	8.5	8.4	9.6	0.1	0.1	0.2	. . .	. . .	. . .
Azerbaijan	1.1	−2.4	1.4	4.0	10.2	8.5	−0.4	0.7	3.1	6.0	6.0	6.0
Turkmenistan	6.5	5.4	5.4	6.4	5.5	5.0	−10.3	−18.5	−18.0	. . .	. . .	. . .
Net Energy Importers	**−5.7**	**0.7**	**2.1**	**29.4**	**11.9**	**9.9**	**−3.0**	**−4.0**	**−4.2**	. . .	. . .	. . .
Ukraine	−9.9	1.5	2.5	48.7	15.1	11.0	−0.3	−1.5	−2.1	9.1	9.0	8.7
Belarus	−3.9	−3.0	−0.5	13.5	12.7	12.0	−3.8	−4.9	−4.8	1.5	1.5	1.5
Georgia	2.8	3.4	5.2	4.0	2.6	3.6	−11.7	−12.1	−12.0	12.0	. . .	. . .
Armenia	3.0	3.2	3.4	3.7	−0.5	2.5	−2.7	−2.5	−3.0	17.7	17.9	18.0
Tajikistan	6.0	6.0	4.5	5.8	6.3	7.3	−6.0	−5.0	−5.0	. . .	. . .	. . .
Kyrgyz Republic	3.5	2.2	2.3	6.5	1.1	7.4	−10.4	−15.0	−14.9	7.5	7.4	7.3
Moldova	−0.5	2.0	3.0	9.6	6.8	4.4	−4.7	−2.8	−3.4	4.9	4.7	4.5
Memorandum												
Caucasus and Central Asia[5]	3.2	1.3	2.6	6.2	9.8	8.3	−3.0	−4.1	−2.8	. . .	. . .	. . .
Low-Income CIS Countries[6]	6.1	5.0	5.2	7.3	6.3	7.7	−3.0	−3.0	−3.1	. . .	. . .	. . .
Net Energy Exporters Excluding Russia	3.1	1.0	2.4	6.4	10.8	8.7	−2.4	−3.5	−2.0	. . .	. . .	. . .

Note: Data for some countries are based on fiscal years. Please refer to Table F in the Statistical Appendix for a list of countries with exceptional reporting periods.
[1]Movements in consumer prices are shown as annual averages. Year-end to year-end changes can be found in Table A7 in the Statistical Appendix.
[2]Percent of GDP.
[3]Percent. National definitions of unemployment may differ.
[4]Georgia, Turkmenistan, and Ukraine, which are not members of the Commonwealth of Independent States (CIS), are included in this group for reasons of geography and similarity in economic structure.
[5]Caucasus and Central Asia comprises Armenia, Azerbaijan, Georgia, Kazakhstan, the Kyrgyz Republic, Tajikistan, Turkmenistan, and Uzbekistan.
[6]Low-Income CIS Countries comprise Armenia, Georgia, the Kyrgyz Republic, Moldova, Tajikistan, and Uzbekistan.

Annex Table 1.1.5. Middle East, North Africa, Afghanistan, and Pakistan: Real GDP, Consumer Prices, Current Account Balance, and Unemployment

(Annual percent change, unless noted otherwise)

	Real GDP			Consumer Prices[1]			Current Account Balance[2]			Unemployment[3]		
		Projections			Projections			Projections			Projections	
	2015	2016	2017	2015	2016	2017	2015	2016	2017	2015	2016	2017
Middle East, North Africa, Afghanistan, and Pakistan	2.3	3.4	3.4	5.8	5.1	6.0	−4.0	−4.6	−2.6	...	...	...
Oil Exporters[4]	1.6	3.3	2.9	5.4	4.7	4.2	−3.8	−4.4	−1.8	...	...	...
Saudi Arabia	3.5	1.2	2.0	2.2	4.0	2.0	−8.3	−6.6	−2.6	5.6	...	...
Iran	0.4	4.5	4.1	11.9	7.4	7.2	2.1	4.2	3.3	10.8	11.3	11.2
United Arab Emirates	4.0	2.3	2.5	4.1	3.6	3.1	3.3	1.1	3.2	...	...	...
Algeria	3.9	3.6	2.9	4.8	5.9	4.8	−16.5	−15.1	−13.7	11.2	9.9	10.4
Iraq	−2.4	10.3	0.5	1.4	2.0	2.0	−7.2	−10.8	−3.6	...	...	...
Qatar	3.7	2.6	3.4	1.8	3.0	3.1	8.2	−1.8	0.0	...	...	...
Kuwait	1.1	2.5	2.6	3.2	3.4	3.8	5.2	3.6	8.4	2.1	2.1	2.1
Oil Importers[5]	3.8	3.6	4.2	6.7	5.9	9.9	−4.5	−4.8	−4.7	...	...	...
Egypt	4.2	3.8	4.0	11.0	10.2	18.2	−3.7	−5.8	−5.2	12.9	12.7	12.3
Pakistan	4.0	4.7	5.0	4.5	2.9	5.2	−1.0	−0.9	−1.5	5.9	6.0	6.0
Morocco	4.5	1.8	4.8	1.5	1.3	1.3	−1.9	−1.2	−1.4	9.7	10.2	10.1
Sudan	4.9	3.1	3.5	16.9	13.5	16.1	−7.8	−5.9	−4.9	21.6	20.6	19.6
Tunisia	0.8	1.5	2.8	4.9	3.7	3.9	−8.8	−8.0	−6.9	15.0	14.0	13.0
Lebanon	1.0	1.0	2.0	−3.7	−0.7	2.0	−21.0	−20.4	−20.6	...	...	...
Jordan	2.4	2.8	3.3	−0.9	−0.5	2.3	−9.0	−9.0	−8.9	13.1	...	...
Memorandum												
Middle East and North Africa	2.1	3.2	3.2	6.0	5.4	6.1	−4.4	−5.0	−2.8	...	...	...
Israel[6]	2.5	2.8	3.0	−0.6	−0.6	0.8	4.6	3.1	2.9	5.2	5.2	5.2
Maghreb[7]	2.8	2.3	4.3	4.7	5.0	4.5	−14.4	−13.8	−12.7	...	...	...
Mashreq[8]	3.9	3.6	3.8	9.1	8.7	16.0	−6.3	−7.9	−7.7	...	...	...

Note: Data for some countries are based on fiscal years. Please refer to Table F in the Statistical Appendix for a list of countries with exceptional reporting periods.
[1]Movements in consumer prices are shown as annual averages. Year-end to year-end changes can be found in Tables A6 and A7 in the Statistical Appendix.
[2]Percent of GDP.
[3]Percent. National definitions of unemployment may differ.
[4]Includes Bahrain, Libya, Oman, and Yemen.
[5]Includes Afghanistan, Djibouti, and Mauritania. Excludes Syria because of the uncertain political situation.
[6]Israel, which is not a member of the economic region, is included for reasons of geography. Note that Israel is not included in the regional aggregates.
[7]The Maghreb comprises Algeria, Libya, Mauritania, Morocco, and Tunisia.
[8]The Mashreq comprises Egypt, Jordan, and Lebanon. Syria is excluded because of the uncertain political situation.

Annex Table 1.1.6. Sub-Saharan Africa: Real GDP, Consumer Prices, Current Account Balance, and Unemployment
(Annual percent change, unless noted otherwise)

	Real GDP			Consumer Prices[1]			Current Account Balance[2]			Unemployment[3]		
		Projections			Projections			Projections			Projections	
	2015	2016	2017	2015	2016	2017	2015	2016	2017	2015	2016	2017
Sub-Saharan Africa	3.4	1.4	2.9	7.0	11.3	10.8	−5.9	−4.5	−3.9	...	...	...
Oil Exporters[4]	2.4	−1.7	0.8	9.1	19.1	19.3	−4.8	−2.1	−1.8	...	...	...
Nigeria	2.7	−1.7	0.6	9.0	15.4	17.1	−3.1	−0.7	−0.4	9.0	12.1	...
Angola	3.0	0.0	1.5	10.3	33.7	38.3	−8.5	−5.4	−5.4	...	...	...
Gabon	4.0	3.2	4.5	0.1	2.5	2.5	−2.3	−5.3	−4.7	...	...	...
Chad	1.8	−1.1	1.7	3.7	0.0	5.2	−12.4	−8.7	−7.8	...	...	...
Republic of Congo	2.3	1.7	5.0	2.0	4.0	3.7	−21.0	−8.2	−2.1	...	...	...
Middle-Income Countries[5]	2.6	1.9	2.9	5.4	7.0	5.7	−4.3	−3.9	−3.6	...	...	...
South Africa	1.3	0.1	0.8	4.6	6.4	6.0	−4.3	−3.3	−3.2	25.4	26.3	27.0
Ghana	3.9	3.3	7.4	17.2	17.0	10.0	−7.5	−6.3	−6.0	...	...	...
Côte d'Ivoire	8.5	8.0	8.0	1.2	1.0	1.5	−1.8	−1.8	−2.1	...	...	...
Cameroon	5.8	4.8	4.2	2.7	2.2	2.2	−4.2	−4.2	−4.0	...	...	...
Zambia	3.0	3.0	4.0	10.1	19.1	9.1	−3.5	−4.5	−2.2	...	...	...
Senegal	6.5	6.6	6.8	0.1	1.0	1.8	−7.6	−8.4	−8.2	...	...	...
Low-Income Countries[6]	5.8	5.4	5.8	5.7	5.8	5.9	−10.1	−8.8	−7.4	...	...	...
Ethiopia	10.2	6.5	7.5	10.1	7.7	8.2	−12.0	−10.7	−9.3	...	...	...
Kenya	5.6	6.0	6.1	6.6	6.2	5.5	−6.8	−6.4	−6.1	...	...	...
Tanzania	7.0	7.2	7.2	5.6	5.2	5.0	−8.8	−8.8	−8.8	...	...	...
Uganda	4.8	4.9	5.5	5.5	5.5	5.1	−9.4	−8.7	−8.9	...	...	...
Madagascar	3.1	4.1	4.5	7.4	6.7	6.9	−1.9	−2.3	−3.7	...	...	...
Democratic Republic of the Congo	6.9	3.9	4.2	1.0	1.7	2.7	−3.7	−0.8	5.2	...	...	...
Memorandum												
Sub-Saharan Africa Excluding South Sudan	3.4	1.5	2.9	6.7	10.2	10.4	−5.8	−4.5	−3.9	...	...	...

Note: Data for some countries are based on fiscal years. Please refer to Table F in the Statistical Appendix for a list of countries with exceptional reporting periods.
[1]Movements in consumer prices are shown as annual averages. Year-end to year-end changes can be found in Table A7 in the Statistical Appendix.
[2]Percent of GDP.
[3]Percent. National definitions of unemployment may differ.
[4]Includes Equatorial Guinea and South Sudan.
[5]Includes Botswana, Cabo Verde, Lesotho, Mauritius, Namibia, Seychelles, and Swaziland.
[6]Includes Benin, Burkina Faso, Burundi, the Central African Republic, Comoros, Eritrea, The Gambia, Guinea, Guinea-Bissau, Liberia, Malawi, Mali, Mozambique, Niger, Rwanda, São Tomé and Príncipe, Sierra Leone, Togo, and Zimbabwe.

Special Feature: Commodity Market Developments and Forecasts, with a Focus on Food Security and Markets in the World Economy

Commodity prices have rebounded since the release of the April 2016 World Economic Outlook *(WEO) in spite of rising uncertainty following the Brexit vote—the June 23, 2016, U.K. referendum result in favor of leaving the European Union. Supply outages in various countries have led to tighter oil markets. The announcement of China's stimulus package increased metal demand prospects and prices. Unfavorable weather conditions have put upward pressure on food prices. This special feature includes an in-depth analysis of food security and markets in the world economy.*

The IMF's Primary Commodities Price Index has rebounded 22 percent since February 2016, the reference period for the April 2016 WEO (Figure 1.SF.1, panel 1). Oil prices have rallied, by 44 percent, due to involuntary outages. Natural gas prices have declined. With strong supply from Russia, natural gas prices in Europe are at their lowest in 12 years. Asian markets show weaker demand from Japan, which is reactivating its nuclear power plants. Coal prices have rebounded. Nonfuel commodity prices have increased, with metals and agricultural commodities prices increasing by 12 percent and 9 percent, respectively.

Oil markets are in midstream. On the supply side, the market has been hit by a few outages. Some had a short-term impact on production, including the labor dispute in Kuwait and the Fort McMurray wildfires in Canada, but others, such as the geopolitical unrest in Iraq, Libya, Nigeria, and Yemen, could have a long-term impact. These disruptions temporarily brought balance to the oil market. On the policy front, the Organization of the Petroleum Exporting Countries (OPEC) did not reach its production target agreement in June. However, some observers expect OPEC members to set a new target in November once the Islamic Republic of Iran's production reaches its presanction level.

The recent oil price rebound has helped shale producers, leading to a bottoming of rig count. In addition, drilled-but-uncompleted wells can be completed at current price levels, which will add to U.S. oil

The authors of this feature are Rabah Arezki (team leader), Claudia Berg, Christian Bogmans, and Akito Matsumoto, with research assistance from Rachel Yuting Fan and Vanessa Diaz Montelongo.

Figure 1.SF.1. Commodity Market Developments

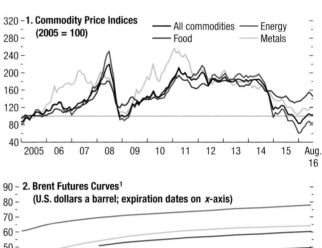

1. Commodity Price Indices (2005 = 100)
All commodities — Energy — Food — Metals

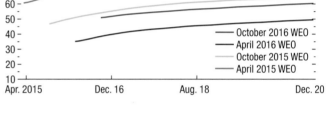

2. Brent Futures Curves[1] (U.S. dollars a barrel; expiration dates on *x*-axis)
October 2016 WEO — April 2016 WEO — October 2015 WEO — April 2015 WEO

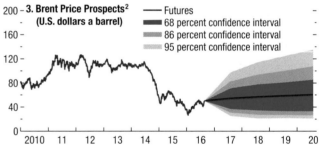

3. Brent Price Prospects[2] (U.S. dollars a barrel)
Futures — 68 percent confidence interval — 86 percent confidence interval — 95 percent confidence interval

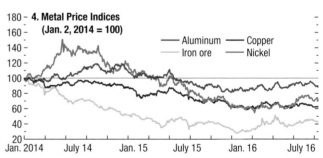

4. Metal Price Indices (Jan. 2, 2014 = 100)
Aluminum — Copper — Iron ore — Nickel

Sources: Bloomberg, L.P.; IMF, Primary Commodity Price System; Thomson Reuters Datastream; and IMF staff estimates.
Note: WTI = West Texas Intermediate.
[1] *World Economic Outlook* (WEO) future prices are baseline assumptions for each WEO and derived from future prices. October WEO prices are based on August 18, 2016, closing.
[2] Derived from prices of futures options on August 18, 2016.

production. Tighter credit conditions could, however, limit the recovery in investment. Canada's oil production is strong, but new investment in oil sand fields is limited. In sum, uncertainties over supply stem from the persistence of involuntary outages, OPEC policy, and investment in unconventional oil fields.

After strong global oil demand growth last year—at 1.6 million barrels a day—on account of lower oil prices for the most part, the International Energy Agency expects growth in demand slightly above trend at 1.3 million barrels a day in 2016 and 1.2 million barrels a day in 2017. Given robust oil demand, the continued erosion of high-cost producers, and severe unplanned outages, markets expect the oil market to rebalance during the course of next year.

Natural gas prices are declining—with a key natural gas price index (the price average for Europe, Japan, and the United States) down by 6 percent since February 2016. Falling oil prices, abundant natural gas production from Russia, and weak demand in Asia have contributed to that decline. In the United States, natural gas prices have instead edged higher on account of stronger demand from the power sector, reflecting hotter-than-expected weather. The coal price index of average Australian and South African prices has also increased 32 percent since February 2016 in line with other energy and metal prices.

Oil futures contracts point to rising prices (Figure 1.SF.1, panel 2). Baseline assumptions for the IMF's average petroleum spot prices, which are based on futures prices, suggest average annual prices of $43.0 a barrel in 2016—a decline of 15 percent from 2015—and $50.6 a barrel in 2017 (Figure 1.SF.1, panel 3). There remains substantial uncertainty around the baseline assumptions for oil prices. Although geopolitical tensions in the Middle East could cause oil market disruptions, high inventory and a rapid response from U.S. shale producers should mitigate a sharp rise in prices in the near future. Oil demand could weaken if the consequences of Brexit for global aggregate demand are more severe than anticipated. In the medium term, the oil market is expected to remain quite tight in light of supply constraints, considering that the decline in oil prices has dramatically reduced investment in extraction, unless shale production can be boosted or global demand falters. In that environment, geopolitical events could trigger oil price hikes.

Metal prices have rebounded 12 percent since February 2016 (Figure 1.SF.1, panel 4). Prices have been gradually declining since 2011 because of a slowdown and a shift away from commodity-intensive investment in China. However, the recent stimulus program announcement directed toward the construction sector has provided some support to prices. Metal prices are projected to decline by 8 percent in 2016 and to increase by 2 percent in 2017. Futures prices point to continued low prices.

Prices of agricultural commodities have increased by 9 percent overall since February 2016. Food prices rose by 7 percent, with increases in most food items, except a few, such as wheat and corn. International prices have not fully reflected the adverse weather shock until recently, but El Niño and a potential La Niña took a toll on international food markets. In addition, Brazil—a big producer of corn, soybeans, coffee, beef, and other food products—has been suffering a prolonged drought. In the past two years, other regions have made up the difference, but global stocks of corn and soybeans are now expected to decline. Wheat stocks are expected to rise due to favorable production in the United States, the European Union, and Russia, pushing prices down.

Annual food prices are projected to increase next year on account of changing weather conditions. Food prices are projected to increase by 2 percent in 2016 and to remain broadly unchanged in 2017; current price levels are already 3 percent above 2015 levels. Over the next two years, prices for major food products, such as rice, are expected to increase slightly from current levels. Risks to food prices are associated with weather variability, particularly concerns over La Niña, which typically has a stronger negative impact on harvests than does El Niño.

The following section takes a longer view and explores the evolution of food markets over the past decades.

Food Security and Markets in the World Economy

The debate over the evolution of food supply relative to population growth dates back at least to the influential theory laid out by Malthus (1798). Since then, a large body of literature has explored the interplay between technology, population, and income per capita and how different growth regimes emerge.[1] A central insight is that the modern era has been characterized

---

[1]See, among others, Galor and Weil 2000; Galor 2005 and 2011; and Gollin, Parente, and Rogerson 2002.

by rapid economic growth and divergence across countries, and that this stands in contrast with most of human history (the so-called Malthusian era), which was characterized by stagnant income per capita.

Today, access to food is mainly seen as an issue facing poor countries. However, developments in food markets are far reaching and indicative of structural developments at the global level.[2] The rapid growth in emerging markets, the demographic transition, and technological developments have and will continue to shape food markets. Furthermore, food markets are segmented and subject to multifaceted distortions to investment and trade. It is thus appropriate to take an in-depth look at the recent and future evolution of food markets and discuss what it means for food security.[3]

This feature answers the following questions related to the evolution of food markets and food security:
- What is special about food markets?
- What are the drivers of food production and consumption?
- How has global food trade evolved?
- What are the risks?

What Is Special about Food Markets?

Food is an edible or potable substance that helps sustain life. Food crops include cereals (for example, wheat, maize, and rice); fruits and vegetables (for example, oranges, and potatoes); meat and seafood (for example, pork and shrimp); beverages (for example, coffee, tea, and cocoa); oilseeds (for example, soybeans and groundnuts); and sugar.[4] These categories differ in a variety of ways in terms of nutritional value, perishability, and storability. The agricultural sector is a source of livelihood for millions, whether through cash cropping or subsistence farming. Globally, over 750 million individuals work in agriculture—that is, 30 percent of the workforce. In sub-Saharan Africa, 60 percent of the workforce labors in agriculture (see World Bank 2015a). Historically, the process of structural transformation that drove labor from the

agricultural (low-productivity) sector to the industrial (high-productivity) sector can explain most of the fast increase in aggregate productivity (see Duarte and Restuccia 2010).

Unsurprisingly, most food production is consumed domestically—about 85 percent of food is produced in the country where it is consumed, according to the World Bank (2015a). There are important differences across types of food depending, among other things, on whether or not they are cash crops. The transmission of international price variations from the border is often limited by taxes, subsidies, price controls, weak market integration, and local distribution costs. In advanced economies, the average long-term pass-through of a 1 percent food price shock to domestic food prices is about 0.10 percent and about 0.15 percent in emerging market economies (see Chapter 3, Box 3.3).[5] For these reasons, and because most food production is consumed domestically, local agricultural and weather conditions are influential, alongside global market developments.[6]

Food has been a long-standing sticking point in trade negotiations, including over tariff and nontariff barriers, even though it is a relatively small portion of global trade—8 percent of merchandise in value terms according to the World Trade Organization (2015). Tariff and nontariff barriers often result from concerns over food sovereignty and the protection of domestic farmers. The Doha Round trade negotiations stalled in July 2008 over disagreements on agriculture. More recently, the special safeguard mechanism proposal to allow temporary tariff hikes when food imports surge was opposed by exporters—in both advanced and developing market economies.

The rationale for a special safeguard has been to counterbalance official agricultural support in exporting countries. Direct agricultural support in countries

---

[2]See Arezki and others 2016 and references therein for a discussion on food price fluctuations and their consequences.

[3]According to the World Food Summit 1996 declaration, "Food security exists when all people, at all times, have physical and economic access to sufficient, safe and nutritious food that meets their dietary needs and food preferences for an active and healthy life."

[4]Some of the aggregate figures presented in this special feature also include nonedible agricultural commodities such as cotton, rubber, wool, and hides.

[5]See also Furceri and others 2016.

[6]Changes in transportation technology and costs have shaped the degree of integration of commodity markets, including for food, which initially had very limited geographical reach. These changes occurred in two stages (see Radetzki 2011). The first took place in the latter half of the 19th century and included the introduction of refrigerated ships permitting long-distance shipment of meat and fruit. The second stage began in the 1950s, but came to fruition in the 1970s. This stage involved the introduction of huge specialized bulk carriers, along with their harbor loading and unloading facilities, which allowed economical shipment of low-value products across much greater distances. The result was a further dramatic decline in the cost of shipping—particularly across vast transoceanic shipping routes—which led in turn to convergence of prices across regional markets.

of the Organisation for Economic Co-operation and Development has declined, while emerging markets have ramped up their support (Figure 1.SF.2). Historically, in developed economies, the distortions tended to favor farmers, whereas in developing economies they tended to favor urban consumers at the expense of small farmers (Anderson 2016). Over the past two decades, high-income countries have generally reduced the distortions in their agricultural sectors. Most developing regions, especially in Asia, have switched from taxing their farmers to providing them with support. All countries continue to have a strong antitrade bias in the structure of assistance to their agricultural sector (Anderson 2016).[7] Trade-policy instruments, such as export and import tariffs, subsidies, and quotas, have serious distributional consequences for consumers. Markets that are specially distorted include those for soybeans, sugar, rice, wheat, beef, pork, and poultry (Anderson, Rausser, and Swinnen 2013).[8]

What Are the Drivers of Food Production and Consumption?

Production and consumption centers for food are concentrated in a few countries, but the location of production centers varies considerably with the type of food under consideration (Figure 1.SF.3). The main production and consumption centers, however, often overlap. For example, China is both a large consumer and producer of rice and pork, as well as a large importer of soybeans—a key animal feed. The United States is a large producer and consumer of both corn and beef, as is the European Union for wheat. Of course, many raw food products are key intermediate inputs to the agricultural industry, which in turn produces and exports processed products.

Population growth is a key factor behind food consumption. Income growth reorients the composition of demand, for instance, toward meat, dairy,

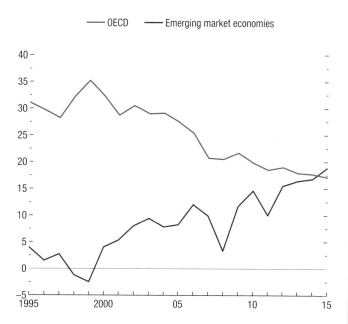

Figure 1.SF.2. Producer Support Estimate
(Percentage of gross farm receipts)

Source: Organisation for Economic Co-operation and Development (OECD), Producer and Consumer Support Estimates, Agriculture Statistics (database).
Note: OECD country classification is based on current membership. Emerging market economies comprise Brazil, China, Colombia, Indonesia, Kazakhstan, Russia, South Africa, Ukraine, and Vietnam. Vietnam is included from 2000 onward.

vegetables, and fresh fruits (Figure 1.SF.4).[9] A case in point is China's remarkable economic growth over the past 30 years, which brought sustained increases in consumer income. Chinese consumers have moved away from staples (such as grains and rice) toward a more diversified and higher-quality diet.[10] There are of course important differences in preferences across countries that lead to a differentiated effect of income growth on the composition of food demand. India is a major exception to the trend toward higher meat

---

[7]Available data from the World Bank's World Integrated Trade Solution on the evolution of import tariffs on food products indicate that they fell from 22 percent to 11.5 percent between 1991 and 2014. Tariffs did not increase in any region. However, tariffs remained especially high in east Asia at 30 percent. In North America, tariffs were the lowest at about 8–9 percent. These results are based on effectively applied average import tariff data for food products (in percent) calculated by aggregating, over all trading partners, the lowest applicable tariff for each partner.

[8]Cotton markets are also severely distorted.

[9]Tilman and Clark (2014 and 2015) show that there is a strong relationship between income per capita and consumption of (1) meat protein; (2) refined sugars and animal fats, oils, and alcohol; and (3) total calories. Global food demand could double by 2050 compared with 2005, with dietary shifts responsible for about 70 percent and global population growth responsible for the remaining 30 percent (Tilman and Clark 2015).

[10]In China, per capita food consumption of cereals decreased by 7 percent, while consumption of sugar and vegetable oils increased by 14 percent and 16 percent, respectively. Consumption of protein increased as well: meat by 37 percent and seafood by 42 percent. The increases in fruit and milk consumption were especially dramatic, both increasing by 115 percent.

Figure 1.SF.3. World Food Production and Consumption by Country, 2015

(Percent of world production or consumption)

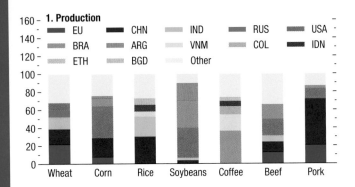

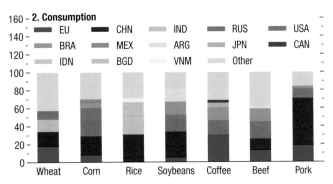

Sources: U.S. Department of Agriculture; and IMF staff calculations.
Note: Data labels in the figure use International Organization for Standardization (ISO) country codes.

Figure 1.SF.4. Population and World Food Consumption

(Index 1995 = 100)

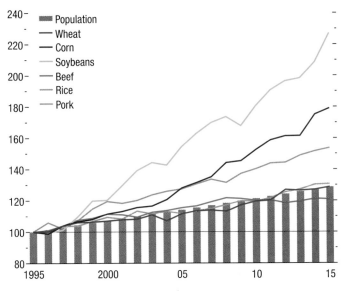

Sources: U.S. Department of Agriculture; World Bank, *World Development Indicators*; and IMF staff calculations.

has been blamed for food price increases (Chakravorty, Hubert, and Marchand 2015).

Land and technology availability are key drivers of food production. Most of the available land suitable for agriculture is located in developing regions—mostly sub-Saharan Africa and South America, as shown in Table 1.SF.1. Growing population, especially in Africa and Asia, will require an increase in food calorie production by 70 percent by 2050 (IFPRI 2016).[12] Putting all unused land into service, assuming everything

consumption, due to religious traditions.[11] Besides population and income growth, the advent of some types of biofuels—whose share has doubled over the past decade—can put pressure on food markets and

[11]See Anand and Cashin (2016) and Tulin and Anand (2016) for additional details on India's changing food demand.

[12]The global population is forecast to reach 9.7 billion by 2050, up from 7.3 billion as of 2015 (United Nations 2015). More than half of this increase—that is 1.3 billion—is expected to occur in Africa, the fastest growing region, and Asia is estimated to contribute 0.9 billion.

Table 1.SF.1. Used-to-Available Land Suitable for Agriculture by Region, 2013

(Thousand hectares)

	North Africa	Sub-Saharan Africa	South America	North America	Europe	Oceania	Asia	World
Used land (2013)	46,151	221,805	192,393	205,091	292,457	48,912	568,454	1,575,263
Unused suitable land	46,595	162,198	130,946	7,242	27,189	15,628	13,392	403,190
Total available land	92,746	384,003	323,339	212,333	319,646	64,540	581,846	1,978,453
Ratio used/available	0.50	0.58	0.60	0.97	0.91	0.76	0.98	0.80

Sources: Food and Agriculture Organization of the United Nations (FAO), FAOSTAT and Global Agro-Ecological Zones (GAEZ); and IMF staff calculations.
Note: Used land is the total of arable land and land under permanent crops, from FAOSTAT. Unused suitable land is calculated from GAEZ. Land is considered suitable if the land is ranked by GAEZ as highly or very highly suitable in one crop out of five (maize, soybean, wheat, sugarcane, palm oil). Oceania includes American Samoa, Australia, Cook Islands, Fiji, French Polynesia, Guam, Kiribati, Marshall Islands, Melanesia, Micronesia, Nauru, New Caledonia, New Zealand, Niue, Norfold Island, Northern Mariana Islands, Pacific Islands Trust Territory, Palau, Papua New Guinea, Pitcairn Islands, Polynesia, Samoa, Solomon Islands, Tokelau, Tonga, Tuvalu, Vanuatu, and Wallis and Futuna Islands.

Table 1.SF.2. Food Exports
(Share of global exports)

Region	1990	2000	2013
OECD	0.7766	0.7406	0.6240
Non-OECD	0.2234	0.2594	0.3760
Brazil	0.0236	0.0292	0.0661
China	0.0370	0.0411	0.0393
India	0.0051	0.0103	0.0263
Argentina	0.0258	0.0281	0.0262
Indonesia	0.0046	0.0108	0.0224

Source: Food and Agriculture Organization of the United Nations (FAO); and IMF staff calculations.
Note: Food refers to food excluding fish aggregate from FAO. OECD = Organisation for Economic Co-operation and Development. OECD and Non-OECD country classification is based on current membership.

else remains equal, would help feed 9 billion people—less than the 9.7 billion who will need to be fed by midcentury. It is important to note that this back-of-the-envelope calculation leaves aside other factors, such as potential technological innovations, reductions in food waste, and land degradation.

Future food supply increases—necessary to feed the growing global population—ought to come mostly from productivity increases. Expanded use of land for agriculture should be limited to the extent possible in the interest of the environment and social concerns: biodiversity loss, ecosystem degradation, increased carbon emissions, and traditional land-use rights. The challenge therefore, is to find a way to increase the productivity of currently cultivated land and slow the rate of land degradation and deforestation. The potential to increase agricultural productivity is especially high in sub-Saharan Africa, where yields are 50 percent below their potential level (Fischer and Shah 2011).

How Has Global Food Trade Evolved?

Over the past decades, the global pattern of food demand has shifted relatively more than it has for sup-

ply. Demand has shifted from west to east on account of differences in population growth, as well as changes in income affecting the composition of demand. The supply shift from north to south for food has been more modest than for other commodities, such as minerals and metals. While some emerging markets have increased their shares, the lion's share of global food trade is still sourced from advanced economies (Table 1.SF.2). This is true despite potentially high returns on capital in the agricultural sector in many developing economies, which would justify capital flowing into that sector (for example, see Gollin, Lagakos, and Waugh 2014a and 2014b).

There are wide gaps across countries in agricultural yield—defined as crop production per unit of land cultivation, which is a measure of land productivity (Table 1.SF.3). These gaps reflect multifaceted impediments to investment and technology transfers in the agricultural sectors of developing economies. There is limited evidence of catching up in productivity between advanced economies and low-income countries. The example of maize shows a huge divergence in agricultural yields between North America and sub-Saharan Africa (Figure 1.SF.5). While a recent spurt in large-scale cross-border land acquisitions following food price hikes suggests that capital has started to flow from north to south, it has also revealed important fault lines between investors and recipient countries (see Box 1.SF.1).

There are many impediments to investment in the agricultural sector. Scant net capital flows to developing economies, contrary to what neoclassical theory would suggest, are not unique to the agricultural sector (Alfaro, Kalemli-Ozcan, and Volosovych 2008). The many factors that deter investment in agriculture are emblematic of the challenges these countries face in improving their institutions. There is ample evidence of the role of technology adoption (or the lack thereof), and of

Table 1.SF.3. Agricultural Yield
(Ratio relative to highest producer)

	North Africa	Sub-Saharan Africa	Latin America and the Caribbean	North America	Europe	Oceania	Asia
Maize	0.60	0.19	0.43	1.00	0.56	0.77	0.48
Rice	0.88	0.22	0.48	0.81	0.59	1.00	0.44
Soybeans	0.82	0.40	0.88	1.00	0.63	0.68	0.42
Wheat	0.63	0.60	0.65	0.71	1.00	0.48	0.73

Sources: Food and Agriculture Organization of the United Nations; and IMF staff calculations.
Note: The above table reports the weighted average yield of crops by region, normalized relative to the highest producer. The average yield is weighted by the area of harvested land. Oceania includes Australia, Fiji, Guam, Micronesia, New Caledonia, New Zealand, Pacific Islands Trust Territory, Papua New Guinea, Solomon Islands, and Vanuatu.

Figure 1.SF.5. Maize Yield
(Kilogram per hectare)

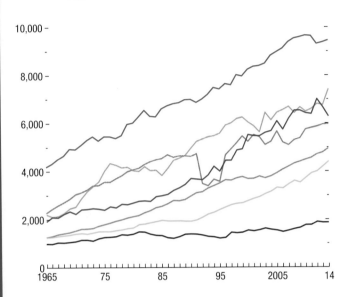

Sources: Food and Agriculture Organization of the United Nations; and IMF staff calculations.
Note: Yield refers to a five-year moving average. Oceania includes Australia, Fiji, Guam, Micronesia, New Caledonia, Vanuatu, New Zealand, and Papua New Guinea.

human capital and credit constraints, in agricultural development (see for instance, Besley and Case 1993, Foster and Rosenzweig 1995, and Dercon and Christiaensen 2011). Other factors, such as lack of adequate infrastructure (Donaldson and Hornbeck, forthcoming), expropriation risk (Jacoby, Li, and Rozelle 2002), and questions of land tenure (Besley and Burgess 2000), also limit investment in the sector.

What Are the Risks?

Amartya Sen (1981) was the first to point out that hunger was not necessarily caused by a lack of food, but by a lack of the capability to buy that food. Food security is a multidimensional concept. The Food and Agriculture Organization of the United Nations (FAO) (2015) identified four pillars for food security:

- *Availability*—The supply side, determined by production, stocks, and trade in food
- *Access*—Economic access (the ability to purchase with disposable income) and physical access (the ability to reach food sources via the transportation infrastructure)
- *Utilization*—Through diet diversity, intrahousehold distribution of food, and food preparation and consumption
- *Stability*—The constancy of the other three dimensions over time

Rapid urbanization and galloping population growth—especially in sub-Saharan Africa and Asia—not matched with increases in domestic food supply, have led to growing dependence on imports (Table 1. SF.4). An overwhelming majority of countries around the world are net importers of food (Table 1.SF.5). Despite the high concentration of countries that have always been food importers, 27 have switched from being net exporters to importers since 1990. These are countries in east Asia, Latin America, and sub-Saharan Africa and include Honduras, the Philippines, Vietnam, and Zimbabwe. These four countries experienced major declines in net food exports of more than 7 percentage points of GDP.

These switches have led to further concerns over food security. Countries can achieve food security through imports, provided that they are able to finance the imports. Economically prosperous countries are

Table 1.SF.4. Urban Population by Region
(Percent of total population)

Region	1990	2014	2050	Change 1990–2014	Change 1990–2050
Africa	31.3	40.0	55.9	8.7	24.7
Asia	32.3	47.5	64.2	15.3	31.9
Europe	70.0	73.4	82.0	3.5	12.0
Latin America and the Caribbean	70.5	79.5	86.2	9.0	15.7
Northern America	75.4	81.5	87.4	6.0	12.0
Oceania	70.7	70.8	73.5	0.1	2.8

Sources: United Nations, World Urbanization Prospects: The 2014 Revision; and IMF staff calculations.
Note: Oceania includes American Samoa, Australia, Cook Islands, Fiji, French Polynesia, Guam, Kiribati, Marshall Islands, Micronesia, Nauru, New Caledonia, New Zealand, Niue, Northern Mariana Islands, Palau, Papua New Guinea, Samoa, Solomon Islands, Tokelau, Tonga, Tuvalu, Vanuatu, and Wallis and Futuna Islands.

Table 1.SF.5. Net Food Exporters and Importers
(1990 versus 2013, number of countries)

Region	Always Exporter	Always Importer	Exporter --> Importer	Importer --> Exporter	Total
East Asia and Pacific	6	17	7	2	32
Europe and Central Asia	9	13	1	1	24
Latin America and Caribbean	12	14	8	0	34
Middle East and North Africa	0	17	2	0	19
North America	2	1	0	0	3
South Asia	1	6	0	1	8
Sub-Saharan Africa	4	29	9	3	45
Total	34	97	27	7	165

Sources: Food and Agriculture Organization of the United Nations; World Bank: World Development Indicators; and IMF staff calculations.

able to finance their food imports, while impoverished countries struggle to do so.[13] Over the past few years, the commodity price bust (except food) has exposed developing economies to food price shocks by reducing export receipts and fiscal space.[14]

Climate change affects agriculture—through large economic losses such as reduced crop yields and livestock productivity—through changes in average temperatures and patterns of precipitation and extreme weather events such as heat waves.[15] There are a host of other effects too, including changes in pests, diseases, and atmospheric concentrations of carbon dioxide (Porter and others 2014). Generally, research has stressed unequal exposure across countries, with countries closer to the equator being more vulnerable to climate change than countries at higher latitudes (Rosenzweig and others 2014).[16] For example, Ethiopia recently experienced one of the worst droughts in decades. Strikingly, the country's two main rainy seasons supply over 80 percent of its agricultural yield. The agricultural sector employs 85 percent of the population. The lack of rainfall and subsequent drought associated with the El Niño weather phenomenon, therefore, caused a massive spike in humanitarian needs, which are expected to continue through much of 2016 (see Government of Ethiopia 2015).[17]

Such extreme weather events and their threats to food security are expected to continue to worsen and increase in frequency (IFPRI 2016; UNEP 2016; World Bank 2015a).[18] So-called climate-smart agriculture can help mitigate the effects of climate change on agriculture by offering opportunities for smallholder farmers to produce more nutritious crops, sustainably and efficiently (IFPRI 2016).[19] In addition, the FAO and the United States Agency for International Development have established early warning systems to anticipate and prevent famines. The FAO hosts the Global Information and Early Warning System, which monitors the world food situation in 190 FAO member countries and warns of impending crises within countries (Groskopf 2016). The Famine Early Warning Systems Network (FEWS NET, www.fews.net), set up by the United States Agency for International Development, helps anticipate and plan for humanitarian crises in 29 countries.

Volatility in food prices and outright food shortages have a crucial impact on the most basic aspect of welfare in poor countries—namely, survival. As shown in Table 1.SF.6, the share of food consumption in the overall consumption basket is dramatically high for many low-income countries. It is even higher for fragile states such as Guinea and Burundi. For middle-income countries, the share is somewhat lower but still significant—reaching up to about 50 percent

[13]The poorest segments of the population in some rich countries may, however, be subject to food insecurity.

[14]In principle, food terms-of-trade shocks can also drive a country to go from food exporter to importer. In practice, fast population growth and urbanization, stagnating productivity, and poor infrastructure are key elements explaining many developing economies' dependence on food imports (Rakotoarisoa, Iafrate, and Paschali 2011).

[15]See IMF (2016) for a discussion of the effect of natural disasters and climate change on sub-Saharan African countries.

[16]There is evidence to suggest that climate change affects different crops differently.

[17]Beyond Africa, the impact of the 2015–16 El Niño could be even more severe in Asia in locations such as the uplands of Cam-

bodia, central and southern India, eastern Indonesia, the central and southern Philippines, central and northeast Thailand, Papua New Guinea, and other Pacific island countries. In India, severe floods were reported in several parts of Tamil Nadu during November and December 2015, inundating most areas of Chennai (United Nations 2015).

[18]In Latin America and southeast Asia, floods and droughts during recent El Niño/La Niña episodes, which have already caused heavy losses in agriculture, are likely to double in frequency (World Bank 2015b).

[19]For example, C4 rice has been found to increase yields by 50 percent as a result of doubling water use efficiency and increasing nitrogen use efficiency by 30 percent (IFPRI 2016).

Table 1.SF.6. Share of Food and Beverages in Total Consumption, 2010

Area	Share
High-income countries	21.0
Middle-income countries	43.7
Low-income countries	56.6
Burundi	71.0
Democratic Republic of the Congo	69.5
Guinea	71.1

Sources: World Bank, Global Consumption Database; Organisation for Economic Co-operation and Development, National Accounts database; and IMF staff calculations.
Note: Includes processed food such as alcoholic beverages and catering services.

Figure 1.SF.6. Food Prices and Violent Events
(Number of events, unless noted otherwise)

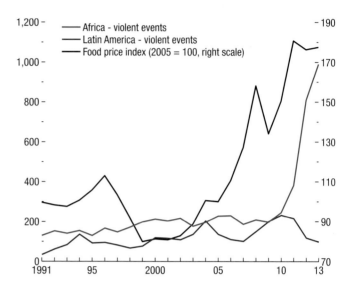

Sources: IMF, Primary Commodity Price System; Social Conflict Analysis Database (SCAD) 3.1; and IMF staff calculations.

of total consumption. Existing econometric evidence (see Arezki and Brueckner 2014; and Bellemare 2015) suggests that food price volatility can cause enormous distributional challenges within and between countries and lead to conflicts (Figure 1.SF.6).[20] Existing indices of food insecurity (Figure 1.SF.7) show that as a region, Africa is the most prone to such food insecurity, but that pockets of vulnerability also exist in Asia, Central America, and South America.

Policy interventions can at times magnify food price spikes. The price volatility of weather-dependent commodities, such as food, is exacerbated by the tendency for both developed and developing economies to alter their trade and domestic policies from year to year in an effort to stabilize prices and quantities in domestic food markets (Anderson 2016; FAO 2015). During periods of elevated food prices, as in 2008, net food exporting countries frequently implemented export restrictions, and net food importers lowered import barriers. Both measures were aimed at increasing domestic food supplies. Taken together, these two policy responses exacerbated the food price spike (Anderson, Rausser, and Swinnen 2013; Anderson 2016). To avoid such outcomes, ensuring higher agricultural sector productivity and improved supply chains, as well as regional coordination—including through maintaining and managing

regional grain reserves—have proved effective in hedging against the consequences of food price volatility in developing Asia (Jha and Rhee 2012).[21]

Overall, food markets are segmented, owing to distortions in trade and domestic impediments to investment in the sector. Demand for food has and will continue to grow at a fast pace on account of population growth. Income growth also affects the composition of food demand. Fast urbanization trends in Africa and Asia will make even more countries dependent on trade. To meet these challenges and reduce food insecurity, all countries alike must continue to dismantle barriers to trade. Low-income countries should also raise productivity in the agricultural sector by attracting capital flows, but for that to occur, multifaceted institutional improvements are needed.

---

[20]Food production is endogenous to civil conflict; country examples indicate that the presence of civil war may be associated with an increase of domestic food prices. For example, in Darfur, prices of the main food staples increased rapidly after widespread violence started in late 2003 and early 2004 (see, for example, Brinkman and Hendrix 2010).

[21]Other avenues to alleviate food shortages in the long term include: (1) reducing excessive food consumption, which leads to obesity and associated negative health outcomes, and (2) reducing food waste. The FAO estimates that one-third of food produced for human consumption is lost or wasted globally, which amounts to about 1.3 billion tons a year.

Figure 1.SF.7. Global Food Security Index, 2016
(Overall score 0–100, 100 = best environment)

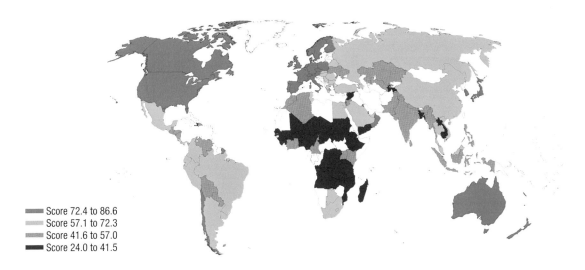

Score 72.4 to 86.6
Score 57.1 to 72.3
Score 41.6 to 57.0
Score 24.0 to 41.5

Source: Economist Intelligence Unit, *Global Food Security Index 2016*.

Box 1.SF.1. A Global Rush for Land

Against the backdrop of increasing demand for food, there has been a growing interest by governments, agribusinesses, and investment funds in acquiring long-term property rights or leases over large areas of farmland, mostly in developing economies (Arezki, Deininger, and Selod 2015). Most of the land acquisitions have been in food-insecure countries that are in dire need of investment in the agricultural sector. These deals could lead to positive or negative outcomes. This box presents evidence related to these transnational land acquisitions and discusses policy implications.

What Is Driving Large-Scale Land Deals?

In this box, the term "land deal" refers to a large-scale cross-border acquisition of land, typically at the expense of smallholder production or greenspace.[1] The food crisis of 2007–08 led to a massive increase in food prices, thereby raising farmland value and the option value of securing land for food production to insure against the next food crisis. While the benefits of cultivating vacant land today remain small, increased uncertainty in the wake of the crisis may have increased the future profitability for private investors (Collier and Venables 2012).

Figure 1.SF.1.1 shows a sharp increase in the annual number of land deals in the years leading up to the 2007–08 financial crisis and peaking shortly thereafter. In 2009, at the height of the rush for land, an average size of 223 square miles a deal was negotiated almost every day, an area more than five times the size of Paris, France. In the years that follow, investors' and governments' appetite for farmland has receded.

The boom-bust pattern in Figure 1.SF.1.1 is consistent with the idea of rapidly changing farmland (option) value fueled by substantial shifts in food prices and uncertainty. Evidence suggests that much of the acquired land has been left idle, raising concern about the motive behind these large-scale land invest-

The authors of this box are Christian Bogmans and Vanessa Diaz Montelongo.

[1]A deal is defined as an intended, concluded, or failed attempt to acquire land through purchase, lease, or concession that meets the following criteria: It (1) entails a transfer of rights to use, control, or ownership of land through sale, lease, or concession; (2) occurred after the year 2000; (3) covers an area of 200 hectares or more; and (4) implies the potential conversion of land from smallholder production, local community use, or important ecosystem service provision to commercial use. The analysis presented in this box focuses on cross-border deals only.

Figure 1.SF.1.1. Evolution of Deals over Time by Target Region
(Number of deals)

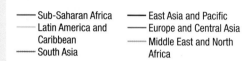

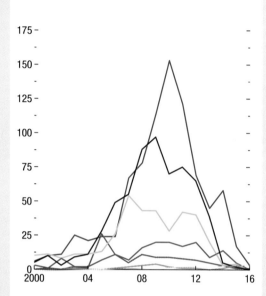

Sources: Land Matrix; and IMF staff calculations.

ments and hinting at potential obstacles to bringing their agricultural projects to fruition. According to the Land Matrix database, to date only 49 percent of the acquired land has been cultivated to some extent, and this fraction is significantly smaller in sub-Saharan Africa (37 percent).[2]

What Do the Data Tell Us about Land Investments?

As of May 2016, the Land Matrix database has information on 2,152 transnational deals. Slightly more than two thirds are linked to agricultural projects, with a cumulative size of almost 59 million hectares in 88 countries worldwide. This expanse roughly corresponds to an area the size of France or Ukraine. While the amount of land that changed hands is substantial, it is still fairly modest compared with the total stock of uncultivated and (nonforest) suitable land, which amounts to roughly 400 million hect-

[2]The Land Matrix Global Observatory. Accessed May 7, 2016. http://landmatrix.org/en/get-the-detail/.

Box 1.SF.1 *(continued)*

ares—one billion hectares when including forestland. Sub-Saharan Africa (884 deals) and east Asia (611 deals) have been the most important target regions for investment, followed by Latin America (368 deals).

To explore the determinants of interest in transnational farmland deals, we use a bilateral Poisson regression to model the occurrence and count of projects in origin-destination pairs. Let N_{ij} be the expected number of projects undertaken in host country j by investors from country i. The regression pools all land deals between 2000 and 2016.

Following the standard gravity model from the trade literature, land investment is attributed to origin and destination country characteristics, $VarOrig_i$ and $VarDest_j$, respectively, and bilateral variables, $VarBilat_{ij}$. The baseline specification is:

$$N_{ij} = c + \alpha_i \cdot$$
$$VarOrig_i + \beta_j \cdot VarDest_j + \gamma_{ij} \cdot VarBilat_{ij} + \varepsilon_{ij}, (1.SF.1.1)$$

in which α_i, β_j and γ_{ij} are the parameters of interest, and ε_i is an error term. With a large number of zeros in the data, the ordinary least squares estimator may be biased and inconsistent. To overcome this issue, a Poisson pseudo-maximum-likelihood estimator is used (Silva and Tenreyro 2006).

The analysis uses a novel measure of uncultivated nonforest land that takes into account proximity to market. Data are obtained from the FAO's *Global Agro-Ecological Zones* (FAO 2016). To analyze the relationship between this type of foreign direct investment and governance, data on law and order from the *International Country Risk Guide* (ICRG 2009), a measure of investor protection from the World Bank's Doing Business dataset, and an index of tenure security (de Crombrugghe and others 2009) are included. Physical distance and a dummy variable for former colonial ties are included as proxies for trade costs. Finally, an index of food security from the Economist Intelligence Unit is included.

The results of the regressions based on equation (1.SF.1.1) are presented in Table 1.SF.1.1. They confirm the importance of trade costs and an abundant supply of uncultivated arable land. Interestingly, and in contrast with the existing literature on capital flows, we find that poor land governance is associated with more land deals (see Table 1.SF.1.1, column 1). As weak land governance and food insecurity are highly correlated (with a correlation coefficient of $\rho = 0.77$), this finding suggests that food-insecure regions are associated with more land investment. Governments of

Table 1.SF.1.1. Impact of Land Governance and Food Security on Land Deals

	(1)	(2)
Bilateral Variables		
Distance (log)	−0.838***	−1.061***
	(0.0669)	(0.0793)
Former Colonial Relationship	1.529***	0.874***
	(0.269)	(0.253)
Origin Country Variables		
Net Food Exports (over GDP)	8.199***	
	(1.180)	
Food Security Index		0.0403***
		(0.00447)
Destination Country Variables		
Landlocked	0.234	0.0575
	(0.220)	(0.192)
Suitable Nonforest Land	0.525***	0.810***
	(0.0748)	(0.0936)
Land Governance	−0.572***	−0.165
	(0.0957)	(0.108)
Law and Order	−0.265***	−0.152
	(0.0827)	(0.0958)
Weak Investor Protection	−0.00606**	−0.00913***
	(0.00243)	(0.00256)
Net Food Exports (over GDP)	5.757***	
	(1.384)	
Food Security Index		−0.0539***
		(0.00639)
Number of Observations	19,186	10,044
Pseudo R^2	0.217	0.283

Note: Robust standard errors in parentheses.
*** $p < 0.01$, ** $p < 0.05$, * $p < 0.1$.

food-insecure countries, while eager to host large-scale land investments, often face the challenge of ensuring that such outside investments actually help alleviate domestic hunger. This is especially difficult in light of weak land governance.

What Are the Implications for Food Security?

Land deals may have either positive or negative effects. On the one hand, these deals signal that capital in the agricultural sector is flowing from rich to poor countries' investors and hence help transfer new technology and agronomic knowledge to local farmers. On the other hand, the clustering of these deals in food insecure countries can potentially amplify the detrimental effects of a future food crisis. Host-country governments can remedy these risks by investing in monitoring capacity to ensure that land is leased to investors who (1) promote integration of local producers into value chains, (2) coinvest in local public goods, and (3) compensate displaced land users.

References

Alfaro, Laura, Sebnem Kalemli-Ozcan, and Vadym Volosovych. 2008. "Why Doesn't Capital Flow from Rich to Poor Countries? An Empirical Investigation." *Review of Economics and Statistics* 90 (2): 347–68.

Aiyar, Shekhar, and Ashoka Mody. 2011. "The Democratic Dividend: Evidence from the Indian States." IMF Working Paper 11/38, International Monetary Fund, Washington.

Anand, Rahul, and Paul Cashin. 2016. *Taming Indian Inflation.* Washington: International Monetary Fund.

Anderson, Kym. 2009. *Distortions to Agricultural Incentives: A Global Perspective, 1955–2007.* London: Palgrave Macmillan and Washington: World Bank.

———. 2016. "National and Global Price-and-Trade-Distorting Policies." Working Paper 2016/07, Australian National University, Canberra.

———, Gordon Rausser, and Johan Swinnen. 2013. "Political Economy of Public Policies: Insights from Distortions to Agricultural and Food Markets." *Journal of Economic Literature* 51 (2): 423–77.

Anseeuw, Ward, Liz Alden Wily, Lorenzo Cotula, and Michael Taylor. 2012. *Land Rights and the Rush for Land: Findings of the Global Commercial Pressures on Land Research Project.* Rome: International Land Coalition.

Arezki, Rabah, and Markus Brueckner. 2014. "Effects of International Food Price Shocks on Political Institutions in Low-Income Countries: Evidence from an International Food Net-Export Price Index." *World Development* 61 (C): 142–53.

———, Klaus Deininger, and Harris Selod. 2015. "What Drives the Global 'Land Rush'?" *World Bank Economic Review* 29 (2): 207–33.

———, Karim El Aynaoui, Yaw Nyarko, and Francis Teal. 2016. "Food Price Volatility and Its Consequences: Introduction." *Oxford Economic Papers* 68 (3): 655–64.

Bellemare, Marc F. 2015. "Rising Food Prices, Food Price Volatility, and Social Unrest." *American Journal of Agricultural Economics* 97 (1): 1–21.

Berden, Koen G., Joseph Francois, Saara Tamminen, Martin Thelle, and Paul Wymenga. 2009. "Non-Tariff Measures in EU–US Trade and Investment: An Economic Analysis." ECORYS, Rotterdam.

Besley, Timothy, and Robin Burgess. 2000. "Land Reform, Poverty Reduction, and Growth: Evidence from India." *Quarterly Journal of Economics* 115 (2): 389–430.

Besley, Timothy, and Anne Case. 1993. "Modeling Technology Adoption in Developing Countries." *American Economic Review* 83 (2): 396–402.

Blanchard, Olivier, Eugenio Cerutti, and Lawrence Summers. 2015. "Inflation and Activity—Two Explorations and Their Monetary Policy Implications." IMF Working Paper 15/230, International Monetary Fund, Washington.

Brinkman, Henk-Jan, and Cullen S. Hendrix. 2010. "Food Insecurity and Conflict: Applying the WDR Framework." Background paper for the World Bank's *World Development Report 2011*, World Bank, Washington.

Byrne, David M., John G. Fernald, and Marshall B. Reinsdorf. 2016. "Does the United States Have a Productivity Slowdown or a Measurement Problem?" https://www.brookings.edu/bpea-articles/does-the-united-states-have-a-productivity-slow-down-or-a-measurement-problem/.

Chakravorty, Ujjayant, Marie-Helene Hubert, and Beyza Ural Marchand. 2015. "Food for Fuel: The Effect of the U.S. Biofuel Mandate on Poverty in India." Working Paper, University of Caen and University of Rennes.

Collier, Paul, and Anthony J. Venables. 2012. "Land Deals in Africa: Pioneers and Speculators." *Journal of Globalization and Development* 3 (1): Article 3.

Dave, Donaldson, and Richard Hornbeck. Forthcoming. "Railroads and American Economic Growth: A 'Market Access' Approach." *Quarterly Journal of Economics.*

de Crombrugghe, Denis, Kristine Farla, Nicolas Meisel, Chris de Neubourg, Jacques Ould Aoudia, and Adam Szirmai. 2009. "Institutional Profiles Database III. Presentation of the Institutional Profiles Database 2009 (IPD 2009)." Documents de Travail de la DGTPE, No. 2009/14. Treasury Directorate General of the French Ministry of the Economy, Industry and Employment, Paris.

Dercon, Stefan, and Luc Christiaensen. 2011. "Consumption Risk, Technology Adoption and Poverty Traps: Evidence from Ethiopia." *Journal of Development Economics* 96 (2): 159–73.

Duarte, Margarida, and Diego Restuccia. 2010. "The Role of the Structural Transformation in Aggregate Productivity." *Quarterly Journal of Economics* 125 (1): 129–73.

Egger, Peter, Joseph Francois, Miriam Manchin, and Douglas Nelson. 2015. "Non-Tariff Barriers, Integration, and the Trans-Atlantic Economy." *Economic Policy* 30 (83): 541–73.

Fernald, John. 2015. "Productivity and Potential Output before, during, and after the Great Recession." In *NBER Macroeconomics Annual 2014.* Cambridge, Massachusetts: National Bureau of Economic Research.

Food and Agriculture Organization of the United Nations (FAO). 2015. *The State of Agricultural Commodity Markets: Trade and Food Security: Achieving a Better Balance between National Priorities and the Collective Good.* Rome: FAO.

———. 2016. *Global Agro-Ecological Zones.* Rome: FAO. http://gaez.fao.org/Main.html#.

Foster, Andrew, and Mark Rosenzweig. 1995. "Learning by Doing and Learning from Others: Human Capital and Technical Change in Agriculture." *Journal of Political Economy* 103 (6): 1176–209.

Fischer, Günther, and Mahendra Shah. 2011. "Farmland Investments and Food Security." Report prepared under World Bank and International Institute for Applied Systems Analysis contract, Laxenburg.

Furceri, Davide, Prakash Loungani, John Simon, and Susan M. Wachter. 2016. "Global Food Prices and Domestic Inflation: Some Cross-Country Evidence." *Oxford Economic Papers* 68 (3): 665–87.

Galor, Oded. 2005. "From Stagnation to Growth: Unified Growth Theory." In *Handbook of Economic Growth,* edited by Phillipe Aghion and Steven N. Durlauf. Amsterdam: Elsevier.

———. 2011. *Unified Growth Theory.* Princeton: Princeton University Press.

———, and David N. Weil. 2000. "Population, Technology, and Growth: From Malthusian Stagnation to the Demographic Transition and Beyond." *American Economic Review* 90 (4): 806–28.

Gollin, Douglas, David Lagakos, and Michael E. Waugh. 2014a. "Agricultural Productivity Differences across Countries." *American Economic Review* 104 (5): 165–70.

———. 2014b. "The Agricultural Productivity Gap." *Quarterly Journal of Economics* 129 (2): 939–93.

Gollin, Douglas, Stephen Parente, and Richard Rogerson. 2002. "The Role of Agriculture in Development." *American Economic Review* 92 (2): 160–64.

Government of Ethiopia, Ethiopia Humanitarian Country Team. 2015. "Ethiopia Humanitarian Requirements Document 2016." Addis Ababa.

Groskopf, Christopher. 2016. "Science Is Warning Us That a Food Crisis Is Coming to Southern Africa. Will We Stop It?" *Quartz Africa.* March 5. http://qz.com/620499/science-is-warning-us-that-a-food-crisis-is-coming-to-southern-africa-will-we-stop-it/.

Gruss, Bertrand. 2014. "After the Boom—Commodity Prices and Economic Growth in Latin America and the Caribbean." IMF Working Paper 14/154, International Monetary Fund, Washington.

HM Treasury. 2016. "HM Treasury Analysis: The Long-Term Economic Impact of EU Membership and the Alternatives." Presented to Parliament by the Chancellor of the Exchequer by command of Her Majesty, April.

Hördahl, Peter, Jhuvesh Sobrun, and Philip Turner. 2016. "Low Long-Term Interest Rates as a Global Phenomenon." BIS Working Paper 574, Bank for International Settlements, Basel.

International Country Risk Guide. 2009. http://epub.prsgroup.com/products/icrg. Political Risk Services, New York.

International Food Policy Research Institute (IFPRI). 2016. *Global Food Policy Report.* Washington: IFPRI. http://dx.doi.org/10.2499/9780896295827.

International Monetary Fund. 2016. "Enhancing Resilience to Natural Disasters in Sub-Saharan Africa." Chapter 3 of the October 2016 *Regional Economic Outlook: Sub-Saharan Africa,* Washington.

Jacoby, Hanan G., Guo Li, and Scott Rozelle. 2002. "Hazards of Expropriation: Tenure Insecurity and Investment in Rural China." *American Economic Review* 92 (5): 1420–447.

Jha, Shikha, and Changyong Rhee. 2012. "Distributional Consequences and Policy Responses to Food Price Inflation in Developing Asia." In *Commodity Price Volatility and Inclusive Growth in Low-Income Economies,* edited by Rabah Arezki, Catherine Pattillo, Marc Quintyn, and Min Zhu. Washington: International Monetary Fund.

Laubach, Thomas, and John C. Williams. 2015. "Measuring the Natural Rate of Interest Redux." Federal Reserve Bank of San Francisco Working Paper 2015–16.

Malthus, Thomas. R. 1798. *An Essay on the Principle of Population.* London: J. Johnson.

Organisation for Economic Co-operation and Development (OECD). 2016. *Agricultural Policy Monitoring and Evaluation 2016.* OECD Publishing: Paris. http://dx.doi.org/10.1787/agr_pol-2016-en.

Ottaviano, Gianmarco, João Paulo Pessoa, Thomas Sampson, and John Van Reenen. 2014. "The Costs and Benefits of Leaving the EU." London School of Economics and Political Science, Centre for Economic Performance. Unpublished.

Pescatori, Andrea, and Jarkko Turunen. 2015. "Lower for Longer: Neutral Rates in the United States." IMF Working Paper 15/135, International Monetary Fund, Washington.

Porter, J.R., L. Xie, A.J. Challinor, K. Cochrane, S.M. Howden, M.M. Iqbal, D.B. Lobell, and M.I. Travasso. 2014. "Food Security and Food Production Systems." In *Climate Change 2014: Impacts, Adaptation, and Vulnerability. Part A: Global and Sectoral Aspects. Contribution of Working Group II to the Fifth Assessment Report of the Intergovernmental Panel on Climate Change,* edited by C.B. Field, V.R. Barros, D.J. Dokken, K.J. Mach, M.D. Mastrandrea, T.E. Bilir, M. Chatterjee, K.L. Ebi, Y.O. Estrada, R.C. Genova, B. Girma, E.S. Kissel, A.N. Levy, S. MacCracken, P.R. Mastrandrea, and L.L. White. Cambridge, United Kingdom and New York: Cambridge University Press.

Radetzki, Marian. 2011. "Primary Commodities: Historical Perspectives and Prospects." In *Beyond the Curse Policies to Harness the Power of Natural Resources,* edited by Rabah Arezki, Thorvaldur Gylfason, and Amadou Sy. Washington: International Monetary Fund.

Rakotoarisoa, Manitra A., Massimo Iafrate, and Marianna Paschali. 2011. "Why Has Africa Become a Net Food Importer? Explaining Africa Agricultural and Food Trade Deficits." Trade and Markets Division, Food and Agriculture Organization of the United Nations, Rome.

Reifschneider, Dave, William Wascher, and David Wilcox. 2015. "Aggregate Supply in the United States: Recent Developments and Implications for the Conduct of Monetary Policy." *IMF Economic Review* 63 (1): 71–109.

Rosenzweig, Cynthia, Joshua Elliott, Delphine Deryng, Alex C. Ruane, Christoph Müller, Almut Arneth, Kenneth J. Boote, Christian Folberth, Michael Glotter, Nikolay Khabarov, Kathleen Neumann, Franziska Piontek, Thomas A. M. Pugh, Erwin Schmid, Elke Stehfest, Hong Yang, and James W. Jones. 2014. "Assessing Agricultural Risks of Climate Change in the 21st Century in a Global Gridded Crop Model Intercomparison." *Proceedings of the National Academy of Sciences of the United States of America 2014* 111 (9): 3268–273. Published ahead of print, December 16, 2013.

Sen, Amartya. 1981. "Ingredients of Famine Analysis: Availability and Entitlements." *The Quarterly Journal of Economics* 96 (3): 433–64.

Silva, J. M. C. Santos, and Silvana Tenreyro. 2006. "The Log of Gravity." *Review of Economics and Statistics* 88 (4): 641–58.

Syverson, Chad. 2016. "Challenges to Mismeasurement Explanations for the U.S. Productivity Slowdown," NBER Working Paper No. 21974, February, National Bureau of Economic Research, Cambridge, Massachusetts.

Tilman, David, and Michael Clark. 2014. "Global Diets Link Environmental Sustainability and Human Health." *Nature* 515: 518–22.

———. 2015. "Food, Agriculture and the Environment: Can We Feed the World and Save the Earth?" *Daedalus* 144: 8–23.

Tulin, Volodymyr, and Rahul Anand. 2016. "Understanding India's Food Inflation Through the Lens of Demand and Supply." In *Taming Indian Inflation*, edited by Rahul Anand and Paul Cashin. Washington: International Monetary Fund.

United Kingdom Office for National Statistics. 2015. "National Population Projections: 2014-Based Statistical Bulletin." http://www.ons.gov.uk/peoplepopulationandcommunity/populationandmigration/populationprojections/bulletins/nationalpopulationprojections/2015-10-29/pdf.

United Nations, Department of Economic and Social Affairs, Population Division. 2015. "World Population Prospects: The 2015 Revision, Key Findings and Advance Tables." Working Paper ESA/P/WP.241. United Nations, Department of Economic and Social Affairs, Population Division, New York.

United Nations Environment Program (UNEP). 2016. *UNEP Frontiers 2016 Report: Emerging Issues of Environmental Concern.* Nairobi: UNEP.

Williams, John C. 2016. "Monetary Policy in a Low R-Star World." *Federal Reserve Bank of San Francisco Economic Letter* 2016–23, August 15.

World Bank. 2015a. *Ending Poverty and Hunger by 2030: An Agenda for the Global Food System.* Washington: World Bank Group.

———. 2015b. *Future of Food: Shaping a Climate-Smart Global Food System.* Washington: World Bank Group.

World Food Summit. 1996. *Rome Declaration on World Food Security.* Rome: Food and Agriculture Organization of the United Nations.

World Resources Institute. 2014. "Creating a Sustainable Food Future: Interim Findings." World Resources Institute, Washington.

World Trade Organization (WTO). 2015. *International Trade Statistics 2015.* Geneva: WTO. https://www.wto.org/english/res_e/statis_e/its2015_e/its2015_e.pdf.

CHAPTER 2

GLOBAL TRADE: WHAT'S BEHIND THE SLOWDOWN?

Trade growth has slowed since 2012 relative both to its strong historical performance and to overall economic growth. This chapter finds that the overall weakness in economic activity, in particular in investment, has been the primary restraint on trade growth, accounting for up to three-fourths of the slowdown. However, other factors are also weighing on trade. The waning pace of trade liberalization and the recent uptick in protectionism are holding back trade growth, even though their quantitative impact thus far has been limited. The decline in the growth of global value chains has also played an important part in the observed slowdown. The findings suggest that addressing the general weakness in economic activity, especially in investment, will stimulate trade, which in turn could help strengthen productivity and growth. In addition, given the subdued global growth outlook, further trade reforms that lower barriers, coupled with measures to mitigate the cost to those who shoulder the burden of adjustment, would boost the international exchange of goods and services and revive the virtuous cycle of trade and growth.

Global trade growth has decelerated significantly in recent years. After its sharp collapse and even sharper rebound in the aftermath of the global financial crisis, the volume of world trade in goods and services has grown by just over 3 percent a year since 2012, less than half the average rate of expansion during the previous three decades. The slowdown in trade growth is remarkable, especially when set against the historical relationship between growth in trade and global economic activity (Figure 2.1). Between 1985 and 2007, real world trade grew on average twice as fast as global GDP, whereas over the past four years, it has barely kept pace. Such prolonged sluggish growth in trade

volumes relative to economic activity has few historical precedents during the past five decades.

The reasons for the weakness in global trade growth are still not clearly understood, yet a precise diagnosis is necessary to assess if and where policy action may help.[1] Is the waning of trade simply a symptom of the generally weak economic environment, or is it a consequence of a rise in trade-constricting policies? Private investment remains subdued across many advanced and emerging market and developing economies (see Chapter 4 of the April 2015 *World Economic Outlook* [WEO]), and China has embarked on a necessary and welcome process of rebalancing away from investment and toward more consumption-led growth.[2] Many commodity exporters have cut capital spending in response to persistently weak commodity prices. Since investment relies more heavily on trade than consumption, Freund (2016) argues that an investment slump would inevitably lead to a slowdown in trade growth (see also Boz, Bussière, and Marsilli 2015 and Morel 2015, for example).

Additional contributors to the trade slowdown are also possible. The waning pace of trade liberalization over the past few years and the recent uptick in protectionist measures could be limiting the sustained policy-driven reductions in trade costs achieved during 1985–2007, which provided a strong impetus to trade growth (Evenett and Fritz 2016; Hufbauer and Jung 2016). Lower trade costs, as well as advances in transportation and communication, also supported the spread of global value chains, in which the fragmentation of production processes boosted trade growth as intermediate goods crossed borders multiple times. The formation of cross-border production chains may have slowed—possibly because their growth matured or because the cost of trade fell more modestly, or both—implying a slower expansion

The main authors of this chapter are Aqib Aslam, Emine Boz (co–team leader), Eugenio Cerutti, Marcos Poplawski-Ribeiro, and Petia Topalova (co–team leader), with support from Ava Yeabin Hong, Hao Jiang, Evgenia Pugacheva, Rachel Szymanski, Hong Yang, and Marina Topalova Cole, and contributions from Jaebin Ahn, Diego Cerdeiro, Romain Duval, and Christian Henn. Andrei Levchenko was the external consultant. The chapter benefited from comments and suggestions by Brent Neiman.

[1]See Hoekman (2015) and papers therein for an analysis of the global trade slowdown. Relative to the studies in Hoekman (2015), the chapter's approach allows for a more comprehensive horse race among the various hypotheses for a large number of economies and using a range of analytical approaches.

[2]Chapter 4 of this WEO report discusses the global spillovers from China's rebalancing, including through trade.

Figure 2.1. World Real Trade and GDP Growth in Historical Perspective
(Percent)

The decline in real trade growth since 2012 has been remarkable, especially when set against the historical relationship between growth in trade and global economic activity.

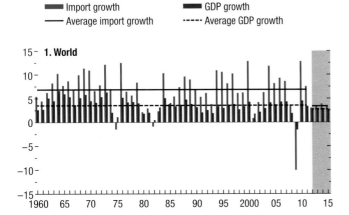

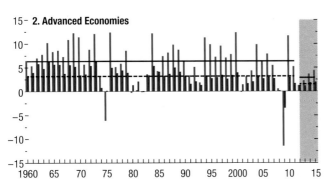

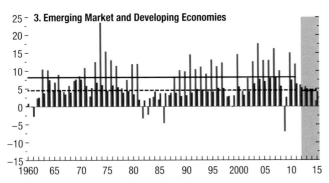

Source: IMF staff calculations.
Note: Imports include goods and services. The charts are based on an unbalanced sample of 100 countries in 1960 and 189 in 2015. Annual aggregate import (GDP) growth is calculated as the weighted average of country-specific real import (GDP) growth rates, where nominal import (GDP at market exchange rates) shares are the weights used.

in such supply chain-related trade (Constantinescu, Mattoo, and Ruta 2015).[3,4] Other causes of a decline in goods trade growth could be more evolutionary in nature, such as an increase in the relative demand for nontradables in response to growing wealth or aging populations.

The 1985–2007 period witnessed substantial globalization and rapid economic growth. There is strong consensus among economists that international trade contributed to the rise in overall prosperity, notwithstanding the often considerable adjustment costs faced by some workers. International trade allows economies to specialize in producing goods and services in which they have a comparative advantage and to exploit the resulting economies of scale and scope. But trade can also boost economic growth by spreading knowledge and technology and by fostering the development of new products and, ultimately, productivity.[5] In light of the synchronized slowdown in productivity growth in many economies, there may be a strong case for reviving the virtuous cycle of trade and growth through a concerted effort by policymakers to open markets and reduce trade costs further.[6]

To contribute to our understanding of the drivers of the sharp slowdown in trade since the end of 2011 and the design of an appropriate policy response, the chapter focuses on the following questions:

- How widespread is the post-2011 decline in the growth of international trade? Have the dynamics of trade differed among economies? Has the trade slowdown varied by type of trade and product group?
- How much of the slump in trade growth reflects weakness in economic activity and changes in the composition of growth? In particular, how much of

[3]Constantinescu, Mattoo, and Ruta (2015) argue that the growth of global supply chains, particularly those involving China, had weakened even before the global financial crisis. See Kee and Tang (2016) for further evidence on the evolution of China's value chains during 2000–07.

[4]If, indeed, the observed slowdown in trade simply marks the end of a period of unusually rapid trade growth, due to some of the factors listed above, then the global economy could be returning to a steady state in which, as theory predicts, trade grows at the same rate as output. In such a steady state, trade costs, the structure of individual economies, and production, sourcing, and trade patterns across countries would be constant. See, for example, Dixit and Norman (1980) or Ethier (1985).

[5]See, for example, Krugman (1979), Grossman and Helpman (1991), Young (1991), Lee (1993), Frankel and Romer (1999), and Bernard and others (2003), among others.

[6]See Goldberg and Pavcnik (2016) for a review of the literature on the effects of trade policy on trade volumes, productivity, labor markets, and growth.

the 2012–15 slowdown in trade growth relative to the period before the global financial crisis can be attributed to subdued growth? To what extent is the trade slowdown relative to GDP growth attributable to compositional changes in demand?
- What role have other factors—beyond output— played in holding back trade growth? Is the slowdown a consequence of policy distortions, such as a deceleration in trade liberalization or a rise in protectionism? Or does it reflect a maturation of global supply chains?

The chapter starts by documenting the evolution of trade growth across various dimensions. It then employs three complementary analytical approaches to analyze the factors behind the recent slowdown. The first part uses a standard empirical model of import demand to determine whether import growth at the country level has slowed by more than changes in aggregate demand components and relative prices would predict in recent years. The second part complements the empirical analysis by estimating a structural multicountry, multisector model, which quantifies the importance of changes in the composition of demand and other factors, such as trade costs. The third part of the analysis uses highly disaggregated data to shed light on the role of trade policies and global value chain participation.

The chapter's main findings are as follows:
- The decline in real trade growth has been broad based. Few countries were spared the 2012–15 slowdown in trade growth, either in absolute terms or relative to GDP growth. Likewise, trade growth fell for both goods and services, although services trade slowed less. Among goods, trade growth fell for 85 percent of product lines, with the sharpest slowdown observed in trade in capital and intermediate goods.
- The overall weakness in economic activity and, in particular, the slowdown in investment growth appear to be key restraints on trade growth since 2012. Empirical analysis suggests that, for the world as a whole, up to three-fourths of the decline in real goods import growth between 2003–07 and 2012–15 can be traced to weaker economic activity, most notably subdued investment growth. A general equilibrium model similarly finds that changes in the composition of demand explain about 60 percent of the slowdown in the growth rate of the nominal goods imports-to-GDP ratio.

- Other factors, however, are also weighing on trade growth. The slowdown in the pace of trade liberalization and the recent uptick in protectionist measures are holding back international trade in goods, even if their quantitative impact thus far has been relatively limited. The apparent decline in the growth of global value chains has also played an important part in the observed slowdown. Overall, factors beyond the level and composition of economic activity have shaved about 1¾ percentage points off global annual real import growth since 2012.

The key finding of the chapter—that weak trade growth is largely a symptom of the synchronized slowdown in economic activity across advanced and emerging market and developing economies—implies that policies to address the constraints to growth, and in particular investment where it is depressed, should take center stage in the effort to improve global economic health. Such policies, by lifting trade indirectly, will generate positive spillovers as trade linkages transmit and mutually reinforce each country's economic expansion. Yet, precisely because trade can strengthen productivity and boost growth, policies directly aimed at reducing trade costs and reinvigorating trade remain important in light of the subdued global outlook and unfavorable productivity trends. Many emerging market and developing economies maintain or face trade barriers that inhibit their entry into global markets and participation in global production chains; a coordinated effort to remove such barriers could kick off a new round of integration and global value chain development and provide firms with greater incentives to invest (Freund 2016). More broadly, avoiding protectionist measures and reviving the process of trade liberalization through trade reforms that lower barriers, coupled with measures that mitigate the cost to those who shoulder the burden of adjustment, would boost growth in the international exchange of goods and services and ultimately strengthen global activity.

It is important to emphasize from the outset that providing a precise quantification of the role of economic activity, trade policies, and global value chains in the evolution of trade flows is inherently a difficult task. Demand for traded goods is clearly a function of economic growth, but international trade and trade policies can also shape economic activity by influencing firms' investment decisions, their access to intermediate inputs, production processes, and productivity.

For example, the fading pace of trade liberalization since the early 2000s may have contributed to slow productivity growth, weak investment, and lackluster output growth in recent years. As in the vast majority of the trade literature, this chapter's empirical analysis focuses only on part of this complex web of relationships, as its primary goal is to establish whether recent trade dynamics are consistent with the observed level and composition of output growth, the evolution of trade policies, and global value chain integration given historical patterns of association. The structural analysis takes a more holistic approach as, in general equilibrium, the level of economic activity, production structure, and trade patterns are jointly determined by trade costs, preferences, and productivity. However, due to its stylized representation of the real world, the model is unable to capture all the channels through which trade may affect output.

The Implications of Trade for Productivity and Welfare: A Primer

While the primary focus of the chapter is to diagnose the drivers of the recent decline in trade growth, understanding its potential implications for productivity and growth is important in the context of a subdued global outlook and unfavorable productivity trends. To this end, this section provides a brief review of the key channels through which the opening of a closed economy to trade or further boosting international trade by reducing trade barriers can benefit the macroeconomy as well as the challenges it may pose.[7]

Trade liberalization can improve productivity, raise overall living standards, and promote economic growth through a number of channels. The best-known benefit from trade is that it induces factors of production, such as capital and labor, to be used more efficiently. When economies open up to international trade, they can specialize in the goods and services for which they have comparative advantage, thereby improving their overall productivity (Ricardo 1817). Trade liberalization could also enhance productivity in each sector by reallocating resources toward more productive firms that are better placed to expand their activities in

export markets (Melitz 2003) and exploit the resulting economies of scale (Box 2.1).[8]

Beyond the productivity gains from reallocation, trade can also lead to productivity improvements for individual firms. Exporting offers businesses the opportunity to learn from foreign markets, for example, through their relationship with particular buyers (De Loecker 2013), and the expanded market access provides greater incentives for investment in technology (Bustos 2011; Lileeva and Trefler 2010). Firms that face foreign competition in domestic markets may be forced to lower price-cost margins and move down their average cost curve (Helpman and Krugman 1985), focus on their core competency products (Bernard, Redding, and Schott 2011), and reduce managerial slack and generate efficiency gains (Hicks 1935). Trade liberalization has also been found to stimulate innovation by firms as reflected in their research and development spending and patenting as they attempt to increase their presence in the world marketplace (Bloom, Draca, and Van Reenen 2016). Finally, firms benefit from the larger variety, cheaper, and potentially higher-quality intermediate inputs international trade can offer (Grossman and Helpman 1991; Rivera-Batiz and Romer 1991).

Both consumers and producers broadly benefit from the international exchange of goods and services and the efficiencies it creates. Trade lowers the prices faced by consumers and producers, thereby raising real incomes. It also increases the variety of products available to consumers and producers (Broda and Weinstein 2006). Both of these channels can significantly boost welfare (Box 2.3). Economic theory also suggests that the consumption gains and the more efficient use of resources generated by trade should boost GDP even if a robust causal relationship between trade and growth is difficult to detect in cross-country data.[9]

---

[7]It is important to note that, in most cases, theory predicts benefits from trade to arise from the removal of distortions that limit greater trade flows. The Council of Economic Advisers (2015) provides a comprehensive review of the benefits from trade in the case of the United States.

[8]For a discussion of the impact of trade on intra-industry reallocation and productivity, see, for example, Melitz (2003); Bernard, Jensen, and Schott (2006); and Melitz and Ottaviano (2008). Lileeva and Trefler (2010) and Bustos (2011) present evidence of export-induced technology investments, while De Loecker (2007, 2013) and Atkin, Khandelwal, and Osman (2014) study the "learning-by-exporting" channel. Pavcnik (2002), Erdem and Tybout (2003), Amiti and Konings (2007), and Topalova and Khandelwal (2011) examine the productivity effects of trade liberalization, including through the intermediate inputs channel.

[9]Frankel and Romer (1999) provide some of the first estimates of the causal effects of trade on income; for a more recent analysis, see Feyrer (2009a, 2009b). Rodríguez and Rodrik (2001) instead conclude that the nature of the relationship between trade policy and economic growth remains ambiguous on empirical grounds.

However, while trade increases the size of the pie, its benefits may not often be evenly distributed—a source of much of the public opposition against increased trade openness. Trade has a distributional impact within an economy through two distinct channels. It differentially affects the earnings of workers across sectors and skills (see, for example, Stolper and Samuelson 1941).[10] It can also differentially impact the cost of living faced by different consumers through its effects on the relative prices of goods and services.

Numerous studies have examined the effect of trade on the distribution of earnings.[11] On one hand, sectors and firms that expand in response to greater foreign market access create new and often higher-quality employment opportunities.[12] On the other hand, the earnings and employment prospects of workers in sectors and firms competing with foreign imports may be adversely affected, and these adverse effects could be long lasting if expanding firms and sectors cannot promptly absorb the dislocated workers due to the nature of their skills or geographical location. A widely cited study by Autor, Dorn, and Hanson (2013) on the impact of Chinese import competition on the U.S. labor market finds that rising imports from China have led to higher unemployment, lower labor force participation, and reduced wages in local labor markets with import-competing manufacturing industries.[13]

Trade can also have a distributional effect as consumers enjoy different baskets of goods whose prices are differentially affected by trade-induced relative price changes. In a recent study, Fajgelbaum and Khandelwal (2016) develop a framework to isolate precisely this effect and simulate the gains from reducing trade costs in a large number of economies. They find that the benefits of trade from lower prices tend to favor those at the bottom of the income distribution because the poor spend a larger share of their income on heavily traded goods.

In sum, greater trade integration can strengthen productivity and growth, raising overall welfare. However, there are winners and losers from increasing trade openness, especially in the short term. The adjustment costs that further trade liberalization entails for certain workers should not be underestimated and call for complementary policy measures to ensure trade integration works for all (see also Box 2.2).

The Slowdown in Trade Growth: Key Patterns

An investigation into the evolution of global trade in recent years yields two strikingly different pictures, depending on whether trade is measured in real or nominal U.S. dollar terms. In real terms, world trade growth has slowed since the end of 2011; in nominal U.S. dollar terms, it has collapsed since the second half of 2014 (Figure 2.2, panels 1 and 2). The value of goods and services trade fell by 10½ percent in 2015, driven by a 13 percent drop in the import deflator as oil prices fell sharply and the U.S. dollar appreciated; the pace of decline has moderated in recent months.[14] The volume of goods and services trade continued to grow throughout this period, albeit at the relatively low rate of just over 3 percent a year, with no sign of acceleration.[15] Because much of the decline in nominal trade is due to the sharp drop in the price of oil and the strength of the U.S. dollar, the rest of the stylized facts and several of the analytical approaches focus on the evolution of trade volumes—that is, trade in real terms.[16]

Across economies, the slowdown in real trade growth is widespread, both in absolute terms and

---

[10]See also Jones (1971) and Mussa (1974) for discussions of the Stolper-Samuelson theorem and the specific-factors model of trade. Levchenko and Zhang (2013) provide a quantitative assessment of the differential effects of the trade integration of China, India, and central and eastern Europe on real wages across countries and sectors.

[11]See Goldberg and Pavcnik (2004, 2007) and World Bank (2010), and references therein, for a review of the evidence on the distributional consequences of trade in developing economies. For the United States, see Ebenstein and others (2014). For recent theory and evidence on the link between inequality and trade, see Helpman and others (forthcoming).

[12]A large number of studies document the higher wages paid to workers employed in exporting industries or exporting plants in the United States, with estimates for this export wage premium ranging from 1¾ percent to 18 percent (see, for example, Bernard and Jensen 1995, Bernard and others 2007, and Table 4 of Council of Economic Advisers 2015).

[13]See also Lawrence (2014), who argues that while manufactured imports from China have significantly raised the standard of living overall in the United States, for some U.S. workers and regions, the expansion of Chinese trade has meant costly and painful adjustment. In Europe, rising Chinese import competition also led to declines in employment and the share of unskilled workers (Bloom, Draca, and Van Reenen 2016).

[14]See Chapter 3 of this WEO for a discussion of the effect of import prices on global inflation.

[15]In fact, according to the CPB *World Trade Monitor*, as of July 2016, global merchandise trade volumes have remained almost flat since the end of 2014.

[16]The general equilibrium analysis examines the evolution of nominal values of trade relative to nominal GDP. Similarly, the gravity model, also discussed in this chapter, studies nominal bilateral sectoral trade flows.

Figure 2.2. World Trade in Volumes, Values, and across Countries

In real terms, world trade continued to grow since the end of 2011, albeit at a much lower rate, whereas in nominal U.S. dollar terms, it has collapsed since the second half of 2014. Across economies, the slowdown in real trade growth is widespread, both in absolute terms and relative to GDP growth.

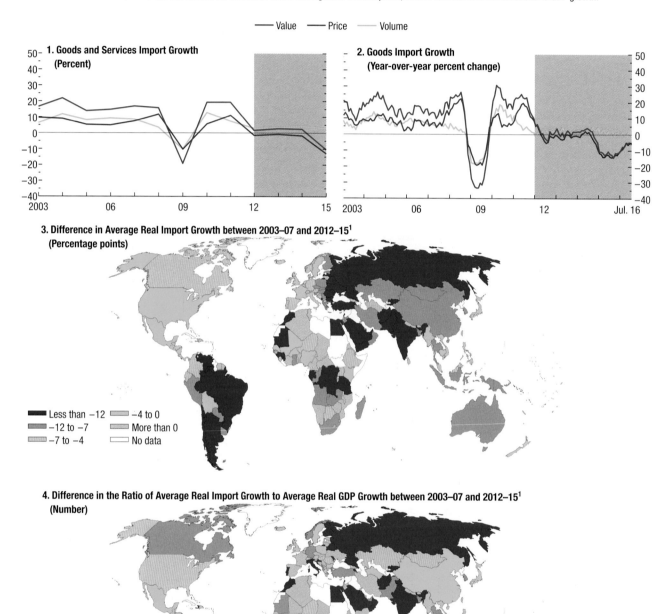

Sources: CPB Netherlands Bureau for Economic Policy Analysis; and IMF staff calculations.
[1]Different intervals, shown as different shades, correspond to quartile ranges that are calculated based on the distribution across countries that experienced a decline in real import growth (panel 3) or in the ratio of average real import growth to average real GDP growth (panel 4).

relative to GDP growth (Figure 2.2, panels 3 and 4). Compared with the five years leading up to the global financial crisis, growth of goods and services imports during 2012–15 slowed in 143 of 171 countries. When measured relative to GDP growth, the slowdown occurred in 116 countries.

The contours of the 2012–15 slowdown in the growth of real imports varied by broad country group (Figure 2.3) and sector (Figure 2.4). For advanced economies, the slowdown was sharp at the outset of the period following the euro area debt crises, but import growth picked up thereafter in line with the modest recovery in those economies. In emerging market and developing economies, the slowdown was initially milder, but became more severe during the past two years. This was driven by weaker imports in China and macroeconomic stress in a number of economies, including commodity exporters affected by sharp declines in their export prices (see also Chapter 1 of the April 2016 WEO).

As was the case during the global financial crisis, services trade has been more resilient than trade in goods (Figure 2.4, panel 1). Services and goods trade volumes grew at an annual rate of about 9½ percent and 9 percent, respectively, during 2003–07, but during 2012–15 the growth rate for services fell to 5½ percent. For goods, it dropped much more, to just under 3 percent.[17] Many have argued that the growth in services trade may be even stronger than is reflected in these numbers.[18] New business models and advances in information and communications technology have rapidly expanded trade in digital services, including in digitally enabled data and services delivered free of charge (for example, e-mail, social media, maps, and search engine services). Measuring such trade, however, will remain a challenge until important conceptual and methodological issues are resolved.[19]

Across goods, the trade slowdown during the past four years has been broad based (Figure 2.4, panels 2

and 3). The analysis for this chapter uses a novel data set to separately compute import price and volume indices by product and end-use categories using disaggregated data for about 5,300 products for 52 countries.[20] This novel data set suggests that the entire distribution of trade volume growth across the roughly 100 separately analyzed product lines shifted to the left during 2012–15 relative to the distribution of growth rates observed in 2003–07. More than 85 percent of product lines experienced a decline in the average trade volume growth rates between the two periods, including oil-related products, which account for more than 10 percent of total trade.

However, the severity of the slowdown in goods trade growth varied across types of products. Trade in nondurable consumption goods held up relatively well. Trade growth in capital goods declined the most, followed by primary intermediate goods, durable consumption goods, and processed intermediate goods (Figure 2.4, panel 4). The sharper slowdown of trade in capital and durable consumption goods (including cars and other nonindustrial transportation equipment), which is a large part of investment expenditures, points to the potential role of investment weakness in holding back global trade growth in recent years.

Understanding the Slowdown in Trade Growth

Assessing the appropriate policy responses to the weakness in trade requires a clear diagnosis of its causes. Has trade growth been held back primarily by the protracted weakness in the global economic environment? If so, policymakers may best focus their attention on reinvigorating growth, and in particular on strengthening investment where it is particularly depressed. Or do the causes lie with other types of impediments, such as a slower pace of trade reform, which would suggest a different set of actions?

This analysis starts by quantifying the influence of the overall economic environment and the composition of growth in the trade growth slowdown, using both an empirical and a model-based approach. Since both methodologies suggest that output, and its composition, cannot fully predict the observed weakness in trade since 2012, the analysis moves on in the subse-

[17]Services trade has remained relatively robust compared with goods trade since 2012, so trade refers specifically to goods trade for the remainder of the chapter, unless specified otherwise.

[18]A closer examination of nominal services trade across sectors reveals that trade in information and communication technologies, travel, and financial services has been significantly more resilient than trade in other services. (See Annex 2.1.)

[19]Magdeleine and Maurer (2016) provide an overview of the statistical challenges of measuring trade in "digitized ideas." A recent report by the McKinsey Global Institute (Manyika and others 2016) also discusses the impact of an increasingly digital era of globalization on trade, arguing that cross-border data flows generate more economic value than traditional flows of traded goods.

[20]United Nations Comtrade International Trade Statistics provide information on the nominal value and quantity of goods imports, so it is possible to compute unit value changes for each product over time. (See Annex 2.2 and Boz and Cerutti (forthcoming) for more details.)

Figure 2.3. Trade Dynamics across Broad Country Groups
(Percent)

Not all economies experienced the slowdown in trade at the same time. In advanced economies, import growth fell sharply in 2012. In emerging market and developing economies, the decline in import growth became more severe in 2014 and 2015.

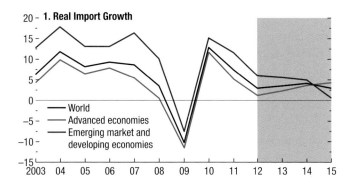

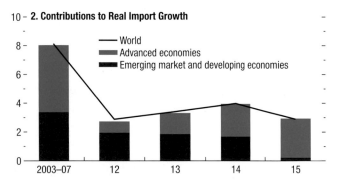

Source: IMF staff calculations.
Note: Imports include goods and services. Annual aggregate import growth is calculated as the weighted average of country-specific real import growth rates, where nominal import shares are the weights used.

quent sections to disentangle the role of other factors—trade policies and changes in the pace of global value chain expansion—using disaggregated product and bilateral-sectoral trade flows.

The Role of Output and Its Composition: Insights from an Empirical Investigation

To gauge the role of economic activity and shifts in its composition, this section examines the historical relationship between import volumes of goods and services and aggregate demand during 1985–2015 to predict a country's import growth from observed fluctuations in its domestic expenditures, exports, and relative prices. This predicted import growth is then compared with actual trade dynamics to assess whether

Figure 2.4. Trade Dynamics across Types of Trade and Products

Services trade has been more resilient than goods trade. Among goods, the trade slowdown has been broad based with imports of capital goods experiencing the most pronounced decline in growth.

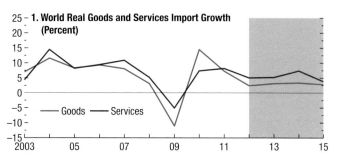

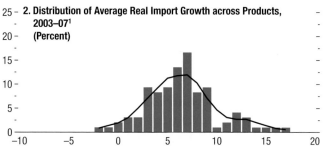

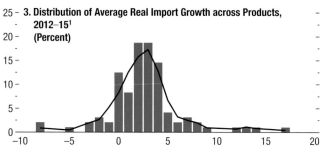

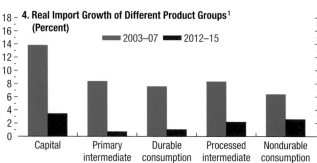

Sources: United Nations Comtrade; and IMF staff calculations.
Note: Panels 2–4 are computed using import volume indices constructed from quantity and value trade data at HS 6-digit level for 52 economies. See Boz and Cerutti (forthcoming) and Annex 2.2 for more details.
[1]Goods only.

trade has been unusually weak since 2012 given its historical relationship with economic activity.

For each of the 150 countries in the sample, the chapter estimates a standard import demand model that links import volume growth of goods and services separately to growth in demand, controlling for relative import prices.[21] Most studies use a country's GDP as a proxy for absorption. In contrast, the analysis here follows the innovation of Bussière and others (2013) and computes the import-intensity-adjusted aggregate demand (IAD) as a weighted average of traditional aggregate demand components (investment, private consumption, government spending, and exports). The weights used are the import content of demand computed from input-output tables.[22,23] The approach explicitly accounts for differences in the import content of the various aggregate demand components and captures the effect of changes in the overall strength of economic activity and across its drivers. The latter is especially important. Investment, together with exports, has a particularly rich import content, and it has been weak in many advanced economies still recovering from the global financial and European debt crises. It has also decelerated significantly in many emerging market and developing economies, including

in China, which is undergoing a necessary and welcome rebalancing of its economy away from investment as discussed in Chapter 4 of this WEO.

In addition to the measure proposed by Bussière and others (2013), the chapter estimates two alternative models of import demand using: (1) IAD including only the domestic components of aggregate demand (domestic IAD) and (2) domestic IAD and exports predicted by trading partners' domestic IAD. These alternative models are useful given the global nature of the trade slowdown: they help focus more precisely on the dynamics of import growth driven only by domestic demand at home and domestic demand in trading partners (rather than exports, which are the sum of the imports of trading partners). A single country can take external demand for its goods and services as given, but for the world as a whole, only the sum of individual countries' domestic demand determines global import growth.

The empirical model closely tracks the dynamics of import growth (Figure 2.5), particularly when predicted values are calculated using the IAD measure based on all four aggregate demand components instead of only those for domestic demand. This is to be expected as country-level imports and exports are increasingly linked given the rise in the internationalization of production (Bussière and others 2013).

The model does reveal, however, that predicted versus actual trade growth for goods differed from that of services during 2012–15. For services, the actual and predicted import growth series are close to each other for the entire estimation period. In contrast, the annual growth of goods imports was, on average, significantly lower than predicted for 2012–15. For the average economy, the "missing" goods import growth averaged 1 percentage point over the past four years according to the model using all four components of aggregate demand to predict imports. The two alternative models suggest an even larger gap between actual and predicted goods import growth, of about 2¼ and 1¾ percentage points, respectively (Figure 2.6, panel 1).[24]

The results are also consistent with the time profile of the trade slowdown across countries discussed in the previous section. For advanced economies, the unpre-

---

[21]An import demand equation, which relates growth in real imports to changes in absorption and relative price levels, can be derived from virtually any international real business cycle model. The exact empirical specification estimated is

$$\Delta \ln M_{c,t} = \delta_c + \beta_{D,c} \Delta \ln D_{c,t} + \beta_{P,c} \Delta \ln P_{c,t} + \varepsilon_{c,t},$$

in which $M_{c,t}$, $D_{c,t}$, and $P_{c,t}$ denote, respectively, real imports, aggregate demand, and relative import prices of country c in year t. As in Bussière and others (2013), the baseline specification assumes that import growth depends only on contemporaneous growth of the explanatory variables; however, the findings discussed in the chapter are robust to the inclusion of lags of the dependent and explanatory variables growth rates to allow for richer dynamics. See Annex 2.3 for the estimation results.

[22]Import-intensity-adjusted demand is computed as $IAD_t = C_t^{\omega_C} G_t^{\omega_G} I_t^{\omega_I} X_t^{\omega_X}$, in which ω_k is the import content of each of the expenditure components for $k \in \{C, G, I, X\}$, normalized to sum to 1. Import content is computed from the Eora Multi-Region Input-Output country-specific tables, averaged over 1990–2011. Note that if import intensity were perfectly measured in each period and the import intensity weights were allowed to vary over time, the model would be able to fully account for the level of imports (although not their growth rates). This chapter uses the 1990–2011 average import intensity, recognizing that the change in import intensity over time may be a consequence of changing trade costs and international production fragmentation, factors that are examined separately in this chapter.

[23]See Hong and others (2016), IMF (2015e), Jääskelä and Mathews (2015), Martinez-Martin (2016), and Morel (2015) for further examples of analysis of trade growth based on IAD, with substantially smaller samples of countries.

[24]These findings are robust to controlling for the role of uncertainty, global financial conditions, and financial stress in the economy when analyzing the import demand model residuals. (See Annex 2.3.)

Figure 2.5. Empirical Model: Actual and Predicted Evolution of Real Import Growth

(Percent)

Post 2012, predicted import growth is consistently above actual for trade in goods, especially in emerging market and developing economies. For services, actual and predicted import growth track each other closely.

— Actual
— Predicted based on domestic import-intensity-adjusted demand
— Predicted based on import-intensity-adjusted demand
— Predicted based on domestic and partner's domestic import-intensity-adjusted demand

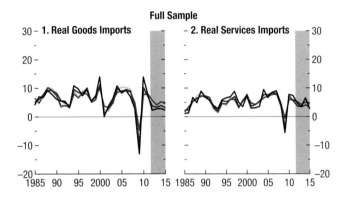

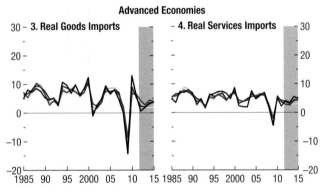

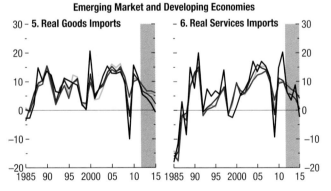

Source: IMF staff calculations.
Note: Actual and predicted lines display the average of country real import growth rates, weighted by import shares. Predictions are based on an import demand model, estimated country by country, linking real import growth to growth in import-intensity-adjusted demand and relative import prices. See Annex 2.3.

dicted slowdown in import growth occurred in 2012. Since then, goods import growth has recovered and is close to model-predicted values on average (Figure 2.6, panel 2). For emerging market and developing economies, the missing goods import growth is larger and has become more pronounced over time (Figure 2.6, panel 3).

Overall, these results suggest that the strength of economic activity and its composition are unable to fully account for the slowdown in goods import growth beginning in 2012, especially in emerging market and developing economies.

But how large is the missing goods import growth compared with the overall decline in import growth? To answer this question, the chapter decomposes the observed slowdown in goods import growth rates prior to and following the global financial crisis. The analysis takes both a long view (1985–2007) and a short view (2003–07) of the precrisis period, comparing each of these intervals with the 2012–15 period to establish what share of the slowdown the empirical model could and could not match (Figure 2.7). It further allocates the predicted slowdown into the shares attributable to the different aggregate demand components. Two findings stand out:

- From an individual country's perspective, the unpredicted portion of the goods import growth slowdown is relatively small when compared with the overall decline in import growth. Comparing 2012–15 with 2003–07, the model, using all four aggregate demand components to predict import growth, can account for 85 percent of the slowdown for the average economy in the full sample.[25]

- The declines in investment and export growth account for the lion's share of the slowdown in trade growth, especially relative to 2003–07, when capital spending in many emerging market and developing economies, including China, was growing at an unusually brisk pace.

Regarding the second result, the extent to which the decline of exports underlies the slowdown of import growth in individual economies reflects two factors: (1) the tight linkages between a country's imports and exports as production processes become increasingly fragmented across borders and (2) the

[25]The unpredicted portion is larger if the change in import growth relative to 1985–2007 is considered, especially for emerging market and developing economies.

Figure 2.6. Empirical Model: Difference between Actual and Predicted Growth of Real Goods Imports
(Percent)

In advanced economies, "missing" goods import growth during 2012–15 is smaller than in emerging market and developing economies. For the former, the largest unpredicted component occurred in 2012, with real goods import growth subsequently recovering to levels predicted by the model. For the latter, missing goods import growth has instead become more pronounced over time.

■ Predicted based on domestic import-intensity-adjusted demand
■ Predicted based on import-intensity-adjusted demand
■ Predicted based on domestic and partners' domestic import-intensity-adjusted demand

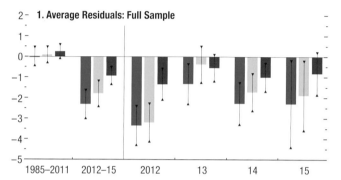

1. Average Residuals: Full Sample

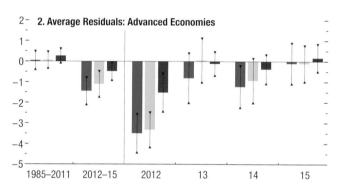

2. Average Residuals: Advanced Economies

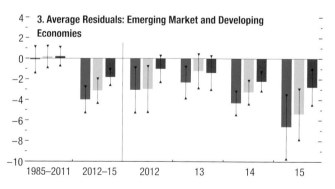

3. Average Residuals: Emerging Market and Developing Economies

Source: IMF staff calculations.
Note: Bars display the average residuals, weighted by import shares, from an import demand model, estimated country by country, linking real import growth to growth in import-intensity-adjusted demand and relative import prices. Black markers denote the 90 percent confidence interval. See Annex 2.3.

Figure 2.7. Empirical Model: Decomposing the Slowdown in Real Goods Import Growth
(Percentage points)

The empirical model can predict a sizable fraction of the difference in average real goods import growth between 1985–2007 or 2003–07 and 2012–15. The lion's share of the slowdown in import growth can be attributed to the weakness in investment and external demand.

■ Predicted by consumption and relative prices
■ Predicted by investment
■ Predicted by exports
■ Predicted by own and partners' domestic import-intensity-adjusted demand
■ Unpredicted

Full Sample

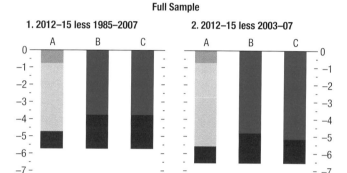

Advanced Economies

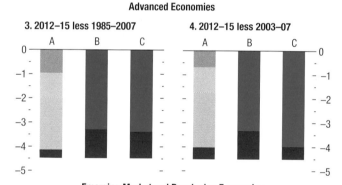

Emerging Market and Developing Economies

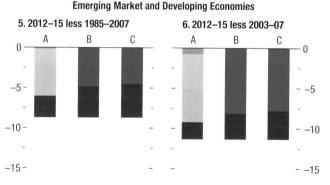

Source: IMF staff calculations.
Note: Bar A decomposes the difference in average real goods import growth between the two periods into portions predicted by consumption and relative prices, investment, exports, and an unpredicted residual. Bar B apportions the component predicted by exports into what can and cannot be predicted by domestic demand from trading partners, using an iterative procedure. Bar C decomposes the difference into the sum of domestic demand and external demand predicted by trading partners' domestic demand.

globally synchronized weakness in economic growth in recent years. These two factors have contributed to the widespread nature of the trade growth slowdown across countries and have amplified its magnitude.

To trace the role of domestic demand in the global trade slowdown, the analysis breaks down for each country the share of the decline in import growth accounted for by its exports into: (1) the predicted value of its trading partners' import demand, attributable to domestic demand; (2) the predicted value of its trading partners' import demand, attributable to exports; and (3) a residual portion unaccounted for by the model. Iterating in this fashion, it is possible to fully allocate the global goods import slowdown to domestic demand components and an unpredicted portion as depicted in the middle bar of each panel of Figure 2.7. This procedure reveals that, for the world as a whole, changes in economic activity can account for about three-fourths of the decline in the global goods import growth rate. The unpredicted portion of the slowdown in global goods import growth is larger than for the average economy, as impediments to trade at the individual country level are compounded in the aggregate. Using the import demand model based on domestic IAD and exports predicted by partners' domestic IAD yields a very similar pattern, as revealed in the right bar of the panels in Figure 2.7.

Ultimately, the slowdown in goods import growth during 2012–15 is not just a symptom of weak activity. About three-fourths of the global trade slowdown can be traced to the combined effect of slower overall growth, a change in the composition of economic activity away from more import-intensive components—namely, investment—and the synchronized nature of the growth slowdown across countries, which may be in part effected via trade. However, at the global level, goods import growth rates during 2012–15 have fallen short by about 1¾ percentage points on average relative to what would be expected based on the historical relationship between trade flows and economic activity. This is not a trivial amount: the level of real global goods trade would have been 8 percent higher in 2015 had it not been for this missing trade growth.

The empirical approach described above is well established in the literature, but carries two important caveats.[26] First, as previously discussed, it focuses

narrowly on only one side of the relationship between economic activity and trade: the link from the former to the latter. Other factors can simultaneously affect economic activity and trade, in particular, trade policies. Not taking these into account would likely lead to an upward bias in the estimated role of economic activity in predicting trade flows. As demonstrated in Annex 2.3, this bias, however, is relatively small.[27]

Second, as a partial equilibrium analysis—the empirical model takes each country's external demand as given—it is insufficient on its own to analyze a synchronized trade slowdown across many countries. To overcome the second limitation, the chapter uses a multicountry general equilibrium structural model, which is described in the next section. The general equilibrium approach also allows for an endogenous response of the level of economic activity and output to changes in trade patterns and trade costs through their effect on intermediate and consumption goods' prices, thus addressing partially the first limitation of the empirical approach as well.[28]

The Role of Demand Composition and Trade Costs: Insights from a Structural Investigation

This section examines the slowdown in the growth of trade in goods relative to GDP growth in nominal terms by adapting the multisector, multicountry, static model of production and trade in Eaton and others (2010).[29] Since this is a general equilibrium

---

[26]Some recent examples of studies that recover trade wedges—that is, components of trade growth that cannot be explained by models of trade demand, based on the one-way relationship from demand and relative prices to imports—include Levchenko, Lewis, and Tesar (2010); Alessandria, Kaboski, and Midrigan (2013); and Alessandria and Choi (2016). See also Bussière and others (2013); Constantinescu, Mattoo, and Ruta (2015); Ollivaud and Schwellnus (2015); and the studies cited in footnote 23.

[27]Purging growth in aggregate demand components from the effects of policy-driven changes in trade costs before constructing IAD yields slightly larger "missing" trade growth during 2012–15. For the average economy, the share of the decline in import growth predicted by changes in economic activity—by construction orthogonal to trade policies—and relative prices is 79 percent, compared to the 85 percent using the baseline specification.

[28]As is the case with most general equilibrium models of trade, certain channels through which trade affects output, for example, the dynamic productivity gains from greater trade openness, are not captured.

[29]This model incorporates the canonical Ricardian trade model of Eaton and Kortum (2002). Eaton and others (forthcoming) extend the static model of their 2010 work to explicitly model the role of investment in a dynamic framework. However, the dynamic version of the model has a heavier data and computational requirement, making its estimation for a large number of emerging market and developing economies not feasible for this study.

model, which endogenously computes equilibrium wages and prices, the main object of interest is nominal import growth in relation to GDP growth. In this framework, countries trade to exploit their comparative advantage in goods production. However, international trade is costly: it involves transportation costs and man-made trade barriers, such as tariffs. Countries weigh these trade-related costs against the efficiency gains from trade to determine whether and how much to produce, export, and import. The model also includes a rich input-output structure allowing the output from each sector—durable, nondurable manufacturing, and commodities and a residual sector that mostly includes nontradables—to be used as an input to other sectors.

According to the model, observed trade dynamics can be attributed to changes in four specific factors, or "wedges": (1) composition of demand, (2) trade costs (or frictions), (3) productivity, and (4) trade deficits. These time-varying wedges act as shocks to preferences, cost of trade, productivity, and trade deficits, thereby influencing agents' economic decisions, including whether to trade. When the observed patterns of sectoral trade, production, and prices are analyzed through the lens of the model, the model endogenously allocates changes in actual trade flows to these four wedges so that the implied trade dynamics match those in the data exactly. The four factors are sector and country specific and are identified within the framework as follows:

- The *demand composition* wedge captures changes in the share of a sector's output in total final demand. For example, if weak investment reduces demand for durable manufactured goods disproportionately more than the demand for other goods, changes in trade flows will be attributed to this wedge.

- The *trade costs* wedge accounts for changes in preferences between domestically produced and imported goods that are not due to relative price changes. For example, if prices in all countries remain fixed, but a country consumes more domestically produced durables than imported durables, this would be attributed to rising trade costs. These trade costs may include tariffs, subsidies for domestic production, nontariff barriers, cross-border transportation costs, and so forth.[30]

- The *productivity* wedge reflects countries' comparative advantage. As a country becomes more productive in a particular sector, it exports more output from this sector to its trading partners and consumes more of this sector's output domestically.

- The *trade deficit* wedge is necessary to ensure that the model can perfectly match imports and exports for countries that run trade deficits or surpluses.

Many of the key hypotheses about the causes of the slowdown in global trade relative to GDP can be mapped to these factors. A slowdown in trade growth, which mostly reflects shifts in the composition of economic activity, will be captured in the demand composition wedge. On the other hand, if the erection of trade barriers or a slower pace of trade liberalization underpins the slowdown, the model would attribute this to a rise in the trade cost wedge. By generating counterfactual scenarios in which only one factor is allowed to change, the model can quantify the role of these wedges in the current trade slowdown in a general equilibrium setting. For example, in the scenario with only the demand composition wedge active, the model allows the demand composition to change as observed in the data but keeps trade costs, productivity, and trade deficits constant. For the purposes of this chapter, only the results of the counterfactual scenarios for the first two wedges (demand composition and trade costs) are presented.[31]

The analysis here uses annual sectoral data on production, bilateral trade, and producer prices for 2003–15 to apply the accounting procedure for 34 advanced and emerging market and developing economies (accounting for 75 percent of world trade), thus extending both the geographical and temporal coverage of Eaton and others (2010).[32] Furthermore, the chapter enriches the model's structure by explicitly modeling a commodity sector in addition to the

---

[30]The model does not feature any nominal rigidities or variations in the length of global value chains. This implies that observed fluctuations in trade flows due to these two factors will be imperfectly attributed to one of the four wedges. For example, the recent depreciation of stressed emerging market and developing economies'

currencies appears to have boosted the trade cost wedge as trade values declined more than domestic absorption and production in U.S. dollars due to incomplete exchange rate pass-through. Similarly, changes in global value chain growth also tend to be absorbed by the trade cost wedge as exemplified by significant declines in measured trade costs for Vietnam.

[31]The trade deficit wedge played a negligible role during the recent trade slowdown. The productivity wedge exhibits some interesting dynamics, but they can be ascribed mostly to the recent supply-side-induced price changes in the commodity sector.

[32]The very large data requirement precludes the application of the procedure over a longer historical period for a large number of economies. See Annex 2.4 for a description of the data and parameters used in this exercise.

three sectors included in the original setup. This is an essential addition in light of recent price shifts in this sector, which affect the ratio of trade growth to GDP growth.[33] However, the model does not separate investment from consumption, and the findings on the role of demand composition should be interpreted in light of this limitation.

Comparing the results from the two counterfactual scenarios with the actual data on the gross growth of nominal imports-to-GDP ratio for 2003–15 (Figure 2.8, panels 1, 3, and 5) yields the following insights:

- During 2003–07, nominal goods trade grew faster relative to GDP because of both shifts in the composition of demand and reduced trade costs. In advanced economies, these two factors were about equal in importance; in emerging market and developing economies, falling trade costs took a leading role, particularly for China, which is consistent with its accession to the World Trade Organization in 2001.
- The 2012–15 slowdown in the growth of the nominal goods import-to-GDP ratio was characterized by a shift in demand toward nontradables and by a shift within tradables toward nondurable manufactured goods. For the world, the expenditure shares of all three tradable sectors declined; the share of commodities fell more than others given that sector's price declines. The further decline in 2015 in the ratio of nominal import growth to GDP growth was mostly due to the decline in commodity prices.
- The model attributes that largely to wedges in the commodity sector. However, other wedges played a role, too, with their relative contribution varying across countries. For example, China stands out in terms of a rise in trade costs. Although it is difficult to pinpoint the driver of this finding, it may be indicative of the flattening of global value chains. Brazil experienced a significant decline in the share of durable manufacturing goods in its expenditures, which depressed the growth of imports.

Comparing results of the alternative scenarios for 2003–07 with those for 2012–15 reveals that changes in demand composition alone accounted for almost 60 percent of the slowdown in world trade

growth relative to GDP growth (Figure 2.8, panels 2, 4, and 6). In addition, the shift in the composition of demand has been more important in advanced economies than in emerging market and developing economies. For the world, trade costs also played a nonnegligible role: the model attributes close to 25 percent of the slowdown in the growth of nominal imports-to-GDP ratio to changes in this factor. Reductions in trade costs boosted trade in 2003–07, while their pace of decline fell considerably in 2012–15. When combined—that is, when changes in the composition of demand and in trade costs are allowed to shape trade flows simultaneously—the model can account for close to 80 percent of the slowdown.[34]

Despite their significant differences, the two analytical approaches deliver a consistent message. The global slowdown in trade reflects to a significant extent, but not entirely, the weakness of the overall economic environment and compositional shifts in aggregate demand. According to both methodologies, demand composition shifts have played a larger role in the slowdown in advanced economies' trade, relative to that in emerging market and developing economies. And, finally, both the structural model and the reduced-form approach suggest a role for other factors, including trade costs, in the observed slowdown in trade.

The Role of Trade Costs and Global Value Chains: Insights from Disaggregated Trade Data

Motivated by the findings of the first two analytical exercises of the chapter, this section examines the role of trade costs and changes in global production processes in the recent trade slowdown. Since many trade policies—for example, tariffs and nontariff barriers—are set at the product level, and global value chain participation varies significantly across sectors within the same economy, properly disentangling their role requires the use of disaggregated data.[35] To do so, this section follows a three-step approach.

[33]In this Ricardian model of trade, trade in commodities occurs as a result of differences in the efficiency of production. This can be mapped to the real world—for example, oil importers have reservoirs deep underground and extraction is more inefficient than for oil exporters.

[34]Adding up the results under four counterfactual scenarios, each featuring a different wedge, does not necessarily yield the scenario containing all wedges at the same time. The wedges can amplify or dampen each other when they are present simultaneously, so that the sum of the fraction of the data they can account for individually can be greater or less than one.
[35]Analysis performed at the aggregate (country) level may fail to uncover the association between these factors and trade growth since it cannot account for a large part of the variation in the data (across products and sectors).

Figure 2.8. Structural Model: Actual and Model-Implied Evolution of Nominal Import-to-GDP Ratio

During 2003–07, nominal imports grew faster than GDP due to both shifts in the composition of demand and reductions in trade costs. During the slowdown period of 2012–15, however, changes in demand composition played a more prominent role relative to trade costs, particularly in advanced economies.

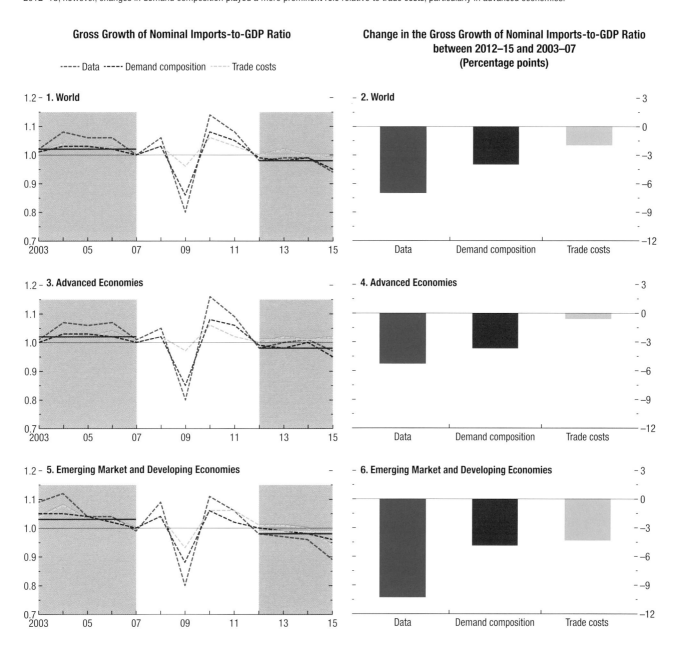

Source: IMF staff calculations.
Note: Actual and simulated lines in panels 1, 3, and 5 display the ratio of gross growth of nominal goods imports to gross growth of nominal world GDP, $(M_t/M_{t-1})/(Y_t/Y_{t-1})$, and their period averages (solid lines). A value of 1 indicates that nominal imports and GDP grow at the same rate. The simulated effect of demand composition and trade costs are obtained through counterfactual exercises in which only the corresponding wedge is allowed to operate, holding all other factors affecting production and trade constant. A decline in trade costs corresponds to an increase in the depicted trade wedge as it boosts model-implied trade values. Bars in panels 2, 4, and 6 display the difference in the average growth of the imports-to-GDP ratio described above between 2003–07 and 2012–15 implied by: (1) the data; (2) the model with the demand composition wedge only; and (3) the model with the trade cost wedge only, that is, the differences in the period averages depicted in panels 1, 3, and 5. See Annex 2.4 for further details of country coverage, data sources, and methodology.

First, it presents comprehensive evidence on how trade costs and production chains have evolved over time. Second, it analyzes disaggregated trade flows and measures of trade costs and global value chain participation at the country-product level to estimate the elasticity of real import growth with respect to these factors. Third, the analysis combines the first two steps to obtain an estimate of how much each potential factor can account for in the slowdown in trade growth during 2012–15. It should be emphasized that this analysis does not attempt to identify causation, only association; the ultimate goal is to uncover how much of the import growth decline can be predicted by the behavior of the various correlates.

The Evolution of Trade Costs and Global Value Chains

Overall Trade Costs

The term "trade costs" typically encompasses a broad range of factors that drive a wedge between the producer price of the exporter and the consumer prices in the importing country. Factors can include measurable components, such as transportation costs and tariffs, availability and cost of trade credit, and other harder-to-quantify elements, such as language barriers, regulations, and other informational asymmetries.[36]

To get a bird's eye view of how trade costs in the broadest sense have evolved, the analysis infers them from the patterns of observed bilateral trade, production, and absorption across countries, following Head and Ries (2001) and Novy (2012). Intuitively, if bilateral trade flows increase relative to domestic trade flows (proxied by gross sectoral output less total exports), the methodology concludes that it must have become easier for the two countries to trade with each other, and therefore trade costs must have fallen.[37]

Global average manufacturing trade costs vis-à-vis the world's 10 largest importers declined significantly during 1990–2008, spiked with the retrenchment in international trade during the global financial cri-

sis, and flattened thereafter (Figure 2.9, panel 1).[38] The same pattern can be observed across economies and across sectors (Figure 2.9, panel 2). While more dispersed, the decline in trade costs was substantially larger for emerging market and developing economies—which face significantly higher trade costs—than for advanced economies over this period (Figure 2.9, panels 3 and 4). What halted the decline of trade costs? The following subsections examine the role of some specific influences on trade costs: tariffs, nontariff barriers, free trade agreements, and transportation and logistics.[39]

Tariffs

Import tariffs are the most easily observable and measurable form of trade cost. Trade negotiation and unilateral trade liberalization lowered the import-weighted average tariff rates for all economies by almost 1 percentage point a year between 1986 and the conclusion of the Uruguay Round in 1995, with a significant narrowing in the dispersion of tariffs across countries and products (Figure 2.10, panels 1 and 2). Subsequently, tariff reductions continued, albeit at a more moderate rate of ½ percentage point a year until 2008. In the absence of tariff agreements since then, tariff declines have been minimal.[40]

Nontariff Barriers

Nontariff barriers are arguably the most difficult to measure. As the name suggests, they cover any nontariff measure that restricts trade flows, such as quotas, bailouts, state aid, and trade defense measures, as well as mandated preferences for local over foreign products.

Two complementary sources of data, the Centre for Economic Policy Research Global Trade Alert initiative and the World Bank Temporary Trade Barriers data-

---

[36]Trade costs can be fixed (for example, institutional and behind-the-border barriers, which force a firm to pay a fixed cost to access a new market) or variable (such as transportation costs, import tariffs, costs linked to trade logistics, and facilitation services). See Annex 2.5 for details on the construction of the index of trade costs and Arvis and others (2013) for a discussion of trade costs in the developing world.

[37]Trade costs calculated this way are conceptually the same as the trade cost wedges recovered from the general equilibrium model previously described.

[38]The 10 largest importers include Canada, China, France, Germany, Italy, Japan, Korea, Mexico, the United Kingdom, and the United States.

[39]The availability and cost of trade finance are also an important part of trade costs faced by businesses, and could limit trade growth, as witnessed during the great trade collapse (Chor and Manova 2012). However, anecdotal evidence on the availability of trade finance suggests that it is unlikely to play a major role in the current trade slowdown (International Chamber of Commerce 2015). Annex 2.5 presents some survey data on trends in the availability of trade credit lines offered by banks.

[40]It is important to note that the continuous decline in average tariffs occurred even though the sample of countries grew significantly over time and included increasing numbers of developing economies, which tend to have higher import tariffs.

Figure 2.9. Trade Costs in Historical Perspective: A Top-Down Approach
(Percent)

Trade costs fell somewhat consistently up until the global financial crisis but have since flattened. The same pattern can be observed across advanced and emerging market and developing economies and globally across sectors.

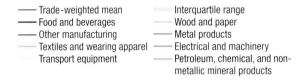

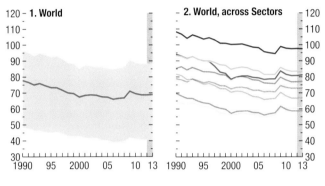

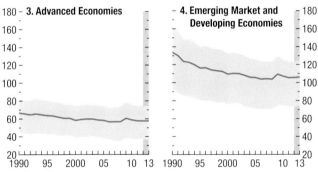

Sources: Eora Multi-Region Input-Output database; and IMF staff calculations.
Note: The index follows the Head and Ries (2001) and Novy (2012) methodology to understand how trade costs in a broad sense have evolved over time. These costs are inferred from the patterns of observed bilateral trade, production, and absorption across countries. See Annex 2.5 for a detailed description of country coverage, data sources, and methodology.

base, show a steady increase in protectionist measures (Figure 2.10, panels 3 and 4).[41] The stock of three

[41]We thank Chad Bown, Simon Evenett, and Johannes Fritz for generously sharing their databases on nontariff barriers. The Global Trade Alert database has the most comprehensive coverage of all types of trade-discriminatory and trade-liberalizing measures, although it only begins in 2008 (Evenett and Fritz 2015). The World Bank data generally cover a longer period but only for national governments' use of three specific policies: antidumping, countervailing duties, and safeguard measures (Bown 2016).

specific temporary trade barriers (antidumping, countervailing duties, and safeguards) suggests that while temporary barriers affect only a small share of products (2½ percent in 2015), the share of products affected by them has grown since 1990, with a significant uptick in 2014 and 2015. The Global Trade Alert, currently the most comprehensive database for all types of trade-related measures imposed since the global financial crisis, also shows a steady increase in protectionist measures since 2012, with 2015 recording the largest number of harmful trade measures. While the limited time coverage of the Global Trade Alert precludes a more rigorous analysis, there is clear evidence that the real import growth of products subject to trade discriminatory measures experienced a deeper decline in 2012–15 relative to 2003–07 (Figure 2.10, panel 5).

An additional indication of the extent to which trade issues have become a concern for businesses can be gleaned from firms' lobbying activity (Ludema, Mayda, and Mishra 2015).[42] According to U.S. firms' mandatory lobbying disclosure reports, there has been a steady increase in lobbying on trade issues since 2009 (Figure 2.10, panel 6). These trends may be part of the reason for the halt in the decline of overall trade costs.[43]

Free Trade Agreements

Free trade agreements can also reduce trade costs, not only by curtailing tariff and nontariff barriers but also by including provisions on various other issues that may impede trade in goods and services, such as, for example, regulatory cooperation. The proliferation of free trade agreements was particularly strong in the 1990s, averaging nearly 30 signed agreements a year according to the Design of Trade Agreements database. In the run-up to the global financial crisis, the number dropped slightly (to 26) but, since 2011, the rate has fallen sharply to about 10 agreements signed a year (Figure 2.10, panel 7).

However, compared with earlier pacts, recent agreements are deeper—they cover a much broader spectrum of measures than tariffs alone. And unlike earlier arrangements, they include more trading partners—

[42]We thank Prachi Mishra for updating and sharing her database on firms' lobbying activity.
[43]Henn and McDonald (2014) find that the trade-restrictive measures captured in the Global Trade Alert database as of 2010 had a sizable adverse effect on product-level trade flows during 2008–10, although their aggregate impact was muted by their limited adoption during the sample period.

Figure 2.10. Trade Policies in Historical Perspective

The pace of tariff reduction and the coverage of free trade agreements has slowed. There are signs that protectionism is on the rise.

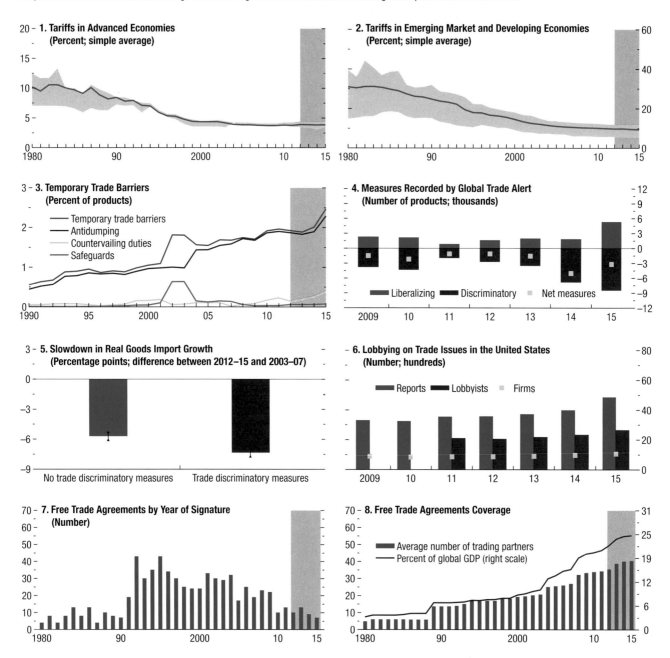

Sources: Bown 2016; Design of Trade Agreements database; Evenett and Fritz 2016; Global Trade Alert database; Ludema, Mayda, and Mishra 2015; United Nations Conference on Trade and Development Trade Analysis and Information System; World Bank Temporary Trade Barriers database; World Trade Organization (WTO) Tariff Download Facility; WTO Regional Trade Agreements database; and IMF staff calculations.
Note: Blue shaded areas in panels 1 and 2 denote the interquartile ranges. See Annex 2.5 for a detailed description of country coverage, data sources, and methodology of each indicator.

for example, the recently concluded megaregional Trans-Pacific Partnership, the Regional Comprehensive Economic Partnership, and the Transatlantic Trade and Investment Partnership, which are still being negotiated. Such arrangements encompass large groups of countries with a major share of world trade and foreign direct investment. Such deeper and larger agreements tend to have a bigger impact on trade growth.[44]

To calculate the coverage of these agreements, the analysis measures the average number of trading partners with which a representative country is in a free trade agreement and the average share of world GDP of those trading partners. On that measure, free trade agreements' coverage continues to increase, albeit at a slightly slower rate more recently (Figure 2.10, panel 8).

Transportation and Logistical Costs of Trade

International transportation costs and costs associated with domestic transportation and border and documentary compliance have been shown to hurt trade flows (Hummels 2007a; Djankov, Freund, and Pham 2010). However, according to most available measures, such costs have been continuously declining since 2006. Both the monetary cost in connection with the logistics of trade, such as documentary compliance fees and movement of goods to ports and borders, and the time involved in this process have significantly fallen in emerging market and developing economies since 2006 (Figure 2.11, panels 1 and 2). These costs have remained flat in advanced economies at their already low levels. Countries are also increasingly connected to global shipping networks, as reflected in such measures as the size of their maritime fleets, container-carrying capacity, and so forth (Figure 2.11, panel 3). An exception to this pattern is air freight costs, which rose more or less steadily between 2002 and 2012, but have since fallen during the trade slowdown on the back of lower oil prices. The decline in oil prices since 2014 has likely lowered the cost of other modes of transport as well. The time pattern of international transportation and logistical costs

of trade suggests that they probably did not contribute to the decline in the growth rate of global trade.

Global Value Chains

In addition to trade costs, some have argued that the dispersion of production across countries in the 1990s and early 2000s, which resulted from the creation or extension of global value chains and boosted gross trade flows, may have run its course.[45] The claim is hard to assess, however. Information on the degree of production sharing is typically available only with a significant time lag.[46] And the cause of any detected slowdown in global value chains would be hard to assign: it could stem from deceleration in the decline in trade costs, higher obstacles to cross-border investment, or inherent maturation.[47]

A standard measure of participation in global value chains calculates the sum of: (1) the domestic content in a country's exports that is reused in the exports of its trading partners and (2) its exports' foreign value added as a share of gross exports (see, for example, Koopman, Wang, and Wei (2014) for a discussion of vertical specialization measurement). On this measure, there is wide variation in participation in global value chains across countries, with many emerging market and developing economies yet to fully integrate into global production processes (IMF 2015a, 2015d). Participation rose steadily across both advanced and emerging market and developing economies until the global financial crisis (Figure 2.12, panels 1, 2, and 3). A notable exception is China, where participation peaked during the second half of the 2000s (Figure 2.12, panel 4). However,

---

[44]For more recent evidence on the trade-creation effect of trade agreements, see, for example, Carrère (2006); Baier and Bergstrand (2007, 2009); and Cipollina and Salvatici (2010) for a meta-analysis. Osnago, Rocha, and Ruta (forthcoming) demonstrate that deeper trade agreements also contribute to greater vertical foreign direct investment between countries, potentially fostering firms' integration into global value chains. More recently, Conconi and others (2016) find evidence that preferential rules of origin embodied in free trade agreements can instead increase the level of protectionism faced by nonmember countries.

[45]See, for example, Constantinescu, Mattoo, and Ruta (2015); Crozet, Emlinger, and Jean (2015); and Gangnes, Ma, and Van Assche (2015).

[46]The timeliest source at publication is the Eora Multi-Region Input-Output set of global input-output matrices, which covers 26 sectors for 173 countries in the IMF World Economic Outlook database sample for 1990–2013. See Lenzen and others (2013) for a detailed description of the database.

[47]An example of maturation would be a rise in productivity and skilled labor in China, which could cause companies to bring back some production that previously took place abroad. Trade barriers, on the other hand, can lead to a similar outcome, as the costs associated with goods that must cross borders many times as part of the supply chain could become prohibitive. Yi (2003, 2010) and Koopman, Wang, and Wei (2014) discuss the magnifying impact of trade costs in multistage production, while Evenett and Fritz (2016) summarize the evidence on the proliferation of trade-diverting localization requirements, which can also restrict the development of cross-border production.

Figure 2.11. Logistics and Transportation Costs of Trade in Historical Perspective

Monetary and time costs associated with domestic transport and border and documentary compliance for importing goods have been continuously declining, particularly in emerging market and developing economies. Countries are increasingly more connected to global shipping networks. Air freight costs have also fallen during the trade slowdown period amid lower oil prices.

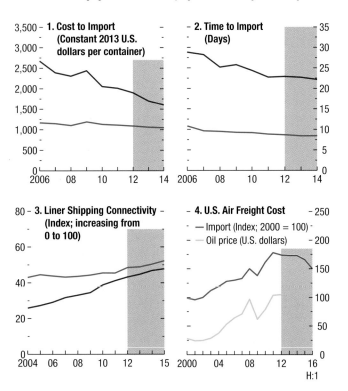

Sources: United Nations Conference on Trade and Development (UNCTAD); U.S. Bureau of Labor Statistics; World Bank, *Doing Business Indicators*; and IMF staff calculations.
Note: The cost and time indicators measure the cost (excluding tariffs) and time associated with three sets of procedures—documentary compliance, border compliance, and domestic transport—within the overall process of importing a shipment of goods across a balanced sample of 161 economies. The UNCTAD Liner Shipping Connectivity Index captures how well countries are connected to global shipping networks based on five components of the maritime transport sector: number of ships, their container-carrying capacity, maximum vessel size, number of services, and number of companies that deploy container ships in a country's ports.

since 2011, participation seems to have leveled off across all country aggregates.

The Role of These Other Factors: Insights from Product-Level Data

To explore the historical association of trade costs and global value chains with trade growth, this section draws on the novel data set described earlier in the

Figure 2.12. Global Value Chains in Historical Perspective
(Percent)

Global value chain participation rose in both advanced and emerging market and developing economies until the global financial crisis. Since 2011, participation appears to have plateaued across both country aggregates.

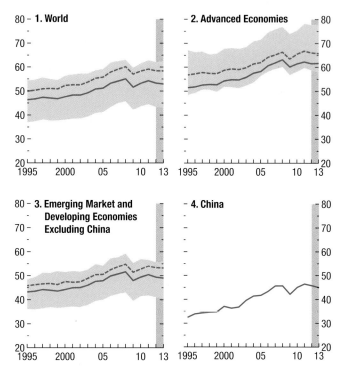

Sources: Eora Multi-Region Input-Output database; and IMF staff calculations.
Note: Global value chain participation denotes the sum of the domestic content in a country's exports—which is reused in the exports of its trading partners—and the foreign value added of its exports as a share of gross exports. See Annex 2.5 for a detailed description of country coverage, data sources, and methodology of each indicator.

chapter for real import flows of 700 products.[48] The analysis estimates the elasticity of import volumes of noncommodity products with respect to four of the factors discussed above—tariffs, free trade agreement coverage (as a share of world GDP), temporary trade barriers, and global value chain participation, con-

---

[48]These volume series were computed for imports starting in 2003 for 52 countries, which, as of 2015, accounted for more than 90 percent of both world imports and GDP. The data set is for products at the four-digit level under Revision 2 of the Standard Industrial Trade Classification. The nominal value of imports of these products was adjusted with import price deflators constructed at the Harmonized System two-digit level, with the same deflator applied to all Standard Industrial Trade Classification four-digit products that map to a particular Harmonized System two-digit code.

trolling for sectoral domestic demand, relative prices of imported goods, and country-product and time fixed effects (see Annex 2.5 for details on estimation, specification, and robustness). Given the steady decline in the logistical costs of trade since 2006 and the limited availability of time-series data on these costs, the chapter does not investigate their role in the trade slowdown.

The estimated elasticities of import growth with respect to the various measures of trade costs are outlined in Table 2.1. The estimates are highly statistically significant and of the expected sign.[49] The greater incidence of trade barriers is associated with lower import volume growth, although the estimated elasticity of imports to tariffs is smaller than estimates from other studies. Likewise, expanding the set of trading partners with which a country is in a free trade agreement is associated with higher growth of import volumes.

Higher participation in global value chains is also associated with higher growth of import volumes: a 10 percentage point increase in participation is associated with a 1 percentage point increase in import growth (Table 2.1, column 5). As noted, whether such participation is also capturing additional policy effects is difficult to know; therefore, this estimate likely represents an upper bound.

As a cross-check of the disaggregated product level analysis, the chapter examines the relationship between the country-specific residuals discussed earlier (the difference between the actual and model-predicted growth of aggregate real imports) and the same four factors. The point estimates are similar to those from the product-level regressions, but not as precisely estimated due to the more aggregated nature of the data (Table 2.1, column 8). Overall, these results suggest that the imposition of trade-distorting policy measures hurts trade growth. At the same time, slower growth in the coverage of free trade agreements and a slower pace of global value chain participation are associated with lower import growth.

Combining the estimated elasticities of import growth with the differences in the growth rate of the different factors between 2012–15 and 2003–07 allows for an estimation of their relative contribution. This exercise reveals that a sizable share of the trade slowdown not accounted for by weak economic activity and its composition is attributable to changes in trade policy and to the slowing expansion of global value chains (Figure 2.13 and Annex 2.5).

The Connection between Trade and Global Value Chains: Insights from the Gravity Model

The final piece of analysis uses a gravity model of trade at the sectoral level to highlight the role of global value chains during the slowdown. The gravity model is widely used to explain the level of bilateral trade flows on the basis of individual characteristics of each country and the characteristics of the country pair that capture trading costs, such as distance between the countries or whether they share a common border, language, or currency.

Estimated at the sectoral level, the gravity model has two advantages that make it an especially useful tool to isolate the importance of global value chain participation in trade growth: (1) it controls for compositional changes in trade flows across sectors and partners (unlike the aggregate import demand analysis reported earlier in the chapter), and (2) it exploits the heterogeneity in the degree of production linkages across trading partners (unlike the product-level analysis reported earlier).

The analysis is performed in three stages (see also Annex 2.6). The first stage involves estimating a gravity model at the sectoral level to provide a benchmark for bilateral-sectoral trade. The model is estimated separately for each year between 2003 and 2014 and for each of the 10 traded sectors in the Eora Multi-Region Input-Output database. In addition to the standard gravity variables, the estimated specification controls for importer and exporter fixed effects.[50] These fixed effects control for all sectoral source and destination characteristics, such as sectoral demand and supply,

[49]The literature provides a very wide range of estimates for the elasticity of trade with respect to trade policy. Studies based on cross-sectional data, typically thought of as capturing the long-term elasticity, tend to find much higher elasticities. Studies based on time-series variation, capturing the short-term effects of changing trade costs, yield much lower estimates for the trade elasticity. The approach used here is in the spirit of the latter strand of literature. See Hillberry and Hummels (2013) and Goldberg and Pavcnik (2016) for a review of the literature.

[50]See Feenstra, Markusen, and Rose (2001) or Feyrer (2009b) for other examples of gravity models estimated separately for different years and sectors. The results from the gravity estimations (available from the authors upon request) are strictly in line with those of the literature. The coefficients on the bilateral measures of trade costs (such as distance, common language, common borders) have the correct signs and are highly significant and stable across time. Such stability indicates that bilateral trade flows have not become more sensitive to bilateral trade costs.

Table 2.1 Historical Association among Real Import Growth at the Product Level, Trade Policies, and Participation in Global Value Chains

	A. Product and Country							B. Country
	Real					Nominal		Import-Intensity-Adjusted Demand Residual
Sample Period	2003–15	2003–15	2003–15	2003–13	2003–13	1990–2013	2003–13	2003–13
Dependent Variable: Import Growth	(1)	(2)	(3)	(4)	(5)	(6)	(7)	(8)
Growth of:								
Temporary Trade Barriers	−0.024*** (0.008)				−0.031*** (0.009)	−0.028*** (0.006)	−0.029*** (0.007)	−0.253 (0.196)
Tariffs		−0.008 (0.007)			−0.016** (0.008)	−0.021*** (0.005)	−0.034*** (0.007)	−0.015 (0.018)
Free Trade Agreement Coverage			0.119** (0.048)		0.106** (0.054)	0.139*** (0.040)	0.205*** (0.055)	0.227*** (0.056)
Global Value Chain Participation				0.066* (0.038)	0.095** (0.041)	0.192*** (0.029)	0.170*** (0.041)	0.083* (0.043)
Country x Product Fixed Effects	Yes	Yes	Yes	Yes	Yes	Yes	Yes	...
Country Fixed Effects	...	...	...	...	...	...	...	Yes
Time Fixed Effects	Yes	Yes	Yes	Yes	Yes	Yes	Yes	Yes
R^2	0.264	0.266	0.265	0.295	0.293	0.324	0.407	0.504
Adjusted R^2	0.193	0.190	0.192	0.212	0.208	0.281	0.338	0.449
Number of Observations	316,840	341,553	371,622	315,636	258,196	472,178	270,587	464

Source: IMF staff calculations.
Note: Global value chain participation is a measure of backward participation: foreign value added in exports as share of gross exports. In the product-country level regressions, this variable is calculated at the sectoral level. Standard errors are clustered at the product-country level for regressions A and at the country level in regression B. Columns (1)–(7) control for growth in sectoral demand and growth in relative prices.
$* p < 0.10; ** p < 0.05; *** p < 0.01.$

Figure 2.13. Contribution of Trade Policies and Global Value Chains to the Slowdown in Real Goods Import Growth
(Percent)

The decline in global value chain participation and changes in trade policy are weighing on trade growth, although their quantitative contribution is limited.

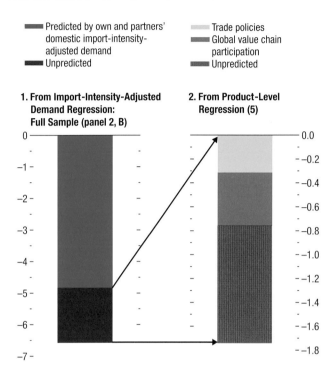

Source: IMF staff calculations.
Note: The figure combines the estimated historical association between real import growth and growth in trade costs and global value chain participation, and the differences in the growth rate of these factors between 2003–07 and 2012–15 to compute their contribution to the observed trade slowdown. See Annex 2.5 for a detailed description of country coverage, data sources, and methodology.

and all country sectoral time-varying characteristics, such as prices and trade costs, that do not vary across trading partners in a particular year. The fixed effects also control for the so-called multilateral resistance term (Anderson 2011)—the barriers to trade that each economy faces with respect to all its trading partners. In the second stage, the residuals obtained from the gravity estimation are collected and differenced when in levels to obtain the growth of bilateral sectoral trade that is unexplained by the gravity model. The third step examines whether the degree of production linkages between the two countries in this particular sector—measured as the share of foreign value-added component in bilateral-sectoral gross exports—is associated with trade growth between the two countries in this sector, after controlling for all standard deter-

minants of trade growth.[51] The findings of the gravity model analysis suggest that greater production linkages between countries are indeed positively associated with growth of trade between them, corroborating the product-level analysis presented earlier.

Indeed, during 2003–07, country-pair trade in sectors that were in the top quartile of global value chain participation grew on average 1¼ percentage points faster than the rest (Figure 2.14). During 2012–14, however, trade in these country-pair sectors was not significantly different from trade in the rest. This further supports the hypothesis that higher-value-chain participation significantly boosted trade growth in the period leading up to the global financial crisis. However, since 2012, there is little evidence of such a boost.

Summary and Policy Implications

The analysis in this chapter suggests that the slowdown in trade growth since 2012 is to a significant extent, but not entirely, consistent with the overall weakness in economic activity. Weak global growth, particularly weak investment growth, can account for a significant part of the sluggish trade growth, both in absolute terms and relative to GDP. Empirical analysis suggests that, for the world as a whole, up to three-fourths of the decline in trade growth since 2012 relative to 2003–07 can be predicted by weaker economic activity, most notably subdued investment growth. While the empirical estimate may overstate the role of output, given the feedback effects of trade policy and trade on growth, a general equilibrium framework suggests that changes in the composition of demand account for about 60 percent of the slowdown in the growth rate of nominal imports relative to GDP.

However, factors beyond the level and composition of demand are also weighing on trade growth, shaving up to 1¾ percentage points off global real import growth during 2012–15. Among those, trade policies and global value chain participation account for a sizable share of the unpredicted shortfall in annual global trade growth since 2012. The pace of new trade policy initiatives at the global level has slowed notably. At the same time, the uptick in protectionism since the global financial crisis is not innocuous. While the quantitative contribution of trade policies to the slowdown in trade growth has been

[51]Rose (2002) takes a similar approach in analyzing estimated residuals from gravity models.

Figure 2.14. Gravity Model: Global Value Chain Participation and Bilateral Sectoral Trade Growth
(Percentage points)

A high degree of production linkages through global value chains between countries in a particular sector was positively associated with trade growth between them in that sector in the period prior to the global financial crisis. However, there is little evidence that high participation in global value chains has provided a boost to trade growth after 2012.

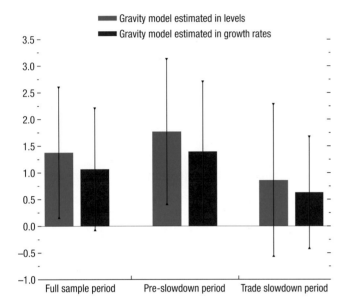

Source: IMF staff calculations.
Note: Bars depict the average difference in bilateral sectoral trade growth residuals between country-sector pairs in the top quartile in terms of global value chain integration and the rest in 2003–13, 2003–07, and 2012–13. The vertical lines are the 90 percentile confidence intervals. Residuals are obtained from gravity models of trade estimated separately for each sector and year, controlling for all standard gravity variables, as well as importer and exporter fixed effects. See Annex 2.6 for a detailed description of country coverage, data sources, and methodology.

limited so far, protectionist measures could significantly weigh on global trade if they become more widespread. The apparent decline in the growth of production fragmentation across countries is also putting the brakes on trade growth, although it is still difficult to judge whether this is a natural maturation of existing global value chains or the result of policy-induced distortions. The general equilibrium framework also suggests that a slower reduction in trade costs, broadly defined, can account for about one-quarter of the decline in the growth rate of nominal imports relative to GDP.

What does this mean for the outlook for global trade? As the findings of the chapter suggest, trade growth and economic growth are closely linked. Current projections anticipate only a limited pickup in global activity and weak investment growth over

the medium term due to both cyclical and structural factors (see Chapter 1 of this WEO), so slow global trade growth will most likely persist. Moreover, even as global growth eventually gathers speed, trade growth is unlikely to achieve the rates seen prior to the global financial crisis when investment growth in many emerging market and developing economies, including China, was unusually high, trade costs were falling due to policy cooperation and technological advances, and global value chains were rapidly developing.[52]

What can be done so that trade can play its role in helping promote productivity and growth in the context of slow and fragile global activity? First, this chapter's findings suggest that much of the trade slowdown appears to be a symptom of the many forces that are holding back growth across countries, possibly including the slower pace of reduction in trade costs and slow trade growth itself as discussed in the section titled "The Slowdown in Trade Growth: Key Patterns" and Box 2.1. Addressing these constraints to growth, and in particular investment, should lie at the heart of the policy response for improving the health of the global economy, which would strengthen trade as a by-product. As discussed in Chapter 1 and Chapter 3 of the April 2016 WEO, a combination of near-term demand support, balance sheet repair to relieve financial constraints where needed, and productivity-enhancing structural reforms, including further progress in trade integration, could help boost global growth and strengthen investment. These policies, by lifting trade growth indirectly, can reinforce each country's economic expansions given trade's role in transmitting economic activity and raising productivity and economic growth.

Second, this chapter's findings also suggest that trade policies, which shape the costs of the international exchange of goods and services, are still relevant. With other factors, notably weak investment, already weighing on trade, resisting all forms of protectionism and reviving the process of trade liberalization to dismantle remaining trade barriers would provide much-needed support for trade growth, including through possibly kicking off a new round of global value chain development. As elaborated in Box 2.2, there is substantial scope to further reduce trade costs through cutting tariffs where they remain elevated, ratifying and fully implementing com-

---

[52]There are reasons for trade growth optimism as well: many emerging market and developing economies have substantial scope to increase trade flows by integrating into global value chains and reducing still-high trade barriers. For a discussion, see IMF (2015a, 2015d).

mitments made under the Trade Facilitation Agreement, and establishing a way forward in the post-Doha trade agenda. Future trade reforms would need to focus on the areas most relevant to the contemporary global economy, such as regulatory cooperation, reducing barriers to trade in services, and leveraging complementarities between investment and trade (see IMF 2016b).

Such initiatives could help strengthen global economic growth and raise overall living standards over time. As discussed in Box 2.3, an illustrative scenario in which existing tariffs are completely eliminated and the Trade Facilitation Agreement is fully implemented could improve welfare. Various trade models deliver an array of possible outcomes (see Costinot and Rodriguez-Clare 2014), but gains in real incomes from lower trade costs could range from less than 1 percent to more than 6 percent in the long term for the average country.[53] Given the relatively low levels of tariffs for

many advanced economies, advancing trade reform in services and other "frontier" areas would likely yield even larger aggregate gains.

But to sustain popular support for trade integration and preserve its economic and welfare benefits, policymakers should be mindful of the adjustment costs that deepening trade integration entails. Although the analysis of these effects is beyond the scope of the chapter, a number of studies document significant and long-lasting adjustment costs for those whose employment prospects were adversely affected by the structural changes associated with trade, even if the gains from trade from lower prices may tend to favor those at the bottom of the income distribution. An increasingly popular narrative that sees the benefits of globalization and trade accrue only to a fortunate few is also gaining traction. Policymakers need to address the concerns of trade-affected workers, including through effective support for re-training, skill building, and occupational and geographic mobility, to mitigate the downsides of further trade integration for the trade agenda to revive.

---

[53]Note that the calculations presented likely underestimate the real income gains from the Trade Facilitation Agreement as they treat nontariff barriers as tariffs.

Box 2.1. Is the Trade Slowdown Contributing to the Global Productivity Slowdown? New Evidence

This box attempts to quantify the effect of the decline in trade growth on productivity. Using an instrumental variable approach to identify the historical impact of trade on productivity in a sample of 18 Organisation for Economic Co-operation and Development economies,[1] the findings suggest that the trade slowdown could weigh significantly on the already weak productivity growth in advanced economies.

As discussed in this chapter, trade can shape the productivity of an economy in a variety of ways. This box focuses on three distinct channels through which international trade can affect productivity:[2]

- *Imports*—Imports can promote productivity by increasing competitive pressure on domestic firms with the entry of foreign producers in domestic markets. This is often referred to as the "procompetition" channel.
- *Imported inputs*—Imported inputs can improve firm-level productivity by expanding the variety and enhancing the quality of the intermediate goods to which firms have access. This is the called the "input" channel.
- *Exports*—Exporting can increase firm-level productivity via learning from foreign markets both directly, through buyer-seller relationships, and indirectly, through increased competition from foreign producers, externalities, and so forth. Together, these form the "export" channel.

These channels operate both through their effect at the firm level, by pushing companies to adopt more efficient production processes, improve product quality, or undertake specific investments, and at the sectoral level, by bringing about reallocation of resources toward more productive firms within a sector. This box focuses on estimating the effects of trade at the sectoral level.

Empirical Analysis

All three different types of trade grew steadily between the mid-1990s and mid-2000s. In line with

The authors of this box are JaeBin Ahn and Romain Duval.
[1] The modern empirical literature on this topic traces to Sachs and Warner (1995) and Frankel and Romer (1999), among others. For a recent study that looks at the growth impact of the recent global trade slowdown, see Constantinescu, Mattoo, and Ruta (2016).
[2] The first two (import) channels are discussed in more detail in Ahn and others (2016), whose summary appears in IMF (2016c). A recent discussion on the export channel can be found in De Loecker (2013).

aggregate trends, trade in most sectors fell during the global financial crisis and has recovered only slowly since then (Figure 2.1.1). An examination of sectoral data reveals wide dispersion in these trends across countries and industries, providing a source of variation that can be used to identify the impact of each trade channel on growth.

To quantify the effect of each of these channels on productivity at the sector level, Ahn and Duval (forthcoming), estimate an econometric specification using data from the WORLD KLEMS and World Input-Output Database covering 18 sectors across 18 advanced economies from 1995 to 2007:

$$\ln TFP_{i,s,t} = \beta_1 IMP_{i,s,t-2} + \beta_2 IMP^{input}_{i,s,t-2} + \beta_2 EXP_{i,s,t-2} + FE_{i,s} + FE_{i,t} + \varepsilon_{i,s,t},$$

in which $TFP_{i,s,t}$ denotes total factor productivity (TFP) in country i and sector s in year t, while $IMP_{i,s,t-2}$, $IMP^{input}_{i,s,t-2}$, and $EXP_{i,s,t-2}$ are the corresponding country-sector-level imports (as a share of total domestic sectoral output), imported inputs (as a share of total input used in the sector), and exports (as a share of total domestic sectoral output), respectively, all lagged two years.[3] The specification also includes country-sector ($FE_{i,s}$) and country-year ($FE_{i,t}$) fixed effects to control for any time-invariant variation that is common to all sectors in a country and all country-specific shocks that may equally affect all industries within the country in a particular year.

Identifying the causal effect of trade on growth is challenging due to potentially severe reverse causality and measurement issues. Several studies have addressed these issues through the use of instrumental variables for overall trade (Frankel and Romer 1999; Noguer and Siscart 2005). Because the analysis in this box attempts to identify the causal effect of the three distinct channels through which trade may shape productivity, it requires a separate instrumental variable for each of them. The following instrumental variables are used:

- *China's import penetration in other countries*—In the absence of a proper instrument for imports from all trading partners, the box focuses on estimating the impact of imports from China. The analysis uses a well-established methodology of instrumenting a country's own imports from China in a particular

[3] All the results reported below are robust to alternative productivity measures (for example, labor productivity) or alternative lags (namely, one- or three-year lags).

Box 2.1 *(continued)*

Figure 2.1.1. The Evolution of Trade across Industries in Major Economies
(Percent)

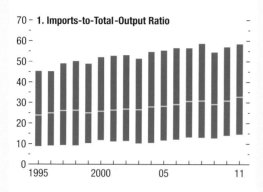

1. Imports-to-Total-Output Ratio

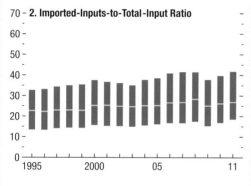

2. Imported-Inputs-to-Total-Input Ratio

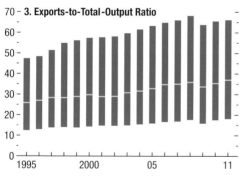

3. Exports-to-Total-Output Ratio

Sources: World Input-Output Database; and IMF staff calculations.
Note: The horizontal line inside each box represents the median value across all country-industry observations; the upper and lower edges of each box show the top and bottom quartiles. They are all expressed in percent. Countries included in the sample are Australia, Austria, Canada, Czech Republic, Finland, France, Germany, Hungary, Ireland, Italy, Japan, Korea, Netherlands, Slovenia, Spain, Sweden, United Kingdom, and United States.

sector with all other countries' imports from China in that particular sector. The identifying assumption is that sector-level import demand shocks are not correlated across sample countries, as confirmed by Autor, Dorn, and Hanson (2013). As such, the analysis estimates the procompetition effect of China's penetration on productivity.

- *Input tariffs*—To the extent that input tariffs, the tariffs applied to imported inputs, are not driven by expected future productivity in the sector considered or by other unobserved factors correlated with it,[4] they can be employed as an instrumental variable for imported inputs. The input tariff in each sector s is computed as a weighted average of tariff rates in all sectors, with weights reflecting the share of inputs imported directly and indirectly from each of these sectors used in the production of sector s's output.[5] Its two-year lagged value is used as an instrument for imported inputs.

- *Export tariffs*—For a given country, the export tariff in each sector s is computed as a weighted average of output tariff rates in major destination countries, with weights equal to the share of total sector s exports to each destination. Its two-year lagged value is a valid instrument for exports insofar as the import tariff applied by the destination country in sector s is not influenced by the overall exports of any particular country in that sector.

Findings

International trade boosts productivity through all of the channels discussed above (Table 2.1.1).[6] Moreover, the instrumental variable strategy employed in this box suggests that the magnitude of its

[4]Such simultaneity bias is more likely for output tariffs, which governments may be more inclined to adjust depending on expected future productivity and competitiveness in the sector considered. For this reason, tariffs are not used as instruments for imports above.
[5]To avoid potential endogeneity issues, we pick one vintage of the input-output table for the country-sector-level weights and keep them constant throughout the sample period.
[6]Compared with ordinary least squares (OLS—columns [1]–[4]), the magnitude of the estimated effects is typically stronger when using instrumental variables (columns [5]–[8]). This suggests that measurement bias—which leads OLS to underestimate the impact of trade on productivity—is in practice a more serious concern than simultaneity bias—which is likely instead to inflate OLS estimates—as already flagged by Frankel and Romer (1999).

Box 2.1 *(continued)*

Table 2.1.1. Baseline Estimation Results

Dependent Variable: ln (TFP)$_{i,s,t}$	OLS			IV		
	(1)	(2)	(3)	(4)	(5)	(6)
(Imports from China/Total Output) $\times$ 100$_{i,s,t-2}$	0.004 (0.004)			0.021*** (0.004)		
(Imports Inputs/Total Input) $\times$ 100$_{i,s,t-2}$		0.005** (0.002)			0.033*** (0.009)	
(Exports/Total Output)*100$_{i,s,t-2}$			0.006*** (0.002)			0.032** (0.015)
First Stage *F*-stats				154.3	4.3	3.7
First Stage *p*-value				0.00	0.04	0.05
Number of Observations	2,634	2,634	2,976	2,634	2,634	2,976

Source: IMF staff calculations.
Note: The dependent variable is log total factor productivity (TFP) in country *i* and sector *s* in year *t*. Independent variables are corresponding country-sector-level imports from China (as a ratio to total domestic output), total imported inputs (as a ratio to total input), and total exports (as a ratio to total domestic output), all lagged two years. Average value of imports from China relative to domestic output in all other countries, input tariff rates, and export tariff rates, all lagged two years, are used as instrumental variables (IVs) in columns (4) and (7), (5) and (8), and (6) and (9), respectively. Coefficient estimates in bold in columns (7)–(9) denote instrumented variables. Country-sector as well as country-year fixed effects are included in all columns. Robust standard errors are provided in parentheses.
* $p < 0.10$; ** $p < 0.05$; *** $p < 0.01$.

productivity-enhancing effect can be sizable. For example, a 1 percentage point increase in China's import penetration in a given sector is associated with a 1.5 percent increase in the level of total factor productivity of that sector. A 1 percentage point increase in the ratio of imported inputs to total inputs, or in the ratio of exports to domestic output, leads to about a

0.9 percent increase in productivity in a given sector. Assuming for simplicity that the recent global trade slowdown has led the trade-to-GDP ratio to level off—and hence that there has been no further increase in the share of imported inputs, imports from China, or exports in output—advanced economies are missing out on the productivity boost from international trade.

Box 2.2. The Role of Trade Policies in Reinvigorating Trade

An ambitious yet achievable trade policy agenda would help reinvigorate trade and bolster global economic growth more generally. At a country and global level, trade reforms complement other reforms in goods and services markets, boosting growth by enhancing efficiency, promoting competition, and encouraging innovation (Melitz and Redding 2014). This box discusses the scope for trade policy to remove existing barriers to the cross-border exchange of goods and services and reduce trade costs.

Trade policy needs to address "frontier" areas, such as services trade barriers, as well as remaining traditional barriers, such as tariffs. Firms' investment, sourcing, and export decisions increasingly reflect many different types of policies, especially in global value chains that link companies in many countries in the production of a single end product. While trade policy priorities vary from country to country, there are a number of elements common to each of the main country income groups (Table 2.2.1).

Traditional Barriers

Traditional barriers—tariffs, subsidies, custom procedures, domestic tax policies, and other regulations that de facto discriminate against imports or provoke unwanted tax competition (IMF 2016a)—still pose an obstacle for trade and remain high in many countries. Recent advances by the World Trade Organization (WTO) illustrate how flexible negotiating approaches can lower remaining barriers:

- *Tariffs*—Despite earlier progress through multilateral, regional, and unilateral liberalization, the process of reducing tariffs remains incomplete, particularly in low-income countries and in some emerging market and developing economies. The WTO's Information Technology Agreement (ITA), which eliminated import duties for participating countries on many information technology products, underscores the sizable gains that countries can achieve through tariff reduction, including by developing export industries (Figure 2.2.1, panel 1). The expansion of the ITA to an additional set of 201 products accounting for about 7 percent of world merchandise trade came into force in July 2016.[1] However, in other areas, namely agricultural

products in some emerging market and developing economies, tariffs remain relatively high.

- *Subsidies*—WTO trade ministers agreed in December 2015 to eliminate outstanding agricultural export subsidies, which should support the exports of agricultural products of low-income and developing countries. Lower trade-distorting domestic subsidies, particularly in agriculture in advanced economies, would strengthen the global trading environment.

- *Trade facilitation*—In every region of the world, delays in customs represent a larger obstacle to trade than tariffs (Hummels 2007b). Studies estimate that a one-day customs delay decreases imports as much as a 1 percent increase in the distance between the importing and exporting countries (Djankov, Freund, and Pham 2010). For exporters, a 10 percent increase in customs delays can reduce foreign sales by nearly 4 percent (Volpe Martincus, Carballo, and Graziano 2015). The 2013 WTO Trade Facilitation Agreement (TFA) contains provisions to lower trade costs by strengthening customs practices (Figure 2.2.1, panel 2).[2] The WTO estimates that its implementation would increase world trade by $1 trillion and developing economies' growth by 0.9 percent (WTO 2015). It will enter into force when two-thirds of WTO members have concluded domestic approval processes; as of September 26, 2016, 93 of the 108 members needed had approved. Once approved, developing economies will have flexibility in the pace of implementation coupled with expanded technical assistance.

Trade Policy "Frontier" Areas

Addressing behind-the-border barriers can complement and augment other structural reforms. The increasing importance of global value chains and services trade—including as catalysts of foreign direct investment (FDI)—has moved policy cooperation in

---

The authors of this box are Diego Cerdeiro and Christian Henn.

[1]Tariff eliminations apply to all WTO members' exports, regardless of whether the exporter is a signatory of the ITA.

However, the ITA is on a positive-list basis, which implies that, to retain a comprehensive coverage, it would need to be updated regularly as new products appear.

[2]Among its disciplines, the TFA includes prearrival processing and electronic payment for clearance of goods (Article 7), a single window for submission of custom forms (Article 10), and provisions to ensure nondiscrimination and transparency in the application of border controls of food products (Article 5)—the latter is particularly relevant for some developing economies. See Table B.1 in WTO 2015 for an overview of TFA disciplines.

Box 2.2 *(continued)*

Table 2.2.1. Trade Policy Challenges Vary across Countries

Advanced Economies	Advanced economies can address remaining protection in traditional trade areas (for example, agriculture and textiles), further open services markets (for example, transport), make their regulatory systems more coherent, and advance trade policy frontiers. The preference should be for nondiscriminatory approaches that will minimize fragmentation and facilitate raising initiatives to the multilateral level.
Emerging Market and Developing Economies	Many emerging market and developing economies, including Latin America and South Asia, can still benefit greatly from integrating via traditional liberalization, including on a unilateral basis; they should strive to anchor their economies to global value chains, moving further away from failed import-substitution policies and avoiding protectionism through opaque nontariff measures. Trade reform would complement the strengthening of policy and institutional frameworks.
Low-Income Countries	To promote the development and growth, most low-income countries need to prioritize trade facilitation in order to integrate with global value chains, especially by upgrading their hard and soft trade infrastructure and improving economic institutions.[1] They should also address traditional trade barriers and promote competition in those service industries that are critical to local participation in global value chains, such as transport and finance services. Technical assistance can support the development of trade infrastructure, address the fiscal implications of reform, and help to sequence and coordinate the reform process.

Source: IMF 2015c.
[1] Hard infrastructure includes quality of ports, airports, roads, rail, and information and communications networks. Soft infrastructure includes border efficiency (for example, number of documents necessary for import/export, speed of customs clearance) as well as other regulations and institutional frameworks directly impinging on trade.

areas previously outside the sphere of trade policy to the forefront of trade policy discussions. Reforms in these areas carry high potential to bolster productivity and increase medium-term growth:

- *Regulatory cooperation*—While WTO rules already contain meaningful provisions, recent regional agreements have put a stronger emphasis on promoting active regulatory cooperation. This can be challenging because it involves multiple domestic agencies, procedures rooted in domestic legal systems, and differences in domestic policy priorities. As such, provisions in trade agreements can range from transparency provisions to recognizing others' regulatory processes (Mavroidis 2016).

- *Leveraging complementarities between investment and trade*—Sales by FDI affiliates are larger than recorded exports of goods and services (Figure 2.2.2, panel 1), with trade and investment increasingly complementary. FDI is one of the most important channels of technology diffusion, but start-up FDI often faces significant policy-related fixed costs (OECD 2015a). Governance is fragmented: there are more than 3,000 bilateral investment treaties and other agreements without a common template (González 2013). Complementary structural reforms promoting competition and opening government procurement policies would bolster the productivity gains of FDI.

- *Reducing barriers to trade in services*—Services comprise some two-thirds of global GDP and employment, but their share in international trade is smaller: cross-border services represent a quarter of global trade. This rises to almost half when considering value-added trade, which can account for services embodied in traded goods. With policy barriers still very large (Figure 2.2.2, panel 2) and even increasing for e-commerce (OECD 2015b), reforms have tremendous potential to promote trade and growth in the services sector. For example, countries could expand specific commitments under the WTO General Agreement on Trade in Services.

The Way Forward

It will be important to build on the ground covered on frontier issues under regional trade agreements by bringing them to the multilateral level. Megaregional agreements recently signed or under negotiation—for example, the Trade in Services Agreement and the Trans-Pacific Partnership—offer such opportunities because they address a number of frontier issues. These agreements must remain open and harnessed accordingly to reinvigorate trade integration more broadly by forging a post-Doha round agenda at the WTO. This would bring them to a global level and reduce the risk of further proliferation of regional trade agreements

Box 2.2 *(continued)*

Figure 2.2.1. Potential Gains from Tackling Traditional Trade Barriers
(Percent)

Figure 2.2.2. Trade Policy Frontier Areas

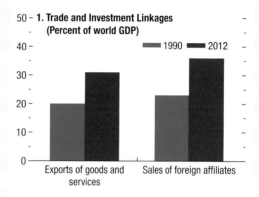

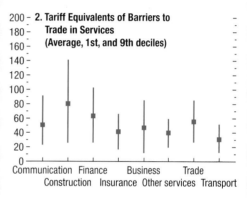

Sources: United Nations Conference on Trade and Development 2013; and Fontagné, Guillin, and Mitaritonna (2011).

Sources: Henn and Mkrtchyan (2015); and World Trade Organization (WTO) Statistics database.
Note: ITA = Information Technology Agreement; TFA = Trade Facilitation Agreement. Panel 1 shows the evolution (pre- and post-WTO ITA accession) of information technology exports of "passive signatories," that is, those countries that joined the agreement as part of a large policy objective rather than due to an established comparative advantage in the sector.

resulting in unintended fragmentation. Meanwhile, at the national level, countries should ensure that the benefits of trade accrue to all. Sufficiently broad social safety nets would likely be most important as trade often only serves as a catalyst of (skill-biased) technological change, although more specific trade

adjustment assistance schemes could also have a role to play in certain cases. In this regard, effective support for re-training, skill building, and occupational and geographic mobility can help those who bear the burden of adjusting.

A successful global agenda on trade policy must address both new and long-standing issues while preserving a focus on economic development. Promoting the resilience of the global trading system also calls for countries to resist recent trends toward protectionism and roll back trade-restrictive measures put in place since the global financial crisis.

Box 2.3. Potential Gains from Jump-Starting Trade Liberalization

Trade liberalization has slowed over the past decade. This box aims to quantify potential welfare gains from stimulating this liberalization process through an experiment in which all existing tariffs are eliminated and the 2013 World Trade Organization Trade Facilitation Agreement, discussed in Box 2.2, is fully ratified and implemented. Average import-weighted tariffs for the world stand at 8 percent. The World Trade Organization estimates that the implementation of the Trade Facilitation Agreement would reduce trade costs by an ad-valorem tariff equivalent of 14 percent (Figure 2.2.1; Box 2.2). Progress on these two fronts, entailing a total of a 22 percent reduction in trade costs, can bring significant benefits by boosting international trade.

The benefits of tariff reductions, computed as changes in real consumption from initial to counterfactual equilibria, depend crucially on the class of model used for the analysis. Following Costinot and Rodriguez-Clare (2014), this box considers a range of gravity models of trade, which differ in their assumptions about market structure, the existence of firm-level heterogeneity, the number of sectors, and the role of intermediate goods. Models assuming perfect competition can typically be solved to capture the impact of tariff reductions at the country level. Models with monopolistic competition are computationally more challenging, hence countries are aggregated to 10 geographic regions. These alternatives on model specification and level of aggregation yield a total of nine different cases; the first three are solved at the country level and the remaining six at the regional level.[1]

The simple average of the welfare gains from eliminating all existing tariffs and implementing the Trade Facilitation Agreement across countries (or regions) ranges from less than 1 percent to more than 6 percent depending on the model at hand (Figure 2.3.1).[2,3]

The author of this box is Emine Boz.

[1]These cases correspond to columns 5–7 of Table 4.2 and all columns of Table 4.3 in Costinot and Rodriguez-Clare (2014).

[2]These numbers likely underestimate the gains for two reasons. First, modeling the Trade Facilitation Agreement as a tariff reduction assumes a tariff revenue loss when the agreement is implemented, but there would be no such revenue loss in reality. Second, the exercise is conducted with a tariff increase of 22 percent (whose implications are interpreted with a negative sign). Computing the negative of the welfare loss from a higher value of consumption to a lower one would lead to a smaller percentage change than computing the welfare gain from a lower base value of consumption.

[3]All the models considered quantify only the static gains from trade reform and are silent on some potentially important

Figure 2.3.1. Gains from Eliminating Tariffs and Implementing the World Trade Organization Trade Facilitation Agreement
(Percent)

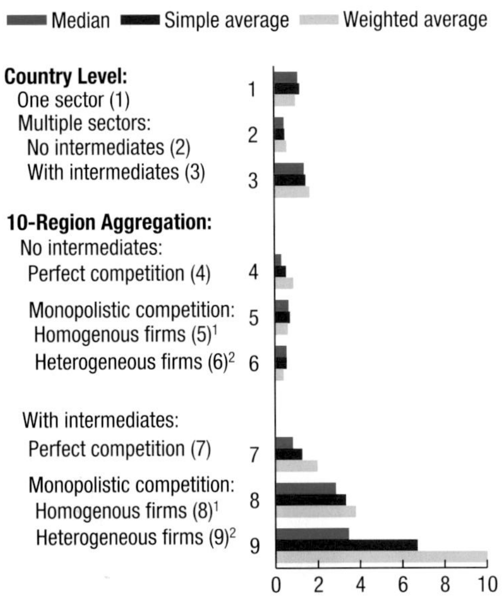

Source: IMF staff calculations.
[1] Krugman (1980).
[2] Melitz (2003).

Weighing countries or regions by their shares in world population in the spirit of utilitarian welfare yields even higher potential gains, while medians suggest that these gains can be more moderate but still sizable, especially considering that they would be permanent. These results highlight that there is potential to improve global well-being through further trade liberalization. However, for these global benefits to be reaped, policymakers would also need to limit the adjustment costs of deeper trade integration, and make the case to an increasingly skeptical public.

benefits and costs. Such elements as technological spillovers through trade or its distributional implications are absent in all cases studied.

Annex 2.1. Data

Data Sources

The primary data sources for this chapter are the IMF's World Economic Outlook, Information Notice System, and Global Assumptions and Economic Environment databases; the United Nations Commodity Trade Statistics database; and the Eora Multi-Region Input-Output database. For each section of the chapter, several other databases are also used. Annex Table 2.1.1 lists all indicators used in the chapter as well as their sources.

The sample of economies included in the various analytical exercises varies due to data constraints. Annex Table 2.1.2 lists the samples of economies used in each exercise. Economies are grouped based on the analytical exercise in which they are included.

Data Definitions

Trade flows are measured using imports denominated in U.S. dollars throughout the chapter, except in the section "The Role of Output and Its Composition: Insights from an Empirical Investigation," where they are denominated in local currency units. Imports are used in both value and volume terms depending on the exercise undertaken and are specified accordingly. Similarly, the chapter indicates whether imports cover both goods and services or only one of these categories.

Services Trade

For imports of services, the chapter investigates the nominal import growth for different categories using the United Nations Service Trade Statistics database. That database contains 11 different sectors of services imports: (1) transport; (2) travel; (3) communication; (4) construction; (5) insurance; (6) financial; (7) computer and information; (8) royalties and license fees; (9) other business; (10) personal, cultural, and recreational; and (11) governmental. Data coverage varies across countries and sectors.

Annex Figure 2.1.1 aggregates these categories in four main broad categories of import services: (1) travel (sectors 1 and 10), (2) information and communication technologies (sectors 3 and 7), (3) financial (sectors 5 and 6), and (4) other (remaining sectors). The figure displays the average annual nominal growth rates for these categories, as well as for total services, for two different periods (2003–07 and 2012–13) for

a balanced sample of 36 economies. This examination reveals that trade in information and communication technologies, travel, and financial services has been more resilient during the recent period while trade in other services has slowed more markedly.

Annex 2.2. Constructing Disaggregated Import Volume and Price Indices

The disaggregated volume data set used in Figure 2.4 and in the subsection on the role of other factors is based on data from the United Nations Commodity Trade Statistics database for about 5,300 products classified according to the Harmonized Commodity Description and Coding Systems (HS) at the six-digit level. Data include information on U.S. dollar values and quantities (for example, units or kilograms) of total goods imports for 52 countries during 2003–15. The disaggregated data are used to construct price and volume indices for products at the HS two-digit level, as well as by end use. The procedure involves three steps: (1) examine growth rates of unit values at the most disaggregate level to eliminate potential outliers, (2) calculate chained Fisher price indices at the HS two-digit level and by end use based on the clean disaggregated unit values, and (3) deflate values of trade at the HS two-digit level or by end use using the constructed Fisher price indices to arrive at trade volumes.

Because value and unit value changes at the six-digit level are noisy, simple procedures to identify outliers are applied to construct these price and volume indices. Boz and Cerutti (forthcoming) document in detail two steps for eliminating outliers for each country individually. First, a cross-section truncation is performed after computing the distribution of annual changes in the log unit value of all six-digit products. Truncating both tails of this distribution eliminates extreme positive and negative values stemming from cases such as typos during recording import values and/or quantities. Second, a time series truncation is applied to the distribution of the standard deviation of unit value changes over time for each product within each HS vintage. This second step is intended to alleviate the unit value bias: unit values capture not only true price changes but also variations in the composition of products, even within narrowly defined HS six-digit categories. Products that suffer from a more severe unit value bias are more likely to have a high standard deviation of unit value changes over

Annex Table 2.1.1. Data Sources

Indicator	Source
Banking Crisis Indicator	Laeven and Valencia (2012)
Bilateral Nominal U.S. Dollar Exchange Rate	IMF, Global Assumptions database
Chicago Board Options Exchange Volatility Index (VIX)	Chicago Board Options Exchange; Haver Analytics
Cost to Import	World Bank, Doing Business Indicators
Discriminatory Trade Measures	Bown 2016; UNCTAD, Trade Analysis Information System
Domestic Value Added Embedded in Exports of Other Countries	OECD–WTO, Trade in Value Added database; Eora MRIO database; IMF staff calculations
Export Prices of Goods and Services	CPB Netherlands Bureau for Economic Policy Analysis; IMF staff calculations using export value divided by export volume
Export Value of Goods and Services	CPB Netherlands Bureau for Economic Policy Analysis; IMF, World Economic Outlook database
Export Volume of Goods and Services	CPB Netherlands Bureau for Economic Policy Analysis; IMF, World Economic Outlook database
Foreign Value Added of Exports	Eora MRIO database; IMF staff calculations; OECD–WTO, Trade in Value Added database
Free Trade Agreements by Year of Signature	DESTA, Free Trade Area Database
Free Trade Agreements Coverage	WTO Regional Trade Agreements Database
Global Value Chain Participation	Eora MRIO database; IMF staff calculations
Industrial Production	CEIC database; Haver Analytics
Import Prices of Goods and Services	CPB Netherlands Bureau for Economic Policy Analysis; IMF staff calculations using import value divided by import volume
Import Prices of Goods at Product Level	United Nations Commodity Trade Statistics (Comtrade) Database; World Bank, World Integrated Trade Solution
Import Value of Goods and Services	CPB Netherlands Bureau for Economic Policy Analysis; IMF, World Economic Outlook database
Import Value of Services by Categories	United Nations Service Trade Statistics Database; IMF staff calculations
Import Volume of Goods and Services	CPB Netherlands Bureau for Economic Policy Analysis; IMF, World Economic Outlook database
Import Volume of Goods at Product Level	Eora MRIO database; United Nations Commodity Trade Statistics (Comtrade) Database; World Bank, World Integrated Trade Solution
Liner Shipping Connectivity Index	UNCTAD, World Maritime Review
Lobbying on Trade Issues in the United States	Ludema, Mayda, and Mishra (2015)
Measures Implemented by Global Trade Alert	Centre for Economic Policy Research, Global Trade Alert Database
Nominal Effective Exchange Rate	IMF, Information Notice System
Nominal GDP	IMF, World Economic Outlook database
Oil Price in U.S. Dollars	IMF, Global Assumptions database
Producer Price Index	Haver Analytics; CEIC database
Real Effective Exchange Rate	IMF, Information Notice System
Real GDP	IMF, World Economic Outlook database
Real Interest Rate	Haver Analytics
Sectoral Gross Production	Eora MRIO database; Haver Analytics; OECD, Structural Analysis Database, Input-Output Tables
Tariffs	UNCTAD, Trade Analysis Information System; WTO Tariff Download Facility; IMF, Structural Reforms database
Nontariff and Temporary Trade Barriers	Bown 2016; Centre for Economic Policy Research, Global Trade Alert Database; UNCTAD, Trade Analysis Information System
Time to Import	World Bank, Doing Business Indicators
Trade Finance Availability	International Chamber of Commerce, Global Trade and Finance Survey; IMF staff calculations
Trade-Weighted Foreign CPI	IMF staff calculations
Trade-Weighted Foreign Demand	IMF, Global Economic Environment database
Trade-Weighted Foreign PPI	IMF staff calculations
U.S. Air Freight Cost	U.S. Bureau of Labor Statistics

Source: IMF staff compilation.
Note: CPI = consumer price index; DESTA = Design of Trade Agreements database; MRIO = Multi-Region Input-Output database; OECD = Organisation for Economic Co-operation and Development; PPI = producer price index; UNCTAD = United Nations Conference on Trade and Development; WTO = World Trade Organization.

Annex Figure 2.1.1. Nominal Import Growth across Categories of Services
(Percent)

Sources: United Nations Service Trade Statistics database; and IMF staff calculations.
Note: ICT = information and communication technologies.

time. Hence, eliminating such products based on the product-specific time series standard deviations can help reduce the bias.[54] The truncation thresholds are set at percentiles 2.5 and 97.5 for the cross-section and at the 80th percentile for the time series, respectively.

Once this procedure is complete, chained Fisher price indices are calculated that are then used to deflate U.S. dollar values.

It is important to note that the aforementioned procedures do not eliminate the products identified as outliers from the volume indices, as they affect only the calculation of price indices. When the unprocessed value index is used in the numerator to compute volume indices as opposed to one that ignores products with missing quantity data or extreme unit value changes, the implicit assumption is that the missing unit values grow at the same rate as the aggregate price index.

---

[54]However, for some products this time series standard deviation may be intrinsically high, which may not be a reflection of the severity of the unit value bias—for example, commodities, which experience fluctuations as a result of discoveries of new reserves, disruptions in supply, and so forth.

Annex Table 2.1.2. Sample of Economies Included in the Analytical Exercises

Group[1]	Economies[2]	Exercise[3] I	II	III	IV
A	Argentina, Australia,* Austria,* Belgium,* Brazil, Canada,* Chile, China, Colombia, Czech Republic,* Denmark,* Finland,* France,* Germany,* Hungary, India, Indonesia, Italy,* Japan,* Korea,* Malaysia, Mexico, Norway,* Philippines, Poland, Russia, South Africa, Spain,* Sweden,* Thailand, Turkey, United Kingdom,* United States,* Vietnam	X	X	X	X
B	Algeria, Estonia,* Greece,* Hong Kong SAR,* Ireland,* Israel,* Kazakhstan, Lithuania,* Netherlands,* New Zealand,* Portugal,* Romania, Saudi Arabia, Singapore,* Slovak Republic,* Slovenia,* Switzerland,* Taiwan Province of China,* Ukraine	X		X	X
C	Albania, Angola, Antigua and Barbuda, Armenia, Bahamas, Bahrain, Barbados, Belarus, Benin, Bolivia, Bosnia and Herzegovina, Botswana, Brunei Darussalam, Burkina Faso, Burundi, Cambodia, Cameroon, Cape Verde, Central African Republic, Chad, Democratic Republic of the Congo, Republic of Congo, Côte d'Ivoire, Croatia, Djibouti, Dominican Republic, Ecuador, Egypt, El Salvador, Eritrea, Ethiopia, Gabon, Gambia, Ghana, Haiti, Honduras, Iceland, Iran, Jordan, Kenya, Lebanon, Lesotho, Luxembourg,* Madagascar, Malawi, Maldives, Mali, Moldova, Mongolia, Montenegro, Morocco, Mozambique, Namibia, Niger, Oman, Pakistan, Papua New Guinea, Peru, Rwanda, Senegal, Serbia, Seychelles, Sierra Leone, Sri Lanka, Suriname, Swaziland, Syria, Togo, Trinidad and Tobago, Uganda, United Arab Emirates, Uruguay, Venezuela, Yemen, Zambia	X			X
D	Afghanistan, Azerbaijan, Bangladesh, Belize, Bhutan, Bulgaria, Cyprus, Fiji, Georgia, Guatemala, Iraq, Jamaica, Kuwait, Kyrgyz Republic, Lao P.D.R., Latvia,* Libya, Macedonia, Malta,* Mauritania, Nepal, Nicaragua, Nigeria, Panama, Paraguay, Samoa, São Tomé and Príncipe, Tajikistan, Tunisia, Uzbekistan, Vanuatu				X
E	Guinea, Mauritius, Myanmar, Tanzania		X		

Source: IMF staff compilation.
[1] Group of countries according to their use in different analytical exercises.
[2] Asterisk (*) denotes advanced economies as classified by the IMF's World Economic Outlook database.
[3] Analytical exercises performed in the chapter: I = Import Demand Model; II = Structural Model; III = Product-Level Regression Framework; IV = Gravity Model.

Annex Figure 2.2.1. Real Import Growth
(Percent)

———— Processed ----- Unprocessed ———— WEO ———— WTO

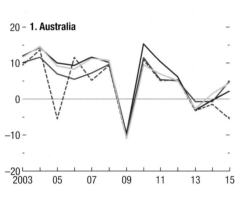

1. Australia

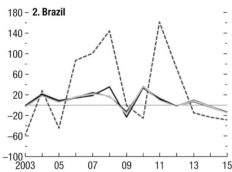

2. Brazil

Sources: IMF, World Economic Outlook (WEO) database; United Nations Comtrade; World Bank World Integrated Trade Solution database; World Trade Organization (WTO) Statistics database; and IMF staff calculations.
Note: "Processed" refers to the index obtained from the truncated data as described in the main text, while the "unprocessed" index is calculated using raw data without any elimination of outliers. Both "processed" and "unprocessed" indices are calculated using chained Fisher price indices.

A comparison of the country-level aggregate import volume indices obtained from the above methodology with those obtained from unprocessed data as well as with those in the IMF's World Economic Outlook database and the World Trade Organization's Statistics database reveals the effectiveness of the proposed methodology (Annex Figure 2.2.1). For Australia, for example, using the cross-section and time series truncations brings the Fisher volume index significantly closer to the two benchmarks relative to the index constructed from unprocessed data. These differences are more striking in the case of emerging market and developing economies, as shown for Brazil.[55]

[55]In addition to these mechanical truncation procedures, all disaggregated indices are thoroughly inspected. In this context,

Annex 2.3. Analysis Using an Empirical Model of Import Demand

This annex provides further details on the empirical model of import demand, which is used to quantify the role of economic activity and its composition in the slowdown of trade in the section "The Role of Output and Its Composition: Insights from an Empirical Investigation." The analysis in that section estimates a standard model of import demand that links real imports growth to growth in absorption and growth in relative prices. Such an import demand equation can be derived from virtually any international real business cycle model. The estimated equation is

$$\Delta \ln M_{c,t} = \delta_c + \beta_{D,c} \Delta \ln D_{c,t} + \beta_{P,c} \Delta \ln P_{c,t} + \varepsilon_{c,t},$$
(A.2.3.1)

in which $M_{c,t}$, $D_{c,t}$ and $P_{c,t}$ denote, respectively, real imports, absorption, and relative import prices of country c in year t. Relative import prices are defined as the ratio of the import price deflator to the GDP deflator. The baseline specification assumes that import growth depends only on the contemporaneous growth rate of the explanatory variables; however, the findings discussed in the chapter are robust to the inclusion of lags of the dependent and explanatory variables' growth rates to allow for richer dynamics. The model is estimated separately for each country and separately for imports of goods and services, as well as for overall imports. The period of analysis is 1985–2015, though data are not available for all countries in all years.

The chapter builds on Bussière and others (2013) and proxies absorption with IAD. Import-intensity-adjusted demand is computed as

$$IAD_{c,t} = C_{c,t}^{\omega_C} G_{c,t}^{\omega_G} I_{c,t}^{\omega_I} X_{c,t}^{\omega_X},$$
(A.2.3.2)

in which ω_k is the import content of each of the expenditure components for $k \in \{C, G, I, X\}$, normalized to sum to 1. Import content is computed from the Eora Multi-Region Input-Output country-specific input-output tables averaged over 1990–2011. Similar to patterns described by Bussière and others (2013), who rely on the Organisation for Economic Co-operation and Development Trade in Value Added database,

some further adjustments are applied in the case of a few countries in which deviations arose with respect to benchmark indices. For example, large spikes in the unit values of product numbers 710,812 (gold) in 2012 in Switzerland and 880,240 (airplanes) in 2015 in Ireland led to adjustments of those unit value changes to better align them with their historical evolution.

Annex Table 2.3.1. Import Content of Aggregate Demand Components

	Mean	Median	25th Percentile	75th Percentile
	(1)	(2)	(3)	(4)
Consumption	23.3	20.7	13.7	27.7
Govt. Spending	14.9	12.1	8.8	17.4
Investment	29.6	26.1	19.0	35.7
Exports	31.7	25.9	14.6	43.0

Sources: Eora Multi-Region Input-Output database; and IMF staff calculations.

Note: The table reports the mean, median, 25th percentile, and 75th percentile of the import content of the four components of aggregate demand across the 150 countries included in the sample. For each country, the import content refers to the average import content over 1990–2011. See Bussière and others 2013 for the exact definition of import content and its computation from national input-output tables.

there are significant differences in the usage of imports across aggregate demand components (Annex Table 2.3.1). Investment and exports have a much richer import content compared with consumption and government spending.

In addition to the measure proposed by Bussière and others (2013), the chapter estimates two alternative models of import demand. In the first alternative model, absorption is proxied by import-intensity-adjusted demand using only the domestic components of aggregate demand, namely

$$DIAD_{c,t} = C_{c,t}\omega^{C^d} G_{c,t}\omega^{G^d} I_{c,t}\omega^{I^d},$$

and the following equation is estimated

$$\Delta \ln M_{c,t} = \delta_c + \beta_{DD,c}\Delta \ln DIAD_{c,t} \\ + \beta_{P,c}\Delta \ln P_{c,t} + \varepsilon_{c,t}. \qquad (A.2.3.3)$$

In the second model, absorption is proxied by *DIAD* and exports are predicted by trading partners' *DIAD*, $\widehat{\Delta \ln X_{c,t}}$. To compute the latter, the chapter first estimates equation (A.2.3.3) and recovers the model-predicted import growth for each country, $\widehat{\Delta \ln M_{c,t,DIAD}}$. It constructs a measure of external demand as the trade-weighted average of partners' $\widehat{\Delta \ln M_{c,t,DIAD}}$ and estimates a model of export demand using this measure as a proxy of the demand for a country's exports:

$$\Delta \ln X_{c,t} = \delta_c^X + \beta_{D,c}^X \sum_{c,t,p} \widehat{\Delta \ln M_{p,t,DIAD}} \\ + \beta_{P,c}^X \Delta \ln P_{c,t}^X + \varepsilon_{c,t}^X. \qquad (A.2.3.4)$$

The procedure then recovers countries' predicted export growth $\widehat{\Delta \ln X_{c,t}}$. Finally, a country's import growth is modeled as

$$\Delta \ln M_{c,t} = \delta_c + \beta_{DD,c}\Delta \ln DIAD_{c,t} + \beta_{DX,c}\widehat{\Delta \ln X_{c,t}} \\ + \beta_{P,c}\Delta \ln P_{c,t} + \varepsilon_{c,t}. \qquad (A.2.3.5)$$

Annex Tables 2.3.2–2.3.4 present the results from estimating equations (A.2.3.1), (A.2.3.3), and (A.2.3.5), for real import growth of goods and services, as well as separately for goods and services. The tables also provide the results from estimating equation A.2.3.1 in a panel framework in columns (1), (5), and (9) for comparison with other studies (in other words, where all the countries in the sample are pooled, and the same elasticities of import growth with respect to its determinants are imposed across countries). The remaining columns report the mean and the interquartile range of the estimated coefficients from a country-by-country estimation.

The results show that estimating the import demand model separately for each country is noticeably superior to estimation in a panel framework (see, for example, column [2] versus column [1]). This is due to the substantial variation in the income elasticity of imports across countries. On average, advanced economies' imports have higher income elasticity than do those of emerging market and developing economies, particularly in the case of goods imports (Annex Table 2.3.3). This finding is in line with Slopek (2015), who demonstrates that the shift in relative growth from advanced toward emerging market and developing economies can account for much of the decline in the global trade elasticity in light of the lower income elasticity of trade of the latter. Moreover, regressions using measures of import demand based solely on the domestic components of aggregate demand (columns [3], [7], and [11]) have a significantly worse fit.

To examine whether there is anything unusual in the 2012–15 period, the chapter pools the residuals from estimating equations (A.2.3.1), (A.2.3.3), and (A.2.3.5) for each country in the sample and estimates the following specification:

$$\widehat{\varepsilon_{c,t}} = \theta Const(1 - D_{2012\text{-}15,t}) \\ + \tau Const(D_{2012\text{-}15,t}) + \varsigma_{c,t}, \qquad (A.2.3.6)$$

where $D_{2012\text{-}15,t}$ is an indicator that takes the value of 1 for $t \in \{2012, 2013, 2014, 2015\}$. The coefficients θ and τ capture the average value of the residuals of the 1985–2011 and 2012–15 periods, respectively. Regressions are weighted by countries' nominal import shares (in U.S. dollars) to more accurately capture the deviations from predicted growth for the world as a whole (or groups of countries).

Annex Table 2.3.2. Empirical Model of Real Imports of Goods and Services

Sample	Full Sample				Advanced Economies				Emerging Market and Developing Economies			
Estimation	Panel	Country-Specific			Panel	Country-Specific			Panel	Country-Specific		
Measure of Import Demand	IAD	IAD	DIAD	DIAD+E	IAD	IAD	DIAD	DIAD+E	IAD	IAD	DIAD	DIAD+E
	(1)	(2)	(3)	(4)	(5)	(6)	(7)	(8)	(9)	(10)	(11)	(12)
Import Demand	0.99 (0.07)	1.31 / 0.94 1.51	1.03 / 0.66 1.29	0.87 / 0.58 1.19	1.33 (0.07)	1.38 / 1.27 1.54	1.08 / 0.92 1.49	0.91 / 0.58 1.06	0.96 (0.07)	1.25 / 0.87 1.50	0.99 / 0.59 1.28	0.86 / 0.58 1.20
Predicted Exports				0.45 / 0.16 0.81				0.61 / 0.36 0.85				0.40 / 0.10 0.78
Relative Prices	−0.24 (0.07)	−0.18 / −0.40 0.04	−0.16 / −0.41 0.07	−0.15 / −0.38 0.00	−0.05 (0.04)	0.04 / −0.15 0.16	0.22 / 0.04 0.43	−0.03 / −0.19 0.15	−0.25 (0.08)	−0.25 / −0.47 −0.05	−0.26 / −0.57 −0.08	−0.23 / −0.42 −0.08
Constant	0.01 (0.00)	0.00 / −0.02 0.01	0.02 / 0.00 0.03	0.00 / −0.03 0.01	0.00 (0.00)	0.00 / −0.01 0.01	0.02 / 0.01 0.04	0.00 / −0.01 0.01	0.01 (0.00)	0.00 / −0.02 0.01	0.01 / −0.01 0.03	−0.01 / −0.03 0.01
R^2	0.53	0.70 / 0.58 0.85	0.57 / 0.43 0.72	0.67 / 0.53 0.80	0.75	0.86 / 0.74 0.88	0.60 / 0.53 0.73	0.72 / 0.64 0.80	0.52	0.65 / 0.52 0.79	0.54 / 0.38 0.72	0.61 / 0.47 0.79

Source: IMF staff calculations.
Note: IAD = import-intensity-adjusted demand; DIAD = import-intensity-adjusted demand using only the domestic components of aggregate demand; DIAD+E = DIAD and exports predicted by trading partners' DIAD. The table presents results from estimating equations (A.2.3.1), (A.2.3.3), and (A.2.3.5). Columns (1), (5), and (9) report point estimates and heteroscedasticity-robust standard errors in parentheses from estimating equation (A.2.3.1) in a panel framework including country fixed effects. The remaining columns report the average point estimates as well as the interquartile range of these estimates from a country-by-country estimation. Absorption is measured as import-intensity-adjusted aggregate demand based on all four components of GDP in columns (1), (2), (5), (6), (9), and (10). In the rest of the columns, absorption is proxied by the import-intensity-adjusted domestic demand. The specifications presented in columns (4), (8), and (12) also control for predicted exports, as estimated according to equation (A.2.3.4).

Annex Table 2.3.3. Empirical Model of Real Imports of Goods

Sample	Full Sample				Advanced Economies				Emerging Market and Developing Economies			
Estimation	Panel	Country-Specific			Panel	Country-Specific			Panel	Country-Specific		
Measure of Import Demand	IAD	IAD	DIAD	DIAD+E	IAD	IAD	DIAD	DIAD+E	IAD	IAD	DIAD	DIAD+E
	(1)	(2)	(3)	(4)	(5)	(6)	(7)	(8)	(9)	(10)	(11)	(12)
Import Demand	0.94	1.32	1.07	0.90	1.52	1.51	1.26	1.00	0.91	1.18	0.93	0.86
	(0.08)	0.95 1.59	0.66 1.37	0.55 1.23	(0.05)	1.38 1.74	1.03 1.58	0.58 1.21	(0.09)	0.77 1.54	0.60 1.32	0.55 1.23
Predicted Exports				0.47				0.66				0.40
				0.12 0.85				0.40 0.94				0.05 0.75
Relative Prices	−0.20	−0.16	−0.06	−0.17	0.01	0.10	0.27	0.01	−0.21	−0.25	−0.24	−0.26
	(0.09)	−0.42 0.13	−0.38 0.20	−0.40 0.03	(0.08)	−0.11 0.25	0.11 0.60	−0.21 0.23	(0.09)	−0.49 0.00	−0.52 0.01	−0.46 0.00
Constant	0.01	0.00	0.02	0.00	0.00	0.00	0.03	0.00	0.01	0.00	0.01	−0.01
	(0.00)	−0.02 0.01	0.00 0.03	−0.03 0.02	(0.00)	−0.01 0.01	0.01 0.03	−0.02 0.01	(0.00)	−0.02 0.02	−0.01 0.03	−0.04 0.02
R^2	0.40	0.66	0.54	0.63	0.72	0.79	0.56	0.72	0.38	0.61	0.52	0.59
		0.50 0.78	0.41 0.69	0.50 0.76		0.71 0.87	0.48 0.73	0.61 0.78		0.45 0.71	0.38 0.65	0.46 0.73

Source: IMF staff calculations.

Note: IAD = import-intensity-adjusted demand; DIAD = import-intensity-adjusted demand using only the domestic components of aggregate demand; DIAD+E = DIAD and exports predicted by trading partners' DIAD. The table presents results from estimating equations (A.2.3.1), (A.2.3.3), and (A.2.3.5). Columns (1), (5), and (9) report point estimates and heteroscedasticity-robust standard errors in parentheses from estimating equation (A.2.3.1) in a panel framework including country fixed effects. The remaining columns report the average point estimates as well as the interquartile range of these estimates from a country-by-country estimation. Absorption is measured as import-intensity-adjusted aggregate demand based on all four components of GDP in columns (1), (2), (5), (6), (9), and (10). In the rest of the columns, absorption is proxied by the import-intensity-adjusted domestic demand. The specifications presented in columns (4), (8), and (12) also control for predicted exports, as estimated according to equation (A.2.3.4).

Annex Table 2.3.4. Empirical Model of Real Imports of Services

Sample	Full Sample				Advanced Economies				Emerging Market and Developing Economies			
Estimation	Panel	Country-Specific			Panel	Country-Specific			Panel	Country-Specific		
Measure of Import Demand	IAD	IAD	DIAD	DIAD+E	IAD	IAD	DIAD	DIAD+E	IAD	IAD	DIAD	DIAD+E
	(1)	(2)	(3)	(4)	(5)	(6)	(7)	(8)	(9)	(10)	(11)	(12)
Import Demand	1.39	1.04	0.89	0.83	1.11	1.03	1.02	0.81	1.41	1.06	0.82	0.83
	(0.33)	0.64 1.69	0.50 1.41	0.31 1.44	(0.13)	0.86 1.26	0.71 1.31	0.29 1.22	(0.35)	0.61 1.92	0.38 1.48	0.37 1.61
Predicted Exports				0.30				0.52				0.17
				-0.02 0.84				0.28 0.83				-0.11 0.86
Relative Prices	0.01	-0.14	-0.19	-0.22	-0.32	-0.07	0.08	-0.06	0.02	-0.25	-0.23	-0.25
	(0.21)	-0.56 0.10	-0.61 0.15	-0.58 0.17	(0.11)	-0.37 0.11	-0.33 0.28	-0.42 0.16	(0.22)	-0.60 0.07	-0.65 0.01	-0.69 0.17
Constant	0.00	0.00	0.02	0.00	0.01	0.01	0.02	0.01	0.00	0.00	0.01	-0.01
	(0.01)	-0.01 0.02	-0.01 0.04	-0.05 0.03	(0.00)	0.00 0.03	0.01 0.04	-0.02 0.02	(0.01)	-0.03 0.02	-0.01 0.04	-0.05 0.03
R^2	0.08	0.38	0.29	0.41	0.24	0.47	0.41	0.46	0.08	0.35	0.26	0.39
		0.16 0.55	0.14 0.48	0.19 0.57		0.30 0.59	0.20 0.50	0.33 0.58		0.15 0.55	0.13 0.45	0.18 0.57

Source: IMF staff calculations.

Note: IAD = import-intensity-adjusted demand; DIAD = import-intensity-adjusted demand using only the domestic components of aggregate demand; DIAD+E = DIAD and exports predicted by trading partners' DIAD. The table presents results from estimating equations (A.2.3.1), (A.2.3.3), and (A.2.3.5). Columns (1), (5), and (9) report point estimates and heteroscedasticity-robust standard errors in parentheses from estimating equation (A.2.3.1) in a panel framework including country fixed effects. The remaining columns report the average point estimates as well as the interquartile range of these estimates from a country-by-country estimation. Absorption is measured as import-intensity-adjusted aggregate demand based on all four components of GDP in columns (1), (2), (5), (6), (9), and (10). In the rest of the columns, absorption is proxied by the import-intensity-adjusted domestic demand. The specifications presented in columns (4), (8), and (12) also control for predicted exports, as estimated according to equation (A.2.3.4).

Annex Table 2.3.5. Residuals: Real Goods Import Growth

	Full Sample			Advanced Economies			Emerging Market and Developing Economies		
	IAD	DIAD	DIAD+E	IAD	DIAD	DIAD+E	IAD	DIAD	DIAD+E
	(1)	(2)	(3)	(4)	(5)	(6)	(7)	(8)	(9)
Indicator 1985–2011	0.003	0.000	0.001	0.003	0.000	0.001	0.002	−0.001	0.002
	(0.002)	(0.003)	(0.002)	(0.002)	(0.003)	(0.002)	(0.005)	(0.007)	(0.006)
Indicator 2012–15	−0.009	−0.023	−0.018	−0.005	−0.014	−0.011	−0.018	−0.040	−0.031
	(0.002)	(0.004)	(0.004)	(0.003)	(0.004)	(0.004)	(0.004)	(0.007)	(0.007)
Number of Observations	3,427	3,427	3,427	910	910	910	2,517	2,517	2,517

Source: IMF staff calculations.
Note: IAD = import-intensity-adjusted demand; DIAD = import-intensity-adjusted demand using only the domestic components of aggregate demand; DIAD+E = DIAD and exports predicted by trading partners' DIAD. The table reports point estimates and heteroscedasticity-robust standard errors in parentheses from estimating equation (A.2.3.6). Regressions are weighted by countries' nominal goods import shares.

Annex Tables A.2.3.5 and A.2.3.6 present the regression results for goods and services real import growth, respectively. On average, for goods imports, the residuals are significantly less than zero across all samples and specifications in the 2012–15 period. The extent of "missing" goods import growth varies across advanced and emerging market and developing economies, with emerging market and developing economies having significantly larger (in absolute value) residuals. According to the baseline specification, which proxies import demand with *DIAD* and exports predicted by trading partners' *DIAD* —equation (A.2.3.5), residuals in columns (3), (6), and (9) in Annex Table 2.3.5—the missing goods import growth amounted to about 1 percentage point in advanced economies, 3 percentage points for emerging market and developing economies, and 1¾ percentage points for the world as a whole.

In the case of services, there is no robust evidence of an unexplained slowdown in import growth during the 2012–15 period for the world as a whole. However, in emerging market and developing economies, services import growth seems to have been lower than predicted in the post-2012 period according to models based on the domestic components of aggregate demand. The findings presented in Annex Tables A.2.3.5 and A.2.3.6 are robust to the inclusion of country fixed effects or to clustering the standard errors by country.

To account for the potential role of uncertainty, global financial conditions and financial stress in shaping countries' import demand, Annex Table 2.3.7 presents the results from the estimation of equation (A.2.3.6) augmented to include these variables. The findings of unexplained negative real goods import growth residuals during 2012–15 are robust to this alternative specification.

Annex Table 2.3.6. Residuals: Real Services Import Growth

	Full Sample			Advanced Economies			Emerging Market and Developing Economies		
	IAD	DIAD	DIAD+E	IAD	DIAD	DIAD+E	IAD	DIAD	DIAD+E
	(1)	(2)	(3)	(4)	(5)	(6)	(7)	(8)	(9)
Indicator 1985–2011	0.003	0.002	0.003	−0.001	−0.002	−0.001	0.015	0.019	0.016
	(0.003)	(0.003)	(0.003)	(0.002)	(0.002)	(0.002)	(0.013)	(0.013)	(0.013)
Indicator 2012–15	0.008	−0.003	−0.003	0.010	0.007	0.006	0.004	−0.024	−0.024
	(0.007)	(0.007)	(0.007)	(0.004)	(0.005)	(0.004)	(0.021)	(0.021)	(0.021)
Number of Observations	3,359	3,359	3,359	909	909	909	2,450	2,450	2,450

Source: IMF staff calculations.
Note: IAD = import-intensity-adjusted demand; DIAD = import-intensity-adjusted demand using only the domestic components of aggregate demand; DIAD+E = DIAD and exports predicted by trading partners' DIAD. The table reports point estimates and heteroscedasticity-robust standard errors in parentheses from estimating equation (A.2.3.6). Regressions are weighted by countries' nominal services import shares.

Annex Table 2.3.7. Residuals: Real Goods Import Growth Controlling for Global Uncertainty, Global Financial Conditions, and Financial Stress

Full Sample	IAD					DIAD+E				
	(1)	(2)	(3)	(4)	(5)	(6)	(7)	(8)	(9)	(10)
Indicator 1985–2011	0.003	0.005	0.005	0.004	0.007	0.001	0.003	0.004	0.002	0.006
	(0.002)	(0.002)	(0.002)	(0.002)	(0.002)	(0.002)	(0.002)	(0.002)	(0.002)	(0.002)
Indicator 2012–15	−0.009	−0.011	−0.006	−0.009	−0.007	−0.018	−0.020	−0.013	−0.018	−0.015
	(0.002)	(0.003)	(0.002)	(0.002)	(0.003)	(0.004)	(0.004)	(0.003)	(0.004)	(0.004)
VIX Growth		−0.015			−0.011		−0.026			−0.024
		(0.006)			(0.007)		(0.007)			(0.008)
Change in Global Real Interest Rate			0.008		0.008			0.013		0.013
			(0.003)		(0.003)			(0.003)		(0.003)
Banking Crisis				−0.022	−0.014				−0.020	−0.005
				(0.007)	(0.009)				(0.008)	(0.010)
Number of Observations	3,427	2,987	2,987	3,427	2,987	3,427	2,987	2,987	3,427	2,987

Source: IMF staff calculations.
Note: IAD = import-intensity-adjusted demand; DIAD = import-intensity-adjusted demand using only the domestic components of aggregate demand; DIAD+E = DIAD and exports predicted by trading partners' DIAD. The table reports point estimates and heteroscedasticity-robust standard errors in parentheses from estimating equation (A.2.3.6) augmented to include the growth rate of the VIX (Chicago Board of Volatility Index), change in real global interest rates, and an indicator for the beginning of a banking crisis from Laeven and Valencia (2012). Regressions are weighted by countries' nominal goods import shares.

Annex Table 2.3.8 decomposes the predicted decline in the growth rate of real goods imports between the 2012–15 period and 1985–2007 and 2003–07 across the various components of import demand for the full sample of economies.[56]

[56]Sectors are aggregated along the lines of Eaton and others (2010) with the exception that mining and quarrying, coke, refined

As mentioned in the main text, other factors can simultaneously affect economic activity and trade, in particular trade policies. If ignored, these would likely lead to an upward bias in the estimated role of economic activity in explaining the slowdown in trade

petroleum products, and nuclear fuel are stripped out from the residual services sector and used to quantify the commodities sector.

Annex Table 2.3.8. Decomposing the Decline in Real Goods Import Growth: Full Sample

	Actual	Import Growth Predicted by IAD Model and Its Components							Import Growth Predicted by DIAD+E Model and Its Components						
		Overall	C	G	I	X	Relative Prices	Constant	Overall	C	G	I	X	Relative Prices	Constant
	(1)	(2)	(3)	(4)	(5)	(6)	(7)	(8)	(9)	(10)	(11)	(12)	(13)	(14)	(15)
1985–2007	8.1	8.0	1.4	0.7	2.7	4.6	0.3	−1.9	7.8	1.5	0.8	2.9	4.6	0.3	−2.3
2003–07	8.9	8.8	1.4	0.7	3.5	4.8	0.2	−1.7	9.2	1.5	0.7	3.7	5.1	0.3	−2.1
2012–15	2.3	3.2	0.9	0.4	1.4	2.0	0.3	−1.7	4.0	1.0	0.4	1.7	3.0	0.1	−2.1
Average Growth in 2012–15 Minus Average Growth															
1985–2007	−5.7	−4.7	−0.6	−0.4	−1.3	−2.7	−0.1	0.2	−3.8	−0.6	−0.4	−1.3	−1.6	−0.2	0.2
2003–07	−6.6	−5.6	−0.6	−0.3	−2.0	−2.9	0.1	0.0	−5.2	−0.6	−0.3	−2.0	−2.1	−0.2	0.0
Fraction of Import Growth Decline Predicted by Model															
1985–2007		0.82							0.66						
2003–07		0.85							0.79						

Source: IMF staff calculations.
Note: IAD = import-intensity-adjusted demand; DIAD = import-intensity-adjusted demand using only the domestic components of aggregate demand; DIAD+E = DIAD and exports predicted by trading partners' DIAD. The table reports actual and predicted real goods import growth rates. Individual economies' growth rates are aggregated using average import shares over the 1985–2015 period to minimize fluctuations in the contribution of the constant to aggregate import growth. Columns (2)–(8) decompose predicted import growth based on equation (A.2.3.2). Columns (9)–(15) decompose predicted import growth based on equation (A.2.3.5), with column (13) denoting the contribution of export growth predicted based on trading partners' import-intensity-adjusted domestic demand.

Annex Table 2.3.9. Residuals: Real Goods Import Growth, Corrected for Potential Effect of Trade Policies on Aggregate Demand

Full Sample	Correcting for Role of Trade Policies	
	IAD*	(DIAD+E)*
Indicator 1985–2011	0.002	0.001
	(0.002)	(0.002)
Indicator 2012–15	−0.012	−0.021
	(0.002)	(0.004)
Number of Observations	2,840	2,817

Source: IMF staff calculations
Note: IAD = import-intensity-adjusted demand; DIAD = import-intensity-adjusted demand using only the domestic components of aggregate demand; DIAD+E = DIAD and exports predicted by trading partners' DIAD. The table reports point estimates and heteroscedasticity-robust standard errors in parentheses from estimating equation (A.2.3.6). Regressions are weighted by countries' nominal goods import shares.

flows. Part of this bias can be corrected by purging the aggregate demand components of the effect of trade policies prior to constructing the measure for import-intensity-adjusted demand. This is done in a first stage regression of these demand components on the factors of interest:

$$\Delta \ln AD_{c,t}^k = \delta_c + \gamma_c{}' \Delta \ln \mathbf{F}_{c,t} + v_{c,t}^k, \quad (A.2.3.7)$$

where $AD_{c,t}^k$ is a component of aggregate demand, $k \in \{C, G, I, X\}$ and $\mathbf{F}_{c,t}$ is the vector of trade policies, in this case tariffs and participation in free trade agreements. The residuals from this first stage regression, $v_{c,t}^k$, which are by construction orthogonal to the trade policy variables, are used to construct the measure

of import-intensity-adjusted demand as in equation (A.2.3.2):

$$IAD_{c,t}^* = \left(v_{c,t}^C\right)^{\omega_C} \left(v_{c,t}^G\right)^{\omega_G} \left(v_{c,t}^I\right)^{\omega_I} \left(v_{c,t}^X\right)^{\omega_X}. \quad (A.2.3.8)$$

The analysis is repeated as before using this measure, as well as for the alternative measures: (1) $DIAD^*$ and (2) absorption proxied by $DIAD^*$ and exports predicted by trading partners' $DIAD^*$.

Annex Table 2.3.9 presents the results from estimating equation (A.2.3.6) using the residuals obtained from the goods import demand model specified in equations (A.2.3.1), (A.2.3.3), and (A.2.3.5) using these alternatives measures of demand. The "missing" trade growth is slightly larger during 2012–15 when changes in aggregate demand have been purged of the role of trade policies.

Annex Table 2.3.10 decomposes the observed decline in trade growth between the 2012–15 and 2003–07 periods into shares predicted and unpredicted by the import demand model. A slightly smaller share of the slowdown is now attributed to changes in economic activity. For example, comparing 2012–15 with 2003–07, the baseline model can predict 85 percent of the decline in import growth for the average economy, while the model based on the import growth predicted by $DIAD^*$ and exports predicted by trading partners' $DIAD^*$ can predict 79 percent of the observed slowdown. The corresponding numbers using the alternative trade-policies-corrected measure are 79 percent and 70 percent, respectively.

Annex Table 2.3.10. Decomposing the Decline in Real Goods Import Growth Controlling for Trade Policies

Full Sample	Actual	Baseline		Baseline Corrected for Trade Policies	
		IAD	DIAD+E	IAD*	(DIAD+E)*
	(1)	(2)	(3)	(4)	(5)
2003–07	8.9	8.8	9.2	8.8	9.1
2012–15	2.3	3.2	4.0	3.6	4.4
Average Growth in 2012–15 Minus Average Growth					
2003–07	−6.6	−5.6	−5.2	−5.2	−4.6
Fraction of Import Growth Decline Predicted by Model					
2003–07		0.85	0.79	0.79	0.70

Source: IMF staff calculations.
Note: IAD = import-intensity-adjusted demand; DIAD = import-intensity-adjusted demand using only the domestic components of aggregate demand; DIAD+E = DIAD and exports predicted by trading partners' DIAD. The table reports actual and predicted real goods import growth rates. Individual economies' growth rates are aggregated using average import shares over the 1985–2015 period to minimize fluctuations in the contribution of the constant to aggregate import growth. Columns (2) and (4) estimate predicted import growth based on equation (A.2.3.3). Columns (3) and (5) estimate predicted import growth based on equation (A.2.3.5).

Annex 2.4. Analysis Using a General Equilibrium Model

The structural analysis presented in the section "The Role of Demand Composition and Trade Costs: Insights from a Structural Investigation" closely follows the model framework of Eaton and others (2010)—a multisector, multicountry, static general equilibrium model of production and trade, which nests the canonical Ricardian trade model of Eaton and Kortum (2002). A full description and derivation of this model can be found in Eaton and others (2010). This annex describes some of the key changes to the model as well as the data sources used.

Framework

One important modification is the inclusion of a fourth sector composed of commodities in addition to two manufacturing sectors (producing durable and nondurable goods) and the residual sector, which covers primarily services.[57] Production and trade in the commodity sector are modeled as for the manufacturing sectors, and so the functional forms of the equations for the latter can be applied to the former. This means there is an additional set of equilibrium conditions that serve to pin down prices, trade shares, and spending in the commodity sector.[58]

As described in the main text, observed trade dynamics can be attributed to changes in four factors in the model framework: (1) composition of demand, (2) trade costs (or frictions), (3) productivity, and (4) trade deficits. Following the business cycle accounting approach of Chari, Kehoe, and McGrattan (2007), these factors are often referred to as "wedges."

The solution method for the model uses the procedure developed by Dekle, Eaton, and Kortum (2007). The key endogenous variables (wages, spending, prices, trade shares) are expressed as a ratio of their end-of-period to beginning-of-period value (gross changes form) given values for the four wedges. Next, the wedges are solved for in a way that the variation in the key endogenous variables implied by the model's equations matches their variation in the actual data. Counter-

factual scenarios—in which certain wedges are turned on and off—rely on the first step of this procedure, in which outcomes are pinned down taking the values of wedges as given. Since the framework is static, the solution procedure is run separately for consecutive year-pairs by feeding in data for two years at a time.

Calibrated parameters include the input-output coefficients, value-added coefficients, and the inverse measure of the dispersion of inefficiencies that governs the strength of comparative advantage in each sector. Following Eaton and others (2010), the inverse measure of the dispersion of inefficiencies is set to 2 and assumed to be the same for all sectors. The literature's estimates for this parameter vary greatly. Setting it to equal 8 as in Eaton and Kortum (2002) yields similar results. The remaining parameters are pinned down using the 2011 Organisation for Economic Co-operation and Development (OECD) Trade in Value database. The only exceptions to this are the value-added coefficients for the "rest of the world" category consisting of countries outside of the sample. Those coefficients are set so as to match the exports-to-production ratio of each sector in the data. The exports-to-production ratios are calculated by aggregating exports and production in 2013 for all countries in the Eora Multi-Region Input-Output database excluding the 34 countries used in the exercise.

Data

The estimation requires sectoral data on absorption, gross production, prices, and bilateral trade—very heavy data input. Numerous data sources were spliced to obtain the necessary time coverage through 2015. The sample consists of 17 advanced economies and 17 emerging market and developing economies listed in Group A of Annex Table 2.1.2. In 2015, six of those countries are excluded (Austria, Belgium, Colombia, Indonesia, Korea, Philippines) due to lack of disaggregated trade data at the time of the analysis. The data sources for the analysis are described in Annex Table 2.1.1.

For sectoral gross production, data through 2009 or 2011 are from the OECD Structural Analysis Database, where available. For countries not included in this database, World KLEMS, OECD Input-Output Tables, and Eora Multi-Region Input-Output database are used. For most advanced economies, national sources provide data through 2014, which are used to extrapolate forward the data from the multinational sources. Remaining gaps in the data are filled using the growth rates of sectoral industrial production and producer price indices. These

---

[57]Sectors are aggregated along the lines of Eaton and others (2010) with the exception that (1) mining and quarrying, and (2) coke, refined petroleum products, and nuclear fuel are stripped out from the residual services sector and used to quantify the commodities sector.

[58]The modified system of equations is available on request from the authors.

indices tend to be more disaggregated than the four sectors considered in the analysis. The weights for this aggregation are based on the latest available production data. For the bilateral sectoral import and export flows, data for Belgium and the Philippines are rescaled such that total import and exports from the United Nations Commodity Trade Statistics database match those from the IMF World Economic Outlook database to adjust for the inclusion of re-exports in the former.

Annex 2.5. Analysis at the Product Level

This annex provides additional details on the empirical analysis carried out in the section "The Role of Trade Costs and Global Value Chains: Insights from Disaggregated Trade Data." It starts with an overview of the data used to construct the measures for the other factors that could be relevant to explaining the trade slowdown (see also Annex Table 2.1.1), followed by a technical overview of the baseline specification used in that section. It also presents alternative specifications that assess the robustness of the main results.

Data

Trade costs—The chapter uses the methodology set out by Novy (2012). (Tariff-equivalent) trade costs, t_{ij}, are derived from a gravity model of trade as a geometric average of bilateral trade flows between countries i and j, $X_{ij} \neq X_{ji}$, relative to domestic trade flows within each country, $X_{ii} \neq X_{jj}$:

$$t_{ij} = \left(\frac{X_{ii}X_{jj}}{X_{ij}X_{ji}}\right)^{\frac{1}{2(\sigma-1)}} - 1. \qquad (A.2.5.1)$$

Countries trading more with each other than they trade with themselves is an indication that international trade costs must be falling relative to domestic trade costs. Trade costs are computed at the sectoral level using bilateral sectoral trade data and domestic shipments (that is, intranational trade), which, following the literature, is proxied by gross sectoral output minus total exports. All the data for this exercise is from the Eora Multi-Region Input-Output (MRIO) database.

Tariffs—Data on tariffs are constructed from two sources with detailed information on tariffs for products at the Harmonized System six-digit level: (1) the United Nations Conference on Trade and Development Trade Analysis and Information System database, and (2) the World Trade Organization (WTO) Tariff Download Facility. To extend the historical cover-

age for average tariffs at the country level, the series on average ad valorem tariffs from United Nations Conference on Trade and Development and WTO is spliced with the country-level series from the IMF Structural Reform database (IMF 2008).

Nontariff barriers—Detailed data on more than 30 different national governments' use of policies, such as antidumping, countervailing duties, and safeguard measures, are obtained from the World Bank Temporary Trade Barriers database for 1990–2015 (see Bown 2016). This data set lists temporary trade barriers at a highly disaggregated level (Harmonized System eight-digit or more detailed), including information on their revocation, which makes it possible to calculate the stock of barriers effective in each year.[59] More comprehensive data on a broader range of nontariff barriers are taken from the Center for Economic and Policy Research Global Trade Alert initiative. This includes not only the trade defense measures, but also other state measures taken since 2009 that are likely to discriminate against foreign commerce—for example, localization requirements, bailouts, and state aid.

Free trade agreements—Data on flows of agreements by year of signature are obtained from the Design of Trade Agreements database. This data set is complemented by the stock of free trade agreements in force from the WTO Regional Trade Agreements database. The former builds on the latter, supplementing it with data from other multilateral institutions and national sources.

Global value chain participation—Input-output matrices from the Eora MRIO database for 173 countries are used. The measure of vertical specialization employed (developed by Hummels, Ishii, and Yi 2001) is computed as the sum of the import content in a country's exports (also known as foreign value added) and the domestic content of a country's exports that is used by trading partners for their own exports (see Koopman, Wang, and Wei 2014). This total is expressed as a ratio of gross exports.

Trade finance—Changes in trade finance availability also directly influence overall trade costs. Data from the International Chamber of Commerce Global Trade and Finance Survey were used to gauge whether the availability for trade credit has been growing or shrinking since the global financial crisis. The proportion of banks reporting a decrease in trade credit lines to both

---

[59]These calculations follow those described in the appendix of Bown (2011).

Annex Figure 2.5.1. Trade Finance Availability
(Percent of responding banks reporting a decrease in trade finance credit lines offered)

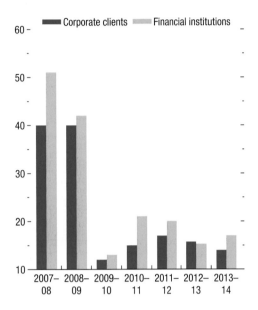

Sources: International Chamber of Commerce, Global Trade and Finance Survey; and IMF staff calculations.
Note: The chart is based on an unbalanced sample of banks comprising 122 banks in 59 countries in 2009 and 482 banks in 112 countries in 2015.

corporate clients and financial institutions has more than halved since 2008–09 (Annex Figure 2.5.1).

Product-Level Regressions

The analysis in the section on the role of trade costs and global value chains uses an augmented model of import demand that relates the product-level growth rate of imports to product, country, or product-country characteristics that are meant to capture factors proposed in the literature that could help explain the recent trade slowdown. The analysis uses data on import volumes across about 780 products, defined using Standard International Trade Classification revision 2, for 52 economies since 2003 (see the list of economies of Groups A and B in Annex Table 2.1.2). The baseline specification is

$$\Delta \ln M_{p,c,t} = \alpha + \delta_{p,c} + \delta_t + \beta_1' \mathbf{X}_{p,c,t} + \beta_2 \Delta \ln D_{s,c,t}$$
$$+ \beta_3 \Delta \ln P_{c,t} + \varepsilon_{p,c,t}, \qquad (A.2.5.2)$$

in which $\Delta \ln M_{p,c,t}$ is the growth rate of real imports of product p by country c in period t; $\delta_{p,c}$ are product-country fixed effects; and δ_t are time fixed effects.

The equation also controls for the demand (or absorption) in sector s to which a particular product can be mapped, $D_{s,c,t}$, and relative import prices at the country level, $P_{c,t}$. In the absence of a measure of demand at the product level, the chapter maps all products to more aggregated sectors. The chapter uses the Eora Multi-Region Input-Output matrices to compute the intensity with which each of the 10 nonservices sectors is used both directly or indirectly in the four components of an economy's aggregate demand. As with the empirical exercise using import-intensity-adjusted demand, these intensities are used as sector-specific weights for aggregate consumption, investment, government spending, and exports to construct a proxy for the absorption of a particular sector.[60] Relative prices are computed as the ratio of the import price deflator to the GDP deflator, as in the analysis discussed in the section "The Role of Output and Its Composition: Insights from an Empirical Investigation."[61]

The variable, $\mathbf{X}_{p,c,t}$, represents a vector of trade policy measures and other factors, which are included in the regression at either the product-country, sector-country, or country level to understand how product-level import growth varies with them. These include: (1) growth in tariff rates at the product level, (2) a dummy variable that captures whether a particular product category was subject to a temporary trade barrier (trade defense measure) in year t, (3) the growth in the share of global GDP that is covered by the free trade agreements a country is party to, and (4) growth in a measure of backward global value chain participation, expressed as the share of foreign value added in sectoral gross exports. Of these, only participation in free trade agreements varies at the country-year level, while participation in global value chains varies at the sector-country-year level. Tariffs and nontariff barriers are measured at the product level.

In addition (and as a cross-check) to the product-level analysis, a similar augmented import demand model is estimated at the aggregate level. In particular, the analysis pools the estimated residuals from the empirical import demand model estimated in the

---

[60]All products within each of the 10 nonservices sectors used in the standardized input-output matrices are assumed to have the same absorption.

[61]Ideally, equation (A.2.5.1) should include sector-level prices. While the import deflator for a particular product can be constructed, disaggregated data on domestic prices are not available. Hence, the same relative price change is applied for all products in an economy.

Annex Table 2.5.1. Alternative Specifications for Real Imports in Product-Level Regressions

Dependent Variable (Real)	A. Product and Country				
	Import Growth			Level of Imports	Imports-to-Sectoral Demand
Sample Period: 2003–13					
	(1)	(2)	(3)	(4)	(5)
Temporary Trade Barriers	−0.031***	−0.037***	−0.036***	−0.033*	−0.031*
	(0.009)	(0.009)	(0.011)	(0.017)	(0.016)
Tariffs	−0.016**	−0.030***	−0.038***	−0.146***	−0.131***
	(0.008)	(0.008)	(0.009)	(0.022)	(0.021)
Free Trade Agreement Coverage	0.106**	0.143***	0.304***	0.134***	0.110***
	(0.054)	(0.053)	(0.060)	(0.013)	(0.012)
Global Value Chain Participation	0.095**	0.474***	0.835***	0.410***	0.322***
	(0.041)	(0.038)	(0.030)	(0.058)	(0.056)
Country x Product Fixed Effects	Yes	Yes	Yes	Yes	Yes
Time Fixed Effects	Yes	No	No	No	No
Control for Demand and Relative Prices	Yes	Yes	No	No	No
R^2	0.293	0.261	0.176	0.978	0.979
Adjusted R^2	0.208	0.173	0.077	0.975	0.977
Number of Observations	258,196	258,196	262,340	292,068	292,068

Source: IMF staff calculations.
Note: Global value chain participation is a measure of backward participation: foreign value added in exports as share of gross exports. In the product-country-level regressions, this variable is calculated at the sectoral level. Standard errors are clustered at the product-country level for regressions A and at the country level in regression B.
* $p < 0.10$; ** $p < 0.05$; *** $p < 0.01$.

section "The Role of Output and Its Composition: Insights from an Empirical Investigation," according to equation (A.2.3.5) (in other words, real goods import growth that cannot be predicted by fluctuations in import-intensity-adjusted demand and relative prices). The product- and sector-level measures for trade policy and global value chain participation are aggregated up to the country level and used as right-hand-side variables in the following regression equation:

$$\widehat{\varepsilon_{c,t}} = \alpha + \phi_c + \phi_t + \beta' \mathbf{X}_{c,t} + \xi_{c,t}, \qquad \text{(A.2.5.3)}$$

where $\widehat{\varepsilon_{c,t}}$ are the estimated residuals and $\mathbf{X}_{c,t}$ are the same trade policy and global value chain factors at the country level.

Decomposing the Slowdown into the Role for Other Factors

The final step of the analysis quantifies how much additional decline in import growth one would have expected based on the historical association between trade policies, global value chain participation and import growth, and the evolution of these other fac-

tors. The elasticities from the country-level equation (A.2.5.3), β, are combined with differences in the growth rate of the different factors at the product level, $X_{p,c,t}$, between 2012–15 and 2003–07 to compute the relative contribution of each factor. Annex Figure 2.5.2 shows the proportion of the estimated country-specific residuals according to equation (A.2.3.5)—that is, that component of import growth not accounted for by import-intensity-adjusted demand—that can be attributed to these other factors, for both real and nominal import growth.

Robustness

The baseline specification in equation (A.2.5.1) for the product-level regressions was subject to a number of robustness tests. In particular, because the relationship between imports and other factors beyond demand was specified in terms of growth rates, it was important to understand whether similar elasticities were recovered using the levels of the same of variables, as is often done in the literature (see, for example, Box

Annex Figure 2.5.2. Contribution of Trade Policies and Global Value Chains to the Slowdown in Real and Nominal Goods Import Growth
(Percent)

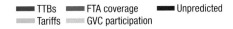

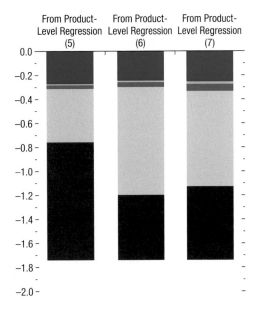

Source: IMF staff calculations.
Note: TTB = temporary trade barrier; FTA = free trade agreement; GVC = global value chain. The figure combines the estimated historical association between real and nominal product-level import growth, and growth in trade costs and global value chain participation, and the differences in the growth rate of these factors between 2003–07 and 2012–15 to compute their contribution to the observed trade slowdown.

2.1). A version using the ratio of real-imports-to-GDP (with the denominator proxied by sectoral demand) on the left-hand side was also estimated.[62] In addition, alternative specifications that omitted the time fixed effects and controls for demand and relative prices were also tested. Omitting time fixed effects can be justified given the synchronicity in the timing of reduction on trade barriers and development of global value chains across countries. In such a setting, including time fixed effects would absorb a large fraction of the variation in trade policies and global value chain measures. To the extent that sectoral demand (and growth) is one

---

[62]At the product level, the ratio used was that of product-level imports to sectoral demand.

---

of the channels through which trade policies affect import growth, a specification that does not control for sectoral demand could also be useful in gauging what is the correct elasticity of import growth with respect to these other factors.

The exercises show that the findings are generally robust to various modifications of the estimated specifications (Annex Table 2.5.1). However, the exclusion of time fixed effects leads to an increase in the role of tariffs and global value chain participation. This is likely due to the fact that the reduction in trade costs and gradual increase in global value chain participation over time was common to all countries.

The same alternative specifications were also run using nominal imports (growth and level and as a ratio of sectoral demand). The results were once again broadly similar, with a stronger role for import tariffs and global value chains once the common time trends were no longer controlled for (Annex Table 2.5.2).

Annex 2.6. Analysis Using Gravity Model of Trade

This annex provides additional details on the empirical analysis carried out in the section "The Role of Trade Costs and Global Value Chains: Insights from Disaggregated Trade Data" using the gravity model of trade. It provides an overview of the data and describes the methodology used.

Data

The data set used in the gravity model is an extension of the bilateral-sectoral database of trade flows from Chapter 2 of the October 2010 *World Economic Outlook*. The data set is extended by using United Nations Commodity Trade Statistics data on bilateral trade flows at the Standard International Trade Classification revision 2, four-digit level. It includes about 780 uniquely identified products and their bilateral trade flows from 1998–2014. To analyze the connection between trade and global value chains, the 780 sectoral trade flows are mapped into the 10 nonservices sectors used in the Eora Multi-Region Input-Output database and aggregated accordingly. Those resulting bilateral-sectoral trade flows are combined with the IMF Direction of Trade Statistics database and the Head, Mayer, and Ries (2010) database on gravity variables. Countries' participation in free trade agreements is

Annex Table 2.5.2. Alternative Specifications for Nominal Imports in Product-Level Regressions

Dependent Variable (Nominal)	A. Product and Country				
	Import Growth			Level of Imports	Imports-to-Sectoral Demand
Sample Period: 2003–13	(1)	(2)	(3)	(4)	(5)
Temporary Trade Barriers	−0.029***	−0.037***	−0.035***	−0.020	−0.018
	(0.007)	(0.009)	(0.011)	(0.019)	(0.018)
Tariffs	−0.034***	−0.057***	−0.067***	−0.205***	−0.167***
	(0.007)	(0.007)	(0.009)	(0.021)	(0.020)
Free Trade Agreement Coverage	0.205***	0.325***	0.534***	0.218***	0.186***
	(0.055)	(0.056)	(0.063)	(0.017)	(0.016)
Global Value Chain Participation	0.170***	0.719***	1.220***	1.109***	0.916***
	(0.041)	(0.043)	(0.031)	(0.065)	(0.061)
Country x Product Fixed Effects	Yes	Yes	Yes	Yes	Yes
Time Fixed Effects	Yes	No	No	No	No
Control for Demand and Relative Prices	Yes	Yes	No	No	No
R^2	0.407	0.337	0.213	0.975	0.977
Adjusted R^2	0.338	0.260	0.122	0.972	0.975
Number of Observations	270,587	270,587	275,424	303,727	297,374

Source: IMF staff calculations.
Note: Global value chain participation is a measure of backward participation: foreign value added in exports as share of gross exports. In the product-country-level regressions, this variable is calculated at the sectoral level. Standard errors are clustered at the product-country level for regressions A and at the country level in regression B.
* $p < 0.10$; ** $p < 0.05$; *** $p < 0.01$.

updated using the World Trade Organization Regional Trade Agreements database.

Methodology

The analysis is performed in the three stages described below.

First and Second Stages: Gravity Model Estimation and Residuals Collection

The first stage of the methodology estimates the gravity model for each year t (between 2003 and 2014) and sector s. The gravity model is first estimated in levels:

$$\forall s,t: \ln M_{i,e,s,t} = \alpha_{i,s,t} + \mu_{e,s,t} + \vec{\beta}_{s,t}\overrightarrow{Gravity}_{i,e,s,t} + \varepsilon_{i,e,s,t}, \quad (A.2.6.1)$$

in which $\ln M_{i,e,s,t}$ is the log of nominal imports between an importer i and an exporter e, $\alpha_{i,s,t}$ denotes importer fixed effects, and $\mu_{e,s,t}$ denotes exporter fixed effects. $\overrightarrow{Gravity}_{i,e,s,t}$ is a vector of standard variables used in gravity models: distance; number of hours differ-

ence between exporters and importers; and indicators for contiguity, common official language, common ethnological language, common colonizer, existence of colonial relationship post-1945, trade from colonizer to colony, trade from colony to colonizer, currently in colonial relationship, regional trade agreement in force, common legal system, common religion, common currency, and generalized system of preferences. Finally, $\varepsilon_{i,e,s,t}$ is the error term, which is collected for the third stage of the analysis.

The gravity model is also estimated in terms of annual growth rates for 2004–14:

$$\forall s,t: \ln M_{i,e,s,t} - \ln M_{i,e,s,t-1} = \sigma_{i,s,t} + \pi_{e,s,t} + \vec{\omega}_{s,t}\overrightarrow{Gravity}_{i,e,s,t} + \varsigma_{i,e,s,t}, \quad (A.2.6.2)$$

in which similarly $\sigma_{i,s,t}$ denotes importer fixed effects, $\pi_{e,s,t}$ denotes exporter fixed effects, $\overrightarrow{Gravity}_{i,e,s,t}$ is the same vector of gravity variables discussed above, and $\varsigma_{i,e,s,t}$ is an independent and identically distributed error term, which is collected for the third stage of the analysis.

Third Stage: Linking Value Chains to the Unexplained Component of Trade Growth

In the third stage, the analysis investigates whether there is an association between the initial value of value chain linkages between two economies in a particular sector and trade growth for that country-pair sector. Using the same notation, the estimated equation is

$$\widehat{\varepsilon_{i,e,s,t}} - \widehat{\varepsilon_{i,e,s,t-1}} = \gamma + \varphi_s GVC_{i,e,s,t-1} + \vartheta_{i,e,s,t}, \quad (A.2.6.3)$$

or

$$\widehat{\varsigma_{i,e,s,t}} = \gamma + \varphi_s GVC_{i,e,s,t-1} + \vartheta_{i,e,s,t}, \quad (A.2.6.4)$$

in which γ is a constant, $GVC_{i,e,s,t-1}$ measures the lagged share of *foreign value added exports to gross exports* in a particular economy-pair-sector, and $\vartheta_{i,e,s,t}$ is an independent and identically distributed error term. The estimation allows for sector-specific effects of GVC, φ_s.

The results of this test are reported in columns (1), (4), (7), (10), and (13) of Annex Tables 2.6.1 (estimation of gravity in levels) and 2.6.2 (estimation of gravity in growth rates) for different country and sectoral samples. They indicate a robust positive association between sectoral trade growth and value chain link linkages over the 2003–14 period.

The second test investigates whether trade in country-pair-sector combinations with high degree of value chain linkages during the 2003–07 period grew more rapidly than trade in country-pair-sector combinations with lower degree of value chain linkages in different sample periods. In this exercise, the analysis considers a time-invariant measure of global value chain linkages, which is an indicator that takes the value of 1 if the average global value chain participation for a particular country-pair-sector over the 2003–07 period is in the top quartile of the distribution of those value chain linkages (*High GVC participation*). The following regression is then estimated:

$$\widehat{\varepsilon_{i,e,s,t}} - \widehat{\varepsilon_{i,e,s,t-1}} = \delta \\ + \theta_s (High\ GVC\ participation)_{i,e,s,2003\text{-}07} \\ + \xi_{i,e,s,t} \quad (A.2.6.5)$$

or

$$\widehat{\varsigma_{i,e,s,t}} = \delta + \theta_s (High\ GVC\ participation)_{i,e,s,2003\text{-}07} \\ + \xi_{i,e,s,t}, \quad (A.2.6.6)$$

in which δ is again a constant and $\xi_{i,e,s,t}$ is the error term. Again, the estimation allows for sector-specific effects of global value chains, θ_s.

The results of this test are reported in the remaining columns of Annex Tables 2.6.1 and 2.6.2. Figure 2.14 displays the results from columns (8) and (9) of those tables, whereas the other columns show the robustness of the findings when using different country and sectoral samples.

Annex Table 2.6.1. Link between Global Value Chain Integration and Yearly Nominal Import Growth Using Gravity Model Estimated in Levels
(Percentage points; year-over-year increase in nominal import growth for country-pair-sectors)

Dependent Variable	Unpredicted Bilateral Import Growth by Year (Gravity Model Estimated on Level of Nominal Imports), 2003–14														
	(Percent, year over year)														
	(1)	(2)[2]	(3)	(4)[2]	(5)[2]	(6)[2]	(7)[3]	(8)[3]	(9)[3]	(10)[4]	(11)[4]	(12)[4]	(13)[5]	(14)[5]	(15)[5]
GVC Participation ($t − 1$)	0.021**			0.027***			0.026***			0.028***			0.032***		
	(0.008)			(0.010)			(0.010)			(0.010)			(0.012)		
High GVC Participation Dummy[1] (2003–14)		1.403***			1.256**			1.379*			0.857			1.103**	
		(0.476)			(0.499)			(0.738)			(0.759)			(0.552)	
High GVC Participation Dummy[1] (pre-2012) [I]			1.185**			1.289**			1.770**			1.251			1.693***
			(0.548)			(0.591)			(0.821)			(0.793)			(0.638)
High GVC Participation Dummy[1] × Post-2012 Dummy [II]			0.547			-0.064			-0.909			-0.929			-1.510*
			(0.838)			(0.874)			(1.351)			(1.442)			(0.900)
Constant	-0.603**	-0.474**	-0.474**	-1.046***	-0.709***	-0.709***	-0.910***	-0.539**	-0.539**	-1.017***	-0.524**	-0.524**	-1.243***	-0.761***	-0.761***
	(0.281)	(0.220)	(0.220)	(0.330)	(0.238)	(0.238)	(0.311)	(0.227)	(0.227)	(0.312)	(0.225)	(0.225)	(0.350)	(0.243)	(0.243)
High GVC Participation Total Effect (2012–14) [I + II]			1.732**			1.225*			0.861			0.322			0.183
			(0.730)			(0.741)			(1.189)			(1.300)			(0.792)
F-Test	3.720***	4.100***	3.240***	3.720***	4.080***	3.290***	4.340***	3.850***	3.010***	4.580***	2.630***	2.210***	3.550***	3.520***	2.890***
Analytical Weights	Yes	Yes	Yes	Yes	Yes	Yes	Yes	Yes	Yes	Yes	Yes	Yes	Yes	Yes	Yes
Country-Pair-Sectors	31,126	31,126	31,126	20,492	20,492	20,492	19,263	19,263	19,263	17,220	17,220	17,220	15,642	15,642	15,642
Number of Observations	364,968	364,968	364,968	252,064	252,064	252,064	229,799	229,799	229,799	204,260	204,260	204,260	202,293	202,293	202,293

Source: IMF staff calculations.
Note: Regressions allow (Eora Multi-Region Input-Output) sector-specific coefficients jointly estimated with standard errors clustered by country-pair-sector. GVC = global value chain. GVC participation is measured as foreign valued added in exports as share of gross exports. Weights are defined as levels of nominal imports.
[1] Dummy equaling 1 for those country-pair-sectors in the top quartile of the distribution of the mean of GVC participation across time (time invariant using period 2003–07 to compute the mean).
[2] Excludes commodity exporters.
[3] Keeps data from importers with national input-output tables; see Lenzen and others (2013).
[4] Uses the same importing-country sample employed in the product level analysis.
[5] Excludes commodity exporters and low-income countries, the commodity sector, and outlier values of GVC participation above 150 percent.
* $p < 0.10$; ** $p < 0.05$; *** $p < 0.01$.

Annex Table 2.6.2. Link between Global Value Chain Integration and Yearly Nominal Import Growth Using Gravity Model Estimated in Growth Rates

(Percentage points; year-over-year increase in nominal import growth for country-pair-sectors)

Dependent Variable	Unpredicted Bilateral Import Growth by Year (Gravity Model Estimated on Growth Rate of Nominal Imports), 2003–14														
	(Percent, year over year)														
	(1)	(2)[2]	(3)	(4)[2]	(5)[2]	(6)[2]	(7)[3]	(8)[3]	(9)[3]	(10)[4]	(11)[4]	(12)[4]	(13)[5]	(14)[5]	(15)[5]
GVC Participation ($t-1$)	0.023***						0.031***			0.032***			0.032***		
	(0.008)						(0.009)			(0.010)			(0.011)		
High GVC Participation Dummy[1] (2003–14)		1.647***			1.202**			1.067			2.131***			0.975*	
		(0.464)			(0.502)			(0.689)			(0.621)			(0.522)	
High GVC Participation Dummy[1] (pre-2012) [I]			1.559***			1.405**			1.397*			2.087***			1.530**
			(0.578)			(0.594)			(0.792)			(0.765)			(0.632)
High GVC Participation Dummy[1] × Post-2012 Dummy [II]			0.229			−0.517			−0.767			0.113			−1.408
			(0.886)			(0.851)			(1.364)			(1.474)			(0.887)
Constant	−0.598*	−0.464**	−0.464**	−0.925**	−0.651**	−0.651**	−1.017***	−0.451*	−0.451*	−1.075***	−0.547**	−0.547**	−1.335***	−0.837***	−0.837***
	(0.308)	(0.230)	(0.230)	(0.372)	(0.273)	(0.273)	(0.341)	(0.254)	(0.254)	(0.344)	(0.256)	(0.256)	(0.349)	(0.241)	(0.241)
High GVC Participation Total Effect (2012–14) [I + II]			1.788**			0.888			0.630			2.200*			0.122
			(0.712)			(0.730)			(1.154)			(1.165)			(0.741)
F-Test	4.810***	4.870***	4.310***	4.450***	3.680***	3.550***	5.210***	2.790***	2.590***	5.370***	2.770***	2.570***	3.890***	3.420***	3.680***
Analytical Weights	Yes	Yes	Yes	Yes	Yes	Yes	Yes	Yes	Yes	Yes	Yes	Yes	Yes	Yes	Yes
Country-Pair-Sectors	48,329	48,341	48,341	29,580	29,589	29,589	28,171	28,176	28,171	24,418	24,420	24,420	20,451	20,458	20,458
Number of Observations	446,968	448,302	448,302	297,500	298,202	298,202	266,479	266,992	266,479	231,657	232,040	232,040	228,559	228,954	228,954

Source: IMF staff calculations.

Note: Regressions allow (Eora Multi-Region Input-Output) sector-specific coefficients jointly estimated with standard errors clustered by country-pair-sector. GVC = global value chain. GVC participation is measured as foreign valued added in exports as share of gross exports. Weights are defined as levels of nominal imports.

[1] Dummy equaling 1 for those country-pair-sectors in the top quartile of the distribution of the mean of GVC participation across time (time invariant using period 2003–07 to compute the mean).

[2] Excludes commodity exporters.

[3] Keeps data from importers with national input-output tables; see Lenzen and others (2013).

[4] Uses the same importing-country sample employed in the product level analysis.

[5] Excludes commodity exporters and low-income countries, the commodity sector, and outlier values of GVC participation above 150 percent.

* $p < 0.10$; ** $p < 0.05$; *** $p < 0.01$.

References

Ahn, JaeBin, Era Dabla-Norris, Romain Duval, Bingjie Hu, and Lamin Njie. 2016. "Reassessing the Productivity Gains from Trade Liberalization: A Sector-Level Approach." IMF Working Paper 16/77, International Monetary Fund, Washington.

Ahn, JaeBin, and Romain Duval. Forthcoming. "Global Trade and Productivity Slowdown: Are They Related?" IMF Working Paper, International Monetary Fund, Washington.

Alessandria, George, and Horag Choi. 2016. "The Dynamics of the U.S. Trade Balance and Real Exchange Rate: The J Curve and Trade Costs?" Unpublished.

Alessandria, George, Joseph Kaboski, and Virgiliu Midrigan. 2013. "Trade Wedges, Inventories and International Business Cycles." *Journal of Monetary Economics* 60: 1–20.

Amiti, Mary, and Jozef Konings. 2007. "Trade Liberalization, Intermediate Inputs, and Productivity: Evidence from Indonesia." *American Economic Review* 97 (5): 1611–38.

Anderson, James E. 2011. "The Gravity Model." *Annual Review of Economics* 3 (1): 133–60.

Arvis, Jean-Francois, Yann Duval, Ben Shepherd, and Chorthip Utoktham. 2013. "Trade Costs in the Developing World, 1995–2010." World Bank Policy Research Working Paper 6309, World Bank, Washington.

Atkin, David, Amit K. Khandelwal, and Adam Osman. 2014. "Exporting and Firm Performance: Evidence from a Randomized Trial." NBER Working Paper 20690, National Bureau of Economic Research, Cambridge, Massachusetts.

Autor, David, David Dorn, and Gordon Hanson. 2013. "The China Syndrome: Local Labor Market Effects of Import Competition in the United States." *American Economic Review* 103 (6): 2121–68.

Baier, Scott L., and Jeffrey H. Bergstrand. 2007. "Do Free Trade Agreements Actually Increase Members' International Trade?" *Journal of International Economics* 71: 72–95.

———. 2009. "Estimating the Effects of Free Trade Agreements on Trade Flows Using Matching Econometrics." *Journal of International Economics* 77 (1): 63–76.

Bernard, Andrew B., Jonathan Eaton, J. Bradford Jensen, and Samuel Kortum. 2003. "Trade Costs, Firms and Productivity." *Journal of Monetary Economics* 53 (5): 917–37.

Bernard, Andrew B., and J. Bradford Jensen. 1995. "Exporters, Jobs, and Wages in U.S. Manufacturing: 1976–87." *Brookings Papers on Activity: Microeconomics*: 67–112.

Bernard, Andrew B., J. Bradford Jensen, Stephen J. Redding, and Peter K. Schott. 2007. "Firms in International Trade." *Journal of Economic Perspectives* 21 (3): 105–30.

Bernard, Andrew B., J. Bradford Jensen, and Peter K. Schott. 2006. "Plants and Productivity in International Trade." *American Economic Review* 93 (4): 1268–90.

Bernard, Andrew B., Stephen Redding, and Peter K. Schott. 2011. "Multi-Product Firms and Trade Liberalization." *Quarterly Journal of Economics* 126 (3): 1271–1318.

Bloom, Nicholas, Mirko Draca, and John Van Reenen. 2016. "Trade Induced Technical Change? The Impact of Chinese Imports on Innovation, IT and Productivity." *Review of Economic Studies* 83 (1): 87–117.

Bown, Chad P. 2011. "Taking Stock of Antidumping, Safeguards and Countervailing Duties, 1990–2009." *The World Economy* 34 (12): 1955–98.

———. 2016. "Temporary Trade Barriers Database." June. World Bank, Washington. http://econ.worldbank.org/ttbd/.

Boz, Emine, Matthieu Bussière, and Clément Marsilli. 2015. "Recent Slowdown in Global Trade: Cyclical or Structural?" Chapter 3 of *The Global Trade Slowdown: A New Normal?* edited by Bernard Hoekman. Vox EU E-book. London: Centre for Economic Policy Research Press. http://www.voxeu.org/article/recent-slowdown-global-trade.

Boz, Emine, and Eugenio Cerutti. Forthcoming. "Dissecting the Global Trade Slowdown: A New Database." Unpublished.

Broda, Christian, and David E. Weinstein. 2006. "Globalization and the Gains from Variety." *Quarterly Journal of Economics* 121 (2): 541–85.

Bussière, Matthieu, Giovanni Callegari, Fabio Ghironi, Giulia Sestieri, and Norihiko Yamano. 2013. "Estimating Trade Elasticities: Demand Composition and the Trade Collapse of 2008–09." *American Economic Journal: Macroeconomics* 5 (3): 118–51.

Bustos, Paula. 2011. "Trade Liberalization, Exports, and Technology Upgrading: Evidence on the Impact of MERCOSUR on Argentinian Firms." *American Economic Review* 101 (1): 304–40.

Carrère, Céline. 2006. "Revisiting the Effects of Regional Trade Agreements on Trade Flows with Proper Specification of the Gravity Model." *European Economic Review* 50: 223–47.

Chari, Varadarajan V., Patrick J. Kehoe, and Ellen McGrattan. 2007. "Business Cycle Accounting." *Econometrica* 75 (3): 781–836.

Chor, Davin, and Kalina Manova. 2012. "Off the Cliff and Back? Credit Conditions and International Trade during the Global Financial Crisis." *Journal of International Economics* 87 (1): 117–133.

Cipollina, Maria, and Luca Salvatici. 2010. "Reciprocal Trade Agreements in Gravity Models: A Meta-Analysis." *Review of International Economics* 18 (1): 63–80.

Conconi, Paola, Manuel García-Santana, Laura Puccio, and Roberto Venturini. 2016. "From Final Goods to Inputs: The Protectionist Effect of Preferential Rules of Origin." CEPR Discussion Paper 11084, Center for Economic and Policy Research, Washington.

Constantinescu, Cristina, Aaditya Mattoo, and Michele Ruta. 2015. "The Global Trade Slowdown: Cyclical or Structural?" IMF Working Paper 15/6, International Monetary Fund, Washington.

———. 2016. "Does the Global Trade Slowdown Matter?" World Bank Policy Research Working Paper 7673, World Bank, Washington.

Costinot, Arnaud, and Andres Rodriguez-Clare. 2014. "Trade Theory with Numbers: Quantifying the Consequences of Globalization." Chapter 4 in *Handbook of International Economics* 4: 197–261.

Council of Economic Advisers. 2015. "The Economic Benefits of U.S. Trade." Chapter 7 of the *Economic Report of the President*, Washington.

Crozet, Matthieu, Charlotte Emlinger, and Sébastien Jean. 2015. "On the Gravity of World Trade's Slowdown." Chapter 9 of *The Global Trade Slowdown: A New Normal?*, edited by Bernard Hoekman. Vox EU E-book. London: Centre for Economic Policy Research Press. http://www.voxeu.org/sites/default/files/file/Global%20Trade%20Slowdown_nocover.pdf.

De Loecker, Jan. 2007. "Do Exports Generate Higher Productivity? Evidence from Slovenia." *Journal of International Economics* 73 (1): 69–98.

———. 2013. "Detecting Learning by Exporting." *American Economic Journal: Microeconomics* 5 (3): 1–21.

Dekle, Robert, Jonathan Eaton, and Samuel Kortum. 2007. "Unbalanced Trade." *American Economic Review: Papers and Proceedings* 67 (4): 351–55.

Dixit, Avinash K., and Victor Norman. 1980. *Theory of International Trade: A Dual, General Equilibrium Approach.* Cambridge: Cambridge University Press.

Djankov, Simeon, Caroline Freund, and Cong S. Pham. 2010. "Trading on Time." *The Review of Economics and Statistics* 92 (1): 166–73.

Eaton, Jonathan, and Samuel Kortum. 2002. "Technology, Geography, and Trade." *Econometrica* 70 (5): 1741–79.

———, Brent Neiman, and John Romalis. 2010. "Trade and the Global Recession." National Bank of Belgium Working Paper Research 196, October, Brussels.

———. Forthcoming. "Trade and the Global Recession." *American Economic Review*.

Ebenstein, Avraham, Ann Harrison, Margaret McMillan, and Shannon Phillips. 2014. "Estimating the Impact of Trade and Offshoring on American Workers Using the Current Population Surveys." *The Review of Economics and Statistics* 96 (3): 581–95.

Erdem, Erkan, and James Tybout. 2003. "Trade Policy and Industrial Sector Responses: Using Evolutionary Models to Interpret the Evidence." NBER Working Paper 9947, National Bureau of Economic Research, Cambridge, Massachusetts.

Ethier, Wifred J. 1985. *Modern International Economics.* New York: W.W. Norton and Company.

Evenett, Simon J., and Johannes Fritz. 2015. "The Tide Turns? Trade Protectionism and Slowing Global Growth." Global Trade Alert, Centre for Economic Policy Research Press.

———. 2016. "Global Trade Plateaus." Global Trade Alert, Centre for Economic Policy Research Press.

Fajgelbaum, Pablo, and Amit Khandelwal. 2016. "Measuring the Unequal Gains from Trade." *Quarterly Journal of Economics* 131(3): 1113–80.

Feenstra, Robert C., James R. Markusen, and Andrew K. Rose. 2001. "Using the Gravity Equation to Differentiate among Alternative Theories of Trade." *Canadian Journal of Economics* 34 (2): 430–47.

Feyrer, James. 2009a. "Distance, Trade, and Income—The 1967 to 1975 Closing of the Suez Canal as a Natural Experiment." NBER Working Paper 15557, National Bureau of Economic Research, Cambridge, Massachusetts.

———. 2009b. "Trade and Income—Exploiting Time Series in Geography." NBER Working Paper 14910, National Bureau of Economic Research, Cambridge, Massachusetts.

Fontagné, Lionel, Amélie Guillin, and Cristina Mitaritonna. 2011. "Estimations of Tariff Equivalents for the Services Sectors." CEPII Document de Travail 2011–24, CEPII, Paris.

Frankel, Jeffrey, and David Romer. 1999. "Does Trade Cause Growth?" *American Economic Review* 89 (3): 379–99.

Freund, Caroline. 2016. "The Global Trade Slowdown and Secular Stagnation." Peterson Institute of International Economics blog. https://piie.com/blogs/trade-investment-policy-watch/global-trade-slowdown-and-secular-stagnation.

Gangnes, Byron, Alyson Ma, and Ari Van Assche. 2015. "Global Value Chains and Trade-Income Relationship: Implications for the Recent Trade Slowdown." Chapter 6 of *The Global Trade Slowdown: A New Normal?*, edited by Bernard Hoekman. Vox EU E-book. London: Centre for Economic Policy Research Press. http://www.voxeu.org/article/recent-slowdown-global-trade.

Goldberg, Pinelopi, and Nina Pavcnik. 2004. "Trade, Inequality, and Poverty: What Do We Know? Evidence from Recent Trade Liberalization Episodes in Developing Countries." *Brookings Trade Forum* 2004, 223–69.

———. 2007. "Distributional Effects of Globalization in Developing Countries." *Journal of Economic Literature* 45 (1): 39–82.

———. 2016. "The Effects of Trade Policy." Chapter 3 in *Handbook of Commercial Policy*, edited by Kyle Bagwell and Robert W. Staiger. New York: Elsevier North Holland.

González, Anabel. 2013. "Executive Summary." In *Foreign Direct Investment as a Key Driver for Trade, Growth and Prosperity: The Case for a Multilateral Agreement on Investment.* Global Agenda Council on Global Trade and FDI, World Economic Forum, Geneva.

Grossman, Gene, and Elhanan Helpman. 1991. *Innovation and Growth in the Global Economy.* Cambridge, Massachusetts: MIT Press.

Head, Keith, Thierry Mayer, and John Ries. 2010. "The Erosion of Colonial Trade Linkages after Independence." *Journal of International Economics* 81 (1): 1–14.

Head, Keith, and John Ries. 2001. "Increasing Returns versus National Product Differentiation as an Explanation for the Pattern of U.S.-Canada Trade." *American Economic Review* 91: 858–76.

Helpman, Elhanan, Oleg Itskhoki, Marc-Andreas Muendler, and Stephen Redding. Forthcoming. "Trade and Inequality: From Theory to Estimation." *The Review of Economic Studies*.

Helpman, Elhanan, and Paul Krugman. 1985. *Market Structure and Foreign Trade: Increasing Returns, Imperfect Competition, and the International Economy*. Cambridge, Massachusetts: MIT Press.

Henn, Christian, and Brad McDonald. 2014. "Crisis Protectionism: The Observed Trade Impact." *IMF Economic Review* 62 (1): 77–118.

Henn, Christian, and Arevik Mkrtchyan. 2015. "The Layers of the IT Agreement's Trade Impact." WTO Staff Working Paper ERSD-2015-01, World Trade Organization, Geneva.

Hicks, John. 1935. "Annual Survey of Economic Theory: The Theory of Monopoly." *Econometrica* 3 (1): 1–20.

Hillberry, Russell, and David Hummels. 2013. "Trade Elasticity Parameters for a Computable General Equilibrium Model." *Handbook of Computable General Equilibrium Modeling* 1: 1213–69.

Hoekman, Bernard, editor. 2015. *The Global Trade Slowdown: A New Normal?* Vox EU E-book. London: Center for Economic and Policy Research Press. http://voxeu.org/sites/default/files/file/Global%20Trade%20Slowdown_nocover.pdf.

Hong, Gee Hee, Jaewoo Lee, Wei Liao, and Dulani Seneviratne. 2016. "China and Asia in the Global Trade Slowdown." IMF Working Paper 16/105, International Monetary Fund, Washington.

Hufbauer, Gary C., and Euijin Jung. 2016. "Why Has Trade Stopped Growing? Not Much Liberalization and Lots of Micro-Protection." Peterson Institute of International Economics blog.

Hummels, David. 2007a. "Transportation Costs and International Trade in the Second Era of Globalization." *Journal of Economic Perspectives* 21 (3): 131–54.

———. 2007b. "Calculating Tariff Equivalents for Time in Trade." USAID Report, U.S. Agency for International Development, Washington, March.

———, Jun Ishii, and Kei-Mu Yi. 2001. "The Nature and Growth of Vertical Specialization in World Trade." *Journal of International Econom*ics 54 (1): 75–96.

International Chamber of Commerce. 2015. "Rethinking Trade and Finance." Paris, France.

International Monetary Fund. 2008. "Structural Reforms and Economic Performance in Advanced and Developing Countries." Research Department paper, Washington. https://www.imf.org/external/np/res/docs/2008/pdf/061008.pdf.

———. 2015a. "Global Value Chains: Where Are You? The Missing Link in Sub-Saharan Africa's Trade Integration." Chapter 3 of the April 2015 *Regional Economic Outlook: Sub-Saharan Africa*, Washington. https://www.imf.org/external/pubs/ft/reo/2015/afr/eng/pdf/chap3.pdf.

———. 2015b. "Private Investment: What's the Holdup?" Chapter 3 of the *World Economic Outlook*, Washington, April.

———. 2015c. "Review of the Role of Trade in the Work of the Fund." IMF Staff Report, Washington.

———. 2015d. "Trade Integration in Latin America and the Caribbean: Hype, Hope, and Reality." Chapter 4 of the *Regional Economic Outlook: Western Hemisphere*, Washington, October. http://www.imf.org/external/pubs/ft/reo/2015/whd/eng/wreo1015.htm.

———. 2015e. "Understanding the Role of Cyclical and Structural Factors in the Global Trade Slowdown." Box 1.2 of the *World Economic Outlook*, Washington, April.

———. 2016a. "Is the WTO a World Tax Organization? A Primer on WTO Rules for Tax Policymakers." IMF Technical Notes and Manuals, 16/03, International Monetary Fund, Washington.

———. 2016b. "Reinvigorating Trade to Support Growth: A Path Forward." Note for Ministers and Governors for the July G-20 Ministerial.

———. 2016c. "The Potential Productivity Gains from Further Trade and Foreign Direct Investment Liberalization." Box 3.3 of the April 2016 *World Economic Outlook*, Washington.

Jääskelä, Jarkko, and Thomas Mathews. 2015. "Explaining the Slowdown in Global Trade." Reserve Bank of Australia Bulletin, September, 39–46.

Jones, Ronald W. 1971. "A Three-Factor Model in Theory, Trade and History." Chapter 1 in *Trade, Balance of Payments and Growth*, edited by Jagdish Bhagwati, Ronald Jones, Robert Mundell, and Jaroslav Vanek. Amsterdam: North-Holland.

Kee, Hiau Looi, and Heiwai Tang. 2016. "Domestic Value Added in Exports: Theory and Firm Evidence from China." *American Economic Review* 106 (6): 1402–36.

Koopman, Robert, Zhi Wang, and Shang-Jin Wei. 2014. "Tracing Value-Added and Double Counting in Gross Exports." *American Economic Review* 104 (2): 459–94.

Krugman, Paul. 1979. "A Model of Innovation, Technology Transfer, and the World Distribution of Income." *Journal of Political Economy* 87 (2): 253–66.

———. 1980. "Scale Economies, Product Differentiation, and the Pattern of Trade." *American Economic Review* 70 (5): 950–59.

Laeven, Luc, and Fabián Valencia. 2012. "Systemic Banking Crises Database: An Update." IMF Working Paper 12/163, International Monetary Fund, Washington.

Lawrence, Robert Z. 2014. "Adjustment Challenges for US Workers." Chapter 3 in *Bridging the Pacific: Toward Free Trade and Investment between China and the United States*, edited by C. Fred Bergsten, Gary Clyde Hufbauer, and Sean Miner. Washington: Peterson Institute for International Economics.

Lee, Jong-Wha. 1993. "International Trade, Distortions, and Long-Run Economic Growth." *IMF Staff Papers* 40 (2): 299–328.

Lenzen, Manfred, Daniel Moran, Keiichiro Kanemoto, and Arne Geschke. 2013. "Building EORA: A Global Multi-Region Input-Output Database at High Country and Sector Resolution." *Economic Systems Research* 25 (1): 20–41.

Levchenko, Andrei, Logan Lewis, and Linda Tesar. 2010. "The Collapse of International Trade during the 2008–09 Crisis: In

Search of the Smoking Gun." *IMF Economic Review* 58 (2): 214–53.

Levchenko, Andrei, and Jing Zhang. 2013. "The Global Labor Market Impact of Emerging Giants: A Quantitative Assessment." *IMF Economic Review* 61 (3): 479–519.

Lileeva, Alla, and Daniel Trefler. 2010. "Improved Access to Foreign Markets Raises Plant-Level Productivity…For Some Plants." *The Quarterly Journal of Economics* 125 (3): 1051–99.

Ludema, Rodney, Anna Maria Mayda, and Prachi Mishra. 2015. "Information and Legislative Bargaining: The Political Economy of U.S. Tariff Suspensions." Unpublished manuscript, Georgetown University, Washington.

Magdeleine, Joscelyn, and Andreas Maurer. 2016. "Understanding Trade in Digitized Idea – What are the Statistical Challenges?" WTO Working Paper ERSD-2016-11, World Trade Organization.

Manyika, James, Susan Lund, Jacques Bughin, Jonathan Woetzel, Kalin Stamenov, and Dhruv Dhingra. 2016. "Digital Globalization: The New Era of Global Flows." McKinsey Global Institute.

Martinez-Martin, Jaime. 2016. "Breaking Down World Trade Elasticities: A Panel ECM Approach." Bank of Spain Working Paper 1614, Bank of Spain, Madrid.

Mavroidis, Petros. 2016. "Regulatory Cooperation." Policy Options Paper for the E15 Initiative.

Melitz, Marc J. 2003. "The Impact of Trade on Intra-Industry Reallocations and Aggregate Industry Productivity." *Econometrica* 71 (6): 1695–1725.

———, and Gianmarco Ottaviano. 2008. "Market Size, Trade, and Productivity." *Review of Economic Studies* 75: 295–316.

Melitz, Marc J., and Stephen J. Redding. 2014. "Heterogeneous Firms and Trade." *Handbook of International Economics* 1–54.

Morel, Louis. 2015. "Sluggish Exports in Advanced Economies: How Much is Due to Demand?" Bank of Canada Discussion Paper 2015–3, Bank of Canada, Ottawa.

Mussa, Michael. 1974. "Tariffs and the Distribution of Income: The Importance of Factor Specificity, Substitutability, and Intensity in the Short and Long Run." *Journal of Political Economy* 82 (6): 1191–203.

Noguer, Marta, and Marc Siscart. 2005. "Trade Raises Income: A Precise and Robust Result." *Journal of International Economics* 65: 447–60.

Novy, Dennis. 2012. "Gravity Redux: Measuring International Trade Costs with Panel Data." *Economic Inquiry* 51 (1): 101–21.

Ollivaud, Patrice, and Cyrille Schwellnus. 2015. "Does the Post-Crisis Weakness in Global Trade Solely Reflect Weak Demand?" OECD Economics Department Working Paper No. 1216, OECD, Paris.

Organisation for Economic Co-operation and Development (OECD). 2015a. *Business and Finance Outlook 2015*. Paris: OECD.

———. 2015b. "Emerging Policy Issues: Localising Data in a Globalised World – Methodology." TAD/TC/WP (2015) 7. Paris: OECD.

Osnago, Alberto, Nadia Rocha, and Michele Ruta. Forthcoming. "Do Deep Trade Agreements Boost Vertical FDI?" *World Bank Economic Review*.

Pavcnik, Nina. 2002. "Trade Liberalization, Exit, and Productivity Improvements: Evidence from Chilean Plants." *Review of Economic Studies* 69 (1): 245–76.

Ricardo, David. 1817. *On the Principles of Political Economy and Taxation*. In *The Works and Correspondence of David Ricardo*, 11 vols, edited by Piero Sraffa, with the collaboration of M. H. Dobb. Cambridge: Cambridge University Press.

Rivera-Batiz, Luis A., and Paul M. Romer. 1991. "Economic Integration and Endogenous Growth." *Quarterly Journal of Economics* 106 (2): 531–55.

Rodríguez, Francisco R., and Dani Rodrik. 2001. "Trade Policy and Economic Growth: A Skeptic's Guide to the Cross-National Evidence." *NBER Macroeconomics Annual* 2000 15: 261–338.

Rose, Andrew K. 2002. "Estimating Protectionism through Residuals from the Gravity Model." Background paper for the October 2002 *World Economic Outlook*. http%3A%2F%2F-faculty.haas.berkeley.edu%2Farose%2FWEO.pdf&usg=AFQjCNH9us3oDmhsUdLt274yVtFyaw-bQA-&sig2=uJfzpfrxQLFSmdB5E-Jtsg&bvm=bv.126130881,d.dmo.

Sachs, Jeffrey, and Andrew Warner. 1995. "Economic Reform and the Process of Global Integration." *Brookings Papers on Economic Activity* 1: 1–95.

Slopek, Ulf. 2015. "Why Has the Income Elasticity of Global Trade Declined?" Deutsche Bundesbank, Economics Department, unpublished manuscript.

Stolper, Wolfgang F., and Paul A. Samuelson. 1941. "Protection and Real Wages." *The Review of Economic Studies* 9 (1): 58–73.

Topalova, Petia, and Amit Khandelwal. 2011. "Trade Liberalization and Firm Productivity: The Case of India." *The Review of Economics and Statistics* 93 (3): 995–1009.

United Nations Conference on Trade and Development. 2013. "Global Value Chains: Investment and Trade for Development." *World Investment Report 2013*, New York and Geneva.

Volpe Martincus, Christian, Jerónimo Carballo, and Alejandro Graziano. 2015. "Customs." *Journal of International Economics* 96: 119–37.

World Bank. 2010. *Trade Adjustment Costs in Developing Countries: Impacts, Determinants and Policy Responses*, edited by Guido Porto and Bernard M. Hoekman. Washington: World Bank.

World Trade Organization. 2015. "World Trade Report 2015: Speeding Up Trade: Benefits and Challenges of Implementing the WTO Trade Facilitation Agreement." Geneva: World Trade Organization.

Yi, Kei-Mu. 2003. "Can Vertical Specialization Explain the Growth of World Trade?" *Journal of Political Economy* 111 (1): 52–102.

———. 2010. "Can Multistage Production Explain the Home Bias in Trade?" *American Economic Review* 100 (1): 364–93.

Young, Alwyn. 1991. "Learning by Doing and the Dynamic Effects of International Trade." *Quarterly Journal of Economics* 106 (2): 369–405.

3

GLOBAL DISINFLATION IN AN ERA OF CONSTRAINED MONETARY POLICY

Inflation has declined markedly in many economies over the past few years. This chapter finds that disinflation is broad based across countries, measures, and sectors—albeit larger for tradable goods than for services. The main drivers of recent disinflation are persistent economic slack and softening commodity prices. Most of the available measures of medium-term inflation expectations have not declined substantially so far. However, the sensitivity of expectations to inflation surprises—an indicator of the degree of anchoring of inflation expectations—has increased in countries where policy rates have approached their effective lower bounds. While the magnitude of this change in sensitivity is modest, it does suggest that the perceived ability of monetary policy to combat persistent disinflation may be diminishing in these economies.

Inflation rates in many economies have steadily declined toward historically low levels in recent years (Figure 3.1). By 2015, inflation rates in more than 85 percent of a broad sample of more than 120 economies were below long-term expectations, and about 20 percent were in deflation—that is, facing a fall in the aggregate price level for goods and services (Figure 3.2). While the recent decline in inflation coincided with a sharp drop in oil and other commodity prices, core inflation—which excludes the more volatile categories of food and energy prices—has remained below central bank targets for several consecutive years in most of the major advanced economies.

Disinflation can have multiple explanations and is not necessarily a cause for concern. For instance, a temporary decline in inflation due to a supply-driven decline in energy prices can be beneficial to the overall economy. Even when low demand is behind a temporary disinflation, its negative implications may not

necessarily go beyond those of depressed demand itself. However, if persistently low inflation leads firms and households to revise down their beliefs about the future path of inflation, it can have negative implications. In particular, if medium-term inflation expectations drift down significantly, a deflationary cycle may emerge in which weak demand and deflation reinforce each other. Eventually, the economy may end up in a deflation trap—a state of persistent deflation that prevents the real interest rate from decreasing to the level consistent with full employment. Moreover, even if deflation is avoided, a persistent downward shift in inflation to very low levels would not be desirable: lower nominal interest rates would leave little room to ease monetary policy if needed, the economy would still not be far from slipping into deflation and, given stickiness in wages, a weakening in demand would be more likely to cause large job losses.

The risk of disinflation potentially leading to a deflation trap or to persistently weak inflation is closely related to whether monetary policy is perceived to be effective in ensuring that inflation converges to its objective once temporary effects fade. At the current juncture, the ability of central banks to keep inflation expectations anchored could be challenged by several factors. First, the scope of monetary policy to further stimulate demand is perceived to be increasingly constrained in many advanced economies where policy rates are not far from their effective lower bounds. Second, in many countries, the weakness in inflation to some extent reflects price developments abroad—in particular substantial slack in tradable goods–producing sectors in several large economies.[1] Although domestic monetary policy can do little to combat deflation pressure from abroad, its credibility may end up undermined if weakness in import prices combines with weak demand at home to keep inflation

The authors of this chapter are Samya Beidas-Strom, Sangyup Choi, Davide Furceri (lead author), Bertrand Gruss, Sinem Kılıç Çelik, Zsoka Koczan, Ksenia Koloskova, and Weicheng Lian, with contributions from Jaebin Ahn, Elif Arbatli, Luis Catão, Juan Angel Garcia Morales, Keiko Honjo, Benjamin Hunt, Douglas Laxton, Niklas Westelius, and Fan Zhang, and support from Hao Jiang and Olivia Ma. Refet Gürkaynak was the external consultant for the chapter. Comments from Jesper Linde and Signe Krogstrup are gratefully acknowledged.

[1]Investment in tradable goods sectors in some large economies, notably China, grew strongly in the aftermath of the global financial crisis, in part because of a sizable macroeconomic policy stimulus. The increase in investment was underpinned by a path of projected global and domestic demand that subsequently fell short of expectations, leaving several manufacturing sectors with substantial overcapacity (see IMF 2016b).

Figure 3.1. Oil Prices and Consumer Price Inflation
(Percent)

Inflation has steadily declined toward historically low levels in recent years, both in advanced and emerging market economies.

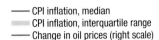

— CPI inflation, median
▨ CPI inflation, interquartile range
— Change in oil prices (right scale)

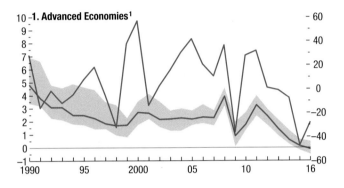

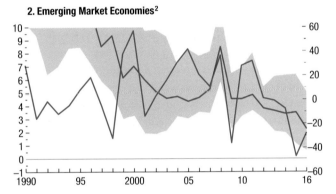

Sources: Haver Analytics; and IMF staff calculations.
Note: CPI = consumer price index.
[1] Australia, Austria, Belgium, Canada, Czech Republic, Denmark, Estonia, Finland, France, Germany, Greece, Hong Kong SAR, Iceland, Ireland, Israel, Italy, Japan, Korea, Latvia, Lithuania, Luxembourg, Netherlands, New Zealand, Norway, Portugal, Singapore, Slovak Republic, Slovenia, Spain, Sweden, Switzerland, United Kingdom, United States.
[2] Argentina, Brazil, Bulgaria, Chile, China, Colombia, Dominican Republic, Ecuador, Egypt, Hungary, India, Indonesia, Jordan, Kazakhstan, Malaysia, Mexico, Morocco, Peru, Philippines, Poland, Romania, Russia, South Africa, Thailand, Turkey, Venezuela.

rates persistently below target. After a long period of stability, certain measures of medium-term inflation expectations have indeed fallen in some advanced economies—especially after the decline in oil prices in 2014 (Figure 3.3).[2] Against this backdrop, there is a growing concern that further disinflationary shocks

---

[2]As measured by inflation compensation embedded in long-maturity nominal bonds or swaps.

Figure 3.2. Share of Countries with Low Inflation
(Percent)

A large number of countries are currently facing low inflation or even deflation.

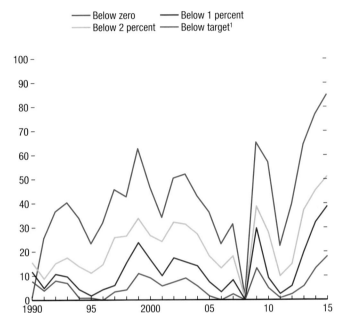

— Below zero   — Below 1 percent
— Below 2 percent   — Below target[1]

Sources: Consensus Economics; and IMF staff calculations.
Note: The figure is based on an unbalanced sample of 120 countries.
[1] Target refers to long-term inflation expectations from Consensus Economics (10-year inflation expectations) or inflation forecasts from the World Economic Outlook database (5-year inflation expectations).

could keep inflation persistently low and eventually lead to deflation trap conditions.

To assess these risks and contribute to the policy debate, this chapter investigates the following questions:

- How widespread is the recent decline in inflation across countries? Does the extent of the decline vary by type of measure—headline, core, wages—and by sector?

- Can the weakening in commodity prices and economic slack explain recent inflation dynamics? What is the role of other factors, including cross-border spillovers from industrial slack in large economies?[3]

---

[3]Industrial slack in light and heavy industries (including commodities)—generated either by weak demand or an excess of supply stemming from previous overinvestment—results in lower producer prices and, in the case of traded goods, lower export prices. Several studies point to marked overcapacity in a range of industrial sectors (National Association of Manufacturers 2016; Organisation for Economic Co-operation and Development 2015). Estimates presented in Box 3.1 suggest that industrial slack in the first quarter of 2016

Figure 3.3. Medium-Term Inflation Expectations and Oil Prices
(Percent, unless noted otherwise)

Medium-term inflation expectations have fallen over the recent past, especially since the sharp drop in oil prices in 2014.

—— Oil prices (year-over-year percent change, right scale)
—— Medium-term inflation expectations[1]

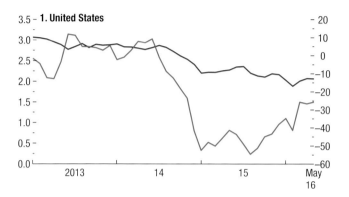

1. United States

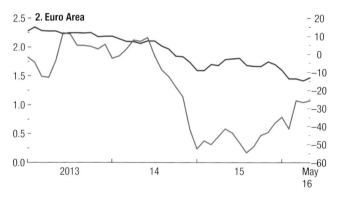

2. Euro Area

Sources: Bloomberg L.P.; and IMF staff calculations.
[1] Medium-term inflation expectations are based on five-year/five-year inflation swaps.

- Have inflation expectations become more sensitive to inflation outturns in recent years, especially in countries where monetary policy is perceived as being constrained? How large is the risk that a decline in inflation will lead to lower inflation expectations? How do monetary policy frameworks affect the degree of anchoring of inflation expectations?

The chapter starts by discussing the potential costs of persistently low inflation and deflation. Next, it examines the evolution of inflation across countries

stood at about 5.5 percent in China, 5 percent in Japan, and 3 percent in the United States.

and the factors driving it during the past decade. It then explores the sensitivity of inflation expectations to changes in inflation and the role of monetary policy frameworks in affecting this sensitivity.

The key findings of the chapter suggest that persistently below-target inflation poses downside risks and calls for a number of policy responses. Specifically,

- Disinflation is a broad-based phenomenon. Inflation has declined across many countries and regions, in both headline and core measures, but more markedly in tradable goods sectors than in services.

- Economic slack and changes in commodity prices are the main drivers of lower inflation since the Great Recession. In addition, industrial slack in large exporters (such as Japan, the United States, and especially China) may also have contributed to lower inflation by putting downward pressure on global prices of tradable goods (Box 3.1).[4] However, the recent decline in inflation goes beyond what these factors can explain—suggesting that inflation expectations may have dropped more than implied by available measures or that economic slack is greater than estimated in some countries.

- The response of inflation expectations to inflation surprises has been decreasing over the past couple of decades in both advanced and emerging market economies, partly as a result of improvements in monetary policy frameworks. The sensitivity remains larger among the latter, suggesting further scope for improvements in emerging market economies.

- However, in countries where monetary policy is constrained, inflation expectations have recently become more responsive to oil price changes or unexpected movements in inflation itself.

Many advanced economies with low inflation and persistent economic slack run the risk of chronically undershooting their inflation targets, which would erode the credibility of monetary policy. To avoid this risk, policymakers in these economies need to boost demand and firm up expectations. With limited policy space, a comprehensive and coordinated approach that exploits the complementarities among all available tools to boost demand and that amplifies the effects of individual policy actions through

[4] Industrial production in China, Japan, and the United States accounts for a significant share of total world industrial production (about 45 percent), which is even larger than the share of these economies in global GDP (about 38 percent).

positive cross-border spillovers would be the most effective (Gaspar, Obstfeld, and Sahay forthcoming). This approach should be centered on continued monetary policy accommodation to help keep medium-term inflation expectations anchored—including a transparent commitment to more aggressive accommodation where there are signs that expectations are becoming unanchored.[5] But monetary stimulus should be complemented with a combination of a more growth-friendly composition of fiscal policy, an expansionary fiscal stance in countries with credible medium-term fiscal frameworks and available fiscal space, and structural reforms that stimulate consumption and investment through higher expected incomes and profits. Income policies could be used in countries where wages are stagnant and deflation expectations appear entrenched (IMF 2016a). Distortionary policies that perpetuate overcapacity should be avoided as they not only worsen resource allocation—and weaken asset quality in the banking system where financed by credit—but also exert disinflationary pressures on other economies.

Although low inflation is a less pervasive phenomenon among emerging market economies, improving monetary policy frameworks is also a policy priority in many of these countries. Additional efforts to strengthen the credibility, independence, and effectiveness of central banks would improve the degree of anchoring of inflation expectations, enhancing the ability to fight deflationary forces in some cases and above-target inflation in others.

A Primer on the Costs of Disinflation, Persistently Low Inflation, and Deflation

Like high inflation, persistently low inflation, disinflation, and deflation can potentially have a severe impact on an economy. Whether they entail costs, and how large these costs are, depends on their underlying sources, their extent and duration, and,

most importantly, the degree of anchoring of inflation expectations.

Unexpected Disinflation

An unexpected decline in the inflation rate can harm demand in an economy with high debt by increasing the real debt burden of borrowers and the real interest rate they face—a phenomenon called "debt deflation"—and increase difficulties in achieving deleveraging (see the October 2016 *Fiscal Monitor*). The increase in the real burden of servicing debt would be more severe under outright deflation. While creditors' wealth rises with debt deflation, they are unlikely to increase their spending enough to offset the macroeconomic consequences of debtors' losses, meaning that debt deflation has a net negative effect on the economy (Fisher 1933). The reduction in collateral values—including house prices—that tends to accompany deflation can result in lower or negative equity, magnifying the problem through costly defaults. Debt deflation not only affects mortgage holders, firms, and banks, but also governments that hold long-maturity debt.[6]

Persistent Disinflation and the Deflation Trap

Persistently low inflation increases the possibility that an adverse shock will reduce the aggregate price level and tip the economy into a deflation trap. But falling into this trap is far from automatic. Inflation expectations would need to drop significantly for this to happen.

In periods of low inflation, even small disinflationary shocks can lead to a fall in the level of prices of goods and services. If economic agents expect prices to continue to fall, they can become less willing to spend—particularly on durable goods whose purchases can be postponed—since the ex-ante real interest rate increases and holding cash generates a positive real yield. Consumption and investment would be deferred farther into the future, leading to a contraction in aggregate demand that would in turn exacerbate deflation pressures. A deflation cycle would then emerge, with weak demand and deflation reinforcing each other, and the economy could end up in a deflation trap. In this context, the behavior of prices and output

---

[5]Several empirical studies have documented that certain unconventional monetary policies adopted in the aftermath of the Great Recession had significant impacts on inflation expectations or asset prices that convey information about these. In particular, a number of recent papers have found significant effects on break-even inflation rates (Guidolin and Neely 2010; Krishnamurthy and Vissing-Jorgensen 2011), survey-based inflation expectations (Hofmann and Zhu 2013), and firms' inflation expectations (Cloyne and others 2016), as well as on interest rates and asset prices (Krishnamurthy and Vissing-Jorgensen 2011; Swanson 2016; Wright 2012; Yu 2016).

[6]The effect on governments is especially important in the current environment because as debt rises, fiscal space is reduced. Persistently weak growth in the GDP deflator, and hence in nominal GDP, worsens the interest-rate-growth differential and contributes to a higher debt burden. See End and others (2015) for further details.

Figure 3.4. Effect of Disinflationary Shocks in Advanced Economies under Constrained Monetary Policy and Unanchored Inflation Expectations

(Years after the shock on x-axis)

Demand-driven deflationary shocks can have particularly large and persistent negative effects if monetary policy is constrained and inflation expectations become unanchored.

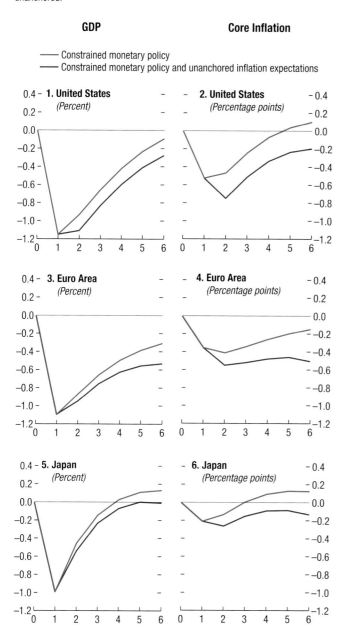

Source: IMF staff estimates.
Note: The figure reports the deviation of output and core inflation from their baseline path after a temporary decline in domestic demand. It is assumed that conventional monetary policy in all countries is constrained at the effective lower bound on nominal interest rates. The alternative scenario (red line) also assumes that inflation expectations are affected by inflation shocks in line with the empirical evidence presented in the chapter. See Annex 3.2 for further details.

could become unstable if monetary policy is constrained by the effective lower bound on interest rates (see, for instance, Benhabib, Schmitt-Grohé, and Uribe 2002; Cochrane 2016).[7] These difficulties are aggravated if fiscal policy cannot be readily and efficiently deployed to stimulate demand.

The capacity of monetary authorities to maintain medium-term inflation expectations anchored at the target (that is, persuade agents that inflation will eventually converge to the target once the effect of temporary factors fades out) is critical to mitigate such concerns. Indeed, model simulations in Annex 3.2 illustrate that even with constrained monetary policy, an economy would escape the deflation trap induced by a negative demand shock as long as medium-term inflation expectations were well anchored. But if expectations drifted down, it could take a very long time for the economy to emerge from deflation (Figure 3.4).[8]

Persistently Low Inflation

An environment of subdued but positive inflation could carry significant economic costs even if a deflation trap is avoided. A prolonged period of below-target inflation may lead to a belief that the central bank is willing to accept low inflation for longer, effectively reducing inflation expectations for the medium term to positive but below-target levels.

The main cost of this low-inflation environment is reduced effectiveness of monetary policy. Low inflation constrains the ability of monetary policy to respond to depressed demand. In a severe downturn, real interest

---

[7]Estimates of the probability of a situation of constrained monetary policy with unstable output and price dynamics vary substantially depending on the shocks considered. Previous studies find this probability to be nonnegligible and as high as 5–10 percent when inflation is around 2 percent and financial shocks similar to those in 2007–08 are considered (Blanco 2015; Chung and others 2012; Coibion, Gorodnichenko, and Wieland 2012; Williams 2014). While the probability associated with an episode of monetary policy at the effective lower bound lasting several years—as in the current juncture—is more difficult to estimate with existing models, it is likely to be larger than previous estimates and associated with greater economic costs.

[8]Many theoretical studies have examined the behavior of the economy in a long-lasting liquidity trap in a context in which prices are slow to move—or sticky—and have proposed distinct solutions to escape from it (Buiter and Panigirzoglous 1999; Cochrane 2016; Eggertsson and Woodford 2003; Svensson 2001; Werning 2012). The solutions range from a combination of devaluation, prolonged monetary policy accommodation, and price level targeting to more aggressive approaches, including negative interest rates or "helicopter money."

rates (the nominal rate minus the expected inflation rate) must decrease significantly to restore full employment and bring output back to its potential. With normal levels of inflation, a central bank can accomplish that by reducing the nominal policy interest rate, but when the economy is experiencing low inflation and nominal interest rates, the central bank would have little room to reduce real interest rates, even if it resorted to unconventional tools.[9]

A low-inflation environment may also lead to higher unemployment in the face of adverse demand shocks. When the demand for goods and services declines, firms seek to reduce costs. In this context, inflation facilitates adjustment because it pushes down real wages—even in the presence of downward nominal wage rigidity. Real wages would be less flexible under lower average inflation. In the context of low inflation, cost reduction by firms is more likely to take the form of job cuts (Akerlof, Dickens, and Perry 1996; Bernanke 2002; Calvo, Coricelli, and Ottonello 2012), because it is typically difficult to lower costs by reducing nominal wages.[10]

In Sum: Slow Growth?

While the above economic costs are difficult to quantify, the Great Depression and the more recent Japanese deflation experience (IMF 2003, Box 3.2) suggest that prolonged weak inflation and, especially, persistent deflation may dampen medium-term growth prospects.

Inflation Dynamics: Patterns and Recent Drivers

How Widespread Is the Decline in Inflation?

The evidence points to a broad-based decline in inflation across countries and regions as well as among different measures of inflation, but more markedly in manufacturing than in services. The breadth of the decline in inflation across countries and the fact that it is stronger in the tradable goods sectors underscore the global nature of disinflationary forces.

Headline Inflation

Inflation was surprisingly stable during the Great Recession (2008–10). Indeed, while previous recessions were usually associated with marked disinflation,

[9]Even if unconventional monetary policies such as quantitative easing are adopted, their effects on long-term interest rates and output are uncertain (Williams 2014).

[10]Bernanke and Bewley (1999) suggest that an important reason for the reluctance of firms to cut nominal wages is their belief that such cuts would harm workers' morale.

inflation proved broadly resilient among advanced economies even as unemployment rates climbed to multidecade highs.[11]

However, since 2011, inflation rates began to decline across many advanced and emerging market economies. Headline inflation—the change in the prices of a broad range of goods and services, including food and energy—recently reached historical lows in many countries (Figure 3.5; Box 3.3).[12] Moreover, many advanced economies—notably in the euro area—experienced outright deflation in 2015, and price declines became more widespread in the first quarter of 2016. In many emerging market economies, headline inflation also declined sharply following the drop in oil prices, despite large currency depreciations in some of these economies—even though in some of these economies inflation actually has recently increased, as evidenced by a relatively wider interquartile range in the past year (Figure 3.5, panels 2, 4, and 6).[13] Some emerging market economies with close links to the euro area or with exchange rates pegged to the euro also experienced some deflation. The evidence of a broad-based decline in headline inflation is supported by principal component analysis (Figure 3.6). The results of this analysis show that the contribution of the first common factor—a proxy for the "global" component—to the variation in headline inflation was broadly similar before and after the Great Recession for an entire sample of about 120 countries. However, the contribution increased substantially (from 47 percent to 60 percent) in advanced economies during 2009–15,

[11]Headline inflation did decline during the crisis, but rebounded quickly. A number of hypotheses were put forward to explain the resilience of inflation, or the missing disinflation—"*the dog that did not bark.*" These include improved credibility of central banks, which helped stabilize inflation outcomes by anchoring inflation expectations (Bernanke 2010); a more muted relationship between cyclical unemployment and inflation—implying a flatter Phillips curve (Chapter 3 of the April 2013 *World Economic Outlook*); and increased wage rigidity that prevented nominal wages from falling as much as during previous recessions. In addition, low inflation contributed to holding up real wages (Daly, Hobijn, and Lucking 2012), and the increase in commodity prices in 2011 may have partly offset the disinflationary impact of increased cyclical unemployment (Coibion and Gorodnichenko 2015).

[12]Box 3.3 explores the role of food price inflation and shows that in some economies, particularly emerging market and developing economies, the global deflation pressure from tradables was mitigated by low pass-through of international food prices to domestic headline inflation.

[13]In emerging market economies, headline inflation has been on a downward trend—in part due to improved monetary policy frameworks. Globalization may have helped reduce inflation in emerging market economies (IMF 2006) by limiting the ability of central banks to temporarily stimulate the economy (Rogoff 2003) and increasing the cost of imprudent macroeconomic policies through the adverse response of international capital flows (Tytell and Wei 2004).

Figure 3.5. Consumer Price Inflation
(Percent)

Inflation declined substantially during the global financial crisis in many countries but quickly rebounded afterward. Since 2011, however, there has been a broad - based slowdown in inflation across advanced and emerging market economies.

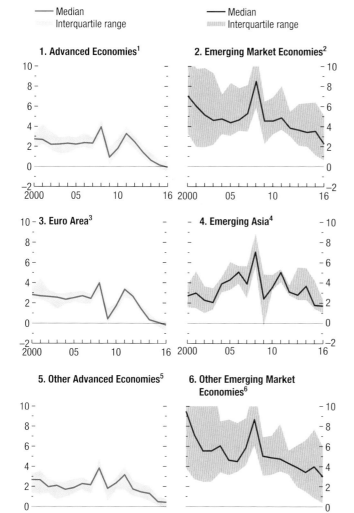

Sources: Haver Analytics; and IMF staff calculations.
Note: Labels in footnotes 1–6 below use International Organization for Standardization (ISO) country codes.
[1] AUS, AUT, BEL, CAN, CHE, CZE, DEU, DNK, ESP, EST, FIN, FRA, GRC, HKG, ISL, ITA, IRL, ISR, JPN, KOR, LVA, LTU, LUX, NLD, NOR, NZL, PRT, SGP, SVK, SVN, SWE, GBR, USA.
[2] ARG, BGR, BRA, CHN, CHL, COL, DOM, ECU, EGY, HUN, IND, IDN, JOR, KAZ, MAR, MEX, MYS, PER, PHL, POL, ROU, RUS, THA, TUR, VEN, ZAF.
[3] AUT, BEL, DEU, ESP, EST, FIN, FRA, GRE, IRL, ITA, LTU, LUX, LVA, NLD, PRT, SVK, SVN.
[4] CHN, IDN, IND, MYS, PHL, THA.
[5] AUS, CAN, CHE, CZE, DNK, GBR, ISL, ISR, JPN, KOR, NOR, NZL, SGP, SWE, USA.
[6] ARG, BGR, BRA, CHL, COL, DOM, ECU, EGY, HUN, JOR, KAZ, MAR, MEX, PER, POL, ROU, RUS, TUR, VEN, ZAF.

Figure 3.6. Share of Consumer Price Inflation Variation Explained by First Common Factor
(Percent)

The share of consumer price inflation variation across advanced economies that can be attributed to global factors increased during 2009–15.

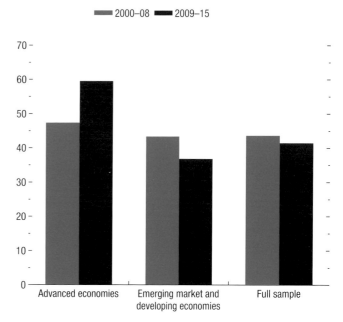

Source: IMF staff calculations.
Note: The figure reports the share of variation in headline consumer price inflation explained by the first common factor based on a principal component analysis. The sample comprises 120 economies, including 31 advanced economies.

likely reflecting the importance of large movements in commodity prices for headline inflation in largely net commodity importers and the synchronized increase in economic slack since the Great Recession (Annex 3.3).[14]

Core Inflation, Wages, and Sectoral Developments

Core inflation—the change in the prices of goods and services excluding food and energy—has also declined widely across countries and regions (Figure 3.7). This measure, which captures the underlying trend in inflation better than headline inflation, has recently been higher than headline inflation given the sharp decline in energy prices. However, core inflation has declined in all advanced economies to rates below central banks' targets and, since 2016, it has also done so in several emerging market economies.

[14]Additional analyses using Bayesian modeling average and weighted least squares confirm that commodity prices stand out among several variables as being strongly linked with the first common factor.

Figure 3.7. Core Consumer Price Inflation
(Percent)

The decline in core inflation over the past few years was broad based across regions.

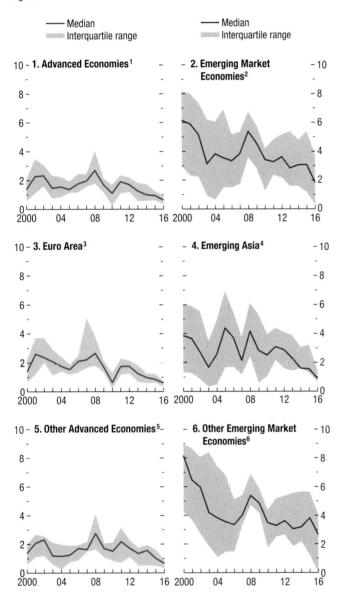

Sources: Haver Analytics; and IMF staff calculations.
Note: Labels in footnotes 1–6 below use International Organization for Standardization (ISO) country codes.
[1] AUS, AUT, BEL, CAN, CHE, CZE, DEU, DNK, ESP, EST, FIN, FRA, GRC, HKG, ISL, ITA, IRL, ISR, JPN, KOR, LVA, LTU, LUX, NLD, NOR, NZL, PRT, SGP, SVK, SVN, SWE, GBR, USA.
[2] ARG, BGR, BRA, CHN, CHL, COL, DOM, ECU, EGY, HUN, IND, IDN, JOR, KAZ, MAR, MEX, MYS, PER, PHL, POL, ROU, RUS, THA, TUR, VEN, ZAF.
[3] AUT, BEL, DEU, ESP, EST, FIN, FRA, GRE, IRL, ITA, LTU, LUX, LVA, NLD, PRT, SVK, SVN.
[4] CHN, IDN, IND, MYS, PHL, THA.
[5] AUS, CAN, CHE, CZE, DNK, GBR, ISL, ISR, JPN, KOR, NOR, NZL, SGP, SWE, USA.
[6] ARG, BGR, BRA, CHL, COL, DOM, ECU, EGY, HUN, JOR, KAZ, MAR, MEX, PER, POL, ROU, RUS, TUR, VEN, ZAF.

Wage growth has been increasing recently but remains subdued in many advanced economies despite some improvements in labor markets (Figure 3.8). One reason for the muted behavior, suggested by Daly and Hobijn (2015) for the United States, may be that many firms were unable to reduce wages enough to avoid job cuts during the 2008–09 recession, but as they resumed hiring thereafter, employers were able to keep a lid on wage gains to effectively work off "pent-up wage cuts." The cyclical slack in labor market participation rates may also have kept wages in check during the postrecession recovery.

Sectoral developments in producer prices in advanced economies show that, although inflation has recently softened in all sectors, the decline has been larger in manufacturing producer prices—a typical proxy for the price of tradable goods (Figure 3.9).[15] This may reflect a larger effect of lower commodity prices and lower import prices in manufacturing—given the larger commodity and imported input content in this sector (Box 3.4)—but, for some large advanced and emerging market economies, it is also associated with an increase in excess manufacturing capacity (Box 3.1).

While distinguishing tradable from nontradable components in consumer price indices is challenging, the comparison of inflation across expenditure categories provides supportive evidence that the recent decline in inflation in advanced economies has been substantially stronger in tradable goods (Figure 3.10). On average, the decline in goods inflation has been steeper than in the case of services. Indeed, there has been a widespread decline in the average price level of nonfood goods across advanced economies over the past two years. Instead, food price inflation has slowed but remains generally positive despite the decline in international food prices over the same period—suggesting a rather low pass-through from international to domestic food prices (Box 3.3).

Explaining the Recent Decline in Inflation

To what extent can declines in oil and other commodity prices and economic slack explain recent inflation patterns? How important is the cross-border transmission

[15]Producer price inflation for manufactured goods has, on average, been lower than total producer price inflation during 1990–2016, while business services inflation has been higher (IMF 2006). Together, manufacturing, business services, and utilities services account for about 70 percent of a typical advanced economy in the sample. The other sectors are agriculture, mining, construction, and social and personal services (including government).

Figure 3.8. Wage Inflation in Advanced Economies
(Year-over-year percent change of nominal wages)

Despite improvements in labor markets, wage growth remains subdued in many advanced economies.

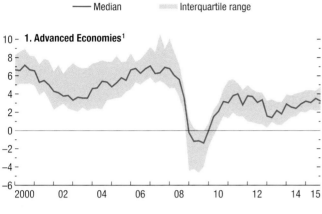

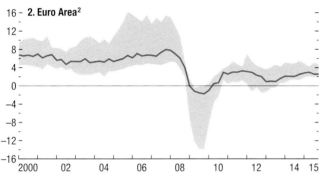

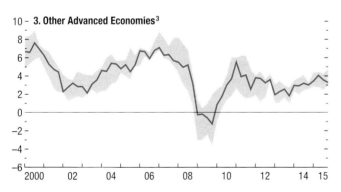

Sources: Organisation for Economic Co-operation and Development; and IMF staff calculations.
[1] Australia, Austria, Canada, Czech Republic, Denmark, Estonia, Finland, France, Germany, Ireland, Israel, Italy, Japan, Latvia, Lithuania, Netherlands, Slovenia, Spain, Sweden, United Kingdom, United States.
[2] Austria, Estonia, Finland, France, Germany, Ireland, Italy, Latvia, Lithuania, Netherlands, Slovenia, Spain.
[3] Australia, Canada, Czech Republic, Denmark, Israel, Japan, Sweden, United Kingdom, United States.

Figure 3.9. Sectoral Producer Prices in Advanced Economies
(Percent change)

While producer price inflation in advanced economies has slowed across sectors, the slowdown has been particularly sharp for manufacturing industries.

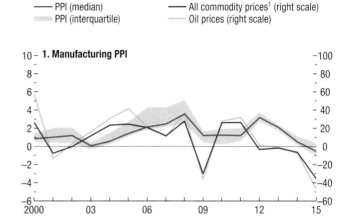

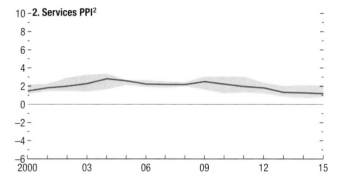

Sources: Haver Analytics; Organisation for Economic Co-operation and Development, Structural Analysis Database; and IMF staff calculations.
Note: The sample includes Australia, Austria, Canada, Denmark, Finland, France, Germany, Italy, Japan, Korea, Luxembourg, Norway, the United Kingdom, and the United States. PPI = producer price index.
[1] Price index using weights based on 2002–04 average world export earnings.
[2] Services comprise wholesale and retail trade; hotels and restaurants; transportation, storage, and communications; and finance, insurance, real estate, and business services.

of deflation pressure from industrial slack in large economies? How large is the portion of disinflation that cannot be attributed to these factors? To answer these questions, an econometric analysis is performed to assess the contribution of various factors to recent inflation developments.

The empirical framework follows the approach of IMF (2013) and Blanchard, Cerutti, and Summers (2015), building on the hybrid New Keynesian Phillips Curve of Fuhrer (1995) and Galí and Gertler (1999). Specifically, the following version of the Phillips curve is estimated:[16]

$$\pi_t = \gamma_t \pi^e_{t+h} + (1 - \gamma_t)\tilde{\pi}_{t-1} + \theta_t u^c_t + \mu_t \pi^m_t + \varepsilon_t, \quad (3.1)$$

in which π_t is headline consumer price inflation; π^e_{t+h} is inflation expectations h years in the future (with 10-year-ahead expectations used in the baseline specification); $\tilde{\pi}_{t-1}$ is the moving average of inflation over the previous four quarters, to allow for inflation persistence; u^c_t is cyclical unemployment—that is, the deviation of the unemployment rate from its level consistent with stable inflation (the nonaccelerating inflation rate of unemployment, or NAIRU); π^m_t is inflation in the relative price of imports—defined as the import-price deflator relative to the GDP deflator—to account for the impact of import prices, including commodity prices, on domestic consumer prices; and ε_t captures the impact of other factors, such as fluctuations in inflation driven by temporary supply shocks, or measurement error in other variables in the specification—particularly in unobservable variables, such as inflation expectations and cyclical unemployment.[17] The coefficient γ captures the degree to which inflation is driven by long-term inflation expectations as opposed to lagged inflation; θ denotes the strength of the relationship between cyclical unemployment and

---

[16]There is a vast literature on the ability of alternative Phillips curve specifications to fit the data, particularly for advanced economies (see, for instance, Ball and Mazumder 2011; Fuhrer 1995; Stock and Watson 2007). The specification used here aims for sufficient versatility to accommodate a large sample of heterogeneous economies over a long period.

[17]Some studies use core inflation, producer price inflation, or GDP deflator inflation when estimating a Phillips curve. However, because for many countries measures of expectations are available only for consumer price inflation, which also tends to be the focus of central bank targets, equation (3.1) is estimated for consumer price inflation. The expectation term in the equation should ideally capture the expectations of firms that set prices for consumer goods and services. Since firms' inflation forecasts are not widely available, the analysis uses long-term inflation projections—at a 10-year horizon—from professional forecasters reported by Consensus Economics (Annex 3.4 discusses the choice of forecast horizon and the robustness of results to using different measures).

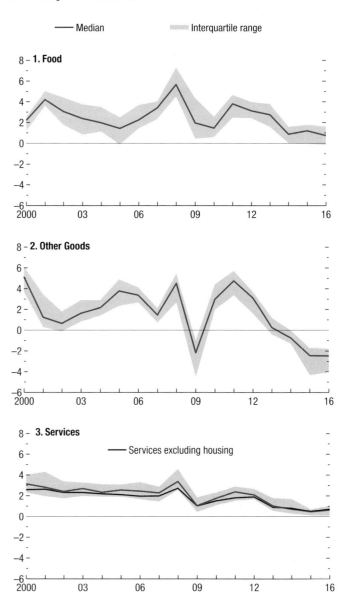

Figure 3.10. Sectoral Consumer Prices in Advanced Economies
(Percent change)

Consumer price inflation declined more for goods than for services, with deflation for nonfood goods in most advanced economies.

Sources: Haver Analytics; and IMF staff calculations.
Note: "Food" comprises food and beverages. "Other goods" comprises fuels, purchases of vehicles, and all categories under the following expenditure groups: clothing and footwear; electricity, gas, and other fuels; and furnishings, household equipment, and routine maintenance. All other consumer price categories are in "Services." Country sample includes Austria, Belgium, Canada, Czech Republic, Cyprus, Denmark, Estonia, Finland, France, Germany, Greece, Iceland, Ireland, Italy, Japan, Korea, Latvia, Lithuania, Luxembourg, Malta, the Netherlands, Norway, Portugal, Slovakia, Slovenia, Spain, Sweden, Switzerland, the United Kingdom, and the United States.

inflation—the slope of the Phillips curve; and μ is the effect of relative import prices on inflation.

The estimation allows for time variation in all the parameters to capture possible changes in the structure of each economy.[18] The model is estimated for each advanced and emerging market economy for which data are available, yielding estimates for a set of 44 countries from the first quarter of 1990 to the first quarter of 2016. The estimates are then used to assess the contribution of labor market slack and import prices to recent inflation dynamics in each country.[19]

Before turning to examine which factors have contributed to the recent decline in inflation, it is useful to assess whether the parameters of the Phillips curve have changed over time. The results suggest that the parameters are broadly stable and, in particular, there is no strong evidence that the slope of the Phillips curve has declined since the mid-1990s (Figure 3.11).[20] A notable exception, particularly for advanced economies, is the degree to which inflation is driven by long-term inflation expectations as opposed to past inflation. The estimated coefficient on expected inflation (γ) steadily increased up to the Great Recession but has been declining since then and now stands at levels comparable to those in the early 1990s (about 0.6).[21] The consequent increase in the coefficient on lagged inflation (1 - γ) implies that inflation has become more backward looking. This implies that the effect of cyclical unemployment and import prices on inflation has become more persistent in the recent period.

Despite some heterogeneity across countries, the results of the country-by-country decompositions show that unemployment slack and weaker import prices are, on average, the most important factors in explaining deviations of inflation from inflation targets in advanced economies since the Great Recession (Figure 3.12). Instead, changes in long-term inflation expectations (as measured by 10-year-ahead expectations by professional forecasters) have played a limited role—although repeating the exercise with expectations at shorter horizons suggests a larger contribution from inflation expectations (see Annex 3.4).

Although parameters are allowed to vary over time—therefore capturing possible nonlinearities (Swamy and Mehta 1975)—the model residuals ("others" in Figure 3.12) have increasingly contributed to the decline in inflation over the past few years. This could reflect a host of factors, including measurement errors in some of the explanatory variables. In particular, expectations of actual price setters may have dropped more than those of professional forecasters (Coibion and Gorodnichenko 2015). Also, underestimation of the extent of unemployment slack could be reflected in larger residuals.[22]

As an aside, the results also suggest that the reason inflation in advanced economies did not fall more between 2008 and 2012 is that the positive effect on inflation of import prices, notably oil prices, partly offset the disinflationary effect stemming from high labor market slack.[23] Accordingly, as import prices started to fall in 2012, inflation began to weaken and undershoot targets.

The decomposition for emerging market economies shows significant heterogeneity. In countries where inflation has recently fallen below long-term inflation expectations, labor market slack, import prices, and, to a lesser extent, currency appreciations explain, on average, the bulk of the recent decline (Figure 3.13, panel 1). In contrast, currency depreciations—notably in commodity exporters—contributed to the increase in inflation in those emerging market economies with inflation currently above long-term expectations. The model residuals over the recent years are particularly large in these economies (Figure 3.13, panel 2), possibly reflecting greater measurement error on inflation expectations as well as changes in administered prices in some cases.[24] Similar to the case of advanced economies, the roles played by these factors vary across countries (Figure 3.13, panels 3 and 4).

---

[18]For example, improvements in the conduct of monetary policy and structural factors—such as globalization and changes in rigidities in product and labor markets—may have affected the sensitivity of inflation to fluctuations in domestic production (April 2006 *World Economic Outlook*, Chapter 3, and references therein; Rogoff 2003).

[19]The decomposition of inflation dynamics is conducted in a manner similar to that in Yellen (2015). See Annex 3.4 for details.

[20]This finding is in line with that of the April 2013 *World Economic Outlook*, Chapter 3, and Blanchard, Cerutti, and Summers (2015), which document that the flattening of the Phillips curve from the 1960s to the 2000s was largely completed by the mid-1990s.

[21]The finding that the parameter increased during the 1990s is consistent with earlier research, including IMF (2013). That study also finds that the link between current and past inflation started to strengthen since the Great Recession.

[22]The exercise reported in Annex 3.4 shows that the results are typically robust to using alternative measures of cyclical unemployment but somewhat sensitive to using inflation expectations at different horizons.

[23]Coibion and Gorodnichenko (2015) and Yellen (2015) find similar results for the United States.

[24]Indeed, robustness exercises in Annex 3.4 show that the residuals vary considerably across different measures of inflation expectations and are much smaller when using inflation expectations at shorter horizons.

Figure 3.11. Estimated Phillips Curve Parameters

Estimation results suggest that the degree of anchoring of inflation to long-term expectations increased in the 1990s and early 2000s but declined more recently toward the level attained in the early 1990s. Other parameters, including the slope of the Phillips curve, have been broadly stable.

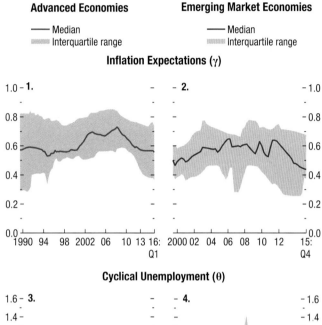

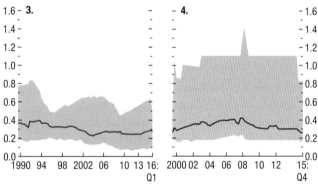

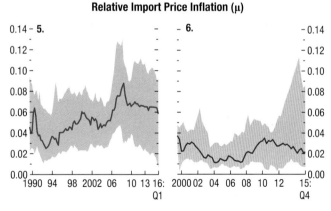

Sources: Consensus Economics; Haver Analytics; Organisation for Economic Co-operation and Development; and IMF staff calculations.
Note: The sample is defined in Annex Table 3.1.1. Venezuela is excluded because of missing data.

Figure 3.12. Contribution to Inflation Deviations from Targets: Advanced Economies

(Percent)

Cyclical unemployment and weaker import prices can account for the bulk of the deviation of inflation from targets in advanced economies since the global financial crisis, but other unexplained factors have been playing an increasingly larger role more recently.

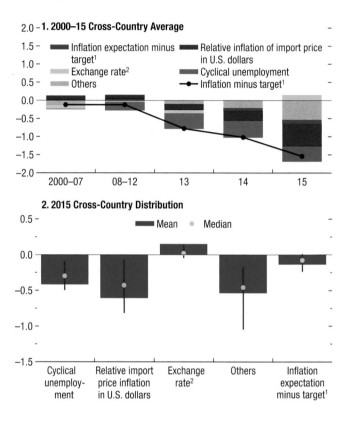

Sources: Consensus Economics; Haver Analytics; Organisation for Economic Co-operation and Development; and IMF staff calculations.
Note: Vertical lines in panel 2 denote interquartile ranges. The sample is defined in Annex Table 3.1.1. Estonia, Latvia, Lithuania, the Slovak Republic, and Slovenia are excluded as outliers.
[1] Target refers to the average of long-term inflation expectations in 2000–07, which are from Consensus Economics (10-year inflation expectations) or *World Economic Outlook* inflation forecasts (5-year inflation expectations).
[2] Exchange rate is defined as currency value per U.S. dollar.

Figure 3.13. Contribution to Inflation Deviations from Targets: Emerging Market Economies

Economic slack and weak import prices also account for a large share of the observed disinflation in emerging market economies with inflation below long-term inflation expectations over the recent past. In contrast, exchange rate depreciations and other unexplained factors played a key role in emerging market economies in which inflation has been above long-term expectations.

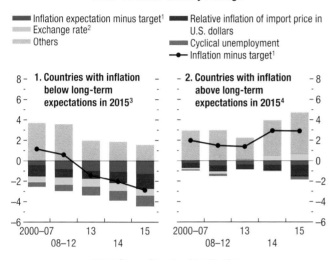

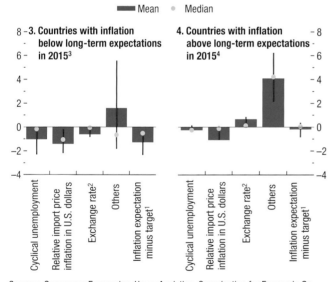

Sources: Consensus Economics; Haver Analytics; Organisation for Economic Co-operation and Development; and IMF staff calculations.

Note: Vertical lines in panels 3 and 4 denote interquartile ranges. The sample is defined in Annex Table 3.1.1. Venezuela is excluded because of missing data. Ukraine is excluded as an outlier.

[1] Target refers to the average of long-term inflation expectations in 2000–07, which are from Consensus Economics (10-year inflation expectations) or *World Economic Outlook* inflation forecasts (5-year inflation expectations).

[2] Exchange rate is defined as currency value per U.S. dollar.

[3] Bulgaria, China, Hungary, Malaysia, Mexico, Philippines, Poland, Romania, Thailand.

[4] Argentina, Brazil, Chile, Columbia, India, Indonesia, Peru, Russia, Turkey.

Given the important role played by import prices, the rising slack in tradables sectors in large economies and systemic trading partners (such as China, Japan, and the United States; Box 3.1) raises an interesting question: are spillovers from industrial slack in large economies an important factor in the decline in import prices and inflation?[25] Further analysis provides suggestive evidence that this may be the case. In many advanced and emerging market economies, the contribution of import prices to inflation over time is correlated with manufacturing slack in China, Japan, and the United States. The average correlation with manufacturing slack in all three countries is important, but is particularly strong in the case of China (Figure 3.14, panel 1; Annex Figure 3.4.3).[26,27]

Causal relationships cannot be inferred from this simple exercise, as many factors could drive manufacturing slack in each of these large economies (including weak demand elsewhere) or be associated with it (for instance, lower international oil prices) and could therefore bias the results. Indeed, the conditional correlation between manufacturing slack and the contribution of import prices to inflation is significantly lower when other global variables—such as oil prices and global demand conditions—are also taken into account (Figure 3.14, panel 2; Annex Figures 3.4.3 and 3.4.4). Nonetheless, the correlation with manufacturing slack in China remains significant and economically meaningful: the recent widening in manufacturing slack of about 5 percentage points would be associated, on average, with a decline in inflation in advanced and emerging market economies of about 0.2 percentage point—down from 0.5 percentage point when the estimation does not control for global conditions.[28]

[25]A single country can take the price of its imports as given, but the world as a whole does not have import prices. Changes in import prices depend on the degree of excess supply or excess demand in globally integrated markets for tradable goods and services.

[26]The impact of industrial slack cannot be directly tested in the empirical framework because reliable estimates for it are available only from the mid-2000s (as discussed in Box 3.1). To avoid shortening the Phillips curve estimation period, the analysis instead regresses, country by country, the contribution of import prices on measures of industrial slack in China, Japan, and the United States. See Annex 3.4 for details on the estimation framework as well as robustness checks.

[27]The association between import price contributions and China's manufacturing slack appears to be stronger for advanced economies than emerging market economies (see Annex Figure 3.4.3).

[28]The correlation of the contribution of import prices to inflation and manufacturing slack in China is negative for 84 percent of the sample, and additional results from panel regressions confirm the statistical significance of this result (see Annex 3.4). Further analysis finds that this correlation is higher in countries with stronger trade links with China, providing additional evidence of direct spillover effects through tradable goods. However, slack in China could exert disinflationary pressure on the price of domestic tradable goods

Figure 3.14. Correlation of Manufacturing Slack in China, Japan, and the United States with Import Price Contribution to Inflation in Other Economies
(Percentage points)

Subdued inflation across a large number of countries is associated with manufacturing slack in Japan, the United States, and especially China.

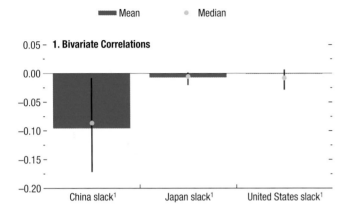

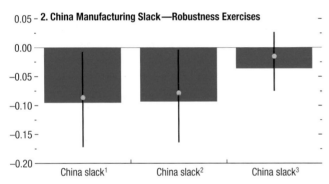

Sources: Consensus Economics; Haver Analytics; Organisation for Economic Co-operation and Development; and IMF staff calculations.
Note: Vertical lines denote interquartile ranges. The figure shows the means, medians, and interquartile ranges of coefficients of manufacturing slack from country-specific regressions. See Annex 3.4 for the regression specifications.
[1] No controls.
[2] Controlling for manufacturing slack in the other two economies, change in oil prices, and global output gap.
[3] Controlling for global output gap and change in oil prices in current and previous four quarters.

In sum, while an accounting of the drivers of global manufacturing slack is beyond the scope of this chapter, these findings suggest that manufacturing slack in large economies may add deflation pressure in other economies.

in other countries—when these prices are set in global markets—beyond what is captured through import prices. Indeed, the correlation of model residuals with manufacturing slack in China is statistically significant.

How Well Anchored Are Inflation Expectations?

The previous results suggest that economic slack and the sharp drop in the global price of tradable goods explain a large fraction of the undershooting of inflation targets observed in many countries over the past few years. The contribution of long-term inflation expectations to recent inflation dynamics has been much smaller—although the results are somewhat sensitive to the inflation expectations horizon. But if inflation expectations drift down substantially even as a result of temporary shocks, this would lead to a protracted period of disinflation—especially in the context of constrained monetary policy.[29]

Therefore, a key question in the current juncture is how well anchored inflation expectations are. In particular, is there evidence that recent inflation developments are affecting inflation expectations? To explore that question, the analysis investigates the sensitivity of inflation expectations to changes in actual inflation, examines the role of monetary policy frameworks in influencing this sensitivity, and assesses whether this sensitivity has increased in countries with policy rates at, or close to, their lower bound.

Measuring Inflation Expectations

The link between inflation and economic activity stems in part from the pricing decisions of firms and their beliefs about future macroeconomic outcomes. Because firms' inflation expectations are not generally known, they are approximated by: (1) surveys of inflation expectations of professional forecasters or households and (2) market-based measures of inflation expectations, such as estimates of inflation compensation embedded in the returns of financial instruments.

Survey-based and market-based measures of inflation expectations measure somewhat different concepts and have different statistical properties. Surveys collect one measure of central tendency—the mean, median, or mode—of the believed distribution of individual professional forecasters or households, and different individuals may report a different measure of their believed distribution. It is customary to use the median of this distribution of individual responses as a summary statistic of survey-based expectations to reduce the distortionary

[29]See Annex 3.2 for simulations on the effect of temporarily subdued import prices—stemming from a decline in oil prices and industrial slack in a key large economy—under constrained monetary policy and unanchored inflation expectations.

effect of outliers. The dispersion of expectations in the survey is a measure of heterogeneity of beliefs rather than a measure of uncertainty—although these tend to move together (Gürkaynak and Wolfers 2007). Survey-based measures of professional forecasters' inflation expectations (such as those from *Consensus Economics*) are available at different horizons for a large set of countries while surveys on the expectations of households (such as the University of Michigan survey for the United States) are available only for a few advanced economies.

Market-based measures of inflation expectations can be extracted from inflation compensation embedded in long-maturity inflation-linked and nominal bonds or from inflation-linked swaps.[30] The break-even inflation rate measured by the yield spread between conventional bonds and comparable inflation-linked bonds provides an estimate of the level of expected inflation at which a (risk-neutral) investor would be indifferent between holding either type of bond. It is widely used as a timely measure of investors' inflation expectations, although it is effectively based on the pricing of the marginal investor and includes a liquidity premium and an inflation risk premium.[31]

It is thus not surprising to observe differences in the behavior of survey- and market-based measures over time, including during the most recent period of disinflation. Inflation expectations from professional forecasters for horizons of up to three years vary over time, but expectations for horizons of five years or more are remarkably stable. Households' expectations are also highly stable over longer horizons. In contrast, historical market-based measures of inflation expectations exhibit more variation over time.

Turning to the most recent period, medium-term market-based expectations (five years or more) in the United States and the euro area have fallen by about 0.9 percentage point and 0.8 percentage point, respectively, since 2009—and by about 0.6 percentage point and 0.5 percentage point, respectively, since the sharp drop in oil prices in 2014—and are now significantly below their historical averages and survey-based measures (Figure 3.15, panels 1 and 2). Survey-based inflation expectations have instead declined by much less—about 0.15 percentage point on average since 2009.[32] But, although survey-based medium-term expectations have remained near central banks' targets since the Great Recession, the deviations of inflation expectations from targets in key advanced economies after the crisis have become large even at relatively long horizons such as three years—while under well-anchored inflation expectations these deviations should be zero (Figure 3.15, panels 3 and 4).[33]

Empirical Analysis

The sensitivity of inflation expectations is estimated empirically in a framework that relates changes in inflation expectations to inflation surprises. In particular, the following equation is estimated:

$$\Delta \pi^e_{t+h} = \beta^h_t \pi^{news}_t + \epsilon_{t+h}, \tag{3.2}$$

in which $\Delta \pi^e_{t+h}$ denotes the first difference in expectations of inflation h years in the future, and π^{news}_t

[30]Inflation-linked bonds are now issued in more than 20 countries. In addition to the United Kingdom, the United States, and four large euro area countries, these countries include Brazil, South Africa, Korea, and Turkey. For a historical overview of international inflation-linked bond markets, see Garcia and van Rixtel (2007) and references therein. Inflation-linked swaps are derivatives through which one party pays a fixed rate of inflation in exchange for actual inflation over the length of the contract. The rate of inflation quoted as the fixed leg of the swap can be used to provide an alternative measure of inflation compensation. Inflation-linked swaps are less prone to incorporate a liquidity premium than inflation-linked and nominal bonds because the swaps do not require an upfront payment and are settled by the net exchanges of flows at the end of the contract.

[31]The liquidity premium may arise from factors unrelated to inflation expectations, such as trading frictions or insufficient market activity and could be gauged by looking at relative trade volumes or asset-swap spreads (see, for example, Celasun, Mihet, and Ratnovski 2012; Gürkaynak, Sack, and Wright 2010). The inflation risk premium captures markets' pricing of risk surrounding inflation expectations and is much more difficult to estimate than the liquidity premium. Estimates of the inflation risk premium are typically taken from term-structure models. But, even for a single country, estimates vary significantly over time, across maturities, and across specifications, which makes the interpretation of changes in inflation compensation far from straightforward. For term-structure models applied to the United States, see, for example, Abrahams and others (2012); Christensen, Lopez, and Rudebusch (2010); and D'Amico, Kim, and Wei (2014). For the euro area, see, for example, Garcia and Werner (2014).

[32]Although the expectations of professional forecasters and households have barely declined since the precrisis period, the skew of the distributions has changed. Evidence for the United States suggests that for both of those measures, the share of respondents expecting 1–2 percent inflation has increased, while most of the declines reflect a reduction in expectations for above-target inflation. Inflation expectations based on professional forecasts show a marked reduction in the upper tail, whereas those based on household forecasts point to a reduction in uncertainty.

[33]Empirical evidence for the United States and the euro area suggests that three-year-ahead inflation expectations were not statistically different from inflation targets during the precrisis period but were statistically significantly lower in 2009–15. The analysis controls for the magnitude of inflation shocks in the two periods.

Figure 3.15. Survey- and Market-Based Inflation Expectations
(Percent)

Medium-term market-based inflation expectations have decreased substantially in the United States and the euro area recently. Survey-based inflation expectations fell by much less, but they have deviated significantly from inflation targets even at a three-year horizon.

Survey- and Market-Based Inflation Expectations

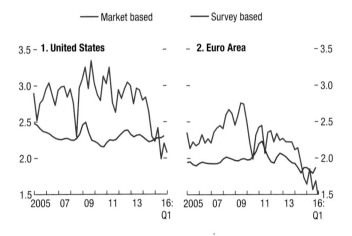

Deviations of Inflation Expectations at Various Horizons from Inflation Targets

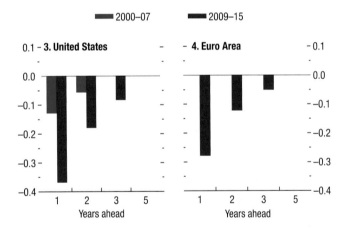

Sources: Bloomberg L.P.; and IMF staff calculations.
Note: Survey-based inflation expectations in panels 1 and 2 correspond to 5-year-ahead inflation forecasts from Consensus Economics; market-based expectations are based on 5-year/5-year inflation swaps. Panels 3 and 4 show the estimated constant in a regression of deviations of survey-based inflation expectation at different horizons from the inflation target (proxied by 10-year-ahead inflation expectation) on deviations from target of actual annualized quarterly inflation. Estimated coefficients are set to zero if they are not significant at the 5 percent confidence level. Euro area forecasts correspond to the GDP-weighted average of the forecasts for France, Germany, Italy, the Netherlands, and Spain.

is a measure of inflation shocks.[34] The coefficient β^h captures the degree of anchoring in h-years-ahead inflation expectations—a term usually referred to as "shock anchoring" (Ball and Mazumder 2011)—and it is allowed to vary over time in some specifications. If monetary policy is credible, the value of this parameter at a sufficiently long horizon should be close to zero. That is, inflation shocks should not lead to changes in medium-term expectations if agents believe that the central bank is able to counteract any short-term developments to bring inflation back to the target over the medium term. Given uncertainty about the relevant horizon for firms' pricing decisions and in light of the previous results, the exercise is performed using inflation expectations at various horizons.

The model is estimated for each advanced and emerging market economy for which data are available, which produces estimates for 44 countries from the first quarter of 1990 to the first quarter of 2016. The specification allows for the parameter β^h to vary over time to capture changes in the sensitivity of inflation expectations due, for instance, to changes in monetary policy frameworks. The analysis is performed for survey-based inflation expectations using data available at quarterly frequency and for market-based inflation expectations using data available at daily frequency.

Results—Survey-Based Inflation Expectations

The analysis starts by using a static framework—that is, β^h is assumed constant over time—to explore how the sensitivity of survey-based inflation expectations varies across countries and how this is related to characteristics of monetary policy frameworks.[35] The

[34]Inflation shocks are defined as the quarterly difference between actual inflation and short-term expectations for the analysis based on survey forecast–based measures of inflation expectations and as the daily change in oil price futures for the analysis using market-based expectations. The quarterly forecast error is used as a baseline measure of inflation shocks for the analysis based on survey-based measures of inflation expectations because it is less subject to reverse causality than other measures, such as changes in inflation or deviations of inflation from target. The results using these two alternative measures are, however, not statistically significantly different. Measures of inflation surprises are not available at daily frequency, so changes in oil price futures are used as proxies for inflation shocks for the analysis based on market-based expectations. While the scope of this measure is clearly narrower, inflation expectations have been shown to be strongly related to oil price developments (see Coibion and Gorodnichenko 2015).

[35]This part of the analysis is carried out using a static framework since data for several characteristics of monetary policy frameworks, such as transparency and independence, are available only for a

Figure 3.16. Sensitivity of Inflation Expectations to Inflation Surprises
(Years on x-axis)

Inflation expectations are less sensitive to inflation surprises in advanced economies than in emerging market economies.

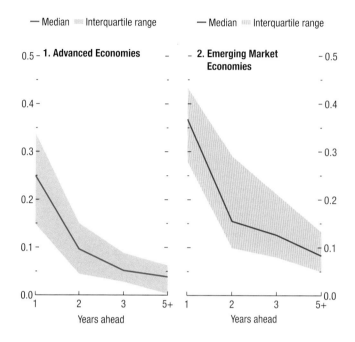

Sources: Consensus Economics; Haver Analytics; and IMF staff calculations.
Note: The figure shows the response of inflation expectations at various horizons to a 1 percentage point unexpected increase in inflation based on coefficients from country-specific static regressions. The sensitivity for 5+ years corresponds to the average of estimations using 5- and 10-year-ahead inflation expectations.

economies, and of 0.13 percentage point in emerging market economies.

The average lower sensitivity of inflation expectations to inflation shocks in advanced economies points to the credibility of monetary policy frameworks as a possible determinant of the cross-country heterogeneity. An exploration of the differences in estimated sensitivities shows that they are related to measures of central bank independence and transparency—two key areas of central bank governance that have improved dramatically over the past few decades and are positively associated with monetary policy performance (Crowe and Meade 2007).

Medium-term inflation expectations—that is, inflation expectations at three years and at five or more years—are typically better anchored in countries where the central bank is more independent. On average, a 1 unit increase in an index based on the turnover of the central bank's governor—a de facto measure of central bank independence, with higher values associated with a lower degree of independence—is associated with an increase of about 0.3 unit in the sensitivity of inflation expectations (Figure 3.17, panels 1 and 2).[36] This suggests that if a country moves from the 25th percentile to the 75th percentile in terms of turnover—which is similar to the average gap in this independence indicator between the United States and Indonesia in the past 20 years—the sensitivity will increase by 0.03, a nontrivial change considering that the median sensitivity across countries is 0.08.

Analogously, the sensitivity of medium-term inflation expectations to inflation surprises is lower the more transparent the central bank is about its objectives and policy decisions. The results show that, on average, a 1 unit increase in an index of central bank transparency is associated with a 0.16 unit decrease in the sensitivity of three-year-ahead inflation expectations (Figure 3.17, panels 3 and 4).[37] The magnitude

estimates show that the sensitivity of inflation expectations is significantly lower in advanced economies than in emerging market economies (Figure 3.16). This is particularly true for inflation expectations at short-term horizons—for example, a 1 percentage point increase in inflation results in a 0.25 percentage point increase in inflation expectations one year ahead for advanced economies, whereas this increase is 0.37 percentage point for emerging market economies. The difference in sensitivity is present, albeit to a lesser degree, even at longer horizons—a 1 percentage point increase in inflation leads to an increase of 0.05 percentage point in three-year-ahead inflation expectations in advanced

[36]The central bank governor's term in office shortens relative to that of the executive as turnover increases, making the governor more vulnerable to political interference from the government and reducing the degree of independence of the central bank. Cukierman, Webb, and Neyapti (1992) find that the link between central bank independence and inflation outcomes is stronger when using the de facto measure based on governor turnover than in the case of de jure metrics based on legal measures. Therefore, the analysis uses the governor turnover index from Crowe and Meade (2007), which extended Cukierman, Webb, and Neyapti's (1992) index up to 2004 and includes a large number of emerging market and developing economies.

[37]The central bank transparency index is taken from Crowe and Meade (2007) and corresponds to 1998.

few points in time. The sensitivity of inflation expectations for the survey-based forecast is normalized to measure how much inflation expectations are updated in response to a 1 percentage point change in inflation. See Annex 3.5 for details on the estimation and the computation of inflation shocks.

Figure 3.17. Sensitivity of Inflation Expectations to Inflation Surprises and Monetary Policy Frameworks

Medium- and long-term inflation expectations are less sensitive to inflation surprises in countries with more independent and transparent central banks.

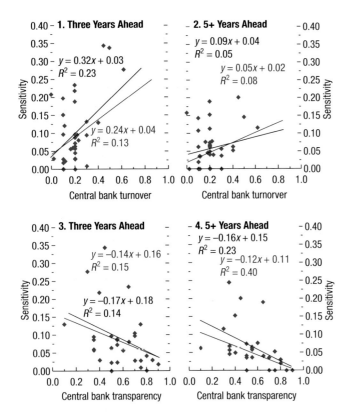

Sources: Consensus Economics; Crowe and Meade (2007) data set; Haver Analytics; and IMF staff calculations.
Note: The sensitivity is measured as the response of inflation expectations at various horizons to a 1 percentage point unexpected increase in inflation based on coefficients from country-specific static regressions. The sensitivity for 5+ years corresponds to the average of estimations using 5- and 10-year-ahead inflation expectations. Black lines denote the fitted lines for the entire sample. Red lines denote the fitted lines excluding outliers.

Figure 3.18. Sensitivity of Inflation Expectations to Inflation Surprises before and after Adoption of Inflation Targeting

Inflation targeting is associated with lower sensitivity of medium- and long-term inflation expectations to inflation surprises.

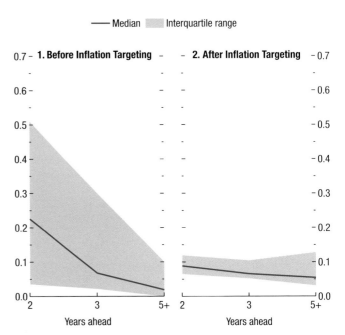

Sources: Consensus Economics; Haver Analytics; *World Economic Outlook* (2011, Chapter 3); and IMF staff calculations.
Note: The figure shows the response of inflation expectations at various horizons to a 1 percentage point unexpected increase in inflation based on coefficients from country-specific static regressions. The sensitivity for 5+ years corresponds to the average of estimations using 5- and 10-year-ahead inflation expectations.

of the estimated coefficient suggests that if a country moves from the 25th percentile to the 75th percentile in terms of transparency—which is similar to the average gap in the transparency indicator between Peru and Canada over the past 20 years—the sensitivity would decline by 0.05.

Many central banks have adopted inflation targeting over the past few decades precisely to make their decision-making process more transparent. Comparing the sensitivity of inflation expectations to inflation surprises in each country before and after the adoption of inflation targeting suggests that those monetary reforms are associated with a considerable decrease in sensitivity (Figure 3.18). The drop in sensitivity is

observed for all countries in the sample, as evidenced by a relatively narrow interquartile range.[38]

Overall, the results using a static framework suggest that stronger monetary policy frameworks are associated with better-anchored inflation expectations. Allowing the estimate of the sensitivity of inflation expectations (β^b) to vary over time shows that it has declined steadily in both advanced and emerging market economies over the past two decades (Figure 3.19). The decline was steeper at the beginning of the sample period, precisely when many economies significantly improved their frameworks, including

[38]See Levin, Natalucci, and Piger (2004) for a similar finding. Clarida and Waldman (2008) find that higher-than-expected inflation leads to an appreciation of the nominal exchange rate in countries with inflation targeting regimes—but not in others—suggesting that inflation targeters are successful in anchoring expectations of inflation and the monetary path required to meet the target.

Figure 3.19. Sensitivity of Inflation Expectations to Inflation Surprises over Time

The sensitivity of inflation expectations to inflation surprises has been steadily declining over time. But this downward trend seems to have come to a halt more recently, especially among advanced economies.

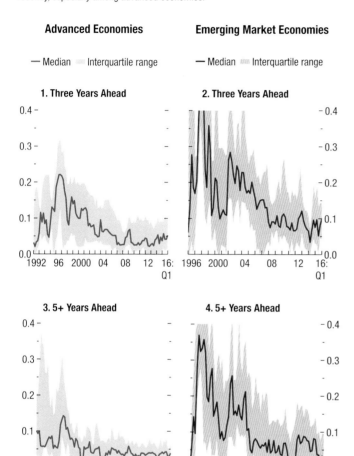

Sources: Consensus Economics; Haver Analytics; and IMF staff calculations.
Note: The figure shows the response of inflation expectations at various horizons to a 1 percentage point unexpected increase in inflation based on time-varying coefficients from country-specific estimations using a Kalman filter. The sensitivity for 5+ years corresponds to the average of estimations using 5- and 10-year-ahead inflation expectations.

that the sensitivity of inflation expectations to inflation surprises remains lower in advanced economies than among emerging market economies suggests there is scope for further improvements in the monetary policy frameworks in the latter group.

However, the downward trend in the sensitivity of expectations seems to have come to a halt in the mid-2000s, especially among advanced economies. In addition, the sensitivity of medium-term inflation expectations over the recent past has been increasing steadily faster in countries with policy rates at, or close to, their lower bound than in other countries (Figure 3.20).[40] This has happened even though many of these economies adopted unconventional monetary policies during this period, suggesting that constrained monetary policy may be affecting the degree of anchoring of inflation expectations.

An analysis of the response of inflation expectations to positive and negative inflation shocks also points to constrained monetary policy as the underlying cause of a possible unanchoring of expectations. If constraints on monetary policy are the source of the increased sensitivity of inflation expectations, this sensitivity should be higher for negative shocks than for positive ones—a central bank constrained by the effective lower bound on policy rates can always respond to higher inflation by raising the policy interest rate, but has little scope to reduce it when inflation is declining. This creates an unavoidable asymmetry in the ability of the monetary authority to handle downward and upward inflation shocks.

Indeed, most of the increased sensitivity for countries with constrained monetary policy seems to stem from negative inflation shocks (Figure 3.21). After 2009, when policy rates approached their effective lower bounds, the response of medium-term inflation expectations to negative shocks exceeded the response to positive shocks, while the response to positive shocks was larger

by adopting inflation targeting regimes.[39] It has also been broad based across countries, as illustrated by the evolution of the interquartile range. The observation

[39]For example, in 1996 only about 20 percent of countries in the sample had an inflation-targeting regime; by 2015 the proportion had increased to about 75 percent. Similarly, the sample average of the transparency indicator increased from 0.55 in 1998 to 0.61 in 2006, and the turnover indicator decreased from 0.29 in 1980–89 to 0.20 in 1995–2004.

[40]In this analysis, the effective-lower-bound constraint refers to the policy rate being equal to or less than 50 basis points. The monetary authorities of the following 19 advanced economies faced this constraint at some point during 2009–15: Canada, the Czech Republic, Estonia, France, Germany, Hong Kong SAR, Italy, Japan, Latvia, Lithuania, the Netherlands, Singapore, the Slovak Republic, Slovenia, Spain, Sweden, Switzerland, the United Kingdom, and the United States. Singapore does not use an interest rate as a monetary policy instrument, but the level of short-term market interest rates is at the effective lower bound. The statistical significance of the difference is tested using Mood's median test. The difference between the two groups is statistically significant for expectations at a three-year horizon and, to a lesser extent, for inflation expectations at a five-year horizon.

Figure 3.20. Change in Sensitivity of Inflation Expectations to Inflation Surprises

The sensitivity of medium-term inflation expectations to inflation surprises is higher in countries whose monetary policy is constrained.

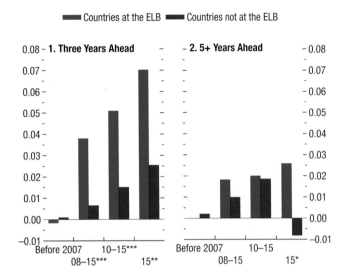

Sources: Consensus Economics; Haver Analytics; and IMF staff calculations.
Note: ELB = effective lower bound. ***,**,* denote that the differences in the change in sensitivity of inflation expectations between countries at the ELB and the rest are significant at the 1, 5, and 10 percent confidence level, respectively, using Mood's median test. The sensitivity of inflation expectations corresponds to the response of inflation expectations to a 1 percentage point unexpected increase in inflation based on time-varying coefficients from country-specific estimations using a Kalman filter. The sensitivity for 5+ years corresponds to the average of estimations using 5- and 10-year-ahead inflation expectations. The change in sensitivity is constructed as the average deviation of the median sensitivity across countries from a linear trend (an exponential trend) fitted over the period 1997–2007 for countries at the ELB (not at the ELB). Countries at the ELB are defined as those with policy rates or short-term nominal interest rates of 50 basis points or lower at some point during 2008–15 and include: Canada, the Czech Republic, Estonia, France, Germany, Hong Kong SAR, Italy, Japan, Latvia, Lithuania, the Netherlands, Singapore, the Slovak Republic, Slovenia, Spain, Sweden, Switzerland, the United Kingdom, and the United States.

before 2009.[41] The estimates imply that if countries with policy rates currently at the effective lower bound faced inflation surprises comparable to those observed over the past two years, long-term inflation expectations would on average drift further down by about 0.15 percentage point. This is not particularly large in absolute terms but still three times larger than if their sensitivity had remained unchanged—while under well-anchored expectations, there should be no impact at all.

The sharp drop in oil prices played an important role in global inflation dynamics over the past few

[41]The difference between the sensitivity for positive and negative shocks is generally not statistically significant, probably due to the limited number of observations (Annex 3.5).

Figure 3.21. Average Sensitivity of Inflation Expectations to Inflation Surprises in Countries at the Effective Lower Bound

In countries whose monetary policy is constrained, medium-term inflation expectations are more sensitive to negative than to positive inflation surprises.

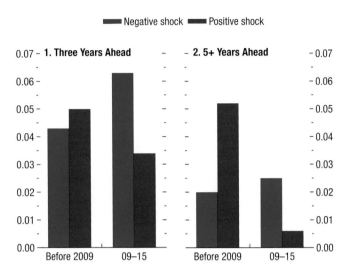

Sources: Consensus Economics; Haver Analytics; and IMF staff calculations.
Note: The figure shows the response of inflation expectations at various horizons to a 1 percentage point unexpected positive or negative change in inflation based on coefficients from country-specific time-varying estimation. The sensitivity for 5+ years corresponds to the average of estimations using 5- and 10-year-ahead inflation expectations. Countries at the Effective Lower Bound (ELB) are defined as those with policy rates or short-term nominal interest rates of 50 basis points or lower at some point during 2008–15 and include: Canada, the Czech Republic, Estonia, France, Germany, Hong Kong SAR, Italy, Japan, Latvia, Lithuania, the Netherlands, Singapore, the Slovak Republic, Slovenia, Spain, Sweden, Switzerland, the United Kingdom, and the United States. Japan is excluded from the analysis, because it reached the ELB much earlier than 2009.

years, and potentially also in the increase in the sensitivity of medium-term inflation expectations to inflation surprises. However, an additional exercise decomposing inflation surprises into oil and non-oil price movements suggests that the latter also contributed to the increase in expectations sensitivity. This result implies that positive inflation shocks stemming from a faster-than-expected recovery in oil prices would only lead to a partial rebound in inflation expectations if economic slack remains significant.[42]

[42]For countries with policy rates at their effective lower bound, the sensitivity of inflation expectations to shocks is decomposed between those driven by changes in oil price inflation and those driven by news on core inflation—proxied by the residuals in the regression of inflation shocks on the oil price (see Annex 3.5). The results suggest that, since 2009, the sensitivities of inflation expectations to oil price shocks and core inflation shocks are comparable.

Taken together, this set of results suggests that it is not just the characteristics of recent inflation outcomes—such as the large negative inflation surprises related to the drop in oil prices—that have led to some unanchoring of medium-term inflation expectations. It is rather the combination of such persistent negative inflation surprises and the perception that monetary policy is constrained and may be less effective in bringing inflation back to the central banks' targets that is behind this apparent unanchoring of medium-term inflation expectations.[43]

Results—Market-Based Inflation Expectations

The analysis so far provides evidence that: (1) the sensitivity of inflation expectations to inflation surprises depends on monetary policy frameworks and (2) this sensitivity has increased during the most recent period in countries with policy rates close to their effective lower bound, particularly in the case of negative inflation surprises. An analysis using high-frequency data for the United States and the euro area further underscores the relevance of constraints to monetary policy for the unanchoring of inflation expectations. Long-term market-based inflation expectations (approximated by five-year/five-year inflation swaps) are affected by inflation surprises proxied by changes in oil price futures (Figure 3.22). The responses are statistically significant—albeit economically small—both in the United States and in the euro area.[44] Splitting the sample around the time monetary policy rates reached their effective lower bounds shows that the sensitivity of inflation expectations was actually indistinguishable from zero before reaching the lower bound on interest rates, but increased substantially thereafter. The higher elasticities imply that surprises in oil prices can account for about one-third of the decline in market-based inflation

Figure 3.22. Sensitivity of Longer-Term Inflation Expectations to Changes in Oil Prices

The sensitivity of market-based inflation expectations to inflation surprises in the United States and the euro area increased after policy rates reached their effective lower bounds.

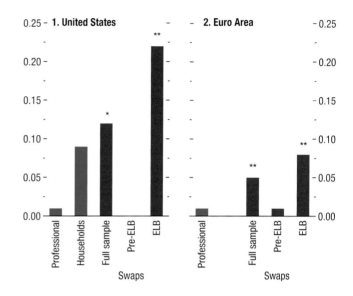

Sources: Bloomberg L.P.; Consensus Economics; University of Michigan Consumer Survey; and IMF staff calculations.
Note: **,* denote significance at the 5 and 10 percent confidence level, respectively. The figure shows coefficient estimates of inflation expectations on changes in oil price futures (simple average of 1-year-ahead Brent and West Texas Intermediate) controlling for changes in the Chicago Board Options Exchange Volatility Index and scaled by a 50 percent drop in oil price futures. Blue bars denote estimation results using survey-based inflation expectations: "Professional" denotes the results using 5-year-ahead inflation forecasts from Consensus Economics; while "Households" denotes results using inflation expectations (5–10 years) from the Michigan survey. Red bars denote results using market-based inflation expectations based on five-year/five-year inflation swaps. The effective lower bound (ELB) is defined as starting in 2009. The full sample refers to the period 2004–16.

expectations since June 2014 in the United States and almost one-fifth in the euro area.[45]

All in all, these empirical findings underscore vulnerabilities at the current juncture, as inflation shocks are predominantly negative and central banks have little space to respond. While the economic significance of the current degree of unanchoring of inflation expectations is still modest, the steady increase in their sensitivity to inflation surprises in cases where monetary policy is constrained is a reason for concern if the undershooting of inflation targets persists.

---

[43]An additional estimation was used to explore whether inflation surprises have a larger impact on inflation expectations when they occur after a long period of relatively large and negative inflation outcomes. There is indeed some evidence that, under constrained monetary policy, protracted deviations of inflation from the target can be associated with increased sensitivity of inflation expectations to inflation surprises. However, the results are somewhat sensitive to the sample periods.

[44]The responses of professional and household survey-based long-term inflation expectations to changes in oil price futures over the same period are in both cases smaller and statistically insignificant.

[45]The results are robust to alternative measures of market-based inflation expectations: inflation compensation embedded in Treasury inflation-protected securities and Treasury inflation-protected securities break-even inflation rates cleaned of a liquidity premium, following Celasun, Mihet, and Ratnovski (2012).

Summary and Policy Implications

Inflation rates have declined substantially in a large number of countries in recent years, with several advanced economies experiencing outright deflation. The decline in inflation is widespread across sectors, but stronger for tradable goods. Its main drivers are persistent labor market slack and weaker import price growth. The results in the chapter suggest the latter are associated with falling commodity prices and widening industrial slack in a few key large economies, particularly in China. At the same time, the part of disinflation not explained by the Phillips curve has tended to become larger in the past few years, especially in advanced economies. This shortfall in inflation relative to model-based predictions could be a sign that price setters' inflation expectations have declined more than what is captured by survey-based measures used in the econometric analysis or that economic slack is larger in some countries.

The chapter finds that monetary policy frameworks play an important role in influencing the sensitivity of inflation expectations to inflation surprises. Improvements in these frameworks over the past few decades have led inflation expectations to be much better-anchored than in the past—although there is scope for further improvements in some emerging market economies.

However, the chapter's analysis also suggests that medium-term inflation expectations in advanced economies with constrained monetary policy have recently become more sensitive to unexpected movements in actual inflation or in commodity prices. Although the increase in this sensitivity is small, it does suggest that faith in central banks' ability to combat persistent disinflationary forces might be diminishing—this sensitivity should be zero if medium-term expectations are perfectly anchored. An implication of this finding is that in advanced economies where perceived monetary policy space is limited, medium-term inflation expectations could become unanchored in the event of further unexpected declines in inflation.

What do these findings imply for the inflation outlook in countries that have experienced sizable disinflation over the past few years? Since most measures of medium-term inflation expectations have not declined significantly and commodity prices are projected to gradually recover, the most likely outcome is a gradual recovery of inflation toward central bank targets as slack diminishes and the effect of past

declines in commodity prices fades. But the increase in the sensitivity of inflation expectations to downside inflation surprises, the finding that inflation has become more persistent, and the possibility that slack might be larger than currently estimated in some countries, suggest downside risks to that central forecast. The possibility of a gradual further downward drift in medium-term inflation expectations and consequent prolonged period of low inflation is more than trivial in some countries.

The main findings of the chapter—the broad reach of the disinflation across countries, evidence of cross-border spillovers of disinflationary forces, the increased sensitivity of medium-term expectations to news, as well as the confluence of slack in many large economies—call for a comprehensive and coordinated effort to tackle the risks of low inflation. Given limited policy space in many economies, exploiting synergies between all available policy levers and across countries will be essential.[46]

- In countries with persistent economic slack and inflation consistently below central bank targets, it is crucial to maintain an appropriate degree of monetary accommodation to help keep medium-term inflation expectations anchored and ease the perception that monetary policy has become ineffective. While unconventional monetary policy actions taken in the aftermath of the Great Recession lifted inflation expectations (see footnote 5), estimates of natural interest rates have been revised down substantially over time, suggesting that monetary policy more recently may have been providing less accommodation than previously thought (see Chapter 1 of this WEO for a further discussion). Where medium-term inflation expectations appear to have shifted down, a more aggressive approach should be considered. In particular, a credible and transparent commitment to a modest and temporary overshooting of the inflation target would provide valuable insurance against deflationary and recessionary risks by reducing longer-term real rates even if the nominal policy rate is at the effective lower bound, generating a path of stronger demand and bringing inflation to target sooner (see Box 3.5; IMF 2016c; and Gaspar, Obstfeld, and Sahay forthcoming).
- Other policy levers need to be aligned with accommodative monetary policy in boosting demand.

[46]See Gaspar, Obstfeld, and Sahay (forthcoming) for a further discussion and case studies.

Given the broad-based nature of the disinflation and the corresponding fact that many countries are easing monetary policy at the same time, dampening the downward pressure that monetary policy easing exerts on the exchange rate, monetary policy stimulus on its own may not be sufficient to keep medium-term inflation expectations anchored at central bank targets. A comprehensive package consisting of a more growth-friendly composition of fiscal policy, an expansionary fiscal stance where fiscal space is available, demand-supportive structural reforms, and measures aimed at addressing weaknesses in bank and corporate balance sheets should play a complementary role in mitigating the risk of protracted weak demand and low inflation. Income policies could also be considered in countries with stagnant wages and entrenched deflationary dynamics to set in motion a healthy upward wage-price spiral.

- Distortionary policies that perpetuate overcapacity in tradables sectors should be avoided: they not only worsen resource allocation and, where financed by credit, weaken asset quality in the banking system, but they also exert disinflation pressure in the domestic economy that could spill over to other countries via import prices, reinforcing global disinflation pressures.[47]

- Finally, the breadth of the disinflation and evidence of meaningful cross-border spillovers of disinflationary forces through import prices also point to the value of a coordinated approach to supporting demand across the larger economies. Through positive spillovers, simultaneous action across countries would amplify the effects of each individual country's actions. A coordinated effort to simultaneously tackle weak demand and inflation in advanced economies and to redouble ongoing efforts to reduce overcapacity in countries with elevated industrial slack would be more impactful than a go-it-alone approach.

[47]In China, the authorities have already signaled their intent to address overcapacity, starting with the coal and steel sectors where capacity reduction targets have been set, together with the establishment of a fund to absorb the welfare costs for affected workers. Restructuring has begun at the local level in provinces with relatively strong public finances and more diverse economies (IMF 2016b).

Box 3.1. Industrial Slack and Producer Price Inflation

The recent decline in inflation has been much more pronounced in the manufacturing sector than in services. Consistent with this trend, an increasing body of evidence points to marked overcapacity in a range of industrial sectors, with industrial output growth decelerating significantly (National Association of Manufacturers 2016; Organisation for Economic Co-operation and Development 2015).[1] This box presents estimates of slack in the industrial sector in three large economies: China, Japan, and the United States.[2] All three economies have recently experienced outright declines in the producer price index (PPI) and generally subdued trends in consumer price inflation—although to varying extents (Figure 3.1.1). Estimates of slack—output gaps—for each economy as a whole, and separately for the industrial sector, are obtained through an extended multivariate filter that includes information on GDP, consumer price inflation, PPI inflation, and industrial production. The identification strategy relies on equations, for each economy separately, relating inflation to the estimated gaps.[3] The key equation resembles the standard Phillips curve but is confined to the industrial sector. It expresses PPI inflation as a function of the estimated industrial sector output gap; expected inflation; and leads and lags in headline inflation.

The results suggest that the industrial slack in the first quarter of 2016 stood at about 5.5 percent in China, 5 percent in Japan, and 3 percent in the United States (Figure 3.1.2). For China, the estimates incorporate a disaggregated treatment of light and heavy industry, derived from electricity consumption in the two subsectors. This shows a marked difference between slack in light industry (about 4.5 percent)

The authors of this box are Kevin Clinton, Zoltan Matyas Jakab, Douglas Laxton, and Fan Zhang.

[1]Industrial production comprises manufacturing, mining, and utilities (with relative weights in the United States of 78 percent, 12 percent, and 10 percent, respectively). Total industrial output is used instead of manufacturing output because of limited data. Annual average industrial production growth in the United States fell from about 2.5 percent in 2011–13 to 0.3 percent during 2014:H2–2016:H1. In Japan and China, the growth rate decreased from 0.3 percent to –2.5 percent and from 10.7 percent to 6.3 percent, respectively, over the same period.

[2]Industrial production in China, Japan, and the United States accounts for 45 percent of total world industrial production (as of 2014 and at constant 2005 prices, according to the United Nations National Accounts Main Aggregates Database): United States (19 percent), China (18 percent), and Japan (8 percent).

[3]For details see Alichi and others (2015).

Figure 3.1.1. Producer Price and Consumer Price Inflation in China, Japan, and the United States
(Percent)

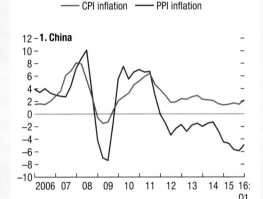

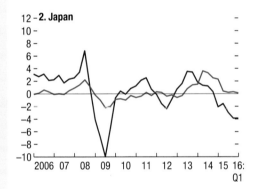

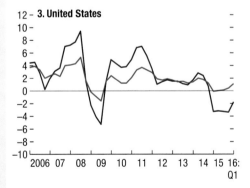

Source: IMF staff estimates.
Note: CPI = consumer price index; PPI = producer price index.

Box 3.1 *(continued)*

Figure 3.1.2. Industrial Slack in China, Japan, and the United States
(Percent)

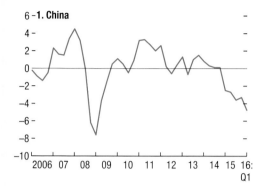

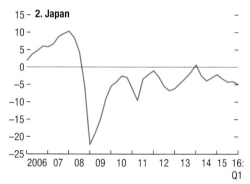

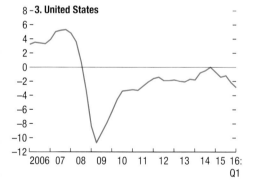

Source: IMF staff estimates.

Figure 3.1.3. Decomposition for Total Producer Price Inflation for China, Japan, and the United States
(Annualized percentage points)

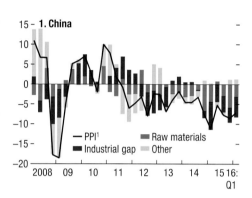

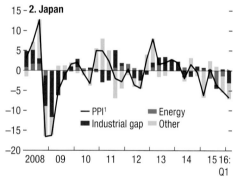

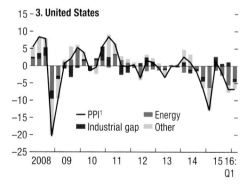

Source: IMF staff estimates.
Note: PPI = producer price index.
[1] Historical contribution of all shocks (difference between actual values and an unconditional forecast estimated using a vector autoregression model).

Box 3.1 *(continued)*

and in heavy industry (about 10.5 percent). In all three countries, the size of industrial slack correlates with the change in PPI inflation.

Although the filtering approach yields estimates of industrial slack consistent with the steep drop in PPI inflation rates, it does not allow for a decomposition of the relative contributions of various factors. For this purpose, the analysis uses structural vector autoregression models for PPI inflation that include the estimated industrial slack and energy or raw materials prices.[4] The historical decompositions

of PPI inflation suggest that the energy shock (or raw material shock in China) has been a key driver of the recent decline in PPI inflation, especially in the United States (Figure 3.1.3). In China and Japan, however, industrial slack has also played an important role. In particular, the estimated contribution of the industrial slack to PPI deflation in China over the past four years is as large as that of raw materials prices.

---

[4]Producer prices for finished consumer energy goods were used as energy prices in the United States; the electric power, gas, and water component of the Domestic Corporate Goods Price Index was used in the case of Japan (both denoted as "Energy" in Figure 3.1.3). In the case of China, the raw materials component of the PPI was used and is denoted "Raw materials" in the figure. The identifying assumptions are that over the long term: (1) the relative price of energy or raw materials prices (vis-à-vis

the PPI) is driven exclusively by energy and raw materials price shocks and not by shocks to industrial slack, (2) industrial slack is affected by both the "Industrial gap" and "Energy" or "Raw materials" shocks, and (3) PPI inflation is driven by all three shocks (Energy, Raw materials, Industrial gap, and by other PPI-specific shocks).

Box 3.2. The Japanese Experience with Deflation

The Japanese economy has experienced weak inflation for most of the past two decades. Inflation measured by the GDP deflator has been particularly low, averaging –0.3 percent between 1990 and 2015 compared with 0.5 percent for consumer price inflation (Figure 3.2.1). Continued efforts to reflate the economy have so far fallen short, highlighting the difficulty in escaping a deflation trap once expectations are anchored around a deflation equilibrium. A great deal of literature has sought to identify the causes and consequences of Japan's deflation experience, offering useful insights into the current disinflation trend in many economies. This box attempts to shed light on the following questions: What drove the Japanese deflation episode that started in the mid-1990s? How has it affected the Japanese economy? How relevant is the Japanese experience to the current disinflation trend?

Drivers of Deflation

The bursting of the asset price bubble in the early 1990s is often mentioned as the initial shock leading Japan into deflation. Inflation and inflation expectations declined gradually as efforts by households, banks, and businesses to strengthen balance sheets and rebuild net worth suppressed demand (IMF 2014; Koo 2008). Supply-side shifts and exchange rate appreciation were also highlighted as factors contributing to deflation momentum during this period (Leigh 2010; Posen 2000). The external shock from the 1997–98 Asian Crisis further weakened demand, and a slow response to the problem of nonperforming loans resulted in a banking crisis, tipping the economy into deflation in 1998. The commodity price boom that started in the early 2000s pushed headline inflation up, offering some temporary relief, but core inflation remained in negative territory (Figure 3.2.1). Further shocks, such as the bursting of the information technology bubble and the 2008–09 global financial crisis, reinforced weak demand, and the output gap remained negative (Figure 3.2.2). The yen appreciation leading up to the introduction of Abenomics in 2013 and the commodity price decline since 2014 have further complicated efforts to reflate the economy.[1] While there has been some recent success in raising core inflation,

The authors of this box are Elif Arbatli, Samya Beidas-Strom, and Niklas Westelius.

[1]See the main chapter text for an analysis of the impact of commodity prices on headline inflation.

Figure 3.2.1. Inflation Dynamics
(Year-over-year percent change)

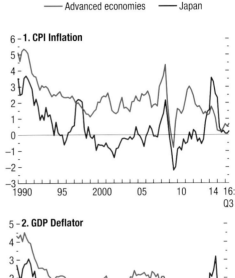
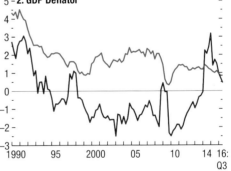

Source: IMF staff calculations.
Note: Quarterly seasonally adjusted data are used and weighted by purchasing-power-parity GDP to aggregate for advanced economies. Advanced economies comprise Australia, Austria, Belgium, Canada, Denmark, Finland, France, Germany, Hong Kong SAR, Iceland, Ireland, Israel, Italy, Japan, Korea, Luxembourg, the Netherlands, New Zealand, Norway, Portugal, Singapore, Spain, Sweden, Switzerland, Taiwan Province of China, the United Kingdom, and the United States. CPI = consumer price index.

deflation risks are rising again amid low demand and declining inflation expectations.

Structural factors exacerbated the effect of demand shocks, feeding into deflation pressure. Several of these factors are relevant for many advanced economies today: a decline in labor's bargaining power and an aging and slow-growing population. The decline in labor's bargaining power—evident in the trend fall in unit labor costs starting in the late 1990s (Figure 3.2.2)—together with firms' sluggishness, as seen in large corporate cash holdings, are argued to have

Box 3.2 *(continued)*

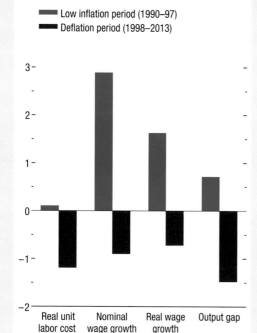

Figure 3.2.2. Cyclical and Structural Indicators in Japan
(Average annual percent change)

Sources: Organisation for Economic Co-operation and Development; and IMF staff calculations.

fed deflation by weakening wage-price dynamics (Porcellacchia 2016). Firms became less likely to hire workers on permanent contracts ("regular workers") in an environment of low expected growth. The share of regular workers among salaried employees fell over this period, contributing to lower unit labor costs, permanent income, and benefits for employees. Japan's aging and declining population growth have also been blamed for deflationary pressure as lower potential growth, and its implication on fiscal sustainability, are cited as holding back demand (Anderson, Botman, and Hunt 2014). At the same time, the aging population could also lead to excess demand and inflation pressure since retirees tend to consume more than they produce (Juselius and Takáts 2015)—even though the net effect of aging on inflation is ambiguous.

The timidity and low credibility of the policy response during the 1990s have also been widely cited as contributors to deflation. In particular, the

pace and extent of the initial monetary easing were likely insufficient, and the fiscal policy response has been criticized as ineffective in stimulating growth (Bernanke and Gertler 1999; Ito and Mishkin 2006; Kuttner and Posen 2002; Leigh 2010). The fiscal position remained broadly accommodative throughout the period of deflation (Figure 3.2.3, panel 1), but periodic attempts at consolidation also led to stop-and-go implementation of fiscal policy (Kuttner and Posen 2002; Syed, Kang, and Tokuoka 2009), and its effectiveness was stymied by lack of coordination with monetary policy (Eggertsson 2006). In addition, the Bank of Japan was moving toward independence and a price stability mandate in the 1990s, with an explicit inflation target introduced only in 2013.[2] As a result, long-term inflation expectations in Japan were not well anchored in the 1990s (Figure 3.2.3, panel 2), making the economy more vulnerable to deflation shocks. Finally, cleaning up weak financial sector balance sheets took long and inhibited financial intermediation, contributing to a prolonged recession and deflation pressure (Ito and Mishkin 2006).

Impact of Deflation and Relevance Today

Sustained deflation is generally believed to have acted as a headwind for the Japanese economy. Firms became more reluctant to invest and hire regular workers, and consumers postponed purchases of durable goods in anticipation of future price declines. A vicious cycle of declining prices, decreasing profits, and wage restraint reinforced weak demand in a "coordination failure" (Kuroda 2013). The increase in borrowers' real debt burden raised default risk and reduced asset prices, collateral valuations, and credit intermediation to the real economy. Deflation supported a shift in portfolio allocations toward so-called safe assets, reducing the supply of risk capital.

Persistently weak growth in the GDP deflator, and hence in nominal GDP, worsened the interest-rate-growth differential and contributed to a higher debt

[2]Measures of central bank credibility (Crowe and Meade 2007; Dincer and Eichengreen 2014) suggest that the Bank of England, the Federal Reserve, and the European Central Bank, for example, ranked higher (on policy transparency) going into the global financial crisis than Japan during both its low-inflation and deflation episodes.

Box 3.2 *(continued)*

Figure 3.2.3. Policy Indicators in Japan

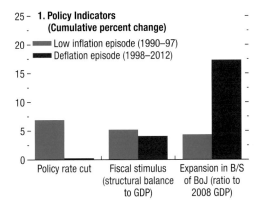

1. Policy Indicators
(Cumulative percent change)

■ Low inflation episode (1990–97)
■ Deflation episode (1998–2012)

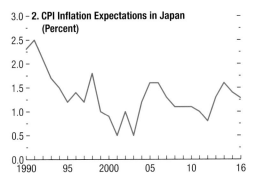

2. CPI Inflation Expectations in Japan
(Percent)

Sources: Consensus Economics; Haver Analytics; and IMF staff calculations.
Note: Inflation expectations are the 10-year forecast from Consensus Economics; the policy rate is the uncollateralized average overnight call rate. BoJ = Bank of Japan; B/S = balance sheet; CPI = consumer price index.

burden (End and others 2015).[3] On the monetary side, as nominal interest rates reached their effective lower bounds and inflation expectations declined, real interest rates could not be lowered sufficiently, contracting the economy further. Despite the large expansion in the Bank of Japan's balance sheet through unconventional monetary operations in recent years, inflation remains stubbornly low.

In sum, the Japanese experience underscores the importance of credible, decisive, and strong policy responses to prevent inflation expectations from becoming unanchored. The impact of persistent deflation can be large, and once deflation expectations emerge, it may be difficult to push the economy out of the liquidity trap. Structural factors in many advanced economies, including a secular decline in labor's bargaining power, could generate additional headwinds.[4]

[3]While it is difficult to quantify the impact of deflation on debt accumulation, a mechanical calculation assuming a zero inflation rate for the years with deflation alone suggests a contribution of about 36 percent of GDP since 1990 through automatic debt dynamics.
[4]IMF (2016a) and Arbatli and others (2016) discuss the potential role for income policies and labor market reforms to strengthen wage-price dynamics in Japan.

Box 3.3. How Much Do Global Prices Matter for Food Inflation?

Bursts of inflation have often been accompanied or preceded by spiraling food prices.[1] This partly reflects the sizable share of food in consumption, particularly in lower-income countries (Figure 3.3.1). Waning global food prices since 2011 have therefore rekindled interest in the extent to which changes in international food prices pass through to domestic food prices and thus put downward pressure on overall consumer price inflation.

Comparing changes in world prices with changes in the domestic price of food in more than 80 economies, however, points to a low correlation between them.[2] Indeed, the patterns of domestic food inflation are strikingly different from inflation patterns in world food markets (which are denominated in U.S. dollars). In many advanced and especially emerging market economies, such a decoupling reflects exchange rate depreciation relative to the U.S. dollar, which has limited or more than offset the decline in world food prices (Figure 3.3.2, panels 1 and 2). By contrast, the exchange rate has played a lesser role in many low-income developing economies. The rapid increases in domestic food prices in these economies were driven by higher inflation in local food production, which is mostly nontradable (Figure 3.3.2, panel 3). Overall, food inflation has been generally higher than nonfood inflation in all country groups, especially in sub-Saharan Africa and emerging market economies (Figure 3.3.3). Thus, domestic food inflation has

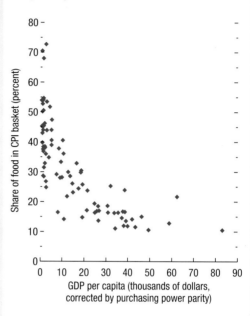

Figure 3.3.1. Food Weights in Consumption and per Capita GDP

Source: IMF staff calculations.
Note: CPI = consumer price index.

generally offset the ongoing nonfood deflationary pressures in many economies.[3]

Evidence of limited pass-through from free-on-board (that is, excluding the transportation cost to the final national market destination) food prices to consumer food prices is corroborated by regression analysis for a sample of 81 countries using monthly data for 2000–15 (Figure 3.3.4).[4] Despite the

The authors of this box are Emre Alper, Luis Catão, Niko Hobdari, Daniel Te Kaat, and Ali Uppal.

[1] A statistical horse race between food and oil prices as leading indicators of worldwide inflation over the past four decades points to a prominent role of food over oil (Catão and Chang 2011). For instance, the great inflation of the 1970s was preceded by a faster pace of food inflation relative to both oil and overall consumer prices. The first post–World War II outburst of global inflation in the 1950s was preceded by rising inflation in food commodities but not in oil. More recently, the widespread rise in consumer price index inflation above central bank targets in 2007–08 was largely due to food rather than oil.

[2] The analysis uses country-specific weights to compute the equivalent world market price of the domestic food consumption basket—that is, the price that consumers of that country would pay if they were to buy that approximate commodity basket in the world market. For sub-Saharan Africa, data availability allowed this computation for 17 of the 41 countries, with mean weights of low-income countries and middle-income countries of that sample applied to the entire sample. The analysis focuses on free-on-board import prices in local currency to control for exchange rate movements.

[3] On average, food inflation exceeded nonfood inflation by 1.4 percentage points a year during 2010–15 in the 41 sub-Saharan African countries comprising the sample. In advanced and emerging market economies, the respective differentials are 0.8 percentage point and 0.5 percentage point during the same period.

[4] The explanatory variables in the individual country regressions are the current and up to six lags of the free-on-board food price inflation index in local currency (computed as the percentage change of the product of the world food price index in U.S. dollars and the country's exchange rate against the U.S. dollar), augmented by lags of domestic food price inflation (with the lag length for each country regression being determined by standard statistical criteria). The pass-through coefficient is then computed as the sum of the coefficients on the free-on-board food inflation divided by 1 minus the sum of the lagged domestic food inflation coefficients (that is, the autoregressive coefficients).

Box 3.3 *(continued)*

Figure 3.3.2. World Food Prices and Consumer Food Prices
(January 2000 = 100)

— Consumer food prices
— World food prices in U.S. dollars
— World food prices in local currency

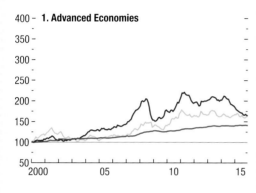

1. Advanced Economies

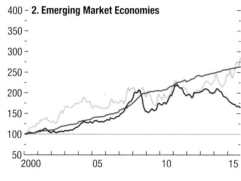

2. Emerging Market Economies

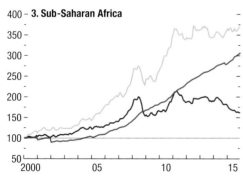

3. Sub-Saharan Africa

Source: IMF staff calculations.

Figure 3.3.3. Food Prices Relative to Nonfood Prices
(January 2000 = 100)

— Advanced economies
— Emerging market economies
— Sub-Saharan Africa

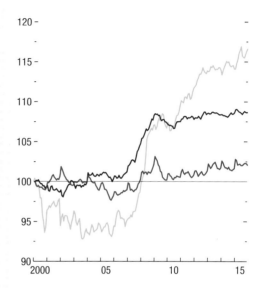

Source: IMF staff calculations.

mass of the distribution of the pass-through coefficients being centered between 0.1 and 0.2 (the median is about 0.12), there is considerable variation across countries. The pass-through is close to 0.4 for some countries and larger than 1 for one outlier (Ethiopia). In general, sub-Saharan Africa not only has a higher average pass-through but also higher cross-country dispersion of pass-through coefficients than advanced and emerging market economies. In addition, when the sample is broken into two subperiods—the first comprising the high food price inflation of 2006–08 and the second the decline in world food prices of 2009 and from 2011 onward—the pass-through appears to be higher on average and more dispersed in the former period (Figure 3.3.5). To explain the dispersion of pass-through coefficients across countries and periods, a regression of the various pass-through coefficients obtained from the full sample period is run on a variety of factors, including those identified by previous studies (for example, Gelos and Ustyugova 2012). The results of this empirical exercise point to the role of

Box 3.3 *(continued)*

Figure 3.3.4. Food Pass-Through Coefficients for Various Country Groups

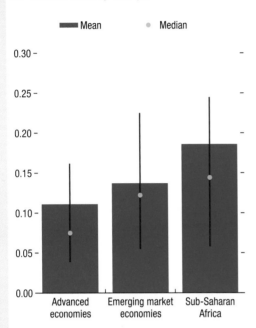

Source: IMF staff calculations.
Note: Vertical lines denote interquartile ranges.

Figure 3.3.5. Distribution of Food Pass-Through Coefficients

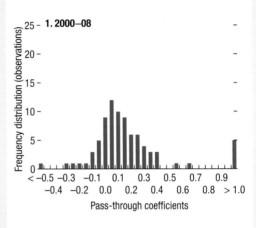

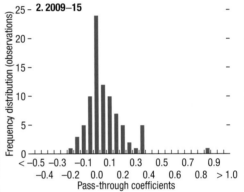

Source: IMF staff calculations.

income levels, exchange rate regimes, openness to food trade, and output volatility in shaping pass-through coefficients (Table 3.3.1):

- *Higher per capita income is associated with lower international food price pass-through.* One explanation for this result is that richer countries on average consume food products with higher value added, for which nontradable components, such as distribution services, represent a larger share of the overall cost.
- *A more stable exchange rate regime is associated with a higher pass-through.* With a fixed exchange rate, free-on-board prices in local currency are a more direct reflection of world prices, mitigating deviations from the law of one price associated with unexpected exchange rate volatility.
- *Countries that are either large net exporters (that is, with food exports exceeding food imports) relative to GDP or larger net importers of food relative to GDP are characterized by higher pass-through.* The rationale for this result is that the tradable component

of domestic food is likely to increase with either net food exports or net food imports.
- *Countries with higher average tariff rates on agricultural products have a lower pass-through*, consistent with the notion that tariffs reduce the tradability of some domestic food items.
- *The pass-through is higher in countries where growth is more volatile.* There may be different explanations for this finding. One straightforward explanation is that more volatile economies display less price stickiness, so the pass-through from higher world food prices to retail food prices is higher.

These findings suggest that a low pass-through of international to domestic food prices might not necessarily enhance welfare. This may be, for instance, the case if the pass-through is low as a result of high

Box 3.3 *(continued)*

Table 3.3.1. Cross-Country Determinants of Pass-Through of Free-on-Board Food Prices to Food Consumer Price Inflation

	(1)	(2)
Log of per Capita GDP	−0.0385***	−0.0333***
	(−3.15)	(−3.31)
Openness	0.0174	
	(0.88)	
Food Trade Balance/GDP	0.00838*	
	(1.71)	
Food Trade Balance/GDP, Squared	0.00124***	0.00151***
	(3.72)	(3.88)
Average CPI Inflation	−0.00135	
	(−1.34)	
Exchange Rate Regime	0.0296**	0.0235*
	(2.3)	(1.96)
Average Agricultural Tariff	−0.00527**	−0.00741***
	(−2.39)	(−4.90)
Growth Volatility	0.0116*	0.0134**
	(1.68)	(2.08)
Quality of Institutions	−0.00484	
	(−0.88)	
Constant	0.168***	0.151***
	(3.32)	(3.06)
Number of Observations	81	81
R^2	0.564	0.517
Adjusted R^2	0.509	0.484

Sources: IMF, National authorities; and IMF staff estimates.
Note: The dependent variable is the estimated pass-through coefficient reported in Figure 3.4. Robust *t*-statistics are in parentheses. CPI = consumer price index. ***, **, * denote significance at the 1, 5, and 10 percent level, respectively.

tariffs that distort resource allocation, or if it reflects a high share of local produce (such as fresh fruits and vegetables) that—given its nontradability—is produced, stored, or transported inefficiently.[5] Indeed, when world prices are falling, low tradability limits the benefits of falling world food prices to consumers. Conversely, when world food prices are rising, low tradability tends to limit the benefits of higher world prices to producers and thus postpone needed adjustments to production, which would eventually benefit domestic consumers as well.

[5]See Chapter 1 for evidence on the share of local produce in domestic food consumption and a broad discussion of the role of food in production and consumption.

Box 3.4. The Impact of Commodity Prices on Producer Price Inflation

The chapter documents a generalized decline in producer price inflation across advanced economies over the past few years, especially in manufacturing. The drop in producer price inflation has been particularly marked among commodity importers, suggesting that international input linkages are a key channel through which deflation pressure spills across countries (Figure 3.4.1). Against this backdrop, this box uses sectoral data from four selected advanced economies—France, Germany, Korea, and the Netherlands—to explore how much of the decline in producer price inflation can be attributed to weakening international commodity prices and other import prices.[1]

The empirical approach used to decompose the contribution of different input prices to sector-level producer price inflation follows the methodology developed in Ahn, Park, and Park (2016). In particular, the following specification is used to estimate the effect of domestic input prices (DOM_{it}), imported input prices (IMP_{it}), and labor costs (ULC_{it}) on domestic producer prices (P_{it}) at the country-sector level:[2]

$$ln(P_{it}) = \beta_1 \alpha_{i,DOM} ln(DOM_{it}) + \beta_2 \alpha_{i,IMP} ln(IMP_{it})$$
$$+ \beta_3 \alpha_{i,ULC} ln(ULC_{it}) + \varepsilon_{it}, \qquad (3.4.1)$$

in which it denotes sector i at time t, ln denotes logs, and $\alpha_{i,X}$ is the share of each type of input in the total cost structure of sector i (with $\sum_X \alpha_{i,X} = 1$), obtained from input-output tables.[3] The degree of pass-through from input prices to producer prices (β) is allowed to vary across inputs to account for a possible heterogeneous response to underlying cost shocks. The equation is estimated separately in panel settings for Korea (including sector fixed effects) and for the three European economies (with country-sector fixed effects). An error correction setup is used to take into account the potential cointegrating relationship between nonstationary producer and input prices.

Following the novel approach in Ahn, Park, and Park (2016) and Auer and Mehrotra (2014),

---

The author of this box is JaeBin Ahn.

[1]The focus on these four advanced economies is based on high-frequency sector-level price data availability.

[2]A possible limitation of the methodology is that prices in other sectors as well as exchange rates—which affect import prices denominated in local currency—are taken as given in the estimation. Also, by relying on a reduced-form specification, the analysis does not take a stand on the underlying source of variation in commodity or other imported input prices.

[3]The source for input shares is the World Input-Output Table (http://www.wiod.org/).

Figure 3.4.1. Commodity Prices and Producer Prices

(January 2014 = 100; simple average by country groups)

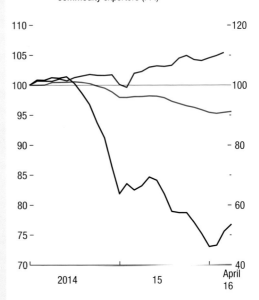

Sources: Bank of Korea; Eurostat; Haver Analytics; and IMF, International Financial Statistics database.
Note: Commodity importers: 18 euro area countries, China, Japan, Korea, United Kingdom, United States; Commodity exporters: Brazil, Chile, Colombia, South Africa. PPI = producer price index.

input-output tables and sector-level price data are combined to construct input price and labor cost indices for each domestic sector i. For instance, the imported input price index for sector i is obtained as:

$$ln(IMP_{it}) = \sum_j (\alpha_{ij,IMP}/\alpha_{i,IMP}) ln(I_{jt}), \qquad (3.4.2)$$

in which $\alpha_{ij,IMP}$ is the share of imported inputs from sector j in total inputs used for sector i's production from input-output tables, and I_{jt} is the price index of sector j imported goods from sector-level import price data.[4] Imported inputs can be further split into

---

[4]All the price series data are available from the Statistics Database at the Bank of Korea (Economic Statistics System), which is publicly accessible on the Web (ecos.bok.or.kr), or from the Eurostat database (http://ec.europa.eu/eurostat/data/database).

Box 3.4 *(continued)*

commodity and noncommodity components, allowing for separate estimation of their contributions to producer price inflation.[5] The sector-specific domestic input price and unit labor cost indices are constructed analogously using input-output tables, sector-level domestic producer price indices, and sector-level unit labor cost indices.

The results suggest that the pass-through from import prices to domestic producer prices is high. The short-term pass-through from commodity to domestic producer prices in Korea is about 40 percent and reaches about 60 percent over the long term. The pass-through from commodity input prices is even higher in the three European countries—90 percent in the short term and almost 100 percent in the long term.[6] The estimated pass-through coefficients from noncommodity import prices are comparable.

Combining these pass-through estimates with actual sector-level import prices over the past two years suggests the following results:

- The sharp drop in commodity prices was a major driver of aggregate producer price deflation in France, Germany, and the Netherlands over the past two years (Figure 3.4.2). Its contribution was somewhat smaller but still important in the case of Korea.

- The differences across countries in the relative contribution of commodity import prices to aggregate producer price inflation are mostly due to variations in input weights—rather than to differences in import price dynamics.

- Most of the impact of commodity prices on aggregate producer price deflation during this period is indirect—stemming from a decline in input prices for domestic noncommodity sectors. The direct contribution—through commodity imports by the domestic commodity sector—is almost zero in all countries except the Netherlands where oil re-exports are significant—and even there it

[5]The commodity sector is defined as the "mining and quarrying" industry at the two-digit industry classification.
[6]The difference in the estimated coefficients across country groups might reflect, among other factors, distinct market structures and degree of competition.

Figure 3.4.2. Contribution to Cumulative Producer Price Inflation
(Percent, January 2014–March 2016)

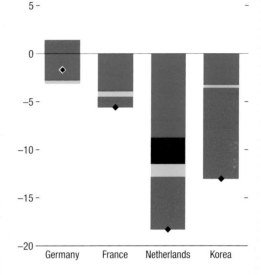

Sources: Bank of Korea; Eurostat; Haver Analytics; IMF, International Financial Statistics database; and IMF staff calculations.
Note: The direct contribution of imported commodity inputs captures the commodity sector's own use of imported commodities, and the indirect contribution reflects other sectors' use of imported commodities as inputs. PPI = producer price index.

accounts for only one-fifth of the total commodity price contribution.

- The contribution of noncommodity import prices to aggregate producer price inflation over the past two years is much smaller. This is mainly due to the fact that international manufacturing prices declined much less than international commodity prices over the past two years—rather than due to differences in pass-through coefficients or differences in the relative weights of commodity versus noncommodity inputs in production.

Box 3.5. A Transparent Risk-Management Approach to Monetary Policy

A risk-management approach to monetary policy seeks to avoid severe outcomes, including deflation. Policymakers do not worry about small deviations from desired outcomes but they attach an increasing marginal cost to inflation and output gap deviations as they grow larger. This implies prompt and aggressive actions to move the economy away from situations in which the risk of conventional policy instruments losing their effectiveness becomes larger—such as in a context of persistent economic slack and low inflation with the policy interest rate at the effective lower bound (ELB).

Expectations play a crucial role in the effectiveness of monetary policy. Adjusting the central bank's conventional policy instrument—a very short-term interest rate—in itself has a negligible effect on the overall economy. Its impact stems from its influence over market expectations about the future path of short-term interest rates which, in turn, affect the medium- and longer-term interest rates at which households and firms invest and borrow.

However, the path for policy interest rates that can bring inflation to the central bank's target is not unique. For example, the central bank may intend to pursue a strategy that returns inflation to target gradually, with small steps in the policy instrument over a period of several quarters. Or it may be planning a quick, aggressive approach. In the absence of direct guidance from policymakers, market expectations will not necessarily match the central bank's intended path for policy rates.

This box presents model simulations to illustrate how a credible and transparent commitment to aggressive monetary accommodation can reduce the risk of recession and deflation even if the monetary policy rate is at the ELB.[1] A standard New Keynesian model of the Canadian economy is used to simulate a counterfactual repeat of the history of the global financial crisis under two alternative policy strategies. In the first strategy, based on the principle of risk management, the central bank minimizes a loss function imposing a steeply increasing marginal cost on output gaps and deviations of inflation from the target. The second policy strategy follows a linear inflation forecast–based policy reaction function—that is, a forward-looking Taylor rule. The counterfactual

The authors of this box are Kevin Clinton, Douglas Laxton, and Hou Wang.
[1]See Obstfeld and others (forthcoming) for further details.

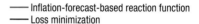

Figure 3.5.1. Forecast as Envisaged at 2009:Q2: Loss Minimization versus Linear Reaction Function
(Percent, unless noted otherwise)

——— Inflation-forecast-based reaction function
——— Loss minimization

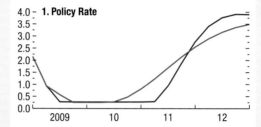

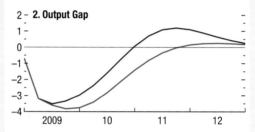

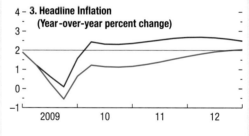

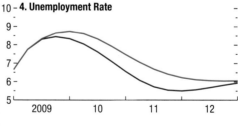

Source: IMF staff estimates.

simulated scenarios start in the second quarter of 2009 and are summarized in Figure 3.5.1:

- The risk-management strategy (red line) implies holding the policy rate at the ELB (assumed here to be 0.25 percent) until the first quarter of 2011, long enough to result in a temporary overshooting

Box 3.5 *(continued)*

of the inflation target. As the public is aware of this intention, expectations for longer-term nominal interest rates shift down and medium-term inflation expectations increase. This reduces real interest rates, which in turn increases asset prices and depreciates the local currency, boosting output and inflation. The inflation overshoot makes up for the initial undesired well-below-target inflation and, on average, inflation ends up being very close to the target.

- The linear policy reaction function plan (blue line), in contrast, implies raising the policy rate already by mid-2010 and a much slower convergence to the target—en route, this means wider output gaps and deviations of inflation from the target and higher unemployment than under the risk-management strategy.

The logic for a more aggressive strategy that deliberately overshoots the inflation target is straightforward. Further negative demand shocks in a context of policy rates already at the ELB pose the risk of pushing the economy into a deflation situation from which escape is increasingly difficult. Relative to this,

the prospect of a short period with inflation above target is acceptable.

But transparency is a key ingredient of this strategy. Publishing the expected path of all the variables used at policy decision meetings, including the projected path for the policy interest rate, would help the central bank give a credible public account of its strategy.[2] This would reinforce public confidence in the central bank's inflation objective and strengthen the transmission of policy actions to the economy: if the published path for policy interest rates is credible, the term structure of interest rates and asset prices, such as the exchange rate, will move in support of the policy objectives. In contrast, forecasting an overshooting of the inflation rate without communicating the whole breadth of the central bank's strategy might undermine confidence in the nominal anchor—it might look as though the central bank is doing "too little, too late" in terms of normalizing interest rates.

---

[2]See Poloz (2014) for arguments in favor of forward guidance, including by publishing the projected path of policy rates, when interest rates are at the effective lower bound but not in normal times.

Annex 3.1. Sample and Data

Country Sample

The broadest sample used for regression analysis in this chapter comprises 44 advanced and emerging market economies, listed in Annex Table 3.1.1. These economies are selected based on the availability of their inflation expectation measures from the Consensus Forecasts database.

Data Sources

The primary data sources for this chapter are the Organisation for Economic Co-operation and Development Economic Outlook and Structural Analysis databases, CEIC China database, Consensus Economics Consensus Forecasts database, Global Data Services database, IMF World Economic Outlook database, World Bank World Development Indicators database, and Haver Analytics and Bloomberg L.P. All variables are of quarterly frequency (with the exception of the variables used in the analysis of market-based inflation expectations, which are available at daily frequency). Medium-term inflation expectations from the Consensus Forecasts database are interpolated to quarterly frequency from biannual surveys. The coverage of GDP and import price deflators is expanded by interpolation from annual data. Annex Table 3.1.2 lists all indicators used in this chapter as well as their sources.

Annex 3.2. Model Simulations

Model simulations are used to assess the deflationary effects of depressed demand and subdued import prices in three large economies—the United States, the euro area, and Japan—when monetary policy is constrained and inflation expectations become unanchored.[48] The simulations are carried out under two alternative macroeconomic environments. In both environments, monetary policy is assumed to be constrained—that is, the policy rate is at its effective lower bound. The second assumes, in addition, that inflation surprises have a direct effect on inflation expectations.[49]

---

[48]Simulations are performed using the IMF's G20MOD model.

[49]The effect of inflation on inflation expectations is introduced in the model via shocks to the expected inflation term that enters the model's reduced-form Phillips curve. An inflation surprise equal to 1 percentage point that occurs in year 1 would shift inflation expectations by 0.25 percentage point in year 2, 0.10 percentage point in year 3, 0.05 percentage point in year 4, and would decline to zero in year 5 and beyond. These magnitudes are based on the empirical evidence in the chapter on the degree to which inflation surprises shift the private sector's inflation expectations at various horizons.

Annex Table 3.1.1. Sample of Advanced and Emerging Market Economies

Advanced Market Economies	Emerging Market Economies
Australia, Canada, Czech Republic, Estonia, France, Germany, Hong Kong SAR, Italy, Japan, Korea, Latvia, Lithuania, Netherlands, New Zealand, Norway, Singapore, Slovak Republic, Slovenia, Spain, Sweden, Switzerland, Taiwan Province of China, United Kingdom, United States	Argentina, Brazil, Bulgaria, Chile, China, Colombia, Hungary, India, Indonesia, Malaysia, Mexico, Peru, Philippines, Poland, Romania, Russia, Thailand, Turkey, Ukraine, Venezuela

Annex Table 3.1.2. Data Sources

Variable	Source
Commodity Prices	Bloomberg L.P., Haver Analytics, IMF Commodity Price System
Consumer Price, Core Consumer Price, Producer Price, and Wage Indices	Haver Analytics; IMF, World Economic Outlook database; Organisation for Economic Co-operation and Development
Import Value, Import Volume, and Import-Price Deflator	CEIC database; Haver Analytics; IMF, World Economic Outlook database; Organisation for Economic Co-operation and Development; World Development Indicators database
Industrial Production Index	IMF, World Economic Outlook database
Nominal and Real GDP, and GDP Deflator	Haver Analytics; IMF, World Economic Outlook database; Organisation for Economic Co-operation and Development; World Development Indicators database
Nominal Effective Exchange Rates	Global Data Services database
Output Gap	IMF, World Economic Outlook database
Unemployment Rate	Bloomberg L.P.; Haver Analytics; IMF, World Economic Outlook database; Organisation for Economic Co-operation and Development; Thomson Reuters Datastream
Inflation Swaps, Stock Market Indices, and Treasury Bill Interest Rates	Bloomberg L.P.; Haver Analytics
Survey-Based Inflation Expectations	Bank of England, Survey of External Forecasters; Consensus Economics; European Commission, Business and Consumer Surveys; IMF, World Economic Outlook database; University of Michigan, Survey of Consumers
Unemployment Expectation	Consensus Economics
Central Bank Transparency and Governor Turnover Rate	Crowe and Meade (2007)
Inflation-Targeting Regime	*World Economic Outlook*, October 2011, Chapter 3

The first shock considered in the simulations is a temporary decline in domestic demand of 1 percent in each of the three economies. The results reported in Figure 3.4 show that even if monetary policy is constrained, the economy would escape from the deflation trap within a reasonable timeframe as long as inflation expectations remained well anchored. But if inflation expectations drifted down, it could take a very long time for the economy to emerge from deflation.

The results in the chapter suggest that reduced import prices have also played an important role in driving inflation down in many economies over the recent past. While in normal circumstances import prices typically have temporary effects on inflation and therefore should not be a source of concern for inflation dynamics going forward, they could be potentially worrisome at the current juncture of constrained monetary policy and evidence of inflation expectations becoming unanchored.

To gauge the possible deflationary consequences of these developments, two shocks to import prices are considered. The first shock is a sharp decline in oil prices.[50] The second shock is a decline in China's export prices—taken as an example of a shock to global prices of tradable goods stemming from manufacturing slack in a key large economy.[51] The results reported in Annex Figures 3.2.1 and 3.2.2 show that shocks to import prices may lead to persistent disinflation pressure when monetary policy is constrained and medium-term inflation expectations become unanchored:

- *Constrained monetary policy*—In countries with constrained monetary policy, lower prices for oil and manufactured goods from China may keep inflation below the baseline—that is, the path in the absence of shocks—for up to four years (Annex Figure 3.2.1). A decline in import prices directly reduces inflation in the short term but also indirectly reduces it through lower demand. The indirect effect arises from lower inflation interacting with the unchanged nominal policy rate: real interest rates rise, putting downward pressure on both consump-

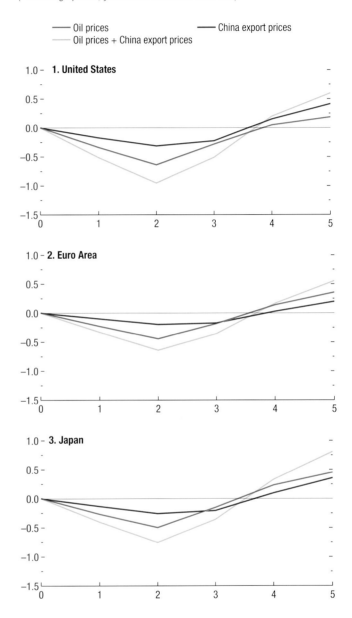

Annex Figure 3.2.1. Effect of Disinflationary Shocks on Core Inflation in Advanced Economies under Constrained Monetary Policy
(Percentage points; years after the shock on x-axis)

Source: IMF staff estimates.
Note: The figure reports the responses of core inflation after a shock to international oil prices and a shock to China's export prices. The model assumes that conventional monetary policy is constrained at the effective lower bound on nominal interest rates in all countries.

[50]The shock to oil prices is calibrated so that its magnitude matches the actual drop in international oil prices in 2014 and its persistence is consistent with prices in the futures market.

[51]The decline in China's export prices has been set to broadly match the impact of excess capacity in China on consumer price inflation in key advanced economies in 2015 documented in the chapter.

tion and investment. However, in the medium term, the decline in import prices raises households' wealth, which stimulates consumption enough to more than offset the downward pressure exerted by higher real interest rates. Higher consumption

Annex Figure 3.2.2. Effect of Disinflationary Shocks on Core Inflation in Advanced Economies under Constrained Monetary Policy and Unanchored Inflation Expectations
(Percentage points; years after the shock on x-axis)

—— Constrained monetary policy
—— Constrained monetary policy + unanchored inflation expectations

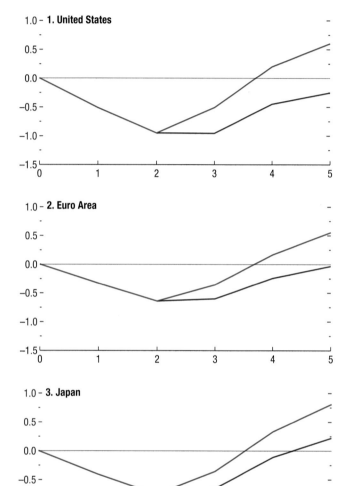

Source: IMF staff estimates.
Note: The figure reports the responses of core inflation after a combined shock to international oil prices and China's export prices. The model assumes that conventional monetary policy is constrained at the effective lower bound on nominal interest rates in all countries. The alternative scenario (red line) assumes also that inflation expectations are affected by inflation shocks.

demand and lower input costs also stimulate investment. The resulting increase in domestic demand is eventually sufficient to halt and then reverse the decline in inflation. The effect of lower import prices on inflation varies by economy depending on (1) its degree of dependence on oil imports, (2) the extent of its trade links with China, (3) the wealth effect generated by lower import prices, and (4) the degree of flexibility in wages and prices.

- *Constrained monetary policy and unanchoring of inflation expectations*—If monetary policy is constrained and inflation expectations become unanchored, lower import prices may lead to persistent disinflation. Inflation rates remain below the baseline for more than five years (Annex Figure 3.2.2). The result is driven by additional deflation pressure stemming from lower inflation expectations, which may more than offset the positive inflation effects associated with increased household wealth effects in the medium term. The results of this scenario suggest that if inflation expectations become unanchored, mitigating the impact of declining import prices on core inflation could be quite challenging without additional measures to stimulate demand.

Annex 3.3. Principal Component Analysis

A principal component analysis is used to assess the extent to which the recent decline in inflation is common across countries.[52] The results of the analysis suggest that the first three common factors explain about 80 percent to 90 percent of the variation in inflation among advanced economies in 2000–08 and 2009–15, respectively, and about 75 percent among emerging market and developing economies in both subperiods. There is, nonetheless, significant heterogeneity across countries in the importance of these factors. For example, common factors play a larger role in France and Spain, while country-specific factors play a larger role in countries such as Iceland, Israel, and South Africa (Annex Figure 3.3.1).

While numerous variables may be correlated with the first three common factors, the evolution over time of the first common factor, for instance, is closely related to changes in commodity prices

[52]The principal component analysis is a statistical procedure that transforms the data into a set of values of linearly uncorrelated variables—principal components. See Rabe-Hesketh and Everitt (2007).

Annex Figure 3.3.1. Share of Consumer Price Inflation Variation Explained by Different Factors
(Percent)

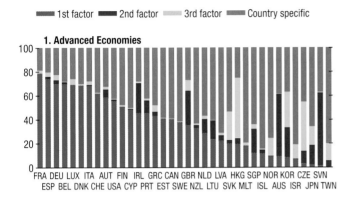
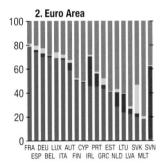
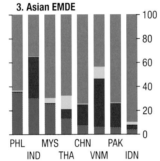
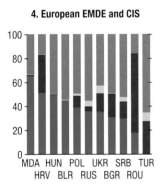
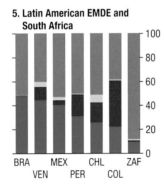

Sources: Haver Analytics; and IMF staff estimates.
Note: CIS = Commonwealth of Independent States; EMDE = emerging market and developing economies. Data labels in the figure use International Organization for Standardization (ISO) country codes.

(Annex Figure 3.3.2).[53] Additional analyses using Bayesian modeling average and weighted least squares find that, indeed, commodity prices stand out among several variables—including slowing global industrial production, growth disappointments in emerging

[53]See the April 2015 *Regional Economic Outlook: Asia and Pacific* and the IMF's *2015 Spillover Report* (IMF 2015) for similar evidence.

Annex Figure 3.3.2. First Common Factor and Commodity Prices
(Percent)

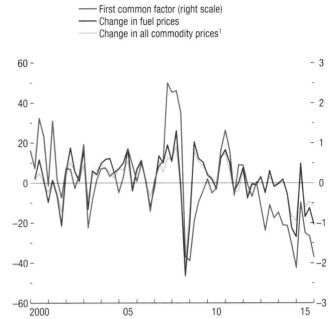

Sources: Haver Analytics; IMF, Primary Commodity Prices database; and IMF staff estimates.
[1] Price index using weights based on 2002–04 average world export earnings.

market economies, and financial market conditions—as being strongly linked with the first common factor.

Annex 3.4. Drivers of the Recent Decline in Inflation

Empirical Framework

The following version of the Phillips curve equation is estimated:

$$\pi_t = \gamma_t \pi^e_{t+h} + (1 - \gamma_t) \tilde{\pi}_{t-1} + \theta_t u^c_t + \mu_t \pi^m_t + \varepsilon_t, \quad (3.4.1)$$

in which π_t denotes annualized quarterly headline consumer price inflation, π^e_{t+h} denotes inflation expectations h years ahead (with 10-year-ahead expectations used in the baseline specification), $\tilde{\pi}_{t-1}$ is the moving average of inflation over the previous four quarters, u^c_t denotes cyclical unemployment, π^m_t denotes the relative price of imports (defined as the import-price deflator relative to the GDP deflator), and ε_t denotes the residual.

The coefficients and the nonaccelerating inflation rate of unemployment (NAIRU) are assumed to follow constrained random walks ($\gamma_t \in (0,1), \theta_t < 0,$

$\mu_t > 0$, and no restrictions on NAIRU). Cyclical unemployment is assumed to follow an AR(1) process: $u_t^c = \rho\, u_{t-1}^c + \varepsilon_t^u$, with $u_c^t = u_t - u_t^*$, in which u_t denotes the unemployment rate, u_t^* denotes the NAIRU, and ε_t^u is assumed to follow $N(0, \sigma_u^2)$.

The model is estimated country-by-country using maximum likelihood based on a constrained nonlinear Kalman filter for a sample of 44 advanced and emerging market economies from the first quarter of 1990 to the first quarter of 2016.

An important feature of the model is that it allows for time variation in all parameters to capture changes in the structure of each economy. The advantages of such a model compared with rolling regressions are fourfold: (1) it uses all observations in the sample to estimate the magnitude of the parameters in each year—which by construction is not possible in rolling regressions; (2) changes in the parameters in a given period come from innovations in the same period, rather than from shocks occurring in neighboring periods; (3) it reflects the fact that economic structures typically change slowly and depend on the immediate past; and (4) it allows for possible nonlinearities (Swamy and Mehta 1975).

Decomposition

The decomposition of inflation dynamics is conducted in a way similar to Yellen (2015). The exercise is constructed in terms of deviations of inflation from inflation targets—using the average of 10-year-ahead inflation expectations during 2000–07 as a proxy for inflation targets. The contribution of each explanatory variable is obtained by setting its value to zero and comparing the model's prediction with that when all explanatory variables are set at their historical values.[54] The contribution of import prices to inflation is further decomposed into the contribution of import prices in U.S. dollars and variations in the domestic exchange rate vis-à-vis the U.S. dollar. The contribution of labor market slack is computed by substituting the cyclical unemployment series estimated with the Kalman filter—and possibly subject to end-sample bias—with a measure derived from output gap estimates in the IMF World Economic Outlook database and country-specific Okun's law coefficient estimates reported in Ball, Furceri, and Loungani (forthcoming);

the residuals are adjusted accordingly. The simulation is dynamic in that the lagged inflation term is set to its simulated values. Therefore, the decomposition incorporates the effects of changes in lagged inflation that are attributable to previous movements in the explanatory variables—which become more relevant as inflation is more persistent.

Robustness Checks

Inflation expectations measure—The baseline specification is estimated using 10-year-ahead inflation expectations from Consensus Economics, for two reasons: (1) long-term inflation expectations are a close proxy for central banks' inflation targets, so that the parameter γ can be interpreted as the degree to which the headline inflation is linked to the central bank's target—a phenomenon typically referred to as "level anchoring" (Ball and Mazumder 2011) and (2) long-term inflation expectations are less correlated with current and lagged inflation and hence are less subject to problems of multicollinearity and reverse causality.

To test for the robustness of the results, two alternative versions of equation (3.4.1) are estimated. The first uses 1-year-ahead inflation expectations instead of 10-year-ahead expectations. The second one uses 1-year-ahead inflation expectations but omits the lagged inflation term. For advanced economies, the results are broadly similar to those obtained in the baseline (Annex Figure 3.4.1, panel 1).[55] In emerging market economies, however, using shorter-term expectations results in substantially smaller residuals, especially in countries with inflation above long-term expectations (Annex Figures 3.4.2, panels 2 and 3).

Cyclical unemployment measure—Estimates of cyclical unemployment are typically subject to large uncertainty. To check the robustness of the results, two alternative estimates of cyclical unemployment are used: (1) the Hodrick-Prescott filtered unemployment rate and (2) deviations of unemployment rates from five-year moving averages. The results presented in Annex Figure 3.4.2 suggest that the contribution of import prices to inflation is robust to alternative proxies of economic slack, but the contribution of slack itself and other factors varies somewhat when different measures are used.

---

[54]The analysis assumes that labor market slack and import prices do not affect 10-year-ahead inflation expectations, which is supported by additional analysis of the effect of these two variables on inflation expectations.

[55]The results of two-year- or three-year-ahead inflation expectations (not reported here due to space constraints) are broadly similar to those of one-year-ahead inflation expectation.

Annex Figure 3.4.1. Contribution to Inflation Deviations from Targets Using Various Measures of Inflation Expectations

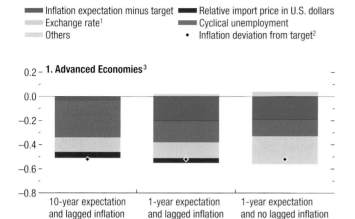

1. Advanced Economies[3]

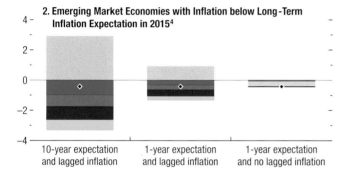

2. Emerging Market Economies with Inflation below Long-Term Inflation Expectation in 2015[4]

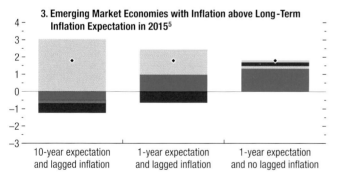

3. Emerging Market Economies with Inflation above Long-Term Inflation Expectation in 2015[5]

Sources: Consensus Economics; Haver Analytics; Organisation for Economic Co-operation and Development, Economic Outlook database; and IMF staff calculations.
Note: The figure reports average contributions in 2008–15. Okun's law coefficients come from Ball and others 2016.
[1] Exchange rate is defined as currency value per U.S. dollar.
[2] The target is defined as the average of 10-year inflation expectation in 2000–07.
[3] Advanced economies in Annex Table 3.1.1. Estonia, Latvia, Lithuania, the Slovak Republic, and Slovenia are excluded as outliers.
[4] Bulgaria, China, Hungary, Malaysia, Mexico, Philippines, Poland, Romania, Thailand.
[5] Argentina, Brazil, Chile, Columbia, India, Indonesia, Peru, Russia, Turkey.

Annex Figure 3.4.2. Contribution to Inflation Deviations from Targets Using Various Measures of Cyclical Unemployment

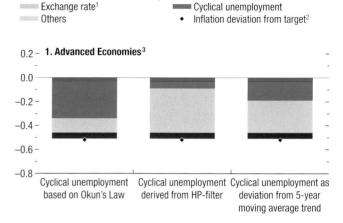

1. Advanced Economies[3]

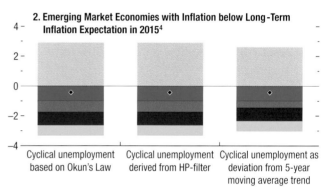

2. Emerging Market Economies with Inflation below Long-Term Inflation Expectation in 2015[4]

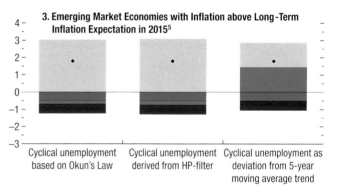

3. Emerging Market Economies with Inflation above Long-Term Inflation Expectation in 2015[5]

Sources: Consensus Economics; Haver Analytics; Organisation for Economic Co-operation and Development, Economic Outlook database; and IMF staff calculations.
Note: The figure reports average contributions in 2008–15. Okun's law coefficients come from Ball and others 2016.
[1] Exchange rate is defined as currency value per U.S. dollar.
[2] The target is defined as the average of 10-year inflation expectation in 2000–07.
[3] Advanced economies in Annex Table 3.1.1. Estonia, Latvia, Lithuania, the Slovak Republic, and Slovenia are excluded as outliers.
[4] Bulgaria, China, Hungary, Malaysia, Mexico, Philippines, Poland, Romania, Thailand.
[5] Argentina, Brazil, Chile, Columbia, India, Indonesia, Peru, Russia, Turkey.

Annex Figure 3.4.3. Correlation of Manufacturing Slack in China, Japan, and the United States with Import Price Contribution to Inflation in Other Economies

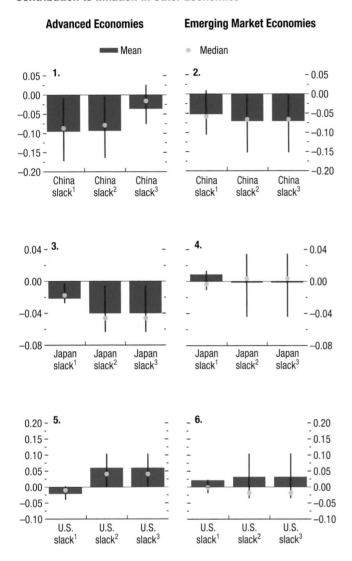

Sources: Consensus Economics; Haver Analytics; Organisation for Economic Co-operation and Development; and IMF staff calculations.
Note: Vertical lines denote interquartile ranges. The figure shows the coefficients of manufacturing slack from regressions of the import price contribution to inflation on manufacturing slack and other variables.
[1] No controls.
[2] Controlling for manufacturing slack in the other two economies, change in oil prices, and global output gap.
[3] Controlling for global output gap and change in oil prices in current and previous four quarters.

Manufacturing Slack in China, Japan, and the United States, and Inflation in Other Economies

To explore the relationship between manufacturing slack in key large economies—China, Japan, and the United States—and inflation developments in other countries, the following equation is estimated for each

of the 44 advanced and emerging market economies in the sample:

$$I_{i,t} = \alpha + \beta S_t^j + \delta X_t + \varepsilon_{i,t}, \tag{3.4.2}$$

in which I is the contribution of import price to inflation as estimated using equation (3.4.1); S denotes manufacturing slack; j refers to China, Japan, or the United States; and X is a set of control variables, including global factors such as current and past changes in oil prices and global output gap—defined as the U.S.-dollar-GDP-weighted average of the output gap across countries.[56]

The results of the analysis suggest that the contribution of import prices to inflation in many advanced and emerging market economies is significantly correlated with manufacturing slack in China, Japan, and the United States. The association is particularly strong, robust, and more precisely estimated for China. In particular, a 1 percentage point increase in manufacturing slack in China is, on average, associated with a decline in inflation in other economies of about 0.04 percentage point to 0.1 percentage point (Figure 3.14), with the relationship being stronger in advanced economies than in emerging market economies (Annex Figure 3.4.3).

Equation (3.4.2) is also estimated in a panel setting with country-fixed effects. The results show that the correlation with manufacturing slack in China is significant at the 90 percent confidence interval and robust to controlling for global variables (Annex Figure 3.4.4). Finally, further analysis finds that this correlation is higher in countries with stronger trade links with China, providing additional evidence of spillover effects through tradable goods.

Annex 3.5. The Effect of Inflation Shocks on Inflation Expectations

The econometric approach to assess the effect of inflation shocks on inflation expectations follows the one used in Levin, Natalucci, and Piger (2004), which relates changes in inflation expectations to changes

---

[56]The contribution of import prices to inflation is used as a dependent variable to provide a direct measure of the association between excess capacity in manufacturing in large economies and inflation rates in other advanced and emerging market economies. Similar results are obtained when import prices are used as the dependent variable (and the effect of manufacturing slack on inflation is computed by rescaling the effect of manufacturing slack on import prices by the effect of import prices on inflation).

Annex Figure 3.4.4. Correlation of China Manufacturing Slack with Import Price Contribution to Inflation in Other Economies: Results from Panel Regressions

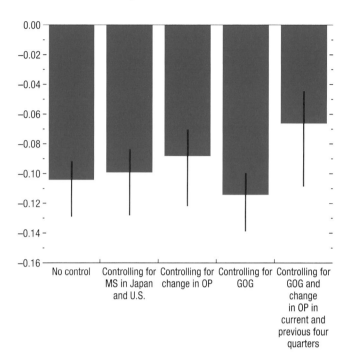

Sources: Consensus Forecasts; Haver Analytics; Organisation for Economic Co-operation and Development, Economic Outlook database; and IMF staff calculations.
Note: The figure reports the coefficients of manufacturing slack in China from panel regressions. Bars denote coefficient median values. Vertical lines denote 90 percent confidence intervals. MS = manufacturing slack; OP = oil prices; GOG = global output gap.

Annex Figure 3.5.1. Change in Inflation Expectations and Inflation Shocks
(Percentage points)

Change in Expectations at 1-, 3-, and 10-Year Horizons

— Median 1-year — Median 3-year — Median 10-year

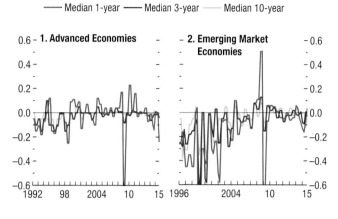

Inflation Shocks

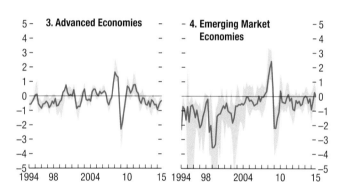

Sources: Consensus Economics; Haver Analytics; and IMF staff calculations.
Note: Data used in this figure are quarterly. In panels 3 and 4, blue lines denote the median of inflation shocks, and shaded areas denote interquartile ranges.

in inflation. In particular, the following equation is estimated country by country:

$$\Delta \pi_{t+h}^e = \beta_t^h \pi_t^{news} + \epsilon_{t+h}, \tag{3.5.1}$$

in which $\Delta \pi_{t+h}^e$ denotes the first difference in expectations of inflation h years in the future; π_t^{news} is a measure of inflation shocks—defined as the difference between actual inflation and short-term inflation expectations from Consensus Economics; and the coefficient β^h captures the degree of anchoring in h-years-ahead inflation expectations—a term usually referred to as "shock anchoring" (Ball and Mazumder 2011).

Annex Figure 3.5.1 shows the evolution of the left-hand-side (top panel) and right-hand-side (bottom panel) variables in equation (3.5.1) for advanced and emerging market economies. Changes in inflation expectations have been more volatile at shorter horizons for both groups of countries. Expectations were

on a downward path throughout the 1990s in both advanced and emerging market economies as monetary frameworks were improving and inflation was falling. This trend was particularly strong in emerging market economies. Inflation expectations have been remarkably stable throughout the 2000s in advanced economies, especially at longer horizons, but recently their volatility has increased. In contrast, for emerging market economies the volatility of expectations during 2009–15 has been lower than in the previous decade.

Inflation shocks have been relatively modest in advanced economies, except for the period surrounding the global financial crisis. These shocks were mostly negative in the 1990s as inflation was declining, but have been close to zero in the 2000s. Since 2011, the median inflation shock in advanced economies was negative. In emerging market economies, inflation shocks were negative on average in the 1990s and early 2000s, but less so more recently.

Robustness Checks

It is possible that changes in current and expected inflation are both driven by changes in expectations about the future state of the economy. For example, if firms and households expect that the economy will be in a recession in the near future and inflation will be lower than today, they will start cutting their consumption and investment expenditures now, putting downward pressure on inflation today. In that case, both inflation expectations and inflation would decline, but this would be driven by a third factor (expectations of future slack), rather than a causal link from inflation shocks to inflation expectations—especially on short-term horizons.

To check whether the results are simply driven by this mechanism, the baseline specification is augmented with the change in expectations about the future state of the economy, proxied by the change in one-year-ahead unemployment rate expectations from Consensus Forecasts (Δu_{t+1}^e):[57]

$$\Delta \pi_{t+h}^e = \beta_t^h \pi_t^{news} + \delta_t \Delta u_{t+1}^e + \epsilon_{t+h}. \qquad (3.5.2)$$

The results reported in Annex Figure 3.5.2 suggest that the sensitivity values obtained controlling for expectations about future slack are not statistically different from those presented in the baseline.

Finally, the results are also robust when considering changes in inflation or deviations of inflation from targets as alternative measures of inflation shocks.

Oil Price Inflation versus Core Inflation

For countries with a zero-lower-bound constraint, the sensitivity of inflation expectations to shocks is further decomposed into those originating from changes in: (1) oil price inflation and (2) core inflation. To do this, inflation surprises are first regressed on oil price inflation country by country:

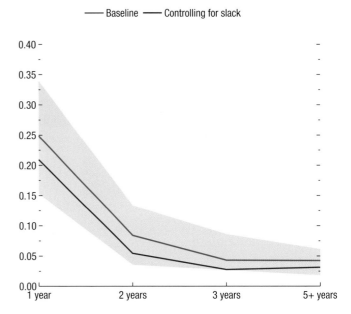

Annex Figure 3.5.2. Sensitivity of Inflation Expectations when Controlling for Slack: Advanced Economies

Sources: Consensus Economics; Haver Analytics; and IMF staff calculations.
Note: The figure shows the response of inflation expectations at various horizons to a 1 percentage point unexpected increase in inflation based on coefficients from country-specific static regressions. The alternative specification (red line) controls for the change in one-year-ahead unemployment rate expectations. The sensitivity for 5+ years corresponds to the average of estimations using 5- and 10-year-ahead inflation expectations. Solid lines denote the median response of inflation expectations across countries while the shaded area denotes the interquartile range of the responses under the baseline specification.

$$\pi_t^{news} = \alpha + \beta \pi_t^{oil} + \epsilon_t, \qquad (3.5.3)$$

in which π_t^{oil} is the oil price inflation. Inflation shocks are then decomposed into the part driven by changes in oil prices (fitted values) and the part unrelated to oil prices (residuals). Finally, the following equation is estimated for countries with policy rates at their effective lower bounds over the period 2009–15:[58]

$$\Delta \pi_{t+h}^e = \alpha + \vartheta \pi_t^{news,oil} + \gamma \pi_t^{news,core} + \epsilon_{t+h}, \qquad (3.5.4)$$

in which $\pi_t^{news,oil}$ denotes the inflation shocks driven by changes in oil prices, and $\pi_t^{news,core}$ is the inflation shocks unrelated to changes in oil prices.

This analysis suggests that the sensitivity of three-year-ahead inflation expectations to oil price shocks over the recent past in countries facing the effective-lower-bound constraint was very similar

---

[57]While it would be preferable to include the change in expectations of the unemployment rate at the same horizon as inflation expectations on the left-hand side, such data are not available. Moreover, even one-year-ahead unemployment rate expectations are collected only for 12 advanced economies; therefore, the sample in this robustness check is smaller than that in the main part of the analysis.

[58]Zero-lower-bound economies are defined as advanced economies whose policy rates or short-term nominal interest rates were 50 basis points or lower at some point during 2009–15.

to that of core inflation shocks. Both sensitivities were around 0.03. The qualitative pattern remains the same when examining inflation expectations at longer-year horizons (five years and beyond) and overall commodity prices instead of oil prices. The results imply that inflation expectations did not become unanchored solely because of the sharp drop in oil and other commodity prices.

References

Abrahams, Michael, Tobias Adrian, Richard K. Crump, and Emanuel Moench. 2012. "Decomposing Real and Nominal Yield Curves." *Federal Reserve Bank of New York Staff Reports* 570, September (revised October 2013).

Ahn, JaeBin, Chang-Gui Park, and Chanho Park. 2016. "Pass-Through of Imported Inputs Prices to Domestic Producer Prices: Evidence from Sector-Level Data." IMF Working Paper 16/23, International Monetary Fund, Washington.

Akerlof, George, William T. Dickens, and George Perry. 1996. "The Macroeconomics of Low Inflation." *Brookings Papers on Economic Activity* (1): 1–59.

Alichi, Ali, Olivier Bizimana, Silvia Domit, Emilio Fernandez Corugedo, Douglas Laxton, Kadir Tanyeri, Hou Wang, and Fan Zhang. 2015. "Multivariate Filter Estimation of Potential Output for the Euro Area and the United States." IMF Working Paper 15/253, International Monetary Fund, Washington.

Anderson, Derek, Dennis Botman, and Ben Hunt. 2014. "Is Japan's Population Aging Deflationary?" IMF Working Paper 14/139, International Monetary Fund, Washington.

Arbatli, Elif, Dennis Botman, Kevin Clinton, Pietro Cova, Vitor Gaspar, Zoltan Jakab, Douglas Laxton, Constant Aime Lonkeng Ngouana, Joannes Mongardini, and Hou Wang. 2016. "Reflating Japan: Time to Get Unconventional?" IMF Working Paper 16/157, International Monetary Fund, Washington.

Auer, Rapahel, and Aaron Mehrotra. 2014. "Trade Linkages and the Globalization of Inflation in Asia and the Pacific." *Journal of International Money and Finance* 49 (A): 129–51.

Ball, Laurence, Davide Furceri, and Prakash Loungani. Forthcoming. "Does One Law Fit All? Okun's Law in Advanced and Developing Economies." IMF Working Paper, International Monetary Fund, Washington.

Ball, Laurence, and Sandeep Mazumder. 2011. "Inflation Dynamics and the Great Recession." *Brookings Papers on Economic Activity*, Spring.

Benhabib, Jess, Stephanie Schmitt-Grohé, and Martín Uribe. 2002. "Avoiding Liquidity Traps." *Journal of Political Economy* 110 (3): 535–63.

Bernanke, Ben. 2002. "Deflation: Making Sure It Doesn't Happen Here." Speech to the National Economists Club, Washington, November 21.

———. 2010. "The Economic Outlook and Monetary Policy." Speech delivered at the Federal Reserve Bank of Kansas City Economic Symposium, Jackson Hole, Wyoming, August 27.

———, and Truman F. Bewley. 1999. "Why Wages Don't Fall during a Recession." Harvard University Press, Cambridge, Massachusetts.

Bernanke, Ben, and Mark Gertler. 1999. "Monetary Policy and Asset Price Volatility," presented at the Federal Reserve Bank of Kansas City's symposium, "New Challenges for Monetary Policy," Jackson Hole, Wyoming, August 26–28.

Blanchard, Olivier, Eugenio Cerutti, and Lawrence Summers. 2015. "Inflation and Activity—Two Explorations and Their Monetary Policy Implications." NBER Working Paper 21726, National Bureau of Economic Research, Cambridge, Massachusetts.

Blanco, Andres. 2015. "Optimal Inflation Target in an Economy with Menu Costs and an Occasionally Binding Zero Lower Bound." Unpublished.

Buiter, Willem, and Nikolaos Panigirtzoglou. 1999. "Liquidity Traps: How to Avoid Them and How to Escape Them." NBER Working Paper 7245, National Bureau of Economic Research, Cambridge, Massachusetts.

Calvo, Guillermo, Fabrizio Coricelli, and Pablo Ottonello. 2012. "Labor Market, Financial Crises and Inflation: Jobless and Wageless Recoveries." NBER Working Paper 18480, National Bureau of Economic Research, Cambridge, Massachusetts.

Catão, Luis A. V., and Roberto Chang. 2011. "Global Food Prices and Inflation Targeting." VoxEU, January 27.

Celasun, Oya, Roxana Mihet, and Lev Ratnovski. 2012. "Commodity Prices and Inflation Expectations in the United States." IMF Working Paper 12/89, International Monetary Fund, Washington.

Christensen, Jens H. E., Jose A. Lopez, and Glenn D. Rudebusch. 2010. "Inflation Expectations and Risk Premiums in Arbitrage-Free Model of Nominal and Real Bond Yields." *Journal of Money, Credit and Banking* 42 (S1): 143–78.

Chung, Hess, Jean-Philippe Laforte, David Reifschneider, and John C. Williams. 2012. "Have We Underestimated the Likelihood and Severity of Zero Lower Bound Events?" *Journal of Money, Credit and Banking* 44: 47–82.

Clarida, Richard H., and Daniel Waldman. 2008. "Is Bad News About Inflation Good News for the Exchange Rate? And, If So, Can That Tell Us Anything about the Conduct of Monetary Policy?" In *Asset Prices and Monetary Policy*, edited by John Y. Campbell. University of Chicago Press: Chicago.

Cloyne, James, Lena Boneva, Martin Weale, and Tomas Wieladek. 2016. "The Effect of Unconventional Monetary Policy on Inflation Expectations: Evidence from Firms in the United Kingdom." External MPC Unit Discussion Paper 47.

Cochrane, John. 2016. "The New-Keynesian Liquidity Trap." Stanford University. Unpublished.

Coibion, Olivier, and Yuriy Gorodnichenko. 2015. "Is the Phillips Curve Alive and Well after All? Inflation Expectations and the Missing Disinflation." *American Economic Journal: Macroeconomics* 7 (1): 197–232.

Coibion, Olivier, Yuriy Gorodnichenko, and Johannes Wieland. 2012. "The Optimal Inflation Rate in New Keynesian Models: Should Central Banks Raise Their Inflation Targets in Light of the Zero Lower Bound?" *Review of Economic Studies* 79 (4): 1371–406.

Crowe, Christopher, and Ellen E. Meade. 2007. "The Evolution of Central Bank Governance around the World." *Journal of Economic Perspectives* 21 (4): 69–90.

Cukierman, Alex, Steven B. Webb, and Bilin Neyapti. 1992. "Measuring the Independence of Central Banks and Its Effect on Policy Outcomes." *World Bank Economic Review* 6 (3): 353–98.

D'Amico, Stefania, Don H. Kim, and Min Wei. 2014. "Tips from TIPS: The Informational Content of Treasury Inflation-Protected Security Prices." Finance and Economics Discussion Series 2014–24, Federal Reserve Board, Washington.

Daly, Mary, and Bart Hobijn. 2015. "Why Is Wage Growth So Slow?" *Federal Reserve Bank of San Francisco Economic Letter* 2015–01, January 5.

Daly, Mary, Bart Hobijn, and Brian Lucking. 2012. "Why Has Wage Growth Stayed Strong?" *Federal Reserve Bank of San Francisco Economic Letter* 2012–10, April 2.

Dincer, N. Nergiz, and Barry Eichengreen. 2014. "Central Bank Transparency and Independence: Updates and New Measures." *International Journal of Central Banking* 10 (1): 189–259.

Eggertsson, Gauti B. 2006. "Fiscal Multipliers and Policy Coordination." *Federal Reserve Bank of New York Staff Reports* 241.

———, and Michel Woodford. 2003. "The Zero Bound on Interest Rates and Optimal Monetary Policy." *Brooking Papers on Economic Activity* 1: 139–211.

End, Nicolas, Sampawende J. A. Tapsoda, Gilbert Terrier, and Renaud Duplay. 2015. "Deflation and Public Finances: Evidence from the Historical Records." IMF Working Paper 15/176, International Monetary Fund, Washington.

Fisher, Irving. 1933. "The Debt-Deflation Theory of Great Depressions." *Econometrica* 1 (4): 337–57.

Fuhrer, Jeffrey. 1995. "The Phillips Curve Is Alive and Well." *New England Economic Review* (March/April).

Galí, Jordi, and Mark Gertler. 1999. "Inflation Dynamics: A Structural Econometric Approach." *Journal of Monetary Economics* 44 (2): 195–222.

Garcia, Juan Angel, and Adrian Van Rixtel. 2007. "Inflation-Linked Bonds from a Central Bank Perspective." Occasional Paper Series No. 62, European Central Bank, Frankfurt.

Garcia, Juan Angel, and Thomas Werner. 2014. "Inflation Compensation and Inflation Risk Premia in the Euro Area Term Structure of Interest Rates." *Developments in Macro-Finance Yield Curve Modelling*, edited by Jagjit S. Chadha, Alain C. J. Durré, Michael A. S. Joyce, and Lucio Sarno. Cambridge: Cambridge University Press.

Gaspar, Vittor, Maurice Obstfeld, and Ratna Sahay. Forthcoming. "Macroeconomic Management when Policy Space Is Constrained: A Comprehensive, Consistent, and Coordinated Approach to Economic Policy." IMF Staff Discussion Note, International Monetary Fund, Washington.

Gelos, Gaston, and Yulia Ustyugova. 2012. "Inflation Responses to Commodity Price Shocks: How and Why Do Countries Differ?" IMF Working Paper 12/225, International Monetary Fund, Washington.

Guidolin, Massimo, and Christopher J. Neely. 2010. "The Effects of Large-Scale Asset Purchases on TIPS Inflation Expectations." *Economic Synopses* 26, Federal Reserve Bank of St. Louis.

Gürkaynak, Refet S., Brian Sack, and Jonathan H. Wright. 2010. "The TIPS Yield Curve and Inflation Compensation." *American Economic Journal: Macroeconomics* 2 (1): 70–92.

Gürkaynak, Refet S., and Justin Wolfers. 2007. "Macroeconomic Derivatives: An Initial Analysis of Market-Based Macro Forecasts, Uncertainty, and Risk." *NBER International Seminar on Macroeconomics 2005* (2): 11–50.

Hofmann, Boris, and Feng Zhu. 2013. "Central Bank Asset Purchases and Inflation Expectation." *BIS Quarterly Review* (March): 23–35.

International Monetary Fund. 2003. "Deflation: Determinants, Risks, and Policy Options—Findings of an Interdepartmental Task Force." Washington, June.

———. 2006. Chapter 3, "How Has Globalization Affected Inflation?" In *World Economic Outlook*. Washington, April.

———. 2013. Chapter 3, "The Dog That Didn't Bark: Has Inflation Been Muzzled or Was It Just Sleeping?" In *World Economic Outlook*. Washington, April.

———. 2014. "Japan: 2014 Article IV Consultation—Staff Report." IMF Country Report 14/236. Washington.

———. 2015. *2015 Spillover Report*. Washington, June.

———. 2016a. "Japan: 2016 Article IV Consultation—Staff Report." IMF Country Report 16/267, Washington.

———. 2016b. "The People's Republic of China: 2016 Article IV Consultation—Staff Report." IMF Country Report 16/270, Washington.

———. 2016c. "United States: 2016 Article IV Consultation—Staff Report." IMF Country Report 16/226, Washington.

Ito, Takatoshi, and Frederic S. Mishkin. 2006. "Two Decades of Japanese Monetary Policy and the Deflation Problem." In *Monetary Policy with Very Low Inflation in the Pacific Rim*. NBER-EASE 15: 131–202. Cambridge, Massachusetts: National Bureau of Economic Research.

Juselius, Mikael, and Előd Takáts. 2015. "Can Demography Affect Inflation and Monetary Policy?" BIS Working Paper 485, Bank for International Settlements, Basel.

Koo, Richard. 2008. *The Holy Grail of Macro Economics: Lessons from Japan's Great Recession*. Singapore: John Wiley & Sons (Asia).

Krishnamurthy, Arvind, and Annette Vissing-Jorgenson. 2011. "The Effects of Quantitative Easing on Interest Rates: Channels and Implications for Policy." *Brookings Papers on Economic Activity* (2).

Kuroda, Haruhiko. 2013. "Overcoming Deflation and After." Speech at the Meeting of Councillors of Nippon Keidanren (Japan Business Federation), Tokyo, December 25.

Kuttner, Kenneth N., and Adam S. Posen. 2002. "Fiscal Policy Effectiveness in Japan." *Journal of the Japanese and International Economies* 16 (4): 536–58.

Leigh, Daniel. 2010. "Monetary Policy and the Lost Decade: Lessons from Japan." *Journal of Money, Credit and Banking* 42 (5): 833–57.

Levin, Andrew T., Fabio M. Natalucci, and Jeremy M. Piger. 2004. "The Macroeconomic Effects of Inflation Targeting."

Federal Reserve Bank of St. Louis Review 86 (July/August): 51–80.

National Association of Manufacturers. 2016. "Global Manufacturing Economic Update: June 2016." http://www.nam.org/Newsroom/eNewsletters/Global-Manufacturing-Economic-Update/2016/Global-Manufacturing-Economic-Update--June-2016.

Obstfeld, Maurice, Kevin Clinton, Douglas Laxton, Ondra Kamenik, Yulia Ustyugova, and Hou Wang. Forthcoming. "How to Improve Inflation Targeting in Canada." IMF Working Paper, International Monetary Fund, Washington.

Organisation for Economic Co-operation and Development. 2015. "Capacity Developments in the World Steel Industry." http://www.oecd.org/sti/ind/Capacity-Developments-Steel-Industry.pdf.

Poloz, Stephen S. 2014. "Integrating Uncertainty and Monetary Policy-Making: A Practitioner's Perspective." Discussion Papers 14–6, Bank of Canada.

Porcellacchia, Davide. 2016. "Wage-Price Dynamics and Structural Reforms in Japan." IMF Working Paper 16/20, International Monetary Fund, Washington.

Posen, Adam S. 2000, "The Political Economy of Deflationary Monetary Policy." In *Japan's Financial Crisis and Its Parallels to U.S. Experience*, edited by Adam S. Posen and Ryoichi Mikitani, 194–208. Washington: Institute for International Economics.

Rabe-Hesketh, Sophia, and Brian Everitt. 2007. *A Handbook of Statistical Analyses Using Stata, Fourth Edition*. Boca Raton, Florida: Chapman & Hall/CRC.

Rogoff, Kenneth. 2003. "Globalization and Global Disinflation." Paper presented at "Monetary Policy and Uncertainty: Adapting to a Changing Economy," Federal Reserve Bank of Kansas City Conference, Jackson Hole, Wyoming, August 29.

Stock, James, and Mark W. Watson. 2007. "Why Has U.S. Inflation Become Harder to Forecast?" *Journal of Money, Credit and Banking* 39 (s1): 3–33.

Svensson, Lars E. O. 2001. "The Zero Bound in an Open Economy: A Foolproof Way of Escaping from a Liquidity Trap." *Monetary and Economic Studies* 277–321.

Swamy, P. A. V. B., and J.S. Mehta. 1975. "Bayesian and Non-Bayesian Analysis of Switching Regressions and a Random Coefficient Regression Model." *Journal of the American Statistical Association* 70: 593–602.

Swanson, Eric T. 2016. "Measuring the Effects of Federal Reserve Forward Guidance and Asset Purchases on Financial Markets." https://www.economicdynamics.org/meetpapers/2016/paper_1222.pdf.

Syed, Murtaza, Kenneth Kang, and Kiichi Tokuoka. 2009. "Lost Decade in Translation: What Japan's Banking Crisis Could Portend about Recovery from the Great Recession." IMF Working Paper 09/282, International Monetary Fund, Washington.

Tytell, Irina, and Shang-Jin Wei. 2004. "Does Financial Globalization Induce Better Macroeconomic Policies?" IMF Working Paper 04/84, International Monetary Fund, Washington.

Werning, Iván. 2012. "Managing a Liquidity Trap: Monetary and Fiscal Policy." Manuscript. Massachusetts Institute of Technology, Cambridge.

Williams, John. 2014. "Monetary Policy at the Zero Lower Bound: Putting Theory into Practice." Brookings Institution, Washington.

Wright, Jonathan H. 2012. "What Does Monetary Policy Do to Long-Term Interest Rates at the Zero Lower Bound?" *The Economic Journal* 122: 447–466.

Yellen, Janet L. 2015. "Inflation Dynamics and Monetary Policy." The Philip Gamble Memorial Lecture, University of Massachusetts, Amherst, September 24.

Yu, Edison. 2016. "Did Quantitative Easing Work?" Economic Insights, Federal Reserve Bank of Philadelphia Research Department, First Quarter.

SPILLOVERS FROM CHINA'S TRANSITION AND FROM MIGRATION

Spillovers are a key factor shaping the path of the global economy and the risks around it, but their nature is changing. The growing clout of emerging markets means that shocks originating there—including those of a noneconomic nature—are playing an increasingly important role around the world. Illustrating these trends, this chapter examines the global impact of China's rebalancing toward a more sustainable growth model, and the effects of increasing migration flows on the originating and recipient economies. While the source and transmission channels of these spillovers vary, a common theme is that, despite the negative short-term impact on recipient economies, they offer potential gains in the long term. If handled well, China's economic transition will eventually result in more sustainable global growth, and migration can help reduce challenges from population aging in recipient countries. Based on recent IMF publications and new analytical work by the IMF Spillover Taskforce, this chapter documents these spillovers and discusses policy implications at the national and multilateral level.[1]

Introduction

As in the past, economic spillovers across national borders continue to shape global prospects, but their

The authors of this chapter are Patrick Blagrave, Sweta Saxena, and Esteban Vesperoni (team leader), with research and editorial support from Chanpheng Fizzarotti, Gabi Ionescu, and Jeffrey Lam. It is based on work by the IMF's Spillover Taskforce, with contributions from Patrick Blagrave, Allan Dizioli, Davide Furceri, Jesus Gonzalez-Garcia, Ermal Hitaj, Ben Hunt, Joao Jalles, Florence Jaumotte, Christina Kolerus, Ksenia Koloskova, Wojciech Maliszewski, Montfort Mlachila, Nkunde Mwase, Papa N'Diaye, Hiroko Oura, Frantisek Ricka, Christian Saborowski, Sweta Saxena, Katya Svirydzenka, Esteban Vesperoni, Arina Viseth, Mustafa Yenice, Aleksandra Zdzienicka, and Yuanyan Zhang.

[1]The IMF introduced specific reports on spillovers in 2011. Until 2013, these reports focused on the external effects of domestic policies in five systemic areas: China, the euro area, Japan, the United Kingdom, and the United States. Since 2014 the reports took a more thematic approach focusing on global, cross-cutting issues centered on economic policies. Beginning with this *World Economic Outlook* report, spillovers analysis will be highlighted in every other report.

scope has expanded. While previous spillover analysis has mostly focused on economic shocks emanating from advanced economies—such as shifting monetary policies in systemic economies—the increasing clout of emerging market economies, which explained the bulk of global growth over the past decade and now represent more than 50 percent of global GDP in purchasing-power-parity terms, suggests that they are a significant source of spillovers shaping the global outlook. In addition, noneconomic shocks are playing a more important role.

The global repercussions of China's welcome transition to a more balanced growth path furnish a case in point. China's rapid, investment-driven growth in the past decade fostered a remarkable expansion of global trade and boosted commodity prices (Figure 4.1). More recently, China's necessary slowdown in investment and its current transition to consumption-led growth has coincided with a very sharp decline in global trade growth.[2] Given the size and openness of the Chinese economy—the sharp increase in its share of global imports over the past decade has made it a main source (top 10) of export demand for over 100 economies that account for about 80 percent of world GDP—the potential for large spillover effects has increased. This suggests that China's transition has the potential to change the global outlook and the risks surrounding it. Not surprisingly, possible bumps around China's transition count among the risks to the global recovery, along with the persistent weak demand and low productivity growth in some key advanced and emerging market economies (see Chapter 1).

The rising trend in migration, compounded by refugees fleeing geopolitical conflicts, is an example of a noneconomic development with significant spillovers. The rapid increase in economic migration has become a pressing issue, and the ongoing refugee crisis in the Middle East and North Africa has added

[2]See Chapter 2 in this *World Economic Outlook* report.

Figure 4.1. China: GDP and Trade Growth
(Percent change, year-over-year)

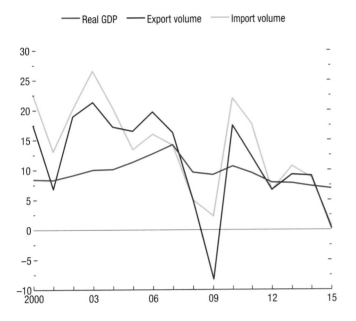

Source: IMF staff calculations.

Figure 4.2. Number of International Migrants and Refugees
(Millions)

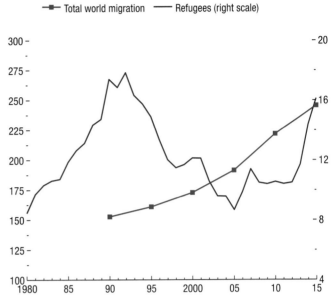

Sources: United Nations High Commissioner for Refugees; and IMF staff calculations.

to this trend.[3] The number of international migrants increased from 150 million in 1990 to 250 million as of the end of 2015 (Figure 4.2). And refugee flows—driven by geopolitical factors, wars, and conflict—have surged over the past couple of years, and continue, with over half a million applications for asylum during the first half of 2016. This surge increased the number of refugees to about 16 million as of the end of 2015—although they still represent a small share in total migration. Large migration, whether triggered by economic or noneconomic forces, has significant repercussions both for sending and for receiving countries. Moreover, against a background of low growth along with rising inequality in many countries, migration can add to anxiety about globalization, and feed a political climate that stalls structural reforms and growth.

The first part of this chapter focuses on the impact of China's transition on the global economy, with an emphasis on the complexities of its diverse transmission channels. The following section focuses on migration issues and their impact on source and recipient econ-

[3]Migrants are defined as individuals who are living in countries other than their country of birth.

omies. Both sections document spillovers and discuss policy issues at the national and multilateral level.

China's Transition

Rapid growth has made China one of the largest economies in the world, and its increasing global links lifted trade and economic activity across the world during its expansion. In this context, China's economic transition toward more balanced growth also has global repercussions, transmitted through trade and commodity markets and amplified by financial markets. These repercussions entail a negative direct impact on global demand, an indirect impact through prices—notably for commodities—and an effect on exchange rates and asset markets. However, some countries stand to gain, such as commodity importers—including some emerging markets—and producers of labor-intensive goods, as China moves up the value chain and imports more consumption goods. A well-managed transition will benefit the global economy in the long term: it will result in more sustainable growth in China, improved resource allocation, and a reduction of risks of a disruptive adjustment—which credit booms have often triggered in other economies. China can help by managing its transition well, notably by accepting the slowdown and by clearly communicating its policy intentions. Globally, it will be important to avoid protectionism and continue to facilitate trade-integration initiatives.

Slowdown, Rebalancing, and Transmission Channels of Spillovers

As the second largest economy in the world, China has become a significant source of global demand. GDP growth averaged 9.6 percent since 2000, increasing China's share of global GDP from about 3 percent to almost 13 percent in 2015 (Figure 4.3, panel 1).[4] Since the early 2000s this growth has been fueled by investment and exports as the economy built infrastructure and housing, and leveraged its abundant labor supply to boost manufacturing. Reinforcing this trend, China's response to the global financial crisis prompted a further push to infrastructure investment in 2009–10—increasing by an average of 17 percent in each of those years. The large size of the economy implies that developments in China had significant spillovers to the global economy through its demand for trade-partner exports. Given the key role of infrastructure investment in China's expansion, commodity exporters also benefited from the boost in prices caused by stronger demand in China, particularly for base metals.

More recently, China has begun to rebalance its economy from investment and exports toward consumption, partly reversing its contribution to global trade growth in previous years.[5] Economic growth has slowed, and rebalancing implies that investment has slowed faster than consumption—between 2010 and 2015, the consumption share of GDP rose from about 49.1 percent to 51.6 percent, while the investment share fell from about 47.2 percent to 46.4 percent, both in real terms (Figure 4.3, panel 2). This implies a sharper decline in demand for imports and commodities than the slowdown in headline GDP growth would suggest, given that investment activity is more import intensive and relies more heavily on commodities. In fact, a striking development of the slowdown in the Chinese economy in 2014–15 is the disproportionate deceleration in exports and imports—GDP growth fell from 7.8 percent in 2013 to 6.9 percent in 2015,

[4]Based on GDP at market exchange rates.
[5]For a richer discussion of China's economic rebalancing, see IMF (2015g).

Figure 4.3. China: Global Clout and Rebalancing

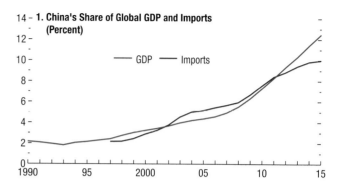

1. China's Share of Global GDP and Imports (Percent)

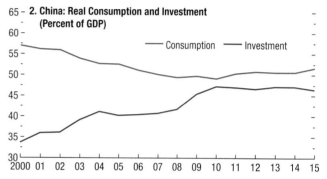

2. China: Real Consumption and Investment (Percent of GDP)

Source: IMF staff calculations.

while export and import growth fell by 7 percentage points and 8 percentage points, respectively, over this same period.

Spillovers from China are transmitted primarily via trade links. A deceleration in China's domestic demand affects imports from trading partners—and more generally, global trade. But this impact differs among countries—creating winners and losers from China's rebalancing—and the analysis of the trade channel is not straightforward, for several reasons:

• China has become deeply integrated into global supply chains, which implies that it often transmits shocks from other countries. The analysis of spillovers needs to differentiate China's direct impact on global demand by disentangling variations in GDP growth due to its own demand from those associated with global shocks.

• Countries have different exposures to China's final demand. While total exposure—the share of exports to China relative to total exports—plays a role, countries differ in terms of sectors of the Chinese economy to which they are exposed. With China's investment demand slowing disproportionately, exporters of investment goods—such as some countries in the euro area—will be more affected than exporters of consumption goods. Finally, China is now producing at home some previously imported intermediate goods (onshoring), adding complexity to the analysis.

- As China moves up the value chain, reducing its production of some labor-intensive goods, opportunities are being created for countries with abundant labor to take its place in the production of these goods, particularly in southeast Asia.

Another important transmission channel relates to China's impact on global prices, particularly in commodity markets. China is both a large producer and consumer of commodities. Its demand for commodities surged since the early 2000s, particularly in energy and base metals markets; by the end of 2014 China's demand for metals accounted for more than 40 percent of global demand. Its large footprint in commodity markets suggests that a slowdown in China's demand can have a material and lasting impact on prices, particularly given short-term price-inelasticity of supply in commodity markets and the additional increases in the supply of metals in recent years.[6] Chinese industries may also be contributing to global "overcapacity" in some sectors, for example, steel and cement. Subsidies on key production inputs—such as energy—as well as credit flows to loss-making enterprises have contributed to an excessive expansion of capacity in these industries and are hindering their adjustment, depressing global prices.

Direct spillovers through financial channels are still limited but will increase, and developments in China are already affecting global asset prices. China's financial integration into global markets remains limited, which suggests that direct financial spillovers from China—for example, through the adoption of domestic financial regulation affecting credit growth or China's foreign assets and liabilities—have been modest so far. However, financial linkages are increasing, and the scope for financial spillovers is likely to increase, as China eases capital-account restrictions. Moreover, developments in China are already affecting volatility in financial markets. For example, policy uncertainty over the past year—related to the exchange rate regime and renminbi depreciation, and the response to a

domestic-equity-market adjustment—was coupled with falling global equity prices and exchange rate depreciation in emerging market economies.

Increasing Clout in Global Trade

As China became a larger and more open economy after its accession to the World Trade Organization, spillovers to the rest of the world increased. Its rapid growth over the past 15 years has made China a key player in global trade—its share in global imports increased from 3 percent in 2000 to approximately 10 percent as of 2015. The gradual increase in China's trade suggests that spillovers could vary over time. Furceri, Jalles, and Zdzienicka (2016) perform time-varying coefficient analysis using local projection methods on a sample of 148 countries over 1990–2014, and show that spillovers from a 1 percentage point negative shock to China's final demand growth have nearly doubled over the past two decades (Figure 4.4). These shocks now have a cumulative impact on global GDP of about 0.25 percent, after one year. This coefficient is broadly in line with those in other studies, which find spillovers between 0.1 percent and 0.2 percent on global GDP, but this new research better exploits rich cross-time dynamics and showcases the increased importance of spillovers from China in recent years and their potential to increase in the future.[7]

Trade links stand out as the main transmission channel of spillovers from China in this recent research, which finds that countries' exports to China, and a larger share of manufacturing exports in total exports, increase the magnitude of spillovers.[8] In particular, a 10 percent rise in exports to China is associated with an increase in the spillover coefficient of about 0.01—that is, close to 5 percent.

Given the importance of this channel, what is the direct impact of China's transition on global

---

[7]Other work on GDP-to-GDP spillovers includes Cashin, Mohaddes, and Raissi (2016); Cesa-Bianchi and Stratford (2016); Dizioli and others (2016); IMF 2014; Hong and others (2016); Duval and others (2014); and Dizioli, Hunt, and Maliszewski (2016).

[8]See Furceri, Jalles, and Zdzienicka 2016, which introduces the countries' time-varying coefficients into a rich panel environment. The panel captures the importance of different factors in explaining the evolution of spillover coefficients, including exports to China, the composition of such exports (commodities and manufacturing), and financial factors—as captured by the Chicago Board Options Exchange Volatility Index (VIX).

[6]See IMF (2015a).

trade? New research (Blagrave and Vesperoni 2016) addresses two critical empirical challenges to answering this question. First, to capture China's direct role as a source of spillovers, China-specific final demand shocks—that is, those not associated with external demand—were estimated. Second, the Organisation for Economic Co-operation and Development (OECD) Trade in Value Added (TiVA) database was used to build country-specific China-demand shocks to account for the impact of rebalancing, which implies that spillovers depend on countries' exposures to various sectors in China, specifically its secondary sector (associated mainly with investment) as opposed to its tertiary sector (mainly consumption).[9]

The evidence suggests that China's transition has played a role in the recent slowdown in global exports and that its impact has differed across countries.[10] Panel vector autoregression estimates for a sample of 46 advanced and emerging market economies show that for a country with an average trade exposure to China, a 1 percentage point negative shock to China's final demand growth (in one quarter) reduces export growth rates by 0.1–0.2 percentage point over the course of a year.[11] This finding suggests that, just as China fostered strong global-trade growth during the expansion, its transition is likely playing a role in the current slowdown. Estimated impacts differ across countries, with those in Asia most affected: in level terms, following a 1 percent shock to China's final demand, exports in these countries are reduced by nearly 1 percent after a year (Figure 4.5). Commodity exporters and countries with stronger trade linkages to China's manufacturing sector are also affected significantly, with much smaller effects in other countries.[12] In line with these results, in-sample projections help

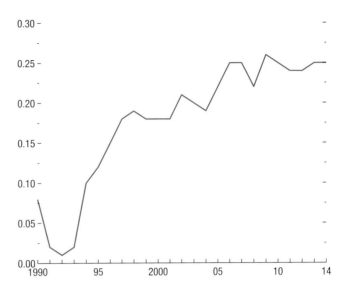

Figure 4.4. Spillovers from China over Time
(Average response of GDP to a 1 percentage point shock to growth in China, percent)

Source: Furceri, Jalles, and Zdzienicka (2016).
Note: Sample includes 148 advanced and emerging market economies.

explain the dynamics of the recent deceleration in global trade (Figure 4.6). These projections suggest that about a sixth of Asia's export-growth slowdown in 2014–15 could be explained by China's transition, with smaller impacts elsewhere.[13]

Demand rebalancing—from public investment to private consumption—has a negative, albeit modest, impact on global activity. Disentangling the impact of a general slowdown from that of demand rebalancing is challenging. Hong and others (2016), using TiVA data, find that the impact of growth-neutral rebalancing is likely to be modest, but stronger in emerging Asia. Using the IMF's Flexible System of Global Models (FSGM), Dizioli, Hunt, and Maliszewski (2016) reach a similar conclusion.[14] Simulating a scenario in which public investment in China declines by 1.5 percent of GDP each year for five years, and transfers to liquidity-constrained households rise by an equivalent amount, demand rebalancing would reduce import demand from China: investment is more import intensive than consumption, and a shift

[9]These data allow for the identification of partners' exports that are directed to specific sectors in China's final demand, even if those exports reach China indirectly, through a third country.

[10]A broader analysis of the determinants of the global trade slowdown (which the China-specific impact provided here complements) is provided in Chapter 2 of this *World Economic Outlook* report. The chapter finds that overall weakness in economic activity has been the primary restraint on trade growth, which is consistent with results suggesting that weaker demand in China played a role in the reduction of global export growth.

[11]The limited availability of TiVA and quarterly trade volume data requires the use of a relatively small sample (2013:Q1–2015:Q3).

[12]Although data limitations prevent an examination of trade spillovers for low-income and developing countries in this analysis, Drummond and Xue Liu (2013) point to an important role for changes in China's investment in explaining export dynamics in sub-Saharan Africa.

[13]Since the first quarter of 2014 China's transition may have depressed average export growth rates in a group of six Asian countries by about 1 percentage point a quarter, and less than half this amount in advanced and other emerging market economies.

[14]For details on the FSGM, see Andrle and others (2015).

Figure 4.5. Impact on Exports of a 1 Percent Shock to China's Demand after One Year

(Percent; GDP-weighted average)

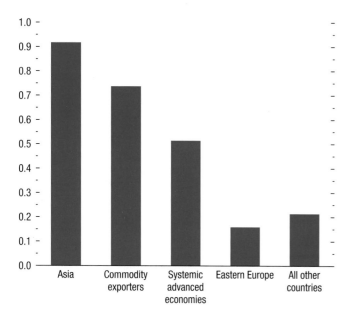

Source: Blagrave and Vesperoni 2016.
Note: Asia = HKG, IDN, KOR, PHL, SGP, THA. Commodity exporters = AUS, BRA, CHL, COL, RUS, ZAF. Eastern Europe = CZE, EST, HUN, LTU, LVA, POL, SVK, SVN, TUR. Systemic advanced economies = DEU, JPN, USA. All other countries = ARG, AUT, BEL, CAN, CHE, DNK, ESP, FRA, FIN, GBR, GRC, ISR, IRL, ISL, ITA, LUX, MEX, NLD, NOR, NZL, PRT, SWE. Data labels in the figure use International Organization for Standardization (ISO) country codes.

Figure 4.6. Decline in Average Export Growth Rate Attributed to China Demand, 2014:Q1–2015:Q3

(Percent)

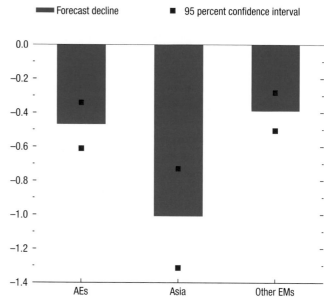

Source: Blagrave and Vesperoni 2016.
Note: Blue bars depict the marginal impact of weaker GDP growth in China (relative to the January 2012 *World Economic Outlook* (WEO) forecast) on average export growth rates from 2014:Q1 to 2015:Q3. They represent the difference between an unconditional forecast (with China's growth rates based on the January 2012 WEO baseline) and a conditional forecast with the same information set, but adding estimated China demand shocks. AE = advanced economy; EM = emerging market economy.

in demand toward the latter triggers a net reduction in imports. The effect on China's GDP depends on assumptions about the impact of public investment on productivity—that is, if the latter is negligible, GDP would fall in the short term but then recover afterward. Assuming some impact on productivity, however, would imply a permanent decline in GDP below baseline. From a global perspective, under both scenarios, GDP falls by less than 0.1 percent after five years, with emerging Asia most affected.

Finally, structural shifts and higher wages in China's transition play a role as well, affecting both trade volumes and global prices. One such shift is China's move to a higher position in the value chain, which prompted a return to domestic production (onshoring) of previously imported intermediate goods, but led to opportunities for some countries. Another shift relates to the persistent buildup of capacity in some sectors of the Chinese economy, which is likely affecting global prices. More specifically,

- *Onshoring*—China is increasingly producing intermediate inputs domestically (Figure 4.7).[15] IMF (2016c) provides evidence that the gradual increase of production of domestic intermediate goods in China has displaced imports from trade partners. This effect has been strongest in recent years and seems to be affecting imports of more sophisticated goods as China increasingly produces more complex medium-high-technology, capital-intensive goods—generally referred to as moving up the value chain. Dizioli, Hunt, and Maliszewski (2016) show that onshoring in China likely entails little change to global GDP, but could have a mild negative

[15]A number of indicators support this conclusion, including recent increases in the domestic-value-added content of China's exports (from about 50 percent in 2000 to just under 60 percent in 2011, according to Organisation for Economic Co-operation and Development–World Trade Organization Statistics on Trade in Value Added data), a steady decline in processing trade, and declining import intensity in some sectors. See Dizioli and others (2016).

effect on countries that trade more with China. To produce a greater share of exported goods domestically, China must increase its capital stock, implying stronger investment. Although China's import demand declines because of onshoring, which depresses activity in Asia and the euro area, the boost to domestic investment offsets these negative spillovers, resulting in little change to global GDP or commodity prices.

- *Market shares in labor-intensive goods*—Some countries stand to benefit from China's move up the value chain. This is the case for economies positioned to replace China's production of labor-intensive goods or to supply consumer goods to the Chinese market. The decline in China's export market shares of some labor-intensive consumer goods suggests a loss of competitiveness in these categories in recent years (see IMF 2016c and Abiad and others 2016). IMF 2016b discusses how countries such as Cambodia, Lao P.D.R., Myanmar, and Vietnam stand to benefit from China's rise up the value chain.

- *Overcapacity*—In the context of economic expansion during the 2000s, China has built up large capacity in certain sectors, notably those associated with infrastructure investment (for example, steel and cement). As the Chinese economy slows, excess capacity in these sectors has the potential to drive down global prices. Measuring overcapacity is complicated, and a thorough analysis of the issue is beyond the scope of this chapter, but a number of economic indicators—including declining profit margins in some sectors, as well as more conventional measures of capacity relative to total demand—point to overcapacity in some industries in China.[16] An analysis of the spillovers to trade-partner inflation from overcapacity in China is provided in Chapter 3 of this *World Economic Outlook* report—it suggests that lower prices across a number of goods have been associated with lower import prices from China.

A Large Footprint in Commodity Markets

As with intermediate and final goods, China's demand for commodities has increased markedly over the past two decades. Since the mid-1990s China's

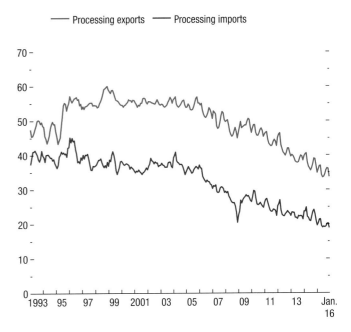

Figure 4.7. China: Processing Trade
(Percent of total exports, three-month moving average)

—— Processing exports   —— Processing imports

Sources: CEIC China database; and IMF staff calculations.

share of global demand for base metals—iron ore, aluminum, copper, and nickel—has risen from about 3 percent to about 40 percent (Figure 4.8, panel 1), while its share of demand for oil has increased from about 1 percent to 11 percent. Some food items show the same pattern—for instance, China's share of demand for soybeans represents 30 percent of global demand.[17] At the same time, China is a major producer of some metals, and domestic supply has increased substantially over the same period.

This large footprint in commodity markets implies that both China's boom and its ongoing economic transition have had a significant impact on commodity markets. China's rapid economic growth in the 2000s likely played a role in the sharp increase in prices. In particular, the infrastructure-investment-led stimulus following the global financial crisis (which arguably created incentives for commodity producers—including China—to build capacity), contributed to higher commodity prices. Subsequently, China's growth transition and the ensuing slowdown in demand for com-

---

[16]See IMF (2016f), IMF (2016i), Morgan Stanley Research (2016a) and (2016b), among others.

[17]For a more thorough discussion of global base metals demand and supply, see IMF (2015a).

Figure 4.8. A Large Footprint in Commodity Markets

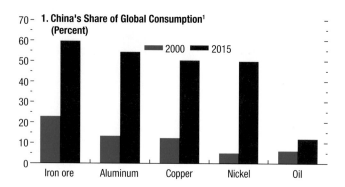

1. China's Share of Global Consumption[1]
(Percent)

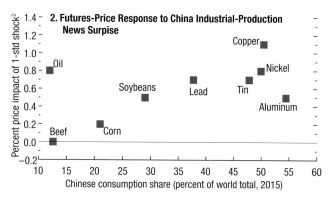

2. Futures-Price Response to China Industrial-Production News Surpise

Sources: Bloomberg L.P.; Kolerus, N'Diaye, and Saborowski 2016; World Bureau of Metal Statistics; U.S. Department of Agriculture; and IMF staff calculations.
[1] Latest available data for oil are from 2014.
[2] 1-std = one standard deviation.

modities have proved suppliers' previous production decisions overly optimistic. The result is oversupply and lower prices in many commodity markets. This has likely affected economies that are beyond production value chains in which China plays a critical role. Moreover, analysis in Nose, Saxegaard, and Torres (2016) indicates that there are spillovers from extractive to nonextractive sectors within these economies, which implies that the effects of negative terms-of-trade shocks are not limited to the extractive sector.

Shocks to economic activity in China have a significant impact on commodity prices, which is stronger in markets in which China's footprint is larger. Kolerus, N'Diaye, and Saborowski (2016) assess this impact under two analytical approaches. One gauges the response of commodity prices in futures markets to surprises in Chinese industrial-production data announcements using high-frequency data, while the other uses a more structural approach to assess the cumulative impact of shocks to China's demand on commodity prices at quarterly

frequency.[18] These are complementary approaches that look both at market pricing of new information and at the economic significance of the price response to activity shocks. Both find that China's shocks have a significant impact on commodity prices; effects are larger in markets in which China represents a greater share of global demand (Figure 4.8, panel 2). Results from a structural vector autoregression also suggest that these effects are economically significant—over a one-year horizon, a 1 percent change in industrial production growth leads to a 5–7 percent increase in metal prices and a rise in fuel prices by about 7 percent.[19] Conversely, high-frequency data offer an additional insight, showing that initial market reactions in commodity futures markets are larger when financial market uncertainty—as proxied by the Chicago Board Options Exchange Volatility Index (VIX)—is higher.

China's commodity price clout has increased over time. Structural vector autoregression estimates of 1-year price elasticities to China's demand estimated over a 10-year rolling window—estimated consecutively for each year, beginning in 1986–95, and ending with the 2006–15 window—show that the sensitivity of commodity prices to China's demand was negligible before China's accession to the World Trade Organization (Figure 4.9). However, since the early 2000s the sensitivity of oil and metal prices to China's demand has become statistically significant and has increased. For instance, the impact of developments in China on the price of iron ore rose throughout the sample period, in line with its increasing footprint in this market—from 3.5 percent of total demand in 1986 to 52 percent in 2015. Similar patterns are observed for copper and aluminum.

In line with these findings, recent IMF research suggests that weak demand in China accounts for a significant portion of the decline in commodity prices since 2013. Analysis in IMF 2016c builds on the strong common factor in commodity-price fluctuations—typically interpreted as a reflection of global economic conditions—and estimates a factor-augmented vector autoregressive model for a sample of about 40 com-

[18]In the first approach, future commodity prices at daily frequency are regressed on China's industrial production announcement surprises—that is, deviations of industrial production growth from the median Bloomberg consensus before the announcement. The second approach employs a structural vector autoregression to estimate the reaction of commodity prices to Chinese demand using quarterly data from 1986 to 2015.
[19]Aastveit and others (2012); Gauvin and Rebillard (2015); Roache (2012); and Roache and Rousset (2015) also find that shocks to China's demand have a significant impact on commodity prices.

modity prices and shocks to economic activity in China and in the rest of the world. The estimates suggest that most of the decline in commodity prices is explained by shocks to economic activity in the rest of the world until 2013, but that China's demand shocks have played a significant role since then, and that the effect on nonfuel commodity prices is larger. These estimates are corroborated by simulations using the IMF's FSGM.[20]

The decline in commodity prices will benefit commodity importers, including some emerging market and developing economies. Lower prices may dampen spillovers from trade in some countries, notably in Asia. Dizioli, Hunt, and Maliszewski (2016) conduct simulations of a gradual slowdown in China over the course of five years that reduces the level of GDP by about 5 percent by 2020 compared with a baseline in which it does not decelerate (Figure 4.10). This shock entails a reduction in investment and consumption in China and thus compression of its demand for imports. Weaker demand also depresses commodity prices—oil and metals prices are lower by about 7 percent. The simulation suggests that oil exporters are significantly worse off: Latin America suffers moderate output losses, and emerging Asia, the euro area, and Japan experience losses in between. Lower commodity prices are behind the positive impact in the United States.[21] An interesting insight from this exercise is that, despite being strongly affected through trade channels, spillovers to emerging Asia are comparable to those in the euro area because the region's heavy reliance on imports of commodities curbs direct spillovers from trade. Indeed, staff calculations indicate that while the impact of lower commodity prices in Asian economies partially offset spillovers through trade, commodity exporters in all regions have experienced negative spillovers from both channels (Figure 4.11).[22]

Financial Markets

Direct transmission of spillovers through financial channels is still limited, but developments in China

[20]Simulations are presented in IMF 2016e.

[21]The impact of lower commodity prices is complex. For exporters, it will reduce export values and negatively impact the terms of trade, but will also affect domestic growth more broadly, by tightening credit conditions and weakening balance sheets, which can also erode the fiscal position (see IMF 2015b, IMF 2015f, and IMF 2016g). The impact on commodity importers depends on the pass-through of lower prices to consumers and their impact on real interest rates in the presence of monetary policy constraints—that is, the zero lower bound.

[22]Calculations are based on the empirical analysis in the previous two sections and on country shares of commodity exports in Gruss (2014).

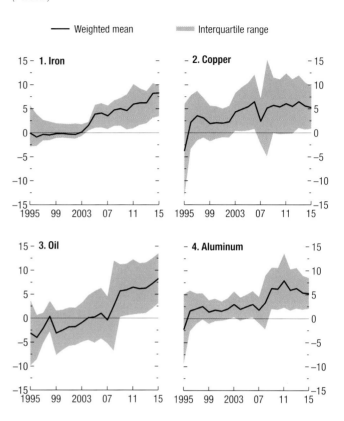

Figure 4.9. Cumulative One-Year Price Impact from a 1 Percent Shock to China's Industrial Production
(Percent)

Source: Kolerus, N'Diaye, and Saborowski 2016.
Note: *x*-axis indicates the last year of a rolling 10-year period.

are increasingly affecting asset prices globally and likely amplifying the impact of real shocks. The relatively limited transmission of financial shocks so far is associated with China's integration into global markets—there are still significant capital-account restrictions, including limitations on inward foreign direct investment, quotas on portfolio flows, and caps on foreign borrowing by domestic residents. However, financial linkages are increasing, and the impact of events in China on financial markets over the past year suggests that they can amplify real shocks by affecting asset prices and hence financing costs, especially in emerging markets. Increasing financial vulnerabilities in China could also lead to a disorderly deleveraging that could trigger contagion in emerging market financial markets and exchange rates by affecting confidence.[23] A closer look at the comovement of China's and global asset prices and the repercus-

[23]See IMF 2016g.

Figure 4.10. China: Slowdown Scenario
(Percent deviation from no-slowdown baseline)

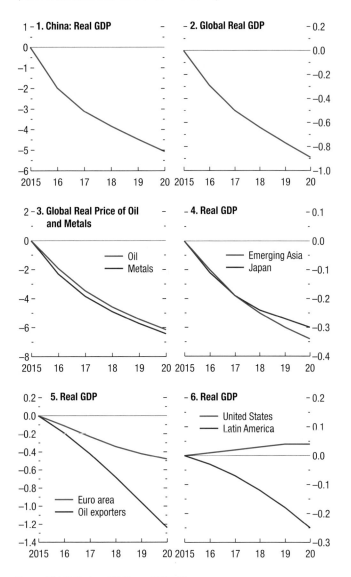

Source: Dizioli, Hunt, and Maliszewski (2016).
Note: This scenario considers a gradual slowdown in China's GDP growth over a five-year period. This slowdown is assumed to be driven by weaker productivity growth, and leaves the level of real GDP 5 percent lower than it would have been if no slowdown occurred.

Figure 4.11. Spillovers from China
(Percent of GDP)[1]

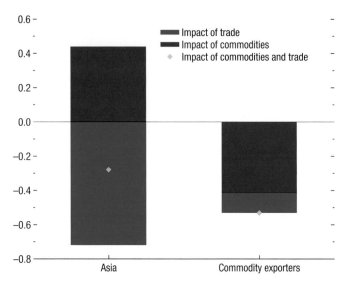

Source: IMF staff calculations.
Note: Asia = HKG, IDN, JPN, KOR, PHL, SGP, THA; Commodity exporters = AUS, BRA, CAN, CHL, COL, ISL, NOR, RUS, ZAF. Data labels in the figure use International Organization for Standardization (ISO) country codes. "Impact of trade" denotes the impact on exports as a percent of GDP from a 1 percent shock to Chinese final demand. "Impact of commodities" denotes the impact on exports as a percent of GDP from a change in commodity prices due to a 1 percent shock to Chinese industrial production. "Impact of commodities and trade" denotes the aggregate spillovers from trade and commodity channels.
[1]Nominal GDP; average 2011–13.

sions of policy uncertainty in China on global financial markets can shed some light on these issues.

Comovement between asset prices in China and elsewhere has strengthened. Mwase and others (2016) assess this comovement using the connectedness indicator proposed by Diebold and Yilmaz (2011).[24]

They show that comovement between stock market returns and exchange rates in China and elsewhere has increased since mid-2015 (Figure 4.12, panel 1), and that the latter is larger in economies with stronger trade links with China—notably in emerging Asia—and in commodity producing countries. The overall magnitude of comovement attributed to China has increased, although it remains relatively modest—it explains about 1 percent of the forecast error variance elsewhere, even during events over the past year.[25] This may in part be related to the inability of Diebold and Yilmaz's (2011) framework to identify structural shocks originating in China.

Developments in China—including policy uncertainty—have an impact on asset prices, particularly in emerging market economies and in countries with stronger trade links to China. Mwase and others (2016) also use a stronger identification strategy of China's shocks

[24]This indicator has also been applied, for example, to assess directional connectedness in IMF (2016d) and Guimaraes-Filho and Hong (2016).

[25]To put this in context, financial market comovements attributed to China are about one-fifth the magnitude of those attributed to the United States but are similar to those attributed to Japan.

developed by Arslanalp and others (2016)—relying on information on asset prices, global developments, and China-specific news—to get further insights into China's role in driving events since early 2015. They find that adverse shocks in China reduce equity prices both in advanced and in emerging market economies, with stronger effects on countries with higher trade exposure to China (Figure 4.12, panel 2).[26] Exchange rates in emerging markets depreciate while those in advanced economies appreciate, in particular in safe haven economies. Arslanalp and others (2016) focus on Asian financial markets and also find that spillovers through financial channels are increasing and are larger for countries with greater trade exposure to China. These results, and the timing of the events, suggest that recent policy uncertainty—related to the exchange rate regime and renminbi depreciation and the policy response to a domestic-equity-market adjustment—affected asset prices elsewhere. The event study evidence is corroborated by structural vector autoregression analysis, which suggests that a decline in equity prices and weak industrial production lead to lower U.S. and emerging market economy stock valuations and weaker oil and metal prices. It also shows that adjustments in China's exchange rate have a large impact on commodity prices, equity prices, and exchange rates in emerging markets. Over the past year, market reactions to renminbi depreciations have been strong because, compared with other asset prices, adjustment in exchange rates have implications beyond financial market developments.

China's large foreign assets and liabilities imply that the financial channel will be more relevant in the future as the capital account opens up. China's international investment position is large, it is long on debt and short on equity, and its main assets are reserve holdings and foreign direct investment.[27] At $3.3 trillion as of June 2016, China's foreign exchange reserves represent about 30 percent of global reserves. Changes in the latter could have a material impact on the price of China's holdings, most of which are U.S. Treasury bonds, although to date there has not been a strong correlation between China's reserve accumulation and U.S. Treasury bond yields.[28] China's foreign direct investment is especially important for low-income countries in particular because it

[26]These findings echo those of IMF (2016d).
[27]Mwase and others (2016).
[28]The recent fall in reserves—$750 billion between June 2014 and June 2016, of which about $240 billion were U.S. Treasury bonds—was met with declining yields, as it took place amid risk-off global conditions.

Figure 4.12. Transmission of Spillovers through Financial Channels

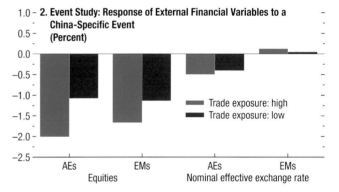

Source: Mwase and others 2016.
Note: AE = advanced economy, EM = emerging market economy.

holds large investments in small emerging Asian and sub-Saharan African economies (see Box 4.1). As for liabilities, cross-border banking linkages are comparable to some Group of Seven economies. Foreign banks' claims on Chinese entities stood at less than $1 trillion as of the first quarter of 2016, declining by more than 25 percent compared with the end of 2014, and is concentrated within a few large systemically important financial institutions. Stress testing suggests that even a substantial shock from Chinese banks would not lower banking system capital below Basel III requirements in countries with exposure to China.

Policy: The Importance of Managing the Transition

China's slowdown has spillover implications, but a smooth transition will benefit the global economy over the long term. Just as rapid growth in China fostered global growth in the past, the ongoing slowdown and rebalancing entail significant spillovers through trade, and a large impact on commodity prices. Spillovers

Figure 4.13. China: Cyclical Slowdown Scenario
(Percent deviation from no-slowdown baseline)

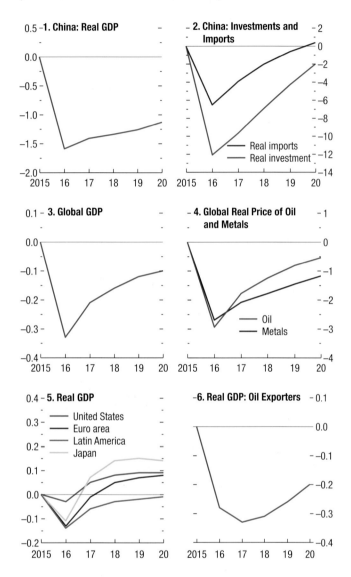

Source: Dizioli, Hunt, and Maliszewski (2016).

boost sentiment and lift investment in trading partners. China's announced capacity reductions in coal and steel production, if implemented, could have a sizable effect on global markets. Moreover, some elements of China's rebalancing—such as its move up the value chain and the prospective boost to domestic consumption growth in the years ahead—will create opportunities for some economies, notably in emerging Asia, and the increase in services trade and China's investment abroad are likely to produce short-term benefits for some countries.[29]

In contrast, a bumpy or incomplete transition may exacerbate spillovers. Policy uncertainty since mid-2015 highlights growing challenges to management of China's slowdown in a highly leveraged economy and may give rise to a disruptive transition. Dizioli, Hunt, and Maliszewski (2016) build a scenario in which a reassessment of risk in China illustrates the possible costs of such a transition (Figure 4.13).[30] A decline in asset prices by 10 percent and an increase in the corporate risk premium by 150 basis points during the first year would reduce investment and private consumption in China by about 10 percent and 2.5 percent, respectively, and real GDP by about 1.5 percent. Despite some offset from lower commodity prices, spillovers would be uniformly negative, and worse than those on the global economy under a smooth transition.

This highlights the benefits of a transition in which China strengthens transparency—especially in communicating policy objectives—and accepts lower growth. Clear communication of policy intentions, including further steps to move toward a floating exchange rate regime, is of the essence. Policy uncertainty and financial sector risk may trigger large adjustments in equity prices and exchange rates, which are destabilizing for global growth. Accepting lower growth entails keeping credit growth in check by tackling its root causes—notably, the pursuit of unsustainably high growth targets—and can produce higher and better-quality growth in the long term. A comprehensive plan to address vulnerabilities in the financial sector is needed, including restructuring or resolving weak firms, requiring banks to recognize and manage impaired assets and

through these channels have become larger over time, as has the impact of events in China on asset prices elsewhere, amplifying spillovers from the real economy. Even a smooth transition will require China's trading partners to adjust to slowing demand in the short term, developing new export markets and reallocating resources away from the most affected sectors. However, a well-managed transition will reduce the risk of a disorderly adjustment with larger spillovers and ensure more sustainable growth with potential gains for the global economy. Sustaining progress on reforms and tackling vulnerabilities will reduce downward risks, which can

---

[29]For a discussion on short-term costs and long-term gains of China's transition, see IMF (2016f) and Hong and others (2016).

[30]This exercise can be thought as one in which China does not rebalance, only to suffer a larger fall in activity later. The reassessment of risk in China would be related to a continued building of vulnerabilities in the financial sector due to rapid credit growth. An explicit risk scenario without reforms in the short term and a larger fall in activity over the medium term is shown in IMF (2015g).

boosting their buffers, hardening budget constraints by reducing access to credit of weak firms, creating a more market-based system to resolve distressed debt, reining in shadow bank and product risks, and dampening excessive housing price growth. On the fiscal front, the large deficit should be reduced over the medium-term to ensure debt sustainability. Temporary, targeted, on-budget, proconsumption fiscal stimulus can be used if growth threatens to fall excessively. Off-budget public investment should be scaled down.

As for recipient economies, efforts to boost trade and integrate them into value chains are called for, as are structural reforms to foster growth or change existing growth models. Policy responses will depend on countries' circumstances—and, in particular, their trade links with China and their export mix. More specifically,

- In countries with significant trade links to China—while available policy space and exchange rate flexibility should be used to cushion the negative impact of weaker external demand—adjustment is needed to permanently lower demand from China. Achieving this goal may imply a reduction in domestic absorption with a possible depreciation of the real exchange rate unless alternative exports markets can be developed (see below).

- Global and regional agreements can bolster trade. These also provide opportunities to push the frontier on such issues as services and regulatory cooperation, and foreign direct investment policies, which can boost efficiency and productivity through greater investment, technology transfer, and integration into global value chains. But it is also important to move ahead with an ambitious agenda in the World Trade Organization, and to leverage its unique reach and well-developed legal and institutional structure to help ensure coherence across the global trading system. Flexible negotiation approaches should allow for different speeds and depths of liberalization among countries.

- Because commodity prices are likely to remain low as a result of weaker demand from China, commodity exporters should use buffers where available, but also plan for adjustment, including through reduced and more efficient public expenditures and stronger fiscal frameworks, and the mobilization of new revenue sources. Some countries may also need to pursue new growth models. Commodity importers stand to benefit from lower prices; the appropriate use of windfall savings in these countries would depend on their cyclical and fiscal positions.

- China's transition creates an opportunity for low-wage, labor-rich countries to increase their production of labor-intensive goods, as well as for producers of consumption goods. To support such an increase, sound structural policies are important, including improvements in infrastructure, governance, the business climate, and trade openness.

From a global perspective, protectionist policies must be avoided, as these would be detrimental to trade over the long term. Spillovers from China's transition may prompt countries to pursue trade restrictions to protect domestic producers against weaker external demand or perceptions that China is contributing to oversupply in some markets. Such protectionist measures—not necessarily in response to developments in China—have likely played some role in depressing global trade over recent years, and could deter it over the long term. In the past, legal commitments, Group of Twenty pledges, and the recognition of potential economic damage from trade restrictions have discouraged countries from imposing new restrictions, particularly during the global financial crisis. Global leadership and a collective effort should promote trade agreements that would counteract movement toward protectionism. Moreover, trade reforms can complement other reforms in goods and services markets as they boost productivity by enhancing efficiency, promoting competition, and encouraging innovation and adoption of existing technologies.

The Challenges and Opportunities of Migration

Geopolitical conflicts and economic disparity are contributing to large migration flows with far-reaching social and economic repercussions and, especially in the case of refugees, humanitarian issues. Migration may stir social tensions and provoke a political backlash in recipient economies, but past experience suggests it may also offer gains in terms of higher growth, productivity, and relief from population aging. Swift labor market integration is key to harnessing the gains in terms of growth, increasing the contribution of migrants to the fiscal accounts, and reducing tensions. In source countries, migration can take a toll on long-term growth prospects as the young and the educated population leave—usually known as "brain drain"—which can be mitigated by remittances. Depending on the underlying drivers of migration, source countries need policies to address brain drain and maximize the benefits from

Figure 4.14. International Migrants and Refugees

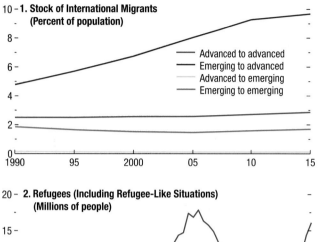

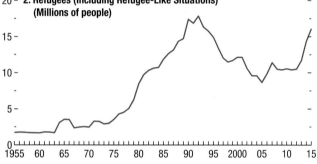

Sources: United Nations High Commissioner for Refugees; and IMF staff calculations.

remittances and diaspora networks. Global cooperation is needed to address humanitarian issues.

Trends, Drivers, and Challenges of Migration

Migration has risen steadily over recent decades. The stock of international migrants increased from 150 million in 1990 to 250 million in 2015.[31] While the number of migrants between emerging market economies is the largest, it comprises a small and stable proportion of their population—about 2 percent. Migration from emerging to advanced economies has been larger in relative terms and more dynamic: the share of migrants in the population of host countries almost doubled from about 5 percent to 10 percent between 1990 and 2015 (Figure 4.14, panel 1), with significant country differences. In 2015, migrants represented about 5 percent of the population in Finland and about 30 percent in Australia. There are two types of migrants: economic (voluntary, in search of better prospects) and humanitarian (refugees, escaping conflict and strife).

[31]This number and the analysis in the chapter exclude illegal migration.

The stock of international migration is dominated by economic migrants, but the recent surge in refugees has raised their number close to record levels. Economic migrants constitute almost 95 percent of the total stock of migrants, and they appear to be on a stable and increasing rise, whereas refugees represent a relatively small share, but their numbers have been volatile. The recent civil war in Syria and unrest throughout the Middle East have raised the number of refugees to the highest level since the 1990s (Figure 4.14, panel 2). The flow of new refugees surged in 2014–15, reaching 4.5 million—about half of the flows of total migration over those years. Jordan, Lebanon, and Turkey were the main recipients, hosting about 2.2 million new refugees over the same period. The European Union also received an unparalleled number of refugees recently—about 1.25 million first-time asylum applications were submitted in 2015, and applications continued to increase in 2016, although at a decreasing rate.

Total international migration is dominated by people of working age but, among refugees, the number of children is much larger. More than 70 percent of the stock of migrants is in the 20–64 age group (Figure 4.15, panel 1). In fact, migrants represent a significant share of the labor force in many advanced economies. Their presence increases the working-age population and reduces dependency ratios; in some countries, they have contributed about half of the growth in the working-age population between 1990 and 2010 (Figure 4.15, panel 2). The stock of refugees has a stronger presence of children; in 2015, for instance, more than half of refugees were under the age of 18.

Increasingly, migrants to advanced economies have high- and medium-level skills, although the number of low-skill migrants is still higher compared with the latter.[32] By 2010, high-skilled migrants constituted about 6 percent of the population across advanced economies—up from 2 percent in the 1990s—while medium- and low-skilled migrants represented about 4 percent and 5 percent, respectively (Figure 4.15, panel 3). This likely reflects in part the global rise in educational attainment over the past decades. Skill-based immigration policies, particularly in some Anglo-Saxon countries, which tend to have a larger proportion of high-skilled migrants, may have played a role as well.

[32]The skill level refers to education level: higher than high school leaving certificate or equivalent (high-skilled); high school leaving certificate or equivalent (medium-skilled); primary or no schooling (low-skilled).

The share of migrants with low skills in continental Europe and medium skills in Nordic countries (Denmark, Finland, Norway, and Sweden) remains relatively high—although skill levels of migrants have been on the rise there as well.

Migration is shaped by a combination of social and economic conditions at home and abroad, raising difficult humanitarian issues and potential tensions in recipient countries. Refugee flows are driven by the need to flee violence and persecution, leaving people no choice but to leave their homes amid political instability and conflicts. As for economic migration, a number of factors are at play. Lack of opportunities and deteriorating economic conditions in source countries can push migrants to greener pastures abroad. Pull factors in recipient economies are more complex and determine not only the extent of migration but also its distribution among host countries (Jaumotte, Koloskova, and Saxena 2016). First, economic conditions in recipient economies are critical. There is a positive association between long-term real GDP per capita growth and the change in the share of migrants (Figure 4.16, panel 1). Second, some structural factors matter. For migrants, the choice to move entails important geographic and cultural factors, such as distance to destination countries, common language, contiguous borders, and common colonial links (Figure 4.16, panel 2). Third, immigration policies in host countries affect migration flows. Reforms that tighten entry laws reduce migration flows, while less restrictive laws—as a result of signing the Maastricht treaty, for example—have the opposite effect (see Ortega and Peri 2009). Despite the opportunities associated with migration, it also poses challenges for both sending and recipient countries, mainly the loss of human capital in the former and potential social tensions with political consequences in the latter.

Recipient Countries: Challenges and Long-Term Gains

International migration is both a boon and a challenge for host countries. Migrants can boost the labor force and have a positive impact on growth and public finances over the long term, especially in countries with aging populations. However, receiving migrants poses challenges. There are concerns about displacement of native workers and short-term fiscal costs, especially in the case of refugees. This can add to possible social tensions related to differences in culture and language—given the compositional effects that migration may have on the population—and security-

Figure 4.15. Migration by Age and Skill

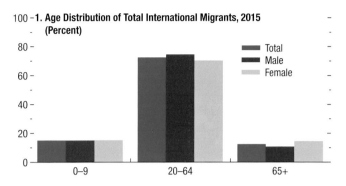

1. Age Distribution of Total International Migrants, 2015 (Percent)

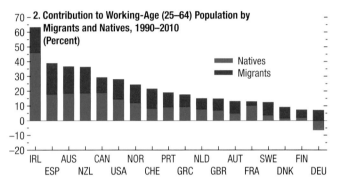

2. Contribution to Working-Age (25–64) Population by Migrants and Natives, 1990–2010 (Percent)

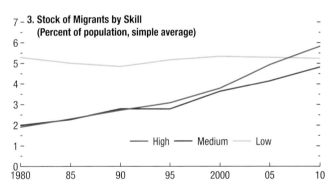

3. Stock of Migrants by Skill (Percent of population, simple average)

Sources: IAB; United Nations Department of Economic and Social Affairs, Population Division 2015 and *World Population Prospects* 2015 Revision; and IMF staff calculations.
Note: Data labels in the figure use International Organization for Standardization (ISO) country codes.

related incidents in some countries.[33] These tensions may prompt a political backlash, as demonstrated by the referendum in the United Kingdom on European Union membership, in which migration played a role.

The speed of integration is key. Past experience suggests that swift integration into labor markets is critical to harness the economic gains from migration, both in

---

[33]See Card, Dustmann, and Preston (2009), who show that people have stronger concerns about migration than trade.

Figure 4.16. Determinants of Migration

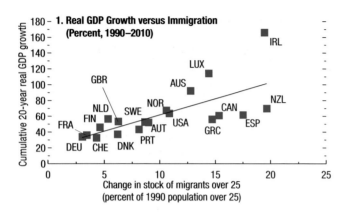

1. **Real GDP Growth versus Immigration**
(Percent, 1990–2010)

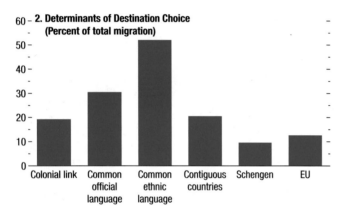

2. **Determinants of Destination Choice**
(Percent of total migration)

Sources: CEPII database; United Nations Global Migration database; and IMF staff calculations.
Note: The numbers are based on total stocks of migrants between all origin and 18 destination countries, that share the listed characteristics. The numbers are expressed as a percent of the total stock of migrants in 18 destination countries. Schengen = Schengen area countries that allow free movement of their citizens across their borders. Data labels in the figure use International Organization for Standardization (ISO) country codes.

the short and the long term. It can also speed up the positive impact on fiscal accounts, bolstering positive spillovers in recipient economies. Arguably, swift economic integration can accelerate and deepen social integration, with positive feedback effects between the two, although it may create tensions in the short term as well, especially when unemployment is high.

Labor Markets: The Central Role of Integration

The impact of migration on labor markets depends on complementarity between migrants and native workers. In principle, migrants with skills similar to those of natives would compete with them in the labor market and affect employment and wages, especially in the short term—before the capital stock adjusts to more labor. However, if migrants' skills complement

those of native workers, the impact could be positive (Aiyar and others 2016). This may be relevant, for instance, in a number of countries where labor market participation of highly skilled native women tends to be greater when there are lower-skilled female labor migrants (Jaumotte, Koloskova, and Saxena 2016; see Figure 4.17). The availability of relatively low-cost workers in the services or health care sector may allow high-skilled women to enter the labor force or work longer hours, increasing productivity.

Past experience suggests that migration has little effect on employment rates and average wages of native workers, although it may have an impact in certain labor market segments. Most of the academic literature suggests that the impact of migration on average wages or employment of native workers is very limited.[34] Instead, the literature suggests that migrants can contribute to labor markets through the complementarities just mentioned, which allow for: (1) natives to move into different segments of labor markets, often performing more complex tasks that promote skill upgrading and hence foster efficient specialization; (2) an increase in female labor market participation; (3) more efficient market functioning, with migrants filling up occupations for which natives are in short supply; (4) contributions of high-skilled migrants to technological progress; and (5) an increase in demand, which is likely to boost consumption in the short term and investment over the medium term.[35] Some studies, though, find a negative impact on wages of low-skilled workers.[36]

The labor market performance of migrants themselves suggests that labor market integration is complex. Aiyar and others (2016) find that migrants have lower participation, employment rates, and wages than natives in advanced economies (Figure 4.18, panel 1). The earnings and employment gaps are pronounced in the initial years and fall as migrants gain language proficiency and obtain more relevant job experience—migrants from

[34]See Peri (2014a), (2014b) for a survey of studies on the impact of immigration on employment and wages of native workers. See also IMF (2015c) and Aiyar and others (2016), and references therein. Some case studies have also found no significant impact of migration on labor markets for natives, for example Card (1990) for the Mariel boatlift in early (1980); and Akgunduz, van den Berg, and Hassink (2015), for the impact of the recent flow of Syrian refugees into Turkey.
[35]See, for example, Alesina, Harnoss, and Rapoport (2015); Cattaneo, Fiorio, and Peri (2015); D'Amuri and Peri (2014); Farré, González, and Ortega (2011); Hunt and Gauthier-Loiselle (2010); Ortega and Peri (2014); Peri, Shih, and Sparber (2015); and Peri and Sparber (2009).
[36]Borjas (2003, 2006) and Aydemir and Borjas (2007, 2011) document a negative impact on low-skilled natives' wages in the U.S. labor market.

Figure 4.17. Females: Low Education versus High Skilled, 2000

(Percent of total)

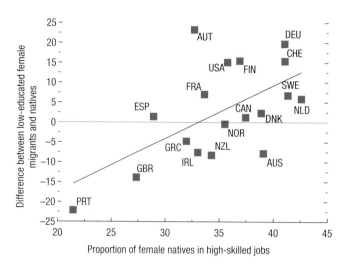

Sources: Organisation for Economic Co-operation and Development; and IMF staff calculations.
Note: Data labels in the figure use International Organization for Standardization (ISO) country codes.

Figure 4.18. Labor Market Performance

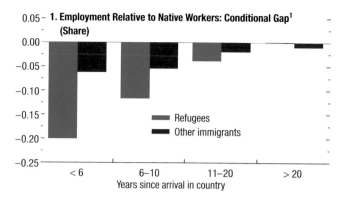

1. **Employment Relative to Native Workers: Conditional Gap[1]** (Share)

Refugees
Other immigrants

Years since arrival in country

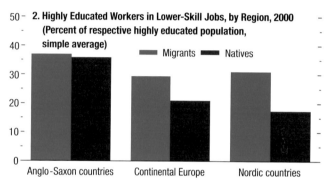

2. **Highly Educated Workers in Lower-Skill Jobs, by Region, 2000** (Percent of respective highly educated population, simple average)

Migrants   Natives

Anglo-Saxon countries   Continental Europe   Nordic countries

Sources: European Social Survey, Rounds 1–6; Organisation for Economic Co-operation and Development; and IMF staff calculations.
[1]Conditional gap measures the difference in the relevant outcome between natives and immigrants; depending on age, sex, years of education, language skills, host country, and time period.

advanced economies or with better initial language skills often do better than other groups. Challenges for female migrants and refugees seem to be particularly acute; their labor market outcomes are worse, especially in the short term (Aldén and Hammarstedt 2014; Ott 2013). The challenges at play include:

- *Skill recognition*—Migrants tend to be under-represented in high-skill jobs and over-represented in low-skill jobs.[37] This may be in part justified by differences in education—for instance, a degree in the country of origin may not be of the same quality as one in host countries—but it may also reflect policies, a lack of recognition of skills, or disadvantages linked to cultural differences. These translate into a missed opportunity for the host country. For example, benchmarking against natives, continental European and Nordic countries have a higher proportion of highly educated migrants employed in lower-skill occupations than other countries. In contrast, the opportunities for highly educated migrants and natives tend to be similar in Anglo-Saxon countries (Figure 4.18, panel 2).

- *Labor market regulations*—Excessive employment protection or high taxes and social security contri-

[37]See, for example, Aleksynska and Tritah (2013) for occupation-educational mismatch of immigrants in Europe.

butions can take a toll on employment, in particular for workers whose productivity is a priori uncertain (see, for example, Blanchard, Jaumotte, and Loungani 2013). Employment rates for migrants are higher in countries with low entry-level wages and less employment protection (Ho and Shirono 2015).

- *Additional challenges for refugees*—Uncertainty about refugees' legal status—the acceptance of their application for asylum—can delay their labor market entry. While their applications are being considered, asylum seekers often face legal barriers to employment (Hatton 2013) and, in European countries, application processing may take from two months to a year. Finally, given that migration drivers for refugees are less determined by pull factors—such as high growth in the host country—arrival in an environment of high unemployment may lower their employment rates and wages for a prolonged period (Åslund and Root 2007),

Figure 4.19. Germany: Present Value of Expected Future Net Fiscal Contribution by Age Group
(Thousands of euros, based on generational account approach; base year = 2012)

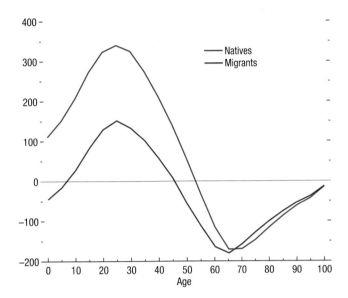

Source: Bonin (2014).

Over their lifetime, migrants tend to contribute less than natives to the fiscal accounts, mainly because they pay less in taxes and social security payments. This points again to the importance of their integration into labor markets—their smaller contributions reflect less time in the labor force and lower-paying jobs.[39] Migrants depend more on some social transfers, but differences between them and natives do not seem to have large budgetary implications. Relative to unemployed native-borns, unemployed migrants are more likely to receive social assistance, but less likely to receive generally more generous unemployment benefits. The case of Germany illustrates that both natives and migrants have an increasing contribution as they approach working age, which diminishes during retirement (Figure 4.19)—the contribution of migrants, though, tends to become positive later, peak at a lower level, and turn negative at an earlier stage (see Aiyar and others 2016 and IMF 2015c).

Past experience suggests that the net fiscal impact of migrants is small for OECD countries. Estimates depend critically on a number of assumptions—notably the many elements that determine the employment prospects of migrants (as noted above), their age profile, and how the analytical approach takes into account the dynamic macroeconomic effects of migration. OECD (2013) presents a cross-country study based on a static accounting (cash flow) model that assesses the tax and social security contributions as well as the receipt of social security benefits and government services of the stock of migrants in 27 OECD countries between 2007 and 2009. The impact, either positive or negative, rarely exceeds 0.5 percent of GDP in a given year and is about zero on average. There is a positive fiscal impact in 19 countries—that is, 70 percent of the sample of countries.

Higher short-term costs of caring for refugees, however, could add fiscal pressure in recipient economies. On arrival, refugees receive housing, subsistence, and integration support. Moreover, as noted above, they are often not allowed to work until their legal status is cleared. This lowers their short-term fiscal contribution relative to that of other migrants and natives. Less developed countries have typically shouldered the largest burden associated with refugees—for instance,

highlighting the importance of the phase of the business cycle in the integration process.

Migration and Fiscal Challenges

Labor market integration also plays a critical role in the fiscal impact in recipient economies. Over time, given their impact on the working-age population and economic activity, migrants can generate additional tax revenues and social contributions. But integration takes time, especially in the case of refugees, which means there will be a delay before they begin making a fiscal contribution. In the short term, they may need recourse to welfare services and claim social benefits—notably, health care and social assistance. Migration may also affect natives' use of fiscal resources to the extent that the presence of migrants increases natives' unemployment rate or lowers their wages.[38] The impact of migration on fiscal accounts depends not only on migrants' income, but also on the generosity of the social security system in host economies.

---

[38]As discussed, most of the literature suggests that such effects are small. These effects could also be mitigated if migration increases the income from capital accruing to natives (Borjas 1999). Conde Ruiz, Ramón Garcia, and Navarro (2008) document such effects for Spain in the early 2000s.

[39]This also explains the rationale of labor migration management systems. In the Australian system, for example, age has a strong weight—up to 38 percent of the pass mark—and there are maximum-age thresholds for admission.

in Jordan, Lebanon, and Turkey, spending on refugees is estimated at 2.4 percent, 3.2 percent, and 1.3 percent of GDP, respectively, during the recent surge.[40] But this is also relevant for many European countries, which have relatively generous welfare systems and a significant number of humanitarian migrants. IMF staff estimates for the euro area suggest that average budgetary expenditures on refugees could reach 0.2 percent of GDP in 2016, with Austria, Finland, Germany, and Sweden expected to shoulder the largest spending increases. For Sweden, expenditure on migration is expected to be 1 percent of GDP in 2016.

Over the longer term, migration has the potential to reduce fiscal pressure related to population aging in recipient countries (Figure 4.20). For example, continued migration in line with current trends could slow the expected increase in the old-age dependency ratio and associated health care and pension spending relative to GDP (Clements and others 2015; European Commission 2015). These effects will be larger, the larger the impact of migration on GDP growth. Migration cannot fully address challenges from population aging, but it can provide time to phase in entitlement and other reforms, which are still necessary in many countries.

Positive Growth Effects over the Longer Term

Migration can boost aggregate income in recipient countries over the long term. It can do so through several channels. First, by expanding the labor force, migration can boost capital accumulation. Second, properly integrated into labor markets, migrants can increase the employment-to-population ratio. Finally, migrants can foster labor productivity through complementarities with native workers and by increasing diversity in productive skills. This section explores the impact of migration on output per capita over the long term.

Past experience suggests that migration could indeed have a positive impact on output per capita in host countries. While much of the literature on migration is microeconomic and focuses on employment, innovation, or productivity, some studies have analyzed the macro relevance of these channels. But such analysis is complicated by the fact that some of the pull factors driving migration can bias the findings—for example, if migrants settle in countries experiencing high GDP growth, it would be easy to conclude that migration is "causing" that growth. To circumvent this complication,

[40]IMF (2015d, 2015e, 2016h).

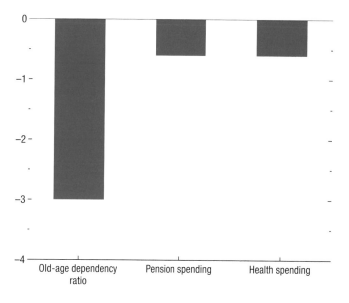

Figure 4.20. Estimated Impact of Migration in More Developed Economies, 2100
(Percent of GDP)

Source: Clements and others (2015).
Note: The impact of migration is calculated as the difference between the baseline scenario, which assumes the continuation of current migration trends, and the zero migration scenario.

Alesina, Harnoss, and Rapoport (2015) and Ortega and Peri (2014) use a gravity model to disentangle the effects of migration driven by push factors. In a cross-sectional setting, they find a large positive impact of migrants on output per capita in recipient countries. They relate this to a positive impact on employment, capital accumulation, and labor productivity from high-skilled migrants, which not only increases productivity on its own, but also fosters diversity in the labor force.

Recent research suggests that migration improves GDP per capita in host countries by boosting investment and increasing labor productivity. Jaumotte, Koloskova, and Saxena (2016) estimate that a 1 percentage point increase in the share of migrants in the working-age population can raise GDP per capita over the long term by up to 2 percent (Figure 4.21, panel 1).[41] While this impact is somewhat lower than previous estimates, it is economically significant. Decomposing these estimates into the effect on employment and on labor productivity, they find that migration has a positive and

[41]To address endogeneity issues, the study uses a pseudo-gravity model to estimate migration caused by push factors from source countries, such as socioeconomic and political conditions, and by bilateral costs of migration, factors that are largely independent of host countries' income levels.

Figure 4.21. Migration: Positive Longer-Term Growth Effects

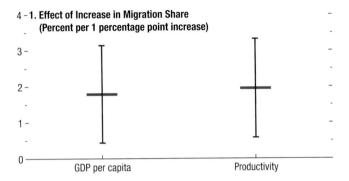

1. Effect of Increase in Migration Share
   (Percent per 1 percentage point increase)

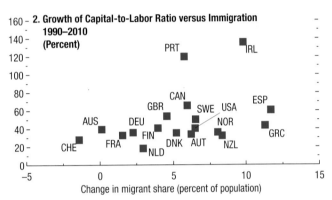

2. Growth of Capital-to-Labor Ratio versus Immigration
   1990–2010
   (Percent)

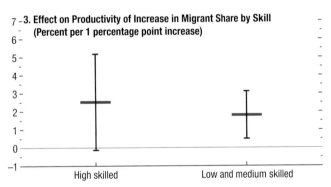

3. Effect on Productivity of Increase in Migrant Share by Skill
   (Percent per 1 percentage point increase)

Sources: Jaumotte, Koloskova, and Saxena (2016); Organisation for Economic Cooperation and Development; United Nations Global Migration database; and IMF staff calculations.
Note: Data labels in the figure use International Organization for Standardization (ISO) country codes. Red lines indicate 95 percent confidence interval.

significant impact on labor productivity.[42] In addition, they find no relationship between the long-term growth in the capital-to-labor ratio and the change in the stock

[42]While these results apply to the panel estimation, labor markets issues and the skill composition of the migrant population vis-à-vis the natives can play a role. For instance, a sudden large increase in the employment of low-skilled immigrants in low productivity sectors—as, for example, during the precrisis boom in Spain—can have a negative impact on aggregate labor productivity (see Kangasniemi and others 2012).

of migrants, consistent with investment adjusting over time to a larger pool of potential workers (Figure 4.21, panel 2). Moreover, the impact is distributed evenly across income groups—that is, migration has a positive effect on the incomes of both the top earners and of those of the rest of the population, although the impact of high-skilled migrants is larger for top earners.

Both high- and low-skilled migrants increase productivity. High-skilled migrants are likely to have a larger impact on GDP per capita through their larger impact on productivity. However, lower-skilled migrants may also increase productivity if their skills are complementary to those of natives. Jaumotte, Koloskova, and Saxena (2016) find that both high- and low-skilled migrants have a positive impact on productivity of a similar magnitude (Figure 4.21, panel 3). They attribute this finding to the "over-qualification of migrants"—as noted above, some countries show a higher proportion of highly educated migrants employed in lower-skill occupations—and to the complementarities mentioned previously. Low-skilled workers allow higher-skilled natives to move into different labor market segments, encouraging them to take higher-skill jobs and obtain additional education. They also promote female labor force participation by taking housekeeping and childcare jobs. This interpretation is supported by evidence on the relationship between low-skilled migrants and female labor participation presented earlier in this chapter. Farré, González, and Ortega (2011) come to a similar conclusion in the case of Spain.

Source Countries: Costs and Mitigating Factors

Migration may impose significant costs in source countries, although there are some mitigating factors. Although push factors for migration can differ—from conflicts (for example, in the Middle East; see Box 4.2) to differences in the economic outlook, such as in eastern Europe during the past decade—the repercussions for source countries are similar. Migration can take a toll on population growth, which is especially costly when migrants are young and educated, damaging prospects for long-term growth. It may also affect the fiscal accounts and increase the challenges posed by population aging. These costs, though, could be mitigated by migrants' remittances, which can increase household income and potentially foster investment. And migrants may facilitate knowledge transfer between host and source countries, which ultimately could promote trade, investment, and growth.

Costs of Brain Drain

While a natural response to demographic trends in some countries, migration may dent population growth in others. Some examples can illustrate these differences:

- Rapid emigration from sub-Saharan Africa has been associated with an ongoing demographic transition involving strong growth in the working-age population. This migration—which is set to continue in coming years—represents a shift in the labor force from countries with young populations to those with aging ones, and should help smooth asynchronous demographic patterns across economies (see Box 4.3).

- However, migration has taken a toll on demographic trends in other regions. For example, Caribbean countries lost between 7 percent and 27 percent of their labor force to the United States in 1965–2000 (Mishra 2006). Since the collapse of the Soviet Union Georgia's and Armenia's populations have contracted by 15 and 27 percent, respectively. In central, eastern, and southeastern Europe, about 5.5 percent of the population left the region during the past 25 years—southeastern European countries have witnessed cumulative outward migration of more than 8 percentage points between 1990 and 2012. Local populations in most countries in the central, eastern, and southeastern Europe have been stagnant or shrinking; the Baltics and Commonwealth of Independent States countries show similar trends (Figure 4.22).

The migration of young and high-skilled people can result in significant losses of human capital. High-skilled people are more likely to migrate than others—they tend to have more resources to relocate and find more favorable conditions in recipient countries.[43] As a result, migration has had a substantial impact on the high-skilled labor force for some countries and regions (Figure 4.23, panel 1). For instance, Caribbean countries lost more than 50 percent of their high-skilled workers between 1965 and 2000 (see Mishra 2006). Atoyan and others (2016) find that, for central, eastern, and southeastern European countries, several decades of migration have exacerbated the shortage of skilled labor. They show that the share of migrants with tertiary education in such countries as the Czech Republic, Hungary, Latvia, and Poland was well above

Figure 4.22. Contributions of Outward Migration to Population Growth

(Percent change from 1993 to 2012)

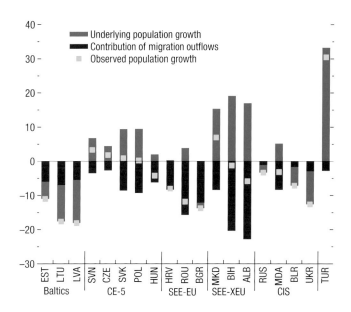

Sources: Organisation for Economic Co-operation and Development, International Migration database; World Bank, *World Development Indicators;* and IMF staff calculations.
Note: Baltics = EST, LTU, LVA; CE-5 = CZE, HUN, POL, SVK, SVN; SEE-EU = Southeast Europe EU members; SEE-XEU = Southeast Europe non-EU members; CIS = Commonwealth of Independent States.
Data labels in the figure use International Organization for Standardization (ISO) country codes.

the equivalent ratio in the general population (Figure 4.23, panel 2).

Brain drain can have profound effects on labor markets and growth prospects in sending countries. Migration dampens working-age population growth and can put upward pressure on wages, as documented in Mishra (2014) in a number of national case studies.[44] At the same time, it can have a negative impact on productivity. Low substitutability between skilled migrants and natives reduces labor productivity, which is compounded by the fact that more educated people usually transfer know-how to others. Atoyan and others (2016) conduct a counterfactual analysis suggesting that cumulative real labor productivity growth in central, eastern, and southeastern European countries between 1995 and 2012 might have been about 5 per-

---

[43]For instance, Atoyan and others (2016) show that in 2010, about three-quarters of migrants in central, eastern, and southeastern European countries were of working age and younger and better educated that the population at large.

[44]Depending on the skill level of migrants, migration can also change relative wages—if migrants are more educated, a decrease in the supply of high-skilled labor can increase the wage gap between high-and low-skill workers. Mishra (2007) finds some evidence of this in the case of Mexico, where emigration has the greatest impact on wages of workers with 12–15 years of schooling.

Figure 4.23. Migration of Population with Tertiary Education

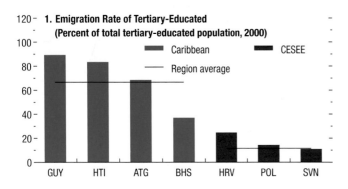

1. Emigration Rate of Tertiary-Educated
(Percent of total tertiary-educated population, 2000)

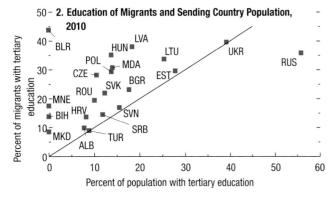

2. Education of Migrants and Sending Country Population, 2010

Sources: Organisation for Economic Co-operation and Development, Database on Immigrants in OECD Countries 2010; World Bank, *World Development Indicators;* and IMF staff calculations.
Note: CESEE = central and southeastern Europe. Data labels in the figure use International Organization for Standardization (ISO) country codes.

centage points higher in the absence of migration. As a consequence, these countries witnessed lower GDP growth not only on account of migration-induced loss of labor but also because of worsening skill composition. Arguably, this has lessened the prospects for income convergence in emerging Europe.

Finally, migration can also affect fiscal accounts. Atoyan and others (2016) argue that emigration has no significant impact on public debt but has led to higher fiscal pressure in central, eastern, and southeastern European countries. This is because labor outflows tend to dampen tax revenue more than they reduce spending. Because migrants are mostly young, health care and pension spending tend to be little affected, which forces governments to increase tax rates or find additional revenue sources.[45] Some case studies have documented that emigration has a negative impact on

[45]See Gibson and McKenzie (2012) on revenue issues, and Clements and others (2015) on pension and health care spending.

fiscal accounts, to a great extent associated with lower revenue.[46]

Remittances and Diasporas

Remittances provide a source of income for a number of small migration source countries, notably for poor households. Remittances to developing countries reached $450 billion in 2015, more than half of foreign direct investment inflows (Figure 4.24, panel 1). For some small countries, remittances can reach over 25 percent of GDP (for example, Tajikistan, Nepal, and Moldova). Caribbean countries provide a clear example of the importance of remittances: after losing a significant portion of their labor force over the past decades, they are now the world's largest recipient of remittances as a percent of GDP as a region—about 7½ percent of the region's GDP in 2015. This can make a significant contribution to poor households' income. A cross-country study of 71 emerging market and developing economies by Adams and Page (2005) has found that a 10 percent increase in remittances per capita leads to a 3.5 percent decline in the share of people living in poverty. Remittances have been shown to increase education and health care spending relative to consumption as well (Ratha 2014).[47]

Remittances may also have macroeconomic effects. As a source of financing, remittances can contribute to investment, financial development, and growth by increasing domestic savings and easing credit constraints. For eastern Europe, Atoyan and others (2016) find a positive impact on private investment, suggesting that remittances ease collateral constraints and lending costs for entrepreneurs. Goschin (2013) also finds a positive impact on growth in central and eastern Europe in 1995–2011. But remittances may have adverse effects on labor markets and exchange rates as well. Atoyan and others (2016) argue that remittances reduce incentives to work due to a relaxation of the budget constraint and an increase in the reservation wage.[48] Remittance flows can also lead to real appre-

[46]See Campos-Vazquez and Sobarzo (2012) for the case of Mexico; Desai, Kapur, and Rogers (2009) for India; and Gibson and McKenzie (2012) for Ghana, Micronesia, New Zealand, Papua New Guinea, and Tonga.

[47]In light of de-risking—the withdrawal of correspondent banking relationships and the closing of bank accounts of remittance service providers—the benefits of remittances are possibly lower in the current environment. See Alwazir and others (forthcoming) for small states in the Pacific.

[48]An increase of 1 percentage point of GDP in remittances is associated with a 2–3 percent increase in the economy-wide inactivity rate in Balkan and central European countries.

ciations and a contraction of the tradable sector, as documented in Magud and Sosa (2013) and Atoyan and others (2016) for Eastern Europe.

Finally, diaspora networks of emigrants may convey knowledge and expertise back to the source country, potentially raising productivity (Figure 4.24, panel 2). Mitra and others (2016) suggest that, by contributing to the curriculum design, diaspora networks can raise the quality of education in their home countries. They can also provide rigorous professional development and leadership training programs. Combining their skills, contacts, and know-how with their insight into global opportunities and local customs, diaspora networks of emigrants may help strengthen the home-country business environment, raise efficiency, and expand into new markets.[49] In the same vein, they can also advise governments and help to improve the quality of public institutions.[50]

Policy: The Importance of Integration

Migration has significant spillovers for recipient and source countries alike, and policy plays an important role in shaping their economic impact. In recipient countries, the degree to which migration increases labor supply and productivity, and contributes to the public finances over the long term, depends on the speed with which migrants integrate into labor markets. For source countries, the right policy response depends on the underlying drivers of migration—that is, whether it is driven by domestic or foreign developments.

Fast integration of migrants is key for recipient economies. Well-designed integration policies are essential for harnessing the benefits of migration and should, in particular,

- *Improve labor market policies.* Simple, affordable, and transparent procedures for hiring foreign workers and recognition of foreign qualifications and work experience can help smooth labor market integration. Proactive job placement and other incentives can reduce entry costs. Any fiscal incentives, such as wage and employment subsidies, should be temporary and targeted.
- *Provide access to education and financing.* Access to education and language and job training can help

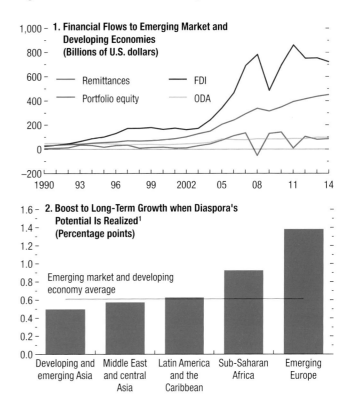

Figure 4.24. Remittances and Diasporas

1. Financial Flows to Emerging Market and Developing Economies
(Billions of U.S. dollars)

Remittances — FDI
Portfolio equity — ODA

2. Boost to Long-Term Growth when Diaspora's Potential Is Realized[1]
(Percentage points)

Emerging market and developing economy average

Developing and emerging Asia | Middle East and central Asia | Latin America and the Caribbean | Sub-Saharan Africa | Emerging Europe

Sources: Mitra and others (2015, 2016); World Bank, *World Development Indicators*; and IMF staff calculations.
[1]Potential growth if diaspora rises to best performers' benchmark. For simulation details see Mitra and others (2016).

achieve a good skill-balance among migrants and minimize the potential for social tension. Ensuring access to financial services—for example, bank accounts and financial transactions—can broaden opportunities.

- *Support migrant entrepreneurs.* Encouraging migrant entrepreneurship could help foster competitiveness and innovation.

Refugees require special attention. A key issue is reducing the time asylum seekers must wait before they are allowed to work. Targeted support can reduce language and skill gaps, and such measures as temporary wage subsidies can create incentives for employers to hire. Improving geographic mobility, including through the availability of affordable housing, will help refugees move where labor demand is high.[51] Where

---

[49]Migrants could also foster trade; see Cohen, Gurun, and Malloy (forthcoming) and Parsons and Vezina (2014); and foreign direct investment (see Burchardi, Chaney, and Hassan 2016).

[50]For example, Indian-born executives working in U.S.-based technology companies played a critical role in giving the latter confidence to outsource work to India.

[51]In the European Union, flexibility built into the Stability and Growth Pact should be allowed for a marginal loosening of fiscal targets to accommodate refugee-related short-term costs.

countries receive refugees from neighboring conflict zones, international support remains crucial—including from donors—to ensure that refugees are appropriately cared for, including through complementary central government assistance.

Source countries should strive to tilt the balance between positive and negative effects of emigration in their favor. If home-grown policy distortions are driving emigration, correcting them is a natural way to avoid brain drain. If emigration is driven by pull factors, the response should stress adjustment and policies to:

- *Retain and re-attract migrants.* Strong institutions and growth-enhancing reforms will foster income convergence and make emigration less attractive—for instance, improvements to the business environment, governance, and the quality of institutions would create greater incentives for people to stay or emigrants to return. Recognition of skills acquired abroad, targeted tax benefits, and portable social security benefits could also persuade migrants to return.
- *Leverage diaspora networks and make remittances count.* This could include, for example, the issuance of diaspora bonds (as, for example, in India, Israel, Nigeria, the Philippines) and outreach to diaspora communities. Reducing the cost of remittances and enhancing incentives for their financial intermediation can also make a difference.
- *Mitigate the effects of migration.* Policies that boost labor supply, including raising female labor force participation, can overcome the labor shrinking effects of migration. Improving the efficiency of social and health care spending can ease possible fiscal pressure, and if there is a need to raise tax

revenue, greater reliance on consumption instead of labor taxes will protect growth.

An effective policy response in postconflict source countries should protect economic institutions, prioritize budget allocations that serve basic needs of the population, and use monetary and exchange rate policies to shore up confidence. Once conflicts subside, successful rebuilding requires well-functioning institutions and robust yet flexible macroeconomic frameworks to absorb capital inflows and maintain debt sustainability. To prevent future violence, postconflict countries should accelerate inclusive growth reforms aimed at reducing inequality.

An enhanced multilateral framework is warranted to better govern international migration. Global efforts should focus on encouraging cooperation between source and recipient countries, including by facilitating remittance flows, protecting labor rights, and promoting a safe and secure working environment for migrants. Cooperation is also vital to address challenges from humanitarian migration, including through enhanced global development diplomacy—aimed at preventing, containing, and responding to humanitarian crises—and more flexible and innovative financing instruments to ensure effective assistance and resources for refugees wishing to return home. Given the increasing flows of refugees over the past years, and the impact that they have on neighboring countries that are shouldering a large share of the cost of receiving them, high-income donor countries (including international institutions, the Group of Seven, the Gulf Cooperation Council, and the European Union) need to coordinate their approach to provide more financial support to improve conditions for refugees.

Box 4.1. China's Ties with Low-Income and Developing Countries

Trade linkages between China and low-income and developing countries have risen markedly in recent years. Exports to China as a share of these countries' total exports have more than doubled, from less than 5 percent before 2000. Although China's share of low-income and developing country exports appears modest, at 13 percent in 2015, it was among the three largest export destination markets for about half of these countries, which tend to trade across a large number of trading partners. As discussed in this chapter, countries with significant trade exposure to China have faced downward pressure on demand for their exports in recent years, and export volume growth in low-income and developing countries has slowed accordingly.

The sectoral composition of trade with China is dominated by fuel, minerals, and metals, which accounted for about 60 percent of total exports in 2014 (Figure 4.1.1, panel 1). The share of commodities, although still high, shows a slight decline relative to the early 2000s, when exports of raw materials represented about 70 percent of the total. Some of the share once occupied by these exports has recently given way to capital-goods exports, which now represent about 10 percent of total exports.

China is a major source of foreign direct investment inflows into low income and developing countries (Figure 4.1.1, panel 2). Although the two largest beneficiaries of Chinese direct investment (Lao P.D.R. and Mongolia) are geographically close to China, China is also a major source of foreign direct investment for several countries in sub-Saharan Africa. As China continues its transition and allows firms to seek new investment opportunities abroad, there may be positive spillovers for these countries. Lower demand for commodities may, however, get in the way somewhat, since foreign direct investment has usually been associated with commodity pro-

The author of this box is Nkunde Mwase.

Figure 4.1.1. China's Ties with Low-Income and Developing Countries

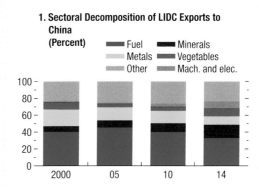

1. Sectoral Decomposition of LIDC Exports to China
(Percent)

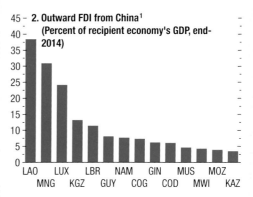

2. Outward FDI from China[1]
(Percent of recipient economy's GDP, end-2014)

Sources: CEIC; and IMF staff calculations.
Note: FDI = foreign direct investment; LIDC = low-income and developing country; Mach. and elec. = machinery and electrical equipment. Data labels in the figure use International Organization for Standardization (ISO) country codes.
[1]Excludes Hong Kong SAR.

duction. In addition, as discussed in IMF 2016j, the recent "One Belt One Road" initiative will involve a further strengthening of foreign direct investment flows from China to the Caucasus and Central Asia, south Asia, and southeast Asia.

Box 4.2. Conflicts Driving Migration: Middle East and North Africa

The Middle East and North Africa is facing a new wave of conflict with significant economic costs and spillovers within the region. Since the end of World War II, countries in this region have suffered more conflicts than those in any other region in the world. Conflicts are more protracted and violent as well—between 1946 and 2014, 12 out of 53 episodes of conflict in the region lasted more than eight years, and a significant number of former conflict countries relapsed into violence within 10 years. The economic costs of conflict are massive for some countries and the spillovers large. GDP in Syria has fallen by half, and growth in Jordan and Lebanon has slowed significantly over recent years.

Based on Rother and others (2016).

The humanitarian and economic costs of conflict are massive. An estimated 10 million refugees from conflict countries have mostly stayed within countries in the region—for example, since 2010, refugees from Iraq and Syria have boosted the populations of Lebanon and Jordan by one-quarter and one-fifth, respectively. More than 1.7 million refugees have reached Europe since July 2014, and Turkey hosts about 3 million. Countries hosting refugees face difficult decisions about access to labor markets and social programs. This highlights the importance both of humanitarian aid aimed at addressing the immediate needs of refugees and those displaced within their own countries, and of scaled-up development assistance to the region as a whole.

Box 4.3. Migration in Sub-Saharan Africa

In the coming decades sub-Saharan African migration will be shaped by a profound demographic transition that has already begun. The working-age population is growing more rapidly than the population overall, which means migration outside the region is set to continue to expand.

Key Trends

Amid rapid population growth, sub-Saharan Africa migration has increased rapidly over the past 20 years. Although the migration rate—migration-to-total population—has remained stable at about 2 percent, the population has doubled over the past 25 years. Until the 1990s intraregional migration dominated and early in that decade represented 75 percent of the total. Over the past 15 years, though, migration outside the region—mainly to Organisation for Economic Co-operation and Development (OECD) countries—has picked up sharply, and represented one-third of the total stock of migrants by 2013 (Figure 4.3.1, panel 1).

Migration from sub-Saharan Africa is set to continue to increase very rapidly. The region is undergoing a demographic transition as a result of strong population growth combined with reduced infant and maternal mortality. The latter implies that the working-age population—which typically feeds migration—is set to increase even more rapidly (Figure 4.3.1, panel 2). IMF staff projections using a gravity model of sub-Saharan African migration to OECD countries indicate that population growth will continue to shape migration. They suggest that the region's migrants in OECD countries could increase from about 7 million in 2013 to about 34 million by 2050. Given the relatively slow population growth expected for OECD countries, the ratio of sub-Saharan African migration as a share of OECD population could increase sixfold, from just 0.4 percent in 2010 to 2.4 percent by 2050 (Figure 4.3.1, panel 3).[1]

Migration is increasingly driven by economic considerations. The flow of refugees—about half of sub-Saharan African migration within and outside the region in 1990—had decreased to only one-tenth of the total in 2013. By 2013 most migrants outside the region—about 85 percent—were in OECD countries.

Based on Gonzalez-Garcia and others (2016).

[1] The determinants of migration to OECD countries are relative per capita income and working-age population, the existing diaspora in OECD countries, distance between countries, public health spending in OECD countries, and indicators of common language, previous colonial relationship, wars in sub-Saharan Africa, and landlocked countries.

Figure 4.3.1. Migration in Sub-Saharan Africa

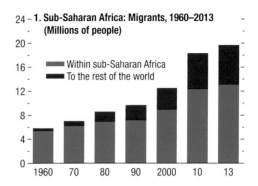

1. Sub-Saharan Africa: Migrants, 1960–2013
(Millions of people)

■ Within sub-Saharan Africa
■ To the rest of the world

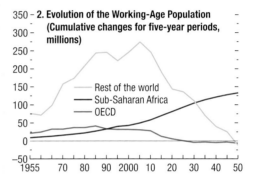

2. Evolution of the Working-Age Population
(Cumulative changes for five-year periods, millions)

Rest of the world
Sub-Saharan Africa
OECD

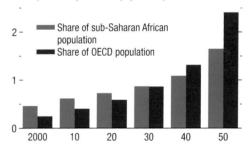

3. Sub-Saharan Africa Migrants in OECD Countries
(Stock as percent of population)

■ Share of sub-Saharan African population
■ Share of OECD population

Sources: United Nations *World Population Prospects;* World Bank, Migration and Remittances database; and IMF staff calculations.
Note: OECD = Organisation for Economic Co-operation and Development.

France, the United Kingdom, and the United States host about half of the total diaspora outside the region. Although a few sub-Saharan African countries—for example, Ethiopia, Nigeria, and South Africa, with close to 0.7 million people each—have a large number of migrants, they represent only a small share of their population. With a relatively small number of migrants, these are proportionately more important for some

Box 4.3 *(continued)*

small economies—such as Cabo Verde (about one-third of its population) and Mauritius, São Tomé and Príncipe, and Seychelles (about 10 percent).

Economic Impact

Brain drain is particularly acute in sub-Saharan Africa. The migration of young and educated workers takes a large toll on a region whose human capital is already scarce. The concentration of migrants among those who are educated is higher than in other developing economies (Figure 4.3.2). The migration of highly skilled workers entails a high social cost, as is evidenced by the departure of doctors and nurses from Malawi and Zimbabwe, which may mean welfare losses beyond those that are purely economic. Nevertheless, recent studies suggest some positive effects: returning migrants bring

back new skills, and prospects for migration motivate human capital accumulation, which may be supported by large remittances from current migrants and returning migrants bringing knowledge and experience.[2]

Remittance inflows represent an important source of foreign exchange and income in several countries in the region. After the global financial crisis, while foreign direct investment entered a clear downward trend, remittances became one of the largest sources of external inflows, currently at a level similar to foreign investment. Remittances represented 25 percent of Liberia's GDP in 2013–15; about 20 percent in Comoros, the Gambia, and Lesotho; and roughly 10 percent in Cabo Verde, São Tomé and Príncipe, Senegal, and Togo (Figure 4.3.3). Remittances provide a relatively stable source of income that helps smooth consumption and support growth in sub-Saharan Africa. They also help alleviate poverty and promote access to financial services—many receiving families develop a relationship with a financial institution, usually a wire transfer company or bank, to receive their funds easily.

[2]For literature on brain gain in sub-Saharan Africa, see Nyarko (2011); Easterly and Nyarko (2008); and Batista, Lacuesta, and Vicente (2007).

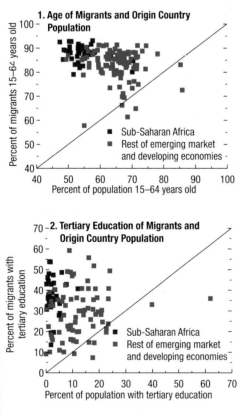

Figure 4.3.2. Age and Education of Migrants and Origin Country Population
(Percent)

Sources: Organisation for Economic Co-operation and Development, International Migration Database; World Bank, *World Development Indicators*; and IMF staff calculations.

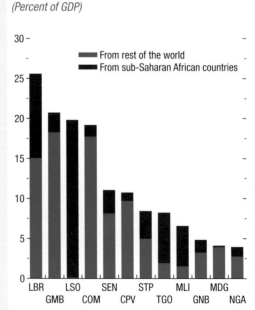

Figure 4.3.3. Top Receivers of Remittances in Sub-Saharan Africa, 2013–15
(Percent of GDP)

Source: World Bank, Migration and Remittances database.
Note: Data labels in the figure use International Organization for Standardization (ISO) country codes.

References

Aastveit, Knut Are, Hilde C. Bjørnland, and Leif Anders Thorsrud. 2012. "What Drives Oil Prices? Emerging versus Developed Economies." Working Paper 2012/11, Norgesbank.

Abiad, Abdul, Madhavi Pundit, Minsoo Lee, and Arief Ramayand. 2016. "Moderating Growth and Structural Change in the People's Republic of China: Implications for Developing Asia and Beyond." ADB Briefs 53, Asian Development Bank, Manila.

Adams Jr., Richard H., and John Page. 2005. "Do International Migration and Remittances Reduce Poverty in Developing Countries?" *World Development* 33 (10): 1645–69.

Aiyar, Shekhar, Bergljot Barkbu, Nicoletta Batini, Helge Berger, Enrica Detragiache, Allan Dizioli, Christian Ebeke, Huidan Lin, Linda Kaltani, Sebastian Sosa, Antonio Spilimbergo, and Petia Topalova. 2016. "The Refugee Surge in Europe: Economic Challenges." IMF Staff Discussion Note 16/02, International Monetary Fund, Washington.

Akgunduz, Yusuf, Marcel van den Berg, and Wolter Hassink. 2015. "The Impact of Refugee Crises on Host Labor Markets: The Case of the Syrian Refugee Crisis in Turkey." IZA Discussion Paper 8841, Institute for the Study of Labor (IZA), Bonn.

Aldén, Lina, and Matts Hammarstedt. 2014. "Integration of Immigrants on the Swedish Labor Market: Recent Trends and Explanations." Centre for Labour Market and Discrimination Study, Linnaeus University, Växjö, Sweden.

Aleksynska, Mariya, and Ahmed Tritah. 2013. "Occupation–Education Mismatch of Immigrant Workers in Europe: Context and Policies." *Economics of Education Review* 36 (C): 229–44.

Alesina, Alberto, Johann Harnoss, and Hillel Rapoport. 2015. "Birthplace Diversity and Economic Prosperity." NBER Working Paper 18699, National Bureau of Economic Research, Cambridge, Massachusetts.

Alwazir, Jihad, Fazurin Jamaludin, Dongyeol Lee, Niamh Sheridan, and Patrizia Tumbarello. Forthcoming. "De-Risking in the Small States of the Pacific: Evidence and Policy Options." IMF Working Paper, International Monetary Fund, Washington.

Amuedo-Dorantes, Catalina, and Susan Pozo. 2006. "Migration, Remittances, and Male and Female Employment Patterns." *American Economic Review* 96 (2): 222–26.

Andrle, Michal, Patrick Blagrave, Pedro Espaillat, Keiko Honjo, Benjamin Hunt, Mika Kortelainen, René Lalonde, Douglas Laxton, Eleonora Mavroeidi, Dirk Muir, Susanna Mursula, and Stephen Snudden. 2015. "The Flexible System of Global Models – FSGM" IMF Working Paper 15/64, International Monetary Fund, Washington.

Arslanalp, Serkan, Wei Liao, Shi Piao, and Dulani Seneviratne. Forthcoming. "China's Growing Influence on Asian Financial Markets." IMF Working Paper, International Monetary Fund, Washington.

Äslund, Olof, and Dan-Olof Rooth. 2007. "Do When and Where Matter? Initial Labor Market Conditions and Immigrant Earnings." *Economic Journal* 117: 422–48.

Atoyan, Ruben, Lone Christiansen, Allan Dizioli, Christian Ebeke, Nadeem Ilahi, Anna Ilyina, Gil Mehrez, Haonan Qu, Faezeh Raei, Alaina Rhee, and Daria Zakharova. 2016. "Emigration and Its Economic Impact on Eastern Europe." IMF Staff Discussion Note 16/07, International Monetary Fund, Washington.

Aydemir, Adburrahman, and George Borjas. 2007. "Cross-Country Variation in the Impact of International Migration: Canada, Mexico, and the United States." *Journal of the European Economic Association* 5 (4): 663–708.

———. 2011. "Attenuation Bias in Measuring the Wage Impact of Immigration." *Journal of Labor Economics* 29 (1): 69–113.

Banerji, Angana, Sergejs Saksonovs, Huidan Lin, and Rodolphe Blavy. 2014. "Youth Unemployment in Advanced Economies in Europe: Searching for Solutions." IMF Staff Discussion Note 14/11, International Monetary Fund, Washington.

Barajas, Adolfo, Ralph Chami, Connel Fullenkamp, Michael Gaspen, and Peter Montiel. 2009. "Do Workers' Remittances Promote Economic Growth?" IMF Working Paper 09/153, International Monetary Fund, Washington.

Batista, Cátia, Aitor Lacuesta, and Pedro C. Vicente. 2007. "Brain Drain or Brain Gain? Micro Evidence from an African Success Story." IZA Discussion Paper 3035, Institute for the Study of Labor (IZA), Bonn.

Blagrave, Patrick, and Esteban Vesperoni. 2016. "China's Slowdown: Implications for International Trade." Spillover Note 4, International Monetary Fund, Washington.

Blanchard, Olivier, Florence Jaumotte, and Prakash Loungani. 2013. "Labor Market Policies and IMF Advice in Advanced Economies during the Great Recession." IMF Staff Discussion Note 13/02, International Monetary Fund, Washington.

Borjas, George. 1999. "The Economic Analysis of Immigration." In *Handbook of Labor Economics*, edited by Orley C. Ashenfelter and David Card, 1697–760. Philadelphia: Elsevier.

———. 2003. "The Labor Demand Curve is Downward Sloping: Reexamining the Impact of Immigration on the Labor Market." *Quarterly Journal of Economics* 118 (4): 1335–74.

———. 2006. "Native Internal Migration and the Labor Market Impact of Immigration." *Journal of Human Resources* XLI (2): 221–58.

Borjas, George J., and Lawrence F. Katz. 2007. "The Evolution of the Mexican-Born Workforce in the United States." In *Mexican Immigration to the United States*, edited by George J. Borjas. Chicago: University of Chicago Press.

Burchardi, Konrad, Thomas Chaney, and Tarek Hassan. 2016. "Migrants, Investors, and Investments." NBER Working Paper 21847, National Bureau of Economic Research, Cambridge, Massachusetts.

Campos-Vazquez, Raymundo, and Horacio Sobarzo. 2012. "The Development and Fiscal Effects of Emigration on Mexico." Migration Policy Institute, Woodrow Wilson Center for Scholars, Washington.

Card, David. 1990. "The Impact of the Mariel Boatlift on the Miami Labor Market." *Industrial and Labor Relations Review* 43 (2): 245–57.

———, Christian Dustmann, and Ian Preston. 2009. "Immigration, Wages, and Compositional Amenities." NBER Working Paper 15521, National Bureau of Economic Research, Cambridge, Massachusetts.

Cashin, Paul, Kamiar Mohaddes, and Mehdi Raissi. 2016. "China's Slowdown and Global Financial Market Volatility: Is World Growth Losing Out?" IMF Working Paper 16/63, International Monetary Fund, Washington.

Cattaneo, Cristina, Carlo V. Fiorio, and Giovanni Peri. 2015. "What Happens to the Careers of European Workers When Immigrants 'Take Their Jobs?'" *Journal of Human Resources* 50 (3): 655–93.

Cesa-Bianchi, Ambrogio, and Kate Stratford. 2016. "How Could a Shock to Growth in China Affect Growth in the United Kingdom?" In *Bank of England Quarterly Bulletin* 56 (1): 4–11.

Chami, Ralph, Adolfo Barajas, Thomas Cosimano, Connel Fullenkamp, Michael Gapen, and Peter Montiel. 2008. "Macroeconomic Consequences of Remittances." IMF Occasional Paper 259, International Monetary Fund, Washington, D.C.

Chami, Ralph, Dalia Hakura, and Peter Montiel. 2009. "Remittances: An Automatic Output Stabilizer?" IMF Working Paper 09/91, International Monetary Fund, Washington.

Christiansen, Lone, Huidan Lin, Joana Pereira, Petia Topalova, and Rima Turk. 2016. "Unlocking Female Employment Potential in Europe: Drivers and Benefits." Departmental Paper; European Department and Strategy, Policy, and Review Department; International Monetary Fund, Washington.

Clements, Benedict, Kamil Dybczak, Vitor Gaspar, Sanjeev Gupta, and Mauricio Soto. 2015. "The Fiscal Consequences of Shrinking Populations." IMF Staff Discussion Note, International Monetary Fund, Washington.

Cohen, Lauren, Umit Gurun, and Christopher Malloy. Forthcoming. "Resident Networks and Corporate Connections: Evidence from World War II Internment Camps." *Journal of Finance.*

Conde Ruiz, J. Ignacio, Juan Ramón Garcia, and Maria Navarro. 2008. "Immigration and Regional Growth in Spain." FEDEA Working Paper 2008–08, Fundación de Estudios de Economía Aplicada, Madrid.

D'Amuri, Francesco, and Giovanni Peri. 2014. "Immigration, Jobs, and Employment Protection: Evidence from Europe before and during the Great Recession." *Journal of the European Economic Association* 12 (2): 432–64.

Desai, Mihir, D. Kapur, J. McHale, and K. Rogers. 2009. "The Fiscal Impact of High-Skilled Emigration: Flows of Indians to the US." *Journal of Development Economics* 88 (1): 32–44.

Diebold, Francis X., and Kamil Yilmaz. 2011. "On the Network Topology of Variance Decompositions: Measuring the Connectedness of Financial Firms." NBER Working Paper 17490, National Bureau of Economic Research, Cambridge, Massachusetts.

Dizioli, Allan, Jaime Guajardo, Vladimir Klyuev, Rui Mano, and Mehdi Raissi. 2016. "Spillovers from China's Growth Slowdown and Rebalancing to the ASEAN-5 Economies." IMF Working Paper 16/170, International Monetary Fund, Washington.

Dizioli, Allan, Ben Hunt, and Wojciech Maliszewski. Forthcoming. "Spillovers from the Maturing of China's Economy: A General Equilibrium Model-Based Analysis." IMF Working Paper, International Monetary Fund, Washington.

Drummond, Paulo, and Estelle Xue Liu. 2013. "Africa's Rising Exposure to China: How Large Are Spillovers through Trade?" IMF Working Paper 13/250, International Monetary Fund, Washington.

Duval, Romain, Nan Li, Richa Saraf, and Dulani Seneviratne. 2016. "Value-Added Trade and Business Cycle Synchronization." *Journal of International Economics* 99: 251–62.

Easterly, William, and Yaw Nyarko. 2008. "Is the Brain Drain Good for Africa?" Brookings Global Economy and Development Working Paper 19, The Brookings Institution, Washington.

Ebeke, Christian Hubert. 2010. "Remittances, Value Added Tax and Tax Revenue in Developing Countries." CERDI Document de travail de la série Etudes et Documents E 2010.30, Centre d'Etudes et de Recherches sur le Développement International, Clermont-Ferrand.

Farré, Lidia, Libertad González, and Francesc Ortega. 2011. "Immigration, Family Responsibility and the Labor Supply of Skilled Native Women." *B.E. Journal of Economic Analysis & Policy* 11 (1), Article 34.

Furceri, Davide, Joao Tovar Jalles, Aleksandra Zdzienicka. 2016. "China Spillovers: New Evidence from Time-Varying Estimates." Spillover Note 7, International Monetary Fund, Washington.

Gauvin, Ludovic, and Cyril Rebillard. 2015. "Towards Recoupling? Assessing the Global Impact of a Chinese Hard Landing through Trade and Commodity Price Channels." Working Paper 562, Banque de France, Paris.

Gibson, John, and David McKenzie. 2012. "The Economic Consequences of 'Brain Drain' of the Best and Brightest: Microeconomic Evidence from Five Countries." *Economic Journal* 122 (560): 339–75.

Gonzalez-Garcia, Jesús, Ermal Hitaj, Montfort Mlachila, Arina Viseth, and Mustafa Yenice. 2016. "Sub-Saharan African Migration: Patterns and Spillovers." Spillover Note 9, International Monetary Fund, Washington.

Guimarães-Filho, Roberto, and Gee Hee Hong. 2016. "Dynamic Interconnectedness of Asian Equity Markets." IMF Working Paper 16/57, International Monetary Fund, Washington.

Gruss, Bertrand. 2014. "After the Boom: Commodity Prices and Economic Growth in Latin America and the Caribbean." IMF Working Paper 14/154, International Monetary Fund, Washington.

Hatton, Timothy J. 2013. "Refugee and Asylum Migration." In *International Handbook on the Economics of Migration*, edited by Amelie F. Constant and Klaus F. Zimmermann. Cheltenham, United Kingdom, and Northampton, Massachusetts: Edward Elgar.

Ho, Giang, and Kazuko Shirono. 2015. "The Nordic Labor Market and Migration." IMF Working Paper 15/254, International Monetary Fund, Washington.

Hong, Gee Hee, Jaewoo Lee, Wei Liao, and Dulani Seneviratne. 2016. "China and Asia in the Global Trade Slowdown." IMF Working Paper 16/105, International Monetary Fund, Washington.

Hunt, Jennifer, and Marjolaine Gauthier-Loiselle. 2010. "How Much Does Immigration Boost Innovation?" *American Economic Journal: Macroeconomics* 2 (2): 31–56.

International Monetary Fund (IMF). 2014. Chapter 3, "Spillovers from a Potential Reversal of Fortune in Emerging Market Economies." In *IMF Multilateral Policy Issues Report*. Washington, July.

———. 2015a. "Special Feature: Commodity Market Developments and Forecasts, with a Focus on Metals in the World Economy." In *World Economic Outlook*. Washington, October.

———. 2015b. "Where Are Commodity Exporters Headed? Output Growth in the Aftermath of the Commodity Boom." In *World Economic Outlook*. Washington, October.

———. 2015c. "International Migration: Recent Trends, Economic Impacts, and Policy Implications." Staff Background Paper for G20 Surveillance Note. Washington.

———. 2015d. *Lebanon: 2015 Article IV Consultation—Staff Report*. IMF Country Report 15/190. Washington.

———. 2015e. *Jordan: Sixth Review under the Stand-By Arrangement, Request for Waivers of Applicability of Performance Criteria, and Rephasing of Access—Staff Report*. IMF Country Report 15/115. Washington.

———. 2015f. *Fiscal Monitor*. Washington, October.

———. 2015g. *People's Republic of China: 2015 Article IV Consultation—Staff Report*. IMF Country Report 15/234. Washington.

———. 2016a. *People's Republic of China—Hong Kong Special Administrative Region: 2015 Article IV Consultation—Staff Report*. IMF Country Report 16/17. Washington.

———. 2016b. "China's Changing Trade and the Implications for the CLMV Economies." Departmental Paper, Asia and Pacific Department. Washington.

———. 2016c. Chapter 3, "China's Evolving Trade with Advanced Upstream Economies and Commodity Exporters." In *Regional Economic Outlook: Asia and Pacific*. Washington, April.

———. 2016d. Chapter 2, "The Growing Importance of Financial Spillovers from Emerging Market Economies." In *Global Financial Stability Report*. Washington, April.

———. 2016e. Chapter 2, "Navigating the Transition: Trade and Financial Spillovers from China." In *Regional Economic Outlook: Asia and Pacific*. Washington, April.

———. 2016f. *People's Republic of China: 2016 Article IV Consultation—Staff Report*. IMF Country Report 16/270. Washington.

———. 2016g. *Global Financial Stability Report*. Washington, April.

———. 2016h. *Turkey: 2016 Article IV Consultation—Staff Report*. IMF Country Report 16/104. Washington.

———. 2016i. Chapter 1, "Too Slow for Too Long: Recent Developments and Prospects." In *World Economic Outlook*. Washington, April.

———. 2016j. *Regional Economic Outlook: Middle East and Central Asia*. Washington, forthcoming October.

Jaumotte, Florence, Ksenia Koloskova, and Sweta C. Saxena. 2016. "Impact of Migration on Income Levels in Advanced Economies." Spillover Note 8, International Monetary Fund, Washington.

Jorda, Oscar. 2005. "Estimation and Inference of Impulse Responses by Local Projections." *American Economic Review* 95 (1): 161–82.

Kangasniemi, Mari, Matilde Mas, Catherine Robinson, and Lorenzo Serrano. 2012. "The Economic Impact of Migration: Productivity Analysis for Spain and the UK." *Journal of Productivity Analysis* 38 (3): 333–43.

Kolerus, Christina, Papa N'Diaye, and Christian Saborowski. 2016. "China's Footprint in Global Commodity Markets." Spillover Note 5, International Monetary Fund, Washington.

Magud, Nicolás, and Sebastián Sosa. 2013. "When and Why Worry About Real Exchange Rate Appreciation? The Missing Link Between Dutch Disease and Growth." *Journal of International Commerce, Economics and Policy* 4 (2).

Mansuri, Ghazala. 2006. "Migration, Sex Bias, and Child Growth in Rural Pakistan." Policy Research Working Paper 3946, World Bank, Washington.

Mishra, Prachi. 2006. "Emigration and Brain Drain: Evidence from the Caribbean." IMF Working Paper 06/25, International Monetary Fund, Washington.

———. 2007. "Emigration and Wages in Source Countries: Evidence from Mexico." *Journal of Development Economics* 82: 180–99.

———. 2014. "Emigration and Wages in Source Countries: A Survey of the Empirical Literature." In *International Handbook of Migration and Economic Development*, edited by Robert E. B. Lucas. Cheltenham, United Kingdom, and Northampton, Massachusetts: Edward Elgar.

Mitra, Pritha, Amr Hosny, Gohar Minasyan, Mark Fischer, and Gohar Abajyan. 2016. "Avoiding the New Mediocre: Raising Long-Term Growth in the Middle East and Central Asia." Departmental Paper 16/01, Middle East and Central Asia Department, International Monetary Fund, Washington.

Morgan Stanley Research. 2016a. "Turnaround in Steel Outlook." China Supply Side Reforms, January 16.

———. 2016b. "Easing Overcapacity Drives Positive Outlook for Machinery Stocks." China Supply Side Reforms, February 16.

Mwase, Nkunde, Papa N'Diaye, Hiroko Oura, Frantisek Ricka, Katsiaryna Svirydzenka, Camilo Ernesto Tovar, and Yuanyan Sophia Zhang. 2016. "Spillovers from China: Financial

Channels." Spillover Note 6, International Monetary Fund, Washington.

Nasser, Razan, and Steven Symansky. 2014. "The Fiscal Impact of the Syrian Refugee Crisis on Jordon." USAID paper, United States Agency for International Development.

Nose, Manabu, M. Saxegaard, and J. Torres. 2016. "The Impact of China's Growth Slowdown and Lower Commodity Prices on South Africa." In *South Africa: Selected Issues*. IMF Country Report 16/218, International Monetary Fund, Washington.

Nyarko, Yaw. 2011. "The Returns to the Brain Drain and Brain Circulation in Sub-Saharan Africa: Some Computations Using Data from Ghana." NBER Working Paper 16813, National Bureau of Economic Research, Cambridge, Massachusetts.

Organisation for Economic Co-operation and Development (OECD). 2013. Chapter 3, "Fiscal Impact of Immigration in OECD Countries." In *International Migration Outlook*. Paris.

Ortega, Francesc, and Giovanni Peri. 2009. "The Causes and Effects of International Migrations: Evidence from OECD Countries 1980–2005." NBER Working Paper 14833, National Bureau of Economic Research, Cambridge, Massachusetts.

_____. 2014. "Openness and Income: The Role of Trade and Migration." *Journal of International Economics* 92: 231–51.

Ott, Eleanor. 2013. "The Labour Market Integration of Resettled Refugees." Evaluation Report 2013/6, United Nations High Commissioner for Refugees Policy Development and Evaluation Services.

Parsons, Christopher, and Pierre-Louise Vezina. 2014. "Migrant Network and Trade: The Vietnamese Boat People as a Natural Experiment." Economic Working Paper 705, University of Oxford, Oxford, United Kingdom.

Peri, Giovanni. 2014. "Do Immigrant Workers Depress the Wages of Native Workers?" *IZA World of Labor* 2014: 42.

_____, Kevin Shih, and Chad Sparber. 2015. "STEM Workers, H-1B Visas, and Productivity in US Cities." *Journal of Labor Economics* 33 (3): S225–55.

_____, and Chad Sparber. 2009. "Task Specialization, Immigration, and Wages." *American Economic Journal: Applied Economics* 1(3): 135–69.

Ratha, Dilip. 2014. "A $100 Billion Idea—Tapping Migrants for Financing Development." "People Move" blog, World Bank.

Roache, Shaun K. 2012. "China's Impact on World Commodity Markets." IMF Working Paper 12/115, International Monetary Fund, Washington.

Roache, Shaun K., and Marina Rousset. 2015. "China: Credit, Collateral, and Commodity Prices." HKIMR Working Paper 27/2015, Hong Kong Institute for Monetary Research, Hong Kong.

Rother, Bjorn, Greg Auclair, Risto Herrala, David Lombardo, Karina Manasseh, Gaelle Pierre, Eric Roos, and Priscilla Toffano. Forthcoming. "The Economic Impact of Conflicts and the Refugee Crisis in the Middle East and North Africa." IMF Staff Discussion Note, International Monetary Fund, Washington.

World Bank. 2015. "Migration and Remittances: Recent Developments and Outlook." *Migration and Development Brief* 24, World Bank, Washington.

STATISTICAL APPENDIX

The Statistical Appendix presents historical data as well as projections. It comprises seven sections: Assumptions, What's New, Data and Conventions, Country Notes, Classification of Countries, Key Data Documentation, and Statistical Tables.

The assumptions underlying the estimates and projections for 2016–17 and the medium-term scenario for 2018–21 are summarized in the first section. The second section presents a brief description of the changes to the database and statistical tables since the April 2016 *World Economic Outlook* (WEO). The third section provides a general description of the data and the conventions used for calculating country group composites. The fourth section summarizes selected key information for each country. The classification of countries in the various groups presented in the WEO is summarized in the fifth section. The sixth section provides information on methods and reporting standards for the member countries' national account and government finance indicators included in the report.

The last, and main, section comprises the statistical tables. (Statistical Appendix A is included here; Statistical Appendix B is available online.) Data in these tables have been compiled on the basis of information available through September 16, 2016. The figures for 2016 and beyond are shown with the same degree of precision as the historical figures solely for convenience; because they are projections, the same degree of accuracy is not to be inferred.

Assumptions

Real effective *exchange rates* for the advanced economies are assumed to remain constant at their average levels measured during the period July 22 to August 19, 2016. For 2016 and 2017, these assumptions imply average U.S. dollar/special drawing right (SDR) conversion rates of 1.398 and 1.403 (the Chinese renminbi, which became an SDR currency on October 1, 2016, is excluded from the calculations), U.S. dollar/euro conversion rates of 1.117 and 1.127, and yen/U.S. dollar conversion rates of 106.8 and 99.9, respectively.

It is assumed that the *price of oil* will average $42.96 a barrel in 2016 and $50.64 a barrel in 2017.

Established *policies* of national authorities are assumed to be maintained. The more specific policy assumptions underlying the projections for selected economies are described in Box A1.

With regard to *interest rates*, it is assumed that the London interbank offered rate (LIBOR) on six-month U.S. dollar deposits will average 1.0 percent in 2016 and 1.3 percent in 2017, that three-month euro deposits will average –0.3 percent in 2016 and –0.4 percent in 2017, and that six-month yen deposits will average 0.0 percent in 2016 and –0.1 percent in 2017.

As a reminder, with respect to *introduction of the euro*, on December 31, 1998, the Council of the European Union decided that, effective January 1, 1999, the irrevocably fixed conversion rates between the euro and currencies of the member countries adopting the euro are as follows:

1 euro	=	13.7603	Austrian schillings
	=	40.3399	Belgian francs
	=	0.585274	Cyprus pound[1]
	=	1.95583	Deutsche marks
	=	15.6466	Estonian krooni[2]
	=	5.94573	Finnish markkaa
	=	6.55957	French francs
	=	340.750	Greek drachmas[3]
	=	0.787564	Irish pound
	=	1,936.27	Italian lire
	=	0.702804	Latvian lat[4]
	=	3.45280	Lithuanian litas[5]
	=	40.3399	Luxembourg francs
	=	0.42930	Maltese lira[1]
	=	2.20371	Netherlands guilders
	=	200.482	Portuguese escudos
	=	30.1260	Slovak koruna[6]
	=	239.640	Slovenian tolars[7]
	=	166.386	Spanish pesetas

[1]Established on January 1, 2008.
[2]Established on January 1, 2011.
[3]Established on January 1, 2001.
[4]Established on January 1, 2014.
[5]Established on January 1, 2015.
[6]Established on January 1, 2009.
[7]Established on January 1, 2007.

See Box 5.4 of the October 1998 WEO for details on how the conversion rates were established.

What's New

No changes have been introduced for the October 2016 WEO database.

Data and Conventions

Data and projections for 191 economies form the statistical basis of the WEO database. The data are maintained jointly by the IMF's Research Department and regional departments, with the latter regularly updating country projections based on consistent global assumptions.

Although national statistical agencies are the ultimate providers of historical data and definitions, international organizations are also involved in statistical issues, with the objective of harmonizing methodologies for the compilation of national statistics, including analytical frameworks, concepts, definitions, classifications, and valuation procedures used in the production of economic statistics. The WEO database reflects information from both national source agencies and international organizations.

Most countries' macroeconomic data presented in the WEO conform broadly to the 1993 version of the *System of National Accounts* (SNA). The IMF's sector statistical standards—the sixth edition of the *Balance of Payments and International Investment Position Manual* (BPM6), the *Monetary and Financial Statistics Manual* (MFSM 2000), and the *Government Finance Statistics Manual 2014* (GFSM 2014)—have been or are being aligned with the SNA 2008. These standards reflect the IMF's special interest in countries' external positions, financial sector stability, and public sector fiscal positions. The process of adapting country data to the new standards begins in earnest when the manuals are released. However, full concordance with the manuals is ultimately dependent on the provision by national statistical compilers of revised country data; hence, the WEO estimates are only partially adapted to these manuals. Nonetheless, for many countries the impact, on major balances and aggregates, of conversion to the updated standards will be small. Many other countries have partially adopted the latest standards and will continue implementation over a period of years.[1]

Composite data for country groups in the WEO are either sums or weighted averages of data for individual countries. Unless noted otherwise, multiyear averages of growth rates are expressed as compound annual rates of change.[2] Arithmetically weighted averages are used for all data for the emerging market and developing economies group except data on inflation and money growth, for which geometric averages are used. The following conventions apply:

- Country group composites for exchange rates, interest rates, and growth rates of monetary aggregates are weighted by GDP converted to U.S. dollars at market exchange rates (averaged over the preceding three years) as a share of group GDP.

- Composites for other data relating to the domestic economy, whether growth rates or ratios, are weighted by GDP valued at purchasing power parity as a share of total world or group GDP.[3]

- Unless noted otherwise, composites for all sectors for the euro area are corrected for reporting discrepancies in intra-area transactions. Annual data are not adjusted for calendar-day effects. For data prior to 1999, data aggregations apply 1995 European currency unit exchange rates.

- Composites for fiscal data are sums of individual country data after conversion to U.S. dollars at the average market exchange rates in the years indicated.

- Composite unemployment rates and employment growth are weighted by labor force as a share of group labor force.

- Composites relating to external sector statistics are sums of individual country data after conversion to U.S. dollars at the average market exchange rates in the years indicated for balance of payments data and at end-of-year market exchange rates for debt denominated in currencies other than U.S. dollars.

- Composites of changes in foreign trade volumes and prices, however, are arithmetic averages of percent changes for individual countries weighted by the

---

[1]Many countries are implementing the SNA 2008 or European System of National and Regional Accounts (ESA) 2010, and a few countries use versions of the SNA older than 1993. A similar adoption pattern is expected for the BPM6 and GFSM 2014. Please refer to Table G, which lists the statistical standards adhered to by each country.

[2]Averages for real GDP and its components, employment, GDP per capita, inflation, factor productivity, trade, and commodity prices are calculated based on the compound annual rate of change, except in the case of the unemployment rate, which is based on the simple arithmetic average.

[3]See "Revised Purchasing Power Parity Weights" in the July 2014 *WEO Update* for a summary of the revised purchasing-power-parity-based weights, as well as Box A2 of the April 2004 WEO and Annex IV of the May 1993 WEO. See also Anne-Marie Gulde and Marianne Schulze-Ghattas, "Purchasing Power Parity Based Weights for the *World Economic Outlook*," in *Staff Studies for the World Economic Outlook* (Washington: International Monetary Fund, December 1993), pp. 106–23.

U.S. dollar value of exports or imports as a share of total world or group exports or imports (in the preceding year).

- Unless noted otherwise, group composites are computed if 90 percent or more of the share of group weights is represented.
- Data refer to calendar years, except in the case of a few countries that use fiscal years. Please refer to Table F, which lists the economies with exceptional reporting periods for national accounts and government finance data for each country.

For some countries, the figures for 2015 and earlier are based on estimates rather than actual outturns. Please refer to Table G, which lists the latest actual outturns for the indicators in the national accounts, prices, government finance, and balance of payments indicators for each country.

Country Notes

- On February 1, 2013, the IMF issued a declaration of censure, and since then has called on *Argentina* to implement specified actions to address the quality of its official GDP data. The new government that took office in December 2015 released a revised GDP series on June 29, 2016. At the IMF Executive Board meeting that took place on August 31, 2016, the revised series was considered to be in line with international standards.
- The consumer price data for *Argentina* before December 2013 reflect the consumer price index (CPI) for the Greater Buenos Aires Area (CPI-GBA), while from December 2013 to October 2015 the data reflect the national CPI (IPCNu). The new government that took office in December 2015 discontinued the IPCNu, stating that it was flawed, and released a new CPI for the Greater Buenos Aires Area on June 15, 2016. Given the differences in geographical coverage, weights, sampling, and methodology of these series, the average CPI inflation for 2014, 2015, and 2016 and end-of-period inflation for 2015 are not reported in the October 2016 *World Economic Outlook*. On February 1, 2013, the IMF issued a declaration of censure and since then has called on Argentina to implement specified actions to address the quality of its official CPI data. At the meeting that took place on August 31, 2016, the IMF Executive Board noted the important progress made in

strengthening the accuracy of the CPI data. The Managing Director will report to the Executive Board on this issue again by November 15, 2016.

- *Argentina's* authorities discontinued the publication of labor market data in December 2015 and released new series starting in the second quarter of 2016.
- *Argentina's* and *Venezuela's* consumer prices are excluded from all WEO group aggregates.
- The series from which the nominal exchange rate assumptions are calculated are not made public for *Egypt* because the nominal exchange rate is a market-sensitive issue in Egypt.
- *India's* growth rates of real GDP calculated from 1998 to 2011 are as per national accounts with base year 2004/05, and thereafter are as per national accounts with base year 2011/12.
- Because of the ongoing IMF program with *Pakistan*, the series from which nominal exchange rate assumptions are calculated are not made public—the nominal exchange rate is a market-sensitive issue in Pakistan.
- Data for *Syria* are excluded from 2011 onward because of the uncertain political situation.
- Projecting the economic outlook in *Venezuela* is complicated by the absence of Article IV consultations since 2004 and delays in the publication of key economic data. General government revenue (1) includes the IMF staff's estimated foreign exchange profits transferred from the central bank to the government (buying U.S. dollars at the most appreciated rate and selling at more depreciated rates in a multitier exchange rate system) and (2) excludes the IMF staff's estimated revenue from PDVSA's sale of PetroCaribe assets to the central bank.

Classification of Countries

Summary of the Country Classification

The country classification in the WEO divides the world into two major groups: advanced economies and emerging market and developing economies.[4] This classification is not based on strict criteria, economic or otherwise, and it has evolved over time. The objective is to facilitate analysis by providing a reasonably

---

[4]As used here, the terms "country" and "economy" do not always refer to a territorial entity that is a state as understood by international law and practice. Some territorial entities included here are not states, although their statistical data are maintained on a separate and independent basis.

meaningful method of organizing data. Table A provides an overview of the country classification, showing the number of countries in each group by region and summarizing some key indicators of their relative size (GDP valued by purchasing power parity, total exports of goods and services, and population).

Some countries remain outside the country classification and therefore are not included in the analysis. Anguilla, Cuba, the Democratic People's Republic of Korea, and Montserrat are examples of countries that are not IMF members, and their economies therefore are not monitored by the IMF. Somalia is omitted from the emerging market and developing economies group composites because of data limitations.

General Features and Composition of Groups in the *World Economic Outlook* Classification

Advanced Economies

The 39 advanced economies are listed in Table B. The seven largest in terms of GDP based on market exchange rates—the United States, Japan, Germany, France, Italy, the United Kingdom, and Canada—constitute the subgroup of *major advanced economies* often referred to as the Group of Seven (G7). The members of the *euro area* are also distinguished as a subgroup. Composite data shown in the tables for the euro area cover the current members for all years, even though the membership has increased over time.

Table C lists the member countries of the European Union, not all of which are classified as advanced economies in the WEO.

Emerging Market and Developing Economies

The group of emerging market and developing economies (152) includes all those that are not classified as advanced economies.

The *regional breakdowns* of emerging market and developing economies are *Commonwealth of Independent States (CIS), emerging and developing Asia, emerging and developing Europe* (sometimes also referred to as "central and eastern Europe"), *Latin America and the Caribbean (LAC), Middle East, North Africa, Afghanistan, and Pakistan (MENAP),* and *sub-Saharan Africa (SSA).*

Emerging market and developing economies are also classified according to *analytical criteria.* The analyti-

cal criteria reflect the composition of export earnings and a distinction between net creditor and net debtor economies. The detailed composition of emerging market and developing economies in the regional and analytical groups is shown in Tables D and E.

The analytical criterion *source of export earnings* distinguishes between categories *fuel* (Standard International Trade Classification [SITC] 3) and *nonfuel* and then focuses on *nonfuel primary products* (SITCs 0, 1, 2, 4, and 68). Economies are categorized into one of these groups when their main source of export earnings exceeded 50 percent of total exports on average between 2011 and 2015.

The financial criteria focus on *net creditor economies, net debtor economies, heavily indebted poor countries* (HIPCs), and *low-income developing countries* (LIDCs). Economies are categorized as net debtors when their latest net international investment position, where available, was less than zero or their current account balance accumulations from 1972 (or earliest available data) to 2015 were negative. Net debtor economies are further differentiated on the basis of *experience with debt servicing.*[5]

The HIPC group comprises the countries that are or have been considered by the IMF and the World Bank for participation in their debt initiative known as the HIPC Initiative, which aims to reduce the external debt burdens of all the eligible HIPCs to a "sustainable" level in a reasonably short period of time.[6] Many of these countries have already benefited from debt relief and have graduated from the initiative.

The LIDCs are countries that were designated as eligible to use the IMF's concessional financing resources under the Poverty Reduction and Growth Trust (PRGT) in the 2013 PRGT eligibility review and had a level of per capita gross national income less than the PRGT income graduation threshold for non–small states (that is, twice the World Bank International Development Association operational threshold, or US$2,390 in 2011 as measured by the World Bank's Atlas method) and Zimbabwe.

---

[5]During 2011–15, 20 economies incurred external payments arrears or entered into official or commercial bank debt-rescheduling agreements. This group is referred to as *economies with arrears and/or rescheduling during 2011–15.*

[6]See David Andrews, Anthony R. Boote, Syed S. Rizavi, and Sukwinder Singh, *Debt Relief for Low-Income Countries: The Enhanced HIPC Initiative,* IMF Pamphlet Series 51 (Washington: International Monetary Fund, November 1999).

Table A. Classification by *World Economic Outlook* Groups and Their Shares in Aggregate GDP, Exports of Goods and Services, and Population, 2015[1]
(Percent of total for group or world)

	Number of Economies	GDP Advanced Economies	GDP World	Exports of Goods and Services Advanced Economies	Exports of Goods and Services World	Population Advanced Economies	Population World
Advanced Economies	**39**	**100.0**	**42.4**	**100.0**	**63.4**	**100.0**	**14.6**
United States		37.2	15.8	17.0	10.8	30.5	4.5
Euro Area	19	28.2	12.0	40.3	25.6	32.0	4.7
Germany		8.0	3.4	11.8	7.5	7.8	1.1
France		5.5	2.3	5.7	3.6	6.1	0.9
Italy		4.5	1.9	4.1	2.6	5.8	0.8
Spain		3.3	1.4	3.0	1.9	4.4	0.6
Japan		10.0	4.2	5.9	3.7	12.0	1.8
United Kingdom		5.6	2.4	5.9	3.7	6.2	0.9
Canada		3.4	1.4	3.7	2.3	3.4	0.5
Other Advanced Economies	16	15.6	6.6	27.2	17.3	15.9	2.3
Memorandum							
Major Advanced Economies	7	74.2	31.5	54.1	34.3	71.7	10.5

	Number of Economies	Emerging Market and Developing Economies (GDP)	World	Emerging Market and Developing Economies (Exports)	World	Emerging Market and Developing Economies (Population)	World
Emerging Market and Developing Economies	**152**	**100.0**	**57.6**	**100.0**	**36.6**	**100.0**	**85.4**
Regional Groups							
Commonwealth of Independent States[2]	12	8.0	4.6	7.7	2.8	4.6	3.9
Russia		5.7	3.3	5.1	1.9	2.3	2.0
Emerging and Developing Asia	29	53.5	30.8	50.4	18.4	57.1	48.8
China		30.0	17.3	31.7	11.6	22.3	19.1
India		12.2	7.0	5.5	2.0	21.0	17.9
Excluding China and India	27	11.3	6.5	13.2	4.8	13.8	11.8
Emerging and Developing Europe	12	5.7	3.3	9.2	3.4	2.8	2.4
Latin America and the Caribbean	32	14.3	8.2	13.8	5.1	9.9	8.4
Brazil		4.9	2.8	2.9	1.1	3.3	2.8
Mexico		3.4	2.0	5.3	1.9	2.0	1.7
Middle East, North Africa, Afghanistan, and Pakistan	22	13.1	7.6	14.4	5.3	10.6	9.1
Middle East and North Africa	20	11.6	6.7	13.9	5.1	7.0	6.0
Sub-Saharan Africa	45	5.4	3.1	4.5	1.7	15.0	12.8
Excluding Nigeria and South Africa	43	2.6	1.5	2.6	1.0	11.2	9.6
Analytical Groups[3]							
By Source of Export Earnings							
Fuel	29	20.1	11.6	21.6	7.9	12.4	10.6
Nonfuel	122	79.9	46.0	78.4	28.7	87.6	74.8
Of Which, Primary Products	30	4.6	2.7	4.6	1.7	7.8	6.7
By External Financing Source							
Net Debtor Economies	118	49.8	28.7	44.3	16.2	67.1	57.3
Net Debtor Economies by Debt-Servicing Experience							
Economies with Arrears and/or Rescheduling during 2011–15	20	3.0	1.8	2.0	0.7	4.6	3.9
Other Groups							
Heavily Indebted Poor Countries	38	2.4	1.4	1.9	0.7	11.2	9.6
Low-Income Developing Countries	59	7.4	4.2	6.5	2.4	22.5	19.2

[1]The GDP shares are based on the purchasing-power-parity valuation of economies' GDP. The number of economies comprising each group reflects those for which data are included in the group aggregates.

[2]Georgia, Turkmenistan, and Ukraine, which are not members of the Commonwealth of Independent States, are included in this group for reasons of geography and similarity in economic structure.

[3]Syria is omitted from the source of export earnings and South Sudan and Syria are omitted from the net external position group composites because of insufficient data.

Table B. Advanced Economies by Subgroup

Major Currency Areas		
United States		
Euro Area		
Japan		

Euro Area		
Austria	Greece	Netherlands
Belgium	Ireland	Portugal
Cyprus	Italy	Slovak Republic
Estonia	Latvia	Slovenia
Finland	Lithuania	Spain
France	Luxembourg	
Germany	Malta	

Major Advanced Economies		
Canada	Italy	United States
France	Japan	
Germany	United Kingdom	

Other Advanced Economies		
Australia	Korea	Singapore
Czech Republic	Macao SAR[2]	Sweden
Denmark	New Zealand	Switzerland
Hong Kong SAR[1]	Norway	Taiwan Province of China
Iceland	Puerto Rico	
Israel	San Marino	

[1]On July 1, 1997, Hong Kong was returned to the People's Republic of China and became a Special Administrative Region of China.

[2]On December 20, 1999, Macao was returned to the People's Republic of China and became a Special Administrative Region of China.

Table C. European Union

Austria	Germany	Poland
Belgium	Greece	Portugal
Bulgaria	Hungary	Romania
Croatia	Ireland	Slovak Republic
Cyprus	Italy	Slovenia
Czech Republic	Latvia	Spain
Denmark	Lithuania	Sweden
Estonia	Luxembourg	United Kingdom
Finland	Malta	
France	Netherlands	

Table D. Emerging Market and Developing Economies by Region and Main Source of Export Earnings

	Fuel	Nonfuel Primary Products
Commonwealth of Independent States		
	Azerbaijan	Uzbekistan
	Kazakhstan	
	Russia	
	Turkmenistan[1]	
Emerging and Developing Asia		
	Brunei Darussalam	Marshall Islands
	Timor-Leste	Mongolia
		Papua New Guinea
		Solomon Islands
		Tuvalu
Latin America and the Caribbean		
	Bolivia	Argentina
	Colombia	Chile
	Ecuador	Guyana
	Trinidad and Tobago	Paraguay
	Venezuela	Suriname
		Uruguay
Middle East, North Africa, Afghanistan, and Pakistan		
	Algeria	Afghanistan
	Bahrain	Mauritania
	Iran	Sudan
	Iraq	
	Kuwait	
	Libya	
	Oman	
	Qatar	
	Saudi Arabia	
	United Arab Emirates	
	Yemen	
Sub-Saharan Africa		
	Angola	Burkina Faso
	Chad	Burundi
	Republic of Congo	Central African Republic
	Equatorial Guinea	Democratic Republic of the Congo
	Gabon	Côte d'Ivoire
	Nigeria	Eritrea
	South Sudan	Guinea
		Guinea-Bissau
		Liberia
		Malawi
		Mali
		Niger
		Sierra Leone
		South Africa
		Zambia

[1]Turkmenistan, which is not a member of the Commonwealth of Independent States, is included in this group for reasons of geography and similarity in economic structure.

Table E. Emerging Market and Developing Economies by Region, Net External Position, and Status as Heavily Indebted Poor Countries and Low-Income Developing Countries

	Net External Position[1]	Heavily Indebted Poor Countries[2]	Low-Income Developing Countries		Net External Position[1]	Heavily Indebted Poor Countries[2]	Low-Income Developing Countries
Commonwealth of Independent States				Bulgaria	*		
Armenia	*			Croatia	*		
Azerbaijan	●			Hungary	*		
Belarus	*			Kosovo	*		
Georgia[3]	*			FYR Macedonia	*		
Kazakhstan	*			Montenegro	*		
Kyrgyz Republic	*		*	Poland	*		
Moldova	*		*	Romania	*		
Russia	●			Serbia	*		
Tajikistan	*		*	Turkey	*		
Turkmenistan[3]	*			**Latin America and the Caribbean**			
Ukraine[3]	*			Antigua and Barbuda	*		
Uzbekistan	●		*	Argentina	●		
Emerging and Developing Asia				The Bahamas	*		
Bangladesh	*		*	Barbados	*		
Bhutan	*		*	Belize	*		
Brunei Darussalam	●			Bolivia	●	●	*
Cambodia	*		*	Brazil	*		
China	●			Chile	*		
Fiji	*			Colombia	*		
India	*			Costa Rica	*		
Indonesia	*			Dominica	*		
Kiribati	●		*	Dominican Republic	*		
Lao P.D.R.	*		*	Ecuador	*		
Malaysia	●			El Salvador	*		
Maldives	*			Grenada	*		
Marshall Islands	*			Guatemala	*		
Micronesia	●			Guyana	*	●	
Mongolia	*		*	Haiti	*	●	*
Myanmar	*		*	Honduras	*	●	*
Nepal	●		*	Jamaica	*		
Palau	●			Mexico	*		
Papua New Guinea	*		*	Nicaragua	*	●	*
Philippines	*			Panama	*		
Samoa	*			Paraguay	*		
Solomon Islands	*		*	Peru	*		
Sri Lanka	*			St. Kitts and Nevis	*		
Thailand	*			St. Lucia	*		
Timor-Leste	●			St. Vincent and the Grenadines	*		
Tonga	*			Suriname	*		
Tuvalu	*			Trinidad and Tobago	●		
Vanuatu	*			Uruguay	*		
Vietnam	*		*	Venezuela	●		
Emerging and Developing Europe							
Albania	*						
Bosnia and Herzegovina	*						

Table E. Emerging Market and Developing Economies by Region, Net External Position, and Status as Heavily Indebted Poor Countries and Low-Income Developing Countries *(continued)*

	Net External Position[1]	Heavily Indebted Poor Countries[2]	Low-Income Developing Countries		Net External Position[1]	Heavily Indebted Poor Countries[2]	Low-Income Developing Countries
Middle East, North Africa, Afghanistan, and Pakistan				Republic of Congo	*	●	*
Afghanistan	●	●	*	Côte d'Ivoire	*	●	*
Algeria	●			Equatorial Guinea	●		
Bahrain	●			Eritrea	*	*	*
Djibouti	*		*	Ethiopia	*	●	*
Egypt	*			Gabon	●		
Iran	●			The Gambia	*	●	*
Iraq	●			Ghana	*	●	*
Jordan	*			Guinea	*	●	*
Kuwait	●			Guinea-Bissau	*	●	*
Lebanon	*			Kenya	*		*
Libya	●			Lesotho	*		*
Mauritania	*	●	*	Liberia	*	●	*
Morocco	*			Madagascar	*	●	*
Oman	●			Malawi	*	●	*
Pakistan	*			Mali	*	●	*
Qatar	●			Mauritius	●		
Saudi Arabia	●			Mozambique	*	●	*
Sudan	*	*	*	Namibia	●		
Syria[4]	...			Niger	*	●	*
Tunisia	*			Nigeria	*		*
United Arab Emirates	●			Rwanda	*	●	*
Yemen	*		*	São Tomé and Príncipe	*	●	*
Sub-Saharan Africa				Senegal	*	●	*
Angola	*			Seychelles	*		
Benin	*	●	*	Sierra Leone	*	●	*
Botswana	●			South Africa	●		
Burkina Faso	*	●	*	South Sudan[4]	...		*
Burundi	*	●	*	Swaziland	*		
Cabo Verde	*			Tanzania	*	●	*
Cameroon	*	●	*	Togo	*	●	*
Central African Republic	*	●	*	Uganda	*	●	*
Chad	*	●	*	Zambia	*	●	*
Comoros	*	●	*	Zimbabwe	*		*
Democratic Republic of the Congo	*	●	*				

[1]Dot (star) indicates that the country is a net creditor (net debtor).
[2]Dot instead of star indicates that the country has reached the completion point.
[3]Georgia, Turkmenistan, and Ukraine, which are not members of the Commonwealth of Independent States, are included in this group for reasons of geography and similarity in economic structure.
[4]South Sudan and Syria are omitted from the net external position group composite for lack of a fully developed database.

Table F. Economies with Exceptional Reporting Periods[1]

	National Accounts	Government Finance
The Bahamas		Jul/Jun
Bangladesh		Jul/Jun
Barbados		Apr/Mar
Belize		Apr/Mar
Bhutan	Jul/Jun	Jul/Jun
Botswana		Apr/Mar
Dominica		Jul/Jun
Egypt	Jul/Jun	Jul/Jun
Ethiopia	Jul/Jun	Jul/Jun
Haiti	Oct/Sep	Oct/Sep
Hong Kong SAR		Apr/Mar
India	Apr/Mar	Apr/Mar
Iran	Apr/Mar	Apr/Mar
Jamaica		Apr/Mar
Lao P.D.R.		Oct/Sep
Lesotho		Apr/Mar
Malawi		Jul/Jun
Marshall Islands	Oct/Sep	Oct/Sep
Micronesia	Oct/Sep	Oct/Sep
Myanmar	Apr/Mar	Apr/Mar
Namibia		Apr/Mar
Nepal	Aug/Jul	Aug/Jul
Pakistan	Jul/Jun	Jul/Jun
Palau	Oct/Sep	Oct/Sep
Puerto Rico	Jul/Jun	Jul/Jun
Samoa	Jul/Jun	Jul/Jun
Singapore		Apr/Mar
St. Lucia		Apr/Mar
Swaziland		Apr/Mar
Thailand		Oct/Sep
Trinidad and Tobago		Oct/Sep

[1]Unless noted otherwise, all data refer to calendar years.

Table G. Key Data Documentation

Country	Currency	National Accounts					Prices (CPI)	
		Historical Data Source[1]	Latest Actual Annual Data	Base Year[2]	System of National Accounts	Use of Chain-Weighted Methodology[3]	Historical Data Source[1]	Latest Actual Annual Data
Afghanistan	Afghan Afghani	NSO	2014	2002/03	SNA 1993		NSO	2015
Albania	Albanian lek	IMF staff	2014	1996	SNA 1993	From 1996	NSO	2015
Algeria	Algerian dinar	NSO	2015	2001	SNA 1993	From 2005	NSO	2015
Angola	Angolan kwanza	MEP	2014	2002	ESA 1995		NSO	2015
Antigua and Barbuda	Eastern Caribbean dollar	CB	2014	2006[6]	SNA 1993		NSO	2014
Argentina	Argentine peso	MEP	2014	2004	SNA 2008		NSO	2015
Armenia	Armenian dram	NSO	2015	2005	SNA 2008		NSO	2015
Australia	Australian dollar	NSO	2015	2013/14	SNA 2008	From 1980	NSO	2015
Austria	Euro	NSO	2015	2010	ESA 2010	From 1995	NSO	2015
Azerbaijan	Azerbaijan manat	NSO	2015	2003	SNA 1993	From 1994	NSO	2015
The Bahamas	Bahamian dollar	NSO	2015	2006	SNA 1993		NSO	2015
Bahrain	Bahrain dinar	MoF	2015	2010	SNA 2008		NSO	2015
Bangladesh	Bangladesh taka	NSO	2013	2005	SNA 1993		NSO	2014
Barbados	Barbados dollar	NSO and CB	2014	1974[6]	SNA 1993		NSO	2015
Belarus	Belarusian ruble	NSO	2015	2009	ESA 1995	From 2005	NSO	2015
Belgium	Euro	CB	2015	2013	ESA 2010	From 1995	CB	2015
Belize	Belize dollar	NSO	2015	2000	SNA 1993		NSO	2015
Benin	CFA franc	NSO	2012	2007	SNA 1993		NSO	2013
Bhutan	Bhutanese ngultrum	NSO	2013/14	2000[6]	SNA 1993		CB	2014/15
Bolivia	Bolivian boliviano	NSO	2015	1990	Other		NSO	2015
Bosnia and Herzegovina	Bosnia convertible marka	NSO	2015	2010	ESA 2010	From 2000	NSO	2015
Botswana	Botswana pula	NSO	2015	2006	SNA 1993		NSO	2015
Brazil	Brazilian real	NSO	2014	1995	SNA 2008		NSO	2014
Brunei Darussalam	Brunei dollar	NSO and GAD	2015	2010	SNA 1993		NSO and GAD	2015
Bulgaria	Bulgarian lev	NSO	2015	2010	ESA 2010	From 1996	NSO	2015
Burkina Faso	CFA franc	NSO and MEP	2014	1999	SNA 1993		NSO	2015
Burundi	Burundi franc	NSO	2015	2005	SNA 1993		NSO	2015
Cabo Verde	Cabo Verdean escudo	NSO	2015	2007	SNA 2008	From 2011	NSO	2015
Cambodia	Cambodian riel	NSO	2013	2000	SNA 1993		NSO	2014
Cameroon	CFA franc	NSO	2014	2000	SNA 1993		NSO	2014
Canada	Canadian dollar	NSO	2015	2007	SNA 2008	From 1980	NSO	2015
Central African Republic	CFA franc	NSO	2012	2005	SNA 1993		NSO	2014
Chad	CFA franc	CB	2013	2005	Other		NSO	2014
Chile	Chilean peso	CB	2015	2008	SNA 2008	From 2003	NSO	2015
China	Chinese yuan	NSO	2015	2010	SNA 2008		NSO	2015
Colombia	Colombian peso	NSO	2015	2005	Other	From 2000	NSO	2015
Comoros	Comorian franc	MEP	2015	2000	Other		NSO	2015
Democratic Republic of the Congo	Congolese franc	NSO	2013	2005	SNA 1993		CB	2015
Republic of Congo	CFA franc	NSO	2014	1990	SNA 1993		NSO	2014
Costa Rica	Costa Rican colón	CB	2015	2012	SNA 1993		CB	2015

Table G. Key Data Documentation (continued)

Country	Government Finance					Balance of Payments		
	Historical Data Source[1]	Latest Actual Annual Data	Statistics Manual in Use at Source	Subsectors Coverage[4]	Accounting Practice[5]	Historical Data Source[1]	Latest Actual Annual Data	Statistics Manual in Use at Source
Afghanistan	MoF	2014	2001	CG	C	NSO, MoF, and CB	2014	BPM 5
Albania	IMF staff	2015	1986	CG,LG,SS,MPC, NFPC	Other	CB	2015	BPM 6
Algeria	CB	2015	1986	CG	C	CB	2015	BPM 5
Angola	MoF	2014	2001	CG,LG	Other	CB	2014	BPM 5
Antigua and Barbuda	MoF	2014	2001	CG	C	CB	2014	BPM 5
Argentina	MEP	2015	1986	CG,SG,LG,SS	C	CB	2014	BPM 5
Armenia	MoF	2015	2001	CG	C	CB	2015	BPM 6
Australia	MoF	2014/15	2001	CG,SG,LG,TG	A	NSO	2015	BPM 6
Austria	NSO	2015	2001	CG,SG,LG,SS	A	CB	2015	BPM 6
Azerbaijan	MoF	2015	Other	CG	C	CB	2015	BPM 5
The Bahamas	MoF	2014/15	2001	CG	C	CB	2015	BPM 5
Bahrain	MoF	2015	2001	CG	C	CB	2014	BPM 6
Bangladesh	MoF	2013/14	Other	CG	C	CB	2013	BPM 6
Barbados	MoF	2015/16	1986	CG,SS,NFPC	C	CB	2015	BPM 5
Belarus	MoF	2015	2001	CG,LG,SS	C	CB	2015	BPM 6
Belgium	CB	2015	ESA 2010	CG,SG,LG,SS	A	CB	2015	BPM 6
Belize	MoF	2015/16	1986	CG,MPC	Mixed	CB	2015	BPM 5
Benin	MoF	2013	2001	CG	C	CB	2012	BPM 5
Bhutan	MoF	2013/14	1986	CG	C	CB	2013/14	BPM 6
Bolivia	MoF	2015	2001	CG,LG,SS,MPC, NMPC,NFPC	C	CB	2015	BPM 5
Bosnia and Herzegovina	MoF	2014	2001	CG,SG,LG,SS	A	CB	2014	BPM 6
Botswana	MoF	2014/15	1986	CG	C	CB	2015	BPM 5
Brazil	MoF	2014	2001	CG,SG,LG,SS, MPC,NFPC	C	CB	2014	BPM 6
Brunei Darussalam	MoF	2015	Other	CG, BCG	C	NSO, MEP, and GAD	2014	BPM 6
Bulgaria	MoF	2015	2001	CG,LG,SS	C	CB	2015	BPM 6
Burkina Faso	MoF	2014	2001	CG	CB	CB	2014	BPM 5
Burundi	MoF	2015	2001	CG	A	CB	2015	BPM 6
Cabo Verde	MoF	2015	2001	CG,SS	A	NSO	2015	BPM 5
Cambodia	MoF	2014	1986	CG,LG	A	CB	2014	BPM 5
Cameroon	MoF	2014	2001	CG,NFPC	C	MoF	2013	BPM 5
Canada	MoF	2015	2001	CG,SG,LG,SS	A	NSO	2015	BPM 6
Central African Republic	MoF	2014	2001	CG	C	CB	2013	BPM 5
Chad	MoF	2014	1986	CG,NFPC	C	CB	2012	BPM 5
Chile	MoF	2015	2001	CG,LG	A	CB	2015	BPM 6
China	MoF	2015	2001	CG,LG	C	GAD	2015	BPM 6
Colombia	MoF	2015	2001	CG,SG,LG,SS	Other	CB and NSO	2015	BPM 5
Comoros	MoF	2015	1986	CG	Mixed	CB and IMF staff	2015	BPM 5
Democratic Republic of the Congo	MoF	2015	2001	CG,LG	A	CB	2015	BPM 5
Republic of Congo	MoF	2014	2001	CG	A	CB	2012	BPM 5
Costa Rica	MoF and CB	2015	1986	CG	C	CB	2015	BPM 5

Table G. Key Data Documentation *(continued)*

Country	Currency	National Accounts					Prices (CPI)	
		Historical Data Source[1]	Latest Actual Annual Data	Base Year[2]	System of National Accounts	Use of Chain-Weighted Methodology[3]	Historical Data Source[1]	Latest Actual Annual Data
Côte d'Ivoire	CFA franc	NSO	2012	2009	SNA 1993		NSO	2015
Croatia	Croatian kuna	NSO	2015	2010	ESA 2010		NSO	2015
Cyprus	Euro	NSO	2015	2005	ESA 2010	From 1995	NSO	2015
Czech Republic	Czech koruna	NSO	2015	2010	ESA 2010	From 1995	NSO	2015
Denmark	Danish krone	NSO	2015	2010	ESA 2010	From 1980	NSO	2015
Djibouti	Djibouti franc	NSO	2014	1990	Other		NSO	2015
Dominica	Eastern Caribbean dollar	NSO	2014	2006	SNA 1993		NSO	2014
Dominican Republic	Dominican peso	CB	2015	2007	SNA 2008	From 2007	CB	2015
Ecuador	U.S. dollar	CB	2015	2007	SNA 1993		NSO and CB	2015
Egypt	Egyptian pound	MEP	2014/15	2011/12	SNA 1993		NSO	2014/15
El Salvador	U.S. dollar	CB	2015	1990	Other		NSO	2015
Equatorial Guinea	CFA franc	MEP and CB	2013	2006	SNA 1993		MEP	2014
Eritrea	Eritrean nakfa	IMF staff	2006	2005	SNA 1993		NSO	2009
Estonia	Euro	NSO	2015	2010	ESA 2010	From 2010	NSO	2015
Ethiopia	Ethiopian birr	NSO	2014/15	2010/11	SNA 1993		NSO	2015
Fiji	Fijian dollar	NSO	2014	2008[6]	SNA 1993/ 2008		NSO	2015
Finland	Euro	NSO	2015	2010	ESA 2010	From 1980	NSO	2015
France	Euro	NSO	2015	2010	ESA 2010	From 1980	NSO	2015
Gabon	CFA franc	MoF	2013	2001	SNA 1993		MoF	2014
The Gambia	Gambian dalasi	NSO	2013	2004	SNA 1993		NSO	2015
Georgia	Georgian lari	NSO	2015	2000	SNA 1993	From 1996	NSO	2015
Germany	Euro	NSO	2015	2010	ESA 2010	From 1991	NSO	2015
Ghana	Ghanaian cedi	NSO	2015	2006	SNA 1993		NSO	2015
Greece	Euro	NSO	2015	2010	ESA 2010	From 1995	NSO	2015
Grenada	Eastern Caribbean dollar	NSO	2014	2006	SNA 1993		NSO	2013
Guatemala	Guatemalan quetzal	CB	2015	2001	SNA 1993	From 2001	NSO	2015
Guinea	Guinean franc	NSO	2011	2003	SNA 1993		NSO	2015
Guinea-Bissau	CFA franc	NSO	2013	2005	SNA 1993		NSO	2015
Guyana	Guyanese dollar	NSO	2015	2006[6]	SNA 1993		NSO	2015
Haiti	Haitian gourde	NSO	2014/15	1986/87	SNA 2008		NSO	2014/15
Honduras	Honduran lempira	CB	2015	2000	SNA 1993		CB	2015
Hong Kong SAR	Hong Kong dollar	NSO	2015	2014	SNA 2008	From 1980	NSO	2015
Hungary	Hungarian forint	NSO	2015	2005	ESA 2010	From 2005	IEO	2015
Iceland	Icelandic króna	NSO	2015	2005	ESA 2010	From 1990	NSO	2015
India	Indian rupee	NSO	2015/16	2011/12	SNA 1993		NSO	2015/16
Indonesia	Indonesian rupiah	NSO	2015	2010	SNA 2008		NSO	2015
Iran	Iranian rial	CB	2014/15	2004/05	SNA 1993		CB	2014/15
Iraq	Iraqi dinar	NSO	2014	2007	SNA 1968		NSO	2014
Ireland	Euro	NSO	2015	2014	ESA 2010	From 1995	NSO	2015

Table G. Key Data Documentation *(continued)*

Country	Government Finance					Balance of Payments		
	Historical Data Source[1]	Latest Actual Annual Data	Statistics Manual in Use at Source	Subsectors Coverage[4]	Accounting Practice[5]	Historical Data Source[1]	Latest Actual Annual Data	Statistics Manual in Use at Source
Côte d'Ivoire	MoF	2015	1986	CG	A	CB	2012	BPM 6
Croatia	MoF	2015	2001	CG,LG	A	CB	2015	BPM 6
Cyprus	NSO	2015	ESA 2010	CG,LG,SS	Other	NSO	2015	BPM 6
Czech Republic	MoF	2015	2001	CG,LG,SS	A	NSO	2015	BPM 6
Denmark	NSO	2015	2001	CG,LG,SS	A	NSO	2015	BPM 6
Djibouti	MoF	2015	2001	CG	A	CB	2015	BPM 5
Dominica	MoF	2013/14	1986	CG	C	CB	2014	BPM 5
Dominican Republic	MoF	2015	2001	CG,SG,LG,SS,NMPC	Mixed	CB	2015	BPM 6
Ecuador	CB and MoF	2015	1986	CG,SG,LG,SS,NFPC	C	CB	2014	BPM 5
Egypt	MoF	2014/15	2001	CG,LG,SS,MPC	C	CB	2014/15	BPM 5
El Salvador	MoF	2015	1986	CG,LG,SS	C	CB	2015	BPM 6
Equatorial Guinea	MoF	2014	1986	CG	C	CB	2013	BPM 5
Eritrea	MoF	2008	2001	CG	C	CB	2008	BPM 5
Estonia	MoF	2015	1986/2001	CG,LG,SS	C	CB	2015	BPM 6
Ethiopia	MoF	2014/15	1986	CG,SG,LG,NFPC	C	CB	2014/15	BPM 5
Fiji	MoF	2015	2001	CG	C	CB	2014	BPM 6
Finland	MoF	2015	2001	CG,LG,SS	A	NSO	2015	BPM 6
France	NSO	2015	2001	CG,LG,SS	A	CB	2015	BPM 6
Gabon	IMF staff	2014	2001	CG	A	CB	2014	BPM 5
The Gambia	MoF	2015	2001	CG	C	CB and IMF staff	2014	BPM 4
Georgia	MoF	2015	2001	CG,LG	C	NSO and CB	2015	BPM 5
Germany	NSO	2015	2001	CG,SG,LG,SS	A	CB	2015	BPM 6
Ghana	MoF	2015	2001	CG	C	CB	2015	BPM 5
Greece	MoF	2015	2014	CG,LG,SS	A	CB	2015	BPM 6
Grenada	MoF	2014	2001	CG	CB	CB	2013	BPM 5
Guatemala	MoF	2015	1986	CG	C	CB	2015	BPM 5
Guinea	MoF	2015	2001	CG	Other	CB and MEP	2015	BPM 6
Guinea-Bissau	MoF	2014	2001	CG	A	CB	2014	BPM 6
Guyana	MoF	2014	2001	CG,SS	C	CB	2014	BPM 5
Haiti	MoF	2014/15	2001	CG	C	CB	2014/15	BPM 5
Honduras	MoF	2015	1986	CG,LG,SS,NFPC	A	CB	2015	BPM 5
Hong Kong SAR	NSO	2015/16	2001	CG	C	NSO	2015	BPM 6
Hungary	MEP and NSO	2015	ESA 2010	CG,LG,SS,NMPC	A	CB	2015	BPM 6
Iceland	NSO	2015	2001	CG,LG,SS	A	CB	2015	BPM 6
India	MoF and IMF staff	2014/15	2001	CG,SG	A	CB	2015/16	BPM 6
Indonesia	MoF	2015	2001	CG,LG	C	CB	2015	BPM 6
Iran	MoF	2014/15	2001	CG	C	CB	2014/15	BPM 5
Iraq	MoF	2014	2001	CG	C	CB	2014	BPM 5
Ireland	MoF	2015	2001	CG,LG,SS	A	NSO	2015	BPM 6

Table G. Key Data Documentation *(continued)*

Country	Currency	National Accounts					Prices (CPI)	
		Historical Data Source[1]	Latest Actual Annual Data	Base Year[2]	System of National Accounts	Use of Chain-Weighted Methodology[3]	Historical Data Source[1]	Latest Actual Annual Data
Israel	New Israeli shekel	NSO	2015	2010	SNA 2008	From 1995	Haver Analytics	2015
Italy	Euro	NSO	2015	2010	ESA 2010	From 1980	NSO	2015
Jamaica	Jamaican dollar	NSO	2015	2007	SNA 1993		NSO	2015
Japan	Japanese yen	GAD	2015	2005	SNA 1993	From 1980	GAD	2015
Jordan	Jordanian dinar	NSO	2015	1994	Other		NSO	2015
Kazakhstan	Kazakhstani tenge	NSO	2015	2007	SNA 1993	From 1994	CB	2015
Kenya	Kenya shilling	NSO	2015	2009	SNA 2008		NSO	2015
Kiribati	Australian dollar	NSO	2014	2006	SNA 2008		NSO	2015
Korea	South Korean won	CB	2015	2010	SNA 2008	From 1980	MoF	2015
Kosovo	Euro	NSO	2015	2015	ESA 2010		NSO	2015
Kuwait	Kuwaiti dinar	MEP and NSO	2014	2010	SNA 1993		NSO and MEP	2015
Kyrgyz Republic	Kyrgyz som	NSO	2015	1995	SNA 1993		NSO	2015
Lao P.D.R.	Lao kip	NSO	2013	2002	SNA 1993		NSO	2013
Latvia	Euro	NSO	2015	2010	ESA 2010	From 1995	NSO	2015
Lebanon	Lebanese pound	NSO	2013	2010	SNA 2008	From 2010	NSO	2015
Lesotho	Lesotho loti	NSO	2014	2004	Other		NSO	2014
Liberia	U.S. dollar	CB	2014	1992	SNA 1993		CB	2015
Libya	Libyan dinar	MEP	2014	2003	SNA 1993		NSO	2014
Lithuania	Euro	NSO	2015	2010	ESA 2010	From 2005	NSO	2015
Luxembourg	Euro	NSO	2015	2010	ESA 2010	From 1995	NSO	2015
Macao SAR	Macanese pataca	NSO	2015	2014	SNA 2008	From 2001	NSO	2015
FYR Macedonia	Macedonian denar	NSO	2015	2005	ESA 2010		NSO	2015
Madagascar	Malagasy ariary	NSO	2015	2000	SNA 1968		NSO	2015
Malawi	Malawian kwacha	NSO	2011	2010	SNA 2008		NSO	2015
Malaysia	Malaysian ringgit	NSO	2015	2010	SNA 2008		NSO	2015
Maldives	Maldivian rufiyaa	MoF and NSO	2014	2003[6]	SNA 1993		CB	2014
Mali	CFA franc	MoF	2013	1999	SNA 1993		MoF	2015
Malta	Euro	NSO	2015	2010	ESA 2010	From 2000	NSO	2015
Marshall Islands	U.S. dollar	NSO	2013/14	2003/04	Other		NSO	2013
Mauritania	Mauritanian ouguiya	NSO	2014	2004	SNA 1993		NSO	2014
Mauritius	Mauritian rupee	NSO	2015	2006	SNA 1993	From 1999	NSO	2015
Mexico	Mexican peso	NSO	2015	2008	SNA 2008		NSO	2015
Micronesia	U.S. dollar	NSO	2013	2004	Other		NSO	2013
Moldova	Moldovan leu	NSO	2015	1995	SNA 1993		NSO	2015
Mongolia	Mongolian tögrög	NSO	2015	2010	SNA 1993		NSO	2015
Montenegro	Euro	NSO	2014	2006	ESA 1995		NSO	2015
Morocco	Moroccan dirham	NSO	2015	2007	SNA 1993	From 1998	NSO	2015
Mozambique	Mozambican metical	NSO	2015	2009	SNA 1993		NSO	2015
Myanmar	Myanmar kyat	MEP	2014/15	2010/11	Other		NSO	2015/16
Namibia	Namibia dollar	NSO	2014	2000	SNA 1993		NSO	2014
Nepal	Nepalese rupee	NSO	2014/15	2000/01	SNA 1993		CB	2014/15
Netherlands	Euro	NSO	2015	2010	ESA 2010	From 1980	NSO	2015
New Zealand	New Zealand dollar	NSO	2015	2009/10	Other	From 1987	NSO	2015
Nicaragua	Nicaraguan córdoba	IMF staff	2015	2006	SNA 1993	From 1994	CB	2015

Table G. Key Data Documentation *(continued)*

Country	Government Finance					Balance of Payments		
	Historical Data Source[1]	Latest Actual Annual Data	Statistics Manual in Use at Source	Subsectors Coverage[4]	Accounting Practice[5]	Historical Data Source[1]	Latest Actual Annual Data	Statistics Manual in Use at Source
Israel	MoF	2015	2001	CG,LG,SS	Other	Haver Analytics	2015	BPM 6
Italy	NSO	2015	2001	CG,LG,SS	A	NSO	2015	BPM 6
Jamaica	MoF	2015/16	1986	CG	C	CB	2015	BPM 5
Japan	GAD	2014	2001	CG,LG,SS	A	MoF	2015	BPM 6
Jordan	MoF	2015	2001	CG,NFPC	C	CB	2015	BPM 5
Kazakhstan	IMF staff	2015	2001	CG,LG	A	CB	2015	BPM 6
Kenya	MoF	2015	2001	CG	A	CB	2015	BPM 6
Kiribati	MoF	2013	1986	CG,LG	C	NSO	2014	BPM 6
Korea	MoF	2015	2001	CG	C	CB	2015	BPM 6
Kosovo	MoF	2015	Other	CG,LG	C	CB	2015	BPM 5
Kuwait	MoF	2014	1986	CG	Mixed	CB	2015	BPM 5
Kyrgyz Republic	MoF	2015	Other	CG,LG,SS	C	MoF	2015	BPM 5
Lao P.D.R.	MoF	2012/13	2001	CG	C	CB	2013	BPM 5
Latvia	MoF	2015	1986	CG,LG,SS,NFPC	C	CB	2014	BPM 6
Lebanon	MoF	2014	2001	CG	C	CB and IMF staff	2014	BPM 5
Lesotho	MoF	2014/15	2001	CG,LG	C	CB	2014	BPM 5
Liberia	MoF	2015	2001	CG	A	CB	2013	BPM 5
Libya	MoF	2014	1986	CG,SG,LG	C	CB	2014	BPM 5
Lithuania	MoF	2015	2014	CG,LG,SS	A	CB	2015	BPM 6
Luxembourg	MoF	2015	2001	CG,LG,SS	A	NSO	2015	BPM 6
Macao SAR	MoF	2015	2001	CG	C	NSO	2015	BPM 6
FYR Macedonia	MoF	2015	1986	CG,SG,SS	C	CB	2015	BPM 6
Madagascar	MoF	2015	1986	CG,LG	C	CB	2015	BPM 5
Malawi	MoF	2014/15	1986	CG	C	NSO and GAD	2014	BPM 5
Malaysia	MoF	2015	1986	CG,SG,LG	C	NSO	2015	BPM 6
Maldives	MoF	2014	1986	CG	C	CB	2014	BPM 5
Mali	MoF	2015	2001	CG	Mixed	CB	2013	BPM 5
Malta	NSO	2015	2001	CG,SS	A	NSO	2015	BPM 6
Marshall Islands	MoF	2012/13	2001	CG,LG,SS	A	NSO	2013	BPM 6
Mauritania	MoF	2014	1986	CG	C	CB	2013	BPM 5
Mauritius	MoF	2015	2001	CG,LG,NFPC	C	CB	2015	BPM 5
Mexico	MoF	2015	2001	CG,SS,NMPC,NFPC	C	CB	2015	BPM 5
Micronesia	MoF	2013/14	2001	CG,SG,LG,SS	Other	NSO	2013	Other
Moldova	MoF	2015	1986	CG,LG,SS	C	CB	2014	BPM 5
Mongolia	MoF	2015	2001	CG,SG,LG,SS	C	CB	2015	BPM 5
Montenegro	MoF	2015	1986	CG,LG,SS	C	CB	2014	BPM 5
Morocco	MEP	2015	2001	CG	A	GAD	2015	BPM 5
Mozambique	MoF	2015	2001	CG,SG	Mixed	CB	2015	BPM 6
Myanmar	MoF	2015/16	2001	CG,NFPC	Mixed	IMF staff	2015/16	BPM 5
Namibia	MoF	2014/15	2001	CG	C	CB	2013	BPM 5
Nepal	MoF	2014/15	2001	CG	C	CB	2014/15	BPM 5
Netherlands	MoF	2015	2001	CG,LG,SS	A	CB	2015	BPM 6
New Zealand	MoF	2014/15	2001	CG	A	NSO	2015	BPM 6
Nicaragua	MoF	2015	1986	CG,LG,SS	C	IMF staff	2015	BPM 6

Table G. Key Data Documentation *(continued)*

Country	Currency	National Accounts Historical Data Source[1]	Latest Actual Annual Data	Base Year[2]	System of National Accounts	Use of Chain-Weighted Methodology[3]	Prices (CPI) Historical Data Source[1]	Latest Actual Annual Data
Niger	CFA franc	NSO	2014	2000	SNA 1993		NSO	2015
Nigeria	Nigerian naira	NSO	2015	2010	SNA 2008		NSO	2015
Norway	Norwegian krone	NSO	2015	2013	ESA 2010	From 1980	NSO	2015
Oman	Omani rial	NSO	2015	2010	SNA 1993		NSO	2015
Pakistan	Pakistan rupee	NSO	2014/15	2005/06[6]	SNA 1968/1993		NSO	2014/15
Palau	U.S. dollar	MoF	2013/14	2005	Other		MoF	2013/14
Panama	U.S. dollar	NSO	2015	2007	SNA 1993	From 2007	NSO	2015
Papua New Guinea	Papua New Guinea kina	NSO and MoF	2013	1998	SNA 1993		NSO	2013
Paraguay	Paraguayan guaraní	CB	2015	1994	SNA 1993		CB	2015
Peru	Peruvian nuevo sol	CB	2015	2007	SNA 1993		CB	2015
Philippines	Philippine peso	NSO	2015	2000	SNA 2008		NSO	2015
Poland	Polish zloty	NSO	2015	2010	ESA 2010	From 1995	NSO	2015
Portugal	Euro	NSO	2015	2011	ESA 2010	From 1980	NSO	2015
Puerto Rico	U.S. dollar	MEP	2014/15	1954	SNA1968		MEP	2015
Qatar	Qatari riyal	NSO and MEP	2014	2013	SNA 1993		NSO and MEP	2015
Romania	Romanian leu	NSO	2015	2010	ESA 2010	From 2000	NSO	2015
Russia	Russian ruble	NSO	2015	2011	SNA 2008	From 1995	NSO	2015
Rwanda	Rwanda franc	MoF	2014	2011	SNA 1993		NSO	2015
Samoa	Samoa tala	NSO	2014/15	2009/10	SNA 1993		NSO	2014/15
San Marino	Euro	NSO	2014	2007	Other		NSO	2015
São Tomé and Príncipe	São Tomé and Príncipe dobra	NSO	2015	2000	SNA 1993		NSO	2015
Saudi Arabia	Saudi riyal	NSO and MEP	2015	2010	SNA 1993		NSO and MEP	2015
Senegal	CFA franc	NSO	2015	2000	SNA 1993		NSO	2015
Serbia	Serbian dinar	NSO	2015	2010	ESA 2010	From 2010	NSO	2015
Seychelles	Seychellois rupee	NSO	2014	2006	SNA 1993		NSO	2014
Sierra Leone	Sierra Leonean leone	NSO	2014	2006	SNA 1993	From 2010	NSO	2015
Singapore	Singapore dollar	NSO	2015	2010	SNA 1993	From 2010	NSO	2015
Slovak Republic	Euro	NSO	2015	2010	ESA 2010	From 1997	NSO	2015
Slovenia	Euro	NSO	2015	2010	ESA 2010	From 2000	NSO	2015
Solomon Islands	Solomon Islands dollar	CB	2014	2004	SNA 1993		NSO	2015
South Africa	South African rand	CB	2015	2010	SNA 1993		NSO	2015
South Sudan	South Sudanese pound	NSO	2014	2010	SNA 1993		NSO	2014
Spain	Euro	NSO	2015	2010	ESA 2010	From 1995	NSO	2015
Sri Lanka	Sri Lankan rupee	NSO	2015	2002	SNA 1993		NSO	2015
St. Kitts and Nevis	Eastern Caribbean dollar	NSO	2014	2006[6]	SNA 1993		NSO	2014
St. Lucia	Eastern Caribbean dollar	NSO	2014	2006	SNA 1993		NSO	2015

Table G. Key Data Documentation (continued)

	Government Finance					Balance of Payments		
Country	Historical Data Source[1]	Latest Actual Annual Data	Statistics Manual in Use at Source	Subsectors Coverage[4]	Accounting Practice[5]	Historical Data Source[1]	Latest Actual Annual Data	Statistics Manual in Use at Source
Niger	MoF	2015	1986	CG	A	CB	2014	BPM 6
Nigeria	MoF	2015	2001	CG,SG,LG,NFPC	C	CB	2015	BPM 5
Norway	NSO and MoF	2014	2014	CG,LG,SS	A	NSO	2015	BPM 6
Oman	MoF	2015	2001	CG	C	CB	2015	BPM 5
Pakistan	MoF	2014/15	1986	CG,SG,LG	C	CB	2014/15	BPM 5
Palau	MoF	2013/14	2001	CG	Other	MoF	2013/14	BPM 6
Panama	MoF	2015	1986	CG,SG,LG,SS,NFPC	C	NSO	2015	BPM 5
Papua New Guinea	MoF	2013	1986	CG	C	CB	2013	BPM 5
Paraguay	MoF	2015	2001	CG,SG,LG,SS,MPC, NMPC,NFPC	C	CB	2015	BPM 5
Peru	MoF	2015	1986	CG,SG,LG,SS	C	CB	2015	BPM 5
Philippines	MoF	2015	2001	CG,LG,SS	C	CB	2015	BPM 6
Poland	MoF and NSO	2015	ESA 2010	CG,LG,SS	A	CB	2015	BPM 6
Portugal	NSO	2014	2001	CG,LG,SS	A	CB	2015	BPM 6
Puerto Rico	MEP	2014/15	2001	Other	A	...	...	...
Qatar	MoF	2015	1986	CG	C	CB and IMF staff	2014	BPM 5
Romania	MoF	2015	2001	CG,LG,SS	C	CB	2015	BPM 6
Russia	MoF	2014	2001	CG,SG,SS	Mixed	CB	2014	BPM 6
Rwanda	MoF	2014	2001	CG,LG	Mixed	CB	2015	BPM 6
Samoa	MoF	2014/15	2001	CG	A	CB	2014/15	BPM 6
San Marino	MoF	2014	Other	CG	Other	...	...	...
São Tomé and Príncipe	MoF and Customs	2015	2001	CG	C	CB	2015	BPM 6
Saudi Arabia	MoF	2015	1986	CG	C	CB	2015	BPM 5
Senegal	MoF	2015	1986	CG	C	CB and IMF staff	2015	BPM 5
Serbia	MoF	2015	1986/2001	CG,SG,LG,SS	C	CB	2015	BPM 6
Seychelles	MoF	2015	1986	CG,SS	C	CB	2015	BPM 6
Sierra Leone	MoF	2014	1986	CG	C	CB	2014	BPM 5
Singapore	MoF	2014/15	2001	CG	C	NSO	2015	BPM 6
Slovak Republic	NSO	2015	2001	CG,LG,SS	A	CB	2015	BPM 6
Slovenia	MoF	2015	1986	CG,SG,LG,SS	C	NSO	2015	BPM 6
Solomon Islands	MoF	2014	1986	CG	C	CB	2014	BPM 6
South Africa	MoF	2015/16	2001	CG,SG,SS	C	CB	2015	BPM 6
South Sudan	MoF and MEP	2015	Other	CG	C	MoF, NSO, and MEP	2015	BPM 5
Spain	MoF and NSO	2015	ESA 2010	CG,SG,LG,SS	A	CB	2015	BPM 6
Sri Lanka	MoF	2015	2001	CG,SG,LG,SS	C	CB	2015	BPM 5
St. Kitts and Nevis	MoF	2014	1986	CG	C	CB	2014	BPM 5
St. Lucia	MoF	2013/14	1986	CG	C	CB	2014	BPM 5

Table G. Key Data Documentation *(continued)*

Country	Currency	National Accounts					Prices (CPI)	
		Historical Data Source[1]	Latest Actual Annual Data	Base Year[2]	System of National Accounts	Use of Chain-Weighted Methodology[3]	Historical Data Source[1]	Latest Actual Annual Data
St. Vincent and the Grenadines	Eastern Caribbean dollar	NSO	2014	2006[6]	SNA 1993		NSO	2015
Sudan	Sudanese pound	NSO	2010	2007	Other		NSO	2015
Suriname	Surinamese dollar	NSO	2014	2007	SNA 1993		NSO	2015
Swaziland	Swazi lilangeni	NSO	2015	2011	SNA 1993		NSO	2015
Sweden	Swedish krona	NSO	2015	2015	ESA 2010	From 1993	NSO	2015
Switzerland	Swiss franc	NSO	2015	2010	ESA 2010	From 1980	NSO	2015
Syria	Syrian pound	NSO	2010	2000	SNA 1993		NSO	2011
Taiwan Province of China	New Taiwan dollar	NSO	2015	2011	SNA 2008		NSO	2015
Tajikistan	Tajik somoni	NSO	2014	1995	SNA 1993		NSO	2014
Tanzania	Tanzania shilling	NSO	2015	2007	SNA 1993		NSO	2015
Thailand	Thai baht	MEP	2015	2002	SNA 1993	From 1993	MEP	2015
Timor-Leste	U.S. dollar	MoF	2014	2010[6]	Other		NSO	2015
Togo	CFA franc	MoF and NSO	2014	2000	SNA 1993		NSO	2015
Tonga	Tongan pa'anga	CB	2014	2010	SNA 1993		CB	2015
Trinidad and Tobago	Trinidad and Tobago dollar	NSO	2012	2000	SNA 1993		NSO	2015
Tunisia	Tunisian dinar	NSO	2014	2004	SNA 1993	From 2009	NSO	2015
Turkey	Turkish lira	NSO	2015	1998	ESA 1995		NSO	2015
Turkmenistan	New Turkmen manat	NSO	2015	2005	SNA 1993	From 2000	NSO	2015
Tuvalu	Australian dollar	PFTAC advisors	2012	2005	SNA 1993		NSO	2013
Uganda	Ugandan shilling	NSO	2014	2010	SNA 1993		CB	2015/16
Ukraine	Ukrainian hryvnia	NSO	2015	2010	SNA 2008	From 2005	NSO	2015
United Arab Emirates	U.A.E. dirham	NSO	2014	2007	SNA 1993		NSO	2014
United Kingdom	Pound sterling	NSO	2015	2013	ESA 2010	From 1980	NSO	2015
United States	U.S. dollar	NSO	2015	2009	Other	From 1980	NSO	2015
Uruguay	Uruguayan peso	CB	2014	2005	SNA 1993		NSO	2014
Uzbekistan	Uzbek sum	NSO	2014	1995	SNA 1993		NSO	2014
Vanuatu	Vanuatu vatu	NSO	2014	2006	SNA 1993		NSO	2015
Venezuela	Venezuelan bolívar fuerte	CB	2015	1997	SNA 2008		CB	2015
Vietnam	Vietnamese dong	NSO	2015	2010	SNA 1993		NSO	2015
Yemen	Yemeni rial	IMF staff	2008	1990	SNA 1993		NSO,CB, and IMF staff	2009
Zambia	Zambian kwacha	NSO	2014	2010	SNA 1993		NSO	2015
Zimbabwe	U.S. dollar	NSO	2013	2009	Other		NSO	2014

Table G. Key Data Documentation (continued)

Country	Government Finance					Balance of Payments		
	Historical Data Source[1]	Latest Actual Annual Data	Statistics Manual in Use at Source	Subsectors Coverage[4]	Accounting Practice[5]	Historical Data Source[1]	Latest Actual Annual Data	Statistics Manual in Use at Source
St. Vincent and the Grenadines	MoF	2014	1986	CG	C	CB	2015	BPM 5
Sudan	MoF	2015	2001	CG	Mixed	CB	2015	BPM 5
Suriname	MoF	2015	1986	CG	CB	CB	2015	BPM 5
Swaziland	MoF	2015/16	2001	CG	A	CB	2015	BPM 5
Sweden	MoF	2015	2001	CG,LG,SS	A	NSO	2015	BPM 6
Switzerland	MoF	2013	2001	CG,SG,LG,SS	A	CB	2015	BPM 6
Syria	MoF	2009	1986	CG	C	CB	2009	BPM 5
Taiwan Province of China	MoF	2015	1986	CG,LG,SS	C	CB	2015	BPM 6
Tajikistan	MoF	2015	1986	CG,LG,SS	C	CB	2014	BPM 5
Tanzania	MoF	2015	1986	CG,LG	C	CB	2015	BPM 5
Thailand	MoF	2014/15	2001	CG,BCG,LG,SS	A	CB	2015	BPM 6
Timor-Leste	MoF	2015	2001	CG	C	CB	2015	BPM 6
Togo	MoF	2014	2001	CG	C	CB	2015	BPM 5
Tonga	CB and MoF	2014	2001	CG	C	CB and NSO	2015	BPM 6
Trinidad and Tobago	MoF	2014/15	1986	CG,NFPC	C	CB and NSO	2012	BPM 5
Tunisia	MoF	2015	1986	CG	C	CB	2015	BPM 5
Turkey	MoF	2015	2001	CG,LG,SS	A	CB	2015	BPM 6
Turkmenistan	MoF	2015	1986	CG,LG	C	NSO and IMF staff	2013	BPM 5
Tuvalu	IMF staff	2013	Other	CG	Mixed	IMF staff	2013	BPM 6
Uganda	MoF	2015	2001	CG	C	CB	2015	BPM 6
Ukraine	MoF	2015	2001	CG,SG,LG,SS	C	CB	2015	BPM 6
United Arab Emirates	MoF	2014	2001	CG,BCG,SG,SS	C	CB	2014	BPM 5
United Kingdom	NSO	2015	2001	CG,LG	A	NSO	2015	BPM 6
United States	MEP	2015	2001	CG,SG,LG	A	NSO	2015	BPM 6
Uruguay	MoF	2014	1986	CG,LG,SS,MPC,NFPC	A	CB	2014	BPM 6
Uzbekistan	MoF	2014	Other	CG,SG,LG,SS	C	MEP	2014	BPM 5
Vanuatu	MoF	2015	2001	CG	C	CB	2014	BPM 5
Venezuela	MoF	2010	2001	CG,LG,SS,BCG,NFPC	C	CB	2015	BPM 5
Vietnam	MoF	2014	2001	CG,SG,LG	C	CB	2015	BPM 5
Yemen	MoF	2013	2001	CG,LG	C	IMF staff	2009	BPM 5
Zambia	MoF	2015	1986	CG	C	CB	2015	BPM 6
Zimbabwe	MoF	2014	1986	CG	C	CB and MoF	2013	BPM 4

Note: BPM = *Balance of Payments Manual* (number following abbreviation signifies edition); CPI = consumer price index; ESA = European System of National and Regional Accounts; SNA = System of National Accounts.

[1]CB = Central Bank; FEO = Foreign Exchange Office; GAD = General Administration Department; IEO = International Economic Organization; MEP = Ministry of Economy, Planning, Commerce, and/or Development; MoF = Ministry of Finance and/or Treasury; NSO = National Statistics Office; PFTAC = Pacific Financial Technical Assistance Centre.

[2]National accounts base year is the period with which other periods are compared and the period for which prices appear in the denominators of the price relationships used to calculate the index.

[3]Use of chain-weighted methodology allows countries to measure GDP growth more accurately by reducing or eliminating the downward biases in volume series built on index numbers that average volume components using weights from a year in the moderately distant past.

[4]For some countries, the structures of government consist of a broader coverage than specified for the general government. Coverage: BCG = Budgetary Central Government; CG = Central Government; EUA = Extrabudgetary Units/Accounts; LG = Local Government; MPC = Monetary Public Corporation, including Central Bank; NMPC = Nonmonetary Financial Public Corporations; NFPC = Nonfinancial Public Corporations; SG = State Government; SS = Social Security Funds; TG = Territorial Governments.

[5]Accounting Standard: A = accrual accounting; C = cash accounting; CB = commitments basis accounting; Mixed = combination of accrual and cash accounting.

[6]Nominal GDP is not measured in the same way as real GDP.

Box A1. Economic Policy Assumptions Underlying the Projections for Selected Economies

Fiscal Policy Assumptions

The short-term fiscal policy assumptions used in the *World Economic Outlook* (WEO) are based on officially announced budgets, adjusted for differences between the national authorities and the IMF staff regarding macroeconomic assumptions and projected fiscal outturns. The medium-term fiscal projections incorporate policy measures that are judged likely to be implemented. For cases in which the IMF staff has insufficient information to assess the authorities' budget intentions and prospects for policy implementation, an unchanged structural primary balance is assumed unless indicated otherwise. Specific assumptions used in regard to some of the advanced economies follow. (See also Tables B5 to B9 in the online section of the Statistical Appendix for data on fiscal net lending/borrowing and structural balances.)[1]

Argentina: Fiscal projections are based on the available information regarding budget outturn for the federal government, fiscal measures announced by the authorities, and budget plans for provinces and on IMF staff macroeconomic projections.

Australia: Fiscal projections are based on Australian Bureau of Statistics data, the 2016–2017 budget, and IMF staff estimates.

Austria: For 2014, the creation of a defeasance structure for Hypo Alpe Adria is assumed to increase the general-government-debt-to-GDP ratio by 4.2 percentage points, and the deficit effect arising from Hypo is assumed to be 1.4 percentage points.

Belgium: Projections reflect the IMF staff's assessment of policies and measures laid out in the 2016 budget and the 2016–19 Stability Programme, incorporated into the IMF staff's macroeconomic framework.

---

[1] The output gap is actual minus potential output, as a percentage of potential output. Structural balances are expressed as a percentage of potential output. The structural balance is the actual net lending/borrowing minus the effects of cyclical output from potential output, corrected for one-time and other factors, such as asset and commodity prices and output composition effects. Changes in the structural balance consequently include effects of temporary fiscal measures, the impact of fluctuations in interest rates and debt-service costs, and other noncyclical fluctuations in net lending/borrowing. The computations of structural balances are based on IMF staff estimates of potential GDP and revenue and expenditure elasticities. (See Annex I of the October 1993 WEO.) Net debt is calculated as gross debt minus financial assets corresponding to debt instruments. Estimates of the output gap and of the structural balance are subject to significant margins of uncertainty.

Brazil: For 2015, outturn estimates are based on the information available as of April 2016. Fiscal projections for the end of 2016 take into account budget performance through June 30, 2016, and the deficit target revision announced by the authorities in May 2016.

Canada: Projections use the baseline forecasts in the Update of Economic and Fiscal Projections 2015 (November 2015), Backgrounder: Canadian Economic Outlook (February 2016), 2015 provincial budget updates, and 2016 provincial budgets as available. The IMF staff makes adjustments to these forecasts for differences in macroeconomic projections. The IMF staff forecast also incorporates the most recent data releases from Statistics Canada's Canadian System of National Economic Accounts, including federal, provincial, and territorial budgetary outturns through the second quarter of 2015.

Chile: Projections are based on the authorities' budget projections, adjusted to reflect the IMF staff's projections for GDP and copper prices.

China: The pace of fiscal consolidation is likely to be more gradual, reflecting reforms to strengthen social safety nets and the social security system announced as part of the Third Plenum reform agenda.

Denmark: Estimates for 2015 are aligned with the latest official budget estimates and the underlying economic projections, adjusted where appropriate for the IMF staff's macroeconomic assumptions. For 2016–20, the projections incorporate key features of the medium-term fiscal plan as embodied in the authorities' Convergence Programme 2016 submitted to the European Union (EU).

France: Projections for 2016 reflect the budget law. For 2017–19, they are based on the multiyear budget and the April 2016 Stability Programme, adjusted for differences in assumptions on macro and financial variables, and revenue projections. Historical fiscal data reflect the statistical institute's September 2016 revision and update of the fiscal accounts and national accounts.

Germany: The IMF staff's projections for 2016 and beyond reflect the authorities' adopted core federal government budget plan and the German Stability Programme: 2016 Update, adjusted for the differences in the IMF staff's macroeconomic framework. The estimate of gross debt includes portfolios of impaired assets and noncore business transferred to institutions that are winding up, as well as other financial sector and EU support operations.

Box A1 *(continued)*

Greece: The fiscal projections reflect the IMF staff's assessment, assuming full implementation of the authorities' fiscal policy package under the European Stability Mechanism–supported program.

Hong Kong SAR: Projections are based on the authorities' medium-term fiscal projections on expenditures.

Hungary: Fiscal projections include IMF staff projections of the macroeconomic framework and of the impact of recent legislative measures, as well as fiscal policy plans announced in the 2016 budget.

India: Historical data are based on budgetary execution data. Projections are based on available information on the authorities' fiscal plans, with adjustments for IMF staff assumptions. Subnational data are incorporated with a lag of up to two years; general government data are thus finalized well after central government data. IMF and Indian presentations differ, particularly regarding divestment and license auction proceeds, net versus gross recording of revenues in certain minor categories, and some public sector lending.

Indonesia: IMF projections are based on moderate tax policy and administration reforms, fuel subsidy pricing reforms introduced in January 2015, and a gradual increase in social and capital spending over the medium term in line with fiscal space.

Ireland: Fiscal projections are based on the 2016 Summer Economic Statement, adjusted for differences between the IMF staff's macroeconomic projections and those of the Irish authorities.

Italy: IMF staff estimates and projections are based on the fiscal plans included in the government's 2016 budget and 2016 Economic and Financial Document, published in April of this year. Estimates of the cyclically adjusted balance include the expenditures to clear capital arrears in 2013, which are excluded from the structural balance. After 2016, the IMF staff projects convergence to a structural balance in line with the authorities' declared policy intentions, which implies corrective measures in some years, as yet unidentified.

Japan: The projections include fiscal measures already announced by the government, including the fiscal year 2016 supplementary budget, the upcoming fiscal stimulus package for 2017, and the consumption tax hike in October 2019.

Korea: The medium-term forecast incorporates the government's announced medium-term consolidation path.

Mexico: Fiscal projections for 2016 are broadly in line with the approved budget; projections for 2017 onward assume compliance with rules established in the Fiscal Responsibility Law.

Netherlands: Fiscal projections for the period 2016–21 are based on the authorities' Bureau for Economic Policy Analysis budget projections, after differences in macroeconomic assumptions are adjusted for. Historical data were revised following the June 2014 Central Bureau of Statistics release of revised macro data because of the adoption of the European System of National and Regional Accounts (ESA 2010) and the revisions of data sources.

New Zealand: Fiscal projections are based on the authorities' 2016–17 budget and on IMF staff estimates.

Portugal: The estimate for 2015 reflects the cash outturn and January through September data on a national accounts basis; the projections for 2016 reflect the authorities' approved budget, adjusted to reflect the IMF staff's macroeconomic forecast and the first-half cash outturn. Projections thereafter are based on the assumption of unchanged policies.

Puerto Rico: Fiscal projections are based on the Puerto Rico Fiscal and Economic Growth Plan (FEGP), which was prepared in 2015 pursuant to Governor Alejandro García Padilla's executive order, with subsequent further updates on debt data in 2016. In line with assumptions of this plan, IMF projections assume that Puerto Rico will lose federal funding for the Affordable Care Act (ACA) starting in 2018. Likewise, projections assume federal tax incentives, which were neutralizing the effects of Puerto Rico's Act 154 on foreign companies, will no longer be available, starting in 2018, leading to additional revenue losses. In terms of policy assumptions, FEGP presents a scenario without measures and an alternative scenario with various revenue and expenditure measures; IMF projections assume full implementation of the FEGP measures. On the revenue side, the main measures are (1) an increase in the corporate tax base and (2) improvement in tax administration and enforcement. These are in addition to full transition to a value-added tax, which is an ongoing measure and is expected to be completed by the end of 2016. On the expenditure side, measures include extension of Act 66, which freezes much government spending, through 2021; reduction of operating costs; decreases in government subsidies; and spending cuts in education and health care. Although IMF policy assumptions are

Box A1 *(continued)*

exactly as in the FEGP scenario with full measures, the IMF's projections of fiscal revenues, expenditures, and balance are different from FEGP's. This stems from two main differences in methodologies: first and foremost, while IMF projections are on an accrual basis, FEGP's are on a cash basis. Second, the IMF and FEGP make very different macroeconomic assumptions.

Russia: Projections for 2016–18 are IMF staff estimates. Projections for 2019–21 are based on the oil-price-based fiscal rule introduced in December 2012, with adjustments by the IMF staff.

Saudi Arabia: IMF staff projections of oil revenues are based on WEO baseline oil prices. On the expenditure side, wage bill estimates incorporate 13th-month pay awards every three years in accordance with the lunar calendar. Expenditure projections take the 2016 budget as a starting point and assume that, to adjust to lower oil prices, capital spending falls as a percentage of GDP over the medium term.

Singapore: For fiscal years 2015/16 and 2016/17, projections are based on budget numbers. For the remainder of the projection period, the IMF staff assumes unchanged policies.

South Africa: Fiscal projections are based on the authorities' 2016 Budget Review.

Spain: For 2016 and beyond, fiscal estimates and projections are based on the measures specified in the Stability Programme Update 2016–19 and the IMF staff's macroeconomic projections.

Sweden: Fiscal projections take into account the authorities' projections based on the 2016 Spring Budget. The impact of cyclical developments on the fiscal accounts is calculated using the Organisation for Economic Co-operation and Development's 2005 elasticity to take into account output and employment gaps.

Switzerland: The projections assume that fiscal policy is adjusted as necessary to keep fiscal balances in line with the requirements of Switzerland's fiscal rules.

Turkey: Fiscal projections assume that both current and capital spending will be in line with the authorities' 2016–18 Medium Term Programme based on current trends and policies.

United Kingdom: Fiscal projections are based on the 2016 budget, published in March 2016, with revenue projections adjusted for the actual fiscal year 2015/16 outturn and with revenue and expenditure projections adjusted for differences between IMF staff forecasts of macroeconomic variables (such as

GDP growth and inflation) and the forecasts of these variables assumed in the authorities' fiscal projections. IMF staff data exclude public sector banks and the effect of transferring assets from the Royal Mail Pension Plan to the public sector in April 2012. Real government consumption and investment are part of the real GDP path, which, according to the IMF staff, may or may not be the same as projected by the U.K. Office for Budget Responsibility.

United States: Fiscal projections are based on the March 2016 Congressional Budget Office baseline adjusted for the IMF staff's policy and macroeconomic assumptions. The baseline incorporates the key provisions of the Bipartisan Budget Act of 2015, including a partial rollback of the sequester spending cuts in fiscal year 2016. In fiscal years 2017 through 2021, the IMF staff assumes that the sequester cuts will continue to be partially replaced, in proportions similar to those already implemented in fiscal years 2014 and 2015, with back-loaded measures generating savings in mandatory programs and additional revenues. Projections also incorporate the Protecting Americans from Tax Hikes Act of 2015, which extended some existing tax cuts for the short term and some permanently. Finally, fiscal projections are adjusted to reflect the IMF staff's forecasts for key macroeconomic and financial variables and different accounting treatment of financial sector support and of defined-benefit pension plans and are converted to a general government basis. Historical data start at 2001 for most series because data compiled according to the 2001 *Government Finance Statistics Manual* (GFSM 2001) may not be available for earlier years.

Monetary Policy Assumptions

Monetary policy assumptions are based on the established policy framework in each country. In most cases, this implies a nonaccommodative stance over the business cycle: official interest rates will increase when economic indicators suggest that inflation will rise above its acceptable rate or range; they will decrease when indicators suggest that inflation will not exceed the acceptable rate or range, that output growth is below its potential rate, and that the margin of slack in the economy is significant. On this basis, the London interbank offered rate (LIBOR) on six-month U.S. dollar deposits is assumed to average 1.0 percent in 2016 and 1.3 percent in 2017 (see Table 1.1). The rate on three-month euro

Box A1 *(continued)*

deposits is assumed to average –0.3 percent in 2016 and –0.4 percent in 2017. The interest rate on six-month Japanese yen deposits is assumed to average 0.0 percent in 2016 and –0.1 percent in 2017.

Australia: Monetary policy assumptions are in line with market expectations.

Brazil: Monetary policy assumptions are consistent with gradual convergence of inflation toward the middle of the target range over the relevant horizon.

Canada: Monetary policy assumptions are in line with market expectations.

China: Monetary policy will remain broadly unchanged from its current status, consistent with the authorities' announcement of maintaining stable economic growth.

Denmark: The monetary policy is to maintain the peg to the euro.

Euro area: Monetary policy assumptions for euro area member countries are in line with market expectations.

Hong Kong SAR: The IMF staff assumes that the currency board system remains intact.

India: The policy (interest) rate assumption is consistent with an inflation rate within the Reserve Bank of India's targeted band.

Indonesia: Monetary policy assumptions are in line with the maintenance of inflation within the central bank's targeted band by the end of 2016.

Japan: Monetary policy assumptions are in line with market expectations.

Korea: Monetary policy assumptions are in line with market expectations.

Mexico: Monetary assumptions are consistent with attaining the inflation target.

Russia: Monetary projections assume increasing exchange rate flexibility as part of the new inflation-targeting regime, with policy rates falling over the next year as inflation continues to decline and second-round effects are subdued.

Saudi Arabia: Monetary policy projections are based on the continuation of the exchange rate peg to the U.S. dollar.

Singapore: Broad money is projected to grow in line with the projected growth in nominal GDP.

South Africa: Monetary projections are consistent with South Africa's 3–6 percent inflation target range.

Sweden: Monetary projections are in line with Riksbank projections.

Switzerland: The projections assume no change in the policy rate in 2016–17.

Turkey: Broad money and the long-term bond yield are based on IMF staff projections. The short-term deposit rate is projected to evolve with a constant spread against the interest rate of a similar U.S. instrument.

United Kingdom: Projections assume no change in the Bank Rate over the forecast period, consistent with market expectations.

United States: Following the Federal Reserve's 25 basis point rate hike in mid-December, financial conditions have tightened more than expected, and wage growth has yet to exert significant price pressure. The IMF staff expects the federal funds target rate to increase by 50 basis points in 2016 and rise gradually thereafter.

List of Tables

Table A1. Summary of World Output[1]
(Annual percent change)

	Average 1998–2007	2008	2009	2010	2011	2012	2013	2014	2015	Projections 2016	2017	2021
World	**4.2**	**3.0**	**−0.1**	**5.4**	**4.2**	**3.5**	**3.3**	**3.4**	**3.2**	**3.1**	**3.4**	**3.8**
Advanced Economies	**2.8**	**0.1**	**−3.4**	**3.1**	**1.7**	**1.2**	**1.2**	**1.9**	**2.1**	**1.6**	**1.8**	**1.7**
United States	3.0	−0.3	−2.8	2.5	1.6	2.2	1.7	2.4	2.6	1.6	2.2	1.6
Euro Area	2.4	0.4	−4.5	2.1	1.5	−0.9	−0.3	1.1	2.0	1.7	1.5	1.5
Japan	1.0	−1.0	−5.5	4.7	−0.5	1.7	1.4	0.0	0.5	0.5	0.6	0.6
Other Advanced Economies[2]	3.6	1.0	−2.0	4.6	2.9	1.9	2.2	2.8	1.9	1.9	1.9	2.3
Emerging Market and Developing Economies	**5.8**	**5.8**	**2.9**	**7.5**	**6.3**	**5.3**	**5.0**	**4.6**	**4.0**	**4.2**	**4.6**	**5.1**
Regional Groups												
Commonwealth of Independent States[3]	6.2	5.3	−6.3	4.7	4.7	3.5	2.1	1.1	−2.8	−0.3	1.4	2.4
Emerging and Developing Asia	7.6	7.2	7.5	9.6	7.9	7.0	7.0	6.8	6.6	6.5	6.3	6.4
Emerging and Developing Europe	4.2	3.1	−3.0	4.7	5.4	1.2	2.8	2.8	3.6	3.3	3.1	3.2
Latin America and the Caribbean	3.1	4.0	−1.8	6.1	4.6	3.0	2.9	1.0	0.0	−0.6	1.6	2.7
Middle East, North Africa, Afghanistan, and Pakistan	5.3	4.8	1.5	4.9	4.5	5.0	2.4	2.7	2.3	3.4	3.4	3.9
Middle East and North Africa	5.3	4.8	1.5	5.2	4.6	5.1	2.2	2.6	2.1	3.2	3.2	3.6
Sub-Saharan Africa	5.2	5.9	3.9	7.0	5.0	4.3	5.2	5.1	3.4	1.4	2.9	4.2
Memorandum												
European Union	2.7	0.6	−4.3	2.1	1.7	−0.4	0.3	1.6	2.3	1.9	1.7	1.7
Low-Income Developing Countries	6.0	5.7	5.7	7.4	5.3	5.2	6.2	6.0	4.6	3.7	4.9	5.4
Analytical Groups												
By Source of Export Earnings												
Fuel	5.6	5.1	−1.5	5.2	5.0	4.8	2.5	2.3	0.0	0.8	1.8	2.7
Nonfuel	5.9	6.0	4.2	8.1	6.6	5.4	5.6	5.2	5.0	5.0	5.3	5.6
Of Which, Primary Products	3.8	4.1	−0.8	6.8	4.8	2.6	4.0	1.6	2.8	1.1	2.8	3.7
By External Financing Source												
Net Debtor Economies	4.7	4.5	2.3	6.9	5.1	4.3	4.6	4.2	3.8	3.9	4.6	5.4
Net Debtor Economies by Debt-Servicing Experience												
Economies with Arrears and/or Rescheduling during 2011–15	5.6	5.1	−0.1	3.8	2.3	1.9	2.5	0.7	0.1	2.6	3.5	5.0
Memorandum												
Median Growth Rate												
Advanced Economies	3.5	0.8	−3.8	2.3	2.0	1.1	1.4	2.2	1.6	1.7	1.9	2.0
Emerging Market and Developing Economies	4.6	4.9	1.7	4.5	4.5	4.0	4.0	3.7	3.1	3.0	3.5	4.0
Low-Income Developing Countries	4.7	5.6	3.8	6.2	5.6	5.2	5.4	5.0	4.4	3.9	4.5	5.4
Output per Capita												
Advanced Economies	2.1	−0.6	−4.0	2.5	1.2	0.7	0.7	1.2	1.5	1.0	1.3	1.2
Emerging Market and Developing Economies	4.4	4.3	1.7	6.3	5.1	4.0	3.8	3.5	3.0	3.1	3.6	4.2
Low-Income Developing Countries	3.8	3.6	3.6	5.3	4.1	2.8	4.0	3.9	2.6	1.7	2.9	3.5
World Growth Rate Based on Market Exchange Rates	**3.2**	**1.5**	**−2.1**	**4.2**	**3.0**	**2.5**	**2.5**	**2.7**	**2.6**	**2.4**	**2.8**	**3.0**
Value of World Output (billions of U.S. dollars)												
At Market Exchange Rates	40,468	63,422	60,048	65,643	72,769	74,092	76,075	78,042	73,599	75,213	79,536	98,632
At Purchasing Power Parities	58,618	83,179	83,479	88,997	94,486	99,270	104,153	109,554	114,137	119,097	125,774	158,562

[1]Real GDP.
[2]Excludes the United States, euro area countries, and Japan.
[3]Georgia, Turkmenistan, and Ukraine, which are not members of the Commonwealth of Independent States, are included in this group for reasons of geography and similarity in economic structure.

Table A2. Advanced Economies: Real GDP and Total Domestic Demand[1]

(Annual percent change)

	Average 1998–2007	2008	2009	2010	2011	2012	2013	2014	2015	Projections 2016	Projections 2017	Projections 2021	Fourth Quarter[2] 2015:Q4	Projections 2016:Q4	Projections 2017:Q4
Real GDP															
Advanced Economies	**2.8**	**0.1**	**−3.4**	**3.1**	**1.7**	**1.2**	**1.2**	**1.9**	**2.1**	**1.6**	**1.8**	**1.7**	**1.8**	**1.7**	**1.8**
United States	3.0	−0.3	−2.8	2.5	1.6	2.2	1.7	2.4	2.6	1.6	2.2	1.6	1.9	2.0	1.9
Euro Area	2.4	0.4	−4.5	2.1	1.5	−0.9	−0.3	1.1	2.0	1.7	1.5	1.5	2.0	1.6	1.6
Germany	1.7	0.8	−5.6	4.0	3.7	0.7	0.6	1.6	1.5	1.7	1.4	1.2	1.3	1.7	1.6
France	2.4	0.2	−2.9	2.0	2.1	0.2	0.6	0.6	1.3	1.3	1.3	1.8	1.3	1.3	1.5
Italy	1.5	−1.1	−5.5	1.7	0.6	−2.8	−1.7	−0.3	0.8	0.8	0.9	0.8	1.1	0.7	1.2
Spain	3.9	1.1	−3.6	0.0	−1.0	−2.6	−1.7	1.4	3.2	3.1	2.2	1.6	3.5	2.6	2.1
Netherlands	2.8	1.7	−3.8	1.4	1.7	−1.1	−0.2	1.4	2.0	1.7	1.6	1.6	1.1	2.0	1.7
Belgium	2.4	0.7	−2.3	2.7	1.8	0.2	0.0	1.3	1.4	1.4	1.4	1.5	1.5	1.3	1.4
Austria	2.6	1.5	−3.8	1.9	2.8	0.8	0.3	0.4	0.9	1.4	1.2	1.1	1.1	1.4	1.0
Greece	3.9	−0.3	−4.3	−5.5	−9.1	−7.3	−3.2	0.7	−0.2	0.1	2.8	1.8	−0.8	0.7	3.7
Portugal	2.1	0.2	−3.0	1.9	−1.8	−4.0	−1.1	0.9	1.5	1.0	1.1	1.2	1.3	1.2	1.1
Ireland	6.6	−4.4	−4.6	2.0	0.0	−1.1	1.1	8.5	26.3	4.9	3.2	2.8	27.4	5.7	6.0
Finland	3.8	0.7	−8.3	3.0	2.6	−1.4	−0.8	−0.7	0.2	0.9	1.1	1.6	0.6	1.1	0.9
Slovak Republic	4.9	5.7	−5.5	5.1	2.8	1.5	1.4	2.5	3.6	3.4	3.3	3.7	4.0	3.1	3.3
Lithuania	6.6	2.6	−14.8	1.6	6.0	3.8	3.5	3.0	1.6	2.6	3.0	3.3	2.1	3.2	2.4
Slovenia	4.3	3.3	−7.8	1.2	0.6	−2.7	−1.1	3.1	2.3	2.3	1.8	1.5	2.1	2.9	0.8
Luxembourg	5.1	−0.8	−5.4	5.7	2.6	−0.8	4.3	4.1	4.8	3.5	3.1	3.0	3.6	2.3	3.7
Latvia	7.7	−3.6	−14.3	−3.8	6.2	4.0	2.9	2.0	2.7	2.5	3.4	4.0	2.3	6.3	−2.1
Estonia	6.7	−5.4	−14.7	2.5	7.6	5.2	1.6	2.9	1.1	1.5	2.5	3.3	1.0	1.9	2.7
Cyprus	4.3	3.7	−2.0	1.4	0.4	−2.4	−6.0	−2.5	1.5	2.8	2.2	2.0	2.8	2.8	2.2
Malta	2.2	3.3	−2.4	3.5	1.8	2.8	4.5	3.5	6.2	4.1	3.4	3.0	6.2	3.3	3.3
Japan	1.0	−1.0	−5.5	4.7	−0.5	1.7	1.4	0.0	0.5	0.5	0.6	0.6	0.8	0.8	0.8
United Kingdom	2.9	−0.6	−4.3	1.9	1.5	1.3	1.9	3.1	2.2	1.8	1.1	1.9	1.8	1.4	0.8
Korea	4.8	2.8	0.7	6.5	3.7	2.3	2.9	3.3	2.6	2.7	3.0	3.0	3.1	2.5	3.1
Canada	3.2	1.0	−2.9	3.1	3.1	1.7	2.2	2.5	1.1	1.2	1.9	1.9	0.3	1.5	1.9
Australia	3.6	2.6	1.8	2.3	2.7	3.6	2.0	2.7	2.4	2.9	2.7	2.8	2.8	2.5	3.3
Taiwan Province of China	5.0	0.7	−1.6	10.6	3.8	2.1	2.2	3.9	0.6	1.0	1.7	2.7	−0.7	1.3	2.1
Switzerland	2.4	2.2	−2.1	2.9	1.9	1.1	1.8	1.9	0.8	1.0	1.3	1.7	0.3	1.2	1.2
Sweden	3.5	−0.6	−5.2	6.0	2.7	−0.3	1.2	2.3	4.2	3.6	2.6	2.0	4.8	3.4	1.2
Singapore	5.5	1.8	−0.6	15.2	6.2	3.7	4.7	3.3	2.0	1.7	2.2	2.6	1.7	1.0	2.7
Hong Kong SAR	3.8	2.1	−2.5	6.8	4.8	1.7	3.1	2.7	2.4	1.4	1.9	2.9	2.0	1.7	1.8
Norway	2.4	0.4	−1.6	0.6	1.0	2.7	1.0	2.2	1.6	0.8	1.2	2.1	0.2	0.7	2.3
Czech Republic	3.7	2.7	−4.8	2.3	2.0	−0.8	−0.5	2.7	4.5	2.5	2.7	2.2	4.0	2.3	2.4
Israel	3.8	3.0	1.4	5.7	5.1	2.4	4.4	3.2	2.5	2.8	3.0	2.9	2.3	2.8	3.0
Denmark	2.0	−0.7	−5.1	1.6	1.2	−0.1	−0.2	1.3	1.0	1.0	1.4	1.8	0.1	2.4	−1.4
New Zealand	3.5	−0.4	0.3	2.0	1.8	2.8	1.7	3.0	3.0	2.8	2.7	2.6	2.9	2.2	3.3
Puerto Rico	2.5	−1.8	−2.0	−0.4	−0.4	0.0	−0.3	−1.4	0.0	−1.8	−1.4	−0.5	...	...	...
Macao SAR	5.0	3.4	1.3	25.3	21.7	9.2	11.2	−0.9	−20.3	−4.7	0.2	2.6	...	...	...
Iceland	4.6	1.5	−4.7	−3.6	2.0	1.2	4.4	2.0	4.0	4.9	3.8	2.6	2.7	7.6	3.3
San Marino	...	1.7	−12.8	−4.6	−9.5	−7.5	−3.0	−1.0	0.5	1.0	1.2	1.3	...	...	...
Memorandum															
Major Advanced Economies	2.4	−0.3	−3.8	2.9	1.6	1.4	1.3	1.7	1.9	1.4	1.7	1.5	1.5	1.6	1.6
Real Total Domestic Demand															
Advanced Economies	**2.8**	**−0.3**	**−3.7**	**3.0**	**1.4**	**0.8**	**0.9**	**1.9**	**2.2**	**1.7**	**2.0**	**1.7**	**2.1**	**1.8**	**2.0**
United States	3.4	−1.3	−3.8	2.9	1.6	2.1	1.3	2.4	3.2	1.8	2.5	1.6	2.5	2.3	2.1
Euro Area	2.4	0.3	−4.0	1.5	0.7	−2.3	−0.6	1.1	1.9	1.8	1.6	1.5	2.3	1.4	1.6
Germany	1.0	1.0	−3.2	2.9	3.0	−0.8	1.0	1.5	1.4	1.9	1.7	1.6	2.0	1.4	1.8
France	2.7	0.5	−2.5	2.1	2.0	−0.3	0.7	1.1	1.5	1.7	1.3	1.8	2.2	0.8	1.9
Italy	1.8	−1.2	−4.1	2.0	−0.6	−5.6	−2.6	−0.4	1.1	1.0	1.0	0.7	1.8	0.7	1.6
Spain	4.9	−0.4	−6.0	−0.5	−3.1	−4.7	−3.1	1.6	3.8	3.0	2.1	1.5	4.3	2.6	1.9
Japan	0.6	−1.3	−4.0	2.9	0.4	2.6	1.7	0.0	0.1	0.6	0.8	0.7	0.9	1.0	0.9
United Kingdom	3.4	−1.7	−4.9	2.5	−0.6	2.2	2.1	3.4	2.5	1.8	0.1	2.1	1.9	1.3	0.2
Canada	3.4	2.6	−3.0	5.1	3.4	2.0	1.9	1.3	0.0	1.5	2.1	2.0	−1.4	3.1	1.7
Other Advanced Economies[3]	3.4	1.5	−2.7	6.1	3.1	2.0	1.4	2.5	2.1	1.7	2.6	2.8	2.3	1.3	3.4
Memorandum															
Major Advanced Economies	2.5	−0.8	−3.7	2.8	1.4	1.2	1.1	1.7	2.2	1.6	1.8	1.5	1.9	1.8	1.7

In this and other tables, when countries are not listed alphabetically, they are ordered on the basis of economic size.
From the fourth quarter of the preceding year.
Excludes the G7 (Canada, France, Germany, Italy, Japan, United Kingdom, United States) and euro area countries.

Table A3. Advanced Economies: Components of Real GDP

(Annual percent change)

| | Averages | | 2008 | 2009 | 2010 | 2011 | 2012 | 2013 | 2014 | 2015 | Projections | |
	1998–2007	2008–17									2016	2017
Private Consumer Expenditure												
Advanced Economies	**2.9**	**1.2**	**0.1**	**−1.2**	**1.9**	**1.4**	**1.0**	**1.1**	**1.8**	**2.2**	**2.2**	**2.1**
United States	3.7	1.7	−0.3	−1.6	1.9	2.3	1.5	1.5	2.9	3.2	2.9	2.7
Euro Area	2.1	0.4	0.3	−1.1	0.8	0.0	−1.1	−0.6	0.8	1.8	1.6	1.5
Germany	0.9	1.0	0.5	0.3	0.3	1.3	1.3	0.9	1.0	1.9	1.5	1.5
France	2.7	0.8	0.4	0.2	1.8	0.5	−0.2	0.5	0.7	1.5	1.6	1.4
Italy	1.4	−0.4	−1.1	−1.5	1.2	0.0	−4.0	−2.4	0.6	0.9	1.0	1.0
Spain	3.9	−0.3	−0.7	−3.6	0.3	−2.4	−3.5	−3.1	1.2	3.1	3.3	2.3
Japan	0.9	0.5	−0.9	−0.7	2.8	0.3	2.3	1.7	−0.9	−1.2	0.5	1.2
United Kingdom	3.5	0.8	−0.7	−3.2	0.6	−0.5	1.7	1.6	2.2	2.5	2.7	0.8
Canada	3.5	2.2	2.9	0.0	3.6	2.3	1.9	2.4	2.5	1.9	2.2	2.0
Other Advanced Economies[1]	3.5	2.2	1.1	0.0	3.7	3.0	2.2	2.2	2.3	2.6	2.3	2.6
Memorandum												
Major Advanced Economies	2.7	1.2	−0.2	−1.2	1.8	1.4	1.1	1.2	1.8	2.1	2.2	2.0
Public Consumption												
Advanced Economies	**2.2**	**1.0**	**2.3**	**3.0**	**0.9**	**−0.6**	**0.1**	**−0.3**	**0.4**	**1.6**	**1.5**	**1.0**
United States	2.0	0.3	2.5	3.7	0.1	−2.7	−0.9	−2.4	−0.7	1.6	0.7	0.8
Euro Area	1.9	1.0	2.4	2.4	0.8	−0.1	−0.3	0.2	0.6	1.4	1.7	1.1
Germany	0.9	2.0	3.4	3.0	1.3	0.9	1.0	1.2	1.2	2.8	3.5	1.9
France	1.4	1.4	1.1	2.4	1.3	1.0	1.6	1.5	1.2	1.4	1.4	1.0
Italy	1.4	−0.2	1.0	0.4	0.6	−1.8	−1.4	−0.3	−1.0	−0.7	0.6	0.5
Spain	4.9	0.7	5.9	4.1	1.5	−0.3	−4.5	−2.8	0.0	2.7	0.9	0.4
Japan	2.1	1.1	−0.1	2.3	1.9	1.2	1.7	1.9	0.1	1.2	1.7	−0.8
United Kingdom	3.2	1.1	2.1	1.1	0.2	0.2	1.7	0.3	2.3	1.4	0.8	0.6
Canada	2.4	1.6	3.8	2.7	2.3	1.3	0.7	0.3	0.3	1.7	1.6	1.9
Other Advanced Economies[1]	2.8	2.5	2.9	3.4	2.8	1.5	2.0	2.2	2.3	2.3	3.1	2.2
Memorandum												
Major Advanced Economies	1.9	0.8	2.1	2.9	0.7	−1.0	0.1	−0.7	0.0	1.5	1.2	0.8
Gross Fixed Capital Formation												
Advanced Economies	**3.1**	**0.3**	**−2.7**	**−11.1**	**1.8**	**2.9**	**2.4**	**1.2**	**2.9**	**2.5**	**1.4**	**2.4**
United States	3.7	0.7	−4.8	−13.1	1.1	3.7	6.3	3.1	4.2	3.7	1.1	3.0
Euro Area	3.3	−0.7	−0.7	−11.2	−0.3	1.6	−3.3	−2.4	1.5	3.1	2.9	2.5
Germany	1.3	1.0	0.8	−9.9	5.0	7.4	−0.1	−1.1	3.5	1.2	2.2	1.5
France	3.9	0.0	0.8	−9.1	2.1	2.1	0.2	−0.8	−0.3	1.0	2.4	1.7
Italy	3.0	−3.2	−3.1	−9.9	−0.5	−1.9	−9.3	−6.6	−3.4	0.8	1.4	1.8
Spain	6.9	−2.7	−3.9	−16.9	−4.9	−6.9	−7.1	−2.5	3.5	6.4	4.2	3.0
Japan	−1.1	−0.5	−4.1	−10.6	−0.2	1.4	3.4	2.5	1.3	0.0	0.5	1.6
United Kingdom	3.3	−0.2	−6.5	−15.2	5.0	1.9	2.3	3.2	6.7	3.3	1.0	−2.0
Canada	5.1	0.5	1.5	−11.8	11.4	4.6	4.9	−0.4	0.7	−4.4	−1.4	1.1
Other Advanced Economies[1]	3.7	1.7	−0.1	−5.1	6.0	4.0	2.9	2.4	2.1	1.1	1.2	2.6
Memorandum												
Major Advanced Economies	2.7	0.2	−3.4	−12.0	2.0	3.2	3.4	1.5	3.0	2.2	1.1	2.0

Table A3. Advanced Economies: Components of Real GDP *(continued)*
(Annual percent change)

	Averages		2008	2009	2010	2011	2012	2013	2014	2015	Projections	
	1998–2007	2008–17									2016	2017
Final Domestic Demand												
Advanced Economies	**2.8**	**1.0**	**−0.2**	**−2.6**	**1.7**	**1.3**	**1.1**	**0.9**	**1.8**	**2.2**	**2.0**	**2.0**
United States	3.4	1.3	−0.9	−3.1	1.5	1.7	1.9	1.2	2.6	3.1	2.2	2.5
Euro Area	2.3	0.3	0.5	−2.7	0.5	0.3	−1.4	−0.8	0.9	2.0	1.9	1.6
Germany	1.0	1.2	1.1	−1.4	1.4	2.5	1.0	0.5	1.5	1.9	2.0	1.5
France	2.6	0.8	0.7	−1.5	1.8	0.9	0.3	0.4	0.6	1.4	1.7	1.4
Italy	1.8	−0.9	−1.2	−2.9	0.7	−0.8	−4.5	−2.7	−0.4	0.6	1.0	1.0
Spain	4.9	−0.8	−0.5	−5.9	−0.7	−3.0	−4.5	−2.9	1.4	3.7	3.0	2.1
Japan	0.6	0.4	−1.6	−2.3	2.0	0.7	2.4	1.9	−0.3	−0.4	0.8	0.9
United Kingdom	3.4	0.7	−1.2	−4.4	1.1	0.0	1.8	1.6	2.9	2.4	2.1	0.3
Canada	3.7	1.7	2.8	−2.2	5.0	2.6	2.4	1.3	1.6	0.3	1.2	1.8
Other Advanced Economies[1]	3.3	2.1	1.1	−0.7	4.3	2.9	2.2	2.2	2.3	2.3	2.2	2.5
Memorandum												
Major Advanced Economies	2.6	0.9	−0.5	−2.7	1.6	1.3	1.4	0.9	1.7	2.0	1.8	1.8
Stock Building[2]												
Advanced Economies	**0.0**	**0.0**	**−0.2**	**−1.1**	**1.3**	**0.1**	**−0.2**	**0.0**	**0.1**	**0.1**	**−0.2**	**0.0**
United States	0.0	0.0	−0.5	−0.8	1.5	−0.1	0.1	0.2	−0.1	0.2	−0.4	0.0
Euro Area	0.0	−0.1	−0.2	−1.3	0.9	0.4	−0.9	0.2	0.2	−0.1	−0.1	0.0
Germany	0.0	−0.2	−0.1	−1.7	1.4	0.5	−1.6	0.4	−0.1	−0.5	−0.2	0.1
France	0.1	0.0	−0.2	−1.1	0.3	1.1	−0.6	0.2	0.5	0.1	0.0	0.0
Italy	0.0	0.0	−0.1	−1.2	1.3	0.2	−1.1	0.2	0.0	0.5	−0.1	0.0
Spain	0.0	0.0	0.1	−0.2	0.2	−0.1	−0.3	−0.3	0.3	0.1	0.0	0.0
Japan	0.0	0.0	0.2	−1.5	0.9	−0.2	0.2	−0.2	0.2	0.5	−0.1	0.0
United Kingdom	0.0	0.1	−0.5	−0.5	1.5	−0.6	0.2	0.3	0.7	−0.2	0.2	−0.2
Canada	0.0	−0.1	0.0	−0.7	0.1	0.7	−0.3	0.5	−0.4	−0.3	−0.4	0.1
Other Advanced Economies[1]	0.1	−0.1	0.3	−1.9	1.9	0.2	−0.3	−0.8	0.3	0.0	−0.4	0.1
Memorandum												
Major Advanced Economies	0.0	0.0	−0.3	−1.0	1.2	0.0	−0.2	0.2	0.0	0.1	−0.2	0.0
Foreign Balance[2]												
Advanced Economies	**−0.1**	**0.2**	**0.5**	**0.3**	**0.1**	**0.3**	**0.4**	**0.3**	**0.0**	**−0.2**	**−0.2**	**−0.1**
United States	−0.5	0.1	1.1	1.2	−0.5	0.0	0.1	0.3	−0.2	−0.7	−0.3	−0.4
Euro Area	0.0	0.3	0.1	−0.6	0.7	0.9	1.4	0.4	0.0	0.2	0.0	0.0
Germany	0.6	0.1	−0.1	−2.6	1.1	0.9	1.4	−0.3	0.3	0.1	0.0	−0.2
France	−0.3	−0.1	−0.3	−0.4	−0.1	0.0	0.5	−0.1	−0.5	−0.3	−0.4	0.0
Italy	−0.3	0.3	0.2	−1.3	−0.3	1.2	2.8	0.8	0.1	−0.3	−0.2	0.0
Spain	−0.9	1.0	1.6	2.8	0.5	2.1	2.1	1.4	−0.2	−0.5	0.1	0.1
Japan	0.4	−0.1	0.2	−2.0	2.0	−0.8	−0.8	−0.2	0.3	0.4	−0.1	−0.2
United Kingdom	−0.4	0.1	0.9	0.3	−0.8	1.4	−0.7	−0.8	−0.4	−0.5	−0.1	1.2
Canada	−0.3	−0.2	−1.9	0.0	−2.1	−0.3	−0.4	0.4	1.1	1.0	0.3	−0.1
Other Advanced Economies[1]	0.6	0.4	0.4	1.5	0.1	0.5	0.5	0.9	0.4	−0.2	−0.1	0.1
Memorandum												
Major Advanced Economies	−0.2	0.0	0.5	−0.1	0.0	0.1	0.2	0.1	0.0	−0.3	−0.2	−0.2

[1]Excludes the G7 (Canada, France, Germany, Italy, Japan, United Kingdom, United States) and euro area countries.
[2]Changes expressed as percent of GDP in the preceding period.

Table A4. Emerging Market and Developing Economies: Real GDP

(Annual percent change)

	Average 1998–2007	2008	2009	2010	2011	2012	2013	2014	2015	Projections 2016	2017	2021
Commonwealth of Independent States[1,2]	**6.2**	**5.3**	**−6.3**	**4.7**	**4.7**	**3.5**	**2.1**	**1.1**	**−2.8**	**−0.3**	**1.4**	**2.4**
Russia	5.8	5.2	−7.8	4.5	4.0	3.5	1.3	0.7	−3.7	−0.8	1.1	1.5
Excluding Russia	7.5	5.6	−2.4	5.1	6.2	3.6	4.3	2.0	−0.5	0.9	2.3	4.4
Armenia	10.4	6.9	−14.1	2.2	4.7	7.1	3.3	3.6	3.0	3.2	3.4	4.0
Azerbaijan	14.1	10.8	9.3	5.0	0.1	2.2	5.8	2.8	1.1	−2.4	1.4	3.2
Belarus	7.3	10.3	0.1	7.7	5.5	1.7	1.0	1.7	−3.9	−3.0	−0.5	1.8
Georgia	6.7	2.4	−3.7	6.2	7.2	6.4	3.4	4.6	2.8	3.4	5.2	4.8
Kazakhstan	8.1	3.3	1.2	7.3	7.5	5.0	6.0	4.3	1.2	−0.8	0.6	4.6
Kyrgyz Republic	4.2	7.6	2.9	−0.5	6.0	−0.9	10.9	4.0	3.5	2.2	2.3	4.3
Moldova	3.4	7.8	−6.0	7.1	6.8	−0.7	9.4	4.8	−0.5	2.0	3.0	3.8
Tajikistan	7.9	7.9	3.9	6.5	7.4	7.5	7.4	6.7	6.0	6.0	4.5	6.0
Turkmenistan	14.4	14.7	6.1	9.2	14.7	11.1	10.2	10.3	6.5	5.4	5.4	6.9
Ukraine[3]	5.8	2.2	−15.1	0.3	5.5	0.2	0.0	−6.6	−9.9	1.5	2.5	4.0
Uzbekistan	5.6	9.0	8.1	8.5	8.3	8.2	8.0	8.1	8.0	6.0	6.0	6.0
Emerging and Developing Asia	**7.6**	**7.2**	**7.5**	**9.6**	**7.9**	**7.0**	**7.0**	**6.8**	**6.6**	**6.5**	**6.3**	**6.4**
Bangladesh	5.7	5.5	5.3	6.0	6.5	6.3	6.0	6.3	6.8	6.9	6.9	6.5
Bhutan	7.8	10.8	5.7	9.3	9.7	6.4	3.6	3.8	5.2	6.0	6.4	5.2
Brunei Darussalam	2.0	−2.0	−1.8	2.7	3.7	0.9	−2.1	−2.3	−0.6	0.4	3.9	13.2
Cambodia	9.3	6.7	0.1	6.0	7.1	7.3	7.4	7.1	7.0	7.0	6.9	6.3
China	9.9	9.6	9.2	10.6	9.5	7.9	7.8	7.3	6.9	6.6	6.2	5.8
Fiji	2.3	1.0	−1.4	3.0	2.7	1.4	4.7	5.3	4.3	2.5	3.9	3.6
India[4]	7.1	3.9	8.5	10.3	6.6	5.6	6.6	7.2	7.6	7.6	7.6	8.1
Indonesia	2.7	7.4	4.7	6.4	6.2	6.0	5.6	5.0	4.8	4.9	5.3	6.0
Kiribati	1.9	−1.8	0.3	−1.6	0.5	5.2	5.8	2.4	3.5	3.1	2.5	1.8
Lao P.D.R.	6.3	7.8	7.5	8.1	8.0	7.9	8.0	7.5	7.6	7.5	7.3	7.1
Malaysia	4.2	4.8	−1.5	7.5	5.3	5.5	4.7	6.0	5.0	4.3	4.6	5.0
Maldives	8.8	12.7	−5.3	7.2	8.7	2.5	4.7	6.5	1.5	3.0	4.1	4.7
Marshall Islands	1.8	−1.7	6.2	1.3	4.0	1.9	−1.1	0.4	1.4	1.7	1.8	1.3
Micronesia	1.0	−2.2	1.0	3.5	1.8	−0.5	−3.6	−3.4	−0.2	1.1	0.7	0.6
Mongolia	5.7	7.8	−2.1	7.3	17.3	12.3	11.6	7.9	2.4	0.0	1.0	5.5
Myanmar	12.0	3.6	5.1	5.3	5.6	7.3	8.4	8.7	7.0	8.1	7.7	7.7
Nepal	3.8	6.1	4.5	4.8	3.4	4.8	4.1	6.0	2.7	0.6	4.0	3.8
Palau	...	−5.6	−9.1	3.3	5.0	3.2	−2.4	4.2	9.4	0.0	5.0	2.0
Papua New Guinea	2.6	3.6	2.9	11.6	3.7	6.1	4.7	7.4	6.6	2.5	3.0	3.4
Philippines	4.2	4.2	1.1	7.6	3.7	6.7	7.1	6.2	5.9	6.4	6.7	7.0
Samoa	3.7	2.9	−6.4	−1.4	5.4	0.4	−1.9	1.2	1.6	3.0	1.5	2.1
Solomon Islands	1.1	7.1	−4.7	6.9	12.9	4.7	3.0	2.0	3.3	3.0	3.3	3.2
Sri Lanka	4.3	6.0	3.5	8.0	8.4	9.1	3.4	4.9	4.8	5.0	5.0	5.5
Thailand	3.8	1.7	−0.7	7.5	0.8	7.2	2.7	0.8	2.8	3.2	3.3	3.0
Timor-Leste[5]	...	14.2	13.0	10.2	8.3	5.8	2.9	5.9	4.3	5.0	5.5	5.5
Tonga	1.2	2.7	3.0	3.2	1.8	−1.1	−0.6	2.9	3.4	2.7	2.4	1.8
Tuvalu	...	8.0	−4.4	−2.7	8.5	0.2	1.3	2.2	2.6	4.0	2.3	2.1
Vanuatu	2.5	6.5	3.3	1.6	1.2	1.8	2.0	2.3	−0.8	4.0	4.5	3.0
Vietnam	6.8	5.7	5.4	6.4	6.2	5.2	5.4	6.0	6.7	6.1	6.2	6.2
Emerging and Developing Europe	**4.2**	**3.1**	**−3.0**	**4.7**	**5.4**	**1.2**	**2.8**	**2.8**	**3.6**	**3.3**	**3.1**	**3.2**
Albania	7.0	7.5	3.4	3.7	2.5	1.4	1.0	1.8	2.8	3.4	3.7	4.1
Bosnia and Herzegovina	6.2	5.6	−0.8	0.8	0.9	−0.9	2.4	1.1	3.2	3.0	3.2	4.0
Bulgaria	5.3	5.6	−4.2	0.1	1.6	0.2	1.3	1.5	3.0	3.0	2.8	2.5
Croatia	3.7	2.1	−7.4	−1.7	−0.3	−2.2	−1.1	−0.4	1.6	1.9	2.1	2.0
Hungary	3.7	0.8	−6.6	0.7	1.8	−1.7	1.9	3.7	2.9	2.0	2.5	2.1
Kosovo	...	4.5	3.6	3.3	4.4	2.8	3.4	1.2	4.0	4.1	3.3	4.0
FYR Macedonia	3.4	5.5	−0.4	3.4	2.3	−0.5	2.9	3.5	3.7	2.2	3.5	3.8
Montenegro	...	6.9	−5.7	2.5	3.2	−2.7	3.5	1.8	3.2	5.1	3.6	4.8
Poland	4.2	3.9	2.6	3.7	5.0	1.6	1.3	3.3	3.6	3.1	3.4	3.0
Romania	4.0	8.5	−7.1	−0.8	1.1	0.6	3.5	3.0	3.8	5.0	3.8	3.3
Serbia	3.8	5.4	−3.1	0.6	1.4	−1.0	2.6	−1.8	0.7	2.5	2.8	4.0
Turkey	4.0	0.7	−4.8	9.2	8.8	2.1	4.2	3.0	4.0	3.3	3.0	3.5

Table A4. Emerging Market and Developing Economies: Real GDP *(continued)*
(Annual percent change)

	Average 1998–2007	2008	2009	2010	2011	2012	2013	2014	2015	Projections 2016	2017	2021
Latin America and the Caribbean	**3.1**	**4.0**	**−1.8**	**6.1**	**4.6**	**3.0**	**2.9**	**1.0**	**0.0**	**−0.6**	**1.6**	**2.7**
Antigua and Barbuda	4.6	1.5	−10.7	−8.5	−1.9	3.6	1.5	4.2	2.2	2.0	2.4	2.7
Argentina[6]	2.6	4.1	−5.9	10.1	6.0	−1.0	2.4	−2.5	2.5	−1.8	2.7	3.3
The Bahamas	2.8	−2.3	−4.2	1.5	0.6	3.1	0.0	−0.5	−1.7	0.3	1.0	1.3
Barbados	2.2	0.4	−4.0	0.3	0.8	0.3	−0.1	0.2	0.9	1.7	1.7	2.4
Belize	5.7	3.2	0.8	3.3	2.1	3.7	1.3	4.1	1.0	0.0	2.6	1.7
Bolivia	3.3	6.1	3.4	4.1	5.2	5.1	6.8	5.5	4.8	3.7	3.9	3.5
Brazil	3.0	5.1	−0.1	7.5	3.9	1.9	3.0	0.1	−3.8	−3.3	0.5	2.0
Chile	4.0	3.2	−1.1	5.7	5.8	5.5	4.0	1.8	2.3	1.7	2.0	3.4
Colombia	3.1	3.5	1.7	4.0	6.6	4.0	4.9	4.4	3.1	2.2	2.7	4.0
Costa Rica	5.5	2.7	−1.0	5.0	4.5	5.2	1.8	3.0	3.7	4.2	4.3	4.0
Dominica	2.4	7.1	−1.2	0.7	−0.2	−1.1	0.8	4.2	−1.8	1.5	2.9	1.7
Dominican Republic	5.6	3.1	0.9	8.3	2.8	2.6	4.8	7.3	7.0	5.9	4.5	4.5
Ecuador	3.0	6.4	0.6	3.5	7.9	5.6	4.6	3.7	0.3	−2.3	−2.7	1.5
El Salvador	2.9	1.3	−3.1	1.4	2.2	1.9	1.8	1.4	2.5	2.4	2.4	2.0
Grenada	4.8	0.9	−6.6	−0.5	0.8	−1.2	2.4	7.3	6.2	3.0	2.7	2.7
Guatemala	3.8	3.3	0.5	2.9	4.2	3.0	3.7	4.2	4.1	3.5	3.8	4.0
Guyana	1.4	2.0	3.3	4.4	5.4	4.8	5.2	3.8	3.2	4.0	4.1	3.8
Haiti	0.9	0.8	3.1	−5.5	5.5	2.9	4.2	2.8	1.2	1.5	3.2	3.5
Honduras	4.4	4.2	−2.4	3.7	3.8	4.1	2.8	3.1	3.6	3.6	3.7	3.8
Jamaica	1.3	−0.8	−3.4	−1.4	1.4	−0.5	0.2	0.5	0.9	1.5	2.0	2.8
Mexico	2.9	1.4	−4.7	5.1	4.0	4.0	1.4	2.2	2.5	2.1	2.3	2.9
Nicaragua	4.0	2.9	−2.8	3.2	6.2	5.6	4.5	4.6	4.9	4.5	4.3	4.0
Panama	5.6	8.6	1.6	5.8	11.8	9.2	6.6	6.1	5.8	5.2	5.8	6.0
Paraguay	1.6	6.4	−4.0	13.1	4.3	−1.2	14.0	4.7	3.1	3.5	3.6	3.8
Peru	4.1	9.1	1.0	8.5	6.5	6.0	5.8	2.4	3.3	3.7	4.1	3.5
St. Kitts and Nevis	3.5	3.4	−3.8	−3.8	−1.9	−0.9	6.2	6.1	5.0	3.5	3.5	2.8
St. Lucia	2.4	4.2	−0.4	−1.7	0.2	−1.4	0.1	0.4	2.4	1.5	1.9	2.1
St. Vincent and the Grenadines	4.0	−0.5	−2.0	−2.3	0.2	1.3	2.5	0.2	0.6	1.8	2.5	3.0
Suriname	3.9	4.1	3.0	5.1	5.3	3.1	2.8	1.8	−0.3	−7.0	0.5	3.0
Trinidad and Tobago	8.2	3.4	−4.4	3.3	−0.3	1.3	2.3	−1.0	−2.1	−2.7	2.3	1.2
Uruguay	1.2	7.2	4.2	7.8	5.2	3.5	4.6	3.2	1.0	0.1	1.2	3.1
Venezuela	2.9	5.3	−3.2	−1.5	4.2	5.6	1.3	−3.9	−6.2	−10.0	−4.5	0.0
Middle East, North Africa, Afghanistan, and Pakistan	**5.3**	**4.8**	**1.5**	**4.9**	**4.5**	**5.0**	**2.4**	**2.7**	**2.3**	**3.4**	**3.4**	**3.9**
Afghanistan	. . .	3.9	20.6	8.4	6.5	14.0	3.9	1.3	0.8	2.0	3.4	6.0
Algeria	4.3	2.4	1.6	3.6	2.8	3.3	2.8	3.8	3.9	3.6	2.9	3.4
Bahrain	5.8	6.2	2.5	4.3	2.0	3.7	5.4	4.4	2.9	2.1	1.8	2.2
Djibouti	2.8	5.8	1.6	4.1	7.3	4.8	5.0	6.0	6.5	6.5	7.0	6.0
Egypt	5.1	7.2	4.7	5.1	1.8	2.2	2.1	2.2	4.2	3.8	4.0	6.0
Iran	5.2	0.9	2.3	6.6	3.7	−6.6	−1.9	4.3	0.4	4.5	4.1	4.3
Iraq	. . .	8.2	3.4	6.4	7.5	13.9	7.6	−0.4	−2.4	10.3	0.5	2.0
Jordan	5.9	7.2	5.5	2.3	2.6	2.7	2.8	3.1	2.4	2.8	3.3	4.0
Kuwait	6.0	2.5	−7.1	−2.4	10.9	7.9	0.4	0.6	1.1	2.5	2.6	2.9
Lebanon	3.2	9.1	10.3	8.0	0.9	2.8	2.5	2.0	1.0	1.0	2.0	3.0
Libya	4.2	2.7	−0.8	5.0	−62.1	104.5	−13.6	−24.0	−6.4	−3.3	13.7	4.8
Mauritania	5.4	1.1	−1.0	4.8	4.7	5.8	6.1	5.4	1.2	3.2	4.3	2.9
Morocco	4.6	5.9	4.2	3.8	5.2	3.0	4.5	2.6	4.5	1.8	4.8	4.9
Oman	2.4	8.2	6.1	4.8	4.1	5.8	3.2	2.9	3.3	1.8	2.6	2.2
Pakistan	4.9	5.0	0.4	2.6	3.6	3.8	3.7	4.1	4.0	4.7	5.0	5.5
Qatar	10.7	17.7	12.0	19.6	13.4	4.9	4.6	4.0	3.7	2.6	3.4	2.0
Saudi Arabia	2.9	6.2	−2.1	4.8	10.0	5.4	2.7	3.6	3.5	1.2	2.0	2.3
Sudan[7]	11.2	3.0	4.7	3.0	−1.3	−3.4	5.2	1.6	4.9	3.1	3.5	3.5
Syria[8]	3.6	4.5	5.9	3.4	. . .	. . .	. . .	. . .	. . .	. . .	. . .	. . .
Tunisia	4.9	4.5	3.1	2.6	−1.9	3.9	2.4	2.3	0.8	1.5	2.8	4.3
United Arab Emirates	5.7	3.2	−5.2	1.6	4.9	7.1	4.7	3.1	4.0	2.3	2.5	3.4
Yemen	4.3	3.6	3.9	7.7	−12.7	2.4	4.8	−0.2	−28.1	−4.2	12.6	5.4

Table A4. Emerging Market and Developing Economies: Real GDP *(continued)*

(Annual percent change)

	Average 1998–2007	2008	2009	2010	2011	2012	2013	2014	2015	Projections 2016	2017	2021
Sub-Saharan Africa	**5.2**	**5.9**	**3.9**	**7.0**	**5.0**	**4.3**	**5.2**	**5.1**	**3.4**	**1.4**	**2.9**	**4.2**
Angola	10.3	13.8	2.4	3.4	3.9	5.2	6.8	4.8	3.0	0.0	1.5	3.5
Benin	4.4	4.9	2.3	2.1	3.0	4.6	6.9	6.5	5.0	4.6	5.4	5.6
Botswana	4.7	6.2	−7.7	8.6	6.0	4.5	9.9	3.2	−0.3	3.1	4.0	4.0
Burkina Faso	5.9	5.8	3.0	8.4	6.6	6.5	6.6	4.0	4.0	5.2	5.9	6.0
Burundi	3.1	4.9	3.8	5.1	4.0	4.4	5.9	4.5	−4.0	−0.5	2.0	4.5
Cabo Verde	7.5	6.7	−1.3	1.5	4.0	1.1	0.8	1.9	1.5	3.6	4.0	4.0
Cameroon	3.8	2.9	1.9	3.3	4.1	4.6	5.6	5.9	5.8	4.8	4.2	4.3
Central African Republic	1.4	2.1	1.7	3.0	3.3	4.1	−36.7	1.0	4.8	5.2	5.5	5.8
Chad	8.2	3.1	4.2	13.6	0.1	8.9	5.7	6.9	1.8	−1.1	1.7	3.5
Comoros	2.0	1.0	1.8	2.1	2.2	3.0	3.5	2.0	1.0	2.2	3.3	4.0
Democratic Republic of the Congo	1.4	6.2	2.9	7.1	6.9	7.1	8.5	9.5	6.9	3.9	4.2	5.5
Republic of Congo	3.3	5.6	7.5	8.7	3.4	3.8	3.3	6.8	2.3	1.7	5.0	2.9
Côte d'Ivoire	0.8	2.5	3.3	2.0	−4.2	10.1	9.3	7.9	8.5	8.0	8.0	7.0
Equatorial Guinea	27.6	17.8	1.3	−8.9	6.5	8.3	−4.1	−0.5	−7.4	−9.9	−5.8	0.1
Eritrea	0.7	−9.8	3.9	2.2	8.7	7.0	3.1	5.0	4.8	3.7	3.3	3.9
Ethiopia	6.5	11.2	10.0	10.6	11.4	8.7	9.9	10.3	10.2	6.5	7.5	7.3
Gabon	0.1	1.7	−2.3	6.3	7.1	5.3	5.6	4.3	4.0	3.2	4.5	4.9
The Gambia	3.8	5.7	6.4	6.5	−4.3	5.6	4.8	−0.2	4.4	2.3	3.3	5.5
Ghana	4.9	9.1	4.8	7.9	14.0	9.3	7.3	4.0	3.9	3.3	7.4	4.5
Guinea	3.1	4.9	−0.3	1.9	3.8	3.7	2.3	1.1	0.1	3.8	4.4	4.7
Guinea-Bissau	0.6	3.2	3.3	4.4	9.4	−1.8	0.8	2.5	4.8	4.8	5.0	5.0
Kenya	3.6	0.2	3.3	8.4	6.1	4.6	5.7	5.3	5.6	6.0	6.1	6.5
Lesotho	3.2	5.1	4.5	6.9	4.5	5.3	3.6	3.4	2.8	2.4	3.8	2.9
Liberia	...	6.0	5.1	6.1	7.4	8.2	8.7	0.7	0.0	2.0	4.0	6.6
Madagascar	3.7	7.2	−4.7	0.3	1.5	3.0	2.3	3.3	3.1	4.1	4.5	5.0
Malawi	3.1	7.6	8.3	6.9	4.9	1.9	5.2	5.7	2.9	2.7	4.5	5.5
Mali	5.2	4.8	4.7	5.4	3.2	−0.8	2.3	7.0	6.0	5.3	5.2	4.7
Mauritius	4.4	5.5	3.0	4.1	3.9	3.2	3.2	3.6	3.5	3.5	3.9	3.9
Mozambique	8.3	6.9	6.4	6.7	7.1	7.2	7.1	7.4	6.6	4.5	5.5	6.8
Namibia	4.2	2.6	0.3	6.0	5.1	5.1	5.7	6.5	5.3	4.2	5.3	4.5
Niger	4.7	9.6	−0.7	8.4	2.2	11.8	5.3	7.0	3.5	5.2	5.0	6.9
Nigeria	7.0	7.2	8.4	11.3	4.9	4.3	5.4	6.3	2.7	−1.7	0.6	3.3
Rwanda	7.7	11.1	6.3	7.3	7.8	8.8	4.7	7.0	6.9	6.0	6.0	7.5
São Tomé and Príncipe	3.8	8.1	4.0	4.5	4.8	4.5	4.0	4.5	4.0	4.0	5.0	6.0
Senegal	4.6	3.7	2.4	4.3	1.9	4.5	3.6	4.3	6.5	6.6	6.8	7.0
Seychelles	2.6	−2.1	−1.1	5.9	5.4	3.7	5.0	6.2	5.7	4.9	3.5	3.3
Sierra Leone	12.0	5.4	3.2	5.3	6.3	15.2	20.7	4.6	−21.1	4.3	5.0	6.5
South Africa	3.7	3.2	−1.5	3.0	3.3	2.2	2.3	1.6	1.3	0.1	0.8	2.2
South Sudan	...	...	...	...	...	−52.4	29.3	2.9	−0.2	−13.1	−6.1	0.5
Swaziland	3.5	4.3	1.9	1.4	1.2	3.0	2.9	2.5	1.7	0.5	0.9	1.0
Tanzania	5.9	5.6	5.4	6.4	7.9	5.1	7.3	7.0	7.0	7.2	7.2	6.5
Togo	1.1	2.4	3.5	4.1	4.8	5.9	5.4	5.4	5.4	5.3	5.0	4.4
Uganda	7.1	10.4	8.1	7.7	6.8	2.6	4.0	4.9	4.8	4.9	5.5	6.4
Zambia	5.5	7.8	9.2	10.3	5.6	7.6	5.1	5.0	3.0	3.0	4.0	5.5
Zimbabwe[9]	...	−16.6	7.5	11.4	11.9	10.6	4.5	3.8	1.1	−0.3	−2.5	1.6

[1]Data for some countries refer to real net material product (NMP) or are estimates based on NMP. The figures should be interpreted only as indicative of broad orders of magnitude because reliable, comparable data are not generally available. In particular, the growth of output of new private enterprises of the informal economy is not fully reflected in the recent figures.
[2]Georgia, Turkmenistan, and Ukraine, which are not members of the Commonwealth of Independent States, are included in this group for reasons of geography and similarity in economic structure.
[3]Data are based on the 2008 System of National Accounts. The revised national accounts data are available beginning in 2000 and exclude Crimea and Sevastopol from 2010 onward.
[4]See country-specific notes for India in the "Country Notes" section of the Statistical Appendix.
[5]In this table only, the data for Timor-Leste are based on non-oil GDP.
[6]See country-specific notes for Argentina in the "Country Notes" section of the Statistical Appendix.
[7]Data for 2011 exclude South Sudan after July 9. Data for 2012 and onward pertain to the current Sudan.
[8]Data for Syria are excluded for 2011 onward owing to the uncertain political situation.
[9]The Zimbabwe dollar ceased circulating in early 2009. Data are based on IMF staff estimates of price and exchange rate developments in U.S. dollars. IMF staff estimates of U.S. dollar values may differ from authorities' estimates. Real GDP is in constant 2009 prices.

Table A5. Summary of Inflation
(Percent)

	Average 1998–2007	2008	2009	2010	2011	2012	2013	2014	2015	Projections 2016	2017	2021
GDP Deflators												
Advanced Economies	**1.7**	**1.9**	**0.7**	**0.9**	**1.3**	**1.2**	**1.2**	**1.4**	**1.2**	**1.0**	**1.5**	**1.8**
United States	2.2	2.0	0.8	1.2	2.1	1.8	1.6	1.8	1.1	1.3	2.1	2.2
Euro Area	1.9	2.0	1.0	0.7	1.1	1.3	1.3	0.8	1.2	1.0	1.0	1.5
Japan	−1.2	−1.3	−0.5	−2.2	−1.9	−0.9	−0.6	1.7	2.0	0.6	0.4	0.9
Other Advanced Economies[1]	2.0	3.0	0.9	2.0	2.0	1.2	1.4	1.3	0.9	0.7	1.6	2.1
Consumer Prices												
Advanced Economies	**2.0**	**3.4**	**0.2**	**1.5**	**2.7**	**2.0**	**1.4**	**1.4**	**0.3**	**0.8**	**1.7**	**2.0**
United States	2.6	3.8	−0.3	1.6	3.1	2.1	1.5	1.6	0.1	1.2	2.3	2.3
Euro Area[2]	2.0	3.3	0.3	1.6	2.7	2.5	1.3	0.4	0.0	0.3	1.1	1.7
Japan	−0.2	1.4	−1.4	−0.7	−0.3	−0.1	0.3	2.8	0.8	−0.2	0.5	1.3
Other Advanced Economies[1]	1.9	3.9	1.4	2.4	3.3	2.1	1.7	1.5	0.6	1.0	1.9	2.1
Emerging Market and Developing Economies[3]	**7.9**	**9.2**	**5.0**	**5.6**	**7.1**	**5.8**	**5.5**	**4.7**	**4.7**	**4.5**	**4.4**	**4.0**
Regional Groups												
Commonwealth of Independent States[4]	19.7	15.4	11.1	7.2	9.7	6.2	6.4	8.1	15.5	8.4	6.3	4.8
Emerging and Developing Asia	4.2	7.6	2.8	5.1	6.5	4.6	4.6	3.5	2.7	3.1	3.3	3.7
Emerging and Developing Europe	18.5	8.0	4.8	5.6	5.4	5.9	4.3	3.8	2.9	3.1	4.2	4.3
Latin America and the Caribbean	7.0	6.4	4.6	4.2	5.2	4.6	4.6	4.9	5.5	5.8	4.2	3.6
Middle East, North Africa, Afghanistan, and Pakistan	5.8	11.8	7.3	6.6	9.2	9.8	9.1	6.8	5.8	5.1	6.0	4.3
Middle East and North Africa	5.7	11.7	6.1	6.2	8.6	9.7	9.3	6.6	6.0	5.4	6.1	4.1
Sub-Saharan Africa	10.2	12.9	9.8	8.2	9.4	9.3	6.6	6.3	7.0	11.3	10.8	7.9
Memorandum												
European Union	2.6	3.7	1.0	2.0	3.1	2.6	1.5	0.5	0.0	0.3	1.3	1.8
Low-Income Developing Countries	9.4	14.6	8.2	9.2	11.7	9.9	8.0	7.3	7.3	8.9	9.1	7.1
Analytical Groups												
By Source of Export Earnings												
Fuel	12.2	12.6	7.6	6.5	8.3	7.8	7.7	6.3	8.6	7.4	6.2	4.7
Nonfuel	6.7	8.2	4.3	5.4	6.8	5.3	4.9	4.3	3.8	3.8	4.0	3.9
Of Which, Primary Products[5]	. . .	. . .	. . .	. . .	. . .	. . .	. . .	. . .	. . .	. . .	. . .	. . .
By External Financing Source												
Net Debtor Economies	9.1	9.4	7.2	6.8	7.7	7.0	6.3	5.7	5.5	5.6	5.7	4.8
Net Debtor Economies by Debt-Servicing Experience												
Economies with Arrears and/or Rescheduling during 2011–15	9.0	15.4	13.0	10.2	10.6	8.2	7.1	11.2	16.8	10.1	14.1	6.5
Memorandum												
Median Inflation Rate												
Advanced Economies	2.1	4.1	0.9	1.9	3.2	2.6	1.3	0.7	0.1	0.5	1.2	2.0
Emerging Market and Developing Economies[3]	4.9	10.3	3.7	4.2	5.4	4.6	4.0	3.2	2.7	3.0	3.5	3.5

Excludes the United States, euro area countries, and Japan.
Based on Eurostat's harmonized index of consumer prices.
Excludes Argentina and Venezuela. See country-specific notes for Argentina in the "Country Notes" section of the Statistical Appendix.
Georgia, Turkmenistan, and Ukraine, which are not members of the Commonwealth of Independent States, are included in this group for reasons of geography and similarity in economic structure.
Data are missing because of Argentina, which accounts for more than 30 percent of the weights of the group. See country-specific notes for Argentina in the "Country Notes" section of the Statistical appendix.

Table A6. Advanced Economies: Consumer Prices[1]

(Annual percent change)

	Average 1998–2007	2008	2009	2010	2011	2012	2013	2014	2015	Projections 2016	Projections 2017	Projections 2021	End of Period[2] 2015	End of Period[2] Projections 2016	End of Period[2] Projections 2017
Advanced Economies	**2.0**	**3.4**	**0.2**	**1.5**	**2.7**	**2.0**	**1.4**	**1.4**	**0.3**	**0.8**	**1.7**	**2.0**	**0.5**	**1.2**	**1.8**
United States	2.6	3.8	−0.3	1.6	3.1	2.1	1.5	1.6	0.1	1.2	2.3	2.3	0.7	1.8	2.6
Euro Area[3]	2.0	3.3	0.3	1.6	2.7	2.5	1.3	0.4	0.0	0.3	1.1	1.7	0.2	0.6	1.0
Germany	1.5	2.8	0.2	1.1	2.5	2.1	1.6	0.8	0.1	0.4	1.5	2.0	0.3	1.2	1.6
France	1.7	3.2	0.1	1.7	2.3	2.2	1.0	0.6	0.1	0.3	1.0	1.7	0.3	0.0	0.2
Italy	2.3	3.5	0.8	1.6	2.9	3.3	1.2	0.2	0.1	−0.1	0.5	1.2	0.1	−0.6	0.8
Spain	3.0	4.1	−0.3	1.8	3.2	2.4	1.4	−0.1	−0.5	−0.3	1.0	1.6	0.0	0.7	0.7
Netherlands	2.3	2.2	1.0	0.9	2.5	2.8	2.6	0.3	0.2	0.1	0.9	1.3	0.2	0.5	1.0
Belgium	1.9	4.5	0.0	2.3	3.4	2.6	1.2	0.5	0.6	2.1	1.6	1.5	1.5	2.5	1.2
Austria	1.7	3.2	0.4	1.7	3.5	2.6	2.1	1.5	0.8	0.9	1.5	2.0	1.1	1.2	1.3
Greece	3.3	4.2	1.3	4.7	3.1	1.0	−0.9	−1.4	−1.1	−0.1	0.6	1.8	0.4	−0.1	1.1
Portugal	2.9	2.7	−0.9	1.4	3.6	2.8	0.4	−0.2	0.5	0.7	1.1	1.8	0.3	2.4	0.0
Ireland	3.3	3.1	−1.7	−1.6	1.2	1.9	0.5	0.3	0.0	0.3	1.2	2.0	0.0	0.7	1.3
Finland	1.5	3.9	1.6	1.7	3.3	3.2	2.2	1.2	−0.2	0.4	1.2	2.0	−0.2	0.9	1.4
Slovak Republic	6.4	4.0	0.9	0.7	4.1	3.7	1.5	−0.1	−0.3	−0.2	1.1	2.0	−0.5	0.3	1.4
Lithuania	2.2	11.2	4.2	1.2	4.1	3.2	1.2	0.2	−0.7	0.5	1.2	2.2	−0.2	0.5	2.2
Slovenia	5.6	5.7	0.9	1.8	1.8	2.6	1.8	0.2	−0.5	−0.3	1.0	2.0	−0.4	0.3	0.8
Luxembourg	2.5	4.1	0.0	2.8	3.7	2.9	1.7	0.7	0.1	0.2	1.0	2.1	0.9	1.8	−1.0
Latvia	4.6	15.3	3.3	−1.2	4.2	2.3	0.0	0.7	0.2	0.2	1.7	2.0	0.4	0.3	1.8
Estonia	4.4	10.6	0.2	2.7	5.1	4.2	3.2	0.5	0.1	0.5	1.4	2.2	−0.2	0.9	2.3
Cyprus[3]	2.5	4.4	0.2	2.6	3.5	3.1	0.4	−0.3	−1.5	−1.0	0.5	1.9	−0.5	0.0	0.5
Malta	2.5	4.7	1.8	2.0	2.5	3.2	1.0	0.8	1.2	1.2	1.5	1.8	1.3	1.8	1.5
Japan	−0.2	1.4	−1.4	−0.7	−0.3	−0.1	0.3	2.8	0.8	−0.2	0.5	1.3	0.2	−0.1	0.7
United Kingdom[3]	1.6	3.6	2.2	3.3	4.5	2.8	2.6	1.5	0.1	0.7	2.5	2.0	0.1	1.5	2.5
Korea	3.2	4.7	2.8	2.9	4.0	2.2	1.3	1.3	0.7	1.0	1.9	2.0	1.3	1.3	2.2
Canada	2.1	2.4	0.3	1.8	2.9	1.5	0.9	1.9	1.1	1.6	2.1	2.0	1.3	1.8	2.1
Australia	2.8	4.3	1.8	2.9	3.4	1.7	2.5	2.5	1.5	1.3	2.1	2.5	1.7	1.6	2.0
Taiwan Province of China	0.9	3.5	−0.9	1.0	1.4	1.9	0.8	1.2	−0.3	1.1	1.1	2.2	0.1	0.6	1.1
Switzerland	0.8	2.4	−0.5	0.7	0.2	−0.7	−0.2	0.0	−1.1	−0.4	0.0	1.0	−1.3	0.0	0.2
Sweden	1.5	3.3	1.9	1.9	1.4	0.9	0.4	0.2	0.7	1.1	1.4	2.1	0.7	1.2	1.6
Singapore	0.7	6.6	0.6	2.8	5.2	4.6	2.4	1.0	−0.5	−0.3	1.1	1.9	−0.7	0.5	1.4
Hong Kong SAR	−0.8	4.3	0.6	2.3	5.3	4.1	4.3	4.4	3.0	2.5	2.6	3.0	3.0	2.5	2.6
Norway	1.9	3.8	2.2	2.4	1.3	0.7	2.1	2.0	2.2	3.2	2.3	2.5	2.3	3.0	2.5
Czech Republic	3.3	6.3	1.0	1.5	1.9	3.3	1.4	0.4	0.3	0.6	1.9	2.0	0.1	1.1	2.2
Israel	2.3	4.6	3.3	2.7	3.5	1.7	1.5	0.5	−0.6	−0.6	0.8	2.0	−1.0	−0.1	1.2
Denmark	2.1	3.4	1.3	2.3	2.8	2.4	0.8	0.6	0.5	0.4	1.1	2.0	0.4	0.4	1.1
New Zealand	2.2	4.0	2.1	2.3	4.0	1.1	1.1	1.2	0.3	0.7	1.6	2.0	0.1	1.4	1.7
Puerto Rico	2.3	5.2	0.3	2.5	2.9	1.3	1.1	0.6	−0.8	−0.2	1.1	1.2	−0.2	−0.2	1.1
Macao SAR	...	8.5	1.2	2.8	5.8	6.1	5.5	6.0	4.6	2.6	2.8	2.8	3.7	2.6	2.8
Iceland	...	12.7	12.0	5.4	4.0	5.2	3.9	2.0	1.6	1.7	3.1	2.5	2.0	2.2	3.5
San Marino	4.2	4.1	2.4	2.6	2.0	2.8	1.3	1.1	0.14	0.6	0.7	1.2	0.4	0.9	1.1
Memorandum															
Major Advanced Economies	1.9	3.2	−0.1	1.4	2.6	1.9	1.3	1.5	0.2	0.8	1.8	2.0	0.5	1.2	1.9

[1]Movements in consumer prices are shown as annual averages.
[2]Monthly year-over-year changes and, for several countries, on a quarterly basis.
[3]Based on Eurostat's harmonized index of consumer prices.

Table A7. Emerging Market and Developing Economies: Consumer Prices[1]

(Annual percent change)

	Average 1998–2007	2008	2009	2010	2011	2012	2013	2014	2015	Projections 2016	2017	2021	End of Period[2] 2015	Projections 2016	2017
Commonwealth of Independent States[3,4]	**19.7**	**15.4**	**11.1**	**7.2**	**9.7**	**6.2**	**6.4**	**8.1**	**15.5**	**8.4**	**6.3**	**4.8**	**13.9**	**7.1**	**5.8**
Russia	21.2	14.1	11.7	6.9	8.4	5.1	6.8	7.8	15.5	7.2	5.0	4.0	12.9	5.9	4.9
Excluding Russia	15.3	19.3	9.5	8.0	13.1	9.0	5.6	8.7	15.3	11.2	9.2	6.6	16.3	9.8	8.1
Armenia	3.2	9.0	3.5	7.3	7.7	2.5	5.8	3.0	3.7	−0.5	2.5	4.0	−0.1	1.0	3.5
Azerbaijan	3.8	20.8	1.6	5.7	7.9	1.0	2.4	1.4	4.0	10.2	8.5	4.0	7.7	12.8	4.2
Belarus	55.3	14.8	13.0	7.7	53.2	59.2	18.3	18.1	13.5	12.7	12.0	9.0	12.0	13.0	11.0
Georgia	7.3	10.0	1.7	7.1	8.5	−0.9	−0.5	3.1	4.0	2.6	3.6	3.0	4.9	3.2	4.0
Kazakhstan	8.3	17.1	7.3	7.1	8.3	5.1	5.8	6.7	6.5	13.1	9.3	7.1	12.0	9.0	9.0
Kyrgyz Republic	9.7	24.5	6.8	7.8	16.6	2.8	6.6	7.5	6.5	1.1	7.4	5.1	3.4	3.3	5.7
Moldova	15.0	12.7	0.0	7.4	7.6	4.6	4.6	5.1	9.6	6.8	4.4	5.0	13.5	3.5	4.7
Tajikistan	20.2	20.4	6.4	6.5	12.4	5.8	5.0	6.1	5.8	6.3	7.3	6.0	5.1	7.0	6.4
Turkmenistan	10.4	14.5	−2.7	4.4	5.3	5.3	6.8	6.0	6.4	5.5	5.0	6.9	6.0	5.0	5.0
Ukraine[5]	12.1	25.2	15.9	9.4	8.0	0.6	−0.3	12.1	48.7	15.1	11.0	5.0	43.3	13.0	8.5
Uzbekistan	18.9	13.1	12.3	12.3	12.4	11.9	11.7	9.1	8.5	8.4	9.6	10.0	8.4	8.0	9.8
Emerging and Developing Asia	**4.2**	**7.6**	**2.8**	**5.1**	**6.5**	**4.6**	**4.6**	**3.5**	**2.7**	**3.1**	**3.3**	**3.7**	**2.7**	**3.2**	**3.3**
Bangladesh	5.7	8.9	4.9	9.4	11.5	6.2	7.5	7.0	6.4	6.7	6.9	5.7	6.5	7.0	7.0
Bhutan	5.1	6.8	6.3	5.7	7.3	9.3	11.3	9.9	6.3	4.4	4.6	4.7	7.4	7.6	6.9
Brunei Darussalam	0.2	2.1	1.0	0.2	0.1	0.1	0.4	−0.2	−0.4	−0.3	0.0	0.1	−1.0	0.4	0.1
Cambodia	3.8	25.0	−0.7	4.0	5.5	2.9	3.0	3.9	1.2	3.1	2.7	0.2	2.8	3.2	2.9
China	1.1	5.9	−0.7	3.3	5.4	2.6	2.6	2.0	1.4	2.1	2.3	3.0	1.6	2.3	2.3
Fiji	3.0	7.7	3.7	3.7	7.3	3.4	2.9	0.5	1.4	3.3	2.8	2.8	1.6	3.3	2.8
India	5.2	9.2	10.6	9.5	9.5	9.9	9.4	5.9	4.9	5.5	5.2	4.9	5.3	5.3	5.3
Indonesia	14.1	9.8	5.0	5.1	5.3	4.0	6.4	6.4	6.4	3.7	4.2	4.0	3.4	3.4	4.4
Kiribati	1.8	13.7	9.8	−3.9	1.5	−3.0	−1.5	2.1	0.6	1.5	2.0	2.5	0.6	1.5	2.0
Lao P.D.R.	24.0	7.6	0.0	6.0	7.6	4.3	6.4	5.5	5.3	−3.3	2.3	3.1	5.5	−4.5	2.3
Malaysia	2.4	5.4	0.6	1.7	3.2	1.7	2.1	3.1	2.1	2.1	3.0	3.0	2.7	2.1	3.0
Maldives	1.8	12.0	4.5	6.2	11.3	10.9	4.0	2.5	1.4	2.1	2.6	4.2	1.9	2.0	3.2
Marshall Islands	. . .	14.7	0.5	1.8	5.4	4.3	1.9	1.1	−2.2	0.6	1.1	2.1	−2.2	0.7	1.1
Micronesia	2.0	6.6	7.7	3.7	4.3	6.3	2.0	0.6	−1.0	1.9	1.3	3.0	−1.0	1.9	1.3
Mongolia	7.3	26.8	6.3	10.2	7.7	15.0	8.6	12.9	5.9	2.4	6.7	6.5	1.1	5.9	5.8
Myanmar	23.4	11.5	2.2	8.2	2.8	2.8	5.7	5.9	11.4	9.8	9.0	6.9	10.7	10.4	7.7
Nepal	5.5	6.7	12.6	9.6	9.6	8.3	9.9	9.0	7.2	10.0	9.9	6.5	7.6	11.5	8.3
Palau	. . .	9.9	4.7	1.1	2.6	5.4	2.8	4.0	2.2	2.0	2.0	2.0	0.8	3.2	0.8
Papua New Guinea	8.6	10.8	6.9	5.1	4.4	4.5	5.0	5.2	6.0	6.9	7.5	6.0	6.3	7.0	7.5
Philippines	5.2	8.2	4.2	3.8	4.7	3.2	2.9	4.2	1.4	2.0	3.4	3.5	1.5	2.9	3.2
Samoa	4.5	11.6	6.3	0.8	5.2	2.0	0.6	−0.4	0.9	0.3	1.0	3.0	0.4	0.3	1.7
Solomon Islands	8.7	17.3	7.1	0.9	7.4	5.9	5.4	5.2	0.9	2.4	4.0	2.9	3.5	4.5	2.7
Sri Lanka	9.8	22.4	3.5	6.2	6.7	7.5	6.9	3.3	0.9	4.1	5.3	5.0	2.8	5.4	5.2
Thailand	2.8	5.5	−0.9	3.3	3.8	3.0	2.2	1.9	−0.9	0.3	1.6	2.5	−0.9	1.3	1.7
Timor-Leste	. . .	7.4	−0.2	5.2	13.2	10.9	9.5	0.7	0.6	−0.6	1.3	4.0	−0.6	−0.6	3.3
Tonga	7.6	7.5	3.5	3.9	4.6	2.0	1.5	1.2	−0.1	0.1	1.5	2.7	−0.4	0.5	2.5
Tuvalu	. . .	10.4	−0.3	−1.9	0.5	1.4	2.0	1.1	3.2	3.5	2.9	2.5	4.4	3.5	2.9
Vanuatu	2.5	4.8	4.3	2.8	0.9	1.3	1.5	0.8	2.5	2.2	2.6	3.0	1.5	2.5	2.7
Vietnam	4.9	23.1	6.7	9.2	18.7	9.1	6.6	4.1	0.6	2.0	3.6	4.0	0.6	3.5	3.8
Emerging and Developing Europe	**18.5**	**8.0**	**4.8**	**5.6**	**5.4**	**5.9**	**4.3**	**3.8**	**2.9**	**3.1**	**4.2**	**4.3**	**3.5**	**3.9**	**3.7**
Albania	4.1	3.4	2.3	3.6	3.4	2.0	1.9	1.6	1.9	1.1	2.2	3.0	2.0	1.8	2.3
Bosnia and Herzegovina	2.4	7.4	−0.4	2.1	3.7	2.0	−0.1	−0.9	−1.0	−0.7	0.5	2.0	−1.2	−0.3	0.7
Bulgaria[6]	7.3	12.0	2.5	3.0	3.4	2.4	0.4	−1.6	−1.1	−1.6	0.6	2.1	−0.9	−0.8	1.4
Croatia	3.4	6.1	2.4	1.0	2.3	3.4	2.2	−0.2	−0.5	−1.0	0.8	2.0	−0.1	−0.1	1.2
Hungary	7.5	6.0	4.2	4.9	3.9	5.7	1.7	−0.2	−0.1	0.4	1.9	3.0	0.5	0.8	2.6
Kosovo	. . .	9.4	−2.4	3.5	7.3	2.5	1.8	0.4	−0.5	0.2	0.9	2.2	−0.1	0.5	1.7
Macedonia	1.9	7.2	−0.6	1.7	3.9	3.3	2.8	−0.1	−0.2	0.1	0.7	2.0	−0.3	0.5	1.0
Montenegro	. . .	9.0	3.6	0.7	3.1	3.6	2.2	−0.7	1.6	0.5	1.3	2.0	1.4	1.0	1.4
Poland	4.6	4.2	3.4	2.6	4.3	3.7	0.9	0.0	−0.9	−0.6	1.1	2.5	−0.5	0.2	1.5
Romania	24.2	7.8	5.6	6.1	5.8	3.3	4.0	1.1	−0.6	−1.5	1.7	2.5	−0.9	−0.3	2.7
Serbia	25.3	12.4	8.1	6.1	11.1	7.3	7.7	2.1	1.4	1.3	3.2	4.0	1.6	2.0	3.5
Turkey	33.9	10.4	6.3	8.6	6.5	8.9	7.5	8.9	7.7	8.4	8.2	6.5	8.8	9.1	6.2

Table A7. Emerging Market and Developing Economies: Consumer Prices[1] *(continued)*
(Annual percent change)

	Average 1998–2007	2008	2009	2010	2011	2012	2013	2014	2015	Projections 2016	2017	2021	End of Period[2] 2015	Projections 2016	2017
Latin America and the Caribbean[7]	**7.0**	**6.4**	**4.6**	**4.2**	**5.2**	**4.6**	**4.6**	**4.9**	**5.5**	**5.8**	**4.2**	**3.6**	**6.2**	**5.1**	**3.9**
Antigua and Barbuda	1.8	5.3	−0.6	3.4	3.5	3.4	1.1	1.1	1.0	1.4	1.8	2.5	0.9	1.4	2.2
Argentina[8]	6.8	8.6	6.3	10.5	9.8	10.0	10.6	...	...	...	23.2	9.7	...	39.4	20.5
The Bahamas	1.9	4.4	1.7	1.6	3.1	1.9	0.4	1.2	1.9	1.0	1.5	1.3	2.0	1.0	1.5
Barbados	2.6	8.1	3.6	5.8	9.4	4.5	1.8	1.9	−1.1	0.3	2.0	2.5	−2.5	1.7	2.3
Belize	1.8	6.4	−1.1	0.9	1.7	1.2	0.5	1.2	−0.9	1.0	2.2	2.0	−0.6	2.0	2.3
Bolivia	4.1	14.0	3.3	2.5	9.9	4.5	5.7	5.8	4.1	3.9	5.1	5.0	3.0	5.1	5.0
Brazil	6.6	5.7	4.9	5.0	6.6	5.4	6.2	6.3	9.0	9.0	5.4	4.5	10.7	7.2	5.0
Chile	3.3	8.7	1.5	1.4	3.3	3.0	1.9	4.4	4.3	4.0	3.0	3.0	4.4	3.5	3.0
Colombia	8.0	7.0	4.2	2.3	3.4	3.2	2.0	2.9	5.0	7.6	4.1	3.0	6.8	6.0	3.7
Costa Rica	10.9	13.4	7.8	5.7	4.9	4.5	5.2	4.5	0.8	0.7	2.6	3.0	−0.8	2.2	3.0
Dominica	1.6	6.4	0.0	2.8	1.1	1.4	0.0	0.8	−0.8	−0.2	1.6	2.2	−0.1	−0.1	1.8
Dominican Republic	12.2	10.6	1.4	6.3	8.5	3.7	4.8	3.0	0.8	2.3	4.0	4.0	2.3	3.0	4.0
Ecuador	22.4	8.4	5.2	3.6	4.5	5.1	2.7	3.6	4.0	2.4	1.1	0.7	3.4	2.9	−0.2
El Salvador	3.1	7.3	0.5	1.2	5.1	1.7	0.8	1.1	−0.7	1.0	1.5	2.0	1.0	0.3	2.0
Grenada	2.3	8.0	−0.3	3.4	3.0	2.4	0.0	−0.8	−0.6	2.3	3.4	2.1	1.0	2.8	2.8
Guatemala	6.9	11.4	1.9	3.9	6.2	3.8	4.3	3.4	2.4	4.5	3.6	4.0	3.1	4.3	4.0
Guyana	6.2	8.1	3.0	4.3	4.4	2.4	2.2	1.0	−0.3	0.2	2.1	3.0	−1.8	2.2	2.0
Haiti	15.1	14.4	3.4	4.1	7.4	6.8	6.8	3.9	7.5	13.3	9.1	5.0	11.3	12.0	7.0
Honduras	9.1	11.4	5.5	4.7	6.8	5.2	5.2	6.1	3.2	3.1	4.1	4.5	2.4	4.7	4.5
Jamaica	9.3	22.0	9.6	12.6	7.5	6.9	9.4	8.3	3.7	4.4	5.2	4.9	3.7	5.2	5.2
Mexico	7.3	5.1	5.3	4.2	3.4	4.1	3.8	4.0	2.7	2.8	3.3	3.0	2.1	3.2	3.1
Nicaragua	9.0	19.8	3.7	5.5	8.1	7.2	7.1	6.0	4.0	6.2	7.3	7.7	3.1	6.2	7.3
Panama	1.5	8.8	2.4	3.5	5.9	5.7	4.0	2.6	0.1	0.7	1.5	2.0	0.3	1.0	1.5
Paraguay	8.8	10.2	2.6	4.7	8.3	3.7	2.7	5.0	3.1	4.1	4.1	4.5	3.1	3.8	4.1
Peru	2.8	5.8	2.9	1.5	3.4	3.7	2.8	3.2	3.5	3.6	2.5	2.5	4.4	2.9	2.5
St. Kitts and Nevis	3.4	5.3	2.1	0.7	7.1	1.4	1.0	0.7	−2.8	−1.3	0.8	1.8	−2.9	0.2	1.3
St. Lucia	2.8	5.5	−0.2	3.3	2.8	4.2	1.5	3.5	−1.0	−1.0	3.2	2.5	−2.6	0.6	4.0
St. Vincent and the Grenadines	2.2	10.1	0.4	0.8	3.2	2.6	0.8	0.2	−1.7	−0.4	1.2	1.5	−2.1	1.0	1.3
Suriname	20.5	14.6	−0.4	6.7	17.8	5.0	1.9	3.4	6.9	67.1	30.7	4.0	25.0	76.7	9.2
Trinidad and Tobago	5.3	12.1	7.0	10.5	5.1	9.2	5.3	5.7	4.7	4.8	5.3	4.6	1.5	5.2	5.3
Uruguay	8.6	7.9	7.1	6.7	8.1	8.1	8.6	8.9	8.7	10.2	8.7	6.3	9.4	9.9	8.8
Venezuela	21.0	30.4	27.1	28.2	26.1	21.1	40.6	62.2	121.7	475.8	1,660.1	4,505.0	180.9	720.0	2,200.0
Middle East, North Africa, Afghanistan, and Pakistan	**5.8**	**11.8**	**7.3**	**6.6**	**9.2**	**9.8**	**9.1**	**6.8**	**5.8**	**5.1**	**6.0**	**4.3**	**5.1**	**6.1**	**5.8**
Afghanistan	...	26.4	−6.8	2.2	11.8	6.4	7.4	4.7	−1.5	4.5	6.0	7.0	0.1	4.7	7.2
Algeria	2.9	4.9	5.7	3.9	4.5	8.9	3.3	2.9	4.8	5.9	4.8	4.0	4.4	5.9	4.8
Bahrain	0.8	3.5	2.8	2.0	−0.4	2.8	3.3	2.7	1.8	3.6	3.0	2.4	0.7	4.4	2.5
Djibouti	2.3	12.0	1.7	4.0	5.1	3.7	2.4	2.9	2.1	3.0	3.5	3.0	1.9	3.0	3.0
Egypt	5.1	11.7	16.2	11.7	11.1	8.6	6.9	10.1	11.0	10.2	18.2	7.1	11.4	14.0	16.5
Iran	14.9	25.3	10.7	12.4	21.2	30.8	34.7	15.6	11.9	7.4	7.2	5.0	8.3	8.0	6.5
Iraq	...	2.7	−2.2	2.4	5.6	6.1	1.9	2.2	1.4	2.0	2.0	2.0	2.3	2.0	2.0
Jordan	2.7	14.0	−0.7	4.8	4.2	4.5	4.8	2.9	−0.9	−0.5	2.3	2.5	−1.6	1.2	2.5
Kuwait	2.2	6.3	4.6	4.5	4.9	3.2	2.7	2.9	3.2	3.4	3.8	3.6	3.2	3.4	3.8
Lebanon	1.7	10.8	1.2	4.0	5.0	6.6	4.8	1.9	−3.7	−0.7	2.0	2.0	−3.4	2.0	2.0
Libya	−0.7	10.4	2.4	2.5	15.9	6.1	2.6	2.8	14.1	14.2	12.5	7.3	23.3	7.4	16.9
Mauritania	6.5	7.5	2.1	6.3	5.7	4.9	4.1	3.8	0.5	1.3	4.2	5.1	−2.8	3.5	4.2
Morocco	1.8	3.9	1.0	1.0	0.9	1.3	1.9	0.4	1.5	1.3	1.3	2.0	0.6	1.2	1.3
Oman	1.0	12.6	3.5	3.3	4.0	2.9	1.2	1.0	0.1	1.1	3.1	2.8	0.1	1.1	3.1
Pakistan	5.8	12.0	19.6	10.1	13.7	11.0	7.4	8.6	4.5	2.9	5.2	5.0	3.2	4.5	5.0
Qatar	5.1	15.1	−4.9	−2.4	2.0	1.9	3.1	3.4	1.8	3.0	3.1	2.2	...	...	...
Saudi Arabia	0.4	6.1	4.1	3.8	3.7	2.9	3.5	2.7	2.2	4.0	2.0	2.0	2.3	4.0	2.0
Sudan[9]	9.4	14.3	11.3	13.0	18.3	35.4	36.5	36.9	16.9	13.5	16.1	13.7	12.6	16.5	13.7
Syria[10]	2.6	15.2	2.8	4.4	...	...	...	...	...	...	...	...	...	...	...
Tunisia	2.6	4.3	3.7	3.3	3.5	5.1	5.8	4.9	4.9	3.7	3.9	3.5	4.1	4.0	3.9
United Arab Emirates	4.5	12.3	1.6	0.9	0.9	0.7	1.1	2.3	4.1	3.6	3.1	3.6	3.8	3.6	3.1
Yemen	10.6	19.0	3.7	11.2	19.5	9.9	11.0	8.2	39.4	5.0	18.0	9.0	18.8	22.0	15.0

Table A7. Emerging Market and Developing Economies: Consumer Prices[1] *(continued)*
(Annual percent change)

	Average 1998–2007	2008	2009	2010	2011	2012	2013	2014	2015	Projections 2016	Projections 2017	Projections 2021	End of Period[2] 2015	End of Period[2] Projections 2016	End of Period[2] Projections 2017
Sub-Saharan Africa	**10.2**	**12.9**	**9.8**	**8.2**	**9.4**	**9.3**	**6.6**	**6.3**	**7.0**	**11.3**	**10.8**	**7.9**	**8.2**	**12.8**	**10.0**
Angola	93.1	12.5	13.7	14.5	13.5	10.3	8.8	7.3	10.3	33.7	38.3	17.8	14.3	48.0	32.0
Benin	2.9	7.4	0.9	2.2	2.7	6.7	1.0	−1.1	0.3	0.6	2.2	2.3	2.3	2.2	2.3
Botswana	8.1	12.6	8.1	6.9	8.5	7.5	5.9	4.4	3.0	3.2	3.5	4.5	3.1	3.3	3.6
Burkina Faso	2.1	10.7	0.9	−0.6	2.8	3.8	0.5	−0.3	0.9	1.6	2.0	2.0	1.3	1.6	2.0
Burundi	8.9	24.4	10.6	6.5	9.6	18.2	7.9	4.4	5.6	6.3	9.4	5.0	7.1	11.6	7.6
Cabo Verde	2.1	6.8	1.0	2.1	4.5	2.5	1.5	−0.2	0.1	0.1	1.3	2.0	−0.5	1.0	1.5
Cameroon	2.2	5.3	3.0	1.3	2.9	2.4	2.1	1.9	2.7	2.2	2.2	2.2	2.8	2.2	2.2
Central African Republic	1.8	9.3	3.5	1.5	1.2	5.9	6.6	11.6	4.5	4.0	3.5	3.0	4.8	4.0	3.5
Chad	1.3	8.3	10.1	−2.1	1.9	7.7	0.2	1.7	3.7	0.0	5.2	3.0	−0.3	5.0	3.0
Comoros	3.6	4.8	4.8	3.9	2.2	5.9	1.6	1.3	2.0	2.2	2.2	2.2	3.3	6.4	1.5
Democratic Republic of the Congo	79.5	18.0	46.1	23.5	14.9	0.9	0.9	1.2	1.0	1.7	2.7	3.0	0.9	2.5	3.0
Republic of Congo	2.5	6.0	4.3	5.0	1.8	5.0	4.6	0.9	2.0	4.0	3.7	3.6	2.2	4.6	3.5
Côte d'Ivoire	2.8	6.3	1.0	1.4	4.9	1.3	2.6	0.4	1.2	1.0	1.5	2.0	1.3	1.2	1.7
Equatorial Guinea	5.4	4.7	5.7	5.3	4.8	3.4	3.2	4.3	1.7	1.5	1.4	1.8	1.6	1.4	1.5
Eritrea	15.3	19.9	33.0	11.2	3.9	6.0	6.5	10.0	9.0	9.0	9.0	9.0	9.0	9.0	9.0
Ethiopia	6.6	44.4	8.5	8.1	33.2	24.1	8.1	7.4	10.1	7.7	8.2	8.2	10.0	9.7	8.0
Gabon	0.3	5.3	1.9	1.4	1.3	2.7	0.5	4.5	0.1	2.5	2.5	2.5	0.1	2.5	2.5
The Gambia	6.1	4.5	4.6	5.0	4.8	4.6	5.2	6.2	6.8	8.3	7.6	5.0	6.7	10.0	5.2
Ghana	17.9	16.5	13.1	6.7	7.7	7.1	11.7	15.5	17.2	17.0	10.0	6.0	17.7	13.5	8.0
Guinea	13.7	18.4	4.7	15.5	21.4	15.2	11.9	9.7	8.2	8.2	8.1	5.0	7.3	8.8	7.5
Guinea-Bissau	2.6	10.4	−1.6	1.1	5.1	2.1	0.8	−1.0	1.5	2.6	2.8	3.0	2.4	2.5	2.5
Kenya	5.9	15.1	10.6	4.3	14.0	9.4	5.7	6.9	6.6	6.2	5.5	5.0	8.0	5.6	5.5
Lesotho	7.2	10.7	5.9	3.4	6.0	5.5	5.0	4.0	5.3	8.6	6.0	5.0	6.0	8.5	6.0
Liberia	. . .	17.5	7.4	7.3	8.5	6.8	7.6	9.9	7.7	8.6	8.5	7.5	8.0	8.8	8.2
Madagascar	10.0	9.3	9.0	9.2	9.5	5.7	5.8	6.1	7.4	6.7	6.9	5.4	7.6	7.1	7.1
Malawi	19.5	8.7	8.4	7.4	7.6	21.3	28.3	23.8	21.9	19.8	13.9	8.1	24.9	15.2	10.2
Mali	1.7	9.1	2.2	1.3	3.1	5.3	−0.6	0.9	1.4	1.0	1.3	2.5	1.0	1.0	1.5
Mauritius	6.1	9.7	2.5	2.9	6.5	3.9	3.5	3.2	1.3	1.5	2.1	2.6	1.3	2.0	2.2
Mozambique	9.6	10.3	3.3	12.7	10.4	2.1	4.2	2.3	2.4	16.7	15.5	5.6	11.1	20.0	12.2
Namibia	7.4	9.1	9.5	4.9	5.0	6.7	5.6	5.3	3.4	6.6	6.0	5.7	3.7	7.3	6.0
Niger	1.8	11.3	4.3	−2.8	2.9	0.5	2.3	−0.9	1.0	1.6	2.0	2.0	2.2	1.6	2.2
Nigeria	11.3	11.6	12.5	13.7	10.8	12.2	8.5	8.0	9.0	15.4	17.1	13.4	9.6	18.5	17.0
Rwanda	5.9	15.4	10.3	2.3	5.7	6.3	4.2	1.8	2.5	5.3	4.9	5.0	4.5	4.7	5.0
São Tomé and Príncipe	16.2	32.0	17.0	13.3	14.3	10.6	8.1	7.0	5.3	3.9	3.5	3.0	4.0	4.0	3.0
Senegal	1.8	6.3	−2.2	1.2	3.4	1.4	0.7	−1.1	0.1	1.0	1.8	1.8	0.4	1.4	1.7
Seychelles	3.2	37.0	31.8	−2.4	2.6	7.1	4.3	1.4	4.0	−0.8	2.5	3.0	3.2	0.9	3.1
Sierra Leone	11.6	14.8	9.2	17.8	18.5	13.8	9.8	8.3	9.0	9.7	9.0	6.5	10.1	9.5	9.0
South Africa	5.4	11.5	7.1	4.3	5.0	5.7	5.8	6.1	4.6	6.4	6.0	5.5	5.2	6.7	5.5
South Sudan	. . .	. . .	. . .	. . .	. . .	45.1	0.0	1.7	52.8	476.0	110.7	20.0	109.9	583.9	38.1
Swaziland	7.0	12.7	7.4	4.5	6.1	8.9	5.6	5.7	5.0	7.0	6.1	5.8	4.9	5.5	6.6
Tanzania	6.3	10.3	12.1	7.2	12.7	16.0	7.9	6.1	5.6	5.2	5.0	5.0	6.8	5.0	5.0
Togo	1.9	8.7	3.7	1.4	3.6	2.6	1.8	0.2	1.8	2.1	2.5	2.0	1.8	2.3	2.5
Uganda	5.1	12.0	13.0	3.8	15.1	12.9	5.0	3.1	5.5	5.5	5.1	5.0	8.5	5.2	5.1
Zambia	19.7	12.4	13.4	8.5	8.7	6.6	7.0	7.8	10.1	19.1	9.1	5.0	21.1	9.5	8.7
Zimbabwe[11]	−18.5	157.0	6.2	3.0	3.5	3.7	1.6	−0.2	−2.4	−1.6	4.6	2.0	−2.5	−1.2	6.0

[1]Movements in consumer prices are shown as annual averages.
[2]Monthly year-over-year changes and, for several countries, on a quarterly basis.
[3]For many countries, inflation for the earlier years is measured on the basis of a retail price index. Consumer price index (CPI) inflation data with broader and more up-to-date coverage are typically used for more recent years.
[4]Georgia, Turkmenistan, and Ukraine, which are not members of the Commonwealth of Independent States, are included in the group for reasons of geography and similarity in economic structure.
[5]Starting in 2014 data exclude Crimea and Sevastopol.
[6]Based on Eurostat's harmonized index of consumer prices.
[7]Excludes Argentina and Venezuela.
[8]See country-specific notes for Argentina in the "Country Notes" section of the Statistical Appendix.
[9]Data for 2011 exclude South Sudan after July 9. Data for 2012 and onward pertain to the current Sudan.
[10]Data for Syria are excluded for 2011 onward owing to the uncertain political situation.
[11]The Zimbabwe dollar ceased circulating in early 2009. Data are based on IMF staff estimates of price and exchange rate developments in U.S. dollars. IMF staff estimates of U.S. dollar values may differ from authorities' estimates.

Table A8. Major Advanced Economies: General Government Fiscal Balances and Debt[1]

(Percent of GDP unless noted otherwise)

	Average 1998–2007	2010	2011	2012	2013	2014	2015	Projections 2016	2017	2021
Major Advanced Economies										
Net Lending/Borrowing	−3.2	−8.8	−7.4	−6.4	−4.4	−3.8	−3.2	−3.6	−3.3	−2.5
Output Gap[2]	0.9	−2.7	−2.2	−1.8	−1.7	−1.4	−0.8	−0.7	−0.4	−0.1
Structural Balance[2]	−3.7	−7.4	−6.5	−5.3	−3.9	−3.3	−2.8	−3.2	−3.1	−2.5
United States										
Net Lending/Borrowing[3]	−3.1	−10.9	−9.6	−7.9	−4.4	−4.2	−3.5	−4.1	−3.7	−3.7
Output Gap[2]	2.0	−3.4	−3.1	−2.2	−1.9	−1.3	−0.4	−0.5	0.0	0.1
Structural Balance[2]	−3.7	−9.6	−8.2	−6.4	−4.3	−3.9	−3.3	−3.9	−3.7	−3.7
Net Debt	41.7	69.4	75.9	79.4	80.8	80.3	79.8	82.2	82.3	84.4
Gross Debt	60.7	94.7	99.0	102.5	104.6	104.6	105.2	108.2	108.4	108.3
Euro Area										
Net Lending/Borrowing	−2.0	−6.2	−4.2	−3.7	−3.0	−2.6	−2.1	−2.0	−1.7	−0.6
Output Gap[2]	0.5	−1.5	−0.6	−1.9	−2.7	−2.5	−1.8	−1.2	−0.8	0.2
Structural Balance[2]	−2.4	−4.6	−3.8	−2.1	−1.3	−1.1	−0.9	−1.2	−1.1	−0.6
Net Debt	47.8	57.8	60.2	65.7	67.8	68.3	67.6	67.4	67.0	62.2
Gross Debt	68.1	84.1	86.7	91.3	93.3	94.3	92.5	91.7	91.0	84.2
Germany										
Net Lending/Borrowing	−2.3	−4.2	−1.0	0.0	−0.2	0.3	0.7	0.1	0.1	0.6
Output Gap[2]	−0.2	−1.3	1.0	0.4	−0.3	0.0	0.0	0.4	0.4	0.2
Structural Balance[2]	−2.4	−2.4	−1.3	−0.2	0.0	0.6	0.7	−0.1	−0.2	0.5
Net Debt	44.3	57.1	55.2	54.4	53.4	50.1	47.5	45.4	43.7	36.8
Gross Debt	61.9	81.0	78.3	79.5	77.1	74.5	71.0	68.2	65.9	56.7
France										
Net Lending/Borrowing	−2.5	−6.8	−5.1	−4.8	−4.0	−4.0	−3.5	−3.3	−3.0	−1.0
Output Gap[2]	0.3	−1.9	−0.9	−1.7	−2.2	−2.5	−2.2	−1.8	−1.5	0.2
Structural Balance[2]	−2.8	−5.6	−4.5	−3.6	−2.6	−2.4	−2.0	−2.0	−1.9	−1.1
Net Debt	53.8	73.7	76.4	81.6	84.4	87.4	88.2	89.2	89.8	85.8
Gross Debt	62.4	81.7	85.2	89.6	92.4	95.3	96.1	97.1	97.8	93.8
Italy										
Net Lending/Borrowing	−2.9	−4.2	−3.5	−2.9	−2.9	−3.0	−2.6	−2.5	−2.2	0.0
Output Gap[2]	−0.2	−1.3	−0.5	−2.8	−4.1	−4.1	−3.3	−2.5	−1.7	0.0
Structural Balance[2,4]	−3.5	−3.7	−3.9	−1.6	−0.6	−1.1	−0.8	−1.2	−1.1	0.0
Net Debt	90.0	98.3	100.4	105.0	109.9	112.5	113.3	113.8	113.9	106.7
Gross Debt	103.7	115.4	116.5	123.3	129.0	132.5	132.7	133.2	133.4	125.0
Japan										
Net Lending/Borrowing	−5.8	−9.3	−9.8	−8.8	−8.6	−6.2	−5.2	−5.2	−5.1	−3.1
Output Gap[2]	−0.7	−2.7	−3.4	−2.0	−1.1	−1.5	−1.5	−1.5	−1.3	−1.2
Structural Balance[2]	−5.6	−7.9	−8.4	−7.9	−8.3	−5.8	−4.8	−4.9	−4.8	−2.9
Net Debt	70.0	113.1	127.2	129.0	124.2	126.2	125.3	127.9	130.7	131.5
Gross Debt[5]	162.4	215.8	231.6	238.0	244.5	249.1	248.0	250.4	253.0	253.9
United Kingdom										
Net Lending/Borrowing	−1.6	−9.5	−7.6	−7.7	−5.7	−5.6	−4.2	−3.3	−2.7	−0.7
Output Gap[2]	1.0	−2.5	−2.0	−2.3	−1.7	−0.7	−0.2	−0.1	−0.4	0.0
Structural Balance[2]	−2.2	−7.4	−6.0	−6.0	−4.2	−4.9	−4.0	−3.2	−2.5	−0.7
Net Debt	34.1	68.5	72.9	76.2	77.6	79.5	80.4	80.5	80.3	73.6
Gross Debt	38.4	75.7	81.3	84.8	86.0	87.9	89.0	89.0	88.8	82.1
Canada										
Net Lending/Borrowing	1.1	−4.7	−3.3	−2.5	−1.9	−0.5	−1.3	−2.5	−2.3	−0.9
Output Gap[2]	1.3	−2.4	−1.1	−1.3	−0.9	−0.4	−0.9	−1.1	−0.6	−0.1
Structural Balance[2]	0.4	−3.4	−2.7	−1.8	−1.4	−0.5	−0.8	−1.9	−1.9	−0.8
Net Debt	38.2	26.8	27.1	28.2	29.4	28.1	26.3	26.9	25.3	17.2
Gross Debt	78.1	81.1	81.5	84.8	86.1	86.2	91.5	92.1	90.5	82.2

Note: The methodology and specific assumptions for each country are discussed in Box A1. The country group composites for fiscal data are calculated as the sum of the U.S. dollar values for the relevant individual countries.

[1]Debt data refer to the end of the year and are not always comparable across countries. Gross and net debt levels reported by national statistical agencies for countries that have adopted the System of National Accounts (SNA) 2008 (Australia, Canada, Hong Kong Special Administrative Region, United States) are adjusted to exclude unfunded pension liabilities of government employees' defined-benefit pension plans. Fiscal data for the aggregated Major Advanced Economies and the United States start in 2001, and the average for the aggregate and the United States is therefore for the period 2001–07.

[2]Percent of potential GDP.

[3]Figures reported by the national statistical agency are adjusted to exclude items related to the accrual-basis accounting of government employees' defined-benefit pension plans.

[4]Excludes one-time measures based on the authorities' data and, in the absence of the latter, receipts from the sale of assets.

[5]Includes equity shares; nonconsolidated basis.

Table A9. Summary of World Trade Volumes and Prices

(Annual percent change)

| | Averages | | 2008 | 2009 | 2010 | 2011 | 2012 | 2013 | 2014 | 2015 | Projections | |
	1998–2007	2008–17									2016	2017
Trade in Goods and Services												
World Trade[1]												
Volume	6.8	2.9	2.9	−10.5	12.4	7.0	2.8	3.5	3.8	2.6	2.3	3.8
Price Deflator												
In U.S. Dollars	2.7	−0.3	11.5	−10.4	5.6	11.1	−1.7	−0.6	−1.8	−13.2	−2.8	2.5
In SDRs	1.6	0.6	8.1	−8.2	6.7	7.4	1.3	0.1	−1.7	−5.7	−2.8	2.2
Volume of Trade												
Exports												
Advanced Economies	5.8	2.5	1.9	−11.1	12.0	5.9	2.3	3.2	3.8	3.6	1.8	3.5
Emerging Market and Developing Economies	8.8	3.7	4.8	−8.3	13.6	9.0	3.8	4.5	3.5	1.3	2.9	3.6
Imports												
Advanced Economies	6.2	2.1	0.4	−11.6	11.4	5.1	1.2	2.3	3.8	4.2	2.4	3.9
Emerging Market and Developing Economies	8.9	4.5	9.5	−8.8	14.0	11.0	5.5	5.3	4.5	−0.6	2.3	4.1
Terms of Trade												
Advanced Economies	−0.2	0.1	−2.2	2.6	−1.0	−1.5	−0.7	0.8	0.3	1.8	0.9	0.1
Emerging Market and Developing Economies	1.7	−0.1	3.8	−5.0	1.9	3.3	0.6	−0.1	−0.5	−4.1	−1.0	−0.1
Trade in Goods												
World Trade[1]												
Volume	6.9	2.8	2.5	−11.5	14.3	6.9	2.5	3.2	3.2	2.4	2.3	3.8
Price Deflator												
In U.S. Dollars	2.6	−0.5	12.4	−11.8	6.6	12.5	−1.8	−1.1	−2.5	−14.4	−3.7	2.6
In SDRs	1.5	0.4	8.9	−9.7	7.7	8.7	1.2	−0.4	−2.4	−7.1	−3.6	2.3
World Trade Prices in U.S. Dollars[2]												
Manufactures	1.5	0.4	6.2	−5.3	2.6	6.4	0.9	−1.5	−1.0	−2.9	−2.1	1.4
Oil	14.0	−3.3	36.4	−36.3	27.9	31.6	1.0	−0.9	−7.5	−47.2	−15.4	17.9
Nonfuel Primary Commodities	3.9	−0.7	7.9	−16.0	26.6	18.0	−10.0	−1.4	−4.0	−17.5	−2.7	0.9
Food	2.1	1.2	24.3	−15.2	12.1	20.2	−2.4	0.7	−4.1	−17.1	1.9	−0.3
Beverages	−0.6	3.4	23.3	1.6	14.1	16.6	−18.6	−11.9	20.7	−3.1	−3.3	3.7
Agricultural Raw Materials	0.2	−0.1	−0.7	−17.1	33.2	22.7	−12.7	1.6	1.9	−13.5	−7.6	1.9
Metal	10.4	−4.3	−7.8	−19.2	48.2	13.5	−16.8	−4.3	−10.3	−23.1	−7.5	1.7
World Trade Prices in SDRs[2]												
Manufactures	0.4	1.3	2.9	−3.0	3.7	2.8	4.0	−0.7	−0.9	5.4	−2.0	1.1
Oil	12.7	−2.5	32.2	−34.8	29.3	27.2	4.1	−0.1	−7.5	−42.7	−15.4	17.5
Nonfuel Primary Commodities	2.8	0.2	4.6	−13.9	28.0	14.0	−7.3	−0.6	−3.9	−10.4	−2.7	0.5
Food	1.0	2.1	20.5	−13.1	13.3	16.1	0.6	1.5	−4.1	−10.0	2.0	−0.6
Beverages	−1.6	4.3	19.5	4.1	15.3	12.7	−16.1	−11.2	20.8	5.2	−3.3	3.3
Agricultural Raw Materials	−0.8	0.8	−3.8	−15.1	34.6	18.6	−10.0	2.4	2.0	−6.1	−7.5	1.6
Metal	9.3	−3.4	−10.7	−17.2	49.8	9.7	−14.3	−3.5	−10.2	−16.6	−7.5	1.4
World Trade Prices in Euros[2]												
Manufactures	−0.5	2.4	−1.1	0.1	7.7	1.4	9.2	−4.7	−1.0	16.3	−2.7	0.4
Oil	11.8	−1.4	27.1	−32.7	34.3	25.5	9.3	−4.1	−7.6	−36.8	−16.0	16.8
Nonfuel Primary Commodities	1.9	1.3	0.5	−11.2	32.9	12.5	−2.6	−4.5	−4.0	−1.2	−3.4	−0.1
Food	0.2	3.2	15.8	−10.4	17.7	14.6	5.6	−2.5	−4.2	−0.7	1.3	−1.2
Beverages	−2.4	5.5	14.8	7.3	19.8	11.2	−11.9	−14.7	20.7	16.1	−3.9	2.7
Agricultural Raw Materials	−1.7	1.9	−7.5	−12.5	39.8	17.0	−5.5	−1.6	1.8	3.6	−8.2	0.9
Metal	8.4	−2.4	−14.1	−14.6	55.5	8.3	−10.0	−7.3	−10.3	−7.9	−8.1	0.8

Table A9. Summary of World Trade Volumes and Prices *(continued)*
(Annual percent change)

	Averages										Projections	
	1998–2007	2008–17	2008	2009	2010	2011	2012	2013	2014	2015	2016	2017
Trade in Goods												
Volume of Trade												
Exports												
Advanced Economies	5.9	2.4	1.6	−13.0	14.7	6.0	1.9	2.6	3.4	3.4	1.7	3.5
Emerging Market and Developing Economies	9.1	3.6	4.1	−8.8	15.0	8.1	4.2	4.3	2.8	1.1	3.0	3.4
Fuel Exporters	5.2	2.0	4.2	−7.9	5.5	7.7	3.7	1.3	−0.2	1.7	2.7	2.2
Nonfuel Exporters	10.6	4.2	4.1	−9.2	18.9	8.3	4.4	5.8	4.1	0.9	3.1	3.7
Imports												
Advanced Economies	6.3	2.0	−0.3	−12.8	13.0	5.3	0.4	1.9	3.5	3.9	2.4	4.1
Emerging Market and Developing Economies	8.9	4.3	8.9	−9.0	15.1	10.3	5.3	5.0	2.8	−0.2	2.5	3.9
Fuel Exporters	9.6	2.3	14.3	−13.0	6.5	8.6	9.9	4.8	1.5	−8.1	−2.6	4.4
Nonfuel Exporters	8.8	4.7	7.4	−8.1	17.4	10.7	4.3	5.0	3.1	1.7	3.6	3.8
Price Deflators in SDRs												
Exports												
Advanced Economies	0.8	0.0	5.8	−7.4	4.4	6.4	−0.3	0.5	−1.9	−6.4	−2.0	2.0
Emerging Market and Developing Economies	4.0	1.0	14.6	−12.8	12.9	12.4	2.8	−0.9	−3.2	−8.8	−5.7	3.0
Fuel Exporters	9.1	−0.7	24.7	−24.6	22.5	23.0	3.6	−1.9	−7.0	−28.6	−11.1	10.1
Nonfuel Exporters	2.0	1.5	10.1	−6.9	8.9	8.1	2.4	−0.5	−1.6	−0.9	−4.1	1.1
Imports												
Advanced Economies	1.1	0.0	8.6	−10.7	6.4	8.6	1.0	−0.4	−2.0	−8.0	−3.2	1.8
Emerging Market and Developing Economies	2.4	1.1	10.0	−8.4	11.1	9.0	2.2	−0.9	−2.9	−4.9	−4.7	2.9
Fuel Exporters	2.0	1.6	8.4	−5.5	9.3	9.9	1.9	−1.2	−2.8	−1.9	−2.8	1.8
Nonfuel Exporters	2.4	1.0	10.5	−9.1	11.5	8.8	2.3	−0.9	−2.9	−5.7	−5.2	3.1
Terms of Trade												
Advanced Economies	−0.3	0.0	−2.6	3.7	−1.8	−2.0	−1.3	0.8	0.1	1.8	1.2	0.2
Emerging Market and Developing Economies	1.6	−0.1	4.1	−4.8	1.6	3.1	0.6	0.0	−0.3	−4.0	−1.0	0.1
Regional Groups												
Commonwealth of Independent States[3]	5.3	−1.0	15.5	−16.7	11.7	6.7	1.9	−1.3	−0.5	−20.1	−7.4	6.5
Emerging and Developing Asia	−1.8	0.5	−1.4	3.3	−6.5	−2.5	1.2	1.1	2.6	9.1	1.5	−2.4
Emerging and Developing Europe	0.0	−0.2	−0.5	3.4	−3.9	−1.8	−1.1	1.9	1.0	2.4	0.5	−3.2
Latin America and the Caribbean	2.8	−0.5	4.7	−4.8	8.5	5.4	−1.3	−1.5	−2.7	−10.0	−1.2	−0.3
Middle East, North Africa, Afghanistan, and Pakistan	6.1	−2.3	11.4	−17.6	8.3	12.9	0.3	−0.7	−4.8	−25.7	−6.3	7.2
Middle East and North Africa	6.4	−2.4	12.0	−18.0	8.2	13.0	0.9	−0.7	−4.9	−26.5	−7.0	7.3
Sub-Saharan Africa	3.0	−0.1	8.9	−10.4	12.5	11.0	−1.3	−0.8	−3.6	−14.7	−2.1	3.6
Analytical Groups												
By Source of Export Earnings												
Fuel	6.9	−2.2	15.0	−20.2	12.1	11.9	1.6	−0.7	−4.3	−27.2	−8.6	8.
Nonfuel	−0.4	0.5	−0.4	2.4	−2.4	−0.7	0.1	0.4	1.4	5.1	1.1	−2.
Memorandum												
World Exports in Billions of U.S. Dollars												
Goods and Services	10,172	20,916	19,585	15,722	18,668	22,210	22,442	23,154	23,574	20,920	20,800	22,08.
Goods	8,084	16,476	15,669	12,222	14,891	17,896	18,031	18,458	18,551	16,166	15,937	16,94
Average Oil Price[4]	14.0	−3.3	36.4	−36.3	27.9	31.6	1.0	−0.9	−7.5	−47.2	−15.4	17.
In U.S. Dollars a Barrel	36.40	79.16	97.04	61.78	79.03	104.01	105.01	104.07	96.25	50.79	42.96	50.6
Export Unit Value of Manufactures[5]	1.5	0.4	6.2	−5.3	2.6	6.4	0.9	−1.5	−1.0	−2.9	−2.1	1.

[1]Average of annual percent change for world exports and imports.

[2]As represented, respectively, by the export unit value index for manufactures of the advanced economies and accounting for 83 percent of the advanced economies' trade (export of goods) wei the average of U.K. Brent, Dubai Fateh, and West Texas Intermediate crude oil prices; and the average of world market prices for nonfuel primary commodities weighted by their 2002–04 shares world commodity exports.

[3]Georgia, Turkmenistan, and Ukraine, which are not members of the Commonwealth of Independent States, are included in this group for reasons of geography and similarity in economic struc

[4]Percent change of average of U.K. Brent, Dubai Fateh, and West Texas Intermediate crude oil prices.

[5]Percent change for manufactures exported by the advanced economies.

Table A10. Summary of Current Account Balances

(Billions of U.S. dollars)

	2008	2009	2010	2011	2012	2013	2014	2015	Projections 2016	Projections 2017	Projections 2021
Advanced Economies	**−586.5**	**−87.9**	**0.8**	**−49.0**	**5.9**	**220.9**	**225.0**	**286.9**	**317.5**	**282.6**	**219.2**
United States	−690.8	−384.0	−442.0	−460.4	−446.5	−366.4	−392.1	−463.0	−469.4	−518.5	−612.4
Euro Area	−155.6	24.1	47.9	55.6	165.2	285.8	334.0	365.7	403.0	382.5	394.3
Germany	210.9	196.7	192.3	229.0	248.9	252.9	282.9	284.2	301.4	291.7	297.1
France	−27.6	−22.5	−22.2	−28.3	−32.7	−24.6	−30.3	−4.8	−11.5	−9.7	10.0
Italy	−68.8	−42.5	−72.7	−68.6	−7.5	20.2	41.1	39.9	40.2	35.5	18.3
Spain	−152.0	−64.3	−56.2	−47.4	−3.1	20.7	13.6	16.7	24.3	22.5	27.6
Japan	142.6	145.3	221.0	129.8	59.7	45.9	36.5	135.6	176.1	171.0	185.0
United Kingdom	−101.9	−70.1	−66.6	−46.6	−97.4	−119.6	−140.0	−153.3	−157.3	−112.3	−115.4
Canada	1.5	−40.4	−58.2	−49.6	−65.7	−57.9	−40.6	−49.0	−56.7	−50.1	−48.8
Other Advanced Economies[1]	165.3	210.1	284.9	267.3	276.9	351.0	364.1	372.7	355.8	341.7	338.7
Emerging Market and Developing Economies	**673.9**	**237.7**	**277.5**	**374.9**	**360.7**	**188.5**	**194.8**	**−39.5**	**−78.9**	**−138.3**	**−253.3**
Regional Groups											
Commonwealth of Independent States[2]	108.4	43.0	69.4	108.4	67.5	18.4	56.1	55.0	22.2	36.1	88.1
Russia	103.9	50.4	67.5	97.3	71.3	33.4	57.5	69.0	38.6	50.0	79.9
Excluding Russia	4.4	−7.4	1.9	11.1	−3.7	−15.0	−1.5	−14.0	−16.3	−13.9	8.2
Emerging and Developing Asia	424.4	272.9	231.9	97.1	121.8	99.2	270.6	333.1	253.5	149.9	25.7
China	420.6	243.3	237.8	136.1	215.4	148.2	277.4	330.6	270.9	200.5	138.3
India	−27.9	−38.4	−48.1	−78.2	−87.8	−32.3	−26.8	−22.1	−32.0	−49.2	−79.4
ASEAN-5[3]	29.9	64.6	43.9	48.9	6.5	−3.9	23.0	31.5	26.4	17.3	−9.8
Emerging and Developing Europe	−148.9	−53.9	−86.9	−119.7	−82.0	−72.3	−58.9	−31.9	−33.8	−52.7	−84.0
Latin America and the Caribbean	−42.0	−33.4	−96.6	−115.0	−137.1	−165.8	−187.6	−182.1	−114.0	−125.4	−153.2
Brazil	−30.6	−26.3	−75.8	−77.0	−74.2	−74.8	−104.2	−58.9	−14.1	−25.9	−25.8
Mexico	−20.4	−8.7	−5.2	−14.0	−17.0	−31.0	−26.2	−32.7	−29.0	−31.0	−38.3
Middle East, North Africa, Afghanistan, and Pakistan	328.5	37.5	168.7	411.3	414.1	342.4	176.3	−125.4	−144.0	−88.8	−45.4
Sub-Saharan Africa	3.5	−28.4	−8.8	−7.2	−23.7	−33.5	−61.7	−88.2	−62.8	−57.4	−84.5
South Africa	−15.9	−8.1	−5.6	−9.2	−20.3	−21.6	−18.6	−13.7	−9.4	−9.2	−12.2
Analytical Groups											
By Source of Export Earnings											
Fuel	580.8	132.4	304.6	613.3	589.6	458.2	273.9	−96.7	−110.2	−29.9	74.8
Nonfuel	93.8	106.9	−25.3	−238.5	−228.9	−269.8	−79.0	57.2	31.3	−108.4	−328.1
Of Which, Primary Products	−20.7	−4.8	−11.7	−26.8	−57.2	−67.4	−44.3	−52.1	−42.8	−49.8	−77.2
By External Financing Source											
Net Debtor Economies	−318.5	−179.1	−273.5	−370.0	−415.5	−388.9	−369.4	−312.4	−257.3	−313.5	−429.2
Net Debtor Economies by Debt-Servicing Experience											
Economies with Arrears and/or Rescheduling during 2011–15	−20.4	−21.7	−15.6	−25.5	−39.3	−39.1	−23.3	−31.5	−37.2	−31.6	−31.0
Memorandum											
World	**87.4**	**149.8**	**278.3**	**325.9**	**366.6**	**409.4**	**419.9**	**247.4**	**238.6**	**144.3**	**−34.1**
European Union	−249.8	−21.5	−0.5	74.1	202.1	299.5	302.4	344.3	364.7	385.5	378.4
Low-Income Developing Countries	−10.5	−24.8	−19.2	−28.2	−33.7	−39.5	−49.0	−82.6	−67.4	−67.7	−103.7
Middle East and North Africa	342.1	45.2	171.5	410.0	417.6	343.2	178.9	−123.7	−142.3	−84.3	−40.8

Table A10. Summary of Current Account Balances *(continued)*

(Percent of GDP)

	2008	2009	2010	2011	2012	2013	2014	2015	Projections		
									2016	2017	2021
Advanced Economies	**−1.3**	**−0.2**	**0.0**	**−0.1**	**0.0**	**0.5**	**0.5**	**0.6**	**0.7**	**0.6**	**0.4**
United States	−4.7	−2.7	−3.0	−3.0	−2.8	−2.2	−2.3	−2.6	−2.5	−2.7	−2.7
Euro Area	−1.1	0.2	0.4	0.4	1.3	2.2	2.5	3.2	3.4	3.1	2.8
Germany	5.6	5.7	5.6	6.1	7.0	6.7	7.3	8.4	8.6	8.1	7.2
France	−0.9	−0.8	−0.8	−1.0	−1.2	−0.9	−1.1	−0.2	−0.5	−0.4	0.3
Italy	−2.9	−1.9	−3.4	−3.0	−0.4	0.9	1.9	2.2	2.2	1.9	0.9
Spain	−9.3	−4.3	−3.9	−3.2	−0.2	1.5	1.0	1.4	1.9	1.7	1.8
Japan	2.9	2.9	4.0	2.2	1.0	0.9	0.8	3.3	3.7	3.3	3.3
United Kingdom	−3.5	−3.0	−2.7	−1.8	−3.7	−4.4	−4.7	−5.4	−5.9	−4.3	−3.8
Canada	0.1	−2.9	−3.6	−2.8	−3.6	−3.2	−2.3	−3.2	−3.7	−3.1	−2.5
Other Advanced Economies[1]	3.1	4.2	5.0	4.1	4.2	5.2	5.3	5.9	5.6	5.1	4.3
Emerging Market and Developing											
Economies	**3.4**	**1.3**	**1.2**	**1.4**	**1.3**	**0.6**	**0.6**	**−0.1**	**−0.3**	**−0.4**	**−0.6**
Regional Groups											
Commonwealth of Independent States[2]	4.7	2.5	3.3	4.1	2.4	0.6	2.1	3.0	1.3	1.9	3.6
Russia	5.8	3.8	4.1	4.8	3.3	1.5	2.8	5.2	3.0	3.5	4.5
Excluding Russia	0.9	−1.8	0.4	1.8	−0.6	−2.1	−0.2	−2.6	−3.7	−2.9	1.3
Emerging and Developing Asia	5.7	3.4	2.4	0.8	1.0	0.7	1.8	2.1	1.6	0.8	0.1
China	9.1	4.7	3.9	1.8	2.5	1.5	2.6	3.0	2.4	1.6	0.8
India	−2.3	−2.8	−2.8	−4.3	−4.8	−1.7	−1.3	−1.1	−1.4	−2.0	−2.2
ASEAN-5[3]	2.2	4.8	2.6	2.5	0.3	−0.2	1.1	1.5	1.2	0.7	−0.3
Emerging and Developing Europe	−8.0	−3.5	−5.1	−6.5	−4.6	−3.8	−3.1	−1.9	−2.0	−3.0	−3.8
Latin America and the Caribbean	−1.0	−0.8	−1.9	−2.0	−2.3	−2.8	−3.2	−3.6	−2.3	−2.3	−2.3
Brazil	−1.8	−1.6	−3.4	−2.9	−3.0	−3.0	−4.3	−3.3	−0.8	−1.3	−1.1
Mexico	−1.9	−1.0	−0.5	−1.2	−1.4	−2.5	−2.0	−2.9	−2.7	−2.8	−2.7
Middle East, North Africa, Afghanistan,											
and Pakistan	12.4	1.6	6.1	12.7	12.5	10.1	5.1	−4.0	−4.6	−2.6	−1.0
Sub-Saharan Africa	0.3	−2.6	−0.7	−0.5	−1.5	−2.1	−3.7	−5.9	−4.5	−3.9	−4.6
South Africa	−5.5	−2.7	−1.5	−2.2	−5.1	−5.9	−5.3	−4.3	−3.3	−3.2	−3.6
Analytical Groups											
By Source of Export Earnings											
Fuel	11.4	3.2	6.0	9.9	9.0	6.9	4.2	−1.9	−2.2	−0.6	1.1
Nonfuel	0.6	0.7	−0.1	−1.2	−1.1	−1.2	−0.3	0.2	0.1	−0.4	−0.9
Of Which, Primary Products	−1.9	−0.4	−0.9	−1.7	−3.5	−4.0	−2.7	−3.2	−2.8	−3.0	−3.4
By External Financing Source											
Net Debtor Economies	−3.2	−1.9	−2.4	−2.9	−3.2	−2.9	−2.7	−2.5	−2.0	−2.3	−2.4
Net Debtor Economies by											
Debt-Servicing Experience											
Economies with Arrears and/or											
Rescheduling during 2011–15	−3.7	−4.2	−2.7	−3.9	−5.6	−5.3	−3.2	−4.4	−5.1	−4.5	−3.2
Memorandum											
World	**0.1**	**0.2**	**0.4**	**0.4**	**0.5**	**0.5**	**0.5**	**0.3**	**0.3**	**0.2**	**0.0**
European Union	−1.3	−0.1	0.0	0.4	1.2	1.7	1.6	2.1	2.2	2.3	1.9
Low-Income Developing Countries	−0.9	−2.2	−1.5	−1.9	−2.1	−2.2	−2.5	−4.4	−3.6	−3.4	−3.8
Middle East and North Africa	13.9	2.1	6.7	13.7	13.6	10.9	5.6	−4.4	−5.0	−2.8	−1.0

Table A10. Summary of Current Account Balances *(continued)*
(Percent of exports of goods and services)

	2008	2009	2010	2011	2012	2013	2014	2015	Projections 2016	Projections 2017	Projections 2021
Advanced Economies	**−4.5**	**−0.8**	**0.0**	**−0.3**	**0.0**	**1.5**	**1.5**	**2.2**	**2.4**	**2.0**	**1.3**
United States	−37.5	−24.3	−23.8	−21.6	−20.1	−16.0	−16.5	−20.5	−21.2	−21.6	−19.5
Euro Area	−5.0	1.0	1.7	1.7	5.1	8.4	9.4	11.4	. . .	. . .	. . .
Germany	12.9	15.2	13.3	13.6	15.3	14.8	16.0	18.1	18.6	17.3	14.4
France	−3.3	−3.4	−3.1	−3.4	−4.1	−2.9	−3.5	−0.6	−1.5	−1.2	1.0
Italy	−10.6	−8.6	−13.5	−11.1	−1.3	3.3	6.5	7.3	7.1	6.0	2.5
Spain	−36.5	−18.9	−15.3	−11.0	−0.8	4.7	3.0	4.2	5.8	5.0	4.8
Japan	16.0	21.7	25.4	13.9	6.5	5.5	4.2	17.3	22.2	20.9	19.8
United Kingdom	−13.1	−11.2	−9.7	−5.9	−12.3	−14.8	−16.6	−19.6	−21.4	−14.8	−13.3
Canada	0.3	−10.4	−12.4	−9.1	−11.9	−10.4	−7.2	−10.0	−12.1	−10.0	−8.1
Other Advanced Economies[1]	5.1	7.9	8.7	6.9	7.1	8.6	9.0	10.3	10.0	9.1	7.5
Emerging Market and Developing											
Economies	**9.5**	**4.3**	**4.0**	**4.5**	**3.9**	**2.0**	**2.3**	**−0.3**	**−0.8**	**−1.5**	**−2.3**
Regional Groups											
Commonwealth of Independent States[2]	13.7	8.2	10.4	12.3	7.4	2.0	6.7	9.4	4.3	6.2	12.4
Russia	19.9	14.7	15.3	17.0	12.1	5.6	10.2	17.5	11.2	13.0	17.5
Excluding Russia	1.7	−4.1	0.8	3.6	−1.2	−4.9	−0.5	−7.2	−9.2	−7.2	3.3
Emerging and Developing Asia	16.5	12.4	8.3	2.8	3.3	2.6	6.6	8.6	6.6	3.7	0.5
China	28.1	19.5	14.8	6.8	9.9	6.3	11.0	13.6	11.4	8.2	4.8
India	−9.5	−13.8	−12.6	−17.3	−19.4	−6.9	−5.6	−5.3	−7.3	−10.1	−11.1
ASEAN-5[3]	4.2	10.7	5.9	5.5	0.7	−0.4	2.4	3.5	2.9	1.8	−0.8
Emerging and Developing Europe	−22.8	−10.3	−14.8	−17.3	−11.9	−9.7	−7.5	−4.5	−4.6	−6.8	−8.7
Latin America and the Caribbean	−4.2	−4.2	−9.7	−9.4	−11.0	−13.3	−15.4	−17.2	−11.0	−11.3	−11.0
Brazil	−13.5	−14.6	−32.7	−26.3	−26.4	−26.8	−39.5	−26.3	−6.1	−10.7	−9.3
Mexico	−6.6	−3.6	−1.7	−3.8	−4.4	−7.7	−6.3	−8.1	−7.4	−7.4	−6.8
Middle East, North Africa, Afghanistan, and											
Pakistan	23.0	3.0	13.4	26.9	24.5	20.9	12.6	−9.9	−11.8	−5.9	−1.8
Sub-Saharan Africa	0.9	−9.4	−2.3	−1.5	−4.9	−6.9	−13.4	−25.3	−19.0	−15.5	−18.0
South Africa	−15.5	−9.8	−5.2	−7.3	−17.3	−19.0	−17.0	−14.1	−9.6	−9.0	−10.6
Analytical Groups											
By Source of Export Earnings											
Fuel	25.9	8.5	15.8	24.5	21.7	17.4	11.8	−4.8	−6.0	−0.6	4.5
Nonfuel	2.1	2.8	−0.5	−4.1	−3.8	−4.3	−1.2	1.0	0.5	−1.7	−4.1
Of Which, Primary Products	−5.9	−1.6	−3.1	−6.0	−13.6	−16.0	−10.9	−14.9	−12.3	−13.5	−17.1
By External Financing Source											
Net Debtor Economies	−10.8	−7.4	−9.1	−10.2	−11.2	−10.2	−9.6	−9.2	−7.5	−8.5	−8.8
Net Debtor Economies by											
Debt-Servicing Experience											
Economies with Arrears and/or											
Rescheduling during 2011–15	−10.3	−14.9	−8.8	−12.3	−19.3	−19.3	−12.7	−21.0	−27.6	−20.7	−14.9
Memorandum											
World	**0.3**	**0.9**	**1.4**	**1.4**	**1.5**	**1.7**	**1.8**	**1.3**	**1.2**	**0.7**	**−0.1**
European Union	−3.3	−0.4	0.0	1.0	2.7	3.9	3.8	4.8	5.0	5.0	4.0
Low-Income Developing Countries	−2.9	−8.3	−5.0	−5.8	−6.8	−7.3	−8.9	−16.7	−13.3	−11.9	−12.3
Middle East and North Africa	24.6	3.9	14.0	27.4	25.2	21.4	13.1	−10.0	−12.0	−5.7	−1.6

[1]Excludes the G7 (Canada, France, Germany, Italy, Japan, United Kingdom, United States) and euro area countries.
[2]Georgia, Turkmenistan, and Ukraine, which are not members of the Commonwealth of Independent States, are included in this group for reasons of geography and similarity in economic structure.
[3]Indonesia, Malaysia, Philippines, Thailand, Vietnam.

Table A11. Advanced Economies: Balance on Current Account

(Percent of GDP)

	2008	2009	2010	2011	2012	2013	2014	2015	Projections 2016	Projections 2017	Projections 2021
Advanced Economies	**−1.3**	**−0.2**	**0.0**	**−0.1**	**0.0**	**0.5**	**0.5**	**0.6**	**0.7**	**0.6**	**0.4**
United States	−4.7	−2.7	−3.0	−3.0	−2.8	−2.2	−2.3	−2.6	−2.5	−2.7	−2.7
Euro Area[1]	−1.1	0.2	0.4	0.4	1.3	2.2	2.5	3.2	3.4	3.1	2.8
Germany	5.6	5.7	5.6	6.1	7.0	6.7	7.3	8.4	8.6	8.1	7.2
France	−0.9	−0.8	−0.8	−1.0	−1.2	−0.9	−1.1	−0.2	−0.5	−0.4	0.3
Italy	−2.9	−1.9	−3.4	−3.0	−0.4	0.9	1.9	2.2	2.2	1.9	0.9
Spain	−9.3	−4.3	−3.9	−3.2	−0.2	1.5	1.0	1.4	1.9	1.7	1.8
Netherlands	4.1	5.8	7.4	9.1	10.8	9.8	8.9	8.6	9.1	8.2	6.9
Belgium	−1.0	−1.1	1.8	−1.1	−0.1	−0.2	−0.2	0.0	0.1	0.4	1.5
Austria	4.5	2.6	2.9	1.6	1.5	1.9	1.9	2.6	2.6	2.7	2.3
Greece	−15.1	−12.3	−11.4	−10.0	−3.8	−2.0	−2.1	0.0	0.0	0.0	0.0
Portugal	−12.1	−10.4	−10.1	−6.0	−1.8	1.5	0.1	0.4	0.0	−0.7	−1.6
Ireland	−6.3	−4.7	−1.2	−1.6	−2.6	2.1	1.7	10.2	9.5	9.1	8.6
Finland	2.2	1.9	1.2	−1.8	−1.9	−1.6	−0.9	0.1	0.1	0.2	0.2
Slovak Republic	−6.4	−3.5	−4.7	−5.0	0.9	2.0	0.1	−1.3	−1.0	−0.6	2.1
Lithuania	−13.3	2.1	−0.3	−3.9	−1.2	1.5	3.6	−1.7	−1.6	−2.8	−2.7
Slovenia	−5.3	−0.6	−0.1	0.2	2.6	4.8	6.2	5.2	7.7	7.2	3.7
Luxembourg	7.7	7.4	6.8	6.2	6.1	5.7	5.5	5.5	4.4	4.3	4.4
Latvia	−12.4	8.1	2.3	−2.8	−3.3	−2.4	−2.0	−1.2	−2.0	−1.2	−1.3
Estonia	−8.7	2.5	1.8	1.3	−2.4	−0.1	1.0	2.1	0.6	0.0	−2.4
Cyprus	−15.6	−7.7	−10.7	−4.0	−5.6	−4.5	−4.6	−3.6	−0.9	−3.7	−4.3
Malta	−1.1	−6.6	−4.7	−2.5	1.3	3.6	3.4	9.9	6.2	5.8	5.2
Japan	2.9	2.9	4.0	2.2	1.0	0.9	0.8	3.3	3.7	3.3	3.3
United Kingdom	−3.5	−3.0	−2.7	−1.8	−3.7	−4.4	−4.7	−5.4	−5.9	−4.3	−3.8
Korea	0.3	3.7	2.6	1.6	4.2	6.2	6.0	7.7	7.2	5.9	5.2
Canada	0.1	−2.9	−3.6	−2.8	−3.6	−3.2	−2.3	−3.2	−3.7	−3.1	−2.5
Australia	−4.9	−4.6	−3.6	−2.9	−4.2	−3.4	−2.9	−4.7	−3.5	−3.9	−4.0
Taiwan Province of China	6.6	10.9	8.9	8.2	9.5	10.4	12.0	14.6	15.0	14.4	13.9
Switzerland	3.0	8.0	14.9	7.7	10.3	11.1	8.8	11.4	9.2	9.0	8.5
Sweden	7.8	6.0	6.0	5.5	5.6	5.3	4.6	5.2	5.0	5.3	4.3
Singapore	14.6	17.0	23.8	22.8	18.1	17.9	17.5	19.8	19.3	19.3	15.7
Hong Kong SAR	15.0	9.9	7.0	5.6	1.6	1.5	1.3	3.1	2.8	2.9	3.4
Norway	15.7	10.6	10.9	12.4	12.4	10.2	11.9	9.0	7.0	7.6	7.2
Czech Republic	−1.9	−2.3	−3.6	−2.1	−1.6	−0.5	0.2	0.9	1.5	1.0	−0.8
Israel	1.0	3.5	3.6	2.3	0.5	3.6	4.0	4.6	3.1	2.9	2.0
Denmark	2.7	3.3	5.7	5.7	5.7	7.1	7.7	7.0	6.7	6.6	5.9
New Zealand	−7.8	−2.2	−2.3	−2.8	−3.9	−3.2	−3.1	−3.2	−3.0	−3.5	−4.1
Puerto Rico	. . .	. . .	. . .	. . .	. . .	. . .	. . .	. . .	. . .	. . .	. . .
Macao SAR	16.0	28.2	39.4	41.0	39.3	40.2	34.4	28.0	28.4	29.2	30.4
Iceland	−22.8	−9.7	−6.6	−5.3	−4.2	5.7	3.7	4.2	2.9	1.9	1.1
San Marino	. . .	. . .	. . .	. . .	. . .	. . .	. . .		. . .	. . .	. . .
Memorandum											
Major Advanced Economies	−1.6	−0.7	−0.8	−0.8	−1.0	−0.7	−0.7	−0.6	−0.5	−0.5	−0.6
Euro Area[2]	−0.7	0.4	0.5	0.8	2.2	2.8	3.0	3.8	3.9	3.6	3.3

[1]Data corrected for reporting discrepancies in intra-area transactions.
[2]Data calculated as the sum of the balances of individual euro area countries.

Table A12. Emerging Market and Developing Economies: Balance on Current Account
(Percent of GDP)

	2008	2009	2010	2011	2012	2013	2014	2015	Projections 2016	2017	2021
Commonwealth of Independent States[1]	**4.7**	**2.5**	**3.3**	**4.1**	**2.4**	**0.6**	**2.1**	**3.0**	**1.3**	**1.9**	**3.6**
Russia	5.8	3.8	4.1	4.8	3.3	1.5	2.8	5.2	3.0	3.5	4.5
Excluding Russia	0.9	−1.8	0.4	1.8	−0.6	−2.1	−0.2	−2.6	−3.7	−2.9	1.3
Armenia	−14.2	−16.5	−13.6	−10.4	−10.0	−7.3	−7.6	−2.7	−2.5	−3.0	−4.7
Azerbaijan	35.5	23.0	28.0	26.5	20.2	16.4	13.9	−0.4	0.7	3.1	11.3
Belarus	−8.2	−12.6	−15.0	−8.5	−2.9	−10.4	−6.9	−3.8	−4.9	−4.8	−3.3
Georgia	−22.0	−10.5	−10.2	−12.8	−11.7	−5.8	−10.6	−11.7	−12.1	−12.0	−8.6
Kazakhstan	4.7	−3.6	0.9	5.1	0.5	0.4	2.6	−2.4	−2.2	0.0	3.9
Kyrgyz Republic	−14.3	0.9	−2.2	−2.9	3.7	−1.1	−17.8	−10.4	−15.0	−14.9	−9.5
Moldova	−16.1	−8.2	−7.5	−10.7	−7.5	−5.1	−3.8	−4.7	−2.8	−3.4	−4.5
Tajikistan	−7.7	−5.9	−1.1	−4.8	−2.5	−2.9	−2.8	−6.0	−5.0	−5.0	−3.5
Turkmenistan	16.5	−14.7	−10.6	2.0	0.0	−7.2	−7.5	−10.3	−18.5	−18.0	6.7
Ukraine[2]	−6.8	−1.4	−2.2	−6.3	−8.1	−9.2	−3.9	−0.3	−1.5	−2.1	−2.2
Uzbekistan	8.7	2.2	6.2	5.8	1.8	2.9	0.7	0.1	0.1	0.2	0.5
Emerging and Developing Asia	**5.7**	**3.4**	**2.4**	**0.8**	**1.0**	**0.7**	**1.8**	**2.1**	**1.6**	**0.8**	**0.1**
Bangladesh	1.2	2.4	0.4	−1.0	0.7	1.2	0.9	0.7	−0.1	−0.7	−2.0
Bhutan	−8.6	−6.3	−22.2	−29.8	−21.5	−25.4	−26.4	−28.8	−27.8	−31.5	−5.3
Brunei Darussalam	43.4	32.3	36.6	34.7	29.8	20.9	31.9	12.0	4.3	−4.1	15.1
Cambodia	−6.6	−6.9	−6.8	−10.2	−11.0	−12.3	−12.1	−10.6	−10.2	−9.4	−8.6
China	9.1	4.7	3.9	1.8	2.5	1.5	2.6	3.0	2.4	1.6	0.8
Fiji	−15.1	−4.2	−4.5	−5.1	−1.3	−9.8	−7.5	−5.4	−7.2	−7.0	−5.7
India	−2.3	−2.8	−2.8	−4.3	−4.8	−1.7	−1.3	−1.1	−1.4	−2.0	−2.2
Indonesia	0.0	1.8	0.7	0.2	−2.7	−3.2	−3.1	−2.1	−2.3	−2.3	−2.3
Kiribati	−6.4	−13.3	−2.2	−13.4	−4.5	8.2	24.0	44.9	−7.2	−2.5	2.2
Lao P.D.R.	−19.3	−22.0	−18.8	−18.4	−29.3	−28.9	−22.8	−23.1	−18.0	−17.6	−13.7
Malaysia	16.5	15.0	10.1	10.9	5.2	3.5	4.4	3.0	1.2	1.5	1.5
Maldives	−28.9	−10.5	−8.2	−16.5	−7.3	−4.5	−3.9	−9.5	−11.9	−14.1	−9.8
Marshall Islands	0.5	−14.2	−26.5	1.0	−3.4	−9.9	−4.4	−3.2	−7.6	−9.4	−11.2
Micronesia	−16.5	−18.8	−15.0	−17.8	−12.6	−10.0	6.8	1.0	−0.1	−0.7	−2.9
Mongolia	−8.9	−6.9	−13.0	−26.5	−27.4	−25.4	−11.5	−4.8	−11.1	−19.2	−9.9
Myanmar	−4.2	−1.2	−1.1	−1.8	−4.0	−4.9	−5.6	−7.8	−8.3	−8.1	−5.7
Nepal	2.7	4.2	−2.4	−1.0	4.8	3.3	4.5	5.0	3.9	−0.9	−4.2
Palau	−20.0	−7.7	−6.7	−9.2	−8.7	−9.3	−11.8	−0.5	−5.3	−7.0	−4.9
Papua New Guinea	6.1	−8.4	−20.5	−24.0	−36.1	−31.5	3.0	10.1	7.5	6.1	3.2
Philippines	0.1	5.0	3.6	2.5	2.8	4.2	3.8	2.9	1.8	1.4	0.2
Samoa	−5.8	−4.7	−7.6	−5.1	−8.5	−0.2	−7.3	−3.7	−3.3	−3.0	−3.1
Solomon Islands	−18.2	−21.9	−33.4	−8.7	1.8	−3.5	−4.3	−2.6	−4.4	−7.7	−3.3
Sri Lanka	−9.5	−0.5	−2.2	−7.8	−6.7	−3.8	−2.7	−2.5	−1.5	−2.8	−3.3
Thailand	0.3	7.3	2.9	2.4	−0.4	−1.2	3.8	7.8	9.6	7.7	2.2
Timor-Leste	45.5	37.9	39.3	39.4	40.2	42.4	26.2	8.3	−9.9	−11.6	−8.4
Tonga	−11.5	−20.9	−19.1	−15.1	−8.6	−6.2	−9.4	−8.0	−7.6	−11.5	−8.7
Tuvalu	7.1	6.9	−11.9	−36.5	17.2	1.2	19.3	7.6	−4.0	−5.7	−1.9
Vanuatu	−10.8	−7.9	−5.4	−8.1	−6.5	−3.3	−0.3	−11.1	−16.6	−21.1	−5.6
Vietnam	−11.0	−6.5	−3.8	0.2	6.0	4.5	5.1	0.5	0.4	0.1	0.7
Emerging and Developing Europe	**−8.0**	**−3.5**	**−5.1**	**−6.5**	**−4.6**	**−3.8**	**−3.1**	**−1.9**	**−2.0**	**−3.0**	**−3.8**
Albania	−15.8	−15.9	−11.3	−13.2	−10.1	−10.8	−12.9	−11.2	−13.3	−13.8	−10.9
Bosnia and Herzegovina	−14.1	−6.4	−6.1	−9.5	−8.7	−5.3	−7.5	−5.6	−5.1	−6.0	−5.0
Bulgaria	−22.0	−8.4	−1.7	0.3	−0.9	1.3	0.9	1.4	0.8	0.0	−1.7
Croatia	−8.8	−5.1	−1.1	−0.8	−0.1	0.8	0.9	5.2	3.0	2.2	−0.7
Hungary	−7.1	−0.8	0.3	0.7	1.8	4.0	2.0	4.4	4.9	4.6	1.4
Kosovo	−16.2	−9.2	−11.7	−13.7	−7.5	−6.4	−7.9	−8.7	−9.6	−9.1	−8.8
FYR Macedonia	−12.8	−6.8	−2.0	−2.5	−3.2	−1.6	−0.8	−1.4	−1.8	−2.4	−3.0
Montenegro	−49.8	−27.9	−22.7	−17.6	−18.5	−14.5	−15.2	−9.7	−10.3	−11.8	−6.8
Poland	−6.8	−4.1	−5.4	−5.2	−3.7	−1.3	−2.0	−0.2	−0.1	−1.0	−2.6
Romania	−11.8	−4.8	−5.1	−4.9	−4.8	−1.1	−0.5	−1.1	−2.0	−2.8	−3.2
Serbia	−21.0	−6.2	−6.4	−8.6	−11.5	−6.1	−6.0	−4.8	−4.2	−3.9	−3.9
Turkey	−5.4	−1.8	−6.1	−9.6	−6.1	−7.7	−5.5	−4.5	−4.4	−5.6	−5.6

Table A12. Emerging Market and Developing Economies: Balance on Current Account *(continued)*
(Percent of GDP)

	2008	2009	2010	2011	2012	2013	2014	2015	Projections 2016	2017	2021
Latin America and the Caribbean	**−1.0**	**−0.8**	**−1.9**	**−2.0**	**−2.3**	**−2.8**	**−3.2**	**−3.6**	**−2.3**	**−2.3**	**−2.3**
Antigua and Barbuda	−26.7	−14.0	−14.7	−10.4	−14.6	−14.6	−14.8	−10.2	−9.4	−10.2	−11.4
Argentina[3]	1.8	2.5	−0.3	−0.8	−0.2	−2.0	−1.4	−2.5	−2.3	−3.2	−4.2
The Bahamas	−10.6	−10.3	−10.1	−15.1	−17.9	−17.5	−22.0	−16.0	−11.4	−10.7	−7.3
Barbados	−10.6	−6.6	−5.7	−12.8	−9.3	−9.1	−9.9	−7.2	−5.3	−6.0	−7.5
Belize	−10.6	−4.9	−2.5	−1.1	−1.2	−4.6	−7.4	−9.8	−12.4	−9.9	−8.0
Bolivia	11.9	4.3	3.9	0.3	7.2	2.4	0.2	−5.8	−6.6	−4.9	−2.0
Brazil	−1.8	−1.6	−3.4	−2.9	−3.0	−3.0	−4.3	−3.3	−0.8	−1.3	−1.1
Chile	−3.2	2.0	1.7	−1.2	−3.5	−3.7	−1.3	−2.0	−1.9	−2.4	−2.7
Colombia	−2.6	−2.0	−3.0	−2.9	−3.1	−3.2	−5.1	−6.4	−5.2	−4.2	−3.3
Costa Rica	−9.1	−1.9	−3.4	−5.3	−5.2	−5.0	−4.7	−4.0	−4.5	−4.5	−4.5
Dominica	−28.3	−22.7	−15.9	−14.1	−17.3	−9.7	−11.1	−9.3	−13.1	−14.2	−10.0
Dominican Republic	−9.4	−4.8	−7.4	−7.5	−6.6	−4.1	−3.3	−1.9	−2.4	−2.7	−4.0
Ecuador	2.9	0.5	−2.3	−0.5	−0.2	−1.0	−0.6	−2.2	−1.5	−0.9	−0.9
El Salvador	−7.1	−1.5	−2.5	−4.8	−5.4	−6.5	−5.2	−3.6	−2.1	−2.9	−4.4
Grenada	−29.0	−24.3	−23.7	−23.6	−21.1	−23.2	−16.5	−15.9	−12.7	−14.1	−15.4
Guatemala	−3.6	0.7	−1.4	−3.4	−2.6	−2.5	−2.1	−0.3	−0.5	−0.7	−1.9
Guyana	−13.7	−9.1	−9.6	−13.0	−11.6	−13.3	−10.7	−5.7	2.1	0.4	−3.8
Haiti	−3.1	−1.9	−1.5	−4.3	−5.7	−6.3	−6.3	−2.5	0.4	−1.0	−1.3
Honduras	−15.4	−3.8	−4.3	−8.0	−8.6	−9.6	−7.4	−6.3	−5.7	−5.7	−5.0
Jamaica	−17.7	−11.0	−8.0	−12.2	−11.1	−9.2	−7.7	−3.4	−3.3	−3.6	−3.8
Mexico	−1.9	−1.0	−0.5	−1.2	−1.4	−2.5	−2.0	−2.9	−2.7	−2.8	−2.7
Nicaragua	−17.8	−8.7	−9.0	−12.1	−10.5	−10.9	−7.7	−8.2	−8.0	−8.7	−10.4
Panama	−10.8	−0.8	−10.8	−13.2	−10.5	−9.8	−9.8	−6.5	−5.5	−4.9	−2.3
Paraguay	1.0	3.0	−0.3	0.4	−2.0	1.7	−0.4	−1.7	0.6	−0.5	0.6
Peru	−4.3	−0.5	−2.4	−1.9	−2.7	−4.2	−4.0	−4.4	−3.8	−3.1	−2.2
St. Kitts and Nevis	−26.8	−25.7	−20.8	−15.9	−9.8	−13.4	−12.1	−12.3	−17.2	−19.4	−17.4
St. Lucia	−28.6	−11.6	−16.3	−19.0	−13.6	−11.4	−6.8	−3.7	−6.7	−6.7	−7.4
St. Vincent and the Grenadines	−33.1	−29.2	−30.6	−29.4	−27.6	−30.9	−29.6	−26.2	−23.0	−22.0	−16.0
Suriname	9.2	2.9	13.0	5.7	3.3	−3.8	−8.0	−15.7	−4.2	4.2	1.7
Trinidad and Tobago	30.5	8.5	18.9	11.4	3.2	7.3	4.6	−5.4	−8.7	−7.2	−4.0
Uruguay	−5.7	−1.2	−1.8	−2.7	−5.1	−5.0	−4.5	−3.5	−2.9	−3.1	−3.5
Venezuela	10.8	0.2	1.9	4.9	0.8	2.0	1.7	−7.8	−3.4	−0.9	0.7
Middle East, North Africa, Afghanistan, and Pakistan	**12.4**	**1.6**	**6.1**	**12.7**	**12.5**	**10.1**	**5.1**	**−4.0**	**−4.6**	**−2.6**	**−1.0**
Afghanistan	2.7	13.1	7.5	6.0	5.9	8.7	2.4	4.7	4.5	1.1	−3.9
Algeria	20.1	0.3	7.5	9.9	5.9	0.4	−4.4	−16.5	−15.1	−13.7	−6.3
Bahrain	8.8	2.4	3.0	8.8	8.4	7.4	4.6	−3.1	−4.7	−3.8	−1.9
Djibouti	−24.3	−9.7	0.7	−13.7	−20.3	−23.3	−25.6	−30.7	−17.2	−14.4	−18.5
Egypt	−1.4	−3.8	−1.9	−2.5	−3.7	−2.2	−0.8	−3.7	−5.8	−5.2	−2.2
Iran	5.2	2.2	4.4	10.6	6.1	7.0	3.8	2.1	4.2	3.3	3.8
Iraq	15.9	−6.8	3.0	12.0	6.7	1.4	−0.8	−7.2	−10.8	−3.6	−0.8
Jordan	−9.4	−5.2	−7.1	−10.3	−15.2	−10.3	−6.8	−9.0	−9.0	−8.9	−6.2
Kuwait	40.9	26.7	31.8	42.9	45.5	39.9	33.3	5.2	3.6	8.4	9.2
Lebanon	−10.5	−11.9	−20.7	−15.1	−23.9	−26.7	−28.1	−21.0	−20.4	−20.6	−19.7
Libya	42.5	14.9	19.5	9.1	29.1	13.5	−27.8	−42.1	−47.4	−36.9	−19.0
Mauritania	−12.0	−22.2	−14.6	−10.6	−31.5	−28.6	−33.3	−27.0	−21.9	−24.9	−21.5
Morocco	−7.1	−5.4	−4.4	−7.6	−9.3	−7.6	−5.7	−1.9	−1.2	−1.4	−1.3
Oman	8.5	−1.1	8.6	13.1	10.3	6.7	5.7	−17.5	−21.3	−17.6	−8.3
Pakistan	−8.1	−5.5	−2.2	0.1	−2.1	−1.1	−1.3	−1.0	−0.9	−1.5	−0.9
Qatar	23.1	6.5	19.1	30.7	32.6	29.9	23.5	8.2	−1.8	0.0	0.3
Saudi Arabia	25.5	4.9	12.7	23.7	22.4	18.2	9.8	−8.3	−6.6	−2.6	−1.2
Sudan[4]	−1.6	−9.6	−2.1	−0.4	−9.3	−8.7	−7.0	−7.8	−5.9	−4.9	−3.5
Syria[5]	−1.3	−2.9	−2.8	. . .	. . .	. . .	. . .	. . .	. . .	. . .	. . .
Tunisia	−3.8	−2.8	−4.8	−7.4	−8.3	−8.4	−9.1	−8.8	−8.0	−6.9	−4.0
United Arab Emirates	7.1	3.1	4.3	12.7	19.8	19.1	10.0	3.3	1.1	3.2	2.1
Yemen	−4.6	−10.1	−3.4	−3.0	−1.7	−3.1	−1.7	−5.5	−6.1	−2.8	−3.7

Table A12. Emerging Market and Developing Economies: Balance on Current Account *(continued)*
(Percent of GDP)

	2008	2009	2010	2011	2012	2013	2014	2015	Projections 2016	2017	2021
Sub-Saharan Africa	**0.3**	**−2.6**	**−0.7**	**−0.5**	**−1.5**	**−2.1**	**−3.7**	**−5.9**	**−4.5**	**−3.9**	**−4.6**
Angola	8.5	−10.0	9.1	12.6	12.0	6.7	−2.9	−8.5	−5.4	−5.4	−2.5
Benin	−7.5	−8.3	−8.2	−7.3	−7.4	−8.0	−8.7	−10.5	−10.0	−11.8	−8.8
Botswana	−1.1	−6.3	−2.6	3.1	−1.1	9.3	15.6	7.2	4.1	3.7	11.1
Burkina Faso	−11.5	−4.7	−2.2	−1.5	−7.2	−11.0	−8.0	−6.4	−6.0	−5.0	−8.0
Burundi	−1.0	1.7	−12.2	−14.4	−18.6	−19.3	−18.5	−15.9	−4.6	−9.6	−17.6
Cabo Verde	−13.7	−14.6	−12.4	−16.3	−12.6	−4.9	−9.0	−4.3	−7.7	−9.2	−7.3
Cameroon	−1.2	−3.5	−2.8	−3.0	−3.6	−3.9	−4.3	−4.2	−4.2	−4.0	−4.8
Central African Republic	−9.9	−9.1	−10.2	−7.6	−4.6	−3.0	−5.6	−9.0	−10.0	−9.7	−6.6
Chad	3.7	−9.2	−9.0	−5.6	−8.7	−9.2	−9.0	−12.4	−8.7	−7.8	−5.9
Comoros	−10.4	−6.2	−0.2	−4.9	−7.2	−8.1	−6.3	0.8	−9.0	−9.7	−13.7
Democratic Republic of the Congo	−0.8	−6.1	−10.5	−5.2	−4.6	1.8	4.0	−3.7	−0.8	5.2	7.1
Republic of Congo	−0.5	−14.1	7.5	4.9	17.7	1.6	−3.3	−21.0	−8.2	−2.1	0.5
Côte d'Ivoire	1.9	6.6	1.9	10.4	−1.2	−2.0	1.5	−1.8	−1.8	−2.1	−2.7
Equatorial Guinea	21.9	−8.4	−19.4	6.7	4.1	0.1	−5.6	−16.8	−11.8	−6.7	−3.5
Eritrea	−5.5	−7.6	−5.6	0.6	2.3	−0.1	0.6	−2.2	0.2	0.9	−1.4
Ethiopia	−6.7	−6.7	−1.4	−2.5	−6.9	−5.9	−7.9	−12.0	−10.7	−9.3	−7.8
Gabon	21.6	4.4	14.9	15.2	15.9	11.6	8.1	−2.3	−5.3	−4.7	−2.7
The Gambia	−12.2	−12.5	−16.3	−12.3	−7.9	−10.2	−10.9	−15.2	−12.7	−13.7	−13.7
Ghana	−11.9	−5.5	−8.6	−9.0	−11.7	−11.9	−9.6	−7.5	−6.3	−6.0	−4.3
Guinea	−10.2	−8.2	−9.3	−24.7	−26.0	−16.9	−17.3	−18.7	−13.2	−11.3	−17.7
Guinea-Bissau	−2.5	−5.4	−8.7	−4.2	−11.8	−7.4	−3.3	−1.1	−1.7	−2.8	−2.9
Kenya	−5.5	−4.6	−5.9	−9.1	−8.4	−8.8	−10.3	−6.8	−6.4	−6.1	−5.7
Lesotho	21.1	3.9	−10.0	−14.7	−9.8	−10.3	−7.9	−8.7	−8.0	−9.0	−22.9
Liberia	−46.6	−23.2	−32.0	−27.5	−21.5	−28.4	−32.7	−34.7	−30.5	−26.5	−25.6
Madagascar	−20.6	−21.1	−9.7	−6.9	−6.9	−5.9	−0.3	−1.9	−2.3	−3.7	−4.0
Malawi	−15.1	−10.2	−8.6	−8.6	−9.3	−8.7	−8.5	−8.3	−15.8	−9.3	−8.1
Mali	−13.7	−10.8	−10.7	−5.1	−2.2	−2.9	−4.7	−5.1	−6.0	−5.2	−5.8
Mauritius	−10.1	−7.4	−10.3	−13.8	−7.3	−6.3	−5.7	−4.9	−4.3	−4.5	−4.9
Mozambique	−9.9	−10.9	−16.1	−25.3	−44.7	−42.9	−38.2	−39.0	−33.5	−28.3	−146.4
Namibia	−0.1	−1.5	−3.5	−3.0	−5.7	−4.0	−10.7	−12.9	−12.4	−6.9	−6.9
Niger	−12.0	−24.4	−19.8	−22.3	−14.7	−15.0	−14.1	−17.2	−17.8	−17.5	−12.3
Nigeria	8.8	4.7	3.9	3.0	4.4	3.9	0.2	−3.1	−0.7	−0.4	−0.1
Rwanda	−5.1	−7.1	−7.3	−7.5	−11.4	−7.4	−10.5	−13.5	−16.6	−11.9	−10.7
São Tomé and Príncipe	−33.1	−23.2	−21.7	−25.5	−21.3	−13.8	−22.6	−17.2	−12.7	−13.3	−8.7
Senegal	−14.2	−6.7	−4.4	−8.1	−10.8	−10.4	−8.9	−7.6	−8.4	−8.2	−6.2
Seychelles	−18.5	−14.8	−19.4	−23.0	−21.1	−12.1	−23.0	−18.6	−18.7	−18.3	−16.5
Sierra Leone	−9.0	−13.3	−22.7	−65.0	−31.8	−17.5	−18.2	−15.5	−16.2	−16.3	−15.2
South Africa	−5.5	−2.7	−1.5	−2.2	−5.1	−5.9	−5.3	−4.3	−3.3	−3.2	−3.6
South Sudan	. . .	. . .	. . .	18.4	−15.9	−1.2	2.1	−11.1	−0.5	−8.6	−11.0
Swaziland	−7.1	−11.6	−8.6	−6.8	3.1	5.1	3.3	9.2	−4.9	−2.4	0.6
Tanzania	−7.8	−7.6	−7.7	−10.8	−11.6	−10.6	−9.5	−8.8	−8.8	−8.8	−7.9
Togo	−7.0	−5.6	−6.3	−8.0	−7.5	−13.1	−9.9	−7.1	−8.0	−8.2	−9.1
Uganda	−7.1	−5.7	−8.0	−10.0	−6.8	−7.0	−8.7	−9.4	−8.7	−8.9	−7.2
Zambia	−3.3	6.0	7.5	4.7	5.4	−0.6	2.1	−3.5	−4.5	−2.2	2.9
Zimbabwe[6]	−16.7	−43.6	−13.3	−22.2	−14.6	−18.2	−15.2	−10.7	−7.5	−6.1	−9.6

[1]Georgia, Turkmenistan, and Ukraine, which are not members of the Commonwealth of Independent States, are included in this group for reasons of geography and similarity in economic structure.
[2]Starting in 2014 data exclude Crimea and Sevastopol.
[3]See country-specific notes for Argentina in the "Country Notes" section of the Statistical Appendix.
[4]Data for 2011 exclude South Sudan after July 9. Data for 2012 and onward pertain to the current Sudan.
[5]Data for Syria are excluded for 2011 onward owing to the uncertain political situation.
[6]The Zimbabwe dollar ceased circulating in early 2009. Data are based on IMF staff estimates of price and exchange rate developments in U.S. dollars. IMF staff estimates of U.S. dollar values may differ from authorities' estimates.

Table A13. Summary of Financial Account Balances
(Billions of U.S. dollars)

	2008	2009	2010	2011	2012	2013	2014	2015	Projections 2016	Projections 2017
Advanced Economies										
Financial Account Balance	−699.1	19.3	−86.0	−191.7	−105.2	246.8	437.1	539.7	410.9	272.2
Direct Investment, Net	657.4	311.7	346.1	376.9	133.8	81.8	197.5	6.6	184.4	255.2
Portfolio Investment, Net	−1,212.9	−377.6	−738.5	−904.3	−202.0	−328.8	−143.5	162.1	152.9	−27.8
Financial Derivatives, Net	323.2	−91.9	−118.1	0.7	−89.6	18.4	−50.3	−46.9	−32.6	−42.9
Other Investment, Net	−563.9	−287.8	62.9	−41.9	−222.7	323.2	298.2	190.9	21.7	14.8
Change in Reserves	76.5	469.7	352.8	350.7	274.0	153.2	135.3	227.4	86.4	74.3
United States										
Financial Account Balance	−730.6	−231.0	−437.0	−515.8	−440.5	−391.0	−287.4	−195.2	−377.3	−530.6
Direct Investment, Net	19.0	159.9	95.2	183.0	135.2	117.7	136.1	−30.8	81.0	79.1
Portfolio Investment, Net	−808.0	18.5	−620.8	−226.3	−498.3	−30.7	−119.2	−97.0	−466.0	−600.2
Financial Derivatives, Net	32.9	−44.8	−14.1	−35.0	7.1	2.2	−54.3	−25.4	0.0	−22.4
Other Investment, Net	20.6	−416.9	100.9	−453.4	−89.0	−477.1	−246.3	−35.8	9.0	13.0
Change in Reserves	4.8	52.3	1.8	15.9	4.5	−3.1	−3.6	−6.3	−1.2	0.0
Euro Area										
Financial Account Balance	−470.1	28.5	−69.6	−153.1	150.1	465.1	492.1	304.7	. . .	. . .
Direct Investment, Net	336.6	66.4	83.4	139.0	14.4	−77.7	79.2	120.9	. . .	. . .
Portfolio Investment, Net	−356.0	−350.3	−109.8	−454.5	−181.3	−5.1	150.6	223.4	. . .	. . .
Financial Derivatives, Net	−34.9	15.1	−4.3	5.5	42.0	19.4	56.9	94.2	. . .	. . .
Other Investment, Net	−420.5	239.1	−53.0	142.3	256.0	522.3	199.6	−145.6	. . .	. . .
Change in Reserves	4.7	58.1	14.1	14.7	19.0	6.2	5.8	11.7	. . .	. . .
Germany										
Financial Account Balance	179.9	184.4	123.7	167.7	185.8	291.3	323.9	250.0	301.4	291.7
Direct Investment, Net	67.1	43.0	60.6	10.3	33.6	28.1	105.6	62.6	23.0	23.8
Portfolio Investment, Net	−44.5	119.2	154.1	−51.4	66.8	212.8	180.6	220.3	265.7	257.1
Financial Derivatives, Net	44.0	−7.5	17.6	39.8	30.9	31.9	42.1	28.7	34.6	33.5
Other Investment, Net	110.6	17.4	−110.7	165.1	52.7	17.4	−1.0	−59.2	−21.8	−22.7
Change in Reserves	2.7	12.4	2.1	3.9	1.7	1.2	−3.3	−2.4	0.0	0.0
France										
Financial Account Balance	−26.9	−30.7	−34.2	−74.6	−48.0	−19.2	−10.0	−7.8	−9.2	−7.4
Direct Investment, Net	66.0	70.3	34.3	19.8	19.4	−13.9	47.9	−2.1	2.0	6.1
Portfolio Investment, Net	−37.8	−328.7	−155.0	−333.7	−50.6	−79.3	−23.8	60.1	57.5	51.9
Financial Derivatives, Net	24.1	23.6	−34.8	−19.4	−18.4	−22.3	−31.5	12.0	15.3	19.3
Other Investment, Net	−86.5	212.0	105.1	240.3	−3.6	98.2	−3.6	−85.7	−86.2	−87.1
Change in Reserves	−12.5	−5.5	7.7	−7.7	5.2	−1.9	1.0	8.0	2.3	2.3
Italy										
Financial Account Balance	−45.7	−54.5	−111.2	−89.6	−13.1	16.9	66.8	36.7	42.1	37.4
Direct Investment, Net	76.2	−0.3	21.3	17.2	6.8	0.9	3.3	7.3	7.6	8.0
Portfolio Investment, Net	−110.7	−55.4	58.4	15.9	−31.3	−17.5	1.4	99.4	28.1	10.4
Financial Derivatives, Net	−0.4	−6.9	6.6	−10.1	7.5	4.0	−4.8	3.7	0.0	0.0
Other Investment, Net	−19.0	−0.7	−198.9	−113.9	2.1	27.5	68.1	−74.3	6.4	19.0
Change in Reserves	8.2	8.8	1.4	1.3	1.9	2.0	−1.3	0.6	0.0	0.0

Table A13. Summary of Financial Account Balances *(continued)*
(Billions of U.S. dollars)

	2008	2009	2010	2011	2012	2013	2014	2015	Projections 2016	2017
Spain										
Financial Account Balance	−149.8	−72.8	−58.9	−43.4	0.5	44.1	26.8	24.9	31.2	29.7
Direct Investment, Net	−2.3	2.7	−1.9	12.8	−27.2	−19.1	12.4	26.7	26.8	27.3
Portfolio Investment, Net	1.9	−69.6	−46.6	43.1	53.7	−59.1	−13.0	23.2	−22.8	−21.4
Financial Derivatives, Net	10.4	8.4	−11.4	2.9	−10.7	1.4	1.5	−1.4	0.0	0.0
Other Investment, Net	−160.8	−20.4	0.0	−116.2	−18.2	120.2	20.7	−29.3	27.2	23.8
Change in Reserves	0.9	6.0	1.1	13.9	2.8	0.7	5.2	5.6	0.0	0.0
Japan										
Financial Account Balance	181.6	168.8	247.3	158.4	53.9	−4.3	58.6	174.8	172.8	167.7
Direct Investment, Net	89.1	61.2	72.5	117.8	117.5	144.7	118.3	131.0	116.7	129.9
Portfolio Investment, Net	289.0	211.7	147.9	−162.9	28.8	−280.6	−42.2	131.7	257.6	247.0
Financial Derivatives, Net	−24.9	−10.5	−11.9	−17.1	6.7	58.1	34.0	17.7	−34.6	−18.7
Other Investment, Net	−202.3	−120.9	−5.5	43.4	−61.1	34.8	−60.1	−110.7	−176.4	−200.5
Change in Reserves	30.8	27.2	44.3	177.3	−37.9	38.7	8.5	5.1	9.5	10.0
United Kingdom										
Financial Account Balance	−72.8	−45.4	−46.8	−37.6	−83.7	−122.9	−129.5	−152.1	−158.2	−113.2
Direct Investment, Net	106.9	−61.0	−10.1	53.4	−34.9	−11.2	−193.4	−115.0	−53.0	−13.0
Portfolio Investment, Net	−454.8	−48.5	21.3	11.4	338.3	−86.8	−204.4	−405.8	26.5	52.2
Financial Derivatives, Net	225.5	−45.5	−39.4	4.8	−58.6	18.1	−1.0	−48.6	−15.0	−17.9
Other Investment, Net	52.2	100.6	−28.0	−115.1	−340.6	−50.7	257.5	385.1	−129.2	−147.5
Change in Reserves	−2.5	9.0	9.4	7.9	12.1	7.8	11.7	32.2	12.5	13.0
Canada										
Financial Account Balance	−3.0	−41.6	−58.3	−49.4	−62.7	−54.6	−39.1	−44.2	−56.7	−50.1
Direct Investment, Net	17.7	16.9	6.3	12.5	12.8	−16.9	−2.8	25.0	−7.2	2.1
Portfolio Investment, Net	−47.6	−91.0	−109.6	−104.3	−63.8	−21.4	−17.1	−25.6	−17.8	−13.4
Financial Derivatives, Net	...	...	...	...	...	...	...	...	...	...
Other Investment, Net	25.3	22.3	41.4	34.3	−13.4	−21.1	−24.4	−52.2	−31.7	−38.7
Change in Reserves	1.6	10.2	3.9	8.1	1.7	4.7	5.3	8.5	0.0	0.0
Other Advanced Economies[1]										
Financial Account Balance	62.9	150.7	287.9	295.4	265.7	371.7	368.5	375.7	344.4	329.6
Direct Investment, Net	17.7	21.7	94.3	−6.7	−23.4	18.0	−22.4	−106.2	0.3	7.1
Portfolio Investment, Net	178.4	−106.9	−50.7	42.7	139.7	121.4	184.6	334.4	241.7	211.2
Financial Derivatives, Net	−12.6	20.0	−17.9	41.0	−28.8	−28.8	−33.9	−22.0	−27.5	−30.0
Other Investment, Net	−166.2	−114.0	−17.1	93.4	−97.7	160.8	134.0	−8.2	67.8	93.9
Change in Reserves	44.8	332.5	279.3	125.1	275.3	101.4	106.8	176.7	64.1	48.8
Emerging Market and Developing Economies										
Financial Account Balance	605.8	68.9	136.0	255.8	107.6	80.7	−5.4	−215.9	−30.2	−86.1
Direct Investment, Net	−467.8	−328.0	−455.8	−534.4	−481.6	−470.1	−417.2	−323.4	−246.4	−171.6
Portfolio Investment, Net	124.8	−85.1	−235.1	−142.8	−245.0	−139.4	−118.0	125.3	48.5	−65.0
Financial Derivatives, Net	...	...	...	...	...	...	...	...	...	...
Other Investment, Net	229.2	−40.0	−8.1	183.1	424.6	129.1	414.8	526.9	398.3	188.4
Change in Reserves	713.3	521.1	834.1	749.0	411.8	576.3	118.4	−544.8	−225.5	−29.8

Table A13. Summary of Financial Account Balances *(continued)*
(Billions of U.S. dollars)

	2008	2009	2010	2011	2012	2013	2014	2015	Projections 2016	Projections 2017
Regional Groups										
Commonwealth of Independent States[2]										
Financial Account Balance	111.3	36.7	89.9	116.2	51.2	28.2	−5.4	62.3	32.7	55.2
Direct Investment, Net	−49.4	−17.2	−9.4	−16.1	−27.9	3.6	19.4	4.7	−2.6	3.0
Portfolio Investment, Net	35.8	−6.1	−14.3	17.9	3.5	17.4	23.4	10.9	−0.6	−4.9
Financial Derivatives, Net	...	...	...	...	...	...	...	...	...	...
Other Investment, Net	140.7	46.0	50.9	81.2	61.8	48.8	82.9	86.6	32.6	43.4
Change in Reserves	−17.0	10.8	60.9	31.9	12.2	−42.0	−131.3	−39.5	4.0	14.5
Emerging and Developing Asia										
Financial Account Balance	467.3	211.3	141.9	65.7	9.2	32.9	148.9	129.1	258.7	154.4
Direct Investment, Net	−151.4	−114.1	−224.3	−277.3	−221.7	−273.0	−203.6	−128.8	−35.1	46.6
Portfolio Investment, Net	6.0	−67.0	−93.3	−57.9	−115.5	−64.6	−124.0	82.8	57.4	−41.9
Financial Derivatives, Net	...	...	0.2	−0.3	1.5	−2.0	1.0	−1.6	−0.9	−1.1
Other Investment, Net	114.0	−67.8	−103.5	−28.8	208.5	−78.3	280.0	493.6	401.2	193.0
Change in Reserves	497.5	463.0	563.9	432.0	137.7	450.8	195.9	−316.6	−163.5	−41.3
Emerging and Developing Europe										
Financial Account Balance	−160.6	−51.3	−89.0	−107.1	−65.3	−62.1	−41.7	−0.2	−13.1	−33.9
Direct Investment, Net	−63.3	−30.7	−27.0	−40.0	−27.2	−25.3	−31.1	−24.2	−30.0	−32.0
Portfolio Investment, Net	14.4	−10.1	−45.4	−53.2	−70.2	−39.9	−19.2	26.1	−4.3	−4.2
Financial Derivatives, Net	2.5	0.9	0.0	1.6	−3.0	−1.4	0.3	−1.7	−0.8	−2.5
Other Investment, Net	−120.0	−42.4	−52.5	−30.1	7.2	−14.0	8.6	9.9	8.6	−5.
Change in Reserves	5.9	31.0	35.9	14.6	27.9	18.5	−0.1	−10.3	13.5	10.
Latin America and the Caribbean										
Financial Account Balance	−41.5	−31.7	−123.7	−125.5	−162.9	−205.9	−219.1	−209.9	−115.7	−133.
Direct Investment, Net	−103.0	−72.9	−112.0	−147.5	−150.7	−145.0	−141.7	−134.6	−134.1	−133.
Portfolio Investment, Net	−6.1	−25.4	−106.9	−107.2	−95.3	−107.0	−117.7	−60.3	−33.8	−46.
Financial Derivatives, Net	...	...	...	...	...	...	...	...	...	..
Other Investment, Net	24.9	11.6	4.0	16.3	24.2	38.8	−1.5	11.6	54.4	43.
Change in Reserves	41.5	54.5	90.5	110.5	59.6	6.4	38.2	−32.5	−1.9	3.
Middle East, North Africa, Afghanistan, and Pakistan										
Financial Account Balance	235.0	−46.9	118.4	313.3	291.6	334.0	180.5	−132.8	−137.4	−78.
Direct Investment, Net	−64.3	−64.0	−49.3	−22.9	−25.3	−8.6	−32.8	−12.5	−23.1	−25
Portfolio Investment, Net	51.0	32.0	25.0	73.3	57.3	72.1	132.9	73.9	32.0	32
Financial Derivatives, Net	...	...	...	...	...	...	...	...		
Other Investment, Net	80.1	15.8	59.4	124.6	105.0	142.1	62.0	−61.4	−74.0	−66
Change in Reserves	168.3	−30.7	83.3	138.2	154.7	140.1	24.1	−132.2	−71.0	−17
Sub-Saharan Africa										
Financial Account Balance	−5.7	−49.3	−1.5	−6.8	−16.1	−46.4	−68.6	−64.5	−55.4	−49
Direct Investment, Net	−36.4	−29.2	−33.9	−30.7	−28.8	−21.8	−27.4	−28.0	−21.4	−30
Portfolio Investment, Net	23.8	−8.4	−0.3	−15.7	−24.7	−17.3	−13.5	−8.3	−2.1	0
Financial Derivatives, Net	0.0	−0.2	−0.2	−1.7	−1.7	−0.8	−1.5	−0.4	−0.3	−0
Other Investment, Net	−10.5	−3.3	33.6	19.9	17.8	−8.3	−17.2	−13.5	−24.5	−19
Change in Reserves	17.3	−7.5	−0.4	21.7	19.7	2.5	−8.3	−13.6	−6.7	1

Table A13. Summary of Financial Account Balances *(continued)*
(Billions of U.S. dollars)

	2008	2009	2010	2011	2012	2013	2014	2015	Projections 2016	2017
Analytical Groups										
By Source of Export Earnings										
Fuel										
Financial Account Balance	444.2	14.2	260.9	516.6	445.9	389.5	202.4	−103.4	−109.6	−25.6
Direct Investment, Net	−88.8	−60.7	−31.3	−31.1	−42.8	3.4	−11.8	−12.8	−20.3	−18.2
Portfolio Investment, Net	91.0	9.4	20.2	82.8	43.7	72.4	151.8	82.1	27.5	27.5
Financial Derivatives, Net	...	...	...	...	...	...	...	...	...	...
Other Investment, Net	274.8	114.2	153.4	265.0	222.5	226.7	180.8	42.2	−20.0	−0.3
Change in Reserves	166.1	−51.3	117.1	198.7	221.8	98.1	−113.3	−215.5	−95.1	−32.1
Nonfuel										
Financial Account Balance	157.2	57.2	−123.3	−260.8	−338.3	−308.7	−207.7	−112.4	79.4	−60.5
Direct Investment, Net	−377.6	−264.7	−422.3	−503.4	−438.7	−473.6	−405.4	−310.6	−226.1	−153.5
Portfolio Investment, Net	33.8	−94.7	−255.3	−225.6	−288.7	−211.8	−269.9	43.1	21.0	−92.4
Financial Derivatives, Net	...	...	...	...	...	...	...	...	...	...
Other Investment, Net	−46.4	−154.3	−161.2	−81.9	202.1	−97.6	234.0	484.7	418.2	188.7
Change in Reserves	542.3	572.7	715.9	550.3	189.9	478.2	231.7	−329.4	−130.5	2.3
By External Financing Source										
Net Debtor Economies										
Financial Account Balance	−304.8	−198.6	−290.5	−381.2	−437.4	−401.2	−404.1	−284.4	−213.0	−262.2
Direct Investment, Net	−279.9	−203.0	−222.2	−281.7	−273.7	−257.8	−285.9	−263.7	−283.1	−303.4
Portfolio Investment, Net	33.2	−63.6	−216.6	−185.1	−216.8	−166.6	−203.6	−40.5	−44.8	−81.3
Financial Derivatives, Net	...	...	...	...	...	...	...	...	...	...
Other Investment, Net	−140.5	−78.5	−88.4	−60.4	−61.5	−31.0	−33.3	20.2	54.4	31.6
Change in Reserves	78.1	148.3	237.7	144.7	116.1	57.4	115.2	−2.0	63.4	96.3
Net Debtor Economies by Debt-Servicing Experience										
Economies with Arrears and/or Rescheduling during 2011–15										
Financial Account Balance	−18.5	−17.0	−13.6	−21.5	−41.2	−12.8	−34.1	−20.3	−25.9	−11.9
Direct Investment, Net	−28.7	−16.5	−16.8	−15.3	−19.9	−6.9	−9.0	−10.0	−13.7	−16.2
Portfolio Investment, Net	3.5	14.2	−10.9	1.1	−0.5	8.3	−5.4	−3.3	1.3	−0.1
Financial Derivatives, Net	...	...	...	...	...	...	...	...	...	...
Other Investment, Net	0.4	−0.8	3.0	5.7	−0.9	−11.3	−8.0	−15.2	−13.3	−10.8
Change in Reserves	6.2	−13.6	11.3	−12.4	−21.6	−2.1	−10.9	8.9	0.5	15.6
Memorandum										
World										
Financial Account Balance	−93.3	88.2	50.0	64.1	2.4	327.5	431.7	323.8	380.7	186.1

Note: The estimates in this table are based on individual countries' national accounts and balance of payments statistics. Country group composites are calculated as the sum of the U.S. dollar values for the relevant individual countries. Some group aggregates for the financial derivatives are not shown because of incomplete data. Projections for the euro area are not available because of data constraints.

[1]Excludes the G7 (Canada, France, Germany, Italy, Japan, United Kingdom, United States) and euro area countries.

[2]Georgia, Turkmenistan, and Ukraine, which are not members of the Commonwealth of Independent States, are included in this group for reasons of geography and similarity in economic structure.

Table A14. Summary of Net Lending and Borrowing

(Percent of GDP)

	Averages								Projections		Average
	1998–2007	2002–09	2010	2011	2012	2013	2014	2015	2016	2017	2018–21
Advanced Economies											
Net Lending and Borrowing	−0.7	−0.8	0.0	0.0	0.1	0.5	0.5	0.6	0.7	0.6	0.4
Current Account Balance	−0.7	−0.8	0.0	−0.1	0.0	0.5	0.5	0.6	0.7	0.6	0.4
Savings	22.4	21.4	20.3	20.8	21.2	21.4	21.9	22.1	21.5	21.3	21.5
Investment	22.8	22.2	20.4	20.8	20.8	20.7	20.9	20.9	20.6	20.7	21.1
Capital Account Balance	0.0	0.0	0.0	0.1	0.0	0.0	0.0	−0.1	0.0	0.0	0.0
United States											
Net Lending and Borrowing	−4.3	−4.7	−3.0	−3.0	−2.7	−2.2	−2.3	−2.6	−2.5	−2.7	−2.7
Current Account Balance	−4.3	−4.7	−3.0	−3.0	−2.8	−2.2	−2.3	−2.6	−2.5	−2.7	−2.7
Savings	18.9	17.1	15.1	15.7	17.7	18.3	19.2	19.1	17.6	17.1	17.4
Investment	22.6	21.6	18.4	18.5	19.4	19.8	20.0	20.3	19.8	19.8	20.1
Capital Account Balance	0.0	0.0	0.0	0.0	0.0	0.0	0.0	0.0	0.0	0.0	0.0
Euro Area											
Net Lending and Borrowing	. . .	0.1	0.5	0.6	1.4	2.4	2.7	3.0	. . .	. . .	. . .
Current Account Balance	−0.4	0.0	0.4	0.4	1.3	2.2	2.5	3.2	3.4	3.1	2.8
Savings	23.1	22.8	21.5	22.4	22.3	22.4	22.8	23.6	23.8	23.7	24.0
Investment	22.6	22.4	21.0	21.5	20.1	19.6	19.8	19.8	19.9	20.1	20.6
Capital Account Balance	. . .	0.1	0.1	0.1	0.1	0.2	0.2	−0.1	. . .	. . .	. . .
Germany											
Net Lending and Borrowing	2.0	4.5	5.7	6.1	7.0	6.7	7.3	8.4	8.6	8.1	7.4
Current Account Balance	2.1	4.5	5.6	6.1	7.0	6.7	7.3	8.4	8.6	8.1	7.4
Savings	23.2	24.1	25.2	27.2	26.3	26.2	27.0	27.7	27.9	27.5	27.1
Investment	21.1	19.6	19.6	21.1	19.3	19.5	19.8	19.2	19.3	19.4	19.7
Capital Account Balance	0.0	0.0	0.0	0.1	0.0	0.0	0.0	0.0	0.0	0.0	0.0
France											
Net Lending and Borrowing	1.9	0.5	−0.8	−0.9	−1.2	−0.8	−1.0	−0.1	−0.4	−0.3	0.1
Current Account Balance	1.9	0.5	−0.8	−1.0	−1.2	−0.9	−1.1	−0.2	−0.5	−0.4	0.0
Savings	23.9	22.9	21.1	22.2	21.4	21.4	21.4	22.2	21.9	21.8	22.1
Investment	22.0	22.4	21.9	23.2	22.6	22.3	22.5	22.4	22.4	22.2	22.1
Capital Account Balance	0.0	0.0	0.1	0.1	0.0	0.1	0.1	0.1	0.1	0.1	0.1
Italy											
Net Lending and Borrowing	0.0	−1.2	−3.4	−2.9	−0.1	1.0	2.1	2.4	2.3	2.0	1.3
Current Account Balance	−0.2	−1.3	−3.4	−3.0	−0.4	0.9	1.9	2.2	2.2	1.9	1.2
Savings	20.8	20.0	17.1	17.5	17.5	17.9	18.2	19.0	18.8	18.6	18.6
Investment	21.0	21.3	20.5	20.5	17.9	17.0	16.3	16.8	16.6	16.7	17.4
Capital Account Balance	0.1	0.1	0.0	0.1	0.2	0.0	0.2	0.2	0.1	0.1	0.1
Spain											
Net Lending and Borrowing	−4.5	−5.9	−3.5	−2.8	0.3	2.2	1.4	1.9	2.5	2.3	2.3
Current Account Balance	−5.3	−6.6	−3.9	−3.2	−0.2	1.5	1.0	1.4	1.9	1.7	1.8
Savings	22.5	22.2	19.6	18.7	20.0	20.7	20.8	22.0	22.9	22.9	23.3
Investment	27.8	28.8	23.5	21.9	20.2	19.1	19.8	20.7	21.0	21.2	21.5
Capital Account Balance	0.8	0.7	0.5	0.4	0.5	0.7	0.4	0.6	0.6	0.6	0.6
Japan											
Net Lending and Borrowing	3.1	3.4	3.9	2.2	1.0	0.8	0.8	3.2	3.7	3.3	3.2
Current Account Balance	3.3	3.5	4.0	2.2	1.0	0.9	0.8	3.3	3.7	3.3	3.3
Savings	26.8	25.8	23.8	22.4	21.9	22.2	22.6	25.3	25.3	25.0	25.1
Investment	23.6	22.3	19.8	20.2	20.9	21.2	21.8	22.0	21.5	21.6	21.8
Capital Account Balance	−0.2	−0.1	−0.1	0.0	0.0	−0.2	0.0	−0.1	−0.1	−0.1	−0.1
United Kingdom											
Net Lending and Borrowing	−1.8	−2.2	−2.7	−1.8	−3.7	−4.4	−4.7	−5.4	−6.0	−4.3	−3.8
Current Account Balance	−1.8	−2.2	−2.7	−1.8	−3.7	−4.4	−4.7	−5.4	−5.9	−4.3	−3.8
Savings	16.4	15.2	13.2	14.1	12.4	12.0	12.7	11.9	11.4	12.6	13.5
Investment	18.2	17.4	16.0	15.8	16.0	16.4	17.3	17.2	17.3	16.9	17.3
Capital Account Balance	0.0	0.0	0.0	0.0	0.0	0.0	0.0	−0.1	0.0	0.0	0.0

Table A14. Summary of Net Lending and Borrowing *(continued)*
(Percent of GDP)

	Averages								Projections		
	1998–2007	2002–09	2010	2011	2012	2013	2014	2015	2016	2017	Average 2018–21
Canada											
Net Lending and Borrowing	1.2	0.8	−3.6	−2.5	−3.6	−3.2	−2.3	−3.2	−3.7	−3.1	−2.7
Current Account Balance	1.2	0.8	−3.6	−2.8	−3.6	−3.2	−2.3	−3.2	−3.7	−3.1	−2.7
Savings	22.7	23.1	19.9	21.4	21.3	21.5	22.0	20.4	19.4	19.8	20.4
Investment	21.4	22.3	23.5	24.2	24.9	24.6	24.3	23.6	23.1	22.9	23.1
Capital Account Balance	0.0	0.0	0.0	0.3	0.0	0.0	0.0	0.0	0.0	0.0	0.0
Other Advanced Economies[1]											
Net Lending and Borrowing	3.8	4.0	5.0	4.2	4.2	5.2	5.2	5.8	5.4	4.9	4.4
Current Account Balance	3.9	4.1	5.0	4.1	4.2	5.2	5.3	5.9	5.6	5.1	4.5
Savings	29.7	29.9	31.0	30.7	30.4	30.5	30.7	30.9	30.4	30.1	29.7
Investment	25.7	25.6	25.6	26.3	26.1	25.2	25.3	24.6	24.6	24.9	25.0
Capital Account Balance	−0.1	−0.1	0.0	0.1	0.0	0.1	−0.1	−0.1	−0.2	−0.2	−0.1
Emerging Market and Developing Economies											
Net Lending and Borrowing	2.0	2.9	1.5	1.5	1.3	0.7	0.7	0.1	−0.1	−0.2	−0.4
Current Account Balance	1.9	2.9	1.2	1.4	1.3	0.6	0.6	−0.1	−0.3	−0.4	−0.6
Savings	27.4	30.3	32.4	33.2	33.1	32.4	32.7	32.5	31.7	31.5	31.6
Investment	25.6	27.6	31.2	31.8	31.9	31.9	32.2	32.5	31.8	31.9	32.1
Capital Account Balance	0.2	0.1	0.3	0.1	0.1	0.1	0.0	0.1	0.1	0.1	0.1
Regional Groups											
Commonwealth of Independent States[2]											
Net Lending and Borrowing	6.2	5.1	3.7	4.1	2.2	0.6	0.5	3.0	1.3	1.9	3.1
Current Account Balance	6.5	5.7	3.3	4.1	2.4	0.6	2.1	3.0	1.3	1.9	3.1
Savings	26.5	27.1	24.9	27.6	25.8	22.4	23.9	24.1	24.4	25.0	26.4
Investment	20.3	21.4	21.5	23.5	23.4	21.7	21.7	20.8	22.6	22.7	23.4
Capital Account Balance	−0.4	−0.7	0.4	0.0	−0.2	0.0	−1.5	0.0	0.0	0.0	0.0
Emerging and Developing Asia											
Net Lending and Borrowing	3.2	4.1	2.5	0.9	1.0	0.8	1.8	2.1	1.6	0.9	0.4
Current Account Balance	3.1	4.0	2.4	0.8	1.0	0.7	1.8	2.1	1.6	0.8	0.3
Savings	35.8	40.1	44.4	43.8	43.6	43.1	43.7	42.8	41.3	40.3	39.0
Investment	33.1	36.4	42.0	42.9	42.6	42.3	41.9	40.7	39.7	39.4	38.6
Capital Account Balance	0.1	0.1	0.1	0.1	0.1	0.1	0.0	0.0	0.1	0.0	0.0
Emerging and Developing Europe											
Net Lending and Borrowing	−4.1	−5.0	−4.4	−5.6	−3.6	−2.7	−1.8	−0.5	−0.8	−1.8	−2.5
Current Account Balance	−4.4	−5.3	−5.1	−6.5	−4.6	−3.8	−3.1	−1.9	−2.0	−3.0	−3.5
Savings	18.0	17.1	16.0	17.0	16.8	17.0	18.0	18.6	17.7	17.4	17.1
Investment	21.8	22.0	21.0	23.2	21.1	20.6	20.8	20.2	19.6	20.3	20.5
Capital Account Balance	0.2	0.4	0.7	0.8	1.0	1.2	1.3	1.4	1.2	1.2	1.0
Latin America and the Caribbean											
Net Lending and Borrowing	−0.7	0.3	−1.7	−1.9	−2.3	−2.7	−3.1	−3.5	−2.2	−2.3	−2.4
Current Account Balance	−0.8	0.2	−1.9	−2.0	−2.3	−2.8	−3.2	−3.6	−2.3	−2.3	−2.4
Savings	19.2	20.8	20.3	20.4	19.9	19.2	18.1	18.9	18.6	18.6	19.3
Investment	20.1	20.7	21.7	22.2	22.3	22.3	21.9	22.2	20.7	21.0	21.7
Capital Account Balance	0.1	0.1	0.2	0.0	0.0	0.0	0.0	0.0	0.0	0.0	0.0
Middle East, North Africa, Afghanistan, and Pakistan											
Net Lending and Borrowing	7.1	9.1	6.0	12.8	12.0	10.0	5.6	−3.4	−3.9	−2.0	−1.1
Current Account Balance	7.4	9.4	6.1	12.7	12.5	10.1	5.1	−4.0	−4.6	−2.6	−1.6
Savings	32.1	35.2	33.8	38.4	37.6	35.4	32.1	23.7	21.8	24.0	25.6
Investment	24.9	26.4	29.0	25.6	25.4	24.8	25.5	26.5	25.1	25.4	25.8
Capital Account Balance	0.2	0.2	0.3	0.0	0.0	0.0	0.1	0.1	0.1	0.1	0.1
Sub-Saharan Africa											
Net Lending and Borrowing	1.4	2.2	1.0	0.0	−1.0	−1.7	−3.3	−5.5	−4.1	−3.5	−4.0
Current Account Balance	0.2	0.8	−0.7	−0.5	−1.5	−2.1	−3.7	−5.9	−4.5	−3.9	−4.4
Savings	18.9	20.3	20.0	19.7	19.2	18.7	17.8	14.9	15.4	16.1	16.9
Investment	18.5	19.4	20.4	20.1	20.6	20.9	21.5	20.6	19.9	20.0	21.3
Capital Account Balance	1.2	1.4	1.7	0.5	0.6	0.4	0.3	0.4	0.4	0.4	0.4

Table A14. Summary of Net Lending and Borrowing *(continued)*
(Percent of GDP)

	Averages 1998–2007	Averages 2002–09	2010	2011	2012	2013	2014	2015	Projections 2016	Projections 2017	Projections Average 2018–21
Analytical Groups											
By Source of Export Earnings											
Fuel											
Net Lending and Borrowing	7.9	9.1	6.1	9.9	8.7	6.8	3.8	−1.6	−1.8	−0.2	1.0
Current Account Balance	8.2	9.6	6.0	9.9	9.0	6.9	4.2	−1.9	−2.2	−0.6	0.6
Savings	30.9	32.7	30.6	34.2	32.9	30.0	28.4	24.8	23.4	24.8	26.4
Investment	23.1	23.6	24.7	24.1	24.1	23.2	24.0	25.5	24.4	24.4	24.8
Capital Account Balance	0.0	−0.1	0.3	0.0	−0.1	0.0	−0.7	−0.1	0.0	0.0	0.0
Nonfuel											
Net Lending and Borrowing	0.4	1.1	0.1	−1.0	−0.9	−1.0	−0.2	0.4	0.3	−0.3	−0.7
Current Account Balance	0.2	0.9	−0.1	−1.2	−1.1	−1.2	−0.3	0.2	0.1	−0.4	−0.8
Savings	26.4	29.6	32.9	32.9	33.1	33.1	33.9	34.2	33.4	32.9	32.6
Investment	26.4	28.8	33.0	34.0	34.1	34.2	34.2	33.9	33.3	33.3	33.4
Capital Account Balance	0.2	0.2	0.3	0.2	0.2	0.2	0.2	0.2	0.2	0.1	0.1
By External Financing Source											
Net Debtor Economies											
Net Lending and Borrowing	−1.0	−1.0	−1.9	−2.7	−2.9	−2.6	−2.4	−2.2	−1.8	−2.1	−2.2
Current Account Balance	−1.3	−1.3	−2.4	−2.9	−3.2	−2.9	−2.7	−2.5	−2.0	−2.3	−2.4
Savings	20.8	22.2	22.8	23.0	22.4	21.9	21.8	21.7	21.9	22.2	23.1
Investment	22.3	23.7	25.1	25.7	25.4	24.7	24.4	24.2	23.9	24.4	25.5
Capital Account Balance	0.3	0.3	0.5	0.2	0.3	0.3	0.3	0.3	0.3	0.3	0.2
Net Debtor Economies by Debt-Servicing Experience											
Economies with Arrears and/or Rescheduling during 2011–15											
Net Lending and Borrowing	−0.1	−0.6	−2.3	−3.6	−5.2	−5.2	−3.0	−4.2	−5.0	−4.3	−3.3
Current Account Balance	−0.3	−0.9	−2.7	−3.9	−5.6	−5.3	−3.2	−4.4	−5.1	−4.5	−3.4
Savings	20.8	21.7	18.9	16.6	14.6	13.4	13.9	12.7	11.9	13.0	14.5
Investment	21.2	22.6	21.6	20.4	20.1	18.6	17.1	17.1	16.9	17.4	17.9
Capital Account Balance	0.2	0.3	0.3	0.3	0.4	0.1	0.2	0.2	0.2	0.2	0.2
Memorandum											
World											
Net Lending and Borrowing	0.0	0.2	0.5	0.5	0.5	0.6	0.6	0.4	0.4	0.3	0.1
Current Account Balance	−0.1	0.1	0.4	0.4	0.5	0.5	0.5	0.3	0.3	0.2	0.0
Savings	23.5	23.8	24.4	25.3	25.7	25.7	26.2	26.2	25.4	25.4	25.8
Investment	23.5	23.6	24.1	24.8	25.0	25.0	25.3	25.4	25.0	25.1	25.7
Capital Account Balance	0.0	0.1	0.1	0.1	0.1	0.1	0.0	0.0	0.1	0.1	0.0

Note: The estimates in this table are based on individual countries' national accounts and balance of payments statistics. Country group composites are calculated as the sum of the U.S. dollar values for the relevant individual countries. This differs from the calculations in the April 2005 and earlier issues of the *World Economic Outlook*, in which the composites were weighted by GDP valued at purchasing power parities as a share of total world GDP. The estimates of gross national savings and investment (or gross capital formation) are from individual countries' national accounts statistics. The estimates of the current account balance, the capital account balance, and the financial account balance (or net lending/net borrowing) are from the balance of payments statistics. The link between domestic transactions and transactions with the rest of the world can be expressed as accounting identities. Savings (*S*) minus investment (*I*) is equal to the current account balance (*CAB*) (*S − I = CAB*). Also, net lending/net borrowing (*NLB*) is the sum of the current account balance and the capital account balance (*KAB*) (*NLB = CAB + KAB*). In practice, these identities do not hold exactly; imbalances result from imperfections in source data and compilation as well as from asymmetries in group composition due to data availability.

[1]Excludes the G7 (Canada, France, Germany, Italy, Japan, United Kingdom, United States) and euro area countries.

[2]Georgia, Turkmenistan, and Ukraine, which are not members of the Commonwealth of Independent States, are included in this group for reasons of geography and similarity in economic structure.

Table A15. Summary of World Medium-Term Baseline Scenario

	Averages				Projections		Averages	
	1998–2007	2008–17	2014	2015	2016	2017	2014–17	2018–21
	Annual Percent Change							
World Real GDP	**4.2**	**3.2**	**3.4**	**3.2**	**3.1**	**3.4**	**3.3**	**3.7**
Advanced Economies	2.8	1.1	1.9	2.1	1.6	1.8	1.8	1.7
Emerging Market and Developing Economies	5.8	5.0	4.6	4.0	4.2	4.6	4.3	5.0
Memorandum								
Potential Output								
Major Advanced Economies	2.2	1.2	1.4	1.4	1.3	1.3	1.3	1.5
World Trade, Volume[1]	**6.8**	**2.9**	**3.9**	**2.6**	**2.3**	**3.8**	**3.1**	**4.2**
Imports								
Advanced Economies	6.2	2.1	3.8	4.2	2.4	3.9	3.6	4.1
Emerging Market and Developing Economies	8.9	4.5	4.5	−0.6	2.3	4.1	2.5	4.7
Exports								
Advanced Economies	5.8	2.5	3.8	3.6	1.8	3.5	3.2	3.8
Emerging Market and Developing Economies	8.8	3.7	3.5	1.3	2.9	3.6	2.8	4.5
Terms of Trade								
Advanced Economies	−0.2	0.1	0.3	1.8	0.9	0.1	0.8	0.1
Emerging Market and Developing Economies	1.7	−0.1	−0.5	−4.1	−1.0	−0.1	−1.4	−0.2
World Prices in U.S. Dollars								
Manufactures	1.5	0.4	−1.0	−2.9	−2.1	1.4	−1.2	1.0
Oil	14.0	−3.3	−7.5	−47.2	−15.4	17.9	−16.5	3.3
Nonfuel Primary Commodities	3.9	−0.7	−4.0	−17.5	−2.7	0.9	−6.1	−0.1
Consumer Prices								
Advanced Economies	2.0	1.5	1.4	0.3	0.8	1.7	1.0	2.0
Emerging Market and Developing Economies	7.9	5.6	4.7	4.7	4.5	4.4	4.6	4.1
Interest Rates	*Percent*							
Real Six-Month LIBOR[2]	1.8	−0.6	−1.5	−0.6	−0.4	−0.8	−0.8	0.8
World Real Long-Term Interest Rate[3]	2.4	0.8	0.5	1.3	0.3	−0.5	0.4	0.2
Current Account Balances	*Percent of GDP*							
Advanced Economies	−0.7	0.1	0.5	0.6	0.7	0.6	0.6	0.4
Emerging Market and Developing Economies	1.9	0.9	0.6	−0.1	−0.3	−0.4	−0.1	−0.6
Total External Debt								
Emerging Market and Developing Economies	33.4	27.1	28.4	28.4	28.4	27.6	28.2	26.2
Debt Service								
Emerging Market and Developing Economies	9.3	9.6	11.2	12.1	10.5	9.4	10.8	8.9

[1]Data refer to trade in goods and services.
[2]London interbank offered rate on U.S. dollar deposits minus percent change in U.S. GDP deflator.
[3]GDP-weighted average of 10-year (or nearest-maturity) government bond rates for Canada, France, Germany, Italy, Japan, the United Kingdom, and the United States.

WORLD ECONOMIC OUTLOOK
SELECTED TOPICS

World Economic Outlook Archives

I. Methodology—Aggregation, Modeling, and Forecasting

II. Historical Surveys

III. Economic Growth—Sources and Patterns

IV. Inflation and Deflation and Commodity Markets

V. Fiscal Policy

VI. Monetary Policy, Financial Markets, and Flow of Funds

X. Regional Issues

XI. Country-Specific Analyses

XII. Special Topics

IMF EXECUTIVE BOARD DISCUSSION OF THE OUTLOOK, OCTOBER 2016

The following remarks were made by the Chair at the conclusion of the Executive Board's discussion of the Fiscal Monitor, Global Financial Stability Report, *and* World Economic Outlook *on September 23, 2016.*

Executive Directors broadly shared the assessment of global economic prospects and risks. They observed that global growth is likely to remain modest this year, world trade growth is declining, and low inflation persists in many advanced economies. On the upside, commodity prices have firmed up, and financial market volatility following the U.K. vote to leave the European Union has generally been contained. Directors noted that, while global growth is expected to pick up somewhat next year, downside risks and uncertainty are elevated. The potential for another setback cannot be ruled out. Directors urged policymakers to employ all policy levers—individually and collectively—and enhance global cooperation, to avoid further growth disappointments, strengthen the foundations of the recovery, revive global trade, and ensure that the benefits of globalization are shared more broadly.

Directors noted that growth in advanced economies is projected to weaken this year and edge up slightly next year. Nevertheless, the overall outlook continues to be weighed down by remaining crisis legacy issues, persistently low inflation, weak demand, continued large external imbalances in some countries, low labor productivity growth, and population aging. At the same time, the full macroeconomic implications of the U.K. vote have yet to unfold. In emerging market and developing countries, growth is expected to strengthen gradually, on the back of improved external financing conditions, rising commodity prices, and a gradual stabilization in key economies currently in recession. Many countries have made steady progress in strengthening policy frameworks and resilience to shocks, and market sentiment has recently improved. Notwithstanding these positive developments, emerging market and developing economies remain exposed to spillovers from subdued growth in advanced economies, developments in China during its transition toward more sustainable growth, and volatility in capi-

tal flows and exchange rates, while domestic challenges remain to be addressed. Globally, concerns are growing about political discontent, income inequality, and populist policies, threatening to derail globalization.

Directors observed that, while financial markets have shown resilience to a number of shocks in the past six months, medium-term risks are rising. In advanced economies where weak growth calls for continued accommodative monetary policy, a prolonged period of low growth and low interest rates could add to banks' structural profitability challenges and put at risk the solvency of many life insurance companies and pension funds. These risks and challenges could, in turn, further weaken economic activity and financial stability more broadly. In many emerging market economies, high corporate leverage and the growing complexity of financial products continue to pose challenges.

Against this backdrop, Directors emphasized the urgent need for comprehensive, clearly articulated strategies—combining structural, macroeconomic, and financial policies—to lift actual and potential output, manage vulnerabilities, and enhance resilience. They recognized that the optimal policy mix will vary according to country contexts and the particular priorities. Directors also stressed that intensified multilateral cooperation is crucial to sustain global growth and improvements in living standards. Specifically, concerted efforts are needed to promote strong, sustainable, balanced, and inclusive growth; facilitate cross-border trade and investment flows; implement effective banking resolution frameworks; reduce policy uncertainty, including through clear communication; and sustain progress on global rebalancing. Strong global safety nets are also vital to deal with shocks, including those stemming from refugee flows, climate events, and domestic strife.

Directors broadly concurred that, in most advanced economies, policy action will need to continue to support demand in the short term and boost productivity and potential output in the medium term. Continued monetary accommodation remains appropriate to lift inflation expectations, while being mindful of negative side effects, but monetary policy alone would not be sufficient for closing output gaps and achieving balanced and sustainable growth. Growth-friendly fiscal policy is therefore essential, calibrated to the amount of space available in each country while ensuring long-term debt sustainability, anchored in a credible medium-term framework. Sustained efforts to repair bank and corporate balance sheets would help improve the transmission of monetary policy to real activity, and proactive use of macroprudential policies would safeguard financial stability. Structural reforms need to be prioritized depending on country circumstances, with a focus on raising labor force participation rates, enhancing the efficiency of the labor market, reducing barriers to entry, and encouraging research and development. In the corporate sector, reforms should focus on eliminating debt overhangs, facilitating restructuring, and further improving governance.

Directors acknowledged that circumstances and challenges in emerging market and developing countries vary depending on their level of development and cyclical position. To achieve the common objective of converging to higher levels of income, structural reforms should focus on facilitating technology diffusion and job creation, and enhancing human capital. Directors encouraged taking advantage of the current relatively benign external financial conditions to press ahead with needed corporate deleveraging, through a comprehensive approach, where warranted. This should be complemented by continued efforts to strengthen financial sector oversight, upgrade regulatory and supervisory frameworks, and improve corporate governance practices. Directors stressed that a smooth adjustment in China's corporate and financial sectors is crucial for sustaining growth and stability in China and elsewhere.

Directors stressed the need for financial institutions, particularly in advanced economies, to adapt their business models to new realities and evolving regulatory standards. Greater vigilance by regulators and improved data collection on nonbank financial institutions are essential to preserve their financial health and monitor their role in monetary policy transmission. Policymakers can help reduce uncertainty by completing the regulatory reform agenda, without significantly increasing overall capital requirements, while preserving the integrity of a robust capital framework. Directors broadly agreed that, in countries facing a private sector debt overhang or where the financial system is seriously impaired but fiscal space is available, well-targeted fiscal measures—with the support of strong insolvency and bankruptcy procedures and safeguards to limit moral hazard—could help facilitate private debt restructuring. Many emerging market countries should continue to enhance resilience, including by curbing excessive private debt build-up and strengthening the government balance sheet in upturns.

Directors underscored that policy priorities in low-income countries are to address near-term macroeconomic challenges and make progress toward their Sustainable Development Goals. In commodity-dependent economies, building fiscal buffers will require increasing the contribution of the non-commodity sector to tax revenue, together with spending rationalization. For countries less dependent on commodities, countercyclical macroeconomic policies should be adopted where growth remains robust, and debt management practices strengthened to lower the impact of potential shifts in capital flows. More broadly, achieving robust, sustainable, and inclusive growth requires sustained efforts to diversify the economy, broaden the revenue base, improve the efficiency of government spending, and enhance financial deepening.

New Releases from IMF Publications

**Modernizing China:
Investing in Soft Infrastructure**

$38. Paperback
ISBN 978-1-51353-994-2. Approx. 186pp.

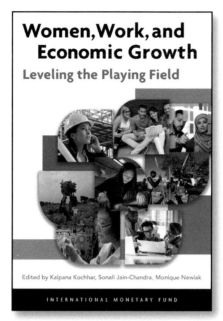

**Women, Work, and Economic Growth:
Leveling the Playing Field**

$30. Paperback
ISBN 978-1-51351-610-3. 180pp.

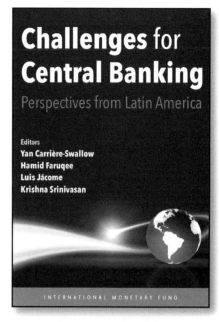

**Challenges for Central Banking:
Perspectives from Latin America**

$30. Paperback
ISBN 978-1-51359-176-6. 280pp.

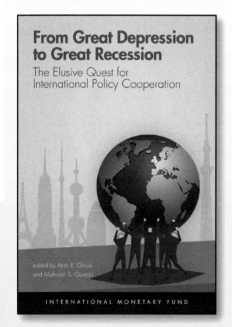

**From Great Depression to
Great Recession: The Elusive Quest
for International Policy Cooperation**

$27. Paperback
ISBN 978-1-51351-427-7. Approx. 196pp.

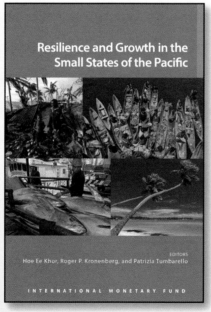

**Resilience and Growth in the Small
States of the Pacific**

$35. Paperback
ISBN 978-1-51350-752-1. 458pp.

**Collapse and Revival: Global
Recessions and Recoveries**

$65. Hardback with DVD
ISBN 978-1-51357-002-0. 292pp.

To order visit bookstore.imf.org/weonro16